Lecture Notes in Computer Science 10184

Commenced Publication in 1973.
Founding and Former Series Editors:
Gerhard Goos, Juris Hartmanis, and Jan van Leeuwen

More information about this series at http://www.springer.com/series/7407

Manuel V. Hermenegildo · Pedro Lopez-Garcia (Eds.)

Logic-Based Program Synthesis and Transformation

26th International Symposium, LOPSTR 2016
Edinburgh, UK, September 6–8, 2016
Revised Selected Papers

Springer

Editors
Manuel V. Hermenegildo ⓘ
IMDEA Software Institute and Universidad
  Politécnica de Madrid
Madrid
Spain

Pedro Lopez-Garcia ⓘ
IMDEA Software Institute and CSIC
Madrid
Spain

ISSN 0302-9743   ISSN 1611-3349 (electronic)
Lecture Notes in Computer Science
ISBN 978-3-319-63138-7   ISBN 978-3-319-63139-4 (eBook)
DOI 10.1007/978-3-319-63139-4

Library of Congress Control Number: 2017945732

LNCS Sublibrary: SL1 – Theoretical Computer Science and General Issues

Printed on acid-free paper

This Springer imprint is published by Springer Nature
The registered company is Springer International Publishing AG
The registered company address is: Gewerbestrasse 11, 6330 Cham, Switzerland

Preface

This volume contains a selection of the papers presented at LOPSTR 2016, the 26th International Symposium on Logic-Based Program Synthesis and Transformation, held during September 6–8, 2016, at the University of Edinburgh, Scotland, UK. It was co-located with two other conferences: PPDP 2016, the 18th International ACM SIGPLAN Symposium on Principles and Practice of Declarative Programming, and SAS 2016, the 23rd Static Analysis Symposium. The co-location of these three related conferences has been shown to be very productive and cross-fertilizing. Previous LOPSTR symposia were held in Siena (2015), Canterbury (2014), Madrid (2013 and 2002), Leuven (2012 and 1997), Odense (2011), Hagenberg (2010), Coimbra (2009), Valencia (2008), Lyngby (2007), Venice (2006 and 1999), London (2005 and 2000), Verona (2004), Uppsala (2003), Paphos (2001), Manchester (1998, 1992, and 1991), Stockholm (1996), Arnhem (1995), Pisa (1994), and Louvain-la-Neuve (1993). More information about the symposium can be found at: http://www.cliplab.org/Conferences/LOPSTR16/.

The aim of the LOPSTR series is to stimulate and promote international research and collaboration in logic-based program development. LOPSTR is open to contributions in all aspects of this area, including all stages of the software life cycle and dealing with issues related to both programming-in-the-small and programming-in-the-large. LOPSTR traditionally solicits contributions, in any language paradigm, in the areas of synthesis, specification, transformation, analysis and verification, specialization, testing and certification, composition, program/model manipulation, optimization, transformational techniques in SE, inversion, applications, and tools. LOPSTR has a reputation for being a lively forum that allows presenting and discussing both finished work and work in progress. Formal proceedings are produced only after the symposium so that authors can incorporate the feedback from the conference presentation and discussions.

In response to the call for papers, 45 abstracts were submitted to LOPSTR 2016, of which 38 resulted in full submissions, from 21 different countries. After the first round of reviewing, the Program Committee accepted two full papers for direct inclusion in the formal proceedings, and 18 full papers presented at the symposium were accepted after a post-conference revision and another round of reviewing. Each submission was reviewed by at least three Program Committee members or external reviewers. The paper "A Hiking Trip Through the Orders of Magnitude: Deriving Efficient Generators for Closed Simply-Typed Lambda Terms and Normal Forms" by Paul Tarau won the best paper award, sponsored by Springer. In addition to the 20 contributed papers, this volume includes the abstracts of the talks by our three outstanding invited speakers: Francesco Logozzo (Facebook, USA) and Greg Morrisett (Cornell University, USA), whose talks were shared with PPDP, and Martin Vechev (ETH Zurich, Switzerland), whose talk was shared with SAS.

We would like to thank the Program Committee members, who worked diligently to produce high-quality reviews for the submitted papers, as well as all the external reviewers involved in the paper selection. We are very grateful to the LOPSTR 2016 Organizing Committee composed by James Cheney (local organizer) and Moreno Falaschi for the wonderful job they did in managing the symposium. Many thanks also to Germán Vidal, the Program Committee chair of PPDP 2016, and Xavier Rival, the Program Committee chair of SAS 2016, with whom we often interacted to coordinate the three events. We would also like to thank Andrei Voronkov for his excellent EasyChair system that automates many of the tasks involved in chairing a conference. Special thanks go to the invited speakers and to all the authors who submitted and presented their papers at LOPSTR 2016. Finally, we also thank our sponsors, the School of Informatics of the University of Edinburgh, the IMDEA Software Institute, the European Association for Programming Languages and Systems, the European Association for Theoretical Computer Science, the Association for Logic Programming, and Springer for their cooperation and support in the organization of the symposium.

April 2017   Manuel V. Hermenegildo
                                                       Pedro Lopez-Garcia

Organization

Program Chairs

Manuel V. Hermenegildo   IMDEA Software Institute and Universidad Politécnica
                           de Madrid, Spain
Pedro Lopez-Garcia   IMDEA Software Institute and CSIC, Spain

Program Committee

Slim Abdennadher   German University in Cairo, Egypt
Maria Alpuente   Universitat Politècnica de València, Spain
Sergio Antoy   Portland State University, USA
Michael Codish   Ben-Gurion University of the Negev, Israel
Jérôme Feret   Inria/École Normale Supérieure, France
Fabio Fioravanti   University of Chieti-Pescara, Italy
Maurizio Gabbrielli   University of Bologna, Italy
Maria Garcia de La Banda   Monash University, Australia
Robert Glück   University of Copenhagen, Denmark
Miguel Gomez-Zamalloa   Complutense University of Madrid, Spain
Gopal Gupta   University of Texas at Dallas, USA
Patricia Hill   University of Leeds, UK and BUGSENG Srl, Italy
Jacob Howe   City University of London, UK
Viktor Kuncak   École Polytechnique Fédérale de Lausanne (EPFL),
                           Switzerland
Michael Leuschel   University of Düsseldorf, Germany
Heiko Mantel   TU Darmstadt, Germany
Jorge A. Navas   SRI International, USA
Naoki Nishida   Nagoya University, Japan
Catuscia Palamidessi   Inria, France
C.R. Ramakrishnan   Stony Brook University, New York, USA
Vítor Santos-Costa   Universidade do Porto, Portugal
Peter Schneider-Kamp   University of Southern Denmark, Denmark
Hirohisa Seki   Nagoya Institute of Technology, Japan

Organizing Committee

James Cheney   University of Edinburgh, Scotland, UK
                           (Local Organizer)
Moreno Falaschi   University of Siena, Italy

Additional Reviewers

Ayala-Rincón, Mauricio
Ballis, Demis
Biernacki, Dariusz
Ceruelo, Víctor Pablos
Comini, Marco
Cristescu, Ioana
Cruz-Filipe, Luís
De Angelis, Emanuele
Denecker, Marc
Escobar, Santiago
Filinski, Andrzej
Fischer, Sebastian
Fortier, Jérôme
Fuhs, Carsten
Grygiel, Katarzyna
Guo, Hai-Feng
Hamann, Tobias
Isabel, Miguel
Kaarsgaard, Robin

Kafle, Bishoksan
Kawabe, Yoshinobu
Kjellerstrand, Håkan
Krings, Sebastian
Krustev, Dimitur
Kuraj, Ivan
Lanese, Ivan
Lescanne, Pierre
Libby, Steven
Lucanu, Dorel
Lämmel, Ralf
Marple, Kyle
Meo, Maria Chiara
Mera, Edison
Nieva, Susana
Ozono, Tadachika
Pettorossi, Alberto
Proietti, Maurizio
Riesco, Adrián

Salazar, Elmer
Sapiña, Julia
Schneider, David
Serrano, Alejandro
Sharaf, Nada
Stuckey, Peter J.
Stulova, Nataliia
Tarau, Paul
Tasch, Markus
Tiezzi, Francesco
Triska, Markus
Tsushima, Kanae
Urban, Caterina
Villanueva, Alicia
Weber, Alexandra
Zaffanella, Enea
Zaki, Amira

Abstracts of Invited Talks

Challenges in Compiling Coq

Greg Morrisett

Cornell University, Ithaca, USA
jgm19@cornell.edu

Abstract. The Coq proof assistant is increasingly used for constructing verified software, including everything from verified micro-kernels to verified databases. Programmers typically write code in Gallina (the core functional language of Coq) and construct proofs about those Gallina programs. Then, through a process of "extraction", the Gallina code is translated to either OCaml, Haskell, or Scheme and compiled by a conventional compiler to produce machine code. Unfortunately, this translation often results in inefficient code, and it fails to take advantage of the dependent types and proofs. Furthermore, it is a bit embarrassing that the process is not formally verified.

Working with Andrew Appel's group at Princeton, we are trying to formalize as much of the process of extraction and compilation as we can, all within Coq. I will talk about both the opportunities this presents, as well as some of the key challenges, including the inability to preserve types through compilation, and the difficulty that axioms present.

Static Analysis for Security at the Facebook Scale

Francesco Logozzo

Facebook, Seattle, USA
logozzo@fb.com

Abstract. The scale and continuous growth of commercial code bases are the greatest challenges for adoption of automated analysis tools in industry. Alas, scale is largely ignored by academic research. We developed a new static analysis tool for security to scale to Facebook scale. It relies on abstract interpretation to focus on the properties that really matter to security engineers and provides fine control on the cost/precision ratio. It was designed from day one for "real world" security and privacy problems at scale. Facebook codebase is huge, and we can analyze it, from scratch in 13 min. This talk will give attendees a peek at some of the secret sauce we use to achieve such amazing performance and precision.

Learning from Programs: Probabilistic Models, Program Analysis and Synthesis

Martin Vechev

ETH Zurich, Zurich, Switzerland
martin.vechev@inf.ethz.ch

Abstract. The increased availability of massive codebases (e.g., GitHub) creates an exciting opportunity for new kinds of programming tools based on probabilistic models. Enabled by these models, tomorrow's tools will provide statistically likely solutions to programming tasks difficult or impossible to solve with traditional techniques. An example is our JSNice statistical program de-minification system (http://jsnice.org), now used by more than 150,000 users in every country worldwide. In this talk, I will discuss some of the latest developments in this new inter-disciplinary research direction: the theoretical foundations used to build probabilistic programming systems, the practical challenges such systems must address, and the conceptual connections between the areas of statistical learning, static analysis and program synthesis.

Contents

Program Transformation

Partial Evaluation of Order-Sorted Equational Programs Modulo Axioms

María Alpuente[1], Angel Cuenca-Ortega[1,3(✉)],
Santiago Escobar[1], and José Meseguer[2]

[1] DSIC-ELP, Universitat Politècnica de València, Valencia, Spain
{alpuente,acuenca,sescobar}@dsic.upv.es
[2] University of Illinois at Urbana-Champaign, Champaign, IL, USA
meseguer@illinois.edu
[3] Universidad de Guayaquil, Guayaquil, Ecuador
angel.cuencao@ug.edu.ec

Abstract. Partial evaluation (PE) is a powerful and general program optimization technique with many successful applications. However, it has never been investigated in the context of expressive rule-based languages like Maude, CafeOBJ, OBJ, ASF+SDF, and ELAN, which support: rich type structures with sorts, subsorts and overloading; and equational rewriting modulo axioms such as commutativity, associativity–commutativity, and associativity–commutativity–identity. In this paper, we illustrate the key concepts by showing how they apply to partial evaluation of expressive rule-based programs written in Maude. Our partial evaluation scheme is based on an automatic unfolding algorithm that computes term *variants* and relies on *equational least general generalization* for ensuring global termination. We demonstrate the use of the resulting partial evaluator for program optimization on several examples where it shows significant speed-ups.

1 Introduction

Partial evaluation (PE) is a semantics-based program transformation technique in which a program is specialized to a part of its input that is known statically (at *specialization* time) [7]. PE has currently reached a point where theory and refinements have matured, substantial systems have been developed, and realistic applications benefit from partial evaluation in a wide range of fields that transcend by far program optimization.

Narrowing-driven PE (NPE) [3,4] is a generic algorithm for the specialization of functional programs that are executed by *narrowing* [10], an extension of rewriting where matching is replaced by unification. Essentially, narrowing

This work has been partially supported by the EU (FEDER) and the Spanish MINECO under grants TIN 2015-69175-C4-1-R and TIN 2013-45732-C4-1-P, and by Generalitat Valenciana under grant PROMETEOII/2015/013, and by NSF grant CNS-1319109. Angel Cuenca-Ortega has been supported by the SENESCYT, Ecuador (scholarship program 2013).

M.V. Hermenegildo and P. Lopez-Garcia (Eds.): LOPSTR 2016, LNCS 10184, pp. 3–20, 2017.
DOI: 10.1007/978-3-319-63139-4_1

consists of computing an appropriate substitution for a symbolic program call in such a way that the program call becomes reducible, and then reduce it: both the rewrite rule and the term can be instantiated. As in logic programming, narrowing computations can be represented by a (possibly infinite) finitely branching tree. Since narrowing subsumes both rewriting and SLD-resolution, it is complete in the sense of both functional programming (computation of normal forms) and logic programming (computation of answers). By combining the functional dimension of narrowing with the power of logic variables and unification, NPE has better opportunities for optimization than the more standard partial evaluation of logic programs (also known as *partial deduction*, PD) and functional programs [4].

Partial evaluation has never been investigated in the context of expressive rule-based languages like Maude, CafeOBJ, OBJ, ASF+SDF, and ELAN, which support: (1) rich type structures with sorts, subsorts and overloading; and (2) equational rewriting modulo axioms such as commutativity, associativity–commutativity, and associativity–commutativity–identity. The key NPE ingredients of [3] have to be further generalized to corresponding (order–sorted) *equational* notions (*modulo* axioms): e.g., *equational unfolding, equational closedness, equational embedding, and equational abstraction*; and the associated partial evaluation techniques become more sophisticated and powerful. In this paper, we illustrate the key concepts by showing how they apply to partial evaluation of expressive rule-based programs written in Maude.

Let us motivate the power of our technique by reproducing the classical specialization of a program parser w.r.t. a given grammar into a very specialized parser [7].

Example 1. Consider the following rewrite theory (written in Maude[1] syntax) that defines a generic parser for the language generated by simple, right regular grammars. We define a symbol _|_|_ to represent the parser configurations, where the first underscore represents the (terminal or non-terminal) symbol being processed, the second underscore represents the current string pending to be recognized, and the third underscore stands for the considered grammar. We provide two non-terminal symbols init and S and three terminal symbols 0, 1, and the finalizing mark eps (for ϵ, the empty string). These are useful choices for this example, but they can be easily generalized to any terminal and non-terminal symbols by defining a Maude parameterized theory. Parsing a string *st* according to a given grammar Γ is defined by rewriting the configuration (init | *st* | Γ) using the rules of the grammar (in the opposite direction) to incrementally transform *st* until the final configuration (eps | eps | Γ) is reached.

---

[1] In Maude 2.7, only equations with the variant attribute are used by the folding variant narrowing strategy, which is the only narrowing strategy considered in this paper. We sometimes remove the variant attribute for saving space.

```
fmod PARSER is
 sorts Symbol NSymbol TSymbol String Production Grammar Parsing .
 subsort Production < Grammar . subsort TSymbol < String .
 subsorts TSymbol NSymbol < Symbol .
 ops 0 1 eps : -> TSymbol . ops init S : -> NSymbol .
 op mt : -> Grammar . op _|_|_ : Symbol String Grammar -> Parsing .
 op __ : TSymbol String -> String [right id: eps].
 op _->_ : NSymbol TSymbol -> Production .
 op _->_._ : NSymbol TSymbol NSymbol -> Production .
 op _;_ : Grammar Grammar -> Grammar [assoc comm id: mt] .
 var E : TSymbol . vars N M : NSymbol . var L : String . var G : Grammar.
 eq (N | eps | ( N -> eps ) ; G)
 = (eps | eps | ( N -> eps ) ; G) [variant] .
 eq (N | E L | ( N -> E . M ) ; G)
 = (M | L | ( N -> E . M ) ; G) [variant] .
endfm
```

Note that this Maude equational[2], program theory contains several novel features that are *unknown territory* for (narrowing-driven) partial evaluation: (1) a subsorting relation TSymbol NSymbol < Symbol, and (2) an associative-commutative with identity symbol _;_ for representing grammars (meaning that they are handled as a multiset of productions), together with the symbol __ with right identity for the input string. The general case of the parser is defined by the second equation that, given the configuration (N | E L | Γ) where (E L) is the string to be recognized, searches for the grammar production (N -> E . M) in Γ to recognize symbol E, and proceeds to recognize L starting from the non-terminal symbol M. Note that the combination of subtypes and equational (algebraic) axioms allows for a very compact definition.

For example, given the following grammar Γ generating the language $(0)^*(1)^*$:

```
init -> eps    init -> 0 . init    init -> 1 . S    S -> eps    S -> 1 . S
```

the initial configuration (init | 0 0 1 1 eps | Γ) is simplified into (init | 0 0 1 1 | Γ) by using right identity and then deterministically rewritten as (init | 0 0 1 1 | Γ) $\rightarrow$ (init | 0 1 1 | Γ) $\rightarrow$ (init | 1 1 | Γ) $\rightarrow$ (S | 1 | Γ) $\rightarrow$ (S | eps | Γ) $\rightarrow$ (eps | eps | Γ).

We can specialize our parsing program to the productions of the given grammar Γ by partially evaluating the input term (init | L | Γ), where L is a logical variable of sort String. By applying our partial evaluator, we aim to obtain the specialized code:

```
eq init || eps = eps || eps .      eq init || 1 = eps || eps .
eq S || eps = eps || eps .         eq init || 0 L = init || L .
eq init || 1 1 L = S || L .        eq S || 1 L = S || L .
```

---

[2] We assume there are no two grammar productions of the form N -> E.M_1 and N -> E.M_2.

which gets rid of the grammar Γ (and hence of costly *ACU-matching* operations) while still recognizing string st by rewriting the simpler configuration (init $\parallel st$) to the final configuration (eps $\parallel$ eps). We have run some test on both the original and the specialized programs with an impressive performance improvement, discussed in Sect. 4.

Our contribution. In this paper, we delve into the essential ingredients of a partial evaluation framework for order sorted equational theories that is able to cope with subsorts, subsort polymorphism, convergent rules (equations), and equational axioms. and state its correctness. We base our partial evaluator Victoria on a suitably extended version of the general NPE procedure of [3], which is parametric w.r.t. the *unfolding rule* used to construct finite computation trees and also w.r.t. an *abstraction operator* that is used to guarantee that only finitely many expressions are evaluated. For unfolding we use *(folding) variant narrowing* [6], a novel narrowing strategy for convergent equational theories that computes *most general variants* modulo algebraic axioms and is efficiently implemented in Maude. For the abstraction we rely on the *(order-sorted) equational least general generalization* recently investigated in [2].

2 Specializing Equational Theories Modulo Axioms

In this section, we introduce a partial evaluation algorithm for an equational theory decomposed as a triple $(\Sigma, B, \overrightarrow{E_0})$, where Σ is the signature, E_0 is a set of convergent (equations that are implicitly oriented as) rewrite rules and B is a set of commonly occurring axioms such as associativity, commutativity, and identity. Let us start by recalling the key ideas of the NPE approach. We assume the reader is acquainted with the basic notions of term rewriting, Rewriting Logic, and Maude (see, e.g., [5]).

2.1 The NPE Approach

Given a set R of rewrite rules and a set Q of program calls (i.e., input terms), the aim of NPE [3] is to derive a new set of rules R' (called a partial evaluation of R w.r.t. Q, or a partial evaluation of Q in R) which computes the same answers and irreducible forms (w.r.t. narrowing) than R for any term that t is inductively covered (*closed*) by the calls in Q. This means that every subterm in the leaves of the execution tree for t in R that can be narrowed (modulo B) in R can also be narrowed (modulo B) in R'. Roughly speaking, R' is obtained by first constructing a *finite* (possibly partial) narrowing tree for the input term t, and then gathering together the set of *resultants* $t\theta_1 \rightarrow t_1, \ldots, t\theta_k \rightarrow t_k$ that can be constructed by considering the leaves of the tree, say $t_1, \ldots, t_k$, and the computed substitutions $\theta_1, \ldots, \theta_k$ of the associated branches of the tree (i.e., a resultant rule is associated to each root-to-leaf derivation of the narrowing tree). Resultants perform what in fact is an n-step computation in R, with $n > 0$, by means of a single step computation in R'. The unfolding process is iteratively repeated for every narrowable subterm of $t_1, \ldots, t_k$ that is not covered by the root nodes of the already deployed narrowing trees. This ensures that resultants cover all calls that may occur at run-time in R'.

Let us illustrate the classical NPE method with the following example that shows its ability to perform *deforestation*, a popular transformation that neither standard PE nor PD can achieve [3]. Essentially, the aim of deforestation is to eliminate useless intermediate data structures, thus reducing the number of passes over data.

Example 2. Consider the following Maude program that computes the mirror image of a (non-empty) binary tree, which is built with the free constructor _{_}_ that stores an element as root above two given (sub-)trees, its left and right children. Note that the program does not contain any equational attributes either for _{_}_ or for flip:

```
fmod FLIP-TREE is protecting NAT .
  sort NatTree . subsort Nat < NatTree . vars R L : NatTree .
  op _{_}_ : NatTree Nat NatTree -> NatTree .
  op flip : NatTree -> NatTree .  var N : Nat .
  eq flip(N) = N [variant] .
  eq flip(L {N} R) = flip(R) {N} flip(L) [variant] .
endfm
```

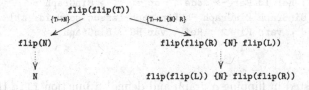

Fig. 1. Folding variant narrowing tree for the goal flip(flip(T)).

By executing flip(flip(T)) this program returns the original tree T back, but first computes an intermediate, mirrored tree flip(T) of T, which is then flipped again.

Let us partially evaluate the input term flip(flip(T)) following the NPE approach. We compute the folding variant narrowing tree depicted[3] in Fig. 1. This tree does not contain, altogether, uncovered calls in its leaves. Thus, after introducing the new symbol dflip we get the following residual program:

```
eq dflip(N) = N .              eq dflip(L {N} R) = dflip(L) {N} dflip(R) .
```

which is completely deforested, since the intermediate tree is not constructed in the residual, specialized program dflip. This is equivalent to the program generated by deforestation but with a much better performance (see Sect. 4). Note

---

[3] We show narrowing steps in solid arrows and rewriting steps in dotted arrows.

that the fact that folding variant narrowing [6] ensures normalization of terms at each step is essential for computing the calls `flip(flip(R))` and `flip(flip(L))` that appear in the rightmost leaf of the tree in Fig. 1, which are closed w.r.t. the tree root.

When we specialize programs that contain sorts, subsorts, rules, and equational axioms, things get considerably more involved, as discussed in the following section.

2.2 Partial Evaluation of Convergent Rules Modulo Axioms

Let us motivate the problem by considering the following variant of the `flip` function of Example 2 for (binary) graphs instead of trees.

Example 3. Consider the following Maude program for flipping binary graphs that are represented as multisets of nodes that may contain explicit, left and right, references (pointers) to their child nodes in the graph. We use symbol ♯ to denote an empty pointer. As expected, the `BinGraph` (set) constructor `_;_` obeys axioms of associativity, commutativity and identity (ACU). For simplicity we consider a fixed set of identifiers.

```
fmod GRAPH is sorts BinGraph Node Id Ref .
  subsort Node < BinGraph . subsort Id < Ref .
  ops 0 1 2 3 4 : -> Id . op # : -> Ref .
  op {___} : Ref Id Ref -> Node .   op mt : -> BinGraph .
  op _;_ : BinGraph BinGraph -> BinGraph [assoc comm id: mt] .
  var I : Id . vars R1 R2 : Ref . var BG : BinGraph .
endfm
```

We are interested in flipping a graph and define[4] a function `flip` that takes a reference and a binary graph and returns the flipped graph.

```
op flip : BinGraph -> BinGraph .
eq [E1] : flip(mt) = mt  [variant] .
eq [E2] : flip({R1 I R2} ; BG) = {R2 I R1} ; flip(BG) [variant] .
```

We can represent the graph shown on the left-hand side of Fig. 2 as the following term BG of sort BinGraph: `{ 1 0 2 } ; { # 1 # } ; { 3 2 4 } ; { # 3 4 } ; { # 4 0 }`. By invoking `flip(BG)`, the graph shown on the right-hand side of Fig. 2 is computed.

In order to specialize the previous program for the call `flip(flip(BG))`, we need several PE ingredients that have to be generalized to the corresponding (order–sorted) equational notions: (i) *equational closedness*, (ii) *equational embedding*, and (iii) *equational generalization*. In the following, we discuss some subtleties about these new notions gradually, through our graph-flipping running example.

---

[4] From now on, we attach a label to each equation.

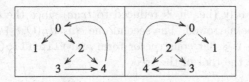

Fig. 2. A binary graph (left) and its flipped version (right).

2.3   Equational Closedness

Roughly speaking, in order to compute a specialization for t in $(\Sigma, B, \overrightarrow{E_0})$, we construct a finite (possibly partial) $(\overrightarrow{E_0}, B)$-narrowing tree for t using the folding variant narrowing strategy [6], and then extract the specialized rules $t\sigma \Rightarrow r$ (resultants) for each narrowing derivation $t \leadsto_{\sigma, \overrightarrow{E_0}, B} r$ in the tree. However, in order to ensure that resultants form a complete description covering all calls that may occur at run-time in the final specialized theory, partial evaluation must rely on a parametric general notion of *equational Q-closedness* (modulo B) that is not a mere syntactic subsumption check (i.e., to be a substitution instance of some term in Q as in the partial deduction of logic programs), but recurses over the algebraic B-structure of the terms.

Definition 1 (equational closedness). *Let $(\Sigma, B, \overrightarrow{E_0})$ be an equational theory decomposition and Q be a finite set of Σ-terms, i.e., terms that are built from Σ and a countably infinite set of variables $\mathscr{X}$. Assume the signature Σ splits into a set $\mathscr{D}_{E_0}$ of defined function symbols and a set $\mathscr{C}_{E_0}$ of constructor symbols (i.e., $\overrightarrow{E_0}, B$-irreducible), so that $\Sigma = \mathscr{D}_{E_0} \uplus \mathscr{C}_{E_0}$. We say that a Σ-term t is* closed *modulo B (w.r.t. Q and Σ), or B–closed, if $closed_B(Q, t)$ holds, where the predicate $closed_B$ is defined as follows:*

$$closed_B(Q, t) \Leftrightarrow \begin{cases} true & \text{if } t \in \mathscr{X} \\ closed_B(Q, t_1) \wedge \ldots \wedge closed_B(Q, t_n) & \text{if } t = c(\overrightarrow{t_n}), \ c \in \mathscr{C}_{E_0}, \ n \geq 0 \\ \bigwedge_{x \mapsto t' \in \theta} closed_B(Q, t') & \text{if } \exists q \in Q, \exists \theta \text{ such that } q\theta =_B t \end{cases}$$

A set T of terms is closed modulo B (w.r.t. Q and Σ) if $closed_B(Q, t)$ holds for each t in T. A set R of rules is closed modulo B (w.r.t. Q and Σ) if so is the set that can be formed by taking the right-hand sides of all the rules in R.

Example 4. In order to partially evaluate the program in Example 3 w.r.t. the input term `flip(flip(BG))`, we set $Q = \{$`flip(flip(BG))`$\}$ and start by constructing the folding variant narrowing tree that is shown[5] in Fig. 3.

When we consider the leaves of the tree, we identify two requirements for Q-closedness, with B being ACU: (i) $closed_B(Q, t_1)$ with $t_1 = $ `mt` and (ii) $closed_B(Q, t_2)$ with $t_2 = \{$`R1 I R2`$\}$; `flip(flip(BG'))`. The call $closed_B(Q, t_1)$

---

[5] To ease reading, the arcs of the narrowing tree are decorated with the label of the corresponding equation applied at the narrowing step.

holds straightforwardly (i.e., it is reduced to *true*) since the mt leaf is a constant and cannot be narrowed. The second one $closed_B(Q, t_2)$ also returns true because {R1 I R2} is a flat constructor term and flip(flip(BG')) is a (syntactic) renaming of the root of the tree.

We now show an example that requires to use *B*-matching in order to ensure equational closedness modulo *B*.

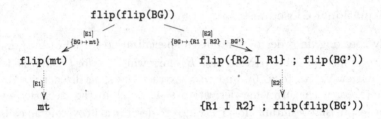

Fig. 3. Folding variant narrowing tree for the goal flip(flip(BG)).

Example 5. Let us introduce a new sort BinGraph? to encode bogus graphs that may contain spurious nodes in a sort Id? and homomorphically extend the rest of symbols and sorts. For simplicity, we just consider one additional constant symbol e in sort Id?.

```
sorts BinGraph? Id? Node? Ref? . subsorts BinGraph Node? < BinGraph? .
subsort Node < Node? . subsort Ref Id? < Ref? .    op e : -> Id? .
op {___} : Ref? Id Ref? -> Node? . op {___} : Ref? Id? Ref? -> Node? .
var BG : BinGraph . var BG? : BinGraph? .
op _;_ : BinGraph? BinGraph? -> BinGraph? [assoc comm id: mt] .
vars I I1 : Id . var I? : Id? . vars R1 R2 : Ref . vars R1? R2? : Ref?.
```

Let us consider a function fix that receives an extended graph BG?, an unwanted node I?, and a new content I, and traverses the graph replacing I? by I.

```
op fix : Id Id? BinGraph? -> BinGraph? .
eq [E3] : fix(I, I?, {R1? I? R2?} ; BG?) = fix(I, I?, {R1? I R2?} ; BG?) [variant] .
eq [E4] : fix(I, I?, {I? I1 R2?} ; BG?) = fix(I, I?, {I I1 R2?} ; BG?) [variant] .
eq [E5] : fix(I, I?, {R1? I1 I?} ; BG?) = fix(I, I?, {R1? I1 I} ; BG?) [variant] .
eq [E6] : fix(I, I?, BG) = BG [variant] .
```

For example, consider the following term t of sort BinGraph? : "{# 1 e} ; {e 0 #} ; {e e 3} ; {e 3 #}" that represents the graph shown on the left-hand side of Fig. 4. We can fix the graph t by invoking fix(2,e,t), which computes the corresponding fixed graph shown on the right-hand side of Fig. 4.

Now assume we want to specialize the above function fix w.r.t. the input term fix(2,e,{R1 I R2} ; BG?), that is, a bogus graph with at least one non-spurious node {R1 I R2} (non-spurious because of the sort of variable I). Following the proposed methodology, we set $Q = \{$fix(2,e,{R1 I R2} ; BG?)$\}$ and start by constructing the folding variant narrowing tree shown in Fig. 5.

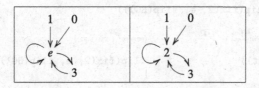

Fig. 4. A binary graph with node e (left) and its fixed version (right).

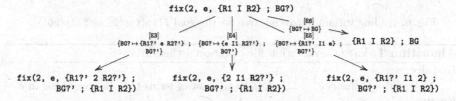

Fig. 5. Folding variant narrowing tree for the goal `fix(2, e, {R1 I R2}; BG?)`.

The right leaf `{R1 I R2}` ; `BG` is a constructor term and cannot be unfolded. The three branches to the left of the tree are closed modulo ACU with the root of the tree in Fig. 5. For instance, for the left leaf $t = \text{fix}(2, e, \{R1?' \ 2 \ R2?'\}; BG?'; \{R1 \ I \ R2\})$, the condition $closed_B(Q, t)$ is reduced[6] to true because t is an instance (modulo ACU) of the root node of the tree, and the subterm $t' = (\{R1?' \ 2 \ R2?'\}; BG?')$ occurring in the corresponding (ACU-)matcher is a constructor term. The other branches can be proved ACU-closed with the tree root in a similar way.

Example 6 (Example 5 continued). Now let us assume that the function flip of Example 2 is replaced by the following definition extended to (bogus graphs of sort) BinGraph?, where the former equation E2 is an instance of the new equation E2a:

```
op flip : BinGraph? -> BinGraph? .
eq [E1x] : flip(mt) = mt   [variant] .
eq [E2a] : flip({R1? I  R2?} ; BG?) = {R2? I  R1?} ; flip(BG?) [variant].
eq [E2b] : flip({R1? I? R2?} ; BG?) = {R2? I? R1?} ; flip(BG?) [variant].
```

We specialize the whole program containing functions flip and fix w.r.t. input term `flip(fix(2,e,flip(BG)))`, that is, take a graph BG, flip it, then fix any occurrence of nodes e, and finally flip it again. Unfortunately, the corresponding folding variant narrowing tree, shown in Fig. 6, does not represent all possible computations for (any ACU-instances of) the input term, since the narrowable redexes occurring in the tree leaves are not a recursive instance of the only partially evaluated call so far. That is, the term `flip(fix(2, e, flip(BG')` ;

---

[6] Note that this is only true because pattern matching modulo ACU is used for testing closedness.

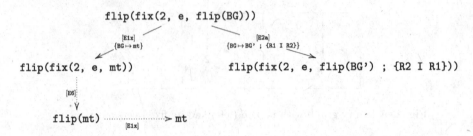

Fig. 6. Folding variant narrowing tree for the goal `flip(fix(2, e, flip(BG)))`.

Algorithm 1. Partial evaluation for equational theories

Require:

An equational theory $\mathscr{E} = (\Sigma, B, \overrightarrow{E_0})$ and a set of terms Q to be specialized in $\mathscr{E}$

Ensure:

A set Q' of terms s.t. UNFOLD$(Q', \mathscr{E}, \mathscr{S})$ is closed modulo B w.r.t. Q'

1: **function** EqNPE$(\mathscr{E}, Q, \mathscr{S})$
2:    $Q := Q \downarrow_{\overrightarrow{E_0}, B}$
3:    **repeat**
4:       $Q' := Q$
5:       $\mathscr{L} \leftarrow$ UNFOLD$(Q', \mathscr{E}, \mathscr{S})$
6:       $Q \leftarrow$ ABSTRACT$(Q', \mathscr{L}, B)$
7:    **until** $Q' =_B Q$
8:    **return** Q'

$\{$R2 I R1$\}$)) of the rightmost leaf is not *ACU*-closed w.r.t. the tree root. As in NPE, we need to recurse (modulo B) over the structure of the terms to augment the set of specialized calls in a controlled way, so as to ensure that all possible calls are covered by the specialization.

3   The Partial Evaluation Scheme for Equational Theories

We are now ready to formulate the backbone of our partial evaluation methodology for equational theories that crystallizes the ideas of the example above. Following the NPE approach, we define a generic algorithm (Algorithm 1) that is parameterized by:

1. a *narrowing relation* (with narrowing strategy $\mathscr{S}$) that constructs search trees,
2. an *unfolding rule*, that determines when and how to terminate building a tree, and
3. an *abstraction operator*, that is used to guarantee that the set of terms obtained during partial evaluation (i.e., the set of deployed narrowing trees) is kept finite.

Informally, the algorithm proceeds as follows. Given the input theory $\mathscr{E}$ and the set of terms Q, the first step consists in applying the unfolding rule

UNFOLD(Q, $\mathcal{E}$, $\mathcal{S}$) to compute a finite (possibly partial) narrowing tree in $\mathcal{E}$ for each term t in Q, and return the set $\mathcal{L}$ of the (normalized) leaves of the tree. Then, instead of proceeding directly with the partial evaluation of the terms in $\mathcal{L}$, an abstraction operator ABSTRACT($Q, \mathcal{L}, B$) is applied that properly combines each uncovered term in $\mathcal{L}$ with the (already partially evaluated) terms of Q, so that the infinite growing of Q is avoided. The abstraction phase yields a new set of terms which may need further specialization and, thus, the process is iteratively repeated while new terms are introduced.

Algorithm 1 does not explicitly compute a partially evaluated theory $\mathcal{E}' = (\Sigma, B, E')$. It does so implicitly, by computing the set of partially evaluated terms Q' (that unambiguously determine E' as the set of resultants $t\sigma \Rightarrow r$ associated to the root-to-leaf derivations $t \leadsto_{\sigma, \overrightarrow{E_0}, B} r$ in the tree, with t in Q'), such that the closedness condition for E' modulo B w.r.t. Q' is satisfied.

3.1 Equational Homeomorphic Embedding

Partial evaluation involves two classical termination problems: the so-called *local* termination problem (the termination of unfolding, or how to control and keep the expansion of the narrowing trees finite, which is managed by an unfolding rule), and the *global* termination (which concerns termination of recursive unfolding, or how to stop recursively constructing more and more narrowing trees).

For local termination, we need to define the notion of *equational homeomorphic embedding* by extending the standard notion of homeomorphic embedding with order-sorted information and reasoning modulo axioms. Embedding is a structural preorder under which a term t is greater than, i.e., it embeds, another term t', written as $t \rhd t'$, if t' can be obtained from t by deleting some parts.

Embedding relations are very popular to ensure termination of *symbolic* transformations because, provided the signature is finite, for every infinite sequence of terms $t_1, t_2, \ldots$, there exist $i < j$ such that $t_i \trianglelefteq t_j$. Therefore, when iteratively computing a sequence $t_1, t_2, \ldots, t_n$, finiteness of the sequence can be guaranteed by using the embedding as a whistle [9]: whenever a new expression t_{n+1} is to be added to the sequence, we first check whether t_{n+1} embeds any of the expressions already in the sequence. If that is the case, we say that $\trianglelefteq$ whistles, i.e., it has detected (potential) non-termination and the computation has to be stopped. Otherwise, t_{n+1} can be safely added to the sequence and the computation proceeds. For instance, if we work modulo commutativity (C), we must stop a sequence where the term $u = \mathsf{s}(\mathsf{s}(\mathsf{s}(X + Y) * (\mathsf{s}(X) + 0))$ occurs after $v = \mathsf{s}(X) * \mathsf{s}(X + Y)$, since v embeds u modulo commutativity of $*$.

Definition 2 ((order-sorted) equational homeomorphic embedding).

Let $(\Sigma, B, \overrightarrow{E_0})$ be an equational theory decomposition. Let us introduce the following signature transformation $\Sigma \ni (f : s_1 \ldots s_n \to s) \mapsto (f : U \overset{n}{\ldots} U \to U) \in \Sigma^u$. Also, for any Σ-term t, t^u leaves the terms unchanged but regards all variables as unsorted. Consider the TRS $Emb(\Sigma)$ that consists of all rewrite rules[7] $f(X_1{:}U, \ldots, X_n{:}U) \rightarrow X_i{:}U$ for $f : A_1, \ldots, A_n \rightarrow A$ in Σ and $i \in \{1, \ldots, n\}$. For terms u and v we write $u \rhd_B v$ if $u \rightarrow^+_{Emb(\Sigma)/B} v'$ and v' is equal to v up to B-renaming (i.e., there is a renaming substitution σ such that $v =_B v'\sigma$). The relation $\unlhd_B$ is called B-embedding (or embedding modulo B).

By using this notion, we stop a branch $t \rightsquigarrow t'$ of a folding variant narrowing tree, if any narrowing redex $t'|_q$ of the leaf t' is embedded (modulo B) by the narrowing redex $u|_p$ of a preceding term u in the branch, i.e., $u|_p \unlhd_B t'|_q$.

Example 7 (Example 6 continued). Consider again the (partial) folding variant narrowing tree of Fig. 6. The narrowing redex $t{=}\texttt{flip(fix(2, e, flip(BG'); \{R2 I R1\}))}$ in the right branch of the tree embeds modulo ACU the tree root $u = \texttt{flip(fix(2, e, flip(BG)))}$, hence the unfolding of this branch is stopped.

3.2 Equational Abstraction via Equational Least General Generalization

For global termination, PE evaluation relies on an abstraction operation to ensure that the iterative construction of a sequence of partial narrowing trees terminates while still guaranteeing that the desired amount of specialization is retained and that the equational closedness condition is reached. In order to avoid constructing infinite sets, instead of just taking the union of the set $\mathscr{L}$ of non-closed terms in the leaves of the tree and the set Q of specialized calls, the sets Q and $\mathscr{L}$ are *generalized*. Hence, the abstraction operation returns a safe approximation A of $Q \cup \mathscr{L}$ so that each expression in the set $Q \cup \mathscr{L}$ is closed w.r.t. A. Let us show how we can define a suitable abstraction operator by using the notion of *equational least general generalization (lgg$_B$)* [2]. Unlike the syntactical, untyped case, there is in general no unique *lgg$_B$* in the framework of [2] but a finite, minimal and complete set of *lgg$_B$*'s for any two terms, so that any other generalizer has at least one of them as a B-instance.

More precisely, given the current set of already specialized calls Q, in order to add a set T of new terms, the function $\textsc{Abstract}^\circlearrowleft(Q, T, B)$ of Algorithm 1 is instantiated with the function of Definition 3 below, which relies on the notion of *best matching terms* (BMT), which is aimed at avoiding loss of specialization due to generalization. Roughly speaking, the function $BMT_B(U, t)$ determines the best matching terms for t in a set U of terms w.r.t. B, i.e., for each u_i in U, we compute the set W_i of *lgg$_B$*'s of t and u_i, and select the subset M of minimal upper bounds of the union $\bigcup_i W_i$. Then, $u_j \in BMT_B(Q, t)$ if at least one lgg element in the corresponding W_j belongs to M.

Example 8. Let $t = g(1) \oplus 1 \oplus g(Y)$, $U = \{1 \oplus g(X), X \oplus g(1), X \oplus Y\}$, and consider B to consist of the associative-commutative (AC) axioms for $\oplus$. To

---

[7] The expression $X{:}S$ represents an explicit definition of a variable X of sort S. It is worth noting that Maude automatically provides B-coherence completion of rules.

compute the best matching terms for t in U, we first compute the sets of lgg_B's of t with each u in U:

$$W_1 = lgg_{AC}(\{g(1) \oplus 1 \oplus g(Y), 1 \oplus g(X)\}) = \{(\{Z \oplus 1\}, \{Z/g(1) \oplus g(Y)\}, \{Z/g(X)\}),$$
$$(\{Z \oplus g(W)\}, \{Z/1 \oplus g(1), W/Y\}, \{Z/1, W/X\})\}$$
$$W_2 = lgg_{AC}(\{g(1) \oplus 1 \oplus g(Y), X \oplus g(1)\}) = \{(\{Z \oplus g(1)\}, \{Z/g(1) \oplus g(Y)\}, \{Z/X\})\}$$
$$W_3 = lgg_{AC}(\{g(1) \oplus 1 \oplus g(Y), X \oplus Y\}) = \{(\{Z \oplus W\}, \{Z/1, W/g(1) \oplus g(Y)\}, \{Z/X, W/Y\})\}$$

Now, the set M of minimal upper bounds of the set $W_1 \cup W_2 \cup W_3$ is $M = \{Z \oplus 1, Z \oplus g(1)\}$ and thus we have: $BMT_{AC}(S, t) = \{1 \oplus g(X), X \oplus g(1)\}$.

Definition 3 (equational abstraction operator). *Let $(\Sigma, B, \overrightarrow{E_0})$ be an equational theory decomposition. Let Q, T be two sets of $\overrightarrow{E_0}, B$-normalized terms. The abstraction function is:*

$$abs_B^{\circlearrowleft}(Q, T) = \begin{cases} abs_B^{\circlearrowleft}(\dots abs_B^{\circlearrowleft}(Q, \{t_1\}), \dots, \{t_n\}) & \text{if } T = \{t_1, \dots, t_n\}, n > 1 \\ Q & \text{if } T = \emptyset \ \text{ or } \ T = \{X\}, \text{with } X \in \mathscr{X} \\ abs_B^{\circlearrowleft}(Q, \{t_1, \dots, t_n\}) & \text{if } T = \{t\}, \text{with } t = c(t_1, \dots, t_n), \ c \in \mathscr{C}_{E_0} \\ generalize_B(Q, Q', t) & \text{if } T = \{t\}, \text{with } t = f(t_1, \dots, t_n), \ f \in \mathscr{D}_{E_0} \end{cases}$$

where $Q' = \{t' \in Q \mid root(t) = root(t') \text{ and } t' \trianglelefteq_B t\}$, and the function generalize is:

$$generalize_B(Q, \emptyset, t) = Q \cup \{t\}$$
$$generalize_B(Q, Q', t) = Q \ \text{if } t \text{ is } Q - closed$$
$$generalize_B(Q, Q', t) = abs_B^{\circlearrowleft}(Q \setminus BMT_B(Q', t), Q'' \downarrow_{\overrightarrow{E_0}, B})$$

where $Q'' = \{l \mid q \in BMT_B(Q', t), \langle w, \{\theta_1, \theta_2\}\rangle \in lgg_B(\{q, t\}), x \in \mathscr{D}om(\theta_1 \cup \theta_2), l \in \{w, x\theta_1, x\theta_2\}\}$.

Example 9 (Example 7 continued). Consider again the (partial) folding variant narrowing tree of Fig. 6 with the leaf $t = $ `flip(fix(2, e, flip(BG'); {R2 I R1}))` at the right branch of the tree and the tree root $u = $ `flip(fix(2, e, flip(BG)))`. We apply the abstraction operator with $Q = \{u\}$ and $T = \{t\}$. Since t is operation-rooted, we call $generalize_{ACU}(Q, Q', t)$ with $Q' = Q$, which calls $abs_{ACU}^{\circlearrowleft}(Q \setminus BMT_{ACU}(Q', t), Q'')$, where $Q'' = \{w, v\}$, $v = \{$`R2' I' R1'`$\}$, and $w = $ `flip(fix(2, e, flip(BG); BG'))` is the only ACU-lgg of u and t. We compute the best matching terms, i.e., $BMT_{ACU}(Q', t) = Q$. Then the call to $abs_{ACU}^{\circlearrowleft}$ returns the set $\{w\}$. However, this means that the previous folding narrowing tree of Fig. 6 is now discarded, since the previous set of input terms $Q = \{u\}$ is now replaced by $Q' = \{w\}$.

We start from scratch and the tree resulting for the new call w is showed in Fig. 7. The right leaf embeds the tree root and is B-closed w.r.t. it. The left leaf mt is a constructor term. For the middle leaf $t'' = $ {R2 I R1}; `flip(BG''')` the whistle `flip(BG'')` $\trianglelefteq_{ACU} t''$ blows and we stop the derivation. However, it is not B-closed w.r.t. w and we have to add it to the set Q', obtaining the new set of input terms $Q'' = \{w, $`flip(BG''')`$\}$. The specialization of the call `flip(BG''')` amounts to constructing the narrowing tree of Fig. 8, which is trivially ACU-closed w.r.t. its root.

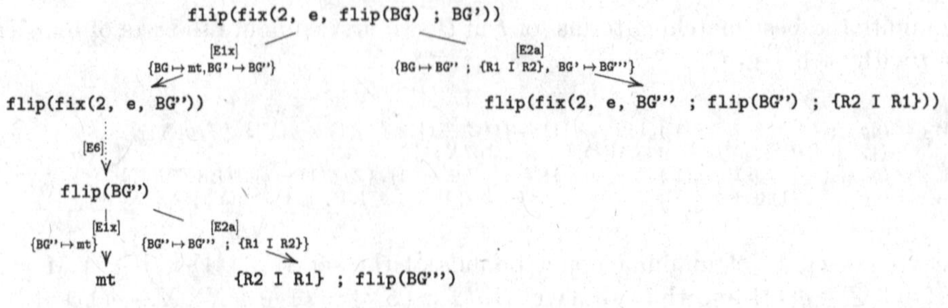

flip(fix(2, e, flip(BG) ; BG'))

[E1x]   {BG ↦ mt, BG' ↦ BG''}   [E2a]   {BG ↦ BG'' ; {R1 I R2}, BG' ↦ BG'''}

flip(fix(2, e, BG''))   flip(fix(2, e, BG''' ; flip(BG'') ; {R2 I R1}))

[E6]

flip(BG'')

[E1x]   {BG'' ↦ mt}   [E2a]   {BG'' ↦ BG''' ; {R1 I R2}}

mt   {R2 I R1} ; flip(BG''')

Fig. 7. Folding variant narrowing tree for the goal flip(fix(2, e, flip(BG); BG')).

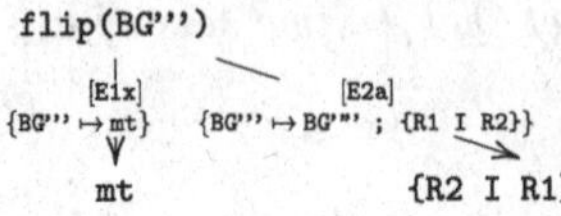

flip(BG''')

[E1x]   {BG''' ↦ mt}   [E2a]   {BG''' ↦ BG'''' ; {R1 I R2}}

mt   {R2 I R1} ; flip(BG'''')

Fig. 8. Folding variant narrowing tree for the goal flip(BG''').

Example 10 (Example 9 continued). Since the two trees in Figs. 7 and 8 do represent all possible computations for (any *ACU*-instance of) u = flip $(fix(2, e, flip(BG)))$, the partial evaluation process ends. Actually u is an instance of the root of the tree in Fig. 7 with {BG' ↦ mt} because of the identity axiom. Now we can extract the set of resultants $t\sigma \Rightarrow r$ associated to the root-to-leaf derivations $t \leadsto_{\sigma, \overrightarrow{E_0}, B} r$ in the two trees:

```
eq flip(fix(2, e, flip(mt))) = mt .
eq flip(fix(2, e, flip({R1 I R2} ; BG')))
 = flip(fix(2, e, flip(BG') ; {R2 I R1})) .
eq flip(fix(2, e, flip(mt) ; mt)) = mt .
eq flip(fix(2, e, flip(mt) ; BG ; {R1 I R2})) = {R2 I R1} ; flip(BG) .
eq flip(fix(2, e, flip({R1 I R2} ; BG) ; BG'))
 = flip(fix(2, e, flip(BG) ; {R2 I R1} ; BG')) .
eq flip(mt) = mt .
eq flip(BG ; {R1 I R2}) = {R2 I R1} ; flip(BG) .
```

The reader may have realized that the specialization call flip(fix(2, e,flip(BG))) should really return the same term BG, since the variable BG is of sort BinGraph instead of BinGraph?, i.e., flip(fix(2,e,flip(BG))) = BG. The resultants above traverse the given graph and return the same graph. Though the code may seem inefficient, we have considered this example to illustrate the different stages of partial evaluation. The following example shows how a better specialization program can be obtained.

Example 11. Let us now overload the flip operator, having simultaneously two declarations for flip that are related in the subsort ordering Bingraph < Bingraph?: "op flip : BinGraph -> BinGraph ." and "op flip : BinGraph? ->

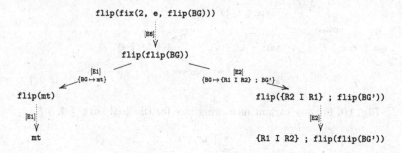

Fig. 9. Folding variant narrowing tree for the goal `flip(fix(2, e, flip(BG)))`.

BinGraph? .", and four equations: E1, E2, E2a, and E2b. By specializing the call
t = flip(fix(2,e,flip(BG))), the subtype definition of flip allows Maude
to simplify the term t using equation E6, which eliminates the occurrence of the
fix symbol. The narrowing tree for t is shown in Fig. 9. The narrowing tree is
B-closed w.r.t. the set of calls {flip(fix(2,e,flip(BG))),flip(flip(BG'))}.
This leads to the following, optimal specialized equations:

```
eq flip(fix(2,e,flip(mt))) = mt .
eq flip(fix(2,e,flip({R1 I R2} ; BG))) = {R1 I R2} ; flip(flip(BG)) .
eq flip(flip(mt)) = mt .
eq flip(flip({R1 I R2} ; BG)) = {R1 I R2} ; flip(flip(BG)) .
```

3.3   Equational Post-processing Renaming

The resulting partial evaluations might be further optimized by eliminating
redundant function symbols and unnecessary repetition of variables. Essentially,
we define a mapping ρ (*independent renaming*) that introduces a new function
symbol for each specialized term and then we replace, by means of a suitable
function $ren_\rho(u)$, each call u in the specialized program by a call to the corresponding renamed function.

Example 12 (Example 11 continued). Consider the following indepen-,
dent renaming for the specialized calls: {flip(flip(BG)) ↦ dflip(BG),
flip(fix(2,e,flip(BG))) ↦ flix(BG)}. The post-processing renaming derives
the renamed program

```
eq flix(mt) = mt .   eq flix({R1 I R2} ; BG) = {R1 I R2} ; dflip(BG) .
eq dflip(mt) = mt .  eq dflip({R1 I R2} ; BG') = {R1 I R2} ; dflip(BG') .
```

Example 13. Consider again the elementary parser defined in Example 1 and
the initial configuration init | L | Γ. The PE algorithm constructs the two
folding variant narrowing trees that are shown in Figs. 10 and 11. Now all leaves
in the trees are closed w.r.t. Q, and by applying the post-partial evaluation
transformation with the independent renaming ρ = {init | L | Γ ↦ finit(L),

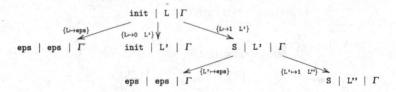

Fig. 10. Folding variant narrowing tree for the goal init | L | Γ.

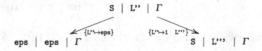

Fig. 11. Folding variant narrowing tree for the goal S | L'' | Γ.

S | L | Γ ↦ fS(L), eps | eps | Γ ↦ feps}, we get the following specialized program

```
eq finit(eps)   = feps .      eq finit(1) = feps .
eq fS(eps)  = feps .          eq finit(0 L)   = finit(L).
eq finit(1 1 L) = fS(L) .     eq fS(1 L)  = fS(L) .
```

that is even more efficient and readable than the specialized program shown in the Introduction. Note that we obtain "finit(1 eps) = feps" but it is simplified to "finit(1) = feps" modulo identity.

3.4 Strong Correctness

In this section we state the strong correctness of our partial evaluation method. Here $VN_{\mathscr{E}}^{\circlearrowleft}(u)$ represents the set of all folding variant narrowing sequences for u in $\mathscr{E}$.

Theorem 1 (Strong correctness). *Let $\mathscr{E} = (\Sigma, B, \overrightarrow{E_0})$ be a decomposition of an equational theory $(\Sigma, E_0 \uplus B)$, u be a Σ-term, and Q be a finite set of Σ-terms. Let ρ be an independent renaming of Q, $u' = ren_\rho(u)$ and $Q' = ren_\rho(Q)$. Let $\mathscr{E}' = (\Sigma, B, \overrightarrow{E_0'})$ be an EqNPE of $\mathscr{E}$ w.r.t. Q (under ρ). If $\overrightarrow{E_0'}$ and u' are closed modulo B w.r.t. Q', then $(u \rightsquigarrow^*_{\sigma, \overrightarrow{E_0}, B} v) \in VN_{\mathscr{E}}^{\circlearrowleft}(u)$ if and only if $(u' \rightsquigarrow^*_{\sigma', \overrightarrow{E_0'}, B} v') \in VN_{\mathscr{E}'}^{\circlearrowleft}(u)$, where $v' =_B ren_\rho(v)$.*

4 Experiments

We have implemented the transformation framework presented in this paper. We do not yet have an automated tool where one can give both a Maude program and an initial call, and the tool returns the specialized program. However, all the independent components are already available and we have performed

Table 1. Experimental results

Benchmark	Data	Original Time (ms)	PE before renaming Time (ms)	Improvement	PE after renaming Time (ms)	Improvement
Parser	100 k	164	39	76,22	33	79,88
	1 M	10.561	411	96,11	348	96,70
	5 M	275.334	2.058	99,25	1.685	99,39
Double-flip	100 k	188	143	23,94	76	59,57
	1 M	1.636	1.427	12,78	759	53,61
	5 M	8.425	7.503	10,94	4.100	51,34
Flip-fix	100 k	203	177	12,81	143	29,56
	1 M	1.955	1.778	9,05	1.427	27,01
	5 M	10.185	9.219	9,48	7.458	26,77
KMP	100 k	401	57	87,79	36	91,02
	1 M	3.872	531	86,29	331	91,45
	5 M	19.932	2.530	87,31	1.661	91,67

various experiments in a semi-automated way, i.e., we make calls to the different components already available without having a real interface yet: equational unfolding (by using folding variant narrowing already available in Maude; see [5]), equational closedness (we have implemented Definition 1 as a Maude program), equational embedding (we have implemented Definition 2 as a Maude program), and equational generalization and abstraction (we have implemented Definition 3 as a Maude program that invokes the lgg_B implementation of [2]).

Table 1 contains the experiments that we have performed using an Intel Core2 Quad CPU Q9300 (2.5 GHz) with 6 Gigabytes of RAM running Maude v2.7 and considering the average of ten executions for each test. These experiments are available at http://safe-tools.dsic.upv.es/victoria. We have considered the three Maude programs discussed in the paper: Parser (Example 1), Double-flip (Example 2), and Flip-fix (Example 3). We have also considered the classical KMP string pattern matcher [3]. For all four Maude programs, we consider input data of three different sizes: one hundred thousand elements, one million elements, and five million elements; elements here refer to graph nodes for Double-flip and Flip-fix, and list elements for Parser and KMP. We have benchmarked three versions of each program on these data: original program, partially evaluated program (before post-processing renaming), and final specialization (with post-processing renaming). The relative speedups that we achieved thanks to specialization are given in the Improvement column(s) and computed as the percentage 100 × (OriginalTime − PETime)/OriginalTime. For all the examples, the partially evaluated programs achieve a significant improvement in execution time when compared to the original program, both with and without renaming, but more noticeable after renaming. The average improvement for these benchmarks is 66.5%. Regarding the KMP test, the average improvement is 91,67%.

That is, the achieved speedup is 12 $(OriginalTime/PETime)$, which is comparable to the average speedup 14 of both the CPD-based partial evaluator ECCE [8] and the PE tool of [1] (actually, the generated residual programs are identical to [1] on this benchmark). This indicates thar our new partial evaluation scheme is a conservative extension of previous approaches on comparable examples. Moreover, matching modulo axioms such as associativity, commutativity, and identity are fairly expensive operations that are massively used in Maude, and can sometimes be drastically reduced after specialization (i.e., the Parser example moves from a program with ACU and Ur operators to a program without axioms). This transformation power can not be achieved by traditional NPE nor by competing on-line partial evaluation techniques, such as CPD or positive supercompilation [4].

5 Conclusion and Future Work

A complete partial evaluator for the entire Maude language requires dealing with some features not considered in this work, and to experiment with more refined heuristics that maximize the specialization power. Future implementation work will focus on automating the entire PE process for a large subset of the language, including conditional rules, memberships, and conditional equations. This, in turn, will necessitate some new developments in the Maude narrowing infrastructure. In this sense, advancing the present PE research ideas will be a significant driver of new symbolic reasoning features in Maude.

References

1. Albert, E., Hanus, M., Vidal, G.: A practical partial evaluation scheme for multi-paradigm declarative languages. J. Funct. Logic Programm. **2002** (2002)
2. Alpuente, M., Escobar, S., Espert, J., Meseguer, J.: A modular order-sorted equational generalization algorithm. Inf. Comput. **235**, 98–136 (2014)
3. Alpuente, M., Falaschi, M., Vidal, G.: Partial evaluation of functional logic programs. ACM Trans. Program. Lang. Syst. **20**(4), 768–844 (1998)
4. Alpuente, M., Falaschi, M., Vidal, G.: A unifying view of functional and logic program specialization. ACM Comput. Surv. **30**(3es), 9es (1998)
5. Clavel, M., Durán, F., Eker, S., Escobar, S., Lincoln, P., Martí-Oliet, N., Meseguer, J., Talcott, C.: Maude Manual (version 2.7), March 2015
6. Escobar, S., Sasse, R., Meseguer, J.: Folding variant narrowing and optimal variant termination. J. Log. Algebr. Program. **81**(7–8), 898–928 (2012)
7. Jones, N.D., Gomard, C.K., Sestoft, P.: Partial Evaluation and Automatic Program Generation. Prentice-Hall, Englewood Cliffs (1993)
8. Jørgensen, J., Leuschel, M., Martens, B.: Conjunctive partial deduction in practice. In: Gallagher, J. (ed.) LOPSTR 1996. LNCS, vol. 1207, pp. 59–82. Springer, Heidelberg (1997). doi:10.1007/3-540-62718-9_5
9. Leuschel, M.: Improving homeomorphic embedding for online termination. In: Flener, P. (ed.) LOPSTR 1998. LNCS, vol. 1559, pp. 199–218. Springer, Heidelberg (1999). doi:10.1007/3-540-48958-4_11
10. Slagle, J.R.: Automated theorem-proving for theories with simplifiers, commutativity and associativity. J. ACM **21**(4), 622–642 (1974)

A Formal, Resource Consumption-Preserving Translation of Actors to Haskell

Elvira Albert[1], Nikolaos Bezirgiannis[2], Frank de Boer[2],
and Enrique Martin-Martin[1(✉)]

[1] Universidad Complutense de Madrid, Madrid, Spain
elvira@sip.ucm.es, emartinm@ucm.es
[2] Centrum Wiskunde & Informatica (CWI), Amsterdam, Netherlands
n.bezirgiannis@cwi.nl, f.s.de.boer@cwi.nl

Abstract. We present a formal translation of an actor-based language with *cooperative scheduling* to the functional language Haskell. The translation is proven correct with respect to a formal semantics of the source language and a high-level operational semantics of the target, i.e. a subset of Haskell. The main correctness theorem is expressed in terms of a simulation relation between the operational semantics of actor programs and their translation. This allows us to then prove that the resource consumption is preserved over this translation, as we establish an equivalence of the cost of the original and Haskell-translated execution traces.

1 Introduction

Abstract Behavioural Specification (ABS) [9] is a formally-defined language for modeling actor-based programs. An actor program consists of computing entities called *actors*, each with a private state, and thread of control. Actors can communicate by exchanging messages asynchronously, i.e. without waiting for message delivery/reply. In ABS, the notion of actor corresponds to the *active object*, where objects are the concurrency units, i.e. each object conceptually has a dedicated thread of execution. Communication is based on asynchronous method calls where the caller object does not wait for the callee to reply with the method's return value. Instead, the object can later use a *future* variable [5,8] to extract the result of the asynchronous method. Each asynchronous method call adds a new *process* to the callee object's process queue. ABS supports *cooperative scheduling*, which means that inside an object, the active process can decide to explicitly suspend its execution so as to allow another process from the queue to execute. This way, the interleaving of processes inside an active object is textually controlled by the programmer, similar to coroutines [10]. However, flexible and state-dependent interleaving is still supported: in particular, a process may suspend its execution waiting for a reply to a method call.

This work was funded partially by the EU project FP7-ICT-610582 ENVISAGE: Engineering Virtualized Services (http://www.envisage-project.eu), by the Spanish MINECO projects TIN2012-38137 and TIN2015-69175-C4-2-R, and by the CM project S2013/ICE-3006.

M.V. Hermenegildo and P. Lopez-Garcia (Eds.): LOPSTR 2016, LNCS 10184, pp. 21–37, 2017.
DOI: 10.1007/978-3-319-63139-4_2

Whereas ABS has successfully been used to model [19], analyze [2], and verify [9] actor programs, the "real" execution of such programs has been a struggle, attributed to the fact that implementing cooperative scheduling efficiently can be hard (common languages as Java and C++ have to resort to instrumentation techniques, e.g. fibers [16]). This led to the creation of numerous ABS backends with different cooperative scheduling implementations:[1] ABS→Maude using an interpreter and term rewriting, ABS→Java using heavyweight threads and manual stack management, ABS→Erlang using lightweight threads and thread parking, ABS→Haskell using lightweight threads and continuations.

The overall contribution of this paper is a formal, resource-consumption preserving translation of the concurrency subset of the ABS language into Haskell, given as an adaptation of the canonical ABS→Haskell backend [4]. We opted for the Haskell backend relying on the hypothesis that Haskell serves as a better middleground between execution speed and most importantly semantic correctness. The translation is based on compiling ABS methods into Haskell functions with *continuations*—similar transformations have been performed in the actor-based Erlang language wrt. rewriting systems [14,18] and rewriting logic [13], in the translation of ABS to Prolog [3] and a subset of ABS to Scala [11]. However, what is unique in our translation and constitutes our main contribution, is that the translation is resource preserving as we prove in two steps:

- *Soundness.* We provide a formal statement of the soundness of this translation of ABS into Haskell which is expressed in terms of a simulation relation between the operational ABS semantics and the semantics of the generated Haskell code. The soundness claim ensures that every Haskell derivation has an equivalent one in ABS. However, since for efficiency reasons, the translation fixes a selection order between the objects and the processes within each object, we do not have a completeness result.
- *Resource-preservation.* As a corollary we have that the transformation preserves the resource consumption, i.e., the cost of the Haskell-translated program is the same as the original ABS program wrt. any *cost model* that assigns a cost to each ABS instruction, since both programs execute the same trace of ABS instructions. This result allows us to ensure that upper bounds on the resource consumption obtained by the analysis of the original ABS program are preserved during compilation and are thus valid bounds for the Haskell-translated program as well.

In Sect. 2 we specify the syntax of the source language and detail its operational semantics. Section 3 describes our target language and defines the compilation process. We present the correctness and resource preservation results in Sect. 4, as well as the intermediate semantics used in this process. In Sect. 5 we show that the runtime environment does not introduce any significant overhead when executing ABS instructions, and show that the upper bounds obtained by the cost analysis are sound. Finally, Sect. 6 contains the conclusions and future work.

---

[1] See http://abs-models.org/documentation/manual/#-abs-backends for more information about ABS backends.

$S ::= x:=E \mid f:=x!m(\bar{y})$
$\quad \mid$ await $f \mid$ skip $\mid$ return z
$\quad \mid S_1;S_2 \mid$ if $B\ \{S\}$ else $\{S\}$
$\quad \mid$ while $B\ \{S\}$
$E ::= V \mid$ new $\mid f.$get $\mid m(\bar{y})$
$V ::= x \mid r \mid I$
$B ::= B \wedge B \mid B \vee B \mid \neg B \mid V \equiv V$
$D ::= m(\bar{r})\{\ S\ \}$
$P ::= \overline{D} : $ main()$\{\ S\ \}$

```
1  main() {                9   r2 = f2.get;
2    node1 = new;          10    r = reduce(r1,r2);
3    node2 = new;          11    return r; }
4    f1 = node1!map(v1);   12
5    f2 = node2!map(v2);   13  map(v) {
6    await f1;             14    ... }
7    await f2;             15  reduce(v1,v2) {
8    r1 = f1.get;          16    ... }
```

Fig. 1. (a) syntax of source language (b) a simplified MapReduce task in ABS

Complete proofs of the theoretical results can be found at http://gpd.sip.ucm. es/enrique/publications/lopstr16_ext.pdf.

2   Source Language

Our language is based on ABS [9], a statically-typed, actor-based language with a purely-functional core (ADTs, functions, parametric polymorphism) and an object-based imperative layer: objects with private-only attributes, and interfaces that serve as types to the objects. ABS extends the OO paradigm with support for *asynchronous* method calls; each call results in a new *future* (placeholder for the method's result) returned to the caller-object, and a new process (stored in the callee-object's process queue) which runs the method's activation. The active process inside an object (only one at any given time) may decide to explicitly suspend its execution so as to allow another process from the same queue to execute.

In this paper, we simplify ABS to its subset that concerns the concurrent interaction of processes (inside and between objects), so as to focus solely on the more challenging part of proving correctness of the cooperative concurrency. In other words, the ABS language is stripped of its functional core, local variables, object groups [15] and types (we assume the input programs are well-typed w.r.t ABS type-system). The formal syntax of the statements S of the subset is shown in Fig. 1(a). Values in our subset are references (object or futures) and integer numbers; values can be stored in method's formal parameters or attributes. We syntactically distinguish between method parameters r and attributes. The attributes are further distinguished for the values they hold: attributes holding object references or integer values (denoted by $x, y, z \ldots$), and future attributes holding future references (denoted by f). An assignment $f:=x!m(\bar{y})$ stores to the future attribute f a new future reference returned by asynchronously calling the method m on the object attribute x passing as arguments the values of object attributes $\bar{y}$. An assignment $x:=E$ stores to an object attribute the result of executing the right-hand side E. A right-hand side can be the value of a method parameter r, an attribute x, an integer expression I (an integer value, addition, subtraction, etc.), a reference to a new object new, the result of a synchronous same-object method call $m(\bar{y})$, or the result of an asynchronous method call f.get stored in the future attribute f. A call to f.get will block the object and all its processes until the result of the asynchronous call is ready. The statement await f may be used (usually before calling f.get) to instead release the current process until the result of f has been computed, allowing another same-object process to execute. Sequential composition of two statements S_1 and S_2 is denoted by $S_1; S_2$. The Boolean condition B in the *if* and *while* statement is a Boolean combination of reference equality between values of attributes. Again, note that, we assume expressions to be well-typed: integer expressions cannot contain futures or object references and boolean equality is between same-type values. The statement return z returns the value of the attribute z both in synchronous and asynchronous method calls. A method declaration D maps a method's name and formal parameters to a statement S (method body). We consider that every method has one return and it is the final statement. Finally, a program P is a set of method declarations $\bar{D}$ and a special method main that has no formal parameters and acts as the program's entry point.

The program of Fig. 1(b) shows a basic version of a MapReduce task [7] implemented using actors in ABS. For clarity the example uses only two *map* nodes and a single *reduce* computation performed in the controller node (the actor running main). First the controller creates two objects node1 and node2 (L2–L3), and invokes asynchronously map with different values v_1 and v_2 (L4–L5). In MapReduce, all map invocations must finish before executing the *reduce* phase: therefore, the await instructions in L6–L7 wait for the termination of the two calls to map, releasing the processor so that any other process in the same object of main can execute. Once they have finished, the get statements in L8-L9 obtain the results from the futures f1 and f2. Although get statements block the object (in this case *main*) and all of its processes until the result is ready, this does not occur in our example because the preceding awaits assure the result is available. Finally, L10 contains a synchronous-method self call to reduce that combines the partial results from the *map* phase.

2.1   Operational Semantics

In order to describe the operational semantics of the language defined above we first introduce the following concepts and assumptions. We consider a set $\mathcal{A}$ of attributes and $\mathcal{P}$ of method parameters. The values considered in this paper are in the *Int* set: integer constants and dynamically generated references to objects and futures. We denote by $\Sigma = \mathcal{A} \rightarrow Int$ the set of assignments of values to the attributes (of an object), with empty element ϵ. A closure consists of a statement S obtained by replacing its free variables by actual values (note that variables are introduced as method parameters and can only appear in E) and a future reference, represented by an integer, for storing the return value. By $S\tau$, where $\tau \in \mathcal{P} \rightarrow Int$, we denote the instantiation obtained from S by replacing each variable x in S by $\tau(x)$. Finally, we represent the global heap h by a triple (n, h_1, h_2) consisting of an integer number n and *partial* functions (with finite disjoint domains) $h_1 : Int \rightarrow \Sigma$ and $h_2 : Int \rightarrow Int_\perp$, where $Int_\perp = Int \cup \{\perp\}$ ($\perp$

$$\text{(Assign)} \frac{\texttt{getVal}(h(n), V) = v \quad h' = h[(n)(x) \mapsto v)]}{\langle n : (\texttt{x:=}V; S, l) \cdot Q, h \rangle \rightarrow \langle n : (S, l) \cdot Q, h' \rangle}$$

$$\text{(New)} \frac{h(count) = m \quad h' = h[(n)(x) \mapsto m, (m) \mapsto \epsilon, count \mapsto m + 1]}{\langle n : (\texttt{x:=new}; S, l) \cdot Q, h \rangle \rightarrow \langle n : (S, l) \cdot Q, h' \rangle}$$

$$\text{(Get)} \frac{h(h(n)(f)) \neq \bot \quad h' = h[(n)(x) \mapsto h(h(n)(f))]}{\langle n : (\texttt{x:=f.get}; S, l) \cdot Q, h \rangle \rightarrow \langle n : (S, l) \cdot Q, h' \rangle}$$

$$\text{(Await I)} \frac{h(h(n)(f)) \neq \bot}{\langle n : (\texttt{await f}; S, l) \cdot Q, h \rangle \rightarrow \langle n : (S, l) \cdot Q, h \rangle}$$

$$\text{(Await II)} \frac{h(h(n)(f)) = \bot}{\langle n : (\texttt{await f}; S, l) \cdot Q, h \rangle \rightarrow \langle n : Q \cdot (\texttt{await f}; S, l), h \rangle}$$

$$\text{(Async)} \frac{\begin{array}{c} h(n)(x) = d \quad h(count) = l' \quad \bar{v} = h(n)(\bar{z}) \\ h' = h[(n)(f) \mapsto l', (l') \mapsto \bot, count \mapsto l' + 1] \end{array}}{\langle n : (\texttt{f:=x!m}(\bar{z}); S, l) \cdot Q, h \rangle \xrightarrow{d.m(l', \bar{v})} \langle n : (S, l) \cdot Q, h' \rangle}$$

$$\text{(Sync)} \frac{(m(\bar{w}) \mapsto S_m) \in D \quad \tau = [\bar{w} \mapsto h(n)(\bar{z})] \quad S' = \widehat{(S_m \tau)}^x}{\langle n : (\texttt{x:=m}(\bar{z}); S, l) \cdot Q, h \rangle \rightarrow \langle n : (S'; S, l) \cdot Q, h \rangle}$$

$$\text{(Return}_A) \frac{h' = h[(l) \mapsto h(n)(x)]}{\langle n : (\textbf{return}^* \texttt{x}; S, l) \cdot Q, h \rangle \rightarrow \langle n : Q, h' \rangle}$$

$$\text{(Return}_S) \frac{h' = h[(n)(z) \mapsto h(n)(x)]}{\langle n : (\textbf{return}^z \texttt{ x}; S, l) \cdot Q, h \rangle \rightarrow \langle n : (S, l) \cdot Q, h' \rangle}$$

Fig. 2. Operational semantics: Local rules

is used to denote "undefined"). The number n is used to generate references to new objects and futures. The function h_1 specifies for each existing object, i.e., a number n such $h_1(n)$ is defined, its *local* state. The function h_2 specifies for each existing future reference, i.e., a number n such $h_2(n)$ is defined, its return value (absence of which is indicated by $\bot$). In the sequel we will simply denote the first component of h by $h(count)$, and write $h(n)(x)$, instead of $h_1(n)(x)$, and $h(n)$, instead of $h_2(n)$. We will use the notation $h[count \mapsto n]$ to generate a heap equal to h but with the counter set to n. A similar notation $h[n \mapsto \bot]$ will be used for future variables, $h[(n)(x) \mapsto v]$ for storing the value v in the variable x in object n and $h[n \mapsto \epsilon]$ for initializing the mapping of an object.

An object's *local* configuration denoted by the (object) reference n consists of a pair $\langle n : Q, h \rangle$ where Q is a list of closures and h is the global heap. We use $\cdot$ to concatenate lists, i.e., $(S, l) \cdot Q$ represents a list where (S, l) is the head and Q is the tail. A *global* configuration—denoted with the letters A and B—is a pair $\langle C, h \rangle$ containing a set of lists of closures $C = \{\overline{Q}\}$ and a global heap h. Figure 2 contains the relation that describes the local behavior of an object (omitting the standard rules for sequential composition, **if** and **while** statements). Note that the first closure of the list Q is the active process of the

$$(\text{INTERNAL})\frac{\langle n:Q,h\rangle \rightarrow \langle n:Q',h'\rangle}{\langle (n:Q)\cup C,h\rangle \rightarrow \langle (n:Q')\cup C,h'\rangle}$$

$$(\text{MESSAGE})\frac{\langle n:Q_n,h\rangle \xrightarrow{d.m(l',\bar{v})} \langle n:Q',h'\rangle \qquad m(\bar{w})\mapsto S_m \in D \qquad \tau = [\bar{w}\mapsto \bar{v}] \qquad S' = \widehat{(S_m\tau)}^*}{\langle (n:Q_n)\cup (d:Q_d)\cup C,h\rangle \rightarrow \langle (n:Q')\cup (d:Q_d\cdot (S',l'))\cup C,h'\rangle}$$

Fig. 3. Operational semantics: Global rules

object, so the different rules process the first statement of this closure. When the active process finishes or releases the object in an `await` statement, the next process in the list will become active, following a FIFO policy. The rule (ASSIGN) modifies the heap storing the new value of variable x of object n. It uses the function $\texttt{getVal}(\Sigma, V)$ to evaluate an expression V involving integer constants and variables in the object's current state Σ. The (NEW) rule stores a new object reference in variable x, increments the counter of objects references and inserts an empty mapping ϵ for the variables of the new object m. Rule (GET) can only be applied if the future is available, i.e., if its value is not $\perp$. In that case, the value of the future is stored in the variable x. Both rules (AWAIT I) and (AWAIT II) deal with `await` statements. If the future f is available, it continues with the same process. Otherwise it moves the current process to the end of the queue, thus avoiding starvation. Note that the `await` statement is not consumed, as it must be checked when the process becomes active again. When invoking the method m asynchronously in rule (ASYNC) the destination object d and the values of the parameters $\bar{r}$ are computed. Then a new future reference l initialized to $\perp$ is stored in the variable f, and the counter is incremented. The information about the new process that must be created is included as the decoration $d.m(l',\bar{v})$ of the step. Synchronous calls—rule (SYNC)—extend the active task with the statements of the method body, where the parameters have been replaced by their value using the substitution τ. In order to return the value of the method and store it in the variable x, the `return` statement of the body is marked with the destination variable x, called *write-back variable*. This marking is formalized in the $\widehat{\cdot}^s$ function, defined as follows (recall that `return` is the last statement of any method):

$$\widehat{S}^s = \begin{cases} S_1;\widehat{S_2}^s & \text{if } S = S_1; S_2, \\ \textbf{return}^s \text{ z} & \text{if } S = \textbf{return z}, \\ S & \text{i.o.c.} \end{cases}$$

Rule (RETURN$_A$) finishes an asynchronous method invocation (in this case the `return` keyword is marked with *, see rule (MESSAGE) in Fig. 3), so it removes the current process and stores the final value in the future l. On the other hand, rule (RETURN$_S$) finishes a synchronous method invocation (marked with the write-back variable), so it behaves like a `z:=x` statement.

Based on the previous rules, Fig. 3 shows the relation describing the global behavior of configurations. The (INTERNAL) rule applies any of the rules in Fig. 2, except (ASYNC), in any of the objects. The (MESSAGE) rule applies the rule (ASYNC) in any of the objects. It creates a new closure $(\widehat{S_m\tau}^*, l')$ for the new process invoking the method m, and inserts it at the back of the list of the destination object d. Note the use of $\widehat{\cdot}^*$ to mark that the return statement corresponds to an asynchronous invocation. Note that in both (INTERNAL) and (MESSAGE) rules the selection of the object to execute is non-deterministic. When needed, we decorate both local and global steps with object reference n and statement S executed, i.e., $\langle n : Q, h \rangle \rightarrow^n_S \langle n : Q', h' \rangle$ and $\langle C, h \rangle \rightarrow^n_S \langle C', h' \rangle$.

We remark that the operational semantics shown in Figs. 2 and 3 is very similar to the foundational ABS semantics presented in [9], considering that every object is a *concurrent object group*. The main difference is the representation of configurations: in [9] configurations are sets of futures and objects that contain their local stores, whereas in our semantics all the local stores and futures are merged in a global heap. Finally, our operational semantics considers a FIFO policy in the processes of an object, whereas [9] left the scheduling policy unspecified.

3 Target Language

Our ABS subset is translated to Haskell with coroutines. A coroutine is a generalization of a subroutine: besides the usual entry-point/return-point of a procedure a coroutine can have other entry/exit points, at intermediate locations of the procedure's body. Simply put, a coroutine does not have to run to completion; the programmer can specify places where a coroutine can suspend and later resume exactly where it left off.

Coroutines can be implemented natively on top of programming languages that support first-class *continuations* (which subsequently require support for closures and tail-call optimization). A continuation with reference to a program's point of execution, is a datastructure that captures what the remaining of the program does (after the point). As an example, consider the Haskell program at Fig. 4(a). The continuation of the call to (even 3) at L2 is $\lambda a \rightarrow$ print a, assuming a is the result of call to even and the continuation is represented as a function. The continuation of (mod x 2) at L1 is the function $\lambda a \rightarrow$ print (eq a 0) where x is bound by the even function and a is the result of (mod x 2). Abstracting over any program, an expression with type expr :: a has a continuation k with type k :: (a → r) with a being the expression's result type and r the program's overall result type. To benefit from continuations (and thus coroutines), a program has to be transformed in the so-called *continuation-passing style* (CPS): a function definition of the program f :: args → a is rewritten to take its current continuation as an extra last argument, as in f ':: args → (a → r) → r. A function call is also rewritten to apply this extra argument with the actual continuation at point.

A CPS transformation can be applied to all functions of a program, as in the example of Fig. 4(b), or (for efficiency reasons) to only the subset that relies

```
1 even x = eq (mod x 2) 0
2 main = print (even 3)
```

```
1 mod' x y k = k (mod x y)
2 eq' x y k = k (eq x y)
3 even' x k = mod' x 2 (λ a → eq' a 0 k)
4 main = even' 3 (λ a → print a)
```

Fig. 4. (a) Example program in direct style and (b) translated to CPS

on continuation support, e.g. only those functions that need to suspend/resume. For our case, ABS is translated to Haskell with CPS applied only to statements and methods, but not (sub)expressions. Continuations have the type k :: a → Stm where Stm is a recursive datatype with each one of its constructors being a statement, and the recursive position being the statement's current continuation. Stm being the program's overall result type (Stm ≡ r), reveals the fact that the translation of ABS constructs a Haskell AST-like datatype "knitted" with CPS (Fig. 5), which will only later be interpreted at runtime (Sect. 3.1): capturing the continuation of an ABS process allows us to save the process' state (e.g. call stack) and rest of statements as data. For technical convenience, our statements and methods do not directly pass results among each other but only indirectly through the state (heap); thus, we can reduce our continuation type to k :: () → Stm and further to the "nullary" function k :: Stm. Accordingly the CPS type of our methods (functions) and statements (constructors) becomes f' :: args → Stm → Stm. Worth to mention in Fig. 5 is that the body of While statement and the two branch bodies of If can be thought of as functions with no args written also in CPS (thus type Stm → Stm) to "tie" each body's last statement to the continuation *after* executing the control structure.

A Method definition is a CPS function that takes as input a list [Ref] of the method's parameters (passed by reference), the callee object named this, a *writeback* reference (Maybe Ref), and last its current continuation Stm. In case of synchronous call the callee method indirectly writes the Return value to the writeback reference of the heap and the execution jumps back to the caller by invoking the method's continuation; in case of asynchronous call the writeback is empty, the return value is stored to the caller's future (destiny) and the method's continuation is invoked resulting to the exit of the ABS process. An object or future reference Ref is represented by an integer index to the program's global heap array; similarly, an object attribute Attr is an integer index to an internal-to-the-object attribute array, hence shallow-embedded (compared to embedding the actual name of the attribute). Values (V) in our language can be this-object attributes (A), parameters to the method (P), integer literals (I), and integer arithmetic on those values (Add, Sub...). The right-hand side (Rhs) of an assignment directly reflects that of the source language. Boolean expressions are only appearing as predicates to If and While and are inductively constructed by the datatype B, that represents reference and integer comparison.

The compilation of statements is shown in Fig. 6. The translation $^s[\![S]\!]_{k,wb}$ takes two arguments: the continuation k and the writeback reference wb.

```
type Method = [Ref] → Ref → Maybe Ref → Stm → Stm
data Stm where  -- (formatted in GADT syntax)
   Skip   :: Stm → Stm
   Await  :: Attr → Stm → Stm
   Assign :: Attr → Rhs → Stm → Stm
   If     :: B → (Stm→Stm) → (Stm→Stm) → Stm → Stm
   While  :: B → (Stm→Stm) → Stm → Stm
   Return :: Attr → Maybe Ref → Stm → Stm
data Rhs = Val V                type Ref = Int
       | New                    type Attr = Int
       | Get Attr               data B = B :∧ B | B :∨ B | :¬ B | V :≡ V
       | Async Attr Method [Attr]  data V = A Ref | P Ref | I Int
       | Sync Method [Attr]        | Add V V | Sub V V ...
```

Fig. 5. The syntax and types of the target language. Continuations are wave-underlined. The program/process final result type is double-underlined

$$^s[\![\text{skip}]\!]_{k,wb} = \text{Skip } k \qquad\qquad ^s[\![\text{x:=}V]\!]_{k,wb} = \text{Assign } x \ ^V[\![V]\!] \ k$$
$$^s[\![\text{await f}]\!]_{k,wb} = \text{Await } f \ k \qquad\quad ^s[\![\text{x:=new}]\!]_{k,wb} = \text{Assign } x \ \text{New } k$$
$$^s[\![\text{return x}]\!]_{k,wb} = \text{Return } x \ wb \ k \qquad ^s[\![\text{x:=f.get}]\!]_{k,wb} = \text{Assign } x \ (\text{Get } f) \ k$$
$$^s[\![\text{return}^*\text{ x}]\!]_{k,wb} = \text{Return } x \ \text{Nothing } k \quad ^s[\![\text{x:=y!m}(\bar{z})]\!]_{k,wb} = \text{Assign } x \ (\text{Async } y \ m \ \bar{z}) \ k$$
$$^s[\![\text{return}^z\text{ x}]\!]_{k,wb} = \text{Return } x \ (\text{Just } z) \ k \quad ^s[\![\text{x:=m}(\bar{z})]\!]_{k,wb} = \text{Assign } x \ (\text{Sync } m \ \bar{z}) \ k$$
$$^s[\![S_1; S_2]\!]_{k,wb} = \ ^s[\![S_1]\!]_{k',wb} \text{ with } k' = \ ^s[\![S_2]\!]_{k,wb}$$
$$^s[\![\text{if } B \ \{S_1\} \text{ else } \{S_2\}]\!]_{k,wb} = \text{If } ^B[\![B]\!] \ (\backslash k' \to \ ^s[\![\ _1]\!]_{k',wb}) \ (\backslash k' \to \ ^s[\![S_2]\!]_{k',wb}) \ k$$
$$^s[\![\text{while } B \ \{S\}]\!]_{k,wb} = \text{While } ^B[\![B]\!] \ (\backslash k' \to \ ^s[\![S]\!]_{k',wb}) \ k$$

$$^m[\![m]\!] = (\text{m l this wb k} = \ ^s[\![S_m]\!]_{k,wb})$$
where $m(\bar{w}) \mapsto S_m \in D$ and l is the Haskell list that contains
the same elements as the sequence $\bar{w}$

Fig. 6. Translation of ABS-subset programs to Haskell AST

Each statement is translated into its Haskell counterpart, followed by the continuation k. The multiple rules for the **return** statement are due to the different uses of the translation: when compiling methods the **return** statement will appear unmarked, so we include the writeback passed as an argument; otherwise it is used to translate runtime configurations, so **return** statements will appear marked and we generate the writeback related to the mark. When omitted, we assume the default values $k = \text{undefined}$ and $wb = \text{Nothing}$ for the $^s[\![S]\!]_{k,wb}$ translation. $^B[\![B]\!]$ represents the translation of a boolean expression B, and $^V[\![V]\!]$ the translation of integer expressions, references or variables. A method definition translates to a Haskell function that includes the compiled body.

3.1 Runtime Execution

The program heap is implemented as the triple: array of objects, array of futures and a Int counter. Every cell in the objects-array designates 1 object holding a

```
1 main, map, reduce :: Method        10   Assign r2 (Get f2) $
2 main [] this wb k =                 11   Assign r (Sync reduce [r1,r2]) $
3   Assign node1 New $                12   Return r wb k
4   Assign node2 New $                13
5   Assign f1 (Async node1 map [v1])$ 14 map [v] this wb k = ...
6   Assign f2 (Async node2 map [v2])$ 15 reduce [a,b] this wb k = ...
7   Await f1 $                        16
8   Await f2 $                        17 -- Position in the attribute array
9   Assign r1 (Get f1) $              18 [node1,node2,f1,f2,r1,r2,r] = [0..]
```

Fig. 7. The Haskell-translated running example of MapReduce

pair of its attribute array and process queue (double-ended) in Haskell `IOVector` (`IOVector Ref, Seq Proc`). A cell in futures-array denotes a future which is either unresolved with a number of listener-objects `awaiting` for it to be completed, or resolved with a final value, i.e. `IOVector (Either [Ref] Ref)`. An ever-increasing counter is used to pick new references; when it reaches the arrays' current size both of the arrays double in size (i.e. dynamic arrays). The size of all attribute arrays, however, is fixed and predetermined at compile-time, by inspecting the source code (as shown in L18 of Fig. 7).

An `eval` function accepts a `this` object reference and the current heap and executes a single statement of the head process in the process queue, returning a new heap and those objects that have become active after the execution (`eval this heap :: IO(Heap, [Ref])`). An `await` executed statement will put its continuation (current process) in the tail of the process queue, effectively enabling cooperative multitasking, whereas all others will keep it as the head. A `Return` executed statement originating from an asynchronous call is responsible for re-activating the objects that are blocked on its resolved future. A global scheduler "trampolines" over a queue of active objects: it calls `eval` on the head object, puts the newly-activated objects in the tail of the queue, and loops until no objects are left in the queue—meaning the ABS program is either finished or deadlocked. At any point in time, the pair of the scheduler's object queue with the heap comprise the program's state.

Comparison. The described target language is an untyped extract of the canonical ABS-Haskell backend [4], with the main difference being that ABS statements are translated to an AST interpreted by `eval` function, while the canonical version compiles statements down to native code, which naturally yields faster execution. However, this deep embedding of an AST allows multiple interpretations of the syntax: debug the syntax tree and have an equivalence result. At runtime, the `eval` function operates in "lockstep" (i.e. executing one CPS statement at a time) whereas the canonical backend applies CPS between release points (`await`, `get` and `return` from asynchronous calls) which benefits in performance but would otherwise make reasoning about correctness and resource preservation for this setup more involved. Another argument for lockstep execution is that we can "simulate" a global Haskell-runtime scheduler (with a N:1 threading model) and include it in our proofs, instead of reasoning for the lower-level C internals of the GHC runtime thread scheduler (with M:N parallelism).

Our target language is also related to *Coroutining Logic Engines* presented in [17] for concurrent Prolog. These engines encapsulate multi-threading by providing entities that evaluate goals and yield answers when requested. They follow a similar coroutining approach, however, logic engines can produce several results, whereas asynchronous methods can be suspended by the scheduler many times but they only generate one result when they finish.

4 Correctness and Resource Preservation

To prove that the translation is correct and resource preserving, we use an intermediate semantics $\rightarrowtail$ closer to the Haskell programs. This semantics, depicted in Fig. 8, considers configurations $(h, [\overline{o_m}])$ where all the information of the objects is stored in a unified heap—concretely $h(o_n)(\mathcal{Q})$ returns the process queue of object o_n. The semantics in Fig. 8 presents two main differences w.r.t. that in Figs. 2 and 3 of Sect. 2. First, the list $[\overline{o_m}]$ is used to apply a *round-robin* policy: the first unblocked object[2] o_n in $[\overline{o_m}]$ is selected using $next(h, [\overline{o_m}])$, the first statement of the active process of o_n is executed and then the list is updated to continue with the object o_{n+1}. The other difference is that process queues do not contain sequences of statements but *continuations*, as explained in the previous section. To generate these continuation rules (ASYNC) and (SYNC) invoke the translation of the methods m with the adequate parameters. Nevertheless, the rules of the $\rightarrowtail$ semantics correspond with the semantic rules in Sect. 2.

Given a list $[\overline{o_m}]$ we use the notation $[\overline{o_{i \to k}}]$ for the sublist $[o_i, o_{i+i}, \ldots, o_k]$, and the operator $(:)$ for list concatenation. In the rules (ASYNC) and (RETURN$_A$), where the object list can increase or decrease one object, we use the following auxiliary functions. $newQ_{add}([\overline{o_m}], o_n, o_y)$ inserts the object o_y into $[\overline{o_m}]$ if it is new (i.e., it does not appear in $[\overline{o_m}]$), and $newQ_{del}([\overline{o_m}], o_n, q_n)$ removes the object o_n from $[\overline{o_m}]$ if its process queue q_n is empty. In both cases they advance the list of objects to o_{n+1}.

$$newQ_{add}([\overline{o_m}], o_n, o_y) = \begin{cases} [\overline{o_{n+1 \to m}}] : [\overline{o_{1 \to n}}] & \text{if } o_y \in [\overline{o_m}] \\ [\overline{o_{n+1 \to m}}] : [\overline{o_{1 \to n}}] : [o_y] & \text{if } o_y \notin [\overline{o_m}] \end{cases}$$

$$newQ_{del}([\overline{o_m}], o_n, q_n) = \begin{cases} [\overline{o_{n+1 \to m}}] : [\overline{o_{1 \to n-1}}] & \text{if } q_n = \epsilon \\ [\overline{o_{n+1 \to m}}] : [\overline{o_{1 \to n}}] & \text{if } q_n \neq \epsilon \end{cases}$$

In order to reason about the different semantics, we define the translation from runtime configurations $\langle C, h \rangle$ of Sect. 2 to concrete Haskell data structures used in the intermediate $\rightarrowtail$ semantics and in the compiled Haskell programs (see Fig. 9). The set of closure lists C is translated into a list of object references, and the process queues inside C are included into the heap related to the special term $\mathcal{Q}$. Although we use the same notation h, we consider that the heap is translated into the corresponding Haskell tuple (*object_vector, future_vector, counter*)

---

[2] Object whose active process is not waiting for a future variable in a `get` statement.

$$\text{(Assign)} \frac{\begin{array}{cc} next(h, [\overline{o_m}]) = o_n & h(o_n)(\mathcal{Q}) = (\texttt{Assign } x \; V \; k', l) \cdot q \\ \texttt{getVal}(h(o_n), V) = v & h' = h[(o_n)(x) \mapsto v, (o_n)(\mathcal{Q}) \mapsto (k', l) \cdot q] \end{array}}{(h, [\overline{o_m}]) \rightarrowtail (h', [\overline{o_{n+1 \to m}}] : [\overline{o_{1 \to n}}])}$$

$$\text{(New)} \frac{\begin{array}{c} next(h, [\overline{o_m}]) = o_n \qquad h(o_n)(\mathcal{Q}) = (\texttt{Assign } x \; \texttt{New } k', l) \cdot q \\ h(count) = o_{new} \qquad h' = h[(o_n)(x) \mapsto o_{new}, count \mapsto o_{new} + 1, \\ (o_{new})(\mathcal{Q}) \mapsto \epsilon, (o_n)(\mathcal{Q}) \mapsto (k', l) \cdot q] \end{array}}{(h, [\overline{o_m}]) \rightarrowtail (h', [\overline{o_{n+1 \to m}}] : [\overline{o_{1 \to n}}])}$$

$$\text{(Get)} \frac{\begin{array}{cc} next(h, [\overline{o_m}]) = o_n & h(o_n)(\mathcal{Q}) = (\texttt{Assign } x \; (\texttt{Get } f) \; k', l) \cdot q \\ h(h(o_n)(f)) = \texttt{Right } v & h' = h[(o_n)(x) \mapsto v, (o_n)(\mathcal{Q}) \mapsto (k', l) \cdot q] \end{array}}{(h, [\overline{o_m}]) \rightarrowtail (h', [\overline{o_{n+1 \to m}}] : [\overline{o_{1 \to n}}])}$$

$$\text{(Await I)} \frac{\begin{array}{cc} next(h, [\overline{o_m}]) = o_n & h(o_n)(\mathcal{Q}) = (\texttt{Await } f \; k', l) \cdot q \\ h(h(o_n)(f)) = \texttt{Right } v & h' = h[(o_n)(\mathcal{Q}) \mapsto (k', l) \cdot q] \end{array}}{(h, [\overline{o_m}]) \rightarrowtail (h', [\overline{o_{n+1 \to m}}] : [\overline{o_{1 \to n}}])}$$

$$\text{(Await II)} \frac{\begin{array}{cc} next(h, [\overline{o_m}]) = o_n & h(o_n)(\mathcal{Q}) = (\texttt{Await } f \; k', l) \cdot q \\ h(h(o_n)(f)) = \texttt{Left } e & h' = h[(o_n)(\mathcal{Q}) \mapsto q \cdot (\texttt{Await } f \; k', l)] \end{array}}{(h, [\overline{o_m}]) \rightarrowtail (h', [\overline{o_{n+1 \to m}}] : [\overline{o_{1 \to n}}])}$$

$$\text{(Async)} \frac{\begin{array}{c} next(h, [\overline{o_m}]) = o_n \qquad h(o_n)(\mathcal{Q}) = (\texttt{Assign } f \; (\texttt{Async } x \; m \; \bar{z}) \; k', l) \cdot q \\ h(count) = l' \qquad h(o_n)(x) = o_x \qquad h(o_x)(\mathcal{Q}) = q_x \qquad (m(\bar{w}) \mapsto S) \in D \\ k'' = \texttt{m } h(o_n)(\bar{z}) \; o_n \; \texttt{Nothing undefined} \qquad newQ_{add}([\overline{o_m}], o_n, o_x) = s \\ h' = h[(o_n)(f) \mapsto l', count \mapsto l' + 1, l' \mapsto \texttt{Left } [\,], \\ (o_n)(\mathcal{Q}) \mapsto (k', l) \cdot q, (o_x)(\mathcal{Q}) \mapsto q_x \cdot (k'', l')] \end{array}}{(h, [\overline{o_m}]) \rightarrowtail (h', s)}$$

$$\text{(Sync)} \frac{\begin{array}{c} next(h, [\overline{o_m}]) = o_n \quad h(o_n)(\mathcal{Q}) = (\texttt{Assign } x \; (\texttt{Sync } m \; \bar{z}) \; k', l) \cdot q \quad (m(\bar{w}) \mapsto S) \in D \\ k'' = \texttt{m } h(o_n)(\bar{z}) \; o_n \; (\texttt{Just } x) \; k' \qquad h' = h[(o_n)(\mathcal{Q}) \mapsto (k'', l) \cdot q] \end{array}}{(h, [\overline{o_m}]) \rightarrowtail (h', [\overline{o_{n+1 \to m}}] : [\overline{o_{1 \to n}}])}$$

$$\text{(Return}_A\text{)} \frac{\begin{array}{cc} next(h, [\overline{o_m}]) = o_n & h(o_n)(\mathcal{Q}) = (\texttt{Return } x \; \texttt{Nothing } \_, l) \cdot q \\ newQ_{del}([\overline{o_m}], o_n, q) = s & h' = h[l \mapsto \texttt{Right } h(o_n)(x), (o_n)(\mathcal{Q}) \mapsto q] \end{array}}{(h, [\overline{o_m}]) \rightarrowtail (h', s)}$$

$$\text{(Return}_S\text{)} \frac{\begin{array}{c} next(h, [\overline{o_m}]) = o_n \qquad h(o_n)(\mathcal{Q}) = (\texttt{Return } x \; (\texttt{Just } z) \; k', l) \cdot q \\ h' = h[(o_n)(z) \mapsto h(o_n)(x), (o_n)(\mathcal{Q}) \mapsto (k', l) \cdot q] \end{array}}{(h, [\overline{o_m}]) \rightarrowtail (h', [\overline{o_{n+1 \to m}}] : [\overline{o_{1 \to n}}])}$$

Fig. 8. Intermediate semantics.

explained in Sect. 3. As usual with heaps, we use the notation $h[(o_n)(\mathcal{Q}) \mapsto q]$ to update the process queue of the object o_n to q. Finally, object attributes and method parameters become Integers and $Int_\perp$ values in the futures become *Either* values. To denote the inverse translation from data structures to runtime configurations we use $^c[\![(h', act)]\!]^{-1} = \langle C, h \rangle$—the same for queues $^q[\![\cdot]\!]^{-1}$ and statements $^s[\![\cdot]\!]^{-1}$. Note that the translation $^c[\![\cdot]\!]_c$ is not deterministic because it generates a list of object references from a set of closures C, so the order of the objects in the list is not defined. On the other hand, the translation of the heap in $^c[\![\cdot]\!]$ and the inverse translation $^c[\![\cdot]\!]^{-1}$ are deterministic.

$$c[[\langle C, h \rangle]] = (h', act), \text{ where}$$
$$act = [o_n \mid (o_n, Q_n) \in C, Q_n \neq \epsilon]$$
$$C = \{(n_1, Q_1), \ldots, (n_m, Q_m)\} \text{ and}$$
$$h' = h[[(n_i)(\mathcal{Q}) \mapsto {}^q[[Q_i]]]]$$

$${}^q[[\epsilon]] = \epsilon$$
$${}^q[[(S, l) \cdot Q]] = ({}^s[[S]], l) \cdot {}^q[[Q]]$$

Fig. 9. Translation from source to target configurations.

Based on the previous definitions we can state the soundness of the traces, i.e., every trace of `eval` steps is a valid trace w.r.t. $\to$. Note that for the sake of conciseness we unify the statements S and their representation as Haskell terms `res`, since there is a straightforward translation between them. We consider the auxiliary function $updL([\overline{o_m}], o_n, l) = [\overline{o_{n+1 \to m}}] : [\overline{o_{1 \to n-1}}] : l$ to update the list of object references.

Theorem 1 (Trace soundness). *Consider an initial state (h_1, s_1) and a sequence of $n - 1$ consecutive `eval` steps defined as: (1) $next(h_i, s_i) = o_i$, (2) `eval` $o_i h_i = (res_i, l_i, h_{i+1})$, (3) $s_{i+1} = updL(s_i, o_i, l_i)$. Then $c[[(h_1, s_1)]]^{-1} \to_{res_1}^{o_1}$ $c[[(h_2, s_2)]]_c^{-1} \to_{res_2}^{o_2} \cdots \to_{res_{n-1}}^{o_{n-1}} c[[(h_n, s_n)]]^{-1}$.*

Note that it is not possible to obtain a similar result about trace completeness since the $\to$-semantics in Fig. 3 selects the next object to execute nondeterministic (random scheduler), whereas the intermediate $\rightarrowtail$-semantics in Fig. 8 follows a concrete *round-robin* scheduling policy. As a final remark notice that the intermediate semantics $\rightarrowtail$ can be seen as a *specification* of the `eval` function. Therefore it can be used to guide the correctness proof of `eval` using proof assistance tools like *Isabelle* [12] or to generate tests automatically using *QuickCheck* [6].

4.1 Preservation of Resource Consumption

A strong feature of our translation is that the Haskell-translated program preserves the *resource consumption* of the original ABS program. As in [1] we use the notion of *cost model* to parameterize the type of resource we want to bound. Cost models are functions from ABS statements to real numbers, i.e., $\mathcal{M} : S \to \mathbb{R}$ that define different resource consumption measures. For instance, if the resource to measure is the number of executed steps, $\mathcal{M} : S \to 1$ such that each instruction has cost one. However, if one wants to measure memory consumption, we have that $\mathcal{M}(new) = c$, where c refers to the size of an object reference, and $\mathcal{M}(instr) = 0$ for all remaining instructions. The resource preservation is based on the notion of *trace cost*, i.e., the sum of the cost of the statements executed. Given a concrete cost model $\mathcal{M}$, an object reference o and a program execution $\mathcal{T} \equiv A_1 \to_{S_1}^{o_1} \cdots \to_{S_{n-1}}^{o_{n-1}} A_n$, the cost of the trace $\mathcal{C}(\mathcal{T}, o, \mathcal{M})$ is defined as:

$$\mathcal{C}(\mathcal{T}, o, \mathcal{M}) = \sum_{S \in \mathcal{T}|_{\{o\}}} \mathcal{M}(S)$$

Notice that, from all the steps in the trace $\mathcal{T}$, it takes into account only those performed in object o (denoted as $\mathcal{T}|_{\{o\}}$), so the cost notion is *object-sensitive*. Since the trace soundness states that the eval function performs the same steps as some trace $\mathcal{T}$, the cost preservation is a straightforward corollary:

Corollary 1 (Consumption Preservation). *Let* (h_1, s_1) *be an initial state and consider a sequence* $\mathcal{T}_E$ *of* $n - 1$ *consecutive* eval *steps defined as: a)* $o_i = next(h_i, s_i)$, *b)* $(res_i, l_i, h_{i+1}) = $ eval o_i h_i, *c)* $s_{i+1} = updL(s_i, o_i, l_i)$. *Then* $\mathcal{T} = {}^c[\![(h_1, s_1)]\!]^{-1} \rightarrow^{o_1}_{res_1} {}^c[\![(h_2, s_2)]\!]^{-1}_c \rightarrow^{o_2}_{res_2} \cdots \rightarrow^{o_{n-1}}_{res_{n-1}} {}^c[\![(h_n, s_n)]\!]^{-1}$ *such that* $\mathcal{C}(\mathcal{T}_E, o, \mathcal{M}) = \mathcal{C}(\mathcal{T}, o, \mathcal{M})$.

As a side effect of the previous result, we know that the upper bounds that are inferred from the ABS programs (using resource analyzers like [1]) are valid upper bounds for the Haskell translated code. We denote by $UB_{main}()|_o$ the upper bound obtained for the analysis of a main method for the computation performed on object o.

Theorem 2 (Bound preservation). *Let* P *be a program,* $\mathcal{T}_E$ *a sequence of* eval *steps from an initial state* (h_1, s_1) *and* $UB_{main}()|_o$ *the upper bound obtained for the program* P *starting from the main block, restricted to the object o. Then* $\mathcal{C}(\mathcal{T}_E, o, \mathcal{M}) \leq UB_{main}()|_o$.

5   Experimental Evaluation

In the previous section we proved that the execution of compiled Haskell programs has the same resource consumption as the original ABS traces wrt. any concrete cost model $\mathcal{M}$, i.e., both programs execute the same ABS statements in the same order and in the same objects. However, cost models are defined in terms of ABS statements so they are unaware of low-level details of the Haskell runtime environment as β-reductions or garbage collection. Studying the relation between cost models and some significant low-level details of the Haskell runtime in a formal way is an interesting line of future work. In this section we address empirically one particular topic: the Haskell runtime does not introduce additional overhead, i.e., the execution of one ABS statement requires only a constant amount of work. In order to evaluate this hypothesis, we have elaborated programs[3] with different asymptotic costs and measured the number of statements executed (steps) and their run-time. The *Primality test* computes the primality of a number n: the program creates n objects and checks every possible divisor of n on each object. The difference is that the *low paralellism* version awaits for the result of one divisor before invoking the next check and the *high parallelism* version does not. Both programs have a $O(n)$ cost. The *Logarithm computation* program computes the integer part n logarithms. It has cost $O(n.log\ n)$. Finally *Primes in a range* computes the prime numbers in the interval $[1..n]$, thus having a $O(n^2)$ cost.

---

[3] The ABS-subset experimental programs and measurements together with the target language & runtime reside at http://github.com/abstools/abs-haskell-formal.

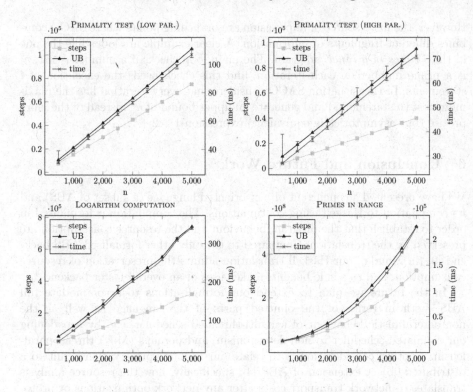

Fig. 10. Execution steps vs. time (Intel® Core™ i7-4790 at 3.60 GHz, 16 GB).

We have tested the programs with n ranging from 500 to 5000, running 20 experiments for every value of n, and measured the time. This is plotted in the cross line (right margin) in Fig. 10. The plot represents the mode times and the minimum and maximum times as *whiskers*. We have also measured the actual number of steps, represented in the square line (left margin) in Fig. 10. These two plots show that the execution time and the number of executed steps grows with a similar rate in all the programs, independently of their asymptotical cost, thus confirming that the compilation does not incur any overhead.

We have also plotted the resource bounds obtained by the SACO tool [2] for the different values of n (triangle line, left margin in Fig. 10). SACO can analyze full ABS programs and thus also the subset considered in this paper, and allows the selection of the cost model of interest. In this case we have analyzed the original ABS programs using the cost model that obtains the number of ABS statements executed. As can be appreciated, the upper bounds are sound and overapproximate the actual number of executed statements. The difference between the upper bounds and the actual number of statements executed is explained for two reasons. First, the SACO tool considers constructor methods, i.e., methods that are invoked on every new object, so the SACO tool will count a constant number of extra statements whenever a new object is created.

However, the main source of imprecision are branching points where SACO combines different fragments of information. A clear example are loops like the one in the *Primes in a range* program. The main loop checks if a number $i \in [1..n]$ is a prime number on each iteration, and this check needs the execution of i statements. In this situation SACO considers that every iteration has the maximum cost (n statements) and generate an upper bound of n^2 instead of the more precise (but asymptotically equivalent) expression $1 + 2 + \ldots + n$.

6   Conclusion and Future Work

We have presented a concurrent object-oriented language (a subset of ABS) and its compilation to Haskell using continuations. The compilation is formalised in order to establish that the program behaviour and the resource consumption are preserved by the translation. Compared to the only other formalised ABS backend [9] (in Maude), our Haskell translation admits the preservation of resource consumption, and as a side benefit, makes uses of an overall faster backend.[4]

In the future we plan to extend our formalisations to accommodate full ABS, both in terms of the omitted parts of the language as well as the non-deterministic behaviour of a multi-threaded scheduler, e.g. by broadening our simulated scheduler to non-determinism, and perhaps (M:N) thread parallelism. Another consideration is to relate our resource-preservation result to a distributed-object extension of ABS [4]; specifically, how the resource analysis translates to network transport costs after any network optimizations or protocol limitations. Finally, we plan to formally relate the ABS cost models used to define the cost of a trace and some of the low-level runtime details of the Haskell runtime like β-reductions, garbage collections or main memory usage. Thus, we could express trace costs and upper bounds in terms closer to the actual running environment.

References

1. Albert, E., Arenas, P., Correas, J., Genaim, S., Gómez-Zamalloa, M., Puebla, G., Román-Díez, G.: Object-sensitive cost analysis for concurrent objects. Softw. Test. Verif. Reliab. **25**(3), 218–271 (2015)
2. Albert, E., Arenas, P., Flores-Montoya, A., Genaim, S., Gómez-Zamalloa, M., Martin-Martin, E., Puebla, G., Román-Díez, G.: SACO: static analyzer for concurrent objects. In: Ábrahám, E., Havelund, K. (eds.) TACAS 2014. LNCS, vol. 8413, pp. 562–567. Springer, Heidelberg (2014). doi:10.1007/978-3-642-54862-8_46
3. Albert, E., Arenas, P., Gómez-Zamalloa, M.: Symbolic execution of concurrent objects in CLP. In: Russo, C., Zhou, N.-F. (eds.) PADL 2012. LNCS, vol. 7149, pp. 123–137. Springer, Heidelberg (2012). doi:10.1007/978-3-642-27694-1_10

---

[4] http://abstools.github.io/abs-bench keeps an up-to-date benchmark of all ABS backends.

4. Bezirgiannis, N., Boer, F.: ABS: a high-level modeling language for cloud-aware programming. In: Freivalds, R.M., Engels, G., Catania, B. (eds.) SOFSEM 2016. LNCS, vol. 9587, pp. 433–444. Springer, Heidelberg (2016). doi:10.1007/978-3-662-49192-8_35

5. Boer, F.S., Clarke, D., Johnsen, E.B.: A complete guide to the future. In: Nicola, R. (ed.) ESOP 2007. LNCS, vol. 4421, pp. 316–330. Springer, Heidelberg (2007). doi:10.1007/978-3-540-71316-6_22

6. Claessen, K., Hughes, J.: QuickCheck: a lightweight tool for random testing of haskell programs. In: Proceedings of the ICFP 2000, pp. 268–279. ACM (2000)

7. Dean, J., Ghemawat, S.: MapReduce: simplified data processing on large clusters. Commun. ACM **51**(1), 107–113 (2008)

8. Flanagan, C., Felleisen, M.: The semantics of future and its use in program optimization. In: Proceedings of the POPL 1995, pp. 209–220. ACM (1995)

9. Johnsen, E.B., Hähnle, R., Schäfer, J., Schlatte, R., Steffen, M.: ABS: a core language for abstract behavioral specification. In: Aichernig, B.K., Boer, F.S., Bonsangue, M.M. (eds.) FMCO 2010. LNCS, vol. 6957, pp. 142–164. Springer, Heidelberg (2011). doi:10.1007/978-3-642-25271-6_8

10. Knuth, D.E.: The Art of Computer Programming. Fundamental Algorithms, 2nd edn, vol. 1. Addison-Wesley Professional, Massachusetts (1973)

11. Nakata, K., Saar, A.: Compiling cooperative task management to continuations. In: Arbab, F., Sirjani, M. (eds.) FSEN 2013. LNCS, vol. 8161, pp. 95–110. Springer, Heidelberg (2013). doi:10.1007/978-3-642-40213-5_7

12. Nipkow, T., Wenzel, M., Paulson, L.C. (eds.): Isabelle/HOL: A Proof Assistant for Higher-order Logic. LNCS, vol. 2283. Springer, Heidelberg (2002)

13. Noll, T.: A rewriting logic implementation of erlang. ENTCS **44**(2), 206–224 (2001). Proc. LDTA '01

14. Palacios, A., Vidal, G.: Towards modelling actor-based concurrency in term rewriting. In: Proceedings of the WPTE 2015. OASICS, vol. 46, pp. 19–29. Dagstuhl Pub. (2015)

15. Schäfer, J., Poetzsch-Heffter, A.: JCoBox: generalizing active objects to concurrent components. In: D'Hondt, T. (ed.) ECOOP 2010. LNCS, vol. 6183, pp. 275–299. Springer, Heidelberg (2010). doi:10.1007/978-3-642-14107-2_13

16. Srinivasan, S., Mycroft, A.: Kilim: isolation-typed actors for Java. In: Vitek, J. (ed.) ECOOP 2008. LNCS, vol. 5142, pp. 104–128. Springer, Heidelberg (2008). doi:10.1007/978-3-540-70592-5_6

17. Tarau, P.: Coordination and concurrency in multi-engine prolog. In: Meuter, W., Roman, G.-C. (eds.) COORDINATION 2011. LNCS, vol. 6721, pp. 157–171. Springer, Heidelberg (2011). doi:10.1007/978-3-642-21464-6_11

18. Vidal, G.: Towards Erlang Verification by Term Rewriting. In: Proc. LOPSTR '13. pp. 109–126. LNCS 8901, Springer (2013)

19. Wong, P.Y., Albert, E., Muschevici, R., Proena, J., Schfer, J., Schlatte, R.: The ABS tool suite: modelling, executing and analysing distributed adaptable object-oriented systems. STTT **14**(5), 567–588 (2012)

Verification of Time-Aware Business Processes Using Constrained Horn Clauses

Emanuele De Angelis[1]($\boxtimes$), Fabio Fioravanti[1]($\boxtimes$), Maria Chiara Meo[1],
Alberto Pettorossi[2,3]($\boxtimes$), and Maurizio Proietti[3]

[1] DEC, University 'G. D' Annunzio', Pescara, Italy
{emanuele.deangelis,fabio.fioravanti,cmeo}@unich.it
[2] DICII, University of Rome Tor Vergata, Rome, Italy
pettorossi@disp.uniroma2.it
[3] IASI-CNR, Rome, Italy
{maurizio.proietti,adp}@iasi.cnr.it

Abstract. We present a method for verifying properties of time-aware business processes, that is, business processes where time constraints on the activities are explicitly taken into account. Business processes are specified using an extension of the Business Process Modeling Notation (BPMN) and durations are defined by constraints over integer numbers. The definition of the operational semantics is given by a set *OpSem* of constrained Horn clauses (CHCs). Our verification method consists of two steps. (Step 1) The specialization of *OpSem* with respect to a given business process and a given temporal property to be verified. This specialization produces a set of CHCs whose satisfiability is equivalent to the validity of the given property. (Step 2) The use of any state-of-the-art solver for CHCs to check the satisfiability of such sets of clauses. We have implemented our verification method using the VeriMAP transformation system and the Z3 solver for CHCs.

1 Introduction

A *business process*, or BP for short, consists of a set of activities, performed in coordination within a single organization, which realize a business goal [31,34]. The *Business Process Model and Notation*, or BPMN for short, is one of the most popular graphical languages proposed for visualizing business processes [27]. The primary goal of BPMN is to provide a standard notation that can be understood by all business stakeholders, which include the business analysts who define and modify the processes, the technical developers in charge of their implementation, and the business managers who monitor and manage the processes.

A BPMN model is a procedural, semi-formal description of the order of execution of the activities of a given process and how these activities must coordinate, abstracting away from many other aspects of the process itself, such as

This work has been partially funded by INdAM-GNCS (Italy).

E. De Angelis, F. Fioravanti, and A. Pettorossi are research associates at IASI-CNR, Rome, Italy.

M.V. Hermenegildo and P. Lopez-Garcia (Eds.): LOPSTR 2016, LNCS 10184, pp. 38–55, 2017.
DOI: 10.1007/978-3-319-63139-4_3

the manipulation of data and the duration of the activities. However, for many analysis tasks these aspects are very significant in practice and should be taken into consideration. In particular, the duration of the activities is crucial when we want to reason about time constraints (such as deadlines or earliest completion times) that should be satisfied by the executions of the process.

Various approaches for BP modeling with duration and time constraints have been proposed in the literature (see [6] for a recent survey). Some of these approaches define the semantics of *time-aware* BPMN models by means of formalisms such as *time Petri nets* [24], *timed automata* [32], and *process algebras* [35]. Properties of these models can then be verified by using very effective reasoning tools available for those formalisms [4,14,22].

However, the above mentioned formalisms and tools may not be adequate if we want to complement time-based reasoning with general purpose logical reasoning, which is often needed if we take into account more complex aspects of knowledge manipulation activities relative to business processes. For instance, some verification approaches make use of ontology-based reasoning about the business domain where processes are executed [30,33], while others combine reasoning on the finite-state process behavior with reasoning on the manipulation of data objects of infinite types such as databases or integers [2,9,29].

Thus, in view of an integration of various reasoning tasks needed to analyze business processes from different perspectives, we propose a logic-based approach to modeling and verifying time-aware business processes.

The main contributions of the paper are the following. We present a logic-based language to specify time-aware BPMN models, where time and duration of activities are explicitly represented. Then we define an operational semantics of time-aware BPMN models by means of deduction rules that allow us to infer the time intervals when a particular activity is in execution or 'is enacting', using the BPMN terminology. Next, in order to prove properties of time-aware BPMN models, we follow a transformational approach similar to the one proposed in [11] for the verification of imperative programs. First, we consider an encoding *OpSem* of the operational semantics of business processes into *Constrained Horn Clauses* (CHCs) [5] (or, equivalently, *Constraint Logic Programs* [20]). Then, we specialize *OpSem* with respect to the time-aware BPMN model under consideration and the temporal property of interest, thereby deriving a new set of CHCs whose satisfiability is equivalent to (and thus implies) the validity of the property to be verified. Finally, we use the state-of-the-art solver Z3 [12] for CHCs to check the satisfiability of such set of clauses.

Since the CHCs are generated in an automatic way by the CHC specializer from the formal definition of the semantics of the BPMN models, and the CHC solvers are general purpose reasoning systems, our approach is, to a large extent, parametric with respect to other extensions of BP models one may want to consider in the future. Moreover, recent advances in the field of CHC solving can be exploited to get very effective reasoning tools for verifying other classes of properties of business processes besides the temporal ones.

The paper is structured as follows. In Sect. 2 we recall some basic notions about Constrained Horn Clauses (CHCs) over integer numbers and Business Process Model and Notation (BPMN). In Sect. 3 we present our logic-based language for specifying time-aware BPMN models and the operational semantics of the language. In Sect. 4 we present the CHC encoding of the semantics and the transformation techniques for specializing *OpSem* with respect to a given time-aware BPMN model and a given property. In Sect. 5 we report on the implementation of the verification technique we have made using the VeriMAP transformation and verification system [10], and the CHC solver Z3. Finally, in Sect. 6 we discuss related work in the field of Business Process verification.

2   Preliminaries

In the next two subsections we recall some basic notions concerning constrained Horn clauses and the Business Process Model and Notation.

We consider time to be a discrete quantity and we consider the 'time line' to be the set of integers. However, our approach applies directly to dense or continuous time as well.

2.1   Constrained Horn Clauses over Integers

First we need the following notions about constraints, constrained Horn clauses, and constraint logic programming. For related notions not familiar to the reader, we refer to [20,23].

Constraints are defined as follows. Let $RelOp$ be the set of predicate symbols $\{=, \neq, \leq, \geq, <, >\}$. If p_1 and p_2 are linear polynomials with integer variables and coefficients, then $p_1 R p_2$, with $R \in RelOp$, is an *atomic constraint*. A *constraint* c is a (possibly empty) conjunction of atomic constraints. An *atom* is a formula of the form $p(t_1, \ldots, t_m)$, where p is a predicate symbol not in $RelOp$ and $t_1, \ldots, t_m$ are terms constructed as usual from variables, constants, and function symbols. In particular, we assume that there are two predicate symbols *true* and *false* of arity 0, and a predicate symbol *eq* denoting identity. A *constrained Horn clause* (or simply, a *clause*) is an implication of the form $A \leftarrow c, G$, where the conclusion (or *head*) A is an atom, and the premise (or *body*) 'c, G' is the conjunction of a constraint c and a (possibly empty) conjunction G of atoms. The empty conjunction is identified with *true*. A *constrained fact* is a clause of the form $A \leftarrow c$, and if c is *true* we will call it simply a *fact*. A *constrained goal* (or simply, a *goal*) is a clause of the form $false \leftarrow c, G$. Given a formula φ, $vars(\varphi)$ denotes the set of variables occurring in φ. A clause C is said to be *ground* if $vars(C) = \emptyset$.

Given a set $\mathcal{P}$ of clauses, a $\mathbb{Z}$-*interpretation* is defined to be an interpretation I of $\mathcal{P}$ such that: (i) *true* holds in I, (ii) *false* does not hold in I, (iii) I is the usual interpretation over the set of the integer numbers $\mathbb{Z}$ for the constraints, and (iv) I is the Herbrand interpretation for predicate and function symbols not in $RelOp \cup \{true, false, +, \times\}$ (in particular, $eq(x, y)$ holds if and only if x and y are identical terms in the Herbrand universe). For any formula φ we write

$\mathbb{Z} \models \varphi$ if φ holds in all $\mathbb{Z}$-interpretations. A $\mathbb{Z}$-*model* of $\mathcal{P}$ is a $\mathbb{Z}$-interpretations M such that every clause of $\mathcal{P}$ holds in M. A set of CHCs is *satisfiable* if it has a $\mathbb{Z}$-*model.* (Note that a set of CHCs may be unsatisfiable if it contains goals.) Every satisfiable set $\mathcal{P}$ of CHCs has a unique *least* $\mathbb{Z}$-*model*, denoted $M(\mathcal{P})$ [20].

2.2 Business Processes Model and Notation

A BPMN model is defined through a diagram drawn by using graphical constructs representing *flow objects* and *sequence flows* (sequence flows will also be called *flows* for short). That diagram can be extended, if so desired, to include information about data flow, resource allocation (for instance, how the work to be done is assigned to the participants in the process), and exception handling (for instance, how erroneous behaviors should be handled).

For reasons of simplicity, in this paper we will only consider a subset of the flow objects and sequence flows that can occur in a BPMN model, but our approach can easily be extended to full BPMN. The flow objects we will consider are of three kinds: either (i) *tasks*, denoted by rounded rectangles, or (ii) *events*, denoted by circles, or (iii) *gateways*, denoted by diamonds. Tasks represent atomic units of work performed within the process. Events denote something that happens during the execution, or the *enactment*, using the BPMN terminology, of a business process. We will only consider the *start event* and the *end event*, which starts and ends the process enactment, respectively. Gateways model the branching and merging of activities. There are several types of gateways in BPMN, each of which can be a *branch* gateway if it has a single incoming flow and multiple outgoing flows, or a *merge* gateway if it has multiple incoming flows and a single outgoing flow. We will consider the following gateways: (i) the *parallel branch* gateway that activates all the outgoing flows at the same time instant, (ii) the *parallel merge* gateway that activates the outgoing flow when all the incoming flows have been activated (that is, the parallel merge synchronizes the incoming flows) (iii) the *exclusive branch* gateway that (non-deterministically) activates exactly one out of the (possibly many) outgoing flows, and (iv) the *exclusive merge* gateway that activates the single outgoing flow upon activation of one of the (possibly many) incoming flows. The diamonds representing parallel and exclusive gateways are labeled by '+' and '×', respectively.

A sequence flow, denoted by an arrow, links two flow objects and denotes a control flow relation, that is, it states that the control flow can pass from the source to the target flow object. If there is a sequence flow from x to y, then x is a *predecessor* of y and y is a *successor* of x. A *path* in a BPMN model is a sequence of flow objects such that every pair of consecutive objects is connected by a sequence flow.

We assume that BPMN models are *well-formed*, that is, they satisfy the following properties: (1) every process contains a unique start event and a unique end event, (2) every flow object occurs on a path from the start event to the end event, (3) the start event has exactly one successor and no predecessor, (4) the end event has exactly one predecessor and no successor, (5) branch gateways

have exactly one predecessor and at least one successor, while merge gateways
have at least one predecessor and exactly one successor, (6) tasks have exactly
one predecessor and one successor, and (7) on every cyclic path there is at least
one occurrence of a task (that is, no cycles through gateways only are allowed).

In Fig. 1 we show the BPMN model of a purchase order process, called *PO*,
describing a interaction pattern between an e-commerce vendor and a customer.

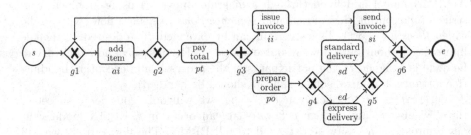

Fig. 1. The BPMN model of the purchase order process *PO*.

At the beginning of the purchase order process the customer adds one or
more items to the shopping cart. Then, he pays for all the items, and the vendor
(i) issues the invoice and sends it to the customer, and also (ii) prepares the
order and ships it by a standard or an express delivery method. The process
terminates when the invoice has been sent and the order has been delivered.

3   Specification and Semantics of Business Processes

In this section we introduce the notion of a Business Process Specification, which
formally represents a business process by means of set of Constrained Horn
Clauses, and we define the operational semantics of a BPS.

3.1   Business Process Specification via CHCs

A *Business Process Specification*, or BPS for short, contains: (i) a set of ground
facts that specify the flow objects and the sequence flows between them, and
(ii) a set of constrained facts that specify the duration of each flow object.

We will use the following predicates: (i) $flow\_object(x)$: x is either a task, or an
event, or a gateway; (ii) $task(x)$: x is a task; (iii) $start(x)$ and $end(x)$: x is a start
event and an end event, respectively; (iv) $exc\_branch(x)$ and $exc\_merge(x)$: x is
an exclusive branch and exclusive merge gateway, respectively; (v) $par\_branch(x)$
and $par\_merge(x)$: x is a parallel branch and a parallel merge gateway, respectively; (vi) $seq(x, y)$: there is a sequence flow from x to y; (vii) $duration(x, d)$: the
enactment of the flow object x takes d units of time to be completed.

In the Business Process Specification we assume that: (i) for every task x
there exists a single clause of the form $duration(x, d) \leftarrow d_{min} \leq d \leq d_{max}$,

where d_{min} and d_{max} are positive integer constants representing the minimal and the maximal time duration of x, respectively, and (ii) for every event and gateway x there exists a single clause of the form $duration(x,0)$ (that is, the enactment of any event or gateway takes no time).

The CHC specification of the BPMN process PO of Fig. 1 is shown in Table 1. Note that a BPS is always satisfiable because it contains no goals, and hence it has a least $\mathbb{Z}$-model.

Table 1. BPS for the purchase order process PO of Fig. 1.

```
task(ai).  task(pt).  task(ii).  task(si).  task(po).  task(sd).  task(ed).
start(s).  end(e).  exc_merge(g1).  exc_branch(g2).  par_branch(g3).
exc_branch(g4).  exc_merge(g5).  par_merge(g6).
seq(s,g1).    seq(g1,ai).  seq(ai,g2).  seq(g2,g1).  seq(g2,pt).  seq(pt,g3).
seq(g3,ii).   seq(g3,po).  seq(ii,si).  seq(si,g6).  seq(po,g4).  seq(g4,sd).
seq(sd,g5).   seq(g4,ed).  seq(ed,g5).  seq(g5,g6).  seq(g6,e).
duration(s,0).      duration(e,0).      duration(g1,0).      duration(g2,0).
duration(g3,0).     duration(g4,0).     duration(g5,0).      duration(g6,0).
duration(ai,D):- D>=1, D=<6.   % add item
duration(pt,D):- D>=1, D=<2.   % pay total
duration(ii,D):- D>=1, D=<2.   % issue invoice
duration(si,D):- D>=1, D=<3.   % send invoice
duration(po,D):- D>=3, D=<5.   % prepare order
duration(sd,D):- D>=2, D=<4.   % standard delivery
duration(ed,D):- D>=1, D=<3.   % express delivery
```

Our formalization of a BPS also includes a set of clauses that represent the *meta-model* of any BPS. In particular, these meta-model clauses express: (i) the disjointness properties of the sets of its flow objects (for instance, we have the clause: *false* ← $task(X), par\_branch(X)$), and (ii) the *well-formedness* properties corresponding to Conditions (1)–(7) of Sect. 2.2. This second set of clauses is as follows:

(c1) $eq(X,Y) \leftarrow start(X), start(Y)$ and $eq(X,Y) \leftarrow end(X), end(Y)$;

(c2) $seqq(S,X) \leftarrow start(S), flow\_object(X)$ and $seqq(X,E) \leftarrow flow\_object(X), end(E)$
 where $seqq$ is the reflexive, transitive closure of seq;

(c3) $eq(Y,Z) \leftarrow start(S), seq(S,Y), seq(S,Z)$ and $false \leftarrow start(S), seq(Y,S)$;

(c4) $eq(Y,Z) \leftarrow end(E), seq(Y,E), seq(Z,E)$ and $false \leftarrow end(E), seq(E,Y)$;

(c5) $eq(Y,Z) \leftarrow par\_branch(X), seq(Y,X), seq(Z,X)$ and
 $eq(Y,Z) \leftarrow par\_merge(X), seq(X,Y), seq(X,Z)$
 and, similarly, for the *exc_branch* and *exc_merge* gateways;

(c6) $eq(Y,Z) \leftarrow task(X), seq(X,Y), seq(X,Z)$ and
 $eq(Y,Z) \leftarrow task(X), seq(Y,X), seq(Z,X)$;

(c7) $false \leftarrow gateway\_path(X,X)$

where $gateway\_path(X,Y)$ is a predicate that holds iff there is a path from X to Y made out of gateways only.

Note that the existence of at least one predecessor and at least one successor for any task or gateway (required by Conditions (5) and (6) of Sect. 2.2) is enforced by the clauses at Point (c2).

A BPS $\mathcal{B}$ is *well-formed* if clauses (c1)–(c7) hold in the least $\mathbb{Z}$-model of $\mathcal{B}$.

3.2   Operational Semantics

We start off by introducing the notion of a *state* at a time instant t. A state s is a pair $\langle F, t \rangle$, where F is a set of terms, called *fluents*, representing the properties that hold at the time instant t in $\mathbb{Z}$. Let *States* be the set of states.

A fluent is a term of one of the following forms, for any flow object x: (i) *begins*(x), which represents the beginning of the execution, or enactment, of x, (ii) *completes*(x), which represents that x has completed its execution, and (iii) *enables*(x, y), which represents that x upon completion of its execution enables the execution of its successor y, and (iv) *enacting*(x, r), which represents that the enactment of x requires r units of time to completion (for this reason r is also called the *residual time* of x). From these definitions it follows that *begins*(x) is equivalent to *enacting*(x, r), where r is the duration of x, and *completes*(x) is equivalent to *enacting*$(x, 0)$. (This redundant representation of fluents allows us to write simpler rules for the operational semantics below.)

The operational semantics is defined by a binary transition relation $\longrightarrow$ which is a subset of *States* $\times$ *States* and is derived according to the rules below. In the rules for $\longrightarrow$, besides the predicates introduced in Sect. 3.1, we use the following ones: (i) *not_par_branch*(x), which holds if x is not a parallel branch, and (ii) *not_par_merge*(x), which holds if x is not a parallel merge.

(S_1)
$$\frac{begins(x) \in F \qquad duration(x, d)}{\langle F, t \rangle \longrightarrow \langle (F \setminus \{begins(x)\}) \cup \{enacting(x, d)\}, \; t \rangle}$$

(S_2)
$$\frac{completes(x) \in F \qquad par\_branch(x)}{\langle F, t \rangle \longrightarrow \langle (F \setminus \{completes(x)\}) \cup \{enables(x, s) \mid seq(x, s)\}, \; t \rangle}$$

(S_3)
$$\frac{completes(x) \in F \qquad not\_par\_branch(x) \qquad seq(x, s)}{\langle F, t \rangle \longrightarrow \langle (F \setminus \{completes(x)\}) \cup \{enables(x, s)\}, \; t \rangle}$$

(S_4)
$$\frac{\forall p \; seq(p, x) \to enables(p, x) \in F \qquad par\_merge(x)}{\langle F, t \rangle \longrightarrow \langle (F \setminus \{enables(p, x) \mid enables(p, x) \in F\}) \cup \{begins(x)\}, \; t \rangle}$$

(S_5)
$$\frac{enables(p, x) \in F \qquad not\_par\_merge(x)}{\langle F, t \rangle \longrightarrow \langle (F \setminus \{enables(p, x)\}) \cup \{begins(x)\}, \; t \rangle}$$

(S_6)
$$\frac{enacting(x, 0) \in F}{\langle F, t \rangle \longrightarrow \langle (F \setminus \{enacting(x, 0)\}) \cup \{completes(x)\}, \; t \rangle}$$

(S_7) $$\frac{no\_other\_premises(F) \qquad \exists x\, \exists r\; enacting(x,r) \in F \qquad m > 0}{\langle F, t \rangle \longrightarrow \langle F \ominus m,\; t+m \rangle}$$

where: (i) $no\_other\_premises(F)$ holds iff none of the rules S_1–S_6 has its premise true, (ii) $m = min\{r \mid enacting(x,r) \in F\}$, and (iii) $F \ominus m$ is the set F of fluents where every $enacting(x,r)$ is replaced by $enacting(x, r-m)$.

Note that rule (S_7) is the only rule that formalizes the flow of time, as it infers transitions of the form $\langle F, t \rangle \longrightarrow \langle F', t+m \rangle$, with $m > 0$. In contrast, rules (S_1)–(S_6) infer instantaneous state transitions of the form $\langle F, t \rangle \longrightarrow \langle F', t \rangle$.

Now let us explain the meaning of rules (S_1)–(S_7).

(S_1) If the execution of a flow object x begins at time t, then, at the same time t, x is enacting and its residual time is the duration d of x;

(S_2) If the execution of the parallel branch x completes at time t, then x enables *all its successors* at time t;

(S_3) If the execution of x completes at time t and x is not a parallel branch, then x enables *precisely one of its successors* at time t (in particular, this case occurs when x is a task);

(S_4) If *all* the predecessors of x have enabled the parallel merge x at time t, then the execution of x begins at time t;

(S_5) If *at least one* predecessor p of x enables x at time t and x is not a parallel merge, then the execution of x begins at time t (in particular, this case occurs when x is a task);

(S_6) If a flow object x is enacting at time t with residual time 0, then the execution of x completes at time t;

(S_7) Let us assume that at time t: (i) none of rules (S_1)–(S_6) can be applied, (ii) there at least one task whose execution requires r (>0) units of time to get to completion (recall that among the flow objects, tasks only may have positive residual time), and (iii) m is the least among the residual times of all the tasks which are in execution (that is, enacting). Then every task x that is in execution at time t with residual time r, is in execution at time $t + m$ with residual time $r - m$.

We say that state $\langle F', t' \rangle$ is *reachable* from state $\langle F, t \rangle$, if $\langle F, t \rangle \longrightarrow^* \langle F', t' \rangle$, where $\longrightarrow^*$ denotes the reflexive, transitive closure of the transition relation $\longrightarrow$. The *initial state* is the pair $\langle \{begins\,(s)\}, 0 \rangle$, where s denotes the start event.

Note that in our formalization we cannot represent multiple, concurrent executions of the same flow object, because a state is a *set* of fluents. However, this limitation can easily be overcome by considering *multisets* of fluents.

4   Encoding Time-Dependent Properties into CHCs

In this section we show the CHC *interpreter* that encodes the operational semantics of business processes and we show how to encode the time-dependent properties to be verified. We also briefly present two transformation techniques:

(RI): a technique for performing the *removal of the interpreter* (see [11,28] for more details), whereby deriving a set of clauses that can be submitted to automatic tools for satisfiability checking such as the Z3 [12] or the ELDARICA [18] solvers for CHCs, and

(PE): a technique for reducing the size of the set of CHCs generated by the RI technique. This PE technique is based on a suitable notion of *predicate equivalence* (see Sect. 4.3) that may be used, if so desired, for improving the time and space efficiency of the satisfiability checking.

4.1 Encoding the Operational Semantics in CHCs

A state $\langle F, t \rangle$ of the operational semantics is encoded by a term of the form s(F,T), where F is a list encoding the set F of fluents and T encodes the time instant t at which the fluents of F hold. The transition relation $\longrightarrow$ between states and its reflexive, transitive closure $\longrightarrow^*$ are encoded by the binary predicates tr and reach, respectively, whose defining clauses are shown in Table 2. In the body of the clauses, we have underlined the atoms that encode the premises of the rules of the operational semantics.

The predicate member(X,L) selects an element X from the list L. The predicate update(F,R,A,FU) holds iff FU is the list obtained from the list F by removing all the elements of R and adding all the elements of A. The predicate no_other_premises(F) holds iff the premise of every rule in $\{S1,\ldots,S6\}$ is false. The predicate mintime(Enacts,M) holds iff Enacts is a list of terms of the form

Table 2. The CHC interpreter for the operational semantics of time-aware BPs.

```
S1. tr(s(F,T), s(FU,T)) :- member(begins(X),F), duration(X,D),
                           update(F,[begins(X)],[enacting(X,D)],FU).
S2. tr(s(F,T), s(FU,T)) :- member(completes(X),F), par_branch(X),
                           findall(enables(X,S),(seq(X,S)),Enbls),
                           update(F,[completes(X)],Enbls,FU).
S3. tr(s(F,T), s(FU,T)) :- member(completes(X),F), not_par_branch(X), seq(X,S),
                           update(F,[completes(X)],[enables(X,S)],FU).
S4. tr(s(F,T), s(FU,T)) :- member(enables(_,X),F), par_merge(X),
                           findall(enables(P,X),(seq(P,X)),Enbls),
                           sublist(Enbls,F), update(F,Enbls,[begins(X)],FU).
S5. tr(s(F,T), s(FU,T)) :- member(enables(P,X),F), not_par_merge(X),
                           update(F,[enables(P,X)],[begins(X)],FU).
S6. tr(s(F,T), s(FU,T)) :- member(enacting(X,R),F), R=0,
                           update(F,[enacting(X,R)],[completes(X)],FU).
S7. tr(s(F,T), s(FU,TU)) :- no_other_premises(F), member(enacting(_,_),F),
                           findall(Y,(Y=enacting(X,R),member(Y,F)),Enacts),
                           mintime(Enacts,M), M>0,
                           decrease_residual_times(Enacts,M,EnactsU),
                           update(F,Enacts,EnactsU,FU), TU=T+M.
R1. reach(S,S).
R2. reach(S,S2) :- tr(S,S1), reach(S1,S2).
```

enacting(X,R) and M is the minimum value of R for the elements of Enacts. The predicate decrease_residual_times(Enacts,M,EnactsU) holds iff EnactsU is the list of terms obtained by replacing every element of Enacts, of the form enacting(X,R), by the term enacting(X,RU) where RU = R-M. The predicates sublist(S,L) and findall(X,G,L) have the usual meaning.

4.2   Encoding Time-Dependent Properties

By using the reach predicate and integer constraints, we can specify many useful time-dependent properties. In particular, we can specify safety properties (stating that 'no unsafe state can be reached'), schedulability properties (stating that a process will be completed within a given deadline), response properties (stating that, whenever a task is executed, another task will be executed within a given time).

In order to see how we encode time-dependent properties of business processes, we consider a property of the process PO stating that, whenever the customer pays and the process PO completes, then completion occurs within 9 time units after payment. By using the reachability relation $\longrightarrow^*$, this property can be written as follows:

Q: if $\langle \{begins(s)\}, 0\rangle \longrightarrow^* \langle \{completes(pt)\}, t_{pt}\rangle \longrightarrow^* \langle \{completes(e)\}, t_e\rangle$,
      then $t_e \leq t_{pt} + 9$

The reader can check that Q holds for the process PO because, in the worst case, the time needed for preparing and delivering the order is actually 9 time units and this time is greater than the time needed for issuing and sending the invoice, which is 5 time units. The property Q is encoded by the following goal (where s(_,_) is the constructor for states, while the constant s of arity 0 denotes the start event):

```
Q.    false :- Ts = 0, Tpt > Ts, Te > Tpt + 9,
                 reach(s([begins(s)],Ts), s([completes(pt)],Tpt)),
                 reach(s([completes(pt)],Tpt), s([completes(e)],Te)).
```

The clauses S1–S7,R1,R2,Q, together with the clauses encoding the process PO, will be collectively referred to as the *interpreter I*. We have that the property Q is valid for the process PO iff the set I of CHCs is satisfiable.

Despite several tools have been developed for checking the satisfiability of constrained Horn clauses, none of them can effectively be leveraged in our example. Constraint logic programming systems [20] are focused on proving the unsatisfiability of sets of clauses, rather then their satisfiability, and they may fail to terminate for the given set I because a clause for reach is recursive (note, in particular that the add_item task can be executed an unbounded number of times). State-of-the-art CHC solvers [12,18] also fail because the predicates in I are defined over lists and structured terms (not just integers) and they depend on the findall predicate, which is not available in those solvers.

In order to be able to effectively use off-the-shelf CHC solvers for checking the validity of time-dependent properties, we apply the so-called *removal of the interpreter* transformation, denoted RI [11, 28]. This transformation is a program specialization strategy based on unfold/fold transformation rules, which takes the program I as input and produces as output a program I_{sp} that is equivalent to I with respect to satisfiability. Indeed, by the correctness of the unfold/fold transformation rules [13], we have that I is satisfiable iff I_{sp} is satisfiable.

A notable effect of applying the transformation RI, which removes the interpreter, is that the program I_{sp} contains no occurrences of the predicates and terms used for encoding the operational semantics and the process PO. In particular, the clauses of I_{sp} will be of the form $A \leftarrow c, G$, where the arguments of the atoms are variables and c is a constraint. For instance, the goal Q expressing the property Q above is transformed into the following goal:

```
Q1.  false :- A=0, B=<2, C=<6, D=<5, E>0, F-E>9, B>=1, C>=1, D>=3,
              new1(C,A,E), new2(B,D,E,F).
```

The new predicates `new1` and `new2` have been introduced by the *definition rule*, and the extra constraints have been derived by the *unfolding rule*. We refer to [11] for the details of the transformation. The whole set of clauses derived by the transformation RI is listed in the online Appendix A.1[1]. The satisfiability of this derived set of clauses can be proved in a fully automatic way by using the Z3 CHC solver, as it will be shown in Sect. 5.

4.3 Predicate Equivalence

Now we present a transformation, called *predicate equivalence*, denoted PE, that allows us to reduce the size of a set of constrained Horn clauses when suitable equivalences between predicates hold. Since predicate equivalence is undecidable in general, we introduce a restricted, decidable notion of equivalence based on constraint equivalence and predicate renaming.

First we need some preliminary notions. Let $\exists Y\,(c_1, G_1)$ and $\exists Z\,(c_2, G_2)$ be two existentially quantified conjunctions of constraints and atoms, where $Y \cap vars(c_2, G_2) = \emptyset$ and $Z \cap vars(c_1, G_1) = \emptyset$ (we extend, in the obvious way, to tuples of variables notions defined for variables and sets of variables). We say that $\exists Y\,(c_1, G_1)$ and $\exists Z\,(c_2, G_2)$ are *equivalent modulo constraints*, if there exists a renaming substitution $\{Y'/Z'\}$ for (c_1, G_1), with $Y' \subseteq Y$ and $Z' \subseteq Z$, such that:

(i) $G_1\{Y'/Z'\} = G_2$, modulo reordering of atoms, and
(ii) $\mathbb{Z} \models \forall (\exists U\, c_1\{Y'/Z'\} \leftrightarrow \exists V\, c_2)$, where $U = Y - Y'$ and $V = Z - Z'$.

For instance, $\exists Y\,(X \geq Y,\ p(X, Y))$ and $\exists V, W\,(X \geq V,\ V \geq W,\ p(X, W))$ are equivalent modulo constraints. Clearly, if $\exists Y\,(c_1, G_1)$ and $\exists Z\,(c_2, G_2)$ are equivalent modulo constraints, then $\mathbb{Z} \models \forall (\exists Y\,(c_1, G_1) \leftrightarrow \exists Z\,(c_2, G_2))$.

Let P be a set of CHCs. By $Pred(P)$ we denote the set of predicate symbols occurring in P. A *predicate renaming* for P is a, possibly not injective, mapping $\pi \colon Pred(P) \to Q$, where Q is a set of predicate symbols. Given a set S of formulas

---

[1] Available at http://map.uniroma2.it/lopstr16/appendix.pdf.

with predicates in $Pred(P)$, $\pi(S)$ is a new set of formulas obtained by replacing, for all predicates $p \in Pred(P)$, every occurrence of p in S by $\pi(p)$.

For every $k \geq 1$, let X be a fixed k-tuple of distinct variables. Without loss of generality, we assume that for every k-ary predicate $p \in Pred(P)$, all clauses are of the form $p(X) \leftarrow B$, where B is a conjunction of constraints and atoms. By $Bodies(p(X), P)$ we denote the set $\{B \mid p(X) \leftarrow B$ is a clause in $P\}$. We write $Bodies(p(X), P) \equiv Bodies(q(X), P)$ if there exists a bijection $\eta : Bodies(p(X), P) \rightarrow Bodies(q(X), P)$ such that, for every $B \in Bodies(p(X), P)$, $\exists Y\, B$ and $\exists Z\, \eta(B)$ are equivalent modulo constraints, where Y is the tuple of variables occurring in B and not in X, and Z is the tuple of variables occurring in $\eta(B)$ and not in X.

Definition 1 (Predicate Equivalence). *Let P be a set of clauses and $E = \{P_1, \ldots, P_n\}$ be a partition of $Pred(P)$. For $i = 1, \ldots, n$, let e_i be a predicate symbol in P_i, and $\pi : Pred(P) \rightarrow \{e_1, \ldots, e_n\}$ be a predicate renaming for P such that, for $i = 1, \ldots, n$, $\pi(p) = e_i$ iff $p \in P_i$.*

The partition E is a cp-equivalence on P if, for $i = 1, ..., n$, given any two predicates p, q in P_i, p and q have the same arity k and, for any fixed k-tuple X of distinct variables, $\pi(Bodies(p(X), P)) \equiv \pi(Bodies(q(X), P))$.

Note that one can compute the coarsest cp-equivalence on P by a greatest fixpoint construction starting from the partition where all predicate symbols belong to the same equivalence class.

Given a cp-equivalence E on P together with the predicate renaming π considered in Definition 1, we can transform P into a set $\widetilde{\pi}(P, E)$ of clauses in two steps: (i) we remove from P all clauses whose head predicate does not appear in the range of π, and (ii) we apply π to the remaining clauses.

Theorem 1. *For any cp-equivalence E on a set P of clauses, P is satisfiable iff $\widetilde{\pi}(P, E)$ is satisfiable.*

Checking the satisfiability of $\widetilde{\pi}(P, E)$ is often more efficient than checking the satisfiability of P, specially when we use solvers, like Z3, that construct a model of each predicate. Indeed, when checking the satisfiability of $\widetilde{\pi}(P, E)$, the solver has to construct, for each equivalence class E, a model of one predicate only.

To see an example of cp-equivalence, let us consider the following subset of the 51 clauses derived by the removal of the interpreter in our PO example (the complete listing of those clauses is given in the online Appendix A.2[2]):

```
new5(A,B,C,D) :- A=0, new21(B,C,D).
new5(A,B,C,D) :- A=0, B=0, E=<3, E>=1, new10(E,C,D).
new5(A,B,C,D) :- B=0, E=<3, E>=1, new7(A,E,C,D).
new5(A,B,C,D) :- E=0, F=-A+B, G=A+C, A-B=<0, A>0, new5(E,F,G,D).
new5(A,B,C,D) :- E=0, F=A-B, G=B+C, B>0, A-B>=0, new5(F,E,G,D).
new4(A,B,C,D) :- A=0, new21(B,C,D).
new4(A,B,C,D) :- A=0, B=0, E=<3, E>=1, new10(E,C,D).
```

---

[2] Available at http://map.uniroma2.it/lopstr16/appendix.pdf.

```
new4(A,B,C,D) :- B=0, E=<3, E>=1, new6(A,E,C,D).
new4(A,B,C,D) :- E=0, F=-A+B, G=A+C, A-B=<0, A>0, new4(E,F,G,D).
new4(A,B,C,D) :- E=0, F=A-B, G=B+C, B>0, A-B>=0, new4(F,E,G,D).
```

The partition $E = \{\{new5, new4\}, \{new7, new6\}, \{new21\}, \{new10\}\}$ of the set of predicates occurring in the above clauses is a cp-equivalence. The predicate renaming associated with E is:

$$\pi(new5) = \pi(new4) = new4 \qquad \pi(new7) = \pi(new6) = new6$$
$$\pi(new21) = new21 \qquad \pi(new10) = new10.$$

By applying the predicate equivalence transformation to the whole set of 51 clauses, we get an equisatisfiable set of 35 clauses. In particular, in the resulting set the clauses for new5 are no longer present and all occurrences of new5 are replaced by new4.

5   Automated Verification

We have implemented the *Removal of the Interpreter* (RI) and the *Predicate Equivalence* (PE) transformations presented in Sects. 4.2 and 4.3, respectively, by using the VERIMAP transformation system [10].

We use these transformations for verifying properties of business processes in the following two different ways:

(i) 'RI; Z3', that is, we execute RI, and then we check the satisfiability of the clauses generated by RI by applying the solver Z3[3] [12], and

(ii) 'RI; PE; Z3', that is, we execute RI, then PE, and finally we check the satisfiability of the clauses generated by PE by applying the solver Z3.

In Table 3 we report the results obtained by using our prototype implementation for the following business processes:

(1) the Purchase Order (*PO*) shown in Fig. 1, consisting of 7 tasks, 6 gateways, and 17 flows,

(2) the Request Day Off Approval (*RDOA*), adapted from [19], consisting of 7 tasks, 4 gateway, 14 flows and representing the activities involving a company's leadership to approve an employee's request for a day off,

(3) the ST-segment Elevation Myocardial Infarction (*STEMI*), adapted from [7], consisting of 11 tasks, 6 gateways, 22 flows and representing an excerpt of the triage process for hospital admission, and

(4) the *STEMI* with Coronary Care Unit admission (*STEMI+CCU*), adapted from [8], consisting of 26 tasks, 18 gateways, and 52 flows and representing an extension of *STEMI* which also includes the activities for admitting a patient to the Coronary Care Unit.

---

[3] v4.4.2, master branch as of 2016-02-18, with the Duality fixed-point engine [25].

For these processes we have considered ten temporal properties (denoted $P1$–$P10$ in Table 3)[4], each one being of the form: *if* some reachability properties between states hold, *then* some constraints between their associated time instants hold.

The experiments have been performed on an Intel Core i5-2467M 1.60 GHz processor with 4 GB of memory under GNU/Linux OS.

Table 3. Columns 'RI.time' and 'RI.cls' denote the time taken by RI and the number of clauses generated by RI, respectively. Column 'Z3.time1' denotes the time taken by Z3 when executed after RI. Column 'answer' tells us whether or not the property holds. Columns 'PE.time' and 'PE.cls' denote the time taken by PE and the number of clauses generated by PE, respectively. Column 'Z3.time2' denotes the time taken by Z3 when executed after PE. The reduction of the number of clauses (cls reduction) is $\frac{\text{RI.cls} - \text{PE.cls}}{\text{RI.cls}}$ and the time speedup is $\frac{\text{Z3.time1}}{\text{Z3.time2}}$. Times are in seconds.

Business process	Property	RI		Z3.time1	Answer	PE		Z3.time2	cls reduction	Time speedup
		time	cls			Time	cls			
PO	$P1$	0.49	51	0.82	True	0.05	35	0.57	0.31	1.44
	$P2$	0.27	51	0.68	True	0.05	37	0.53	0.27	1.28
	$P3$	0.35	12	0.10	False	0.04	12	0.10	0.00	1.00
RDOA	$P4$	0.14	20	0.31	False	0.03	16	0.22	0.20	1.41
STEMI	$P5$	0.34	52	1.04	True	0.05	43	0.88	0.17	1.18
	$P6$	0.31	7	0.09	False	0.02	7	0.09	0.00	1.00
	$P7$	0.36	67	1.62	True	0.06	56	1.60	0.16	1.01
STEMI+	$P8$	1.58	226	10.70	True	0.17	181	9.75	0.20	1.10
CCU	$P9$	0.14	29	30.17	False	0.03	23	11.62	0.21	2.60
	$P10$	0.10	15	2.08	False	0.03	15	2.08	0.00	1.00

In Table 3 we have *not* reported the results of applying the solver Z3 directly to the clauses encoding the given business processes and properties. Indeed, as already mentioned in Sect. 4.2, Z3 is not able to prove the satisfiability of those clauses, if one does not first apply the transformation RI.

The transformation RI is quite efficient and takes less than half a second for all properties with the exception of property $P8$, which generates 226 clauses. The time taken by Z3 for the verification of the properties (with or without the preliminary application of PE) is generally small (indeed, it is not greater than 1.62 s), with the exception of properties $P8$–$P10$ referring to the most complex business process we have considered, which is the $STEMI+CCU$ process.

Note also that the transformation PE often reduces the number of clauses generated by RI and speeds up the satisfiability check performed by Z3. Moreover, in our examples PE never deteriorates the total verification time in any significant way, in the sense that the time taken by 'RI; PE; Z3' is never significantly greater than the time taken by 'RI; Z3'.

---

[4] The VeriMAP tool and the encodings of the examples of Table 3 are available at http://map.uniroma2.it/lopstr16/VeriMAP_lopstr16-linux_x86_64.tar.gz.

6 Related Work

Several papers have proposed approaches to model business processes with time constraints and, in particular, duration [1,7,15,16,35] (see [6] for a recent survey).

The approach of Arbab et al. [1] provides a translation of BPMN into the coordination language Reo. Due to Constraint Automata semantics of Reo, in principle this translation allows formal reasoning about BPMN processes depending on time and resources. However, the paper does not provide any formalized verification technique.

The workflow conceptual model proposed by Combi and Posenato [7] enables the specification and analysis of time constraints in business processes. They propose temporal constructs for expressing various kinds of time constraints, and also introduce the notion of controllability for workflow schemata. Controllability ensures the executability of a workflow for any duration of the tasks performed by the 'external world'. Unfortunately, the algorithms for testing controllability presented in [7] may require a costly, exhaustive exploration of the search space.

del Foyo and Silva consider workflow diagrams extended with task durations and the latest execution deadline of each task [15]. They provide a translation into Time Petri Nets [3] (where clocks are associated with transitions in the net) and use the tool TINA [4] to answer schedulability questions.

The approach proposed by Gagné and Trudel [16] enables the specification of temporal constraints (such as 'As Soon As Possible') and temporal dependencies. However, unlike the approach presented here, no automated verification mechanism of time-dependent properties is provided.

The approach proposed by Wong and Gibbons [35] uses a timed semantic function which takes a diagram describing a collaboration, and returns a CSP process [17] that models the timed behavior of that diagram, by using the notion of a relative time in the form of delays chosen non-deterministically within given intervals. Properties are then verified by using the FDR system [14].

The proposal by Watahiki et al. [32] and other proposals surveyed in [6] use Timed Automata to model business processes with time constraints. They also use the UPPAAL tool [22] for the automatic proof of the properties of interest.

As already mentioned in the Introduction, the translations into formalisms such as Timed Automata, Time Petri Nets, and CSP, may not be adequate when taking into consideration properties of business processes that require general purpose logical reasoning.

Finally, we would like to mention work on modeling and analyzing business processes with explicit time representation based on the *Event Calculus* [21] (see, for instance, [26]). However, the Event Calculus lacks a simple translation into constrained Horn clauses (in particular, it makes use of negation), and hence it cannot be directly handled by CHC solvers.

7   Conclusions

We have presented a logic-based language to specify BPMN models where time and duration of activities are explicitly represented. The language enables the specification of time constraints, given in the form of lower and upper bounds associated with the duration of tasks. These are useful features with an intuitive meaning that allow the specifier to annotate activities with some time restrictions. The language supports the specification of a wide range of time-dependent properties such as the schedulability and the response time.

The main advantage of our approach is that it allows us to automatically generate constrained Horn clauses from the formal definition of the semantics of the BPMN models and the time-dependent properties of interest. Then, by exploiting recent advances in the field of CHC solving, we get very effective reasoning tools for verifying properties of business processes. Finally, since our approach is parametric with respect to the language used for modeling processes, it is possible to incorporate various extensions of that language with little effort.

References

1. Arbab, F., Kokash, N., Meng, S.: Towards using Reo for compliance-aware business process modeling. In: Margaria, T., Steffen, B. (eds.) ISoLA 2008. CCIS, vol. 17, pp. 108–123. Springer, Heidelberg (2008). doi:10.1007/978-3-540-88479-8_9
2. Bagheri Hariri, B., Calvanese, D., De Giacomo, G., Deutsch, A., Montali, M.: Verification of relational data-centric dynamic systems with external services. In: Proceedings of PODS 2013, pp. 163–174 (2013)
3. Berthomieu, B., Diaz, M.: Modeling and verification of time dependent systems using time Petri nets. IEEE Trans. Softw. Eng. **17**(3), 259–273 (1991)
4. Berthomieu, B., Vernadat, F.: Time Petri nets analysis with TINA. In: Proceedings of QEST 2006, pp. 123–124. IEEE Computer Society (2006)
5. Bjørner, N., Gurfinkel, A., McMillan, K., Rybalchenko, A.: Horn clause solvers for program verification. In: Beklemishev, L.D., Blass, A., Dershowitz, N., Finkbeiner, B., Schulte, W. (eds.) Fields of Logic and Computation II. LNCS, vol. 9300, pp. 24–51. Springer, Cham (2015). doi:10.1007/978-3-319-23534-9_2
6. Cheikhrouhou, S., Kallel, S., Guermouche, N., Jmaiel, M.: The temporal perspective in business process modeling: a survey and research challenges. Serv. Oriented Comput. Appl. **9**(1), 75–85 (2015)
7. Combi, C., Posenato, R.: Controllability in temporal conceptual workflow schemata. In: Dayal, U., Eder, J., Koehler, J., Reijers, H.A. (eds.) BPM 2009. LNCS, vol. 5701, pp. 64–79. Springer, Heidelberg (2009). doi:10.1007/978-3-642-03848-8_6
8. Combi, C., Gozzi, M., Posenato, R., Pozzi, G.: Conceptual modeling of flexible temporal workflows. ACM Trans. Auton. Adapt. Syst. **7**(2), 19:1–19:29 (2012)
9. Damaggio, E., Deutsch, A., Vianu, V.: Artifact systems with data dependencies and arithmetic. ACM Trans. Database Syst. **37**(3), 1–36 (2012)
10. de Angelis, E., Fioravanti, F., Pettorossi, A., Proietti, M.: VeriMAP: a tool for verifying programs through transformations. In: Ábrahám, E., Havelund, K. (eds.) TACAS 2014. LNCS, vol. 8413, pp. 568–574. Springer, Heidelberg (2014). doi:10.1007/978-3-642-54862-8_47

11. De Angelis, E., Fioravanti, F., Pettorossi, A., Proietti, M.: Semantics-based generation of verification conditions by program specialization. Science of Computer Programming. Elsevier (2017)
12. de Moura, L., Bjørner, N.: Z3: an efficient SMT solver. In: Ramakrishnan, C.R., Rehof, J. (eds.) TACAS 2008. LNCS, vol. 4963, pp. 337–340. Springer, Heidelberg (2008). doi:10.1007/978-3-540-78800-3_24
13. Etalle, S., Gabbrielli, M.: Transformations of CLP modules. Theor. Comput. Sci. **166**, 101–146 (1996)
14. Formal Systems (Europe) Ltd., Failures-Divergences Refinement, FDR2 User Manual (1998). www.fsel.com
15. del Foyo, P.M.G., Silva, J.R.: Using time Petri nets for modelling and verification of timed constrained workflow systems. In: Proceedings of ABCM Symposium Series in Mechatronics, ABCM, vol. 3(1), pp. 471–478. ABCM, Brazilian Society of Mechanical Sciences and Engineering (2008)
16. Gagné, D., Trudel, A.: Time-BPMN. In: Proceedings of CEC 2009, pp. 361–367. IEEE Computer Society (2009)
17. Hoare, C.A.R.: Communicating sequential processes. Commun. ACM **21**(8), 666–677 (1978)
18. Hojjat, H., Konečný, F., Garnier, F., Iosif, R., Kuncak, V., Rümmer, P.: A verification toolkit for numerical transition systems. In: Giannakopoulou, D., Méry, D. (eds.) FM 2012. LNCS, vol. 7436, pp. 247–251. Springer, Heidelberg (2012). doi:10.1007/978-3-642-32759-9_21
19. Huai, W., Liu, X., Sun, H.: Towards trustworthy composite service through business process model verification. In: Proceedings of UIC-ATC 2010, pp. 422–427. IEEE Computer Society (2010)
20. Jaffar, J., Maher, M.: Constraint logic programming: a survey. J. Logic Program. **19**(20), 503–581 (1994)
21. Kowalski, R.A., Sergot, M.J.: A logic-based calculus of events. New Gener. Comput. **4**(1), 67–95 (1986)
22. Larsen, K.G., Pettersson, P., Yi, W.: Uppaal in a nutshell. Int. J. Softw. Tools Technol. Transfer **1**(1–2), 134–152 (1997)
23. Lloyd, J.W.: Foundations of Logic Programming. Second, Extended Edition. Springer, Heidelberg (1987)
24. Makni, M., Tata, S., Yeddes, M., Ben Hadj-Alouane, N.: Satisfaction and coherence of deadline constraints in inter-organizational workflows. In: Meersman, R., Dillon, T., Herrero, P. (eds.) OTM 2010. LNCS, vol. 6426, pp. 523–539. Springer, Heidelberg (2010). doi:10.1007/978-3-642-16934-2_39
25. McMillan, K., Rybalchenko, A.: Computing relational fixed points using interpolation. Technical Report MSR-TR-2013-6, Microsoft Research, January 2013
26. Montali, M., Maggi, F., Chesani, F., Mello, P., van der Aalst, W.M.P.: Monitoring business constraints with the event calculus. ACM Trans. Intell. Syst. Technol. **5**(1), 17:1–17:30 (2014)
27. OMG. Business Process Model and Notation (2013). www.omg.org/spec/BPMN/
28. Peralta, J.C., Gallagher, J.P., Sağlam, H.: Analysis of imperative programs through analysis of constraint logic programs. In: Levi, G. (ed.) SAS 1998. LNCS, vol. 1503, pp. 246–261. Springer, Heidelberg (1998). doi:10.1007/3-540-49727-7_15
29. Proietti, M., Smith, F.: Reasoning on data-aware business processes with constraint logic. In: Proceedings of SIMPDA 2014, vol. 1293 of CEUR, pp. 60–75 (2014)
30. Smith, F., Proietti, M.: Rule-based behavioral reasoning on semantic business processes. In: Proceedings of ICAART 2013, vol. II, pp. 130–143. SciTePress (2013)

31. ter Hofstede, A.H.M., van der Aalst, W.M.P., Adams, M., Russell, N. (eds.): Modern Business Process Automation: YAWL and its Support Environment. Springer, Heidelberg (2010)

32. Watahiki, K., Ishikawa, F., Hiraishi, K.: Formal verification of business processes with temporal and resource constraints. In: Proceedings of IEEE International Conference on Systems, Man and Cybernetics, pp. 1173–1180. IEEE (2011)

33. Weber, I., Hoffmann, J., Mendling, J.: Beyond soundness: on the verification of semantic business process models. Distrib. Parallel Databases **27**, 271–343 (2010)

34. Weske, M.: Business Process Management: Concepts, Languages, Architectures. Springer, Heidelberg (2007)

35. Wong, P.Y.H., Gibbons, J.: A relative timed semantics for BPMN. Electr. Notes Theor. Comput. Sci. **229**(2), 59–75 (2009)

Constraint Programming

MiniZinc with Strings

Roberto Amadini[1]($\boxtimes$), Pierre Flener[2], Justin Pearson[2], Joseph D. Scott[2],
Peter J. Stuckey[1], and Guido Tack[3]

[1] University of Melbourne, Melbourne, VIC, Australia
roberto.amadini@unimelb.edu.au
[2] Uppsala University, Uppsala, Sweden
[3] Monash University, Melbourne, Australia

Abstract. Strings are extensively used in modern programming languages and constraints over strings of unknown length occur in a wide range of real-world applications such as software analysis and verification, testing, model checking, and web security. Nevertheless, practically no constraint programming solver natively supports string constraints. We introduce string variables and a suitable set of string constraints as builtin features of the MiniZinc modelling language. Furthermore, we define an interpreter for converting a MiniZinc model with strings into a FlatZinc instance relying only on integer variables. This conversion is obtained via rewrite rules, and does not require any extension of the existing FlatZinc specification. This provides a user-friendly interface for modelling combinatorial problems with strings, and enables both string and non-string solvers to actually solve such problems.

1 Introduction

Strings are widely adopted in modern programming languages for representing input/output data as well as actual commands to be executed dynamically. The latter is particularly critical for security reasons: consider, e.g., the dynamic execution of a malicious SQL query that might dump a database or delete entire tables. Apart from security issues, tracking (an approximation of) the possible values of a string variable can also help in bug detection and code optimisation.

String analysis — needed in real-life applications such as test-case generation [13], program analysis [8], model checking [17], web security [5] — is an active and growing field, [11,25,28], and requires the processing of string constraints such as string (in-)equality, concatenation, and so on. Nevertheless, in constraint programming (CP), practically no solver natively supports string constraints. To our knowledge, the only exception is a new extension [33,36] with bounded-length string variables of the GECODE solver [18], here called GECODE+S for convenience, which will become part of the official GECODE release. Empirical results show that GECODE+S is usually better than dedicated string solvers such as HAMPI [23], KALUZA [32], and SUSHI [14].

In this paper we take a further step towards the definition and solving of string constraints. The three contributions of this paper are as follows.

© Springer International Publishing AG 2017
M.V. Hermenegildo and P. Lopez-Garcia (Eds.): LOPSTR 2016, LNCS 10184, pp. 59–75, 2017.
DOI: 10.1007/978-3-319-63139-4_4

First, an extension of the MiniZinc [30] modelling language by string variables of possibly unknown length. MiniZinc enables the specification of constraint problems over (sets of) integers and real numbers, but currently does not allow models containing string variables. Thanks to the extension we describe, a MiniZinc user can now naturally define and solve a MiniZinc model containing string variables and constraints, as well as other constraints on other variable types.

Second, we provide a solver independent conversion of MiniZinc models with strings into equivalent FlatZinc instances containing only integer variables. Thus, every solver supporting FlatZinc can now solve a MiniZinc model with strings. This conversion follows the padding representation advocated in [21] and implemented in [35]. However, we underline that our contribution is orthogonal to [35] and generalises its work (see Sect. 4.2): our MiniZinc formulation does not impose restrictions on the string length (enabling us to express unbounded-length strings), and further allows any solver to use its preferred string representation (e.g., bit vectors or automata), and handles a superset of the constraints of [35].

Third, we provide an experimental evaluation on the NORN string benchmark [1] used in GECODE+S [33,36] and the state-of-the-art constraint solvers CHUFFED [10], GECODE [18], IZPLUS [15], PICAT-SAT [43], MZN/GUROBI [4], MZN/YICES2 [9] and MZN/OSCAR.CBLS [7]. Results indicate that native support for string variables usually pays off, but not always, in which case the technology of the best solver varies. Indeed, we show that — despite longer flattening times — sometimes our conversion is more beneficial than using a dedicated string solver.

Paper Structure. Section 2 gives some background notions about string variables, MiniZinc and FlatZinc. Sections 3 and 4 describe the string extensions we implemented for MiniZinc and FlatZinc. Section 5 presents the experimental results before we discuss related work in Sect. 6 and conclude in Sect. 7.

2   Background

MiniZinc [30] is a flexible and user-friendly modelling language for representing constraint problems. The motto is *model once, solve anywhere*: each MiniZinc model is solver-independent, although it may contain annotations to communicate with the underlying solver.

MiniZinc supports the most common global constraints (constraints defined over an arbitrary number of variables [3]) and allows the separation between model and data: a MiniZinc model can be defined as a generic template to be instantiated by different data.

As an example, consider the n-queens problem, where $n \geq 4$ queens have to be placed on an $n \times n$ chessboard in such a way that they do not attack each other. This problem can be modelled in MiniZinc in terms of an unspecified number n of queens, and then instantiated by providing the value of parameter n.

FlatZinc is a solver-specific target language for MiniZinc. Each MiniZinc model (together with corresponding data, if any) is converted into FlatZinc in the form required by a solver. In other terms, from the same MiniZinc model different FlatZinc instances can be derived according to solver-specific redefinitions.

For example, the n-queens problem can be modelled with the well-known `alldifferent`$([x_1, \ldots, x_n])$ global constraint, which holds if and only if all variables x_i take different values. In this case a solver can decide to keep the constraint as is or to unfold it into the logical conjunction $\bigwedge_{1 \leq i < j \leq n} x_i \neq x_j$.

Following the approach of [23, 32, 33, 35, 36] we focus in this work on constraint solving over *bounded* string variables, i.e., string variables x having a bounded length ℓ, with $|x| \leq \ell \in \mathbb{N}$. We point out that our MiniZinc language extension allows us to express problems with unbounded string variables. Note that, while problems over bounded-length string variables are trivially decidable, satisfiability with unbounded-length strings is not decidable in general [16].

Notation. Given a fixed alphabet Σ, a string $x \in \Sigma^*$ is a finite sequence of $|x| \geq 0$ characters of Σ, where $|x|$ is the length of x. Let ASC denote the set of the ASCII symbols: we define the function $\mathcal{I} \colon \mathsf{ASC} \to [1, 128]$ such that $\mathcal{I}(a) = k$ if and only if a is the k-th ASCII symbol.

The symbols $=$, $\neq$, and $\preceq$ respectively denote string equality, inequality, and lexicographical order on Σ^*. The concatenation of x and y is denoted by $x \cdot y$, while x^n denotes the iterated concatenation of x for n times; x^0 denotes the empty string ϵ, while x^{-1} denotes the reverse of x.

If x is a string (resp., an array), then we denote by $x[i]$ its i-th character (resp., element) and by $x[i..j]$ the subsequence $x[i]x[i + 1] \cdots x[j]$; indices start from 1 in both cases. The symbol $\in$ is used for both set membership and character occurrence within a string.

3 MiniZinc with Strings

MiniZinc supports plenty of builtins (e.g., comparisons, basic and advanced numeric operations, set operations, logical operators, ...) and global constraints. It currently permits four types of variables (i.e., Booleans, integers, floats, and sets of integers) while strings can only be fixed literals, used for formatting output or defining model annotations.

Our first contribution is introducing *string variables*, i.e., variables $x \in \Sigma^*$, where Σ is a given alphabet. As a first step, we assume that the alphabet Σ is always the set ASC of ASCII characters. Although we focus on bounded-length strings, we do not impose any limitation on the maximum string length ℓ.

Figure 1 shows three string variable declarations in a MiniZinc model. Variable x belongs to ASC* but its maximum length is not specified: a solver can choose the preferred upper bound ℓ for its length or consider it unbounded. For example, a solver using automata for representing strings does not need to set a maximum length since it can represent strings of arbitrary length. Conversely, a bounded-length string solver such as GECODE+S has to fix a maximum string

```
1   int: N;
2   var string: x;
3   var string(N): y;
4   var string(500) of {"a", "b", "c"}: z;
```

Fig. 1. Examples of string variable declarations.

Table 1. MiniZinc string constraints, for each $x, y, z \in \mathsf{ASC}^*$, $a, b \in \mathsf{ASC}$, $n, m, q, q_0 \in \mathbb{N}$, $S \subseteq \mathsf{ASC}$, $F \subseteq \mathbb{N}$, $D \in \mathbb{N}^{q \times |S|}$, and $N \in \mathcal{P}(\mathbb{N})^{q \times |S|}$.

Constraint	MiniZinc Syntax	Description
$x = y,\ x \neq y$	x = y, x != y	(in-)equality
$x \prec y,\ x \preceq y,\ x \succeq y,\ x \succ y$	x < y, x < = y, x >= y, x > y	lexicographic order
$x \in S^*$	x in S	character set
$x \overline{\in} S^*$	str_alphabet(x, S)	alphabet
$x \in [a, b]^*$	str_range(x, a, b)	character range
$z = x \cdot y$	z = x ++ y	concatenation
$a = x[n]$	a = x[n]	character access
$y = x[n..m]$	y = str_sub(x, n, m)	sub-string
$y = x^n$	y = str_pow(x, n)	iterated concatenation
$y = x^{-1}$	y = str_rev(x)	reverse
$n = |x|$	n = str_len(x)	length
$x \in \mathcal{L}_\mathrm{D}(q, S, D, q_0, F)$	str_dfa(x, q, S, D, q0,F)	DFA membership
$x \in \mathcal{L}_\mathrm{N}(q, S, N, q_0, F)$	str_nfa(x, q, S, N, q0,F)	NFA membership
$\mathcal{GCC}(x, A, N)$	str_gcc(x, A, N)	global cardinality

length ℓ. This tricky part is analogous to a MiniZinc declaration of the form "var int: i" for an integer variable i: a finite-domain solver assumes the domain of i to be finite and chooses its preferred bounds, while for a MIP solver i is unbounded. The length of y in Fig. 1 can be at most N, where N is an integer parameter to be initialised within the model or in a separate data file. Variable z even has a constrained alphabet: $z \in \{w \in \{"a", "b", "c"\}^* \mid |w| \leq 500\}$.

Given that we now have string variables, inspired by [33,35,36], we introduce the string constraints specified in Table 1. A constraint for membership in a context-free language could be added; it was considered in [33,35,36] for inclusion in GECODE+S, but not implemented for time-reasons as the state-of-the-art propagator of [21] for fixed-length string variables needs work to be generalised to bounded-length string variables.

The constraints $=, \neq, \prec, \preceq, \succeq, \succ$ have the semantics of their standard definitions. Given $S \subseteq \mathsf{ASC}$, the semantics of $x \in S^*$ is $\forall a : a \in x \implies a \in S$, while $x \overline{\in} S$ also enforces the reverse implication, i.e., $\forall a : a \in x \iff a \in S$.

The constraint str_range offers a shortcut for defining a set of strings over a range of characters: $[a, b]^* = \{c \in \mathsf{ASC} \mid a \leq c \leq b\}^*$, so for instance

```
1  int: m;
2  var int: n;
3  var string(m): x;
4  constraint x = str_rev(x);
5  constraint str_range(x, "a", "z");
6  constraint str_len(x) mod 2 = 1;
7  constraint str_gcc(x, ["a", "b", "c"], [n, n, n]);
8  constraint n > 0;
9  solve minimize str_len(x);
```

Fig. 2. A model for finding minimum-odd-length palindromes with the same, positive number of a's, b's, and c's. An optimal solution must have $n = 2 \wedge |x| = 7$.

$["a","d"]^* = \{"a","b","c","d"\}^*$. The function $x[i..j]$ returns the substring $x[n]x[n+1]\cdots x[m]$, where $n = \max(1,i)$ and $m = \min(j,|x|)$. In particular, $i > j$ implies $x[i..j] = \epsilon$.

The constraint $x \in \mathcal{L}_D(q, S, D, q_0, F)$ constrains x to be accepted by the deterministic finite automaton (DFA) $\langle Q, S, \delta, q_0, F \rangle$ where: $Q = \{1, \ldots, q\}$ is the state set, $S = \{a_1, \ldots, a_{|S|}\}$ is the alphabet, $\delta : Q \times S \rightarrow Q$ is the transition function such that $D[i,j] = k \iff \delta(i, a_j) = k$, $q_0 \in Q$ is the initial state, and $F \subseteq Q$ is the set of accepting states. The same applies to the nondeterministic finite automaton (NFA) constraint $x \in \mathcal{L}_N(q, S, N, q_0, F)$, with the only difference that, while $D[i,j] \in Q$, in this case $N[i,j] \subseteq Q$.

Finally, we add a global cardinality constraint $\mathcal{GCC}(x, A, N)$ for strings, stating that each character $A[i] \in \mathsf{ASC}$ must occur exactly $N[i]$ times in string x.

The constraints in Table 1 express all those used in existing string solvers [1, 14, 23, 24, 32, 41] and reflect the most used string operations in modern programming languages. We are not aware of string solvers supporting constraints like lexicographic ordering and global cardinality, but these are natural for a CP solver.

Some constraints are redundant. For example we have that $x[i] = x[i..i]$ and $y = x[i..j] \iff (\exists y_1, y_2 \in \mathsf{ASC}^*) \; x = y_1 \cdot y \cdot y_2 \wedge |y_1| = i - 1 \wedge |y_1 \cdot y| = j$. The rationale behind such redundancy is to ease the model writing and to allow solvers to define a specialised treatment for each constraint in order to optimise the solving process.

The constraint set we added to MiniZinc is intended to be an extensible interface for the definition of string problems to be solved by fixed, bounded, and unbounded-length string solvers.

Consider the MiniZinc model in Fig. 2, encoding the problem of finding a minimum-length palindrome string belonging to $\{"a", \ldots, "z"\}^*$, having an odd length, and containing the same, positive number of occurrences of "a", "b", and "c". We can see in this example the potential of MiniZinc with strings: the model is succinct and readable, it allows the specification of optimisation problems and not just of satisfaction problems, it accepts constraints over different types than just strings, it does not impose any bounds on the lengths of the strings, and it enables expressing the membership of a string variable to a context-*sensitive* language.

```
1  string sql;
2  var int: m; var int: n;
3  var string: pref; var string: suff; var string: expr;
4  constraint sql = pref ++ expr ++ str_pow(" ", m) ++ "=" ++ str_pow(" ", n) ++
       expr ++ suff;
5  constraint str_len(expr) > 0;
6  solve satisfy;
```

Fig. 3. A model for detecting a possible SQL injection.

A more interesting example is provided in Fig. 3, where we show a simplified way to detect a potential SQL injection attack in a script. An *SQL injection* is a technique where a malicious SQL statement is injected into a regular SQL command. A well-known example is the injection of the condition "OR 1=1" into the WHERE clause of an SQL query. Since every Boolean expression containing such a condition evaluates to true, an SQL injection of this type may cause the deletion or communication of tables of a database. The model in Fig. 3 is actually more general, by detecting an injection into the parametric string sql of a substring of the form $expr \cdot b^m = b^n \cdot expr$, where expr can be any non-empty string while b^m and b^n are arbitrary sequences of m and n blanks respectively, where m and n are non-negative integer variables. The prefix pref and the suffix suff of sql can be any string. Clearly, this simplified example is not general enough to cover all the possible SQL injections. Nonetheless, this MiniZinc model is strictly more powerful than when using only regular expressions: the constraint in line 4 cannot be replaced by an equivalent str_dfa or str_nfa constraint, but could alternatively be modelled using the mentioned constraint for membership in a context-free language, which is not considered in this paper.

4   FlatZinc With(out) Strings

MiniZinc is a solver-independent modelling language. In practice, this is achieved by the MiniZinc compiler, which can translate any MiniZinc model into a specialised FlatZinc instance for a particular solver, using a solver-specific library of suitable redefinitions for basic and global constraints.

In order to extend MiniZinc with support for string variables, our second contribution consists of two redefinition libraries to perform different conversions:

- a string-to-string conversion $\mathcal{F}^{str}$ that flattens a model M with string constraints into a FlatZinc instance $\mathcal{F}^{str}(M)$ with all such constraints preserved;
- a string-to-integers conversion $\mathcal{F}^{int}$ that flattens a model M with string constraints into a FlatZinc instance $\mathcal{F}^{int}(M)$ with string constraints transformed into integer constraints.

We now discuss these two conversions in turn.

4.1 The $\mathcal{F}^{\mathrm{str}}$ Conversion

The conversion $\mathcal{F}^{\mathrm{str}}$ is straightforward and we omit its technical details. Each string predicate is preserved in the resulting FlatZinc instance, with a few exceptions in order to be consistent with the FlatZinc syntax. For example, the constraints x = y and x != y are rewritten into str_eq(x, y) and str_neq(x, y) respectively. Similarly, a string function is rewritten into a corresponding Flat-Zinc predicate; e.g., n = str_len(x) is translated into str_len(x, n), while z = x ++ y translates into str_concat(x, y, z).

```
1  array [1..3] of string: X_INTRODUCED_3 = ["a","b","c"];
2  var int: n :: output_var;
3  var string(100): x :: output_var;
4  var string: X_INTRODUCED_0 :: var_is_introduced :: is_defined_var;
5  var int: X_INTRODUCED_1 :: var_is_introduced :: is_defined_var;
6  constraint str_eq(x,X_INTRODUCED_0);
7  constraint str_range(x,"a","z");
8  constraint int_mod(X_INTRODUCED_1,2,1);
9  constraint str_gcc(x,X_INTRODUCED_3,[n,n,n]);
10 constraint int_le(1,n);
11 constraint str_rev(x,X_INTRODUCED_0) :: defines_var(X_INTRODUCED_0);
12 constraint str_len(x,X_INTRODUCED_1) :: defines_var(X_INTRODUCED_1);
13 solve minimize X_INTRODUCED_1;
```

Fig. 4. FlatZinc instance resulting from $\mathcal{F}^{\mathrm{str}}$ applied to the MiniZinc model in Fig. 2.

Figure 4 gives the FlatZinc instance obtained by the $\mathcal{F}^{\mathrm{str}}$ conversion of the MiniZinc model in Fig. 2, assuming that the length-bound parameter m is instantiated with value 100 (see line 3).

$\mathcal{F}^{\mathrm{str}}$ is a straightforward and fast conversion aimed at solvers supporting (some of) the constraints of Table 1. At present, to the best of our knowledge, the only CP solver with such a capability is the new GECODE+S [33,36].

4.2 The $\mathcal{F}^{\mathrm{int}}$ Conversion

When extending MiniZinc with new features, the goal is to be always conservative: the compiler should produce FlatZinc code executable by any current FlatZinc solver, albeit less efficiently than by a solver with native support for the new features. Hence we also develop the $\mathcal{F}^{\mathrm{int}}$ conversion.

The underlying idea of $\mathcal{F}^{\mathrm{int}}$ is to map each string variable x to an integer variable $\ell_x \in [0, n]$ representing the string length $|x|$ and an array $X \in [0, 128]^n$ of n integer variables representing the string itself; we choose $n = \min\left(\overline{|x|}, \ell\right)$, where $\overline{|x|}$ denotes the upper bound on $|x|$ if it is specified in the model and $\overline{|x|} = \ell$ otherwise, as we cannot exceed the maximum string length ℓ. For $i = 1, \ldots, n$ the invariant $i > \ell_x \iff X[i] = 0$ enforces that the end $X[|x| + 1] \cdots X[n]$ of the array X is padded with trailing zeros. The notation $(\forall_{i=1,\ldots,|x|})\, P(i)$ is actually a shortcut for the constraint $(\forall_{i \in [1, \overline{\ell_x}]})\, i \leq |x| \rightarrow P(i)$, and similarly

$$\mathcal{V}_{\text{str}}(x, n, S) \mapsto \{\mathcal{A}(x)\} \tag{1}$$

$$\mathcal{A}(x) \mapsto \langle X \rangle \begin{Bmatrix} n = \min(|\overline{x}|, \ell), \ \mathcal{V}_{\text{arr}}(X, n, 0..\mathcal{I}(\mathcal{D}(x))), \\ \mathcal{V}_{\text{int}}(\ell_x, 0..n), \ell_x = |x|, (\forall_{i \in [1,n]}) \ i > \ell_x \iff X[i] = 0 \end{Bmatrix} \tag{2}$$

$$x \in S^* \mapsto \{(\forall_{i \in [1,|x|]}) \ \mathcal{A}(x)[i] \in \{0\} \cup \mathcal{I}(S)\} \tag{3}$$

$$x \in \overline{S}^* \mapsto \{x \in S, (\forall_{i \in \mathcal{I}(S)})(\exists_{j \in [1,|x|]}) \ \mathcal{A}(x)[j] = i\} \tag{4}$$

$$x \in [a, b]^* \mapsto \{(\forall_{i \in [1,|x|]}) \ \mathcal{A}(x)[i] \in \{0\} \cup [\mathcal{I}(a), \mathcal{I}(b)]\} \tag{5}$$

$$x = y \mapsto \{|x| = |y|, \ (\forall_{i \in [1,|x|]}) \ \mathcal{A}(x)[i] = \mathcal{A}(y)[i]\} \tag{6}$$

$$x \neq y \mapsto \{|x| = |y| \to (\exists_{i \in [1,|x|]}) \ \mathcal{A}(x)[i] \neq \mathcal{A}(y)[i]\} \tag{7}$$

$$x \preceq y \mapsto \{\texttt{lex\_lesseq}(\mathcal{A}(x), \mathcal{A}(y))\} \tag{8}$$

$$\mathcal{GCC}(x, A, N) \mapsto \{\texttt{global\_cardinality}(\mathcal{A}(x), [\mathcal{I}(a) \mid a \in A], N)\} \tag{9}$$

$$|x| \mapsto \langle n \rangle \{\mathcal{V}_{\text{int}}(n, 0..\ell)\} \tag{10}$$

$$x^{-1} \mapsto \langle y \rangle \{\mathcal{V}_{\text{str}}(y), |x| = |y|, (\forall_{i \in [1,|x|]}) \ \mathcal{A}(y)[i] = \mathcal{A}(x)[|x| - i + 1]\} \tag{11}$$

$$x \cdot y \mapsto \langle z \rangle \begin{Bmatrix} \mathcal{V}_{\text{str}}(z), |z| = |x| + |y|, (\forall_{i \in [1,|x|]}) \ \mathcal{A}(z)[i] = \mathcal{A}(x)[i], \\ (\forall_{j \in [1,|y|]}) \ \mathcal{A}(z)[j + |x|] = \mathcal{A}(y)[j] \end{Bmatrix} \tag{12}$$

$$x^n \mapsto \langle y \rangle \begin{Bmatrix} \mathcal{V}_{\text{str}}(y), |y| = n|x|, \\ (\forall_{i \in [1,|x|], j \in [1,|y|]}) \ \mathcal{A}(x)[i] = \mathcal{A}(y)[|x|(j - 1) + i] \end{Bmatrix} \tag{13}$$

$$x[i..j] \mapsto \langle y \rangle \begin{Bmatrix} n = \max(1, i), \ m = \min(|x|, j), \\ \mathcal{V}_{\text{str}}(y), \ |y| = \max(0, m - n + 1), \\ (\forall_{k \in [1,|y|]}) \ \mathcal{A}(y)[k] = \mathcal{A}(x)[k + n - 1] \end{Bmatrix} \tag{14}$$

$$x[i] \mapsto \langle y \rangle \begin{Bmatrix} \mathcal{V}_{\text{str}}(y), \ |y| \leq 1, \\ (i \in [0, |x|] \wedge \mathcal{A}(y)[1] = \mathcal{A}(x)[i]) \vee (i \notin [0, |x|] \wedge y = \epsilon) \end{Bmatrix} \tag{15}$$

$$x \in \mathcal{L}_{\text{D}}(q, S, D, q_0, F) \mapsto$$

$$\begin{Bmatrix} s = |S| + 1, \ D' \in [1, q]^{q \times s}, \ T = \texttt{sort}(\mathcal{I}(S)), \\ (\forall_{i \in [1,q], j \in [1,s]}) \ D'[i, j] = \begin{cases} 0 & \text{if } j = 1 \wedge D[i, j] \notin F \\ D[i, j] & \text{otherwise} \end{cases} \\ \mathcal{V}_{\text{arr}}(X, |x|, 0..|x|), \ \texttt{regular}(X, q, s, D', q_0, F), \\ (\forall_{i \in [1,|x|]}) \ \mathcal{A}(x)[i] = \begin{cases} T[X[i] - 1] & \text{if } X[i] > 1 \\ 0 & \text{otherwise} \end{cases} \end{Bmatrix} \tag{16}$$

Fig. 5. Rewrite rules of $\mathcal{F}^{\text{int}}$.

for existential quantification, where $\overline{\ell_x}$ denotes the current upper bound of the domain of ℓ_x.

The main issue of $\mathcal{F}^{\text{int}}$ is the maximum size ℓ, since FlatZinc does not allow dynamic-length arrays. We set $\ell = 1000$ by default and issue a warning to the user if an unbounded string variable is artificially restricted by this transformation. The user (and in fact each solver) can override this parameter.

The $\mathcal{F}^{\text{int}}$ conversion follows the padding representation advocated in [21] and implemented in [35]: it works through the rewrite rules listed in Fig. 5. This conversion is specified as a library containing the rewrite rules expressed in the MiniZinc language itself and does not require any extension of the existing FlatZinc specification.[1] Each rewrite rule has one of the following forms:

- $P \mapsto \{C_1, \ldots, C_n\}$, meaning that predicate P is rewritten into the constraint conjunction $C_1 \wedge \cdots \wedge C_n$; or
- $F(x_1, \ldots, x_k) \mapsto \langle E \rangle \{C_1, \ldots, C_n\}$, meaning that function F is rewritten into expression E subject to constraint $C_1 \wedge \cdots \wedge C_n$.

We use a more readable meta-syntax instead of using MiniZinc/FlatZinc directly. We denote by $\mathcal{D}(x) \subseteq \mathsf{ASC}$ the auxiliary function that returns the set of characters that may occur in x, and by $\mathcal{I}(S)$ the set $\{\mathcal{I}(a) \mid a \in S\}$ of the ASCII codes for each character of S. Given $D \subseteq \mathbb{N}$ and $S \subseteq \mathsf{ASC}$, the constructs $\mathcal{V}_{\text{int}}(n, D)$, $\mathcal{V}_{\text{str}}(x, m, S)$, and $\mathcal{V}_{\text{arr}}(X, m, D)$ denote respectively: an integer variable declaration `var D: n`, a string variable declaration `var string(m) of S: x`, and an array of integer variables declaration `array[1..m] of var D: X`. If a parameter is omitted, then we assume $D = [0, 128]$, $m = \ell$, and $S = \mathsf{ASC}$.

Rule (1) of Fig. 5 transforms a declaration of a string variable x into the corresponding declaration of an array X of integer variables via the $\mathcal{A}(x)$ function of Rule (2), which enforces the properties of X described above. It is important to note that this transformation relies on the *same* array of integer variables being returned by $\mathcal{A}(x)$ for a variable x, even if the function is called multiple times. This is achieved through the common subexpression elimination mechanism built into MiniZinc functions [37].

Rules (3) to (9) are examples of predicate rewriting. In particular, the latter two rules take advantage of MiniZinc expressiveness by rewriting $x \preceq y$ and $\mathcal{GCC}(x, A, N)$ in terms of the `lex_lesseq` and the `global_cardinality` global constraints over integers. The rewrite rules for predicates $\in$, $\overline{\in}$, $=$, and $\neq$ are intuitive.

Rules (10) to (15) are examples of function rewriting: a string variable is created, constrained, and then returned. We can see that dealing with special cases enables us to reduce the number of generated constraints; e.g., see Rules (14) and (15).

Rule (16) for `str_dfa` predicate is tricky. Indeed, the `regular` global constraint cannot straightforwardly encode $x \in \mathcal{L}_{\text{D}}(q, S, D, q_0, F)$ since the "empty character" 0 might occur in $\mathcal{A}(x)$. In order to agree with the semantics of

---

[1] This library, called `nostrings.mzn`, is publicly available at https://bitbucket.org/jossco/gecode-string.

regular, it is necessary to increment the number s of its symbols (so, the i-th character of S becomes the $(i + 1)$-st symbol of the DFA encoded by regular), and to add a column at the head of D for dealing with the 0 character (matrix D' is the result of this addition — note that the state 0 is always a failing state).[2] If regular is satisfiable, then the accepted sequence X is re-mapped to a corresponding string thanks to the auxiliary array T. The rule for str_nfa is analogous.

We remark that the $\mathcal{F}^{int}$ converter enables the solving of string problems by *any* solver. Clearly, this is achieved at the expense of efficiency. Indeed, several new constraints and reifications are introduced.

Consider for example the model M of Fig. 2: the $\mathcal{F}^{str}(M)$ conversion is instantaneous and produces a FlatZinc instance of only 13 lines, regardless of the maximum length m of string variable x (see Fig. 4). Conversely, the $\mathcal{F}^{int}(M)$ conversion can be considerably less efficient depending on the m parameter. For example, if m = 100, then $\mathcal{F}^{int}(M)$ consists of 4,511 lines; if m = 1000, then a FlatZinc instance of 45,011 lines is produced.

5   Evaluation

Our third contribution is an evaluation of our framework with different solvers. We compared the string CP solver GECODE+S [33,36] against various state-of-the-art constraint solvers, namely:

- CHUFFED [10] is a CP solver with lazy clause generation [31];
- GECODE [18] is a CP solver;
- IZPLUS [15] is a CP solver that also exploits local search;
- PICAT-SAT [43] translates a CP problem into a Boolean satisfiability (SAT) problem, solved by LINGELING;
- MZN/GUROBI [4] translates a MiniZinc (MZN) model into a mixed-integer linear program, solved by GUROBI OPTIMIZER [20];
- MZN/YICES2 [9] translates a MiniZinc model into a SAT modulo theories (SMT) model without string variables, solved by YICES2;
- MZN/OSCAR.CBLS [7] translates a MiniZinc model in a constraint-based local search model and a black-box search procedure, run by OSCAR.CBLS [12].

There is a lack of standardised and challenging string benchmarks [21,33,35,36]. However, we stress that the goal of this paper *is not* an evaluation of solver performance, but the introduction of a framework for modelling string problems easily, with solving by both string and non-string solvers. Moreover, one of the benefits of introducing string variables and constraints in MiniZinc is the possibility of designing and comparing challenging and standard benchmarks.

We picked five problems from the NORN benchmark [1]: $a^n b^n$, ChunkSplit, HammingDistance, Levenshtein, and StringReplace (we use the same names as

---

[2] Details at http://www.minizinc.org/doc-lib/doc-globals-extensional.html.

in [1]). We also used our Palindrome problem of Fig. 2 and our SQL injection problem of Fig. 3. All these problems have no parameters, except for the maximum string length ℓ. For each problem, we:

1. wrote a MiniZinc model M with parametric bound ℓ on string length;
2. obtained FlatZinc instances $F_M(f, \ell)$ by flattening M with $f \in \{\mathcal{F}^{str}, \mathcal{F}^{int}\}$ and $\ell \in \{250, 500, 1000\}$;
3. solved each $F_M(\mathcal{F}^{str}, \ell)$ with GECODE+S (we extended the FlatZinc interpreter of GECODE for handling $\mathcal{F}^{str}$ builtins) and each $F_M(\mathcal{F}^{int}, \ell)$ with the other solvers.

We ran the experiments on Ubuntu 15.10 machines with 16 GB of RAM and 2.60 GHz Intel® i7 CPU. The source code for GECODE+S and the used MiniZinc models are available at https://bitbucket.org/jossco/gecode-string. The versions of the solvers with results in Table 2 are those used by the sunny-cp portfolio solver [2], version 2.2, in the MiniZinc Challenge 2016.[3] We do not compare with the NORN solver, as our results are incomparable with those of an unbounded-length solver such as NORN, which generates the language of all satisfying assignments for each string variable.

Table 2. Runtimes of the solvers. Bold font indicates the best performance for each problem instance.

ℓ	CHUFFED			GECODE			IZPLUS			MZN/GUROBI			PICAT-SAT			GECODE+S		
	250	500	1000	250	500	1000	250	500	1000	250	500	1000	250	500	1000	250	500	1000
$a^n b^n$	0.9	**2**	**4.5**	2.6	16.8	145.2	2.2	6.8	22.7	9.7	20.7	54.7	2.1	3.9	7.2	**0.4**	2.7	28.2
Chunk	4.7	14.9	n/a	3.5	**8**	26	7.2	22.2	**24.8**	t/o	t/o	t/o	46.8	152	291.1	**1.4**	14.2	187.9
Hamm.	25.7	283.6	n/a	84.6	t/o	t/o	t/o	t/o	t/o	363.6	t/o	t/o	46.8	454	t/o	**0.6**	**3.8**	**37.4**
Leven.	1.3	2.6	6	1.2	2.3	5.4	3.7	19.5	8.1	91	345.7	t/o	1.7	3.8	26.8	**0.1**	**0.1**	**0.1**
Str. Rep.	2.4	6.8	23.2	t/o	t/o	t/o	3.1	9.7	44.2	264.2	t/o	t/o	28.3	148.1	t/o	**0.2**	**0.8**	**4.7**
Palind.	1.6	23.4	90	t/o	t/o	t/o	**0.8**	**2.3**	**7.1**	119.5	t/o	t/o	16.6	93.7	504.5	n/a	n/a	n/a
SQLInj.	17.9	399.8	n/a	4.6	10.2	396.3	108.9	431.1	617.9	t/o	t/o	t/o	83.3	148.7	502.6	**0.5**	**0.1**	**0.1**

Table 2 shows the runtimes, in seconds, to conclude the search, i.e., the time needed by a solver to prove the (un-)satisfiability of a problem (for satisfaction problems) or to find and prove an optimal solution (for Palindrome, the only optimisation problem). The 't/o' abbreviation means that the time-out of 600 seconds was reached, while 'n/a' means that a solver failed prematurely (e.g., due to a segmentation fault) or is not applicable. For instance, GECODE+S is not applicable to the Palindrome problem since it does not implement the $\mathcal{GCC}$ constraint, which, to the best of our knowledge, has not been proposed before in the literature. Our MiniZinc extension (see Table 1) covers all the constraints implemented by GECODE+S.

---

[3] sunny-cp is available at https://github.com/CP-Unibo/sunny-cp. We actually took advantage of its architecture for running and evaluating the solvers in Table 2.

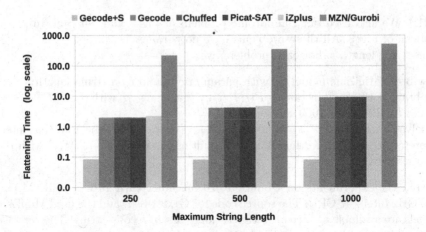

Fig. 6. Average time (in seconds) taken by $\mathcal{F}^{\text{int}}$ or $\mathcal{F}^{\text{str}}$.

The chosen solvers whose results are not listed in Table 2 were not competitive on the chosen problems. Local search, performed by MZN/OSCAR.CBLS, is by design unable to prove unsatisfiability and thus always times out on the unsatisfiable $a^n b^n$, Hamming, and StringReplace problems. Further, the black-box local search performed by MZN/OSCAR.CBLS unfortunately meanders on some of the chosen satisfiable problems and optimisation problems upon flattening by the $\mathcal{F}^{\text{int}}$ conversion: our future work includes integrating the extension [6] for string variables and constraints of OSCAR.CBLS [12] into MZN/OSCAR.CBLS, so that the $\mathcal{F}^{\text{str}}$ conversion can be used instead. Similarly, MZN/YICES2 makes the state-of-the-art SMT solver YICES2 suffer from the result of the composition of the $\mathcal{F}^{\text{int}}$ conversion with the FlatZinc-to-SMT-LIB-format conversion [9], which has not been modernised for a while. We hope that somebody will enable the use of the $\mathcal{F}^{\text{str}}$ conversion so that SMT solvers with a string theory — such as CVC4 [27], S3 [39], and Z3STR2 [41] — can be used instead, though not for optimisation problems.

All the runtimes in Table 2 include the FlatZinc flattening time. As explained at the end of Sect. 4, this time is far greater when the $\mathcal{F}^{\text{int}}$ conversion is used. This is clearly noticeable in Fig. 6, where the average flattening time (in seconds) taken by $\mathcal{F}^{\text{int}}$ (for all the solvers except GECODE+S) or $\mathcal{F}^{\text{str}}$ (for GECODE+S) is shown.[4] As mentioned at the end of Sect. 4, this time is proportional to the maximum string length ℓ.

While GECODE, CHUFFED, PICAT-SAT, and IZPLUS have comparable performance, the flattening time for MZN/GUROBI is remarkably higher. This is due to the fact that the complex reified expressions created by $\mathcal{F}^{\text{str}}$ must be linearized for use with MZN/GUROBI and hence this further expands the resulting FlatZinc. The average percentage of the total solving time (when a problem is

---

[4] We assume a flattening time of $T = 600$ seconds when the conversion time exceeded the time limit T. This happened only for MZN/GUROBI.

solved) taken by $\mathcal{F}^{int}$ is 42.41% for IZPLUS, 47.10% for CHUFFED, 55.97% for GECODE, and 62.36% for MZN/GUROBI. Conversely, the average percentage of the total solving time taken by $\mathcal{F}^{str}$ for GECODE+S is only 6.95%.

The message of this evaluation is twofold. On the one hand, the GECODE+S CP solver is by far the best solver overall, due to its native string support and the short flattening times via $\mathcal{F}^{str}$ to FlatZinc. On the other hand, solvers without native string support sometimes benefit from $\mathcal{F}^{int}$ for being faster than GECODE+S despite longer flattening times. This is interesting and should stimulate further development of native string support in CP solvers.

6   Related Work

GECODE+S [33,36] is currently the only CP solver that handles bounded-length string variables; its representation of string variables improves over the prefix-suffix pairs representation [34] and the open-sequence representation [35]. Fixed-length Boolean string variables, that is bit vectors, are handled in a CP fashion in [29]. Older CP approaches are surveyed in [33].

Apart from these systems, there are a number of string solvers, some custom-made and some others relying on existing solving technologies such as satisfiability modulo theories (SMT). We now discuss three approaches.

Bit-vector solvers map string constraints into bit-vector constraints. Examples of solvers using this approach are HAMPI [23,24] and KALUZA [32]. The effectiveness of this approach appears to be limited when compared with other, more recent string solving techniques [22,41].

Automaton-based solvers rely on regular expressions or (simplified) context-free grammars in order to represent strings and handle string constraints. Examples of these approaches are STRSOLVE [22], STRANGER [40], PASS [26], and PISA [26]. While they can naturally deal with unbounded-length strings, the main drawback of these solvers is their inability to capture other variable types, such as integers. For example, as observed in [41], the PISA solver can provide good performance but cannot model string lengths and symbolic arithmetic operations.

Word-based string solvers, according to [41], are SMT solvers that treat strings without abstractions or representation conversions. They take advantage of already defined theories, and enable a precise modelling of unbounded strings and length constraints. For instance, Z3STR [42], Z3STR2 [41], and Z3STRBV [38] extend the well-known SMT solver Z3. Other SMT-based string solvers are SUSHI [14], CVC4 [27], and NORN [1]. Although it is out of the scope of this paper to provide a comparison with all of them, we remark that GECODE+S provides a better performance than SUSHI in the evaluation reported in [33].

7   Conclusion

We presented an extension of the MiniZinc language that allows users to model and solve combinatorial problems with strings. The framework we propose is expressive enough to encode the most used string operations in modern programming languages, and — via proper FlatZinc translations — it also enables both string and non-string solvers to solve such problems. All the solvers having a FlatZinc interface can now solve string problems without manual intervention.

We took advantage of our framework for evaluating the state-of-the-art constraint solvers — CHUFFED, GECODE, IZPLUS PICAT-SAT, MZN/GUROBI, MZN/YICES2, and MZN/OSCAR.CBLS — on problems with bounded-length strings. The results indicate that, despite longer flattening times, sometimes our FlatZinc decomposition can be more beneficial than using a dedicated string solver.

We are not aware of similar works in CP, and we see our work as a solid starting point for the handling of string variables and constraints with the MiniZinc toolchain. We hope our extension encourages the development of further CP solvers that can natively deal with strings. This will hopefully lead to the creation of new, challenging string benchmarks, and to the development of dedicated search heuristics (e.g., heuristics based on character frequencies in a string).

We are planning to enhance our framework by adding new search annotations, constraints, and features, as well extending the string domain from ASCII to other alphabets, such as Unicode. In particular, the useful missing constraint for membership in a context-free language should at least have a default handling under the $\mathcal{F}^{int}$ conversion, if not a propagator in GECODE+$\mathbb{S}$ used via the $\mathcal{F}^{str}$ conversion.

Finally, non-character alphabets could be useful, such as for the generation of protocol logs [19], where the natural model would use strings of timestamps.

Acknowledgements. The authors from the University of Melbourne are supported by the Australian Research Council (ARC) through Linkage Project Grant LP140100437. The authors in Sweden are supported by the Swedish Research Council (VR) through Project Grant 2015-04910. Many thanks to Gustav Björdal for having run the experiments on his local-search backend [7] for MiniZinc. Many thanks also to all the referees and to the audience of LOPSTR 2016 for their thoughtful feedback.

References

1. Abdulla, P.A., Atig, M.F., Chen, Y.-F., Holík, L., Rezine, A., Rümmer, P., Stenman, J.: Norn: an SMT solver for string constraints. In: Kroening, D., Păsăreanu, C.S. (eds.) CAV 2015. LNCS, vol. 9206, pp. 462–469. Springer, Cham (2015). doi:10.1007/978-3-319-21690-4_29
2. Amadini, R., Gabbrielli, M., Mauro, J.: A multicore tool for constraint solving. In: IJCAI, pp. 232–238. AAAI Press (2015)
3. Beldiceanu, N., Carlsson, M., Demassey, S., Petit, T.: Global constraint catalogue: past, present and future. Constraints **12**(1), 21–62 (2007). http://sofdem.github.io/gccat/
4. Belov, G., Stuckey, P.J., Tack, G., Wallace, M.: Improved linearization of constraint programming models. In: Rueher, M. (ed.) CP 2016. LNCS, vol. 9892, pp. 49–65. Springer, Cham (2016). doi:10.1007/978-3-319-44953-1_4

5. Bisht, P., Hinrichs, T.L., Skrupsky, N., Venkatakrishnan, V.N.: WAPTEC: white-box analysis of web applications for parameter tampering exploit construction. In: CCS, pp. 575–586. ACM (2011)

6. Björdal, G.: String variables for constraint-based local search. Master's thesis, Department of Information Technology, Uppsala University, Sweden, August 2016. http://urn.kb.se/resolve?urn=urn:nbn:se:uu:diva-301501

7. Björdal, G., Monette, J.-N., Flener, P., Pearson, J.: A constraint-based local search backend for MiniZinc. Constraints **20**(3), 325–345 (2015)

8. Bjørner, N., Tillmann, N., Voronkov, A.: Path feasibility analysis for string-manipulating programs. In: Kowalewski, S., Philippou, A. (eds.) TACAS 2009. LNCS, vol. 5505, pp. 307–321. Springer, Heidelberg (2009). doi:10.1007/978-3-642-00768-2_27

9. Bofill, M., Suy, J., Villaret, M.: A system for solving constraint satisfaction problems with SMT. In: Strichman, O., Szeider, S. (eds.) SAT 2010. LNCS, vol. 6175, pp. 300–305. Springer, Heidelberg (2010). doi:10.1007/978-3-642-14186-7_25

10. Chu, G.: Improving Combinatorial Optimization. Ph.D. thesis, Department of Computing and Information Systems, University of Melbourne, Australia (2011)

11. Costantini, G., Ferrara, P., Cortesi, A.: A suite of abstract domains for static analysis of string values. Softw. Pract. Exp. **45**(2), 245–287 (2015)

12. De Landtsheer, R., Ponsard, C.: OscaR.cbls: an open source framework for constraint-based local search. In: ORBEL-27, the 27th Annual Conference of the Belgian Operational Research Society (2013). http://www.orbel.be/orbel27/pdf/abstract293.pdf; The OscaR.cbls solver https://bitbucket.org/oscarlib/oscar/wiki/CBLS

13. Emmi, M., Majumdar, R., Sen, K.: Dynamic test input generation for database applications. In: ISSTA, pp. 151–162. ACM (2007)

14. Fu, X., Powell, M.C., Bantegui, M., Li, C.: Simple linear string constraints. Formal Aspects Comput. **25**(6), 847–891 (2013)

15. Fujiwara, T.: iZplus description (2016). http://www.minizinc.org/challenge2016/description_izplus.txt

16. Ganesh, V., Minnes, M., Solar-Lezama, A., Rinard, M.: Word equations with length constraints: what's decidable? In: Biere, A., Nahir, A., Vos, T. (eds.) HVC 2012. LNCS, vol. 7857, pp. 209–226. Springer, Heidelberg (2013). doi:10.1007/978-3-642-39611-3_21

17. Gange, G., Navas, J.A., Stuckey, P.J., Søndergaard, H., Schachte, P.: Unbounded model-checking with interpolation for regular language constraints. In: Piterman, N., Smolka, S.A. (eds.) TACAS 2013. LNCS, vol. 7795, pp. 277–291. Springer, Heidelberg (2013). doi:10.1007/978-3-642-36742-7_20

18. Gecode Team. Gecode: generic constraint development environment (2016). http://www.gecode.org

19. Grinchtein, O., Carlsson, M., Pearson, J.: A constraint optimisation model for analysis of telecommunication protocol logs. In: Blanchette, J.C., Kosmatov, N. (eds.) TAP 2015. LNCS, vol. 9154, pp. 137–154. Springer, Cham (2015). doi:10.1007/978-3-319-21215-9_9

20. Gurobi Optimization, Inc., Gurobi Optimizer Reference Manual (2016). http://www.gurobi.com

21. He, J., Flener, P., Pearson, J., Zhang, W.M.: Solving string constraints: the case for constraint programming. In: Schulte, C. (ed.) CP 2013. LNCS, vol. 8124, pp. 381–397. Springer, Heidelberg (2013). doi:10.1007/978-3-642-40627-0_31

22. Hooimeijer, P., Weimer, W.: StrSolve: solving string constraints lazily. Autom. Softw. Eng. **19**(4), 531–559 (2012)

23. Kiezun, A., Ganesh, V., Artzi, S., Guo, P.J., Hooimeijer, P., Ernst, M.D.: HAMPI: a solver for word equations over strings, regular expressions, and context-free grammars. ACM Trans. Softw. Eng. Methodol. **21**(4), 25 (2012)

24. Kieżun, A., Ganesh, V., Guo, P.J., Hooimeijer, P., Ernst, M.D.: HAMPI: a solver for string constraints. In: ISSTA 2009, pp. 105–116. ACM (2009)

25. Kim, S.-W., Chin, W., Park, J., Kim, J., Ryu, S.: Inferring grammatical summaries of string values. In: Garrigue, J. (ed.) APLAS 2014. LNCS, vol. 8858, pp. 372–391. Springer, Cham (2014). doi:10.1007/978-3-319-12736-1_20

26. Li, G., Ghosh, I.: PASS: string solving with parameterized array and interval automaton. In: Bertacco, V., Legay, A. (eds.) HVC 2013. LNCS, vol. 8244, pp. 15–31. Springer, Cham (2013). doi:10.1007/978-3-319-03077-7_2

27. Liang, T., Reynolds, A., Tinelli, C., Barrett, C., Deters, M.: A DPLL(T) theory solver for a theory of strings and regular expressions. In: Biere, A., Bloem, R. (eds.) CAV 2014. LNCS, vol. 8559, pp. 646–662. Springer, Cham (2014). doi:10.1007/978-3-319-08867-9_43

28. Madsen, M., Andreasen, E.: String analysis for dynamic field access. In: Cohen, A. (ed.) CC 2014. LNCS, vol. 8409, pp. 197–217. Springer, Heidelberg (2014). doi:10.1007/978-3-642-54807-9_12

29. Michel, L.D., Van Hentenryck, P.: Constraint satisfaction over bit-vectors. In: Milano, M. (ed.) CP 2012. LNCS, pp. 527–543. Springer, Heidelberg (2012). doi:10.1007/978-3-642-33558-7_39

30. Nethercote, N., Stuckey, P.J., Becket, R., Brand, S., Duck, G.J., Tack, G.: MiniZinc: towards a standard CP modelling language. In: Bessière, C. (ed.) CP 2007. LNCS, vol. 4741, pp. 529–543. Springer, Heidelberg (2007). doi:10.1007/978-3-540-74970-7_38

31. Ohrimenko, O., Stuckey, P.J., Codish, M.: Propagation via lazy clause generation. Constraints **14**(3), 357–391 (2009)

32. Saxena, P., Akhawe, D., Hanna, S., Mao, F., McCamant, S., Song, D.: A symbolic execution framework for JavaScript. In: S&P, pp. 513–528. IEEE Computer Society (2010)

33. Scott, J.D.: Other Things Besides Number: Abstraction, Constraint Propagation, and String Variable Types. Ph.D. thesis, Department of Information Technology, Uppsala University, Sweden (2016). http://urn.kb.se/resolve?urn=urn:nbn:se:uu:diva-273311

34. Scott, J.D., Flener, P., Pearson, J.: Bounded strings for constraint programming. In: ICTAI, pp. 1036–1043. IEEE Computer Society (2013)

35. Scott, J.D., Flener, P., Pearson, J.: Constraint solving on bounded string variables. In: Michel, L. (ed.) CPAIOR 2015. LNCS, vol. 9075, pp. 375–392. Springer, Cham (2015). doi:10.1007/978-3-319-18008-3_26

36. Scott, J.D., Flener, P., Pearson, J., Schulte, C.: Design and implementation of bounded-length sequence variables. In: Salvagnin, D., Lombardi, M. (eds.) CPAIOR 2017. LNCS, vol. 10335, pp. 51–67. Springer, Cham (2017). doi:10.1007/978-3-319-59776-8_5

37. Stuckey, P.J., Tack, G.: MiniZinc with functions. In: Gomes, C., Sellmann, M. (eds.) CPAIOR 2013. LNCS, vol. 7874, pp. 268–283. Springer, Heidelberg (2013). doi:10.1007/978-3-642-38171-3_18

38. Subramanian, S., Berzish, M., Zheng, Y., Tripp, O., Ganesh, V.: A solver for a theory of strings and bit-vectors. CoRR, abs/1605.09446 (2016)

39. Trinh, M., Chu, D., Jaffar, J.: S3: a symbolic string solver for vulnerability detection in web applications. In: SIGSAC, pp. 1232–1243. ACM (2014)

40. Yu, F., Alkhalaf, M., Bultan, T.: Stranger: an automata-based string analysis tool for PHP. In: Esparza, J., Majumdar, R. (eds.) TACAS 2010. LNCS, vol. 6015, pp. 154–157. Springer, Heidelberg (2010). doi:10.1007/978-3-642-12002-2_13

41. Zheng, Y., Ganesh, V., Subramanian, S., Tripp, O., Dolby, J., Zhang, X.: Effective search-space pruning for solvers of string equations, regular expressions and length constraints. In: Kroening, D., Păsăreanu, C.S. (eds.) CAV 2015. LNCS, vol. 9206, pp. 235–254. Springer, Cham (2015). doi:10.1007/978-3-319-21690-4_14

42. Zheng, Y., Zhang, X., Ganesh, V.: Z3-str: a Z3-based string solver for web application analysis. In: SIGSOFT, pp. 114–124. ACM (2013)

43. Zhou, N.-F., Kjellerstrand, H.: The Picat-SAT compiler. In: Gavanelli, M., Reppy, J. (eds.) PADL 2016. LNCS, vol. 9585, pp. 48–62. Springer, Cham (2016). doi:10.1007/978-3-319-28228-2_4

Slicing Concurrent Constraint Programs

Moreno Falaschi[1](✉), Maurizio Gabbrielli[2], Carlos Olarte[3],
and Catuscia Palamidessi[4]

[1] Dipartimento di Ingegneria dell'Informazione e Scienze Matematiche,
Università di Siena, Siena, Italy
moreno.falaschi@unisi.it

[2] Dipartimento di Informatica - Scienza e Ingegneria,
Università di Bologna, Bologna, Italy
gabbri@cs.unibo.it

[3] ECT, Universidade Federal do Rio Grande do Norte, Natal, Brazil
carlos.olarte@gmail.com

[4] INRIA and LIX, École Polytechnique, Palaiseau, France
catuscia@lix.polytechnique.fr

Abstract. Concurrent Constraint Programming (CCP) is a declarative model for concurrency where agents interact by telling and asking constraints (pieces of information) in a shared store. Some previous works have developed (approximated) declarative debuggers for CCP languages. However, the task of debugging concurrent programs remains difficult. In this paper we define a dynamic slicer for CCP and we show it to be a useful companion tool for the existing debugging techniques. We start with a partial computation (a trace) that shows the presence of bugs. Often, the quantity of information in such a trace is overwhelming, and the user gets easily lost, since she cannot focus on the sources of the bugs. Our slicer allows for marking part of the state of the computation and assists the user to eliminate most of the redundant information in order to highlight the errors. We show that this technique can be tailored to timed variants of CCP. We also develop a prototypical implementation freely available for making experiments.

Keywords: Concurrent Constraint Programming · Program slicing · Debugging

1 Introduction

Concurrent constraint programming (CCP) [24,26] (see a survey in [22]) combines concurrency primitives with the ability to deal with constraints, and hence, with partial information. The notion of concurrency is based upon the shared-variables communication model. CCP is intended for reasoning, modeling and programming concurrent agents (or processes) that interact with each other and their environment by posting and asking information in a medium, a so-called store. Agents in CCP can be seen as both computing processes (behavioral style)

© Springer International Publishing AG 2017
M.V. Hermenegildo and P. Lopez-Garcia (Eds.): LOPSTR 2016, LNCS 10184, pp. 76–93, 2017.
DOI: 10.1007/978-3-319-63139-4_5

and as logic formulae (declarative style). Hence CCP can exploit reasoning techniques from both process calculi and logic.

CCP is a very flexible model and then, it has been applied to an increasing number of different fields such as probabilistic and stochastic [4], timed [8,18,25] and mobile [23] systems. More recently, CCP languages have been proposed for the specification of spatial and epistemic behaviors as in, e.g., social networks [14,20].

One crucial problem when working with a concurrent language is being able to provide tools to debug programs. This is particularly useful for a language in which a program can generate a large number of parallel running agents. In order to tame this complexity, abstract interpretation techniques have been considered (e.g. in [6,7,11]) as well as (abstract) declarative debuggers following the seminal work of Shapiro [27]. However, these techniques are approximated (case of abstract interpretation) or it can be difficult to apply them when dealing with complex programs (case of declarative debugging). It would be useful to have a semi automatic tool able to interact with the user and filter, in a given computation, the information which is relevant to a particular observation or result. In other words, the programmer could mark the outcome that she is interested to check in a particular computation that she suspects to be wrong. Then, a corresponding depurated partial computation is obtained automatically, where only the information relevant to the marked parts is present.

Slicing was introduced in some pioneer works by Mark Weiser [28]. It was originally defined as a static technique, independent of any particular input of the program. Then, the technique was extended by introducing the so called dynamic program slicing [15]. This technique is useful for simplifying the debugging process, by selecting a portion of the program containing the faulty code. Dynamic program slicing has been applied to several programming paradigms, for instance to imperative programming [15], functional programming [19], Term Rewriting [1], and functional logic programming [2]. The reader may refer to [13] for a survey.

In this paper we present the first formal framework for CCP dynamic slicing and show, by some working examples and a prototypical tool, the main features of this approach. Our aim is to help the programmer to debug her program, in cases where she could not find the bugs by using other debuggers. We proceed with three main steps. First we extend the standard operational semantics of CCP to a "collecting semantics" that adds the needed information for the slicer. Second, we propose several analyses of the faulty situation based on error symptoms, including causality, variable dependencies, unexpected behaviors and store inconsistencies. Thirdly, we define a marking algorithm of the redundant items and define a trace slice. Our algorithm is flexible and it can deal with different variants of CCP. In particular, we show how to apply it to timed extensions of CCP [25].

Organization. Section 2 describes CCP and its operational semantics. In Sect. 3 we introduce a slicing technique for CCP. In Sect. 4 we extend our method to consider timed CCP programs. We present a working prototypical implementation of the slicer available at http://subsell.logic.at/slicer/. We describe an example using the slicer to debug a multimedia interacting system programmed in timed CCP. Due to lack of space, other examples are given only in the web page of the tool as, for instance, a biochemical system specified in timed CCP. Finally, Sect. 5 concludes.

2   Concurrent Constraint Programming

Processes in CCP *interact* with each other by *telling* and *asking* constraints (pieces of information) in a common store of partial information. The type of constraints is not fixed but parametric in a constraint system (CS). Intuitively, a CS provides a signature from which constraints can be built from basic tokens (e.g., predicate symbols), and two basic operations: conjunction ($\sqcup$) and variable hiding ($\exists$). The CS defines also an *entailment* relation ($\models$) specifying inter-dependencies between constraints: $c \models d$ means that the information d can be deduced from the information c. Such systems can be formalized as a Scott information system as in [26], as cylindric algebras [9], or they can be built upon a suitable fragment of logic *e.g.*, as in [18]. Here we follow [9], since the other approaches can be seen as an instance of this definition.

Definition 1 (Constraint System –CS–). *A cylindric constraint system is a structure* $\mathbf{C} = \langle \mathcal{C}, \leq, \sqcup, t, f, Var, \exists, D \rangle$ *s.t.*

- $\langle \mathcal{C}, \leq, \sqcup, t, f \rangle$ *is a complete algebraic lattice with* $\sqcup$ *the lub operation (representing* conjunction*). Elements in* $\mathcal{C}$ *are called* constraints *with typical elements* $c, c', d, d'...$, *and* t, f *the least and the greatest elements. If* $c \leq d$, *we say that* d *entails* c *and we write* $d \models c$. *If* $c \leq d$ *and* $d \leq c$ *we write* $c \cong d$.
- *Var is a denumerable set of variables and for each* $x \in Var$ *the function* $\exists x : \mathcal{C} \to \mathcal{C}$ *is a cylindrification operator satisfying: (1)* $\exists x(c) \leq c$. *(2) If* $c \leq d$ *then* $\exists x(c) \leq \exists x(d)$. *(3)* $\exists x(c \sqcup \exists x(d)) \cong \exists x(c) \sqcup \exists x(d)$. *(4)* $\exists x \exists y(c) \cong \exists y \exists x(c)$. *(5) For an increasing chain* $c_1 \leq c_2 \leq c_3...$, $\exists x \bigsqcup_i c_i \cong \bigsqcup_i \exists x(c_i)$.
- *For each* $x, y \in Var$, *the constraint* $d_{xy} \in D$ *is a* diagonal element *and it satisfies: (1)* $d_{xx} \cong t$. *(2) If* z *is different from* x, y *then* $d_{xy} \cong \exists z(d_{xz} \sqcup d_{zy})$. *(3) If* x *is different from* y *then* $c \leq d_{xy} \sqcup \exists x(c \sqcup d_{xy})$.

The cylindrification operator models a sort of existential quantification for hiding information. As usual, $\exists x.c$ binds x in c. We use $fv(c)$ (resp. $bv(c)$) to denote the set of free (resp. bound) variables in c. The diagonal element d_{xy} can be thought of as the equality $x = y$, useful to define substitutions of the form $[t/x]$ (see the details, e.g., in [11]).

As an example, consider the finite domain constraint system (FD) [12]. This system assumes variables to range over finite domains and, in addition to equality, one may have predicates that restrict the possible values of a variable as in $x < 42$.

2.1   The Language of CCP Processes

In the spirit of process calculi, the language of processes in CCP is given by a small number of primitive operators or combinators as described below.

Definition 2 (Syntax of Indeterminate CCP [26]). *Processes in CCP are built from constraints in the underlying constraint system and the syntax:*

$$P, Q ::= \textbf{skip} \mid \textbf{tell}(c) \mid \sum_{i \in I} \textbf{ask} \ (c_i) \ \textbf{then} \ P_i \mid P \parallel Q \mid (\textbf{local} \, x) \, P \mid p(\overline{x})$$

The process **skip** represents inaction. The process **tell**(c) adds c to the current store d producing the new store $c \sqcup d$. Given a non-empty finite set of indexes I, the process $\sum_{i \in I} \textbf{ask} \ (c_i) \ \textbf{then} \ P_i$ non-deterministically chooses P_k for execution if the store entails c_k. The chosen alternative, if any, precludes the others. This provides a powerful synchronization mechanism based on constraint entailment. When I is a singleton, we shall omit the "$\sum$" and we simply write **ask** (c) **then** P.

The process $P \parallel Q$ represents the parallel (interleaved) execution of P and Q. The process $(\textbf{local} \, x) \, P$ behaves as P and binds the variable x to be local to it. We use $fv(P)$ (resp. $bv(P)$) to denote the set of free (resp. bound) variables in P.

Given a process definition $p(\overline{y}) \stackrel{\Delta}{=} P$, where all free variables of P are in the set of pairwise distinct variables $\overline{y}$, the process $p(\overline{x})$ evolves into $P[\overline{x}/\overline{y}]$. A CCP program takes the form $\mathcal{D}.P$ where $\mathcal{D}$ is a set of process definitions and P is a process.

The Structural Operational Semantics (SOS) of CCP is given by the transition relation $\gamma \longrightarrow \gamma'$ satisfying the rules in Fig. 1. Here we follow the formulation in [10] where the local variables created by the program appear explicitly in the transition system and parallel composition of agents is identified to a multiset of agents. More precisely, a *configuration* γ is a triple of the form $(X; \Gamma; c)$, where c is a constraint representing the store, Γ is a multiset of processes, and X is a set of hidden (local) variables of c and Γ. The multiset $\Gamma = P_1, P_2, \ldots, P_n$ represents the process $P_1 \parallel P_2 \parallel \cdots \parallel P_n$. We shall indistinguishably use both notations to denote parallel composition. Moreover, processes are quotiented by a structural congruence relation $\cong$ satisfying: (STR1) $P \cong Q$ if they differ only by a renaming of bound variables (alpha conversion); (STR2) $P \parallel Q \cong Q \parallel P$; (STR3) $P \parallel (Q \parallel R) \cong (P \parallel Q) \parallel R$; (STR4) $P \parallel \textbf{skip} \cong P$.

Let us briefly explain the rules in Fig. 1. A tell agent **tell**(c) adds c to the current store d (Rule R_{TELL}); the process $\sum_{i \in I} \textbf{ask} \ (c_i) \ \textbf{then} \ P_i$ executes P_k if its corresponding guard c_k can be entailed from the store (Rule R_{SUM}); a local process $(\textbf{local} \, x) \, P$ adds x to the set of hidden variable X when no clashes of variables occur (Rule R_{LOC}). Observe that Rule R_{EQUIV} can be used to do alpha conversion if the premise of R_{LOC} cannot be satisfied; the call $p(\overline{x})$ executes the body of the process definition (Rule R_{CALL}).

$$\frac{}{(X; \textbf{tell}(c), \Gamma; d) \longrightarrow (X; \textbf{skip}, \Gamma; c \sqcup d)} \; \text{R}_{\text{TELL}} \qquad \frac{d \models c_k \quad k \in I}{(X; \sum_{i \in I} \textbf{ask } (c_i) \textbf{ then } P_i, \Gamma; d) \longrightarrow (X; P_k, \Gamma; d)} \; \text{R}_{\text{SUM}}$$

$$\frac{x \notin X \cup fv(d) \cup fv(\Gamma)}{(X; (\textbf{local } x) P, \Gamma; d) \longrightarrow (X \cup \{x\}; P, \Gamma; d)} \; \text{R}_{\text{LOC}} \qquad \frac{p(\bar{y}) \triangleq P \in \mathcal{D}}{(X; p(\bar{x}), \Gamma; d) \longrightarrow (X; P[\bar{x}/\bar{y}], \Gamma; d)} \; \text{R}_{\text{CALL}}$$

$$\frac{(X; \Gamma; c) \cong (X'; \Gamma'; c') \longrightarrow (Y'; \Delta'; d') \cong (Y; \Delta; d)}{(X; \Gamma; c) \longrightarrow (Y; \Delta; d)} \; \text{R}_{\text{EQUIV}}$$

Fig. 1. Operational semantics for CCP calculi

Definition 3 (Observables). *Let* $\longrightarrow^*$ *denote the reflexive and transitive closure of* $\longrightarrow$. *If* $(X; \Gamma; d) \longrightarrow^* (X'; \Gamma'; d')$ *and* $\exists X'.d' \models c$ *we write* $(X; \Gamma; d) \Downarrow_c$. *If* $X = \emptyset$ *and* $d = t$ *we simply write* $\Gamma \Downarrow_c$.

Intuitively, if P is a process then $P \Downarrow_c$ says that P can reach a store d strong enough to entail c, *i.e.*, c is an output of P. Note that the variables in X' above are hidden from d' since the information about them is not observable.

3 Slicing a CCP Program

Dynamic slicing is a technique that helps the user to debug her program by simplifying a partial execution trace, thus depurating it from parts which are irrelevant to find the bug. It can also help to highlight parts of the programs which have been wrongly ignored by the execution of a wrong piece of code.

Our slicing technique consists of three main steps:

S1. *Generating a (finite) trace* of the program. For that, we propose a *collecting semantics* that generates the (meta) information needed for the slicer.
S2. *Marking the final store*, to choose some of the constraints that, according to the symptoms detected, should or should not be in the final store.
S3. *Computing the trace slice*, to select the processes and constraints that were relevant to produce the (marked) final store.

3.1 Collecting Semantics (Step S1)

The slicer we propose requires some extra information from the execution of the processes. More precisely, (1) in each operational step $\gamma \to \gamma'$, we need to highlight the process that was reduced; and (2) the constraints accumulated in the store must reflect, exactly, the contribution of each process to the store.

In order to solve (1) and (2), we propose a collecting semantics that extracts the needed meta information for the slicer. The rules are in Fig. 2 and explained below.

The semantics considers configurations of the shape $(X; \Gamma; S)$ where X is a set of hidden variables, Γ is a sequence of processes with *identifiers* and S is a set of atomic constraints. Let us explain the last two components. We identify the

$$\frac{\langle Y, S_c \rangle = atoms(c, fvars)}{(X; \Gamma, \mathbf{tell}(c) : i, \Gamma'; S) \xrightarrow{[i]} (X' \cup Y; \Gamma, \Gamma'; S \cup S_c)} \text{R}'_{\text{TELL}}$$

$$\frac{\bigsqcup_{d \in S} d \models c_k \quad k \in I}{(X; \Gamma, \sum_{i \in I} \mathbf{ask}\ (c_i)\ \mathbf{then}\ P_i : i, \Gamma'; S) \xrightarrow{[i]_k} (X; \Gamma, P_k : j, \Gamma'; S)} \text{R}'_{\text{SUM}}$$

$$\frac{x' \in Var \setminus fvars}{(X; \Gamma, (\mathbf{local}\ x)\ P : i, \Gamma'; S) \xrightarrow{[i]} (X \cup \{x'\}; \Gamma, P[x'/x] : j, \Gamma'; S)} \text{R}'_{\text{LOC}}$$

$$\frac{p(\bar{y}) \triangleq P \in \mathcal{D}}{(X; \Gamma, p(\bar{x}) : i, \Gamma'; S) \xrightarrow{[i]} (X; \Gamma, P[\bar{x}/\bar{y}] : j, \Gamma'; S)} \text{R}'_{\text{CALL}}$$

Fig. 2. Collecting semantics for CCP calculi. Γ and Γ' are (possibly empty) sequences of processes. $fvars = X \cup fv(S) \cup fv(\Gamma) \cup fv(\Gamma')$. In "$:j$", j is a fresh identifier.

parallel composition $Q = P_1 \parallel \cdots \parallel P_n$ with the *sequence* $\Gamma_Q = P_1 : i_1, \cdots, P_n : i_n$ where $i_j \in \mathbb{N}$ is a unique identifier for P_j. Abusing of the notation, we usually write $Q : i$ instead of Γ_Q when the indexes in the parallel composition are unimportant. Moreover, we shall use ϵ to denote an empty sequence of processes. The context $\Gamma, P : i, \Gamma'$ represents that P is preceded and followed, respectively, by the (possibly empty) sequences of processes Γ and Γ'. The use of indexes will allow us to distinguish, e.g., the three different occurrences of P in "$\Gamma_1, P : i, \Gamma_2, P : j, (\mathbf{ask}\ (c)\ \mathbf{then}\ P) : k$".

Transitions are labeled with $\xrightarrow{[i]_k}$ where i is the identifier of the reduced process and k can be either $\bot$ (undefined) or a natural number indicating the branch chosen in a non-deterministic choice (Rule R'_{SUM}). In each rule, the resulting process has a new/fresh identifier (see e.g., j in Rule R'_{LOC}). This new identifier can be obtained, e.g., as the successor of the maximal identifier in the previous configuration. For the sake of readability, we write $[i]$ instead of $[i]_\bot$. Moreover, we shall avoid the identifier "$:i$" when it can be inferred from the context.

Stores and Configurations. The solution for (2) amounts to consider the store, in a configuration, as a set of (atomic) constraints and not as a constraint. Then, the store $\{c_1, \cdots, c_n\}$ represents the constraint $c_1 \sqcup \cdots \sqcup c_n$.

Consider the process $\mathbf{tell}(c)$ and let $V \subseteq Vars$. The Rule R'_{TELL} first decomposes the constraint c in its atoms. For that, assume that the bound variables in c are all distinct and not in V (otherwise, by alpha conversion, we can find $c' \cong c$ satisfying such condition). We define $atoms(c, V) = \langle bv(c), basic(c) \rangle$ where

$$basic(c) = \begin{cases} c \text{ if } c \text{ is an atom, } \mathbf{t}, \mathbf{f} \text{ or } d_{xy} \\ basic(c') \text{ if } c = \exists x.c' \\ basic(c_1) \cup basic(c_2) \text{ if } c = c_1 \sqcup c_2 \end{cases}$$

Observe that in Rule R'_{TELL}, the parameter V of the function *atoms* is the set of free variables occurring in the context, i.e., $fvars$ in Fig. 2. This is needed to perform alpha conversion of c (which is left implicit in the definition of $basic(\cdot)$) to satisfy the above condition on bound names.

Rule R'_{SUM} signals the number of the branch k chosen for execution. Rule R'_{LOC} chooses a fresh variable x', i.e., a variable not in the set of free variables of the configuration (*fvars*). Hence, we execute the process $P[x'/x]$ and add x' to the set X of local variables. Rule R'_{CALL} is self-explanatory.

It is worth noticing that we do not consider a rule for structural congruence in the collecting semantics. Such rule, in the system of Fig. 1, played different roles. Axioms STR2 and STR3 provide agents with a structure of multiset (commutative and associative). As mentioned above, we consider in the collecting semantics sequences of processes to highlight the process that was reduced in a transition. The sequence Γ in Fig. 2 can be of arbitrary length and then, any of the enabled processes in the sequence can be picked for execution. Axiom STR1 allowed us to perform alpha-conversion on processes. This is needed in R_{LOC} to avoid clash of variables. Note that the new Rule R'_{LOC} internalizes such procedure by picking a fresh variable x'. Finally, Axiom STR4 can be used to simplify **skip** processes that can be introduced, e.g., by a R_{TELL} transition. Observe that the collecting semantics does not add any **skip** into the configuration (see Rule R'_{TELL}).

Example 1. Consider the following toy example. Let $\mathcal{D}$ contain the process definition $A \triangleq \mathbf{tell}(z > x + 4)$ and $\mathcal{D}.P$ be a program where
$P = \mathbf{tell}(y < 7) \parallel \mathbf{ask}\ (x < 0)\ \mathbf{then}\ A \parallel \mathbf{tell}(x = -3)$. The following is a possible trace generated by the collecting semantics.

$$(\emptyset; \mathbf{tell}(y < 7)\!:\!1, \mathbf{ask}\ (x < 0)\ \mathbf{then}\ A\!:\!2, \mathbf{tell}(x = -3)\!:\!3;\ t)$$

$$\xrightarrow{[1]} (\emptyset; \mathbf{ask}\ (x < 0)\ \mathbf{then}\ A\!:\!2, \mathbf{tell}(x = -3)\!:\!3; y < 7)$$

$$\xrightarrow{[3]} (\emptyset; \mathbf{ask}\ (x < 0)\ \mathbf{then}\ A\!:\!2; y < 7, x = -3) \xrightarrow{[2]_1} (\emptyset; A\!:\!4; y < 7, x = -3)$$

$$\xrightarrow{[4]} (\emptyset; \mathbf{tell}(z > x + 4)\!:\!5; y < 7, x = -3) \xrightarrow{[5]} (\emptyset; \epsilon; y < 7, x = -3, z > x + 4)$$

Now we introduce the notion of observables for the collecting semantics and we show that it coincides with that of Definition 3 for the operational semantics.

Definition 4
(Observables Collecting Semantics). *We write* $\gamma \xrightarrow{[i_1,\ldots,i_n]_{k_1,\ldots,k_n}} \gamma'$ *whenever* $\gamma = (X_0; \Gamma_0; S_0) \xrightarrow{[i_1]_{k_1}} \cdots \xrightarrow{[i_n]_{k_n}} (X_n; \Gamma_n; S_n) = \gamma'$. *Moreover, if* $\exists X_n.\ \bigsqcup_{d \in S_n} d \models c$, *then we write* $\gamma \Downarrow_c$. *If* $X_0 = S_0 = \emptyset$, *we simply write* $\Gamma_0 \Downarrow_c$.

Theorem 1 (Adequacy). *For any process* P, *constraint* c *and* $i \in \mathbb{N}$, $P \Downarrow_c$ *iff* $P\!:\!i \Downarrow_c$

Proof (sketch) $(\Rightarrow)$. The proof proceeds by induction on the length of the derivation needed to perform the output c in $P \Downarrow_c$ and using the following results.

Given a set of variables V, a constraint d and a set of constraints S, let us use $\lfloor d \rfloor_V$ to denote (the resulting tuple) $atoms(d, V)$ and $\lceil S \rceil_V$ to denote the constraint $\exists V.\ \bigsqcup_{c_i \in S} c_i$. If $\langle Y, S \rangle = \lfloor d \rfloor_V$, from the definition of *atoms*, we have $d \cong \lceil S \rceil_Y$.

Let Γ (resp. Ψ) be a multiset (resp. sequence) of processes. Let us use $\lfloor \Gamma \rfloor$ to denote any sequence of processes with distinct identifiers built from the processes in Γ and $\lceil \Psi \rceil$ to denote the multiset built from the processes in Ψ. Consider now the transition $\gamma = (X; \Gamma; d) \longrightarrow (X'; \Gamma'; d')$. Let $\langle Y, S \rangle = \lfloor d \rfloor_V$ where $V = X \cup fv(\Gamma) \cup fv(d)$. By choosing the same process reduced in γ, we can show that there exist i, k s.t. the collecting semantics mimics the same transition as $(X \cup Y, \lfloor \Gamma \rfloor, S) \xrightarrow{[i]_k} (X' \cup Y'; \lfloor \Gamma'' \rfloor; S')$ where $d' \cong \lceil S' \rceil_{Y'}$ and $\Gamma'' \cong \Gamma'$.

The ($\Leftarrow$) side follows from similar arguments.

3.2   Marking the Store (Step S2)

From the final store the user must indicate the symptoms that are relevant to the slice that she wants to recompute. For that, she must select a set of constraints that considers relevant to identify a bug. Normally, these are constraints at the end of a partial computation, and there are several strategies that one can follow to identify them.

Let us suppose that the final configuration in a partial computation is $(X; \Gamma; S)$. The symptoms that something is wrong in the program (in the sense that the user identifies some unexpected configuration) may be (and not limited to) the following:

1. *Causality:* the user identifies, according to her knowledge, a subset $S' \subseteq S$ that needs to be explained (i.e., we need to identify the processes that produced S').

2. *Variable Dependencies:* The user may identify a set of variables $V \subseteq fv(S)$ whose constraints need to be explored. Then, one would be interested in marking the following set of constraints

$$S_{sliced} = \{c \in S \mid vars(c) \cap V \neq \emptyset\}$$

3. *Unexpected behaviors:* there is a constraint c entailed from the final store that is not expected from the intended behavior of the program. Then, one would be interested in marking the following set of constraints:

$$S_{sliced} = \bigcup \{S' \subseteq S \mid \bigsqcup S' \models c \text{ and } S' \text{ is set minimal}\}$$

where "S' is set minimal" means that for any $S'' \subset S'$, $S'' \not\models c$.

4. *Inconsistent output:* The final store should be consistent with respect to a given specification (constraint) c, i.e., S in conjunction with c must not be inconsistent. In this case, the set of constraints to be marked is:

$$S_{sliced} = \bigcup \{S' \subseteq S \mid \bigsqcup S' \sqcup c \models \mathbf{f} \text{ and } S' \text{ is set minimal}\}$$

where "S' is set minimal" means that for any $S'' \subset S'$, $S'' \sqcup c \not\models \mathbf{f}$.

We note that "set minimality", in general, can be expensive to compute. However, we believe that in some practical cases, as shown in the examples in Sect. 4.1, this is not so heavy. In any case, we can always use supersets of the minimal ones which are easier to compute but less precise for eliminating useless information.

3.3 Trace Slice (Step S3)

Starting from the set S_{sliced} above we can define a backward slicing step. We shall identify, by means of a backward evaluation, the set of transitions (in the original computation) which are necessary for introducing the elements in S_{sliced}. By doing that, we will eliminate information not related to S_{sliced}.

Notation 1 (Sliced Terms). We shall use the fresh constant symbol $\bullet$ to denote an "irrelevant" constraint or process. Then, for instance, "$c \sqcup \bullet$" results from a constraint $c \sqcup d$ where d is irrelevant. Similarly, **ask** (c) **then** $(P \parallel \bullet) + \bullet$ results from a process of the form **ask** (c) **then** $(P \parallel Q) + \sum$ **ask** (c_l) **then** P_l where Q and the summands in $\sum$ **ask** (c_l) **then** P_l are irrelevant. We also assume that a sequence $\bullet, \dots, \bullet$ with any number (≥ 1) of occurrences of $\bullet$ is equivalent to a single occurrence.

A replacement is either a pair of the shape $[T/i]$ or $[T/c]$. In the first (resp. second) case, the process with identifier i (resp. constraint c) is replaced with T. We shall use θ to denote a set of replacements and we call these sets as "replacing substitutions". The composition of replacing substitutions θ_1 and θ_2 is given by the set union of θ_1 and θ_2, and is denoted as $\theta_1 \circ \theta_2$. If $\Gamma = P_1 : i_1, \dots, P_n : i_n$, for simplicity, we shall write $[\Gamma/j]$ instead of $[P_1 \parallel \cdots \parallel P_n/j]$. Moreover, we shall write, e.g., **ask** (c) **then** Γ instead of **ask** (c) **then** $(P1 \parallel \cdots \parallel P_n)$.

Algorithm 1 computes the slicing. The last configuration in the sliced trace is $(X_n \cap vars(S); \bullet; S)$. This means that we only observe the local variables of interest, i.e., those in $vars(S)$. Moreover, note that the processes in the last configuration were not executed and then, they are irrelevant (and abstracted with $\bullet$). Finally, the only relevant constraints are those in S.

Input: - a trace $\gamma_0 \xrightarrow{[i_1]_{k_1}} \cdots \xrightarrow{[i_n]_{k_n}} \gamma_n$ where $\gamma_i = (X_i; \Gamma_i; S_i)$
        - a set $S \subseteq S_n$
    Output: a sliced trace $\gamma'_0 \longrightarrow \cdots \longrightarrow \gamma'_n$
1 **begin**
2   **let** $\theta = \emptyset$ **in**
3    $\gamma'_n \leftarrow (X_n \cap vars(S); \bullet; S)$;
4   **for** $l = n - 1$ *to 0* **do**
5      $\theta \leftarrow sliceProcess(\gamma_l, \gamma_{l+1}, i_{l+1}, k_{l+1}, \theta, S) \circ \theta$;
6      $\gamma'_l \leftarrow (X_l \cap vars(S) ; \Gamma_l\theta ; S_l \cap S)$
7   **end**
8 **end**

Algorithm 1: Trace Slicer

The algorithm backwardly computes the slicing by accumulating replacing pairs in θ. The new replacing substitutions are computed by the function $sliceProcess$ in Algorithm 2. Suppose that $\gamma \xrightarrow{[i]_k}$. We consider each kind of process. For instance, assume a R'_{TELL} transition $\gamma = (X_\gamma; \Gamma_1, \textbf{tell}(c) :$

```
 1  Function sliceProcess(γ, ψ, i, k, θ, S)
 2    let γ = (X_γ; Γ, P : i, Γ'; S_γ) and ψ = (X_ψ; Γ, Γ_Q, Γ'; S_ψ) in
 3    match P with
 4      case tell(c)
 5        let c' = sliceConstraints(X_γ, X_ψ, S_γ, S_ψ, S) in
 6        if c' = • or c' = ∃x̄.• then return  [•/i] else return  [tell(c')/i];
 7      case ∑ ask (c_l) then Q_l
 8        if Γ_Q θ = • then return  [•/i] else return
             [ask (c_k) then (Γ_Q θ) + • / i];
 9      case (local x) Q
10        let {x'} = X_ψ \ X_γ in
11        if Γ_Q[x'/x]θ = • then return  [•/i] else return
             [(local x') Γ_Q[x'/x]θ/i];
12      case p(ȳ)
13        if Γ_Q θ = • then return  [•/i] else return  ∅;
14    end
15  end
16  Function sliceConstraints(X_γ, X_ψ, S_γ, S_ψ, S)
17    let S_c = S_ψ \ S_γ and θ = ∅ in
18    foreach c_a ∈ S_c \ S do  θ ← θ ∘ [•/c_a] ;
19    return ∃_{X_ψ \ X_γ}. ⊔ S_c θ
20  end
```

Algorithm 2: Slicing Processes and Constraints

$i, \Gamma_2; S_\gamma) \xrightarrow{[i]} (X_\psi; \Gamma_1, \Gamma_2; S_\psi) = \psi$. We note that $X_\gamma \subseteq X_\psi$ and $S_\gamma \subseteq S_\psi$. We replace the constraint c with its sliced version c' computed by the function *sliceConstraints*. In that function, we compute the contribution of **tell**(c) to the store, i.e., $S_c = S_\psi \backslash S_\gamma$. Then, any atom $c_a \in S_c$ not in the relevant set of constraints S is replaced by •. By joining together the resulting atoms, and existentially quantifying the variables in $X_\psi \backslash X_\gamma$ (if any), we obtain the sliced constraint c'. In order to further simplify the trace, if c' is • or $\exists \overline{x}.•$ then we substitute **tell**(c) with • (thus avoiding the "irrelevant" process **tell**(•)).

In a non-deterministic choice, all the precluded choices are discarded ("$+ •$"). Moreover, if the chosen alternative Q_k does not contribute to the final store (i.e., $\Gamma_Q \theta = •$), then the whole process $\sum$ **ask** (c_l) **then** P_l becomes •.

Consider the process (**local** x) Q. Note that x may be replaced to avoid a clash of names (see R'$_{LOC}$). The (new) created variable must be $\{x'\} = X_\psi \backslash X_\gamma$. Then, we check whether $\Gamma_Q[x'/x]$ is relevant or not to return the appropriate replacement. The case of procedure calls can be explained similarly.

Example 2 Let a, b, c, d, e be constraints without any entailment and consider the process $R = $ **ask** (a) **then tell**(c) ∥ **ask** (c) **then** (**tell**(d) ∥ **tell**(b)) ∥ **tell**(a) ∥ **ask** (e) **then skip**.

In any execution of R, the final store is $\{a, b, c, d\}$. If the user selects only $\{d\}$ as slicing criterion, our implementation (see Sect. 4.1) returns the following output (omitting the processes' identifiers):

```
[0; * || ask(c, tell(d) || *) || * || * || * ; *] -->
[0; * || tell(d) || * || * || * || * ; *] -->
[0; * || * || * || * || * || * ; d,*] -->
[0; * || * || * || * || * || * ; d,*] --> stop
```

Note that only the relevant part of the process **ask** (c) **then** $(\mathbf{tell}(d) \parallel \mathbf{tell}(b))$ is highlighted as well as the process **tell**(d) that introduced d in the final store.

Also note that the process $P = \mathbf{ask}$ (a) **then** $\mathbf{tell}(c)$ is not selected in the trace since c is not part of the marked store. However, one may be interested in marking this process to discover the *causality relation* between P and $Q = \mathbf{ask}$ (c) **then** $(\mathbf{tell}(d) \parallel \mathbf{tell}(b))$. Namely, P adds c to the store, needed in Q to produce d.

It turns out that we can easily adapt Algorithm 2 to capture such causality relations as follows. Assume that *sliceProcess* returns both, a replacement θ and a constraint c, i.e., a tuple of the shape $\langle \theta, c \rangle$. In the case of $\sum \mathbf{ask}$ (c_l) **then** P_l, if $\Gamma_Q \theta \neq \bullet$, we return the pair $\langle [\mathbf{ask}\ (c_k)\ \mathbf{then}\ \Gamma_k \theta + \bullet/i], c_k \rangle$. In all the other cases, we return $\langle \theta, \mathbf{t} \rangle$ where θ is as in Algorithm 2. Intuitively, the second component of the tuple represents the guard that was entailed in a "relevant" application of the rule R'_{SUM}. Therefore, in Algorithm 1, besides accumulating θ, we add the returned guard to the set of relevant constraints S. This is done by replacing the line 5 in Algorithm 1 with

$$\mathbf{let} \langle \theta', c \rangle = sliceProcess(\gamma_l, \gamma_{l+1}, i_{l+1}, k_{l+1}, \theta, S) \circ \theta \quad \mathbf{in}$$
$$\theta \leftarrow \theta' \circ \theta$$
$$S \leftarrow S \cup S_{minimal}(S_l, c)$$

where $S_{minimal}(S, c) = \emptyset$ if $c = \mathbf{t}$; otherwise, $S_{minimal}(S, c) = \bigcup \{ S' \subseteq S \mid \bigsqcup S' \models c$ and S' is set minimal$\}$. Therefore, we add to S the minimal set of constraints in S_k that "explains" the entailed guard c of an ask agent.

With this modified version of the algorithm (supporting *causality relations*), the output for the program in Example 2 is:

```
[0 ; ask(a, tell(c)) || ask(c, tell(d) || *) || * || tell(a) || * ; *] [3]
```

where the process **tell**(a) is also selected since the execution of **ask** (a) **then tell**(c) depends on this process.

Soundness. We conclude here by showing that the slicing procedure computes a suitable approximation of the concrete trace. Given two processes P, P', we say that P' approximates P, notation $P \preceq^\sharp P'$, if there exists a (possibly empty) replacement θ s.t. $P' = P\theta$ (i.e., P' is as P but replacing some subterms with $\bullet$). Let $\gamma = (X; \Gamma; S)$ and $\gamma' = (X'; \Gamma'; S')$ be two configurations s.t. $|\Gamma| = |\Gamma'|$. We say that γ' approximates γ, notation $\gamma \preceq^\sharp \gamma'$, if $X' \subseteq X$, $S' \subseteq S$ and $P_i \preceq^\sharp P'_i$ for all $i \in 1..|\Gamma|$.

Theorem 2. *Let* $\gamma_0 \xrightarrow{[i_1]k_1} \cdots \xrightarrow{[i_n]k_n} \gamma_n$ *be a partial computation and* $\gamma'_0 \xrightarrow{[i_1]k_1}$ $\cdots \xrightarrow{[i_n]k_n} \gamma'_n$ *be the resulting sliced trace according to an arbitrary slicing criterion. Then, for all* $t \in 1..n$, $\gamma_t \preceq^\sharp \gamma'_t$. *Moreover, let* $Q = \sum \mathbf{ask}$ (c_k) **then** P_k

and assume that $(X_{t-1}; \Gamma, Q : i_t, \Gamma'; S_{t-1}) \xrightarrow{[i_t]_{k_t}} (X_t; \Gamma, P_{k_t} : j, \Gamma'; S_t)$ *for some* $t \in 1..n$. *If the sliced trace is computed with the Algorithm that supports causality relations, then* $\exists X'_{t-1}(\bigsqcup S'_{t-1}) \models c_{k_t}$.

4 Applications to Timed CCP

Reactive systems [3] are those that react continuously with their environment at a rate controlled by the environment. For example, a controller or a signal-processing system, receives a stimulus (input) from the environment, computes an output and then waits for the next interaction with the environment.

Timed CCP (tcc) [18,25] is an extension of CCP tailoring ideas from Synchronous Languages [3]. More precisely, time in tcc is conceptually divided into *time intervals* (or *time-units*). In a particular time interval, a CCP process P gets an input c from the environment, it executes with this input as the initial *store*, and when it reaches its resting point, it *outputs* the resulting store d to the environment. The resting point determines also a residual process Q that is then executed in the next time-unit. The resulting store d is not automatically transferred to the next time-unit. This way, outputs of two different time-units are not supposed to be related.

Definition 5 (Syntax of tcc [18,25]). *The syntax of tcc is obtained by adding to Definition 2 the processes* **next** P | **unless** (c) **next** P | $!P$.

The process **next** P delays the execution of P to the next time interval. We shall use **next** $^n P$ to denote P preceded with n copies of "**next** " and **next** $^0 P = P$.

The *time-out* **unless** (c) **next** P is also a unit-delay, but P is executed in the next time-unit only if c is not entailed by the final store at the current time interval.

The replication $!P$ means $P \parallel$ **next** $P \parallel$ **next**$^2 P \parallel \dots$, i.e., unboundedly many copies of P but one at a time. We note that in tcc, recursive calls must be guarded by a **next** operator to avoid infinite computations during a time-unit. Then, recursive definitions can be encoded via the ! operator [17].

The operational semantics of tcc considers *internal* and *observable* transitions. The internal transitions correspond to the operational steps that take place during a time-unit. The rules are the same as in Fig. 2 plus:

$$\frac{\bigsqcup S \models c}{(X; \Gamma, \textbf{unless } (c) \textbf{ next } P : i, \Gamma'; S) \xrightarrow{[i]} (X; \Gamma, \Gamma'; S)} \text{R}_{\text{Un}}$$

$$\frac{}{(X; \Gamma, !P, \Gamma'; S) \xrightarrow{[i]} (X; \Gamma, P : j, \textbf{next } !P : j', \Gamma'; S)} \text{R}_!$$

where j and j' are fresh identifiers. The **unless** process is precluded from execution if its guard can be entailed from the current store. The process $!P$ creates a copy of P in the current time-unit and it is executed in the next time-unit. The seemingly missing rule for the **next** operator is clarified below.

The *observable transition* $P \xrightarrow{(c,d)} Q$ ("*P* on input *c*, reduces in one *time-unit* to *Q* and outputs *d*") is obtained from a finite sequence of internal reductions:

$$\frac{(\emptyset; \Gamma; c) \xrightarrow{[i_1,\dots,i_n]_{k_1,\dots,k_n}} (X; \Gamma'; c') \not\longrightarrow}{\Gamma \xrightarrow{(c, \exists X.c')} (\textbf{local } X) \, F(\Gamma')} \text{ R}_{\text{Obs}}$$

The process $F(\Gamma')$ (the continuation of Γ') is obtained as follow:

$$F(R) = \begin{cases} \textbf{skip} & \text{if } R = \textbf{skip} \text{ or } R = \textbf{ask } (c) \textbf{ then } R' \\ F(R_1) \parallel F(R_2) & \text{if } R = R_1 \parallel R_2 \\ Q & \text{if } R = \textbf{next } Q \text{ or } R = \textbf{unless } (c) \textbf{ next } Q \end{cases}$$

The function $F(R)$ (the future of R) returns the processes that must be executed in the next time-unit. More precisely, it unfolds *next* and *unless* expressions. Notice that an *ask* process reduces to **skip** if its guard was not entailed by the final store. Notice also that F is not defined for $\textbf{tell}(c)$, $!Q$, $(\textbf{local } x) \, P$ or $p(\overline{x})$ processes since all of them give rise to an internal transition. Hence these processes can only appear in the continuation if they occur within a **next** or **unless** expression.

4.1 A Trace Slicer for tcc

From the execution point of view, only the observable transition is relevant since it describes the input-output behavior of processes. However, when a tcc program is debugged, we have to consider also the internal transitions. This makes the task of debugging even harder when compared to CCP.

We implemented in Maude (http://maude.cs.illinois.edu) a prototypical version of a slicer for tcc (and then for CCP) that can be found at http://subsell. logic.at/slicer/.

The slicing technique for the internal transition is based on the Algorithm 1 by adding the following cases to Algorithm 2:

1 **case unless** (c) **next** Q **return** $[\bullet/i]$;
2 **case** $!Q$
3 | **if** $\Gamma_Q \theta = \bullet$ **then return** $[\bullet/i]$ **else return** $[!(Q\theta)/i]$;

Note that if an **unless** process evolves during a time-unit, then it is irrelevant. In the case of $!P$, we note that $\Gamma_Q = Q : j, \textbf{next } !Q : j'$. We check whether P is relevant in the current time-unit (Q) or in the following one (**next** $!Q$). If this is not the case, then $!Q$ is irrelevant.

Recall that **next** processes do not exhibit any transition during a time-unit and then, we do not consider this case in the extended version of Algorithm 2.

For the observable transition we proceed as follows. Consider a trace of n observable steps $\gamma_0 \Longrightarrow \cdots \Longrightarrow \gamma_n$ and a set S_{slice} of relevant constraints to be observed in the last configuration γ_n. Let θ_n be the replacement computed during the slicing process of the (internal) trace generated from γ_n. We propagate the replacements in θ_n to the configuration γ_{n-1} as follows:

1. In γ_{n-1} we set $S_{sliced} = \emptyset$. Note that the unique store of interest for the user is the one in γ_n. Recall also that the final store in tcc is not transferred to the next time-unit. Then, only the processes (and not the constraints) in γ_{n-1} are responsible for the final store in γ_n.

2. Let ψ be the last internal configuration in γ_{n-1}, i.e., $\gamma_{n-1} \xrightarrow{[i_1,\ldots,i_m]_{k_1,\ldots,k_m}}$ $\psi \not\longrightarrow$ and $\gamma_n = F(\psi)$. We propagate the replacements in θ_n to ψ before running the slicer on the trace starting from γ_{n-1}. For that, we compute a replacement θ' that must be applied to ψ as follows:
   - If there is a process $R = \textbf{next } P{:}i$ in ψ, then θ' includes the replacement $[\textbf{next } (\Gamma_P\theta_n)/i]$. For instance, if $R = \textbf{next } (\textbf{tell}(c) \parallel \textbf{tell}(d))$ and $\textbf{tell}(c)$ was irrelevant in γ_n, the resulting process in ψ is $\textbf{next } (\bullet \parallel \textbf{tell}(d))$. The case for $\textbf{unless } (c) \textbf{ next } P$ is similar.
   - If there is a process $R = \sum_l \textbf{ask } (c_l) \textbf{ then } P_l{:}i$ in ψ (which is irrelevant since it was not executed), we add to θ' the replacement $[\bullet/i]$.

3. Starting from $\psi\theta$, we compute the slicing on γ_{n-1} (Algorithm 1).

4. This procedure continues until the first configuration γ_0 is reached.

Example 3 Consider the following process definitions:

$$System \triangleq Beat2 \parallel Beat4 \qquad Beat2 \triangleq \textbf{tell}(b2) \parallel \textbf{next }^2 Beat2$$
$$Beat4 \triangleq \textbf{tell}(b4) \parallel \textbf{next }^4 Beat4$$

This is a simple model of a multimedia system that, every 2 (resp. 4) time-units, produces the constraint $b2$ (resp. $b4$). Then, every 4 time-units, the system produces both $b2$ and $b4$. If we compute 5 time-units and choose $S_{slice} = \{b4\}$ we obtain (omitting the process identifiers):

```
{1 / 5 > [System ; *] --> [Beat4 ; *] --> [next^4(Beat4) ; *]} ==>
{2 / 5 > [next~3(Beat4) ; *]} ==>
{3 / 5 > [next~2(Beat4) ; *] } ==>
{4 / 5 > [next(Beat4) ; *]} ==>
{5 / 5 > [Beat4 ; *] --> [tell(b4) || * ; *] --> [* ; b4]}
```

Note that all the executions of *Beat2* in time-units 1, 3 and 5 are hidden since they do not contribute to the observed output $b4$. More interestingly, the execution of $\textbf{tell}(b4)$ in time-unit 1, as well as the recursive call of *Beat4* ($\textbf{next }^4 Beat4$) in time-unit 5, are also hidden.

Now assume that we compute an even number of time-units. Then, no constraint is produced in that time-unit and the whole execution of *System* is hidden:

```
{1/4 > [* ; *]} ==> {2/4 > [* ; *]} ==>
{3/4 > [* ; *]} ==> {4/4 > [* ; *]}
```

As a more compelling example, consider the following process definitions:

$$Beat \triangleq \prod_{i \in I_1} \textbf{next }^i\textbf{tell}(\textbf{beat}) \qquad\qquad Start \triangleq \sum_{i \in I_2} \textbf{next }^i(\textbf{tell}(\textbf{start}))$$
$$Check \triangleq {!}\textbf{ask } (\textbf{start}) \textbf{ then next }^{12}(\textbf{tell}(\textbf{stop})) \quad System \triangleq Beat \parallel Start \parallel Check$$

where $I_1 = \{0, 3, 5, 7, 9, 11, 14, 16, 18, 20, 22\}$, $I_2 = \{0, 3, 5, 7, 9, 11\}$ and Π_i stands for parallel composition. This process represents a rhythmic pattern where groups of "2"-unit elements separate groups of "3"-unit elements, e.g., 3 $\underbrace{2\,2\,2\,2}$ 3 $\underbrace{2\,2\,2\,2\,2}$. Such pattern appears in repertoires of Central African Republic music [5] and were programmed in tcc in [21].

This pattern can be represented in a circle with 24 divisions, where "2" and "3"-unit elements are placed. The "3"-unit intervals are displayed in red in Fig. 3. The important property is *asymmetry*: if one attempts to break the circle into two parts, it is not possible to have two equal parts. To be more precise, the start and stop constraints divide the circle in two halves (see process Start) and it is always the case that the constraint beat does not coincide in a time-unit with the constraint stop. For instance, in Fig. 3(a) (resp. (b)), the circle is divided in time-units 1 –start– to 13 –stop– (resp. 4 –start– to 16 –stop–). The signal beat does not coincide with a stop: in Fig. 3(a) (resp. (b)), the beat is added in time-unit 12 (resp. 15).

If we generate one of the possible traces and perform the slicing processes for the time-unit 13 with $S_{sliced} = \{\text{beat}, \text{stop}\}$, we only observe as relevant process *Check* (since no beat is produced in that time-unit):

```
{1 / 13 > [System ; *] --> [Check ; *] --> [! ask(start, next^12(tell(stop)) ; *]
         --> [ask(start, next^12(tell(stop)) ; *] --> [next^12(tell(stop)) ; *]} ==>
.... ==> ...
{11 / 13 > [next(next(tell(stop))) ; *]} ==>
{12 / 13 > [next(tell(stop)) || * ; *]} ==>
{13 / 13 > [tell(stop) ; *] --> [* ; stop][0]}
```

More interestingly, assume that we wrongly write a process *Check* that is not "well synchronized" with the process *Beat*. For instance, let $I_2' = \{2\}$. In this case, the start signal does not coincide with a beat. Then, in time-unit 15, we (wrongly) observe both beat and stop (i.e., asymmetry is broken!). The trace of that program (that can be found in tool's web page) is quite long and difficult to understand. On the contrary, the sliced one is rather simple:

```
{1 / 15 > [System ; *] --> [Beat || Check ; *] -->
          [next^14(tell(beat)) || next(! ask(start, next^12(tell(stop)); *]} ==>
{2 / 15 > [next^13(tell(beat))|| ! ask(start, next^12(tell(stop))) ; *]} ==>
{3 / 15 > [next^12(tell(beat)))|| ! ask(start, next^12(tell(stop)) ; *]} ==>
{4 / 15 > [next^11(tell(beat))|| next^11(tell(stop)|| * ; *] --> stop} ==>
...
{14 / 15 > [next(tell(beat)) || next(tell(stop)) || * ; *] --> stop} ==>
{15 / 15 > [tell(beat) || tell(stop) || * ; *] --> [tell(stop) || * ; beat] -->
           [* ; beat,stop]}
```

Something interesting in this trace is that the ask in the *Check* process is hidden from the time-unit 4 on (since it is not "needed" any more). Moreover, the only tell(beat) process (from *Beat* definition) displayed is the one that is executed in time-unit 15 (i.e., the one resulting from next [14]tell(beat)). From this trace, it is not difficult to note that the *Start* process starts on time-unit 3 (the process next [11]tell(stop) first appears on time-unit 4). This can tell the user that the process *Start* begins its execution in a wrong time-unit. In order to confirm this hypothesis, the user may compute the sliced trace up to time-unit 3 with $S_{sliced} = \{\text{beat}, \text{start}\}$ and notice that, in that time-unit, start is produced but beat is not part of the store.

The reader may find in the web page of the tool a further example related to biochemical systems. We modeled in tcc the P53/Mdm2 DNA-damage Repair

Mechanism [16]. The slicer allowed us to detect two bugs in the written code. We invite the reader to check in this example the length (and complexity) of the buggy trace and the resulting sliced trace.

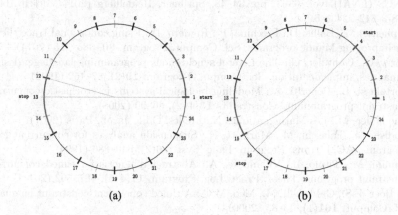

Fig. 3. Pattern of "2" and "3"-unit elements (taken from [5]).

5   Conclusions and Future Work

In this paper we introduced the first framework for slicing concurrent constraint based programs, and showed its applicability for CCP and timed CCP. We implemented a prototype of the slicer in Maude and showed its use in debugging a program specifying a biochemical system and a multimedia interacting system.

Our framework is a good basis for dealing with other variants of CCP such as linear CCP [10], spatial and epistemic CCP [14] as well as with other temporal extensions of it [8]. We are currently working on extending our tool to cope with these languages. We also plan to incorporate into our framework an assertion language based on a suitable fragment of temporal logic. Such assertions will specify invariants the program must satisfy during its execution. If the assertion is not satisfied in a given state, then the execution is interrupted and a concrete trace is generated to be later sliced. For instance, in the multimedia system, the user may specify the invariant stop → (¬beat) (if stop is entailed then beat cannot be part of the store) or stop → ⊖beat (a stop state must be preceded by a beat state).

Acknowledgments. We thank the anonymous reviewers for their detailed comments and suggestions which helped us to improve our paper. The work of Olarte was funded by CNPq and CAPES (Brazil). The work of Palamidessi and Olarte was supported by the Regional Program STIC AMSUD "EPIC: EPistemic Interactive Concurrency".

References

1. Alpuente, M., Ballis, D., Espert, J., Romero, D.: Backward trace slicing for rewriting logic theories. In: Bjørner, N., Sofronie-Stokkermans, V. (eds.) CADE 2011. LNCS (LNAI), vol. 6803, pp. 34–48. Springer, Heidelberg (2011). doi:10.1007/978-3-642-22438-6_5
2. Alpuente, M., Ballis, D., Frechina, F., Romero, D.: Using conditional trace slicing for improving Maude programs. Sci. Comput. Program. **80**, 385–415 (2014)
3. Berry, G., Gonthier, G.: The Esterel synchronous programming language: design, semantics, implementation. Sci. Comput. Program. **19**(2), 87–152 (1992)
4. Bortolussi, L., Policriti, A.: Modeling biological systems in stochastic concurrent constraint programming. Constraints **13**(1–2), 66–90 (2008)
5. Chemillier, M.: Les Mathématiques Naturelles. Odile Jacob, Paris (2007)
6. Codish, M., Falaschi, M., Marriott, K.: Suspension analyses for concurrent logic programs. ACM Trans. Program. Lang. Syst. **16**(3), 649–686 (1994)
7. Comini, M., Titolo, L., Villanueva, A.: Abstract diagnosis for timed concurrent constraint programs. Theor. Pract. Log. Program. **11**(4–5), 487–502 (2011)
8. de Boer, F.S., Gabbrielli, M., Meo, M.C.: A timed concurrent constraint language. Inf. Comput. **161**(1), 45–83 (2000)
9. de Boer, F.S., Di Pierro, A., Palamidessi, C.: Nondeterminism and infinite computations in constraint programming. Theor. Comput. Sci. **151**(1), 37–78 (1995)
10. Fages, F., Ruet, P., Soliman, S.: Linear concurrent constraint programming: operational and phase semantics. Inf. Comput. **165**(1), 14–41 (2001)
11. Falaschi, M., Olarte, C., Palamidessi, C.: Abstract interpretation of temporal concurrent constraint programs. TPLP **15**(3), 312–357 (2015)
12. Van Hentenryck, P., Saraswat, V.A., Deville, Y.: Design, implementation, and evaluation of the constraint language cc(FD). J. Log. Program. **37**(1–3), 139–164 (1998)
13. Josep, S.: A vocabulary of program slicing-based techniques. ACM Comput. Surv. **44**(3), 12:1–12:41 (2012)
14. Knight, S., Palamidessi, C., Panangaden, P., Valencia, F.D.: Spatial and epistemic modalities in constraint-based process calculi. In: Koutny, M., Ulidowski, I. (eds.) CONCUR 2012. LNCS, vol. 7454, pp. 317–332. Springer, Heidelberg (2012). doi:10.1007/978-3-642-32940-1_23
15. Korel, B., Laski, J.: Dynamic program slicing. Inf. Process. Lett. **29**(3), 155–163 (1988)
16. de Maria, E., Despeyroux, J., Felty, A.P.: A logical framework for systems biology. In: Fages, F., Piazza, C. (eds.) FMMB 2014. LNCS, vol. 8738, pp. 136–155. Springer, Cham (2014). doi:10.1007/978-3-319-10398-3_10
17. Nielsen, M., Palamidessi, C., Valencia, F.D.: On the expressive power of temporal concurrent constraint programming languages. In: Proceedings of PPDP 2002, pp. 156–167. ACM (2002)
18. Nielsen, M., Palamidessi, C., Valencia, F.D.: Temporal concurrent constraint programming: denotation, logic and applications. Nord. J. Comput. **9**(1), 145–188 (2002)
19. Ochoa, C., Silva, J., Vidal, G.: Dynamic slicing of lazy functional programs based on redex trails. High. Order Symbol. Comput. **21**(1–2), 147–192 (2008)
20. Olarte, C., Pimentel, E., Nigam, V.: Subexponential concurrent constraint programming. Theor. Comput. Sci. **606**, 98–120 (2015)

21. Olarte, C., Rueda, C., Sarria, G., Toro, M., Valencia, F.D.: Concurrent constraints models of music interaction. In: Assayag, G., Truchet, C. (eds.) Constraint Programming in Music, pp. 133–153. Wiley, Hoboken (2011)
22. Olarte, C., Rueda, C., Valencia, F.D.: Models and emerging trends of concurrent constraint programming. Constraints 18(4), 535–578 (2013)
23. Olarte, C., Valencia, F.D.: Universal concurrent constraint programing: symbolic semantics and applications to security. In: Wainwright, R.L., Haddad, H. (eds.) SAC, pp. 145–150. ACM (2008)
24. Saraswat, V.A.: Concurrent Constraint Programming. MIT Press, Cambridge (1993)
25. Saraswat, V.A., Jagadeesan, R., Gupta, V.: Timed default concurrent constraint programming. J. Symb. Comput. 22(5/6), 475–520 (1996)
26. Saraswat, V.A., Rinard, M.C., Panangaden, P.: Semantic foundations of concurrent constraint programming. In: Wise, D.S. (ed.) POPL, pp. 333–352. ACM Press (1991)
27. Shapiro, E.Y.: Algorithmic Program DeBugging. MIT Press, Cambridge (1983)
28. Weiser, M.: Program slicing. IEEE Trans. Softw. Eng. 10(4), 352–357 (1984)

Compilation and Optimization

A New Functional-Logic Compiler for Curry: SPRITE

Sergio Antoy[(⊠)] and Andy Jost

Department of Computer Science, Portland State University, Portland, OR, USA
antoy@cs.pdx.edu, ajost@pdx.edu

Abstract. We introduce a new native code compiler for Curry code-named SPRITE. SPRITE is based on the Fair Scheme, a compilation strategy that provides instructions for transforming declarative, non-deterministic programs of a certain class into imperative, deterministic code. We outline salient features of SPRITE, discuss its implementation of Curry programs, and present benchmarking results. SPRITE is the first-to-date operationally complete implementation of Curry. Preliminary results show that ensuring this property does not incur a significant penalty.

Keywords: Functional logic programming · Compiler implementation · Operational completeness

1 Introduction

The functional-logic language Curry [16,18] is a syntactically small extension of the popular functional language Haskell. Its seamless combination of functional and logic programming concepts gives rise to hybrid features that encourage expressive, abstract, and declarative programs [5,18].

One example of such a feature is a functional pattern [3], in which functions are invoked in the left-hand sides of rules. This is an intuitive way to construct patterns with syntactically-sugared high-level features that puts patterns on a more even footing with expressions. In Curry, patterns can be composed and refactored like other code, and encapsulation can be used to hide details. We illustrate this with function get, defined below, which finds the values associated with a key in a list of key-value pairs.

```
with x = _ ++ [x] ++ _
get key (with (key, value)) = value
```
(1)

Operation with generates all lists containing x. The anonymous variables, indicated by "_", are place holders for expressions that are not used. Function "++" is the list-appending operator. When used in a left-hand side, as in the rule

This material is based upon work partially supported by the National Science Foundation under Grant No. CCF-1317249.

M.V. Hermenegildo and P. Lopez-Garcia (Eds.): LOPSTR 2016, LNCS 10184, pp. 97–113, 2017.
DOI: 10.1007/978-3-319-63139-4_6

for get, operation with produces a pattern that matches any list containing x. Thus, the second argument to get is a list — any list — containing the pair (key, value). The repeated variable, key, implies a constraint that, in this case, ensures that only values associated with the given key are selected.

By similar means, we may identify keys:

key_of (with (key, _)) = key   (2)

This non-deterministically returns a key of the given list; for example:

```
> key_of [('a',0), ('b',1), ('c',2)]
'a'
'b'                                                                              (3)
'c'
```

This is just one of many features [5,18] that make Curry an appealing choice, particularly when the desired properties of a program result are easy to describe, but a set of step-by-step instructions to obtain the result is more difficult to come by.

This paper describes work towards a new Curry compiler we call SPRITE. SPRITE aims to be the first operationally complete Curry compiler, meaning it should produce every value of a source program (given sufficient time and space resources). This paper does not present new theoretical results. The foundations of our work were previously presented in [7], that sets out rules for compiling a functional-logic program (in the form of a graph rewriting system) into abstract *deterministic* procedures that easily map to the instructions of a low-level programming language. The main contribution of this work is a compiler whose existence and performance prove that the completeness of the strategy presented in [7] can be operationally achieved without incurring noticeable overhead. The compiler generates object code that include several novel ideas. The code, based on an open-source effort [22], is machine-independent and suitable for optimization on various architectures. The graphs rewritten by the code have nodes all of the same size. This allows destructive updates for redex replacement which entirely by-pass the pointer redirection phase of a step and consequently improves the efficiency eases memory management. The code also introduces a very lean pattern matching scheme, specifically designed for functional logic languages, which accommodate non-determinism and consequently is failure tolerant.

Section 2 introduces SPRITE at a high level, and describes the transformations it performs. Section 3 describes the implementation of Curry programs as imperative code. Section 4 contains benchmark results. Section 5 describes other Curry compilers. Section 6 addresses future work, and Sect. 7 contains our concluding remarks.

2   The SPRITE Curry Compiler

SPRITE is a native code compiler for Curry. Like all compilers, SPRITE subjects source programs to a series of transformations. To begin, an external program is used to convert Curry source code into a desugared representation called FlatCurry [17], which SPRITE further transforms into a custom intermediate representation we call ICurry. Then, following the steps laid out in the Fair Scheme, SPRITE converts ICurry into a graph rewriting system that implements the program. This system is realized in a low-level, machine-independent language provided by the open-source compiler infrastructure library LLVM [22]. That code is then optimized and lowered to native assembly, ultimately producing an executable program. SPRITE provides a convenience program, scc, to coordinate the whole procedure.

2.1   ICurry vs FlatCurry

ICurry, where the "I" stands for "imperative," is a form of Curry programs suitable for translation into imperative code. ICurry is inspired by FlatCurry [17], a popular representation of Curry programs that has been very successful for a variety of tasks including implementations in Prolog [19]. FlatCurry provides expressions that resemble those of a functional program — e.g., pattern-matching strategy is made explicit through case expressions that use symbolic variables that have no corresponding element in an imperative language. These case expressions may include local mutually recursive declarations in the form of let blocks and conditionals in the form of nested case constructs which again have no corresponding elements in an imperative language. ICurry's purpose is to represent the program in a more convenient imperative form — more convenient since SPRITE will ultimately implement it in an imperative language. In imperative languages, local declarations and conditionals take the form of statements while expressions are limited to constants and/or calls to subroutines, possibly nested. ICurry provides statements for local declarations and conditionals. It provides expressions that avoid constructs that cannot be directly translated into the expressions of a imperative language.

In ICurry all non-determinism — including the implicit non-determinism in high-level features, such as functional patterns — is expressed through choices. A choice is the archetypal non-deterministic function, indicated by the symbol "?" and defined by the following rules:

$$
\begin{aligned}
x \; ? \; \_ &= x \\
\_ \; ? \; y &= y
\end{aligned}
\tag{4}
$$

The use of only choices is made possible, in part, by a duality between choices and free variables [4,23]: any language feature expressed with choices can be implemented with free variables and vice versa. Algorithms exists to convert one to the other, meaning we are free to choose the most convenient representation in SPRITE.

Finally, as in FlatCurry, the pattern-matching strategy in ICurry is made explicit and guided by a definitional tree [1], a structure made up of stepwise case distinctions that combines all rules of a function. We illustrate this for the zip function, defined as:

```
zip [] _ = []
zip (_:_) [] = []                                         (5)
zip (x:xs) (y:ys) = (x,y) : zip xs ys
```

The corresponding definitional tree is shown below as it might appear in ICurry.

```
zip = \a b -> case a of
    []       -> []
    (x:xs) -> case b of                                   (6)
        []       -> []
        (y:ys) -> (x,y) : zip xs ys
```

2.2   Evaluating ICurry

It is understood how to evaluate the right-hand side of (6) efficiently; the Spineless Tagless G-machine (STG) [28], for instance, is up to the task. But the non-deterministic properties of functional-logic programs complicate matters. To evaluate zip, its first argument must be reduced to head-normal form. In a purely functional language, the root node of a head-normal form is always a data constructor symbol (assuming partial application is implemented by a data-like object), or else the computation fails. But for functional-logic programs, two additional possibilities must be considered, leading to an extended case distinction:

```
zip = \a b -> case a of
    x ? y   -> (pull-tab)    -- implied
    ⊥       -> ⊥             -- implied                    (7)
    []      -> []
    (x:xs) -> case b of ...
```

The infrastructure for executing this kind of pattern matching very efficiently by means of dispatch tables will be described shortly, but for now we note two things. First, there is no need for ICurry to spell out these extra cases, as they can be generated by the compiler. Second, their presence calls for an expanded notion of the computation that allows for additional node states. Because of this, SPRITE hosts computations in a graph whose nodes are taken from four classes: *constructors, functions, choices,* and *failures.* Constructors and functions are provided by the source program; choices are built-in; and failures, denoted "⊥", arise from incompletely defined operations such as head, the function that returns the head of a list. For example, head [] rewrites to "⊥". A simple replacement therefore propagates failure from needed arguments to roots.

Choices execute a special step called a *pull-tab* [2,9]. Pull-tab steps lift non-determinism out of needed positions, where they prevent completion of pattern matches. The result is a choice between two more-definite expressions. A pull-tab step is shown below:

$$\texttt{zip (a ? b) c} \rightarrow \texttt{zip a x ? zip b x where x = c} \tag{8}$$

A pattern match cannot proceed while (a ? b) is the first argument to zip because there is no matching rule in the function definition (one cannot exist because the choice symbol is disallowed on left-hand sides). We do not want to choose between a and b because such a choice would have to be reconsidered to avoid losing potential results. The pull-tab transformation "pulls" the choice to an outermore position, producing two new subexpressions, zip a c and zip b c, that can be evaluated further. The fact that c is shared in the result illustrates a desirable property: that node duplication is minimal and localized. Pull-tabbing involves some technicalities that we address later. The complete details are in [2].

Due to the extra cases, additional node types, and, especially, the unusual mechanics of pull-tabbing steps, we chose to develop in SPRITE a new evaluation machine from scratch rather than augment an existing one such as STG. The property of pull-tabbing that it "breaks-out" of recursively-descending evaluation into nested expressions fundamentally changes the computation so that existing functional strategies are difficult to apply. In SPRITE, we have implemented *de novo* an evaluation mechanism and runtime system based on the Fair Scheme. These are the topic of the next section.

3 Implementation

In this section, we describe the implementation of Curry programs in imperative code. SPRITE generates LLVM code, but we assume most readers are not familiar with that. So, rather than presenting the generated code, we describe the implemented programs in terms of familiar concepts that appear directly in LLVM. In this way, the reader can think in terms of an unspecified target language — one similar to assembly — that implements those concepts. To facilitate the following description, we indicate in parentheses where a similar feature exists in the C programming language.

In the target language, values are strongly typed, and the types include integers, pointers, arrays, structures and functions. Programs are arranged into compilation units called modules that contain symbols. Symbols are visible to other modules, and to control access to them each one is marked internal (static) or external (extern). Control flow within functions is carried out by branch instructions. These include unconditional branches (goto), conditional branches (if, for, while) and indirect branches (goto*). The target of every branch instruction is a function-local address (label). A call stack is provided, and it is manipulated by call and return instructions that enter and exit functions, respectively. Calls are normally executed in a fresh stack frame, but the target language also supports explicit tail recursion, and SPRITE puts it to good use.

3.1 Expression Representation

The expressions evaluated by a program are graphs consisting of labeled nodes having zero or more successors. Each node belongs to one of four classes, as discussed in the previous section. For constructors and functions, node labels are equivalent to symbols defined in the source program. Failures and choices are labeled with reserved symbols. Successors are references to other nodes. The number of successors, which equals the arity of the corresponding symbol, is fixed at compile time. Partial applications are "firstfied", i.e., encoded in first-order rule as per [26].

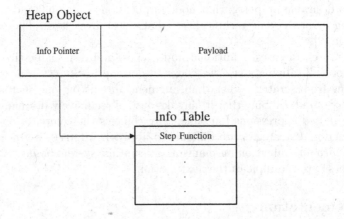

Fig. 1. The heap object layout.

SPRITE implements graph nodes as heap objects. The layout of a heap object is shown in Fig. 1. The label is implemented as a pointer to a static info table that will be described later. SPRITE emits exactly one table for each symbol in the Curry program. Successors are implemented as pointers to other heap objects.

3.2 Evaluation

Evaluation in SPRITE is the repeated execution of rewriting and pull-tabbing steps. Both are implemented by two interleaved activities: replacement and pattern-matching. A replacement produces a new graph from a previous one by replacing a subexpression matching the left-hand side of a rule with the corresponding right-hand side. For instance, $1 + 1$ might be replaced with 2. A replacement is implemented by overwriting the heap object at the root of the subexpression being replaced. The key advantage of this destructive update is that no pointer redirection [12, Definition 8] [15] is required during a rewrite step. Reusing a heap object also has the advantage of saving one memory allocation and deallocation per replacement, but requires that every heap object be capable of storing any node, whatever its arity. SPRITE meets this requirement by providing in heap objects a fixed amount of space capable of holding a small number of successors. For nodes with more successors than would fit in this space, the payload instead contains a pointer to a larger array. This approach simplifies memory management for heap objects: since they are all the same size, a single memory pool suffices. Because arities are known at compile time, no runtime checks are needed to determine whether successor pointers reside in the heap object. Sprite uses a simple mark-and-sweep garbage collector. It can be changed or replaced easily and is not a focus of this work.

Pattern-matching consists of cascading case distinctions over the root symbol of the expression being matched that culminate either in a replacement or in the patter match of a subexpression. The Fair Scheme implements this according to a strategy guided by the definitional trees encoded in ICurry. Case distinction as exemplified in (7) assumes that an expression being matched is not rooted by a function symbol. Thus, when a node needed to complete a match is labeled by a function symbol, the expression rooted by that node is evaluated until it is labeled by a non-function symbol. A function-labeled node, n, is evaluated by a target function called the *step* function that performs a pattern match and replacement at n. Each Curry function gives rise to one target function, a pointer to which is stored in the associated info table (see Fig. 1).

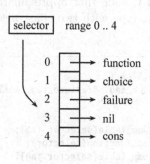

Fig. 2. Schematic representation of the SPRITE tagged dispatching mechanism for a distinction of a List type.

Operationally, pattern-matching amounts to evaluating nested case expressions similar to the one shown in (7). SPRITE implements this through a mechanism we call *tagged dispatch*. With this approach, the compiler assigns each symbol a tag at compile time. Tags are sequential integers indicating which of the four classes discussed earlier the node belongs to. The three lowest tags are reserved for functions, choices, and failures (all functions have the same tag). For constructors, the tag additionally indicates *which* constructor of its type the symbol represents. To see how this works, consider the following type definition:

data ABC = A | B | C   (9)

ABC comprises three constructors in a well-defined order (any fixed order would do). To distinguish between them, SPRITE tags these with sequential numbers starting at the integer that follows the reserved tags. So, the tag of A is one less than the tag of B, which is one less than the tag of C. These values are unique within the type, but not throughout the program: the first constructor of each type, for instance, always has the same tag. Following these rules, it is easy to see that every case selector is a node tagged with one of $3 + N$ consecutive integers, where N is the number of constructors in its type. To compile a case expression, SPRITE emits a jump table that transfers control to a code block appropriate for handling the selector tag. For example, the block that handles failure rewrites to failure, and the block that handles choices executes a pull-tab. This is shown schematically in Fig. 2. It is in general impossible to know at compile time which constructors may be encountered when the program runs, so the jump table must be complete. If a functional logic program does not define a branch for some constructor — i.e., a function is not completely defined — the branch for that constructor is a rewrite to failure.

To implement tagged dispatch, SPRITE creates function-local code blocks as labels, constructs a static jump table containing their addresses, and executes indirect branch instructions — based on the selector tag — through the table. Figure 3 shows a fragment of C code that approximates this. Case distinction occurs over a variable of List type with two constructors, nil and cons. Five

---

```
static void* jump_table[5] = {
    &function_tag, &choice_tag, &failure_tag, &nil_tag, &cons_tag
  };

entry:          goto* jump_table[selector.tag];
function_tag:   call_step_function(selector);
                goto* jump_table[selector.tag];
choice_tag:     /*execute a pull tab*/
failure_tag:    /*rewrite to failure*/
nil_tag:        /*rewrite to []*/
cons_tag:       /*process the nested case expression*/
```

Fig. 3. An illustrative implementation in C of the case expression shown in (7). This code fragment would appear in the body of the step function for zip. Variable selector refers to the case selector. Label entry indicates the entry point into this case expression.

labeled code blocks handle the five tags that may appear at the case selector. A static array of label address implements the jump table. This example assumes the *function, choice, failure, nil,* and *cons* tags take the values zero through four, respectively. The jump table contains one extra case not depicted in (7). When the selector is a *function*, the step function of the selector root label is applied as many times as necessary until the selector class is no longer *function*.

3.3 Completeness and Consistency

SPRITE aims to be the first complete Curry compiler. Informally, complete means the program produces every intended result of the source program. More precisely, and especially for infinite computations, any value will eventually be produced, given enough resources. This is a difficult problem because a non-terminating computation for obtaining one result could block progress of some other computation that would obtain another result. For example, the following program has a result, 1, that can be obtained in only a couple of steps, but existing Curry compilers fail to produce it:

```
loop = loop
main = loop ? (1 ? loop)
```
(10)

The Fair Scheme defines a complete evaluation strategy. It creates a work queue containing in turn any expression that might produce a result. At all times, the expression at the head of the queue is active, meaning it is being evaluated. Initially, the work queue contains only the goal expression. Whenever pull-tabbing places a choice at the root of an expression, that expression forks. It is removed from the queue, and its two alternatives are added. Whenever an expression produces a value, it is removed from the queue. To avoid endlessly working on an expression whose evaluation does not terminate, the program rotates the active expression to the end of the work queue every so often. In so doing, SPRITE guarantees that no expression is ignored forever, hence no potential result is lost.

A proof of correctness of compiled programs is provided in [7] for the abstract formulation of the compiler, the Fair Scheme. In this domain, correctness is the property that an executable program produces all and only the values intended by the corresponding source program. A delicate point is raised by pull-tabbing. A pull-tab step may duplicate or clone a choice, as the following example shows. Cloned choices should be seen as a single choice. Thus when a computation reduces a choice to its right alternative, it should also reduce any other clone of the same choice to the right alternative, and likewise for the left alternative. Computations obeying this condition are called *consistent*.

```
xor x x where x = T ? F
   →pull−tab (xor T x) ? (xor F x) where x = T ? F
```
(11)

In the example above, a pull-tab step applied to the choice in x leads to its duplication. Now, when evaluating either alternative of the topmost choice, a consistent strategy must recognize that the remaining choice (in x) is already made. For instance, when evaluating xor T x, the value of x can only be T, the left alternative, because the left alternative of x has already been selected to obtain xor T x. To keep track of clones, the Fair Scheme annotates choices with identifiers. Two choice nodes with identical identifiers represent the same choice. Fresh identifiers are assigned when new choices arise from a replacement; pull-tab steps copy existing identifiers. Every expression in the work queue owns a finger-print, which is a mapping from choice identifiers to values in the set {*left, right*}. The fingerprint is used to detect and remove inconsistent computations from the work queue.

It is possible to syntactically pre-compute pull-tab steps: that is, a case state-ment such as the one in (7) could implement pull-tabbing by defining an appro-priate right-hand side rule for the choice branch. In fact, a major competing implementation of Curry does exactly that [8]. A disadvantage of that approach is that choice identifiers must appear as first-class citizens of the program and be propagated through pull-tab steps using additional rules not encoded in the source program. We believe it is more efficient to embed choice identifiers in choice nodes as an implementation detail and process pull-tab steps dynami-cally. Section 4.2 compares these two approaches in greater detail.

4 Performance

In this section we present a set of benchmark results. These programs were previous used to compare three implementations of Curry [8]: MCC, PAKCS, and KICS2. We shall use KICS2 to perform direct comparisons with SPRITE[1], since it compares favorably to the others, and mention the relative performance of the others. KICS2 compiles Curry to Haskell and then uses the Glasgow Haskell Compiler (GHC) [13] to produce executables. GHC has been shown to produce very efficient code [20, 21, 27]. Like SPRITE, KICS2 uses a pull-tabbing evaluation strategy, but unlike SPRITE, it does not form a work queue; hence, is incomplete when faced with programs such as (10). Instead, it builds a tree containing all values of the program and executes (lazily and with interleaved steps) a user-selected search algorithm.

A major highlight of KICS2 is that purely functional programs compile to "straight" Haskell, thus incurring no overhead due to the presence of unused logic capabilities. SPRITE, too, enjoys this zero-overhead property, but there is little room to improve upon GHC for functional programs, as it is the beneficiary of exponentially more effort. Our goal for functional programs, therefore, is simply to measure and minimize the penalty of running SPRITE. For programs that utilize logic features KICS2 emits Haskell code that simulates non-determinism. In these cases, there is more room for improvement since, for example, SPRITE can avoid simulation overhead by more directly implementing logic features.

---

[1] Available at https://github.com/andyjost/Sprite-3.

Program	Type	KiCS2	SPRITE	Δ
PaliFunPats	FL	0.64	0.09	-7.1
LastFunPats	FL	1.85	0.30	-6.2
Last	FL	1.90	0.31	-6.1
PermSortPeano	FL	44.04	8.14	-5.4
PermSort	FL	42.72	8.15	-5.3
ExpVarFunPats	FL	5.92	1.29	-4.6
Half	FL	42.31	9.55	-4.4
Reverse	F	0.36	0.21	-1.7
ReverseUser	F	0.34	0.21	-1.6
ReverseBuiltin	F	0.40	0.39	-1.0
ReverseHO	F	0.36	0.39	1.1
Primes	F	0.29	0.32	1.1
ShareNonDet	FL	0.28	0.33	1.2
PrimesBuiltin	F	0.73	1.10	1.5
PrimesPeano	F	0.41	0.66	1.6
QueensUser	F	0.87	1.83	2.1
Queens	F	0.80	1.81	2.3
TakPeano	F	0.84	2.08	2.5
Tak	F	0.32	0.92	2.9

Fig. 4. Execution times for a set of functional (F) and functional-logic (FL) programs taken from the KiCS2 benchmark suite. Times are in seconds. The final column (Δ) reports the speed-up (negative) or slow-down (positive) factor of SPRITE relative to KiCS2. System configuration: Intel i5-3470 CPU at 3.20 GHz, Ubuntu Linux 14.04.

4.1 Functional Programs

The execution times for a set of programs taken from the KiCS2 benchmark suite[2] are shown in Fig. 4. The results are arranged in order from greatest improvement to greatest degradation in execution time. The most striking feature is the clear division between the functional (deterministic) and functional-logic (non-deterministic) subsets, which is consistent with our above-stated expectations. On average, SPRITE produces relatively slower code for functional programs and relatively faster code for functional-logic ones. We calculate averages as the geometric mean, since that method is not strongly influenced by extreme results in either direction. The functional subset runs, on average, 1.4x slower in SPRITE as compared to KiCS2. Figures published by Braßel et al. [8, Figs. 2 and 3] indicate that PAKCS and MCC run 148x and 9x slower than KiCS2, respectively, for these programs. We take these results as an indication that the functional parts of SPRITE — i.e., those parts responsible for pattern-matching, rewriting, memory management, and optimization — although not as finely-tuned as their GHC counterparts, still compare favorably to most mainstream Curry compilers.

We note that SPRITE currently does not perform optimizations such as deforestation [14] or unboxing [21]. These, and other optimizations of ICurry, e.g., [6],

---

[2] Downloaded from https://www-ps.informatik.uni-kiel.de/kics2/benchmarks.

could potentially impact the benchmark results. Inspecting the output of GHC reveals that the `tak` program (incidentally, the worse-case for SPRITE) is optimized by GHC to a fully-unboxed computation. To see how LLVM stacks up, we rewrote the program in C and converted it to LLVM using Clang [11], a C language front-end for LLVM. When we compiled this to native code and measured the execution time, we found that it was identical[3] to the KiCS2 (and GHC) time. We therefore see no fundamental barrier to reducing the SPRITE "penalty" to zero for this program, and perhaps others, too. We have reason to be optimistic that implementing more optimizations at the source and ICurry levels, without fundamentally changing the core of SPRITE, will yield substantive improvements to SPRITE.

4.2   Functional-Logic Programs

For the functional-logic subset, Fig. 4 shows that SPRITE produces relatively faster code: 4.4x faster, on average. Published comparisons [8, Fig. 4] indicate that, compared to KiCS2, PAKCS is 5.5x slower and MCC is 3.5x *faster* for these programs. Our first thought after seeing this result was that SPRITE might enjoy a better algorithmic complexity. We had just completed work to reduce SPRITE's complexity when processing choices, so perhaps, we thought, in doing that work we had surpassed KiCS2. We set out to test this by selecting a program dominated by choice generation and running it for different input sizes, with and without the recent modifications to SPRITE. The results are shown in Fig. 5. Contrary to our expectation, SPRITE and KiCS2 exhibit strikingly similar complexity: both fit an exponential curve with r^2 in excess of 0.999, and their slope coefficients differ by less than 2%. A better explanation, then, for the difference is that some constant factor c exists, such that choice-involved steps in SPRITE are c-times faster than in KiCS2. What could account for this factor? We believe the best explanation is the overhead of simulating non-determinism in Haskell, which we alluded to at the end of Sect. 3.3. To see why, we need to look at KiCS2 in more detail.

KiCS2 uses a few helper functions [8, Sect. 3.1] to generate choice identifiers:

```
thisID       :: IDSupply -> ID
leftSupply  :: IDSupply -> IDSupply                          (12)
rightSupply :: IDSupply -> IDSupply
```

The purpose of these functions is to ensure that choice identifiers are never reused. Here, `ID` is the type of a choice identifier and `IDSupply` is opaque (for our purposes). Any function that might produce a choice is implicitly extended by KiCS2 to accept a supply function. As an example, this program

```
f :: Bool
main = xor f (False ? True)                                  (13)
```

---

[3] Using the Linux `time` command, whose resolution is 0.01 s.

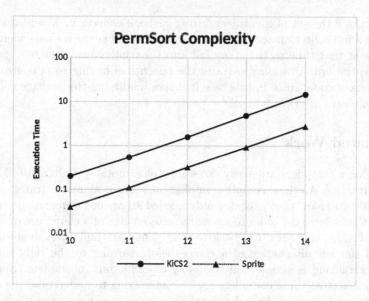

Fig. 5. Complexity analysis of `PermSort`. Execution times are shown for a range of problem sizes. The horizontal axis indicates the number of integers to sort by the permute-and-test method.

is compiled to

```
main s = let s1 = leftSupply s
             s2 = rightSupply s
             s3 = leftSupply s2
             s4 = rightSupply s2
         in xor (f s3) (Choice (thisID s4) False True) s1
```
(14)

Clearly, the conversion to Haskell introduces overhead. The point here is simply to see that the compiled code involves five calls (to helper functions) that were not present in the source program. These reflect the cost of simulating non-determinism in a purely-functional language.

In SPRITE, fresh choice identifiers are created by reading and incrementing a static integer. Compared to the above approach, fewer parameters are passed and fewer functions are called. A similar approach could be used in a Haskell implementation of Curry, but it would rely on impure features, adding another layer of complexity and perhaps interfering with optimizations. By contrast, the SPRITE approach is extreme in its simplicity, as it executes only a few machine instructions. There is a remote possibility that a computation could exhaust the supply of identifiers since the type integer is finite. KICS2 uses a list structure for choice identifiers and so does not suffer from this potential shortcoming. Certainly, the choice identifiers could be made arbitrarily large, but doing so increases memory usage and overhead. A better approach, we believe, would be to compact the set of identifiers during garbage collection. The idea is that whenever a full collection occurs, SPRITE would renumber the n choice identifiers in service at that time so that they fall into the contiguous range $0, \ldots, n-1$. This potential optimization illustrates the benefits of having total control over the implementation, since in this case it makes modifying the garbage collector a viable option.

5   Related Work

Several Curry compilers are easily accessible, most notably PAKCS [19], KiCS2 [8] and MCC [25]. All these compilers implement a lazy evaluation strategy, based on definitional trees, that executes only needed steps, but differ in the control strategy that selects the order in which the alternatives of a choice are executed.

Both PAKCS and MCC use backtracking. They attempt to evaluate all the values of the left alternative of a choice before turning to the right alternative. Backtracking is simple and relatively efficient, but incomplete. Hence, a benchmark against these compilers may be interesting to understand the differences between backtracking and pull-tabbing, but not to assess the efficiency of SPRITE.

By contrast, KiCS2's control strategy uses pull-tabbing, hence the computations executed by KiCS2 are much closer to those of SPRITE. KiCS2's compiler translates Curry source code into Haskell source code which is then processed by GHC [13], a mainstream Haskell compiler. The compiled code benefits from a variety of optimizations available in GHC. Section 4 contains a more detailed comparison between SPRITE and KiCS2.

There exist other functional logic languages, e.g., $\mathcal{TOY}$ [10,24], whose operational semantics can be abstracted by needed narrowing steps of a constructor-based graph rewriting system. Some of our ideas could be applied with almost no changes to the implementation of these languages.

A comparison with graph machines for functional languages is problematic at best. Despite the remarkable syntactic similarities, Curry's syntax extends Haskell's with a single construct, a free variable declaration, the semantic differences are profound. There are purely functional programs whose execution produces a result as Curry, but does not terminate as Haskell [5, Sect. 3]. Furthermore, functional logic computations must be prepared to encounter non-determinism and free variables. Hence, situations and goals significantly differ.

6   Future Work

Compilers are among the most complex software artifacts. They are often bundled with extensions and additions such as optimizers, profilers, tracers, debuggers, external libraries for application domains such as databases or graphical user interfaces. Given this reality, there are countless opportunities for future work. We have no plans at this time to choose any one of the extensions and additions listed above before any other. Some optimizations mentioned earlier, e.g., unboxing integers, are appealing only because they would improve some benchmark, and thus the overall perceived performance of the compiler, but they may contribute very marginally to the efficiency of more realistic programs. Usability-related extensions and additions, such as aids for tracing and debugging an execution, and external libraries may better contribute to the acceptance of our work.

7 Conclusion

We have presented SPRITE, a new native code compiler for Curry. SPRITE combines the best features of existing Curry compilers. Similar to KiCS2, SPRITE's strategy is based on pull-tabbing, hence there is no an inherent loss of completeness of compilers based on backtracking such as PAKCS and MCC. SPRITE compiles to an imperative target language, hence is amenable to low-level machine optimization. It is the only compiler to date designed to ensure operational completeness—all the values of an expression are eventually produced given enough computational resources.

SPRITE's main intermediate language, ICurry, represents programs as graph rewriting systems. We described the implementation of Curry programs in imperative code using concepts of a low-level target language. Graph nodes are represented in memory as heap objects, and an efficient mechanism called tagged dispatch is used to perform pattern matches. Finally, we discussed the mechanisms used by SPRITE to ensure completeness and consistency, and presented empirical data for a set of benchmarking programs. The benchmarks reveal that SPRITE is competitive with a leading implementation of Curry.

References

1. Antoy, S.: Definitional trees. In: Kirchner, H., Levi, G. (eds.) ALP 1992. LNCS, vol. 632, pp. 143–157. Springer, Heidelberg (1992). doi:10.1007/BFb0013825
2. Antoy, S.: On the correctness of pull-tabbing. TPLP **11**(4–5), 713–730 (2011)
3. Antoy, S., Hanus, M.: Declarative programming with function patterns. In: Hill, P.M. (ed.) LOPSTR 2005. LNCS, vol. 3901, pp. 6–22. Springer, Heidelberg (2006). doi:10.1007/11680093_2
4. Antoy, S., Hanus, M.: Overlapping rules and logic variables in functional logic programs. In: Etalle, S., Truszczyński, M. (eds.) ICLP 2006. LNCS, vol. 4079, pp. 87–101. Springer, Heidelberg (2006). doi:10.1007/11799573_9
5. Antoy, S., Hanus, M.: Functional logic programming. Commun. ACM **53**(4), 74–85 (2010)
6. Antoy, S., Johannsen, J., Libby, S.: Needed computations shortcutting needed steps. In: Middeldorp, A., van Raamsdonk, F. (eds.) Proceedings 8th International Workshop on Computing with Terms and Graphs, Vienna, 13 July 2014. Electronic Proceedings in Theoretical Computer Science, vol. 183, pp. 18–32. Open Publishing Association (2015)

7. Antoy, S., Jost, A.: Compiling a functional logic language: the fair scheme. In: 23rd International Symposium on Logic-Based Program Synthesis and Transformation (LOPSTR 2013), Madrid, pp. 129–143. Dpto. de Systems Informaticos y Computation, Universidad Complutense de Madrid, TR-11-13, September 2013

8. Braßel, B., Hanus, M., Peemöller, B., Reck, F.: KiCS2: a new compiler from Curry to Haskell. In: Kuchen, H. (ed.) WFLP 2011. LNCS, vol. 6816, pp. 1–18. Springer, Heidelberg (2011). doi:10.1007/978-3-642-22531-4_1

9. Braßel, B., Huch, F.: On a tighter integration of functional and logic programming. In: Shao, Z. (ed.) APLAS 2007. LNCS, vol. 4807, pp. 122–138. Springer, Heidelberg (2007). doi:10.1007/978-3-540-76637-7_9

10. Caballero, R., Sánchez, J. (eds.): TOY: a multiparadigm declarative language (version 2.3.1) (2007). http://toy.sourceforge.net

11. Clang: a C language family frontend for LLVM (2016). http://www.clang.llvm.org/

12. Echahed, R., Janodet, J.C.: On constructor-based graph rewriting systems. Technical report 985-I, IMAG (1997). ftp://ftp.imag.fr/pub/labo-LEIBNIZ/OLD-archives/PMP/c-graph-rewriting.ps.gz

13. The Glasgow Haskell Compiler (2013). http://www.haskell.org/ghc/

14. Gill, A., Launchbury, J., Jones, S.L.P.: A short cut to deforestation. In: Proceedings of the Conference on Functional Programming Languages and Computer Architecture, pp. 223–232. ACM (1993)

15. Glauert, J.R.W., Kennaway, R., Papadopoulos, G.A., Sleep, M.R.: Dactl: an experimental graph rewriting language. J. Prog. Lang. 5(1), 85–108 (1997)

16. Hanus, M. (ed.): Curry: an integrated functional logic language (Vers. 0.8.2) (2006). http://www-ps.informatik.uni-kiel.de/currywiki/

17. Hanus, M.: Flatcurry: an intermediate representation for Curry programs (2008). http://www.informatik.uni-kiel.de/curry/flat/

18. Hanus, M.: Functional logic programming: from theory to Curry. In: Voronkov, A., Weidenbach, C. (eds.) Programming Logics - Essays in Memory of Harald Ganzinger. LNCS, vol. 7797, pp. 123–168. Springer, Heidelberg (2013). doi:10.1007/978-3-642-37651-1_6

19. Hanus, M. (ed.): PAKCS 1.11.4: The Portland Aachen Kiel Curry system (2014). http://www.informatik.uni-kiel.de/pakcs

20. Jones, S.L.P.: Compiling Haskell by program transformation: a report from the trenches. In: Nielson, H.R. (ed.) ESOP 1996. LNCS, vol. 1058, pp. 18–44. Springer, Heidelberg (1996). doi:10.1007/3-540-61055-3_27

21. Jones, S.P., Santos, A.: Compilation by transformation in the Glasgow Haskell compiler. In: Hammond, K., Turner, D.N., Sansom, P.M. (eds.) Glasgow 1994, pp. 184–204. Springer, London (1995). doi:10.1007/978-1-4471-3573-9_13

22. Lattner, C., Adve, V.: LLVM: a compilation framework for lifelong program analysis and transformation. In: Proceedings of the International Symposium on Code Generation and Optimization: Feedback-Directed and Runtime Optimization (CGO 2004), San Jose, pp. 75–88, March 2004

23. López-Fraguas, F.J., de Dios-Castro, J.: Extra variables can be eliminated from functional logic programs. Electron. Notes Theor. Comput. Sci. 188, 3–19 (2007)

24. López Fraguas, F.J., Sánchez Hernández, J.: TOY: a multiparadigm declarative system. In: Narendran, P., Rusinowitch, M. (eds.) RTA 1999. LNCS, vol. 1631, pp. 244–247. Springer, Heidelberg (1999). doi:10.1007/3-540-48685-2_19

25. Lux, W. (ed.): The Muenster Curry compiler (2012). http://danae.uni-muenster.de/lux/curry/

26. Marlow, S., Jones, S.P.: Making a fast Curry: push/enter vs. eval/apply for higher-order languages. In: Proceedings of the Ninth ACM SIGPLAN International Conference on Functional Programming (ICFP 2004), New York, pp. 4–15. ACM (2004)
27. Partain, W.: The nofib benchmark suite of Haskell programs. In: Launchbury, J., Sansom, P. (eds.) Glasgow 1992, pp. 195–202. Springer, London (1993)
28. Jones, S.L.P., Salkild, J.: The spineless tagless G-machine. In: Proceedings of the Fourth International Conference on Functional Programming Languages and Computer Architecture, pp. 184–201. ACM (1989)

lpopt: A Rule Optimization Tool for Answer Set Programming

Manuel Bichler, Michael Morak$^{(\boxtimes)}$, and Stefan Woltran

TU Wien, Vienna, Austria
{bichler,morak,woltran}@dbai.tuwien.ac.at

Abstract. State-of-the-art answer set programming (ASP) solvers rely on a program called a grounder to convert non-ground programs containing variables into variable-free, propositional programs. The size of this grounding depends heavily on the size of the non-ground rules, and thus, reducing the size of such rules is a promising approach to improve solving performance. To this end, in this paper we announce lpopt, a tool that decomposes large logic programming rules into smaller rules that are easier to handle for current solvers. The tool is specifically tailored to handle the standard syntax of the ASP language (ASP-Core) and makes it easier for users to write efficient and intuitive ASP programs, which would otherwise often require significant hand-tuning by expert ASP engineers. It is based on an idea proposed by Morak and Woltran (2012) that we extend significantly in order to handle the full ASP syntax, including complex constructs like aggregates, weak constraints, and arithmetic expressions. We present the algorithm, the theoretical foundations on how to treat these constructs, as well as an experimental evaluation showing the viability of our approach.

1 Introduction

Answer set programming (ASP) [9,14,16,18] is a well-established logic programming paradigm based on the stable model semantics of logic programs. Its main advantage is an intuitive, declarative language, and the fact that, generally, each answer set of a given logic program describes a valid answer to the original question. Moreover, ASP solvers—see e.g. [1,2,13,15]—have made huge strides in efficiency.

A logic program usually consists of a set of logical implications by which new facts can be inferred from existing ones, and a set of facts that represent the concrete input instance. Logic programming in general, and ASP in particular, have also gained popularity because of their intuitive, declarative syntax. The following example illustrates this:

Example 1. The following rule naturally expresses the fact that two people are relatives of the same generation up to second cousin if they share a great-grandparent.

© Springer International Publishing AG 2017
M.V. Hermenegildo and P. Lopez-Garcia (Eds.): LOPSTR 2016, LNCS 10184, pp. 114–130, 2017.
DOI: 10.1007/978-3-319-63139-4_7

```
uptosecondcousin(X, Y) :-
    parent(X, PX), parent(PX, GPX),
    parent(GPX, GGP), parent(GPY, GGP),
    parent(PY, GPY), parent(Y, PY), X != Y.                    □
```

Rules written in an intuitive fashion, like the one in the above example, are usually larger than strictly necessary. Unfortunately, the use of large rules causes problems for current ASP solvers since the input program is grounded first (i.e. all the variables in each rule are replaced by all possible, valid combinations of constants). This grounding step generally requires exponential time for rules of arbitrary size. In practice, the grounding time can thus become prohibitively large. Also, the ASP solver is usually quicker in evaluating the program if the grounding size remains small.

In order to increase solving performance, we could therefore split the rule in Example 1 up into several smaller ones by hand, keeping track of grandparents and great-grandparents in separate predicates, and then writing a smaller version of the second cousin rule. While this is comparatively easy to do for this example, this can become very tedious if the rules become even more complex and larger, maybe also involving negation or arithmetic expressions. However, since current ASP grounders and solvers become increasingly slower with larger rules, and noting the fact that ASP programs often need expert hand-tuning to perform well in practice, this represents a significant entry barrier and contradicts the fact that logic programs should be fully declarative: in a perfect world, the concrete formulation should not have an impact on the runtime. In addition, to minimize solver runtime in general, it is therefore one of our goals to enable logic programs to be written in an intuitive, fully declarative way without having to think about various technical encoding optimizations.

To this end, in this paper we propose the lpopt tool that automatically optimizes and rewrites large logic programming rules into multiple smaller ones in order to improve solving performance. This tool, based on an idea proposed for very simple ASP programs in [19], uses the concept of tree decompositions of rules to split them into smaller chunks. Intuitively, via a tree decomposition joins in the body of a rule are arranged into a tree-like form. Joins that belong together are then split off into a separate rule, only keeping the join result in a temporary atom. We then extend the algorithm to handle the entire standardized ASP language [11], and also introduce new optimizations for complex language constructs such as weak constraints, arithmetic expressions, and aggregates.

The main contributions of this paper are therefore as follows:

- we extend, on a theoretical basis, the lpopt algorithm proposed in [19] to the full syntax of the ASP language according to the ASP-Core-2 language specification [11];
- we establish how to treat complex constructs like aggregates, and propose an adaptation of the decomposition approach so that it can split up large aggregate expressions into multiple smaller rules and expressions, further reducing the grounding size;

- we implement the lpopt algorithm in C++, yielding the `lpopt` tool for automated logic program optimization, and give an overview of how this tool is
  used in practice; and
- we perform an experimental evaluation of the tool on the encodings and
  instances used in the fifth Answer Set Programming Competition [12] which
  show the benefit of our approach, even for encodings already heavily hand-
  optimized by ASP experts.

2   Preliminaries

General Definitions. We define two pairwise disjoint countably infinite sets of
symbols: a set $\mathbf{C}$ of *constants* and a set $\mathbf{V}$ of *variables*. Different constants
represent different values (*unique name assumption*). By $\mathbf{X}$ we denote sequences
(or, with slight notational abuse, sets) of variables $X_1, \ldots, X_k$ with $k \geqslant 0$. For
brevity, let $[n] = \{1, \ldots, n\}$, for any integer $n \geqslant 1$.

A (*relational*) *schema* $\mathcal{S}$ is a (finite) set of *relational symbols* (or *predicates*).
We write p/n for the fact that p is an n-ary predicate. A *term* is a constant
or variable. An *atomic formula* $\underline{a}$ over $\mathcal{S}$ (called $\mathcal{S}$-*atom*) has the form $p(\mathbf{t})$,
where $p \in \mathcal{S}$ and $\mathbf{t}$ is a sequence of terms. An $\mathcal{S}$-*literal* is either an $\mathcal{S}$-atom (i.e.
a positive literal), or an $\mathcal{S}$-atom preceded by the negation symbol "$\neg$" (i.e. a
negative literal). For a literal ℓ, we write $dom(\ell)$ for the set of its terms, and
$var(\ell)$ for its variables. This notation naturally extends to sets of literals. For
brevity, we will treat conjunctions of literals as sets. For a domain $C \subseteq \mathbf{C}$, a (*total*
or *two-valued*) $\mathcal{S}$-*interpretation* I is a set of $\mathcal{S}$-atoms containing only constants
from C such that, for every $\mathcal{S}$-atom $p(\mathbf{a}) \in I$, $p(\mathbf{a})$ is true, and otherwise false.
When obvious from the context, we will omit the schema-prefix.

A *substitution* from a set of literals L to a set of literals L' is a mapping
$s : \mathbf{C} \cup \mathbf{V} \to \mathbf{C} \cup \mathbf{V}$ that is defined on $dom(L)$, is the identity on $\mathbf{C}$, and
$p(t_1, \ldots, t_n) \in L$ (resp. $\neg p(t_1, \ldots, t_n) \in L$) implies $p(s(t_1), \ldots, s(t_n)) \in L'$
(resp., $\neg p(s(t_1), \ldots, s(t_n)) \in L'$).

Answer Set Programming (ASP). A *logic programming rule* is a universally
quantified reverse first-order implication of the form

$$\mathcal{H}(\mathbf{X}, \mathbf{Y}) \leftarrow \mathcal{B}^+(\mathbf{X}, \mathbf{Y}, \mathbf{Z}, \mathbf{W}) \wedge \mathcal{B}^-(\mathbf{X}, \mathbf{Z}),$$

where $\mathcal{H}$ (the *head*), resp. $\mathcal{B}^+$ (the *positive body*), is a disjunction, resp. conjunction, of atoms, and $\mathcal{B}^-$ (the *negative body*) is a conjunction of negative literals,
each over terms from $\mathbf{C} \cup \mathbf{V}$. For a rule π, let $H(\pi)$, $B^+(\pi)$, and $B^-(\pi)$ denote the
set of atoms occurring in the head, the positive, and the negative body, respec-
tively. Let $B(\pi) = B^+(\pi) \cup B^-(\pi)$. A rule π where $H(\pi) = \emptyset$ is called a *constraint*.
Substitutions naturally extend to rules. We focus on *safe* rules where every vari-
able in the rule occurs in the positive body. A rule is called *ground* if all its terms
are constants. The grounding of a rule π w.r.t. a domain $C \subseteq \mathbf{C}$ is the set of rules
$ground_C(\pi) = \{s(\pi) \mid s$ is a substitution, mapping $var(\pi)$ to elements from $C\}$.

A *logic program* Π is a finite set of logic programming rules. The schema of a program Π, denoted $sch(\Pi)$, is the set of predicates appearing in Π. The *active domain* of Π, denoted $adom(\Pi)$, with $adom(\Pi) \subset \mathbf{C}$, is the set of constants appearing in Π. A program Π is ground if all its rules are ground. The *grounding of a program* Π is the ground program $ground(\Pi) = \bigcup_{\pi \in \Pi} ground_{adom(\Pi)}(\pi)$. The *(Gelfond-Lifschitz) reduct* of a ground program Π w.r.t. an interpretation I is the ground program $\Pi^I = \{H(\pi) \leftarrow B^+(\pi) \mid \pi \in \Pi, B^-(\pi) \cap I = \emptyset\}$.

A $sch(\Pi)$-interpretation I is a *(classical) model* of a ground program Π, denoted $I \vDash \Pi$ if, for every ground rule $\pi \in \Pi$, it holds that $I \cap B^+(\pi) = \emptyset$ or $I \cap (H(\pi) \cup B^-(\pi)) \neq \emptyset$, that is, I satisfies π. I is a *stable model* (or *answer set*) of Π, denoted $I \vDash_s \Pi$ if, in addition, there is no $J \subset I$ such that $J \vDash \Pi^I$, that is, I is subset-minimal w.r.t. the reduct Π^I. The set of answer sets of Π, denoted $AS(\Pi)$, are defined as $AS(\Pi) = \{I \mid I$ is a $sch(\Pi)$-interpretation, and $I \vDash_s \Pi\}$. For a non-ground program Π, we define $AS(\Pi) = AS(ground(\Pi))$. When referring to the fact that a logic program is intended to be interpreted under the answer set semantics, we often refer to it as an *ASP program*.

Tree Decompositions. A *tree decomposition* of a graph $G = (V, E)$ is a pair $\mathcal{T} = (T, \chi)$, where T is a rooted tree and χ is a labelling function over nodes t of T, with $\chi(t) \subseteq V$ called the *bag of* t, such that the following holds: (i) for each $v \in V$, there exists a node t in T, such that $v \in \chi(t)$; (ii) for each $\{v, w\} \in E$, there exists a node t in T, such that $\{v, w\} \subseteq \chi(t)$; and (iii) for all nodes r, s, and t in T, such that s lies on the path from r to t, we have $\chi(r) \cap \chi(t) \subseteq \chi(s)$. The *width* of a tree decomposition is defined as the cardinality of its largest bag minus one. The *treewidth* of a graph G, denoted by $tw(G)$, is the minimum width over all tree decompositions of G. To decide whether a graph has treewidth at most k is NP-complete [3]. For an arbitrary but fixed k however, this problem can be solved (and a tree decomposition constructed) in linear time [6].

Given a non-ground logic programming rule π, we let its *Gaifman graph* $G_\pi = (var(\pi), E)$ such that there is an edge (X, Y) in E iff variables X and Y occur together in the head or in a body atom of π. We refer to a tree decomposition of G_π as a *tree decomposition of rule* π. The treewidth of rule π is the treewidth of G_π.

3 Rule Decomposition

This section lays out the theoretical foundations for our rule decomposition approach. First, we recall the algorithm from [19], and then describe how it can be extended to handle three of the main extensions of the ASP language, namely arithmetic expressions, aggregates, and weak constraints (i.e. optimization statements), as defined in the ASP-Core language standard [11].

As demonstrated in Example 1, rules that are intuitive to write and read are not necessarily the most efficient ones to evaluate in practice. ASP solvers generally struggle with rules that contain many variables since they rely on a grounder-solver approach: first, the grounding of a logic program is computed by a grounder. As per the definition in Sect. 2, the size of the grounding can, in the worst case, be exponential in the number of variables. For large rules, the grounding step can already take a prohibitively large amount of time. However, the solver is also adversely affected by this blowup. In practice, this leads to long runtimes and sometimes the inability of the ASP system to solve a given instance. This also contributes to the fact that, while the syntax of ASP is fully declarative, writing efficient encodings still takes expert knowledge.

It is therefore desirable to have a way to automatically rewrite such large rules into a more efficient representation. One way to do this is the rule decomposition approach, first proposed in [19], which we will briefly recall next.

3.1   Decomposition of Simple Rules

Generally speaking, the approach in [19] computes the tree decomposition of a rule, and then splits the rule up into multiple, smaller rules according to this decomposition. While in the worst case this decomposition may not change the rule at all, in practice it is often the case that large rules can be split up very well. For instance, the large rule in Example 1 will be amenable for such a decomposition.

Let us briefly recall the algorithm from [19] which we will refer to as the lpopt algorithm. For a given rule π, the algorithm works as follows:

Algorithm 1. The lpopt Algorithm [19]

---

1. Compute a tree decomposition $\mathcal{T} = (T, \chi)$ of π with minimal width where all variables occurring in the head of π are contained in its root node bag.

2. For each node n, let $temp_n$ be a fresh predicate, and the same for each variable X in π and predicate dom_X. Let $\mathbf{Y}_n = \chi(n) \cap \chi(p_n)$, where p_n is the parent node of n. For the root node $root$, let $temp_{root}$ be the entire head of π, and, accordingly, $\mathbf{Y}_{root} = var(H(\pi))$. Now, for a node n, generate the following rule:

$$temp_n(\mathbf{Y}_n) \leftarrow \quad \{\underline{a} \in B(\pi) \quad | \ var(\underline{a}) \subseteq \chi(n)\}$$
$$\cup \{dom_X(X) \quad | \ \underline{a} \in B^-(\pi), X \in var(\underline{a}), var(\underline{a}) \subseteq \chi(n),$$
$$\nexists \underline{b} \in B^+(\pi) : var(\underline{b}) \subseteq \chi(n), X \in var(\underline{b})\}$$
$$\cup \{temp_m(\mathbf{Y}_m) \mid m \text{ is a child of } n\}.$$

3. For each $X \in var(B^-(\pi))$, for which a domain predicate dom is needed to guarantee safety of a rule generated above, pick an atom $\underline{a} \in B^+(\pi)$, such that $X \in var(\underline{a})$ and generate a rule

$$dom_X(X) \leftarrow \underline{a}.$$

Step 3 is needed because splitting up a rule may make it unsafe. In order
to remedy this, a domain predicate is generated for each unsafe variable that
arises due to the rule splitting in step 2. The following example illustrates how
the algorithm works.

Example 2. Given the rule

$$\pi = h(X, W) \leftarrow e(X, Y), e(Y, Z), \neg e(Z, W), e(W, X),$$

a tree decomposition of π could look as follows (note that we write in each bag
of the tree decomposition not just the variables as per definition but also all
literals of rule π over these variables which is a more intuitive notation):

$$h(X, W), e(X, Y), e(W, X)$$

$$e(Y, Z), \neg e(Z, W)$$

Applying the lpopt algorithm to π with the tree decomposition above yields the
following set of rules lpopt(π):

$$dom_W(W) \leftarrow e(W, X),$$

$$temp(Y, W) \leftarrow e(Y, Z), \neg e(Z, W), dom_W(W), \text{ and}$$

$$h(X, W) \leftarrow e(X, Y), e(W, X), temp(Y, W),$$

where *temp* is a fresh predicate not appearing anywhere else.   □

Let Π be a logic program. When the above algorithm is applied to all rules in
Π, resulting in a logic program lpopt(Π) as stated in [19], the answer sets of Π
are preserved in the following way: when all temporary atoms are removed, each
answer set of lpopt(Π) coincides with exactly one answer set from the original
program Π. Furthermore, the size of the grounding now no longer depends on
the rule size. In fact, it now only depends on the rule treewidth as the following
result states.

Theorem 1 ([19]). *The size of ground(lpopt(Π)) is bounded by $O(2^k \cdot n)$, where
n is the size of Π, and k is the maximal treewidth of the rules in Π.*

The above theorem implies that the size of the grounding of a program Π,
after optimization via the lpopt algorithm, is no longer exponential in the size of
Π, but only in the treewidth of its rules. As [19] demonstrates, this decomposition
approach already has a significant impact on the size of the grounding in practical
instances.

However, the ASP language standard [11] extends the ASP language with
other useful constructs that the lpopt algorithm proposed in [19] cannot handle.
These include arithmetic expressions, aggregates, and weak constraints. Looking at concrete, practical instances of ASP programs, e.g. the encodings used
in recent ASP competitions [12], a large majority use such constructs. In the
following, we will therefore extend the lpopt algorithm to be able to treat them
in a similar way.

3.2   Treating Arithmetic Expressions

Arithmetic expressions are atoms of the form $X = \varphi(\mathbf{Y})$, that is, an equality with one variable (or constant number) X on the left-hand side, and an expression φ on the right-hand side, where φ is any mathematical expression built using the variables from $\mathbf{Y}$, constant numbers, and the arithmetic connectives "+," "-," "*," and "/." In addition to the positive and negative body, a rule π may also contain a set of such arithmetic expressions describing a relationship between variables with the obvious meaning (that is, after grounding, an arithmetic expression evaluates to true if and only if the mathematical equality between the involved constants is valid). The arithmetic connectives are interpreted according to the usual mathematical preference rules.

Finally, since we require that all rules processed with the lpopt algorithm are safe, we need to extend the definition of safety to include arithmetic expressions. Clearly, the conditions for safety of rules with arithmetic expressions are more involved. In fact, instead of just requiring that each variable appears in the positive body we now have a recursive safety condition: a rule containing arithmetic expressions is safe if and only if every variable X appears (a) in the positive body of the rule, or (b) in an arithmetic expression of the form $X = \varphi(\mathbf{Y})$ where all the variables in $\mathbf{Y}$ are safe.

In order to adapt the lpopt rule decomposition algorithm to rules with arithmetic expressions, we need to extend the definition of the graph representation of π to handle arithmetic expressions. To this end, we simply require it to contain a clique between all variables occurring together in each such expression. The lpopt algorithm then works as described in Algorithm 1 above up to step 2. However, a problem may arise when, in step 3 of the lpopt algorithm, a domain predicate $dom_X(X)$ is to be generated. Consider the following example:

Example 3. Let π be the rule $a(X) \leftarrow \neg b(X,Y), c(Y), d(Z), X = Z + Z$. A simple decomposition according to the lpopt algorithm may lead to the following rules:

$$temp(X) \leftarrow \neg b(X,Y), c(Y), dom_X(X), \text{ and}$$

$$a(X) \leftarrow d(Z), X = Z + Z, temp(X).$$

It remains to define the domain predicate dom_X. According to the original definition of lpopt, we would get

$$dom_X(X) \leftarrow X = Z + Z$$

which is unsafe.   □

As Example 3 shows, in order for such expressions to work with the lpopt algorithm a more general approach to defining the domain predicates is needed in step 3. In fact, instead of choosing a single atom from the rule body to generate the domain predicate, in general a set of atoms and arithmetic expressions must be chosen. It is easy to see that if a rule π is safe then, for each variable $X \in var(B(\pi))$, there is a set A_X of (positive) atoms and arithmetic expressions in

---

Algorithm 2. Domain Predicate Generation Algorithm

Input: A set $\mathbf{X}$ of variables to be made safe, a set $\mathbf{Y}$ of variables already made safe, a rule π, and an upper bound *maxvars*

Output: A set of body elements R from π that has the minimum number of variables not in $\mathbf{X}$ and that, together, defines the domain of the variables in $\mathbf{X}$.

1: **procedure** DOMPRED($\mathbf{X}, \mathbf{Y}, \pi, maxvars$)
2:     Let $R = \emptyset$
3:     Let $A = $ GETBODYELEMENTSWITHONEOF($\mathbf{X}, \pi$)
4:     **while** $A \neq \emptyset$ **do**
5:        Let $\underline{a} = $ GETBESTELEMENT($A, \mathbf{X}, \mathbf{Y}$)
6:        **if** $\underline{a}$ is arithmetic expression $X = \varphi(\mathbf{Z})$ **then**
7:           Let $\mathbf{X}' = (\mathbf{X}\backslash\{X\}) \cup (\mathbf{Z}\backslash\mathbf{Y})$
8:           Let $R' = \{\underline{a}\} \cup $ DOMPRED($\mathbf{X}', \mathbf{Y}, \pi\backslash\{\underline{a}\}, maxvars$)
9:        **else**
10:         Let $\mathbf{X}' = \mathbf{X}\backslash var(\underline{a})$
11:         Let $\mathbf{Y}' = \mathbf{Y} \cup var(\underline{a})$
12:         Let $R' = \{\underline{a}\} \cup $ DOMPRED($\mathbf{X}', \mathbf{Y}', \pi\backslash\{\underline{a}\}, maxvars - |var(\underline{a})\backslash\mathbf{Y}|$)
13:        **end if**
14:        **if** $|var(R')\backslash\mathbf{Y}| \leqslant maxvars$ **then**
15:         Let $R = R'$
16:         Let $maxvars = |var(R)\backslash\mathbf{Y}|$
17:        **end if**
18:        Let $A = A\backslash\{\underline{a}\}$
19:     **end while**
20:     Return R
21: **end procedure**

---

the body of π that makes that variable safe (trivially, if A_X contains all positive body atoms and arithmetic expressions of π the condition is fulfilled). In step 3 of the lpopt algorithm, for a variable X we now choose such a set A_X of body elements to use in the body of the domain predicate rule.

However, since the grounding size of a domain predicate rule is exponential in the number of variables occurring in atoms, we aim to choose a set A_X that contains as few variables in atoms as possible (variables occurring only in arithmetic expressions can be ignored since they don't increase the number of ground instances of a rule). To this end, we devise a depth-first search algorithm that, given a variable X and a rule π, computes a set A_X of positive body atoms and arithmetic expressions that make variable X safe with a minimal number of variables occurring in atoms. Algorithm 2 presents our implementation in pseudocode. It is initially called with the parameters $\mathbf{X} = \{X\}$, $\mathbf{Y} = \emptyset$, π, and $|var(\pi)|$. The function GETBODYELEMENTSWITHONEOF returns, for a given set of variables $\mathbf{X}$ and rule π, the set of all the positive body atoms containing at least one variable from $\mathbf{X}$ and, in addition, all arithmetic expressions of the form $X = \varphi(\mathbf{Y})$, where $X \in \mathbf{X}$; that is, it returns all those body elements from π that can help to make the variables $\mathbf{X}$ safe. The function GETBESTELEMENT returns, for a given set A of atoms and arithmetic expressions, set $\mathbf{X}$ of variables to be made safe, and set $\mathbf{Y}$ of variables already made safe, the element having the minimal number of variables not in $\mathbf{Y}$. If there are multiple such elements, return the atom that contains the maximum number of variables from $\mathbf{X}$. If there are multiple such atoms, pick one at random. If there are no such atoms, return one of the arithmetic expressions. $\pi \backslash \{\underline{a}\}$ denotes rule π with element $\underline{a}$ removed. Note that Algorithm 2 explores the entire search space (that is, each subset of elements from rule π) which may need, at worst, exponential time in the size of π. We optimize this by immediately disregarding all subsets that are worse than the best subset found so far (via variable *maxvars*). Additionally, by using the heuristics implemented in GETBESTELEMENT and since long "chains" of arithmetic expressions are rare (e.g. none of our benchmarks contained any) this does not lead to long runtimes in practice.

Finally, after executing Algorithm 2 and obtaining the set A_X, generate the rule $dom_X(X) \leftarrow A_X$. It is easy to see that, by construction of set A_X, this rule is safe and describes the possible domain of variable X as required. Note that the resulting domain predicate rule may still be amenable to further decomposition. Where this is the case, we recursively call the lpopt algorithm on it. Below, Example 4 shows the output of lpopt when extended with Algorithm 2 above.

Example 4. A correct domain predicate for Example 3 would be defined as follows:

$$dom_X(X) \leftarrow X = Z + Z, d(Z).$$

This ensures the proper safety of all rules generated by the lpopt algorithm. □

Note that the rule generated in Example 4 repeats most of the atoms that the second rule generated in Example 3 already contains. It is not immediately obvious how such situations can be remedied in general. Investigating this issue is part of ongoing work.

3.3   Treating Weak Constraints

As defined in [11], a weak constraint $\pi[k : \mathbf{t}]$ is a constraint π annotated with a term k representing a weight and a sequence of terms $\mathbf{t}$ occurring in π. The intended meaning is that each answer set I is annotated by a total weight $w(I)$, which is the sum over all k for each tuple of constants $\mathbf{c}$ that realize $\mathbf{t}$ in I and satisfy the body of π. Such a weak constraint can easily be decomposed by replacing $\pi[k : \mathbf{t}]$ with the rule $\pi' = temp(k, \mathbf{t}) \leftarrow B(\pi)$, where $temp$ is a fresh predicate, and the weak constraint $\perp \leftarrow temp(k, \mathbf{t})[k : \mathbf{t}]$. Finally, the lpopt algorithm is then applied to rule π'. This allows our rule decomposition approach also to be applied in an optimization context (i.e. where the task for the solver is to find optimal answer sets w.r.t. their weight).

3.4   Treating Aggregate Expressions

An aggregate expression, as defined in [11], is an expression of the form

$$t \preccurlyeq \#agg\{\mathbf{t} : \varphi(\mathbf{X})\},$$

where t is a term; $\preceq\ \in\{<,\leqslant,=,\neq,\geqslant,>\}$ is a built-in relation; agg is one of sum, $count$, max, and min; $\mathbf{t}=\langle t_1,\ldots,t_n\rangle$ is a sequence of terms; and $\varphi(\mathbf{X})$ is a set of literals, arithmetic expressions, and aggregate expressions, called the *aggregate body*. Aggregates may appear in rule bodies, or recursively inside other aggregates, with the following semantic meaning: Given an interpretation I, for each valid substitution s such that $s(\varphi(\mathbf{X}))\subseteq I$, take the tuple of constants $s(\mathbf{t})$. Let us denote this set with T. Now, execute the aggregate function on T as follows: for $\#count$, calculate $|T|$; for $\#sum$, calculate $\Sigma_{t\in T}t_1$, where t_1 is the first term in $\mathbf{t}$; for $\#max$ and $\#min$, take the maximum and minimum term appearing in the first position of each tuple in T, respectively. Finally, an aggregate expression is true if the relation $\preceq$ between term t and the result of the aggregate function is fulfilled.

Extending the lpopt algorithm to aggregate expressions is again straightforward: The rule graph $G_\pi=(V,E)$ of a rule π containing aggregate expressions is defined as follows: Let V be the set of variables occurring in π outside of aggregate expressions. Let E be as before and, in addition, add, for each aggregate expression $\underline{e}$, a clique between all variables $var(\underline{e})\cap V$ to E. Intuitively, the rule graph should contain, for each aggregate expression, a clique between all variables that appear in the aggregate and somewhere else in the rule. Variables appearing only in aggregates are in a sense "local" and are therefore not of interest when decomposing the rule.

While the above transformation is straightforward, we can, however, go one step further and also decompose the inside elements of an aggregate expression. To this end, let $t\preceq\#agg\{\mathbf{t}:\varphi(\mathbf{X},\mathbf{Y})\}$ be an aggregate expression occurring in some rule π, where $\mathbf{X}$ are variables that occur either in $\mathbf{t}$ or somewhere else in π, and $\mathbf{Y}$ are variables occurring inside the aggregate only. Replace the aggregate expression with $t\preceq\#agg\{\mathbf{t}:\psi(\mathbf{X},\mathbf{Z}),temp(\mathbf{t},\mathbf{Z})\}$, and furthermore, generate a rule $temp(\mathbf{t},\mathbf{Z})\leftarrow\overline{\psi}(\mathbf{Y}),\overline{\psi}_{dom}(\mathbf{Y})$, for some fresh predicate $temp$. Here, ψ contains all those atoms from φ that contain a variable from $\mathbf{X}$, and $\overline{\psi}$ contains the rest. $\overline{\psi}_{dom}$ contains domain predicates generated like in step3 of the lpopt algorithm, as needed to make the temporary rule safe. The temporary rule can then be decomposed via lpopt. This is best illustrated by an example:

Example 5. Let π be the following logic programming rule, saying that a vertex is "good" if it has at least two neighbours that, themselves, have a red neighbour:

$$good(X)\leftarrow vertex(X),2\leqslant\#count\{Y:edge(X,Y),edge(Y,Z),red(Z)\}.$$

According to the above approach, the rule can now be split up as follows. Firstly, the aggregate is replaced:

$$good(X)\leftarrow vertex(X),2\leqslant\#count\{Y:edge(X,Y),temp(Y)\},$$

and furthermore, a temporary rule is created as follows:

$$temp(Y)\leftarrow edge(Y,Z),red(Z).$$

The latter rule is now amenable for decomposition via the lpopt algorithm.   □

Note that the above approach allows us to decompose, to a degree, even the insides of an aggregate, which, for large aggregate bodies, can lead to a further significant reduction in the grounding size.

3.5 Correctness

The correctness of the above extensions to the original algorithm follows by the same arguments that prove the correctness of the original algorithm proposed in [19], and trivially from the construction for arithmetic expressions and safety. For the latter, note that for domain predicates of a variable X we explicitly select a set of atoms that make the variable safe, and that such a set always exists, since the original rule is safe. For the former two (namely weak constraints and aggregate expressions), the only thing that needs to be examined is the first step: replacing (part of) the body with a temporary predicate. But correctness of this is easy to see. Instead of performing all joins within the weak constraint or aggregate, we perform the join in a new, separate rule and project only relevant variables into a temporary predicate. The weak constraint or aggregate then only needs to consider this temporary predicate since, by construction, all other variables not projected into the temporary predicate do not play a role w.r.t. optimization or aggregation. Finally, the original algorithm from [19] extended to handle arithmetic expressions, for which correctness has already been established, is then applied to this new, separate rule.

3.6 Further Language Extensions

The ASP-Core language specification [11], as well as the *gringo* grounder[1], allow further constructs like variable pooling, aggregates with multiple bodies, or with upper and lower bounds in the same expression, in addition to various extensions that amount to syntactic sugar. These constructs make the above explanations unnecessarily more tedious. However, from a theoretical point of view, all of these additional constructs can be normalized to one of the forms discussed in the previous subsections. Furthermore, as we shall see in the next section, we have implemented the lpopt algorithm to directly treat all standard ASP language constructs and certain other additions, like variable pooling. More details about this general approach, and the exact, but more tedious, algorithm details, can be found in [4].

4   Implementation

A full implementation of the algorithm and its extensions described in Sect. 3 is now available in the form of the lpopt tool, available with relevant documentation and examples at

http://dbai.tuwien.ac.at/proj/lpopt.

---

[1] http://potassco.sourceforge.net.

The following gives a quick outline of how to use the tool.

lpopt accepts as its input any form of ASP program that follows the ASP input language specification laid out in [11]. The output of the program in its default configuration is a decomposed program that also follows this specification. In addition, the tool guarantees that no language construct is introduced in the output that was not previously present in the input (cf. Sect. 3). Therefore, for example, a program without aggregates will not contain any aggregates as a result of rule decomposition. The following is a description of the parameters of the tool:

```
Usage: lpopt [-idbt] [-s seed] [-f file] [-h alg] [-l file]
   -d       dumb: do not perform optimization
   -b       print verbose and benchmark information
   -t       perform only tree decomposition step
   -i       ignore head variables when decomposing
   -h alg   decomposition algorithm, one of {mcs, mf, miw (def)}
   -s seed  initialize random number generator with seed
   -f file  the file to read from (default is stdin)
   -l file  output infos (treewidth) to file
```

In what follows, we will briefly describe the most important features of the tool.

Tree Decomposition Heuristics. As stated in Sect. 2, computing an optimal tree decomposition w.r.t. width is an NP-hard problem. We thus make use of several heuristic algorithms, namely the *maximum cardinality search (mcs)*, *minimum fill (mf)*, and *minimum induced width (miw)* approaches described in [7], that yield tree decompositions that provide good upper bounds on the treewidth (i.e. on an optimal decomposition). It turns out that in practice, since rules in ASP programs are usually not overly large, these heuristics come close to, and often even yield, an optimal tree decomposition for rules. The heuristic algorithm to use for decomposition can be selected using the -h command line parameter. Since these heuristic approaches rely to some degree on randomization, a seed for the pseudo-random number generator can be passed along with the -s command line parameter.

Measuring the Treewidth of Rules. Theorem 1 allows us to calculate an upper bound on the size of the grounding of the input program. In order to do this, the maximal treewidth of any rule in an ASP program must be known. The -l switch of the lpopt tool allows this to be calculated. It forces the tool to perform tree decompositions on all rules inside an input ASP program, simply outputting the maximal treewidth (or, more accurately, an upper bound; see above) over all of them into the given file, and then exiting. Clearly, when a single ASP rule is given as input, this switch will output a treewidth upper bound of that single rule.

4.1   Recommended Usage

Assuming that a file enc.lp contains the encoding of a problem as an ASP program and that a file instance.db contains a set of ground facts representing a problem instance, the recommended usage of the tool is as follows:

```
cat enc.lp instance.db | lpopt | grounder | solver
```

In the above command, grounder and solver are programs for grounding and for solving, respectively. One established solver that we will use in the next section for our experimental evaluation is *clasp* [15]. If *clasp* is used as a solver together with the lpopt tool, we generally recommend the use of the --sat-prepro flag, which often speeds up the solving process substantially for decomposed rules generated by lpopt (by considering the fact that the truth values of all temporary atoms generated by lpopt are determined exactly by the rule body, and need never be guessed).

5   Experimental Evaluation

We have tested our lpopt tool and benchmarked the performance of grounding and solving of programs preprocessed with lpopt against non-preprocessed ones. All benchmarks were made on the instance sets of the fifth answer set programming competition 2014[2], which, for most problem classes, provides two encodings, one from 2013, and one from 2014. The benchmarks have been run on a 3.5 GHz AMD Opteron Processor 6308 with 192 GB of RAM to its disposal. We used the potassco software suite[3], namely *gringo* verison 4.5.3 as the grounder and *clasp* version 3.1.3 as the solver. A timeout of 300 s was set for solving, and 1000 s for grounding. Furthermore, as suggested in the previous section, *clasp* was called with the --sat-prepro flag enabled. In this paper, we will survey the most important results.

Remark. One central aim of our tool is to improve solving performance for hand-written encodings by non-experts of ASP. In the spirit of a truly declarative language, it shouldn't matter *how* an encoding is written as long as it is correct (i.e. w.r.t. runtime, there should not be a difference between "good" and "bad" encodings). In this respect, the ASP competition does not offer an optimal benchmark set since all encodings are extensively hand-tuned by ASP experts. However, as to the best of our knowledge there is no better-suited comprehensive benchmark set available, we will show that even for these extensively hand-tuned ASP competition encodings our tool can still find decompositions that decrease grounding size and improve solving performance. However, there are also encodings that are so perfectly hand-tuned that only trivial optimizations are possible with the current version of lpopt.

---

[2] https://www.mat.unical.it/aspcomp2014/.
[3] http://potassco.sourceforge.net.

Results. Let us first note that the runtime of lpopt itself, for all encodings in the benchmark set, was always less than what can be accurately measured on a computer system today. Applying our rule decomposition algorithm thus comes virtually for free for hand-written encodings. Out of the 49 encodings provided by the ASP competition, lpopt was able to syntactically rewrite 41 which indicates that, as mentioned above, even extensively hand-tuned programs can be further decomposed in an automated manner. The remaining eight encodings contained rules that were so small that no further decomposition was possible (i.e. their Gaifman graph was a clique of usually 3–4 nodes) and thus the output of lpopt was the original, unmodified encoding in these cases. In 27 of the 41 encodings rewritten by lpopt, the decompositions were trivial and had no significant impact on the solving performance. This is due to the fact that only rules that were already very small (and thus did not contribute much to the grounding size in the first place) could be decomposed. In five cases out of the 41 rewritten encodings, we noticed a decrease in solving performance (see the paragraph on limitations of lpopt below for an explanation) and in the remaining seven cases, the lpopt rewriting was able to speed up the solving process with substantial improvements in three of these seven. Two of those were the stable marriage problem encoding of 2013, and the permutation pattern matching encoding of 2014 which we will take a closer look at below. Full benchmark results for the entire dataset can be found in [4].

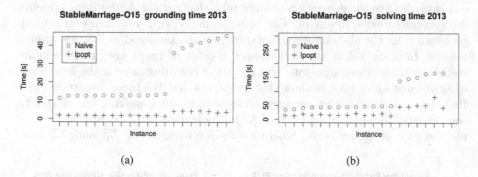

Fig. 1. Benchmark results for the stable marriage 2013 instances. The horizontal axis represents the individual test instances, sorted by runtime without rule decomposition.

Let us look at the stable marriage problem first. As can be seen in Fig. 1, both grounding and solving time decrease dramatically. Notice that the grounding time is, in general, directly correlated with the size of the respective grounding. With lpopt preprocessing, the grounding size decreases dramatically by a factor of up to 65. The grounder is thirty times faster when using preprocessing, and the solver about three times. This is because of the following constraint in the encoding that can be decomposed very well:

```
:- match(M,W1), manAssignsScore(M,W,Smw), W1!=W,
   manAssignsScore(M,W1,Smw1), Smw>Smw1, match(M1,W),
   womanAssignsScore(W,M,Swm), womanAssignsScore(W,M1,Swm1),
   Swm>=Swm1.
```

The constraint rule above is quite intuitive to read: There cannot be a man M and a woman W, such that they would both be better off if they were matched together, instead of being matched as they are (that is, to $W1$ and $M1$, respectively). It encodes, precisely and straightforwardly, the condition of a stable marriage. The 2014 encoding splits this rule up, making the encoding much harder to understand. However, with lpopt preprocessing, the grounding and solving performance matches that of the hand-tuned 2014 encoding. This again illustrates that the lpopt algorithm allows for efficient processing of rules written by non-experts that are not explicitly hand-tuned.

A second example of lpopt's capabilities is the permutation pattern matching problem illustrated in Fig. 2. The grounding time of the largest instance is 980 s without preprocessing and 17 s with preprocessing. This instance was also impossible to solve within the timeout window of 300 s without lpopt preprocessing, but finishing within 88 s when lpopt was run first.

Other Use Cases. lpopt has also been employed in other works that illustrate its performance benefits. In particular, several solvers for other formalisms rely on a rewriting to ASP in order to solve the original problem. Such rewritings can easily lead to the generation of large rules that current ASP solving systems are generally unable to handle. For example, in [17] ASP rewritings for several problems from the abstract argumentation domain, proposed in [10], are implemented. In [4, Sect. 4.6], the performance benefits of lpopt are clearly demonstated for these rewritings. Interestingly, these rewritings also make heavy use of aggregates which goes to show that lpopt also handles these constructs well. Recently, a comprehensive overview of these techniques, making use of lpopt, was accepted for publication at the AAAI conference of 2017 [8]. Another example use case of lpopt is [5], where multiple rewritings for Σ_P^2 and Σ_P^3-hard

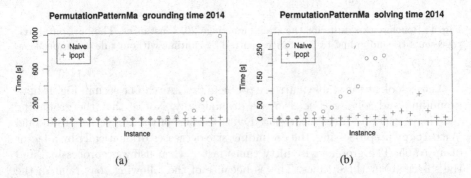

(a)   (b)

Fig. 2. Benchmark results for permutation pattern matching 2014. The horizontal axis represents the individual test instances, sorted by runtime without rule decomposition.

problems are proposed and then benchmarked, again showcasing that without lpopt these rewritings could not be solved by current ASP solvers in all but the most simple cases.

Limitations. However, we also want to point out some limitations of the lpopt algorithm. When a domain predicate is generated by the algorithm, the selection of atoms that generate this domain predicate may not be optimal. In fact, our algorithm picks an optimal set with respect to the number of variables which minimizes the number of ground instances that the rule can give rise to in the mathematical worst case. However, in practice, the number of ground instances depends on other factors. One major factor is the number of tuples (of constants) that can potentially appear in a relation. State-of-the-art grounders exploit this information, but it is not available at the time that the lpopt tool is run (that is, before grounding). For the same reason, it may be the case that the increased grounding size caused by the domain predicate rules may destroy any practical benefit caused by splitting up the main rule, while at the same time the mathematical worst case bound on the grounding size was actually improved by running lpopt. In fact, this is precisely what caused the increase in solving time for the five encodings out of 49 that lpopt was able to rewrite but where solving performance deteriorated. The question of what the best strategy is to select atoms to generate domain predicates (or whether, by integrating the lpopt algorithm into a grounder, these domain predicates can be eliminated entirely) is part of ongoing research.

6 Conclusions

In this paper, we present an algorithm, based on a prototype from [19], that allows the decomposition of large logic programming rules into smaller ones that current state-of-the-art answer set programming solvers are better equipped to handle. Our implementation handles the entire ASP-Core-2 language [11]. Benchmark results show that in practice, even for extensively hand-tuned ASP programs, our rule decomposition algorithm can improve solving performance significantly. Future work will include implementing this approach directly into state-of-the-art grounders like the *gringo* grounder used in our benchmarks, as well as further refining the algorithm w.r.t. selection of domain predicate atoms, as discussed at the end of Sect. 5.

Acknowledgments. Funded by the Austrian Science Fund (FWF): Y698, P25607.

References

1. Alviano, M., Dodaro, C., Faber, W., Leone, N., Ricca, F.: WASP: a native ASP solver based on constraint learning. In: Cabalar, P., Son, T.C. (eds.) LPNMR 2013. LNCS (LNAI), vol. 8148, pp. 54–66. Springer, Heidelberg (2013). doi:10.1007/978-3-642-40564-8_6

2. Alviano, M., Faber, W., Leone, N., Perri, S., Pfeifer, G., Terracina, G.: The disjunctive datalog system DLV. In: Datalog Reloaded. Revised Selected Papers, pp. 282–301 (2010)

3. Arnborg, S., Corneil, D.G., Proskurowski, A.: Complexity of finding embeddings in a k-tree. SIAM J. Algeb. Discr. Meth. **8**(2), 277–284 (1987)

4. Bichler, M.: Optimizing non-ground answer set programs via rule decomposition. BSc Thesis, TU Wien (2015). http://dbai.tuwien.ac.at/proj/lpopt

5. Bichler, M., Morak, M., Woltran, S.: The power of non-ground rules in answer set programming. TPLP **16**(5–6), 552–569 (2016)

6. Bodlaender, H.L.: A linear-time algorithm for finding tree-decompositions of small treewidth. SIAM J. Comput. **25**(6), 1305–1317 (1996)

7. Bodlaender, H.L., Koster, A.M.C.A.: Treewidth computations I. Upper bounds. Inf. Comput. **208**(3), 259–275 (2010)

8. Brewka, G., Diller, M., Heissenberger, G., Linsbichler, T., Woltran, S.: Solving advanced argumentation problems with answer-set programming. In: Proceeding of AAAI, pp. 1077–1083 (2017)

9. Brewka, G., Eiter, T., Truszczynski, M.: Answer set programming at a glance. Commun. ACM **54**(12), 92–103 (2011)

10. Brewka, G., Woltran, S.: GRAPPA: A semantical framework for graph-based argument processing. In: Proceeding of ECAI, pp. 153–158 (2014)

11. Calimeri, F., Faber, W., Gebser, M., Ianni, G., Kaminski, R., Krennwallner, T., Leone, N., Ricca, F., Schaub, T.: ASP-Core-2 Input Language Format v2.03c (2015). https://www.mat.unical.it/aspcomp.2013/ASPStandardization. Accessed 27 Jun 2016

12. Calimeri, F., Gebser, M., Maratea, M., Ricca, F.: Design and results of the fifth answer set programming competition. Artif. Intell. **231**, 151–181 (2016)

13. Elkabani, I., Pontelli, E., Son, T.C.: SMODELS^A — a system for computing answer sets of logic programs with aggregates. In: Baral, C., Greco, G., Leone, N., Terracina, G. (eds.) LPNMR 2005. LNCS, vol. 3662, pp. 427–431. Springer, Heidelberg (2005). doi:10.1007/11546207_40

14. Gebser, M., Kaminski, R., Kaufmann, B., Schaub, T.: Answer Set Solving in Practice. ynthesis Lectures on Artificial Intelligence and Machine Learning. Morgan & Claypool Publishers, San Rafael (2012)

15. Gebser, M., Kaufmann, B., Schaub, T.: Conflict-driven answer set solving: from theory to practice. Artif. Intell. **187**, 52–89 (2012)

16. Gelfond, M., Lifschitz, V.: The stable model semantics for logic programming. In: Proceeding of ICLP/SLP, pp. 1070–1080 (1988)

17. Heißenberger, G.: A system for advanced graphical argumentation formalisms. Master's thesis, TU Wien (2016). www.dbai.tuwien.ac.at/proj/adf/grappavis/

18. Marek, V.W., Truszczyński, M.: Stable models and an alternative logic programming paradigm. In: Apt, K.R., Marek, V.W., Truszczynski, M., Warren, D.S. (eds.) The Logic Programming Paradigm. AI, pp. 375–398. Springer, Heidelberg (1999)

19. Morak, M., Woltran, S.: Preprocessing of complex non-ground rules in answer set programming. In: Proceeding ICLP, pp. 247–258 (2012)

Symbolic Execution and Thresholding for Efficiently Tuning Fuzzy Logic Programs

Ginés Moreno[1]($\boxtimes$), Jaime Penabad[2], José A. Riaza[1], and Germán Vidal[3]

[1] Department of Computing Systems, UCLM, 02071 Albacete, Spain
{Gines.Moreno,JoseAntonio.Riaza}@uclm.es
[2] Department of Mathematics, UCLM, 02071 Albacete, Spain
Jaime.Penabad@uclm.es
[3] MiST, DSIC, Universitat Politècnica de València, Valencia, Spain
gvidal@dsic.upv.es

Abstract. Fuzzy logic programming is a growing declarative paradigm aiming to integrate fuzzy logic into logic programming. One of the most difficult tasks when specifying a fuzzy logic program is determining the right weights for each rule, as well as the most appropriate fuzzy connectives and operators. In this paper, we introduce a symbolic extension of fuzzy logic programs in which some of these parameters can be left unknown, so that the user can easily see the impact of their possible values. Furthermore, given a number of test cases, the most appropriate values for these parameters can be automatically computed. Finally, we show some benchmarks that illustrate the usefulness of our approach.

Keywords: Fuzzy logic programming · Symbolic execution · Tuning

1 Introduction

Logic Programming [17] has been widely used as a formal method for problem solving and knowledge representation. Nevertheless, traditional logic programming languages do not incorporate techniques or constructs to explicitly deal with uncertainty and approximated reasoning. In order to fill this gap, *fuzzy logic programming* has emerged as an interesting—and still growing—research area which aims to consolidate the efforts for introducing fuzzy logic into logic programming.

During the last decades, several fuzzy logic programming systems have been developed. Here, essentially, the classical SLD resolution principle of logic programming has been replaced by a fuzzy variant with the aim of dealing with partial truth and reasoning with uncertainty in a natural way. Most of these

This work has been partially supported by the EU (FEDER), the State Research Agency (AEI) and the Spanish *Ministerio de Economía y Competitividad* under grants TIN2013-45732-C4-2-P, TIN2013-44742-C4-1-R, TIN2016-76843-C4-1-R, TIN2016-76843-C4-2-R (AEI/FEDER, UE) and by the *Generalitat Valenciana* under grant PROMETEO-II/2015/013 (SmartLogic).

M.V. Hermenegildo and P. Lopez-Garcia (Eds.): LOPSTR 2016, LNCS 10184, pp. 131–147, 2017.
DOI: 10.1007/978-3-319-63139-4_8

systems implement (extended versions of) the resolution principle introduced by Lee [15], such as Elf-Prolog [7], F-Prolog [16], generalized annotated logic programming [13], Fril [4], MALP [18], FASILL [11,12], the QLP scheme of [22] and the many-valued logic programming language of [23].

In this paper we focus on the so-called *multi-adjoint logic programming* approach MALP [18], a powerful and promising approach in the area of fuzzy logic programming. Intuitively speaking, logic programming is extended with a *multi-adjoint lattice* L of truth values (typically, a real number between 0 and 1), equipped with a collection of *adjoint pairs* $\langle \&_i, \leftarrow_i \rangle$ and connectives: implications, conjunctions, disjunctions, and other operators called aggregators, which are interpreted on this lattice. Consider, for instance, the following MALP rule:

$$good(X) \leftarrow_{\mathtt{P}} @_{\mathtt{aver}}(nice(X), cheap(X)) \ with \ 0.8$$

where the adjoint pair $\langle \&_{\mathtt{P}}, \leftarrow_{\mathtt{P}} \rangle$ is defined as

$$\&_{\mathtt{P}}(x,y) \triangleq x * y \qquad \leftarrow_{\mathtt{P}}(x,y) \triangleq \begin{cases} 1 & \text{if } y \leq x \\ x/y & \text{if } 0 < x < y \end{cases}$$

and the aggregator $@_{\mathtt{aver}}$ is typically defined as $@_{\mathtt{aver}}(x_1, x_2) \triangleq (x_1 + x_2)/2$. Therefore, the rule specifies that X is good—with a truth degree of 0.8—if X is nice and cheap. Assuming that X is nice and cheap with, e.g., truth degrees n and c, respectively, then X is good with a truth degree of $0.8 * ((n + c)/2)$.

When specifying a MALP program, it might sometimes be difficult to assign weights—truth degrees—to program rules, as well as to determine the right connectives.[1] This is a common problem with fuzzy control system design, where some trial-and-error is often necessary. In our context, a programmer can develop a prototype and repeatedly execute it until the set of answers is the intended one. Unfortunately, this is a tedious and time consuming operation. Actually, it might be impractical when the program should correctly model a large number of test cases provided by the user.

In order to overcome this drawback, in this paper we introduce a symbolic extension of MALP programs called *symbolic multi-adjoint logic programming* (sMALP). Here, we can write rules containing *symbolic* truth degrees and *symbolic* connectives, i.e., connectives which are not defined on its associated multi-adjoint lattice. In order to evaluate these programs, we introduce a symbolic operational semantics that delays the evaluation of symbolic expressions. Therefore, a *symbolic answer* could now include symbolic (unknown) truth values and connectives. We prove the correctness of the approach, i.e., the fact that using the symbolic semantics and then replacing the unknown values and connectives by concrete ones gives the same result as replacing these values and connectives in the original sMALP program and, then, applying the concrete semantics on the resulting MALP program. Furthermore, we show how sMALP programs can

---

[1] For instance, we have typically several adjoint pairs: *Lukasiewicz logic* $\langle \&_{\mathtt{L}}, \leftarrow_{\mathtt{L}} \rangle$, *Gödel logic* $\langle \&_{\mathtt{G}}, \leftarrow_{\mathtt{G}} \rangle$ and *product logic* $\langle \&_{\mathtt{P}}, \leftarrow_{\mathtt{P}} \rangle$, which might be used for modeling *pessimist*, *optimist* and *realistic scenarios*, respectively.

be used to tune a program w.r.t. a given set of test cases, thus easing what is considered the most difficult part of the process: the specification of the right weights and connectives for each rule. We plan to integrate this tuning process into the FLOPER system (*Fuzzy LOgic Programming Environment for Research*); see, e.g., [19,20]. In this paper, we show the results of an experimental evaluation using a prototype implementation of the system, which is available online from http://dectau.uclm.es/tuning/.

The structure of this paper is as follows. After some preliminaries in Sect. 2, we introduce the framework of symbolic multi-adjoint logic programming in Sect. 3 and prove its correctness. Then, in Sect. 4, we show the usefulness of symbolic programs for tuning several parameters so that a concrete program is obtained. Moreover, we show some interesting experiments together with an online implementation which also considers a very efficient tuning method improved with thresholding techniques. Finally, Sect. 5 concludes and points out some directions for further research.

2   Preliminaries

We assume the existence of a multi-adjoint lattice $\langle L, \preceq, \&_1, \leftarrow_1, \ldots, \&_n, \leftarrow_n \rangle$, equipped with a collection of *adjoint pairs* $\langle \&_i, \leftarrow_i \rangle$—where each $\&_i$ is a conjunctor which is intended to be used for the evaluation of *modus ponens* [18]—. In addition, on each program rule, we can have a different adjoint implication $(\leftarrow_i)$, conjunctions (denoted by $\wedge_1, \wedge_2, \ldots$), adjoint conjunctions $(\&_1, \&_2, \ldots)$, disjunctions $(|_1, |_2, \ldots)$, and other operators called aggregators (usually denoted by $@_1, @_2, \ldots$); see [21] for more details. More exactly, a multi-adjoint lattice fulfills the following properties:

- $\langle L, \preceq \rangle$ is a (bounded) complete lattice.[2]
- For each truth function of $\&_i$, an increase in any of the arguments results in an increase of the result (they are *increasing*).
- For each truth function of $\leftarrow_i$, the result increases as the first argument increases, but it decreases as the second argument increases (they are *increasing* in the consequent and *decreasing* in the antecedent).
- $\langle \&_i, \leftarrow_i \rangle$ is an *adjoint pair* in $\langle L, \preceq \rangle$, namely, for any $x, y, z \in L$, we have that: $x \preceq (y \leftarrow_i z)$ if and only if $(x \&_i z) \preceq y$.

The last condition, called the *adjoint property*, could be considered the most important feature of the framework (in contrast with other approaches) which justifies most of its properties regarding crucial results for soundness, completeness, applicability, etc. [18].

---

[2] A complete lattice is a (partially) ordered set $\langle L, \preceq \rangle$ such that every subset S of L has infimum and supremum elements. It is bounded if it has bottom and top elements, denoted by $\perp$ and $\top$, respectively. L is said to be the *carrier set* of the lattice, and $\preceq$ its ordering relation.

Aggregation operators are useful to describe or specify user preferences. An aggregation operator, when interpreted as a truth function, may be an arithmetic mean, a weighted sum or in general any monotone function whose arguments are values of a multi-adjoint lattice L. Although, formally, these connectives are binary operators, we often use them as n-ary functions so that $@(x_1, \ldots, @(x_{n-1}, x_n), \ldots)$ is denoted by $@(x_1, \ldots, x_n)$. By abuse of notation, in these cases, we consider $@$ an n-ary operator. The truth function of an n-ary connective ς is denoted by $[\![\varsigma]\!] : L^n \mapsto L$ and is required to be monotonic and fulfill the following conditions: $[\![\varsigma]\!](\top, \ldots, \top) = \top$ and $[\![\varsigma]\!](\bot, \ldots, \bot) = \bot$.

In this work, given a multi-adjoint lattice L, we consider a first order language $\mathcal{L}_L$ built upon a signature Σ_L, that contains the elements of a countably infinite set of variables $\mathcal{V}$, function and predicate symbols (denoted by $\mathcal{F}$ and Π, respectively) with an associated arity—usually expressed as pairs f/n or p/n, respectively, where n represents its arity—, and the truth degree literals Σ_L^T and connectives Σ_L^C from L. Therefore, a well-formed formula in $\mathcal{L}_L$ can be either:

- A *value* $v \in \Sigma_L^T$, which will be interpreted as itself, i.e., as the truth degree $v \in L$.
- $p(t_1, \ldots, t_n)$, if $t_1, \ldots, t_n$ are terms over $\mathcal{V} \cup \mathcal{F}$ and p/n is an n-ary predicate. This formula is called *atomic* (or just an atom).
- $\varsigma(e_1, \ldots, e_n)$, if $e_1, \ldots, e_n$ are well-formed formulas and ς is an n-ary connective with truth function $[\![\varsigma]\!] : L^n \mapsto L$.

As usual, a *substitution* σ is a mapping from variables from $\mathcal{V}$ to terms over $\mathcal{V} \cup \mathcal{F}$ such that $Dom(\sigma) = \{x \in \mathcal{V} \mid x \neq \sigma(x)\}$ is its domain. Substitutions are usually denoted by sets of pairs like, e.g., $\{x_1/t_1, \ldots, x_n/t_n\}$. Substitutions are extended to morphisms from terms to terms in the natural way. The identity substitution is denoted by id. Composition of substitutions is denoted by juxtaposition, i.e., $\sigma\theta$ denotes a substitution δ such that $\delta(x) = \theta(\sigma(x))$ for all $x \in \mathcal{V}$.

In the following, an $L - expression$ is a well-formed formula of $\mathcal{L}_L$ which is composed only by values and connectives from L, i.e., expressions over $\Sigma_L^T \cup \Sigma_L^C$.

In what follows, we assume that the truth function of any connective ς in L is given by a corresponding definition of the form $[\![\varsigma]\!](x_1, \ldots, x_n) \triangleq E$.[3] For instance, in this work, we will be mainly concerned with the classical set of adjoint pairs (conjunctors and implications) over $\langle[0, 1], \leq\rangle$ shown in Fig. 1, where labels L, G and P mean respectively *Łukasiewicz logic*, *Gödel logic* and *Product logic* (which might be used for modeling *pessimist*, *optimist* and *realistic scenarios*, respectively).

A MALP *rule* over a multi-adjoint lattice L is a formula $H \leftarrow_i \mathcal{B}$, where H is an *atomic formula* (usually called the *head* of the rule), $\leftarrow_i$ is an implication symbol belonging to some adjoint pair of L, and $\mathcal{B}$ (which is called the *body* of the rule) is a well-formed formula over L without implications. A *goal* is a body submitted as a query to the system. A MALP program is a set of expressions R *with* v, where R is a rule and v is a *truth degree* (a value of L) expressing the

---

[3] For convenience, in the following sections, we do not distinguish between the connective ς and its truth function $[\![\varsigma]\!]$.

$$\&_P(x,y) \triangleq x*y \qquad \leftarrow_P (x,y) \triangleq \begin{cases} 1 & \text{if } y \le x \\ x/y & \text{if } 0 < x < y \end{cases} \qquad \textit{Product logic}$$

$$\&_G(x,y) \triangleq \min(x,y) \qquad \leftarrow_G (x,y) \triangleq \begin{cases} 1 & \text{if } y \le x \\ x & \text{otherwise} \end{cases} \qquad \textit{Gödel logic}$$

$$\&_L(x,y) \triangleq \max(0, x+y-1) \qquad \leftarrow_L (x,y) \triangleq \min(x-y+1,1) \qquad \textit{Łukasiewicz logic}$$

Fig. 1. Adjoint pairs of three different fuzzy logics over $\langle [0,1], \le \rangle$.

confidence of a programmer in the truth of rule R. By abuse of the language, we often refer to R *with* v as a rule. See, e.g., [18] for a complete formulation of the MALP framework.

3   Symbolic Multi-adjoint Logic Programming

In this section, we introduce a *symbolic* extension of multi-adjoint logic programming. Essentially, we will allow some undefined values (truth degrees) and connectives in the program rules, so that these elements can be systematically computed afterwards. In the following, we will use the abbreviation sMALP to refer to programs belonging to this setting.

Here, given a multi-adjoint lattice L, we consider an augmented language $\mathcal{L}_L^s \supseteq \mathcal{L}_L$ which may also include a number of symbolic values, symbolic adjoint pairs and symbolic connectives which do not belong to L. Symbolic objects are usually denoted as o^s with a superscript s.

Definition 1 (sMALP program). *Let L be a multi-adjoint lattice. An sMALP program over L is a set of symbolic rules, where each symbolic rule is a formula $(H \leftarrow_i \mathcal{B} \text{ with } v)$ that meets the following conditions:*

- *H is an atomic formula of $\mathcal{L}_L$ (the head of the rule);*
- *$\leftarrow_i$ is a (possibly symbolic) implication from either a symbolic adjoint pair $\langle \&^s, \leftarrow^s \rangle$ or from an adjoint pair of L;*
- *$\mathcal{B}$ (the body of the rule) is a symbolic goal, i.e., a well-formed formula of $\mathcal{L}_L^s$;*
- *v is either a truth degree (a value of L) or a symbolic value.*

Example 1. We consider the multi-adjoint lattice $\langle [0,1], \le, \&_P, \leftarrow_P, \&_G, \leftarrow_G, \&_L, \leftarrow_L \rangle$, where the adjoint pairs are defined in Sect. 2, also including $@_{\text{aver}}$ which is defined as follows: $@_{\text{aver}}(x_1, x_2) \triangleq (x_1 + x_2)/2$. Then, the following is an sMALP program $\mathcal{P}$:

$$\begin{array}{lll} p(X) & \leftarrow^{s_1} \&^{s_2}(q(X), @_{\text{aver}}(r(X), s(X))) & \textit{with} \quad 0.9 \\ q(a) & & \textit{with} \quad v^s \\ r(X) & & \textit{with} \quad 0.7 \\ s(X) & & \textit{with} \quad 0.5 \end{array}$$

where $\langle \&^{s_1}, \leftarrow^{s_1} \rangle$ is a symbolic adjoint pair (i.e., a pair not defined in L), $\&^{s_2}$ is a symbolic conjunction, and v^s is a symbolic value.

The procedural semantics of sMALP is defined in a stepwise manner as follows. First, an *operational* stage is introduced which proceeds similarly to SLD resolution in pure logic programming. In contrast to standard logic programming, though, our operational stage returns an expression still containing a number of (possibly symbolic) values and connectives. Then, an *interpretive* stage evaluates these connectives and produces a final answer (possibly containing symbolic values and connectives). The procedural semantics of both MALP and sMALP programs is based on a similar scheme. The main difference is that, for MALP programs, the interpretive stage always returns a value, while for sMALP programs we might get an expression containing symbolic values and connectives that should be first instantiated in order to compute a value.

In the following, $C[A]$ denotes a formula where A is a sub-expression which occurs in the—possibly empty—context $C[]$. Moreover, $C[A/A']$ means the replacement of A by A' in context $C[]$, whereas $Var(s)$ refers to the set of distinct variables occurring in the syntactic object s, and $\theta[Var(s)]$ denotes the substitution obtained from θ by restricting its domain to $Var(s)$. An sMALP state has the form $\langle Q; \sigma \rangle$ where Q is a symbolic goal and σ is a substitution. We let $\mathcal{E}^s$ denote the set of all possible sMALP states.

Definition 2 (admissible step). *Let L be a multi-adjoint lattice and $\mathcal{P}$ an sMALP program over L. An* admissible step *is formalized as a state transition system, whose transition relation $\rightarrow_{AS} \subseteq (\mathcal{E}^s \times \mathcal{E}^s)$ is the smallest relation satisfying the following transition rules:*[4]

1. $\langle Q[A]; \sigma \rangle \rightarrow_{AS} \langle (Q[A/v \&_i \mathcal{B}])\theta; \sigma\theta \rangle$,
   if $\theta = mgu(\{H = A\}) \neq fail$, $(H \leftarrow_i \mathcal{B} \text{ with } v) \ll \mathcal{P}$ and $\mathcal{B}$ is not empty.[5]
2. $\langle Q[A]; \sigma \rangle \rightarrow_{AS} \langle (Q[A/\perp]); \sigma \rangle$,
   if there is no rule $(H \leftarrow_i \mathcal{B} \text{ with } v) \ll \mathcal{P}$ such that $mgu(\{H = A\}) \neq fail$.

Here, $(H \leftarrow_i \mathcal{B} \text{ with } v) \ll \mathcal{P}$ denotes that $(H \leftarrow_i \mathcal{B} \text{ with } v)$ is a renamed apart variant of a rule in $\mathcal{P}$ (i.e., all its variables are fresh). Note that symbolic values and connectives are not renamed.

Observe that the second rule is needed to cope with expressions like $@_{aver}(p(a), 0.8)$, which can be evaluated successfully even when there is no rule matching $p(a)$ since $@_{aver}(0, 0.8) = 0.4$.

In the following, given a relation $\rightarrow$, we let $\rightarrow^*$ denote its reflexive and transitive closure. Also, an $L^s - expression$ is now a well-formed formula of $\mathcal{L}_L^s$ which is composed by values and connectives from L as well as by symbolic values and connectives.

Definition 3 (admissible derivation). *Let L be a multi-adjoint lattice and $\mathcal{P}$ be an sMALP program over L. Given a goal Q, an* admissible derivation *is*

---

[4] Here, we assume that A in $Q[A]$ is the selected atom. Furthermore, as it is common practice, $mgu(E)$ denotes the *most general unifier* of the set of equations E [14].

[5] For simplicity, we consider that facts $(H \text{ with } v)$ are seen as rules of the form $(H \leftarrow_i \top \text{ with } v)$ for some implication $\leftarrow_i$. Furthermore, in this case, we directly derive the state $\langle (Q[A/v])\theta; \sigma\theta \rangle$ since $v \&_i \top = v$ for all $\&_i$.

a sequence $\langle Q; id \rangle \rightarrow^*_{AS} \langle Q'; \theta \rangle$. When Q' is an L^s-expression, the derivation is called final and the pair $\langle Q'; \sigma \rangle$, where $\sigma = \theta[Var(Q)]$, is called a symbolic admissible computed answer (saca, for short) for goal Q in $\mathcal{P}$.

Example 2. Consider again the multi-adjoint lattice L and the sMALP program $\mathcal{P}$ of Example 1. Here, we have the following final admissible derivation for $p(X)$ in $\mathcal{P}$ (the selected atom is underlined):

$$\langle \underline{p(X)};\ id \rangle \rightarrow_{AS} \langle \&^{s_1}(0.9, \&^{s_2}(\underline{q(X_1)}, @_{\mathrm{aver}}(r(X1), s(X1)))); \{X/X_1\} \rangle$$
$$\rightarrow_{AS} \langle \&^{s_1}(0.9, \&^{s_2}(v^s, @_{\mathrm{aver}}(\underline{r(a)}, s(a)))); \{X/a, X_1/a\} \rangle$$
$$\rightarrow_{AS} \langle \&^{s_1}(0.9, \&^{s_2}(v^s, @_{\mathrm{aver}}(0.7, \underline{s(a)}))); \{X/a, X_1/a, X_2/a\} \rangle$$
$$\rightarrow_{AS} \langle \&^{s_1}(0.9, \&^{s_2}(v^s, @_{\mathrm{aver}}(0.7, \underline{0.5}))); \{X/a, X_1/a, X_2/a, X_3/a\} \rangle$$

Therefore, the associated saca is $\langle \&^{s_1}(0.9, \&^{s_2}(v^s, @_{\mathrm{aver}}(0.7, 0.5))); \{X/a\} \rangle$.

Given a goal Q and a final admissible derivation $\langle Q; id \rangle \rightarrow^*_{AS} \langle Q'; \sigma \rangle$, we have that Q' does not contain atomic formulas. Now, Q' can be *solved* by using the following interpretive stage:

Definition 4 (interpretive step). *Let L be a multi-adjoint lattice and $\mathcal{P}$ be an sMALP program over L. Given a saca $\langle Q; \sigma \rangle$, the interpretive stage is formalized by means of the following transition relation $\rightarrow_{IS} \subseteq (\mathcal{E}^s \times \mathcal{E}^s)$, which is defined as the least transition relation satisfying:*

$$\langle Q[\varsigma(r_1, \ldots, r_n)]; \sigma \rangle \ \rightarrow_{IS} \ \langle Q[\varsigma(r_1, \ldots, r_n)/r_{n+1}]; \sigma \rangle$$

where ς denotes a connective defined on L and $[\![\varsigma]\!](r_1, \ldots, r_n) = r_{n+1}$.

An interpretive derivation of the form $\langle Q; \sigma \rangle \rightarrow^*_{IS} \langle Q'; \theta \rangle$ such that $\langle Q'; \theta \rangle$ cannot be further reduced, is called a final interpretive derivation. In this case, $\langle Q'; \theta \rangle$ is called a symbolic fuzzy computed answer (sfca, for short). Also, if Q' is a value of L, we say that $\langle Q'; \theta \rangle$ is a fuzzy computed answer (fca, for short).

Example 3. Given the saca of Example 2: $\langle \&^{s_1}(0.9, \&^{s_2}(v^s, @_{\mathrm{aver}}(0.7, 0.5))); \{X/a\} \rangle$, we have the following final interpretive derivation (the connective reduced is underlined):

$$\langle \&^{s_1}(0.9, \&^{s_2}(v^s, \underline{@_{\mathrm{aver}}(0.7, 0.5)})); \{X/a\} \rangle \rightarrow_{IS} \langle \&^{s_1}(0.9, \&^{s_2}(v^s, 0.6)); \{X/a\} \rangle$$

with $[\![@_{\mathrm{aver}}]\!](0.7, 0.5) = 0.6$. Therefore, $\langle \&^{s_1}(0.9, \&^{s_2}(v^s, 0.6)); \{X/a\} \rangle$ is a sfca of $p(X)$ in $\mathcal{P}$ since it cannot be further reduced.

Given a multi-adjoint lattice L and a symbolic language $\mathcal{L}^s_L$, in the following we consider *symbolic substitutions* that are mappings from symbolic values and connectives to expressions over $\Sigma^T_L \cup \Sigma^C_L$. Symbolic substitutions are denoted by $\Theta, \Gamma, \ldots$ Furthermore, for all symbolic substitution Θ, we require the following condition: $\leftarrow^s / \leftarrow_i \in \Theta$ iff $\&^s / \&_i \in \Theta$, where $\langle \&^s, \leftarrow^s \rangle$ is a symbolic adjoint pair and $\langle \&_i, \leftarrow_i \rangle$ is an adjoint pair in L. Intuitively, this is required for the substitution to have the same effect both on the program and on an L^s-expression.

Given an sMALP program $\mathcal{P}$ over L, we let $\mathsf{sym}(\mathcal{P})$ denote the symbolic values and connectives in $\mathcal{P}$. Given a symbolic substitution Θ for $\mathsf{sym}(\mathcal{P})$, we denote by $\mathcal{P}\Theta$ the program that results from $\mathcal{P}$ by replacing every symbolic symbol e^s by $e^s\Theta$. Trivially, $\mathcal{P}\Theta$ is now a MALP program.

The following theorem is our key result in order to use sMALP programs for tuning the components of a MALP program:

Theorem 1. *Let L be a multi-adjoint lattice and $\mathcal{P}$ be an* sMALP *program over L. Let $\mathcal{Q}$ be a goal. Then, for any symbolic substitution Θ for* $\mathsf{sym}(\mathcal{P})$, *we have that $\langle v; \theta \rangle$ is a* fca *for Q in $\mathcal{P}\Theta$ iff there exists a* sfca *$\langle Q'; \theta' \rangle$ for Q in $\mathcal{P}$ and $\langle Q'\Theta; \theta' \rangle \rightarrow_{IS}^* \langle v; \theta \rangle$, where θ' is a renaming of θ.*

Proof (Sketch) For simplicity, we consider that the same fresh variables are used for renamed apart rules in both derivations.

Consider the following derivations for goal $\mathcal{Q}$ w.r.t. programs $\mathcal{P}$ and $\mathcal{P}\Theta$, respectively:

$$\mathcal{D}_{\mathcal{P}} \; : \langle Q; id \rangle \rightarrow_{AS}^* \langle Q''; \theta \rangle \; \rightarrow_{IS}^* \langle Q'; \theta \rangle$$
$$\mathcal{D}_{\mathcal{P}\Theta} : \langle Q; id \rangle \rightarrow_{AS}^* \langle Q''\Theta; \theta \rangle \rightarrow_{IS}^* \langle Q'\Theta; \theta \rangle$$

Our proof proceeds now in three stages:

1. Firstly, observe that the sequences of symbolic admissible steps in $\mathcal{D}_{\mathcal{P}}$ and $\mathcal{D}_{\mathcal{P}\Theta}$ exploit the whole set of atoms in both cases, such that a program rule R is used in $\mathcal{D}_{\mathcal{P}}$ iff the corresponding rule $R\Theta$ is applied in $\mathcal{D}_{\mathcal{P}\Theta}$ and hence, the saca's of the derivations are $\langle Q''; \theta \rangle$ and $\langle Q''\Theta; \theta \rangle$, respectively.
2. Then, we proceed by applying interpretive steps until reaching the sfca $\langle Q'; \theta \rangle$ in the first derivation $\mathcal{D}_{\mathcal{P}}$ and it is easy to see that the same sequence of interpretive steps are applied in $\mathcal{D}_{\mathcal{P}\Theta}$ thus leading to state $\langle Q'\Theta; \theta \rangle$, which is not necessarily a sfca.
3. Finally, it suffices to instantiate the sfca $\langle Q'; \theta \rangle$ in the first derivation $\mathcal{D}_{\mathcal{P}}$ with the symbolic substitution Θ, for completing both derivations with the same sequence of interpretive steps until reaching the desired fca $\langle v; \theta \rangle$. $\quad\square$

Example 4. Consider again the multi-adjoint lattice L and the sMALP program $\mathcal{P}$ of Example 1. Let $\Theta = \{\leftarrow^{s_1}/\leftarrow_\mathsf{P}, \&^{s_1}/\&_\mathsf{P}, \&^{s_2}/\&_\mathsf{G}, v^s/0.8\}$ be a symbolic substitution. Given the sfca from Example 3, we have:

$$\langle \&^{s_1}(0.9, \&^{s_2}(v^s, 0.6))\rangle\Theta; \{X/a\} \rangle = \langle \&_\mathsf{P}(0.9, \&_\mathsf{G}(0.8, 0.6)); \{X/a\} \rangle$$

So, we have the following interpretive final derivation for the instantiated sfca:

$$\langle \&_\mathsf{P}(0.9, \underline{\&_\mathsf{G}(0.8, 0.6)}); \{X/a\} \rangle \rightarrow_{IS} \langle \underline{\&_\mathsf{P}(0.9, 0.6)}; \{X/a\} \rangle \rightarrow_{IS} \langle 0.54; \{X/a\} \rangle$$

By Theorem 1, we have that $\langle 0.54; \{X/a\} \rangle$ is also a fca for $p(X)$ in $\mathcal{P}\Theta$.

4   Tuning Multi-adjoint Logic Programs

In this section, we introduce an automated technique for tuning multi-adjoint logic programs using sMALP programs.

Consider a typical Prolog clause "$H : -B_1, \ldots, B_n$". It can be fuzzified in order to become a MALP rule "$H \leftarrow_{label} \mathcal{B}$ with v" by performing the following actions:

1. weighting it with a truth degree v,
2. connecting its head and body with a fuzzy implication symbol $\leftarrow_{label}$ (belonging to a concrete adjoint pair $\langle \leftarrow_{label}, \&_{label} \rangle$) and,
3. linking the set of atoms $B_1, \ldots, B_n$ on its body $\mathcal{B}$ by means of a set of fuzzy connectives (i.e., conjunctions $\&_i$, disjunctions $|_j$ or aggregators $@_k$).

Introducing changes on each one of the three fuzzy components just described above may affect—sometimes in an unexpected way—the set of fuzzy computed answers for a given goal.

Typically, a programmer has a model in mind where some parameters have a clear value. For instance, the truth value of a rule might be statistically determined and, thus, its value is easy to obtain. In other cases, though, the most appropriate values and/or connectives depend on subjective notions and, thus, programmers do not know how to obtain these values. In a typical scenario, we have an extensive set of *expected* computed answers (i.e., *test cases*), so the programmer can follow a "try and test" strategy. Unfortunately, this is a tedious and time consuming operation. Actually, it might even be impractical when the program should correctly model a large number of test cases.

Therefore, we propose an automated technique that proceeds as follows. Here, for simplicity, we only consider the first answer to a goal. Note that this is not a significant restriction since one can encode multiple solutions in a list so that the main goal is always deterministic and all non-deterministic calls are hidden in the computation. Extending the following algorithm for multiple solutions is not difficult, but makes the formalization more cumbersome. Hence, we say that a *test case* is a pair (Q, f) where Q is a goal and f is an fca.

Definition 5 (naive algorithm for symbolic tuning of MALP programs).

Input: *an* sMALP *program* $\mathcal{P}^s$ *and a number of (expected) test cases* $(Q_i, \langle v_i; \theta_i \rangle)$, *where* Q_i *is a goal and* $\langle v_i; \theta_i \rangle$ *is its expected* fca *for* $i = 1, \ldots, k$.
Output: *a symbolic substitution* Θ.

1. *For each test case* $(Q_i, \langle v_i; \theta_i \rangle)$, *compute the* sfca $\langle Q_i', \theta_i \rangle$ *of* $\langle Q_i, id \rangle$ *in* $\mathcal{P}^s$.
2. *Then, consider a finite number of possible symbolic substitutions for* sym$(\mathcal{P}^s)$, *say* $\Theta_1, \ldots, \Theta_n$, $n > 0$.
3. *For each* $j \in \{1, \ldots, n\}$, *compute* $\langle Q_i'\Theta_j, \theta_i \rangle \rightarrow^*_{IS} \langle v_{i,j}; \theta_i \rangle$, *for* $i = 1, \ldots, k$. *Let* $d_{i,j} = |v_{i,j} - v_i|$, *where* $|\_|$ *denotes the absolute value.*
4. *Finally, return the symbolic substitution* Θ_j *that minimizes* $\sum_{i=1}^{k} d_{i,j}$.

Observe that the precision of the algorithm can be parameterized depending on the set of symbolic substitutions considered in step (2). For instance, one can consider only truth values $\{0.3, 0.5, 0.8\}$ or a larger set $\{0.1, 0.2, \ldots, 1.0\}$; one can consider only three possible connectives, or a set including ten of them. Obviously, the larger the domain of values and connectives is, the more precise the results are (but the algorithm is more expensive, of course).

This algorithm represents a much more efficient method for tuning the fuzzy parameters of a MALP program than repeatedly executing the program from scratch (see Table 2, column "Basic").

Let us explain the technique by means of a small, but realistic example. Here, we consider a travel agency that offers booking services on a large number of hotels. The travel agency has a web site where the user can rate every hotel with a value between 1% and 100%. The purpose in this case is to specify a fuzzy model that correctly represents the rating of each hotel.

In order to simplify the presentation, we consider that there are only three hotels, named *sun*, *sweet* and *lux*. In the web site, these hotels have been rated 0.60, 0.77 and 0.85 (expressed as real numbers between 0 and 1), respectively. Our simple model just depends on three factors: the hotel facilities, the convenience of its location, and the rates, denoted by predicates *facilities*, *location* and *rates*, respectively. An sMALP program modelling this scenario is the following:

$$popularity(X) \quad \leftarrow^s \quad |^s(facilities(X), @_{\mathtt{aver}}(location(X), rates(X))) \quad with \ 0.9$$

$facilities(sun)$	$with \ v^s$
$location(sun)$	$with \ 0.4$
$rates(sun)$	$with \ 0.7$
$facilities(sweet)$	$with \ 0.5$
$location(sweet)$	$with \ 0.3$
$rates(sweet)$	$with \ 0.1$
$facilities(lux)$	$with \ 0.9$
$location(lux)$	$with \ 0.8$
$rates(lux)$	$with \ 0.2$

Here, we assume that all weights can be easily obtained except for the weight of the fact $facilities(sun)$, which is unknown, so we introduce a symbolic weight v^s. Also, the programmer has some doubts on the connectives used in the first rule, so she introduced a number of symbolic connectives: the implication and disjunction symbols, i.e. $\leftarrow^s$ and $|^s$.

We consider, for each symbolic connective, the three possibilities shown in Fig. 2 over the lattice $\langle [0,1], \leq \rangle$, which are based on the so-called *Product*, *Gödel* and *Łukasiewicz* logics. Adjectives like *pessimist*, *realistic* and *optimist* are sometimes applied to the *Łukasiewicz*, *Product* and *Gödel* logics, respectively, since conjunctive operators satisfy that, for any pair of real numbers x and y in $[0, 1]$, we have:

$$0 \leq \&_{\mathtt{L}}(x, y) \leq \&_{\mathtt{P}}(x, y) \leq \&_{\mathtt{G}}(x, y) \leq 1$$

$$\&_P(x,y) = x * y \qquad |_P(x,y) = x + y - x * y \qquad \textit{Product logic}$$
$$\&_G(x,y) = \min(x,y) \qquad |_G(x,y) = \max(x,y) \qquad \textit{Gödel logic}$$
$$\&_L(x,y) = \max(x+y-1,0) \qquad |_L(x,y) = \min(x+y,1) \qquad \textit{Łukasiewicz logic}$$

Fig. 2. Conjunctions and disjunctions of three different fuzzy logics over $\langle [0,1], \leq \rangle$.

In contrast, the contrary holds for the disjunction operations, that is:

$$0 \leq |_G(x,y) \leq |_P(x,y) \leq |_L(x,y) \leq 1$$

Note that it is more difficult to satisfy a condition based on a pessimist conjunction/disjunction (i.e., inspired by the *Łukasiewicz* and *Gödel* fuzzy logics, respectively) than with *Product* logic based operators. The optimistic versions of these connectives are less restrictive, obtaining greater truth degrees on fca's. This is a consequence of the following chain of inequalities:

$$0 \leq \&_L(x,y) \leq \&_P(x,y) \leq \&_G(x,y) \leq |_G(x,y) \leq |_P(x,y) \leq |_L(x,y) \leq 1$$

Therefore, it is desirable to tune the symbolic constants $\leftarrow^s$ and $|^s$ in the first rule of our symbolic sMALP program by selecting operators in the previous sequence until finding solutions satisfying in a stronger (or weaker) way the user's requirements.

Focusing on our particular sMALP program, we consider the following three test cases:

$$(popularity(sun), \langle 0.60; id \rangle),$$
$$(popularity(sweet), \langle 0.77; id \rangle),$$
$$(popularity(lux), \langle 0.85; id \rangle)$$

for which the respective three sfca's achieved after applying the first step of our tuning algorithm are:

$$\langle \&^s(0.9, |^s(v^s, 0.55)); id \rangle$$
$$\langle \&^s(0.9, |^s(0.5, 0.65)); id \rangle$$
$$\langle \&^s(0.9, |^s(0.9, 0.5)); id \rangle$$

In the second step of the algorithm, we must provide symbolic substitutions for being applied to this set of sfca's in order to transform them into fca's which are as close as possible to those in the test cases. Table 1 shows the results of the tuning process, where each column has the following meaning:

- The first pair of columns serve for choosing the implication[6] and disjunction connectives of the first program rule (i.e., $\leftarrow^s$ and $|^s$ from each one of the three fuzzy logics considered so far.
- In the third column, we consider three possible truth degrees (0.3, 0.5 and 0.7) as the potential assignment to the symbolic weight v^s. In this example, this set suffices to obtain an accurate solution.

---

[6] It is important to note that, at execution time, each implication symbol belonging to a concrete adjoint pair is replaced by its adjoint conjunction (see again our repertoire of adjoint pairs in Fig. 1 in the preliminaries section).

- Each row represents a different symbolic substitution, which are shown in column four.
- Next, headed by the name of each hotel in the test cases, we have pairs of columns which represent, respectively, the potential truth degree associated to the fca obtained with the corresponding symbolic substitution, and the deviation of such value w.r.t. the expected truth degree, thus summarizing the computations performed on the third step of our algorithm.
- The sum of the three deviations is expressed in the last column of the table, which constitutes the value to be minimized as indicated in the final, fourth step of the algorithm.

According to these criteria, we observe that the cell with the lower value (0.04) in the last column of Table 1 refers to the symbolic substitution

$$\Theta_{13} = \{\leftarrow^s/\leftarrow_\mathrm{P}, \ |^s/ \ |_\mathrm{P}, \ v^s/0.3\}$$

which solve our tuning problem by suggesting that the first pair of rules in our final, tuned MALP program should be the following ones:

$$popularity(X) \ \leftarrow_\mathrm{P} \ |_\mathrm{P}(services(X), @_{\mathtt{aver}}(location(X), rates(X))) \quad with \ 0.9$$
$$facilities(sun) \hspace{8cm} with \ 0.3$$

Unfortunately, the naive algorithm introduced so far might be very inefficient when dealing with many symbolic values and connectives, or when the considered set of their possible substitutions is large. Here, in order to improve its efficiency, we consider *thresholding* techniques—well-known in the fuzzy logic arena—for prematurely disregarding useless computations leading to non-significant answers (see our previous experiences in [2,8,10]).

The improved algorithm is perfectly analogous to the algorithm in Definition 5, but makes use of a threshold τ for determining when a *partial* solution is acceptable. The value of τ is initialized to ∞ (in practice, a very large number). Then, this threshold dinamically decreases whenever we find a symbolic substitution with an associated deviation which is lower that the actual value of τ. Moreover, a partial solution is discarded as soon as the cumulative deviation computed so far is greater than τ. In our running example, τ takes the following values: 0.42, 0.27, 0.05, and 0.04, associated to Θ_1, Θ_3, Θ_4, and Θ_{13}, respectively. In general, the number of discarded solutions grows as the value of τ decreases, improving the pruning power of thesholding. In Table 1, the discarded solutions are shown in bold. They represent a significant percentage of the total computations.

The symbolic execution and tuning methods explained so far can be tested online via the following URL:

Table 1. Table summarizing the results achieved when tuning connectives and weights.

$\leftarrow^s$	$|^s$	v^s	Θ	sun		sweet		lux		z
$\leftarrow_L$	$|_G$	0.3	Θ_1	0.45	0.15	0.55	0.22	0.80	0.05	0.42
		0.5	Θ_2	0.45	0.15	0.55	0.22	0.80	0.05	0.42
		0.7	Θ_3	0.60	0.00	0.55	0.22	0.80	0.05	0.27
	$|_P$	0.3	Θ_4	0.59	0.01	0.73	0.04	0.85	0.00	0.05
		0.5	Θ_5	0.68	0.08	**0.73**	**0.04**	**0.85**	**0.00**	**0.12**
		0.7	Θ_6	0.77	0.17	**0.73**	**0.04**	**0.85**	**0.00**	**0.21**
	$|_L$	0.3	Θ_7	0.75	0.15	**0.90**	**0.13**	**0.90**	**0.05**	**0.33**
		0.5	Θ_8	0.90	0.30	**0.90**	**0.13**	**0.90**	**0.05**	**0.48**
		0.7	Θ_9	0.90	0.30	**0.90**	**0.13**	**0.90**	**0.05**	**0.48**
$\leftarrow_P$	$|_G$	0.3	Θ_{10}	0.50	0.10	**0.59**	**0.18**	**0.81**	**0.04**	**0.32**
		0.5	Θ_{11}	0.50	0.10	**0.59**	**0.18**	**0.81**	**0.04**	**0.32**
		0.7	Θ_{12}	0.63	0.03	0.59	0.18	**0.81**	**0.04**	**0.25**
	$|_P$	0.3	Θ_{13}	0.61	0.01	0.74	0.03	0.85	0.00	0.04
		0.5	Θ_{14}	0.70	0.10	**0.74**	**0.03**	**0.86**	**0.01**	**0.14**
		0.7	Θ_{15}	0.78	0.18	**0.74**	**0.03**	**0.86**	**0.01**	**0.22**
	$|_L$	0.3	Θ_{16}	0.77	0.17	**0.90**	**0.13**	**0.90**	**0.05**	**0.35**
		0.5	Θ_{17}	0.90	0.30	**0.90**	**0.13**	**0.90**	**0.05**	**0.48**
		0.7	Θ_{18}	0.90	0.30	**0.90**	**0.13**	**0.90**	**0.05**	**0.48**
$\leftarrow_G$	$|_G$	0.3	Θ_{19}	0.55	0.05	**0.65**	**0.12**	**0.90**	**0.05**	**0.22**
		0.5	Θ_{20}	0.55	0.05	**0.65**	**0.12**	**0.90**	**0.05**	**0.22**
		0.7	Θ_{21}	0.70	0.10	**0.65**	**0.12**	**0.90**	**0.05**	**0.27**
	$|_P$	0.3	Θ_{22}	0.69	0.09	**0.83**	**0.06**	**0.90**	**0.05**	**0.20**
		0.5	Θ_{23}	0.78	0.18	**0.83**	**0.06**	**0.90**	**0.05**	**0.29**
		0.7	Θ_{24}	0.87	0.27	**0.83**	**0.06**	**0.90**	**0.05**	**0.38**
	$|_L$	0.3	Θ_{25}	0.86	0.26	**0.90**	**0.13**	**0.90**	**0.05**	**0.44**
		0.5	Θ_{26}	0.90	0.30	**0.90**	**0.13**	**0.90**	**0.05**	**0.48**
		0.7	Θ_{27}	0.90	0.30	**0.90**	**0.13**	**0.90**	**0.05**	**0.48**

http://dectau.uclm.es/tuning/

When introducing an sMALP program into the system, symbolic constants must be preceded by the symbol "#". For instance, the first couple of rules in our running example have the following form:

```
popularity(X) #<s1 facilities(X) #|s2 @aver(locatin(X),rates(X)) with 0.9
facilities(sun) with #s3
```

The lattice of truth degrees is encoded as a set of Prolog clauses (see [19,20]) where predicate members/1 contains the list of truth degrees used during the tuning process. Each test case appears in a different line as follows: $r \rightarrow Q$, where r is the desired truth degree for the first fca associated to query Q. For tuning an sMALP program, we have implemented the three methods mentioned so far:

Basic: The basic method is based on applying each symbolic substitution to the original sMALP program and then fully executing the resulting instantiated MALP programs (both the operational and the interpretive stages).

Symbolic: This row refers to the naive algorithm introduced in Definition 5, where the considered substitutions are directly applied to sfca's (thus only the interpretive stage is repeatedly executed).

Thresholded: In this row, we consider the symbolic method improved with thresholding techniques, as explained above.

The system also reports the processing time required by each method and offers an option for applying the best symbolic substitution to the original sMALP program in order to show the final, tuned MALP program.

Table 2. Tuning runtime (in milliseconds).

	Truth degrees			Symbolic constants						
	10	100	1000	5	6	7	8	9	10	11
Basic	120	1130	11360	320	990	3030	9180	28170	86760	264850
Symbolic	30	290	2860	100	290	980	2970	9930	30570	93360
Thresholded	15	130	1300	50	140	420	1580	4390	13460	38310

Table 2 summarizes the results of an experimental evaluation[7] of the three tuning methods described above, varying the number of truth degrees (10, 100 and 1000) used when manipulating our running example. Note that, in the most complex case, 9000 different symbolic substitutions are considered at tuning time, and the thresholded method is about 2 to 3 times more efficient than the symbolic method, and even 6 to 8 times more efficient than the basic method, which witnesses the advantages of our improved tuning mechanism. In the last column, we consider variations of the number of symbolic constants (among connectives and truth degrees) from 5 to 11, thus showing that the thresholded method scales up well and solves the problem in just a few seconds.

5   Discussion

In this paper, we have been concerned with fuzzy programs belonging to the so-called *multi-adjoint logic programming* approach. Our improvements are twofold:

---

[7] Each cell refers to the average of 100 executions using a desktop computer equipped with an i3-2310 M CPU @ 2.10 GHz and 4,00 GB RAM.

- On one side, we have extended their syntax for allowing the presence of symbolic weights and connectives on program rules, which very often prevents the full evaluation of goals. As a consequence, we have also relaxed the operational principle for producing what we call *symbolic fuzzy computed answers*, where all atoms have been exploited and the maximum number of expressions involving connectives of the underlaying lattice of truth degrees have been solved too.
- On the other hand, we have introduced a tuning process for MALP programs that takes as inputs a set of expected test cases and an sMALP program where some connectives and/or truth degrees are unknown. The efficiency of the method has been largely improved by combining it with thresholding techniques, as can be checked online in our prototype implementation.

As future work, we consider the embedding of these techniques in the FLOPER platform, which is freely available from http://dectau.uclm.es/floper/. Currently, the system can be used for compiling MALP programs to standard Prolog code, drawing *derivation trees*, generating declarative traces and executing MALP programs [9,10]. Our last update, described in [11,12], allows the system to cope with *similarity relations* cohabiting with lattices of truth degrees. Extending our tuning method in order to cope with such similarity relations is also an interesting topic for future work.

Another interesting direction for further research consists in combining our approach with recent fuzzy variants of SAT/SMT techniques. Research on SAT (Boolean Satisfiability) and SMT (Satisfiability Modulo Theories) [5] has provided highly efficient solvers based on classical logic. Some recent approaches deal with propositional fuzzy formulae which might contain connectives defined on lattices of truth degrees quite similar to the ones used on MALP programs [3,24].[8] In this context, we think that our tuning method could be significantly improved if the set of sfca's instantiated with symbolic substitutions could be expressed as fuzzy formulae, which are solvable by this kind of fuzzy SAT/SMT solvers.

References

1. Almendros-Jiménez, J.M., Bofill, M., Luna-Tedesqui, A., Moreno, G., Vázquez, C., Villaret, M.: Fuzzy XPath for the automatic search of fuzzy formulae models. In: Beierle, C., Dekhtyar, A. (eds.) SUM 2015. LNCS (LNAI), vol. 9310, pp. 385–398. Springer, Cham (2015). doi:10.1007/978-3-319-23540-0_26
2. Almendros-Jiménez, J.M., Luna, A., Moreno, G.: Fuzzy XPath through fuzzy logic programming. New Gener. Comput. **33**(2), 173–209 (2015)

---

[8] Instead of focusing on satisfiability, (i.e., proving the existence of at least one model) as usually done in a SAT/SMT setting, in [1,6] we have faced the problem of finding the whole set of models for a given fuzzy formula by re-using a previous method based on fuzzy logic programming where the formula is conceived as a goal whose derivation tree, provided by the FLOPER tool, contains in its leaves all the models of the original formula, together with other interpretations.

3. Ansótegui, C., Bofill, M., Manyà, F., Villaret, M.: Building automated theorem provers for infinitely-valued logics with satisfiability modulo theory solvers. In: Proceeding of ISMVL 2012, pp. 25–30 (2012)
4. Baldwin, J.F., Martin, T.P., Pilsworth, B.W.: Fril- Fuzzy and Evidential Reasoning in Artificial Intelligence. Wiley, New York (1995)
5. Barrett, C.W., Sebastiani, R., Seshia, S.A., Tinelli, C.: Satisfiability modulo theories. In: Handbook of Satisfiability, Frontiers in Artificial Intelligence and Applications, 185, pp. 825–885. IOS Press (2009)
6. Bofill, M., Moreno, G., Vázquez, C., Villaret, M.: Automatic proving of fuzzy formulae with fuzzy logic programming and SMT. In: Fredlund, L.A. (ed.) Programming and Computer Languages 2013, vol. 64, p. 19. ECEASST (2013)
7. Ishizuka, M., Kanai, N.: Prolog-ELF incorporating fuzzy logic. In: Proceeding of the IJCAI 1985, pp. 701–703. Morgan Kaufmann (1985)
8. Julián, P., Medina, J., Moreno, G., Ojeda-Aciego, M.: Efficient thresholded tabulation for fuzzy query answering. In: Bouchon-Meunier, B., Magdalena, L., Ojeda-Aciego, M., Verdegay, J.L., Yager, R.R. (eds.) Foundations of Reasoning under Uncertainty. STUDFUZZ, vol. 249, pp. 125–149. Springer, Heidelberg (2010)
9. Julián, P., Moreno, G., Penabad, J.: Operational/interpretive unfolding of multiadjoint logic programs. J. Univ. Comput. Sci. 12(11), 1679–1699 (2006)
10. Julián, P., Moreno, G., Penabad, J.: An improved reductant calculus using fuzzy partial evaluation techniques. Fuzzy Sets Syst. 160, 162–181 (2009). http://dx.doi.org/10.1016/j.fss.2008.05.006
11. Julián-Iranzo, P., Moreno, G., Penabad, J., Vázquez, C.: A fuzzy logic programming environment for managing similarity and truth degrees. In: EPTCS, vol. 173, pp. 71–86 (2015). http://dx.doi.org/10.4204/EPTCS.173.6
12. Julián-Iranzo, P., Moreno, G., Penabad, J., Vázquez, C.: A declarative semantics for a fuzzy logic language managing similarities and truth degrees. In: Alferes, J.J.J., Bertossi, L., Governatori, G., Fodor, P., Roman, D. (eds.) RuleML 2016. LNCS, vol. 9718, pp. 68–82. Springer, Cham (2016). doi:10.1007/978-3-319-42019-6_5
13. Kifer, M., Subrahmanian, V.S.: Theory of generalized annotated logic programming and its applications. J. Logic Program. 12, 335–367 (1992)
14. Lassez, J.L., Maher, M.J., Marriott, K.: Unification revisited. In: Foundations of Deductive Databases and Logic Programming, pp. 587–625. Morgan Kaufmann, Los Altos, CA (1988)
15. Lee, R.: Fuzzy logic and the resolution principle. J. ACM 19(1), 119–129 (1972)
16. Li, D., Liu, D.: A Fuzzy Prolog Database System. Wiley, New York (1990)
17. Lloyd, J.W.: Foundations of Logic Programming. Springer-Verlag, Berlin (1987)
18. Medina, J., Ojeda-Aciego, M., Vojtáš, P.: Similarity-based Unification: a multiadjoint approach. Fuzzy Sets Syst. 146, 43–62 (2004)
19. Morcillo, P.J., Moreno, G., Penabad, J., Vázquez, C.: A practical management of fuzzy truth-degrees using FLOPER. In: Dean, M., Hall, J., Rotolo, A., Tabet, S. (eds.) RuleML 2010. LNCS, vol. 6403, pp. 20–34. Springer, Heidelberg (2010). doi:10.1007/978-3-642-16289-3_4
20. Moreno, G., Vázquez, C.: Fuzzy logic programming in action with FLOPER. J. Softw. Eng. Appl. 7, 237–298 (2014)
21. Nguyen, H.T., Walker, E.A.: A First Course in Fuzzy Logic. Chapman & Hall, Boca Ratón (2006)

22. Rodríguez-Artalejo, M., Romero-Díaz, C.A.: Quantitative logic programming revisited. In: Garrigue, J., Hermenegildo, M.V. (eds.) FLOPS 2008. LNCS, vol. 4989, pp. 272–288. Springer, Heidelberg (2008). doi:10.1007/978-3-540-78969-7_20
23. Straccia, U.: Managing uncertainty and vagueness in description logics, logic programs and description logic programs. In: Baroglio, C., Bonatti, P.A., Małuszyński, J., Marchiori, M., Polleres, A., Schaffert, S. (eds.) Reasoning Web. LNCS, vol. 5224, pp. 54–103. Springer, Heidelberg (2008). doi:10.1007/978-3-540-85658-0_2
24. Vidal, A., Bou, F., Godo, L.: An SMT-based solver for continuous t-norm based logics. In: Hüllermeier, E., Link, S., Fober, T., Seeger, B. (eds.) SUM 2012. LNCS (LNAI), vol. 7520, pp. 633–640. Springer, Heidelberg (2012). doi:10.1007/978-3-642-33362-0_53

Analysis and Verification

Hierarchical Shape Abstraction for Analysis of Free List Memory Allocators

Bin Fang[1,2] and Mihaela Sighireanu[1(✉)]

[1] IRIF, University Paris Diderot and CNRS, Paris, France
{bfang,sighirea}@irif.fr
[2] Shanghai Key Laboratory of Trustworthy Computing, ECNU, Shanghai, China

Abstract. We propose a hierarchical abstract domain for the analysis of free list memory allocators that tracks shape and numerical properties about both the heap and the free lists. Our domain is based on Separation Logic extended with predicates that capture the pointer arithmetics constraints for the heap list and the shape of the free list. These predicates are combined using a hierarchical composition operator to specify the overlapping of the heap list by the free list. In addition to expressiveness, this operator leads to a compositional and compact representation of abstract values and simplifies the implementation of the abstract domain. The shape constraints are combined with numerical constraints over integer arrays to track properties about the allocation policies (best-fit, first-fit, etc.). Such properties are out of the scope of the existing analyzers. We implemented this domain and we show its effectiveness on several implementations of free list allocators.

1 Introduction

A dynamic memory allocator (DMA) is a piece of software managing a reserved region of the heap. It appears in general purpose libraries (e.g., C standard library) or as part of applications where the dynamic allocation shall be controlled to avoid failure due to memory exhaustion (e.g., embedded critical software). A client program interacts with the DMA by requesting blocks of memory of variable size that it may free at any time. To offer this service, the DMA manages the reserved memory region by partitioning it into arbitrary sized blocks of memory, also called *chunks*. When a chunk is allocated to a client program, the DMA can not relocate it to compact the memory region (like in garbage collectors) and it is unaware about the kind (type or value) of data stored. The set of chunks not in use, also called *free chunks*, is managed using different techniques. In this paper, we focus on *free list allocators* [19,27], that records free chunk in a list. This class of DMA includes textbook examples [17,19] and real-world allocators [20].

The automated analysis of DMA faces several challenges. Although the code of DMA is not long (between one hundred to a thousand LOC), it is highly optimised to provide good performance. Low-level code (e.g., pointer arithmetics, bit fields, calls to system routines like sbrk) is used to manage efficiently (i.e.,

© Springer International Publishing AG 2017
M.V. Hermenegildo and P. Lopez-Garcia (Eds.): LOPSTR 2016, LNCS 10184, pp. 151–167, 2017.
DOI: 10.1007/978-3-319-63139-4_9

with low additional cost in memory and time) the operations on the chunks in the reserved memory region. At the same time, the free list is manipulated using high level operations over typed memory blocks (values of C structures) by mutating pointer fields without pointer arithmetic. The analyser has to deal efficiently with this *polar usage of the heap* made by the DMA. The invariants maintained by the DMA are complex. The memory region is organised into a *heap list* based on the size information stored in the chunk header such that chunk overlapping and memory leaks are avoided. The start addresses of chunks shall be aligned to some given constant. The free list may have complex shapes (cyclic, acyclic, doubly-linked) and may be sorted by the start address of chunks to ease free chunks coalescing. A precise analysis shall keep track of both numerical and shape properties to infer specifications implying such invariants for the allocation and deallocation methods of the DMA.

These challenges have been addressed partially by several works in the last ten years [5, 23, 25]. In [23], efficient numerical analyses have been designed to track address alignment and bit-fields. The most important progress has been done by the analysis proposed by Calcagno et al. [5]. It is able to track the free list shape and the numerical properties of chunk start addresses due to an abstract domain built on an extension of Separation Logic (SL) [24] with numerical constraints and predicates specifying memory blocks. However, some properties of the heap and free list can not be tracked, e.g., the absence of memory leaks or the ordering of start addresses of free-chunks. Although the analysis in [25] does not concern DMA, it is the first to propose a hierarchical abstraction of the memory to track properties of linked data structures stored in static memory regions. However, this analysis can not track properties like address sorting of the high level data structures (here the free list) stored in the memory region. Furthermore, its link with a logic theory is not clear. Thus, a precise, logic based analysis for the inference of properties of free list DMA is still a challenge.

In this paper, we propose a static analysis that is able to infer the above complex invariants of DMA on both heap list and free list. We define an abstract domain which uses logic formulas to abstract DMA configurations. The logic proposed extends the fragment of symbolic heaps of SL with a hierarchical composition operator, $\ni$, to specify that the free list covers partially the heap list. This operator provides a hierarchical abstraction of the memory region under the DMA control: the low-level memory manipulations are specified at the level of the heap list and propagated in a way controlled by the abstraction at the level of the free list. The shape specification is combined with a fragment of first order logic on arrays to capture properties of chunks in lists, similar to [3]. This combination is done in an accurate way as regards the logic by including sequences of chunk addresses in the inductive definitions of list segments. The main advantages and contributions of this work are (1) the *high precision of the abstraction* which is able to capture complex properties of free list DMA implementations, (2) the *strong logical basis* allowing to infer invariants that may be used by other verification methods, and (3) the *modularity* of the abstract domain permitting to reuse existing abstract domains for the analysis of linked lists with integer data.

2   Overview

Figure 1 includes excerpts from our running example, a free list DMA implementation proposed in [1]. The type HDR (Fig. 1(a)) defines the information stored by the DMA at the start of chunks. The field size stores the full size of the chunk (in blocks of sizeof(HDR) bytes) and it is used by the heap list to determine the start of the next chunk. The field fnx is valid only for free chunks (i.e., chunks in the free list) and it stores the start address of the next free chunk. To simplify the presentation, we added the ghost field isfree, to mark explicitly free chunks. The memory region managed by the DMA is enclosed within the addresses stored by the global variables _hsta and _hend; they are initialised by minit using sbrk calls. The start of the free list is stored in frhd. An intuitive view of the concrete state of the DMA is shown in Fig. 1(d). The busy chunks are represented in grey. The "next chunk" relation in the heap list (defined using the field size) is represented by the lower arrows; the upper arrows represent the "next free chunk" relation defined by the fnx field. Furthermore, other structural invariants should be maintained after each call of DMA methods: the heap list shall be well formed inside the memory region [_hsta, _hend), consecutive chunks of the heap list are not both free (*early coalescing* policy), the free list shall include only chunks of the heap list, be acyclic and sorted by the start address of chunks. The allocation method searches a chunk with size bigger than the requested nbytes; if the chunk is larger, it is split in two parts such that the last part (the end of the initial chunk) is allocated.

The goal of our analysis is to establish that, if the client uses correctly the DMA methods, these methods (i) preserve the above structural invariants and (ii) are memory safe. In particular, we analyse the DMA methods starting from a client program which initialises the DMA and then calls allocation and deallocation methods (see Sect. 5) in a correct way.

Heap list abstraction. The concrete memory configurations managed by the DMA are abstracted first using an extension of the *symbolic heap graphs* fragment [9] of SL. The logic fragment is parameterised by a set of predicates which capture the properties of the heap list as follows:

- The predicate $\mathsf{blk}(X; Y)$, introduced in [5], specifies an untyped sequence of bytes between the symbolic addresses X and Y. E.g., the configuration obtained at line 20 of minit is abstracted by $\mathsf{blk}(\_\mathtt{hsta}; \_\mathtt{hend})$.
- The predicate $\mathsf{chd}(X; Y)$ specifies a memory block $\mathsf{blk}(X; Y)$ storing a value of type HDR; the fields of this value are represented by the symbolic variables $X.\mathtt{size}$, $X.\mathtt{fnx}$, and $X.\mathtt{isfree}$ respectively.
- The predicate $\mathsf{chk}(X; Y)$ specifies a chunk built from a chunk header $\mathsf{chd}(X; Z)$ followed by a block $\mathsf{blk}(Z; Y)$ such that the full memory occupied, i.e., $Y - X$, has size given by $X.\mathtt{size} \times \mathtt{sizeof}(\mathtt{HDR})$.

```
 1  typedef struct hdr_s {
 2    struct hdr_s *fnx;
 3    size_t size;
 4    //@ghost bool isfree;
 5  } HDR;
 6
 7  static void *_hsta = NULL;
 8  static void *_hend = NULL;
 9  static HDR *frhd = NULL;
10  static size_t memleft;
11
12  void minit(size_t sz)
13  {
14    size_t align_sz;
15    align_sz = (sz+sizeof(HDR)-1)
16              & ~(sizeof(HDR)-1);
17
18    _hsta = sbrk(align_sz);
19    _hend = sbrk(0);
20
21    frhd = _hsta;
22    frhd->size = align_sz / sizeof(HDR);
23    frhd->fnx = NULL;
24    //@ghost frhd->isfree = true;
25
26    memleft = frhd->size;
27  }
```

```
28  void* malloc(size_t nbytes)
29  {
30    HDR *nxt, *prv;
31    size_t nunits =
32      (nbytes+sizeof(HDR)-1)/sizeof(HDR) + 1;
33
34    for (prv = NULL, nxt = frhd; nxt;
35         prv = nxt, nxt = nxt->fnx) {
36      if (nxt->size >= nunits) {
37        if (nxt->size > nunits) {
38          nxt->size -= nunits;
39          nxt += nxt->size;
40          nxt->size = nunits;
41        } else {
42          if (prv == NULL)
43            frhd = nxt->fnx;
44          else
45            prv->fnx = nxt->fnx;
46        }
47        memleft -= nunits;
48        //@ghost nxt->isfree = false;
49        return ((void*)(nxt + 1));
50      }
51    }
52    warning("Allocation Failed!");
53    return (NULL);
54  }
```

(a) Globals and initialisation   (b) Allocation

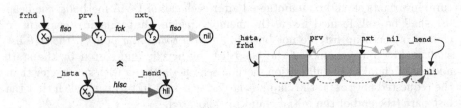

(c) Part of the abstract invariant at line 34 (d) Concrete memory

Fig. 1. Running example with code, concrete memory, and abstract specification

– A well formed heap list segment starting at address X and ending before Y is specified using the predicate $\mathsf{hls}(X;Y)[W]$. The inductive definition of this predicate (see Table 2) requires that chunks do not overlap or leave memory leaks. The variable W registers the sequence of start addresses of chunks in the list segment and it is used to put additional constraints on the fields of these chunks. For DMA with early coalescing of free-chunks (i.e., coalescing at free), we abstract the heap list segments by a stronger predicate, hlsc.

These predicates are combined using the *separation conjunction operator* $*$ of SL, which requires disjointness of memory regions specified by its operands. The bottom of Fig. 1(c) illustrates the heap list abstraction of the concrete memory provided in Fig. 1(d); for readability, the abstraction is represented by its Gaifman graph. The ghost variable hli represents the end of the data segment of the DMA, as returned by sbrk(0).

Hierarchical abstraction of the free list. The first abstraction layer captures the total order of chunks in the heap list. The free list defines a total order over the set of free chunks. The second abstraction layer captures this order using the same SL fragment but over a different set of predicates (see Table 2):

- The predicate $fck(X; Y)$ specifies a chunk $chk(X; ...)$ starting at X, with X.fnx bound to Y and X.isfree set to true.
- The predicate $fls(X; Y)[W]$ specifies a free list segment starting at X, whose last element field fnx points to Y; W registers the sequence of start addresses of free chunks in the list segment. The predicate $flso(X, ...)[W]$ abstracts free list segments sorted by the start address of chunks.

The top of Fig. 1(c) illustrates the free list abstraction by its Gaifman graph.

Finally, the memory shape abstraction is obtained by composing the two abstraction levels using a new operator, denoted by $\ni$, which requires that the set of chunks in the free list abstraction is exactly the sub-set of chunks in the heap list whose field isfree has value true. Notice that the operator $\ni$ can not be replaced by the logical conjunction because we are using the intuitive semantics of SL where spatial formulas fully specify the memory configurations. Or the free list abstraction provides only a partial specification of the heap.

Constraints over sequences of chunk addresses. The predicates presented above specify invariants of DMA independent of parameters of DMA methods. To capture allocation policies that depend on these parameters (e.g., the first-fit policy implemented by the malloc in Fig. 1(b)), we introduce universal constraints over sequences of chunk start addresses W attached to shape atoms, like in [3]. For example, the first-fit policy obtained at line 37 of malloc, is specified by:

$$hlsc(X_0; hli)[W_H] \ni (fls(Y_0; Y_2)[W_1] * fck(Y_2; Y_3) * fls(Y_3; nil)[W_2]) \tag{1}$$
$$\wedge \ Y_2.\texttt{size} \geq \texttt{nunits} \ \wedge \ \forall X \in W_1 \cdot X.\texttt{size} < \texttt{nunits}$$

where Y_2 is the symbolic address stored in the program variable nxt. The general form of universal constraints is $\forall X \in W \cdot A_G \Rightarrow A_U$, where A_G and A_U are arithmetic constraints over X and its fields. To obtain an efficient analysis, we fix A_G and infer A_U. We require that both A_G and A_U belong to a class of constraints supported by some numerical abstract domain (see Sect. 3).

Static analysis with hierarchical shape abstraction. Overall, the analysis algorithm is a standard shape analysis algorithm. To expose fields constrained or assigned by the program statements, it unfolds predicate definitions. To limit the size of the abstraction, the algorithm normalises formulas to maintain only symbolic addresses that are cut-points, i.e., they are stored in the program variables or are sharing points in lists. This transformation of formulas folds back sub-formulas into more general predicates. The set of normalised shape formulas is bounded, so we define the widening operator only for the sequence constraints.

The hierarchical shape requires to solve a number of specific issues (see Sect. 5). The unfolding of shape predicates shall be done at the appropriate level of abstraction. For example, a traversal of the free list requires only unfolding and folding at the free list level. The heap list level may abstract chunks which are explicit in the free list level. Thus, we define protocols for the unfolding and folding operations at each level that are sound as regards the hierarchical composition defined by the operator $\ni$ and with the sequence constraints.

3   Logic Fragment Underlying the Abstract Domain

We formalise in this section a fragment of Separation Logic [24] used to define the values of our abstract domain in Sect. 4.

Syntax. Let AVar be a set of *location variables* representing heap addresses; to simplify the presentation, we consider that AVar contains a special variable nil representing the null address, also denoted by nil. Let SVar be a set of *sequence variables*, interpreted as sequences of heap addresses and IVar be a set of *integer variables*. The full set of *logic variables* is denoted by $\text{Var} = \text{AVar} \cup \text{SVar} \cup \text{IVar}$. The domain of heap addresses is denoted by $\mathbb{A}$ while the domain of values stored in the heap is generically denoted by $\mathbb{V}$, thus $\mathbb{A} \subseteq \mathbb{V}$. To simplify the presentation, we fix HDR, the type of chunk headers, and its fields $\{\texttt{size}, \texttt{fnx}, \texttt{isfree}\}$ typed as declared in Fig. 1. The syntax of formulas is given in Table 1.

Formulas are in disjunctive normal form. Each disjunct is built from a pure formula Π and a spatial formula Σ. Pure formulas Π characterise the values of logic variables using comparisons between location variables, e.g., $X - Y = 0$,

Table 1. Logic syntax

$X, Y \in$ AVar location variables	$W \in$ SVar sequence variables
$i, j \in$ IVar integer variables	$\# \in \{=, \neq, \leq, \geq\}$ comparison operators
$x \in$ Var logic variable	$\vec{x}, \vec{y} \in \text{Var}^*$ vectors of variables
$X.\texttt{f}$ field access term	t, Δ integer term resp. formula

$\varphi ::= \Pi \wedge \Sigma \mid \varphi \vee \varphi \mid \exists x \cdot \varphi$	formulas

$\Pi ::= A \mid \forall X \in W \cdot A \Rightarrow A \mid W = w \mid \Pi \wedge \Pi$	pure formulas
$A ::= X[.\texttt{fnx}] - Y[.\texttt{fnx}] \# t \mid \Delta \mid A \wedge A$	location and integer constraints
$w ::= \epsilon \mid [X] \mid W \mid w.w$	sequence terms

$\Sigma ::= \Sigma_H \ni \Sigma_F$	spatial formulas
$\Sigma_H ::= \texttt{emp} \mid \texttt{blk}(X; Y) \mid \texttt{chd}(X; Y) \mid \texttt{chk}(X; Y) \mid X \mapsto x \mid$	heap formulas
$\quad \texttt{hls}(X; Y)[W] \mid \texttt{hlsc}(X, i; Y, j)[W] \mid \Sigma_H * \Sigma_H$	
$\Sigma_F ::= \texttt{emp} \mid \texttt{fck}(X; Y) \mid \texttt{fls}(X; Y)[W] \mid \texttt{flso}(X, x; Y, y)[W] \mid \Sigma_F * \Sigma_F$	free list formulas

Table 2. Derived predicates

$$\mathsf{chd}(X;Y) \triangleq \mathsf{blk}(X;Y) \wedge \mathtt{sizeof(HDR)} = Y - X \wedge X \equiv_{\mathtt{sizeof(HDR)}} 0$$

$$\mathsf{chk}(X;Y) \triangleq \exists Z \cdot \mathsf{chd}(X;Z) * \mathsf{blk}(Z;Y) \wedge X.\mathtt{size} \times \mathtt{sizeof(HDR)} = Y - X$$

$$\mathsf{fck}(X;Y) \triangleq \exists Z \cdot \mathsf{chk}(X;Z) \wedge X.\mathtt{isfree} = 1 \wedge X.\mathtt{fnx} = Y$$

$$
\begin{aligned}
\mathsf{hls}(X;Y)[W] \triangleq\ & \mathsf{emp} \wedge X = Y \wedge W = \epsilon \\
& \vee\ \exists Z, W' \cdot \mathsf{chk}(X;Z) * \mathsf{hls}(Z;Y)[W'] \wedge W = [X].W'
\end{aligned}
$$

$$
\begin{aligned}
\mathsf{hlsc}(X, f_p; Y, f_\ell)[W] \triangleq\ & \mathsf{emp} \wedge X = Y \wedge W = \epsilon \wedge 0 \leq f_p + f_\ell \leq 1 \\
& \vee\ \exists Z, W', f \cdot \mathsf{chk}(X;Z) * \mathsf{hlsc}(Z, f; Y, f_\ell)[W'] \wedge W = [X].W' \\
& \wedge\ f = X.\mathtt{isfree} \wedge 0 \leq X.\mathtt{isfree} + f_p \leq 1
\end{aligned}
$$

$$
\begin{aligned}
\mathsf{fls}(X;Y)[W] \triangleq\ & \mathsf{emp} \wedge X = Y \wedge W = \epsilon \\
& \vee\ \exists Z, W' \cdot \mathsf{fck}(X;Z) * \mathsf{fls}(Z;Y)[W'] \wedge W = [X].W' \wedge X \neq Y
\end{aligned}
$$

$$
\begin{aligned}
\mathsf{flso}(X, x; Y, y)[W] \triangleq\ & \mathsf{emp} \wedge X = Y \wedge W = \epsilon \wedge x - y \leq 0 \\
& \vee\ \exists Z, W' \cdot \mathsf{fck}(X;Z) * \mathsf{flso}(Z, X; Y, y)[W'] \\
& \wedge\ W = [X].W' \wedge x - X \leq 0
\end{aligned}
$$

constraints Δ over integer terms, and sequence constraints. We let constraints in Δ unspecified, though we assume that they belong to decidable theories, e.g., linear arithmetic. The integer terms t are built over integer variables and field accesses using classic arithmetic operations and constants. We denote by $\Pi_\forall$ (resp. Π_W, $\Pi_\exists$) the set of sub-formulas of Π built from universal constraints (resp. sequence constraints, quantifier free arithmetic constraints).

A spatial formula has two components: Σ_H specifies the heap list and the locations outside this region; Σ_F specifies only the free list. The operator $\ni$ ensures that all locations specified by Σ_F are start addresses of free chunks in the heap list. The atom emp holds iff the domain of the heap is empty. The *points-to atom* $X \mapsto x$ specifies a heap built from one memory block at location X storing the value given by x. The *block atom* $\mathsf{blk}(X;Y)$ holds iff the heap contains a block of memory at location X ending before the location Y. The other predicates are derived from blk and defined in Table 2. Notice that the *chunk header* atom $\mathsf{chd}(X;Y)$ does not expose the fields of the block at location X using the points-to operator of SL. This ease the manipulation of heap list level formulas, e.g., the coalescing of block and chunk atoms into a single block.

Semantics. Formulas φ are interpreted over pairs (I, h) where I is an *interpretation* of logic variables and h is a *heap* mapping a location to a non empty sequence of values stored at this location. Formally, $I \in [(\mathsf{AVar} \cup \mathsf{IVar}) \rightharpoonup \mathbb{V}] \cup [\mathsf{SVar} \rightharpoonup \mathbb{V}^*]$ and $h \in [\mathbb{A} \rightharpoonup \mathbb{V}^+]$ such that $\mathsf{nil} \notin \mathrm{dom}(h)$. Let $h(\ell)[i]$ denote the ith element of $h(\ell)$. Without loss of generality, we consider that a value of type $\mathtt{HDR}$ is a sequence of values indexed by fields. Table 3 provides the most important semantic rules. We following definitions are standard:

Table 3. Logic semantics: main rules

$I, h \models \Sigma_H \ni \Sigma_F$	iff	$I, h \models \Sigma_H$ and $\exists h' \subseteq h$ s.t. $I, h' \models \Sigma_F$
		$\forall \ell \in \mathrm{dom}(h') \cdot h'(\ell)[\texttt{isfree}] = 1$
$I, h \models \mathsf{emp}$	iff	$\mathrm{dom}(h) = \emptyset$
$I, h \models \mathsf{blk}(X; Y)$	iff	$\mathrm{dom}(h) = I(X) \ \wedge \ I(Y) - I(X) = |h(I(X))|$
$I, h \models X \mapsto x$	iff	$\mathrm{dom}(h) = I(X) \ \wedge \ h(I(X))[0] = I(x)$
$I, h \models \Sigma_1 * \Sigma_2$	iff	$\exists h_1, h_2$ s.t. $h = h_1 \uplus h_2$ and $I, h_i \models \Sigma_i$ for $i = 1, 2$
$I, h \models \forall X \in W \cdot A_1 \Rightarrow A_2$	iff	$I(W) = [a_1, \ldots, a_n]$ s.t.
		$\forall i \in (1..n) \ I[X \mapsto a_i], h \models A_1 \Rightarrow A_2$
where		
$h_1 \subseteq h_2$	iff	$\mathrm{dom}(h_1) \subseteq \mathrm{dom}(h_2)$ and $\forall \ell \in \mathrm{dom}(h_1) \cdot h_1(\ell) = h_2(\ell)$
$h_1 \circledast h_2$	iff	$\forall l_1 \in \mathrm{dom}(h_1), l_2 \in \mathrm{dom}(h_2) \cdot l_1 \neq l_2 \wedge$
		$((l_1..l_1 + |h_1(l_1)| - 1) \cap (l_2..l_2 + |h_2(l_2)| - 1) = \emptyset)$
$h = h_1 \uplus h_2$	iff	$h_1 \circledast h_2, \mathrm{dom}(h) = \mathrm{dom}(h_1) \uplus \mathrm{dom}(h_2)$, and
		$(h_1 \uplus h_2)(\ell) \triangleq \begin{cases} h_1(\ell) & \text{if } \ell \in \mathrm{dom}(h_1) \\ h_2(\ell) & \text{if } \ell \in \mathrm{dom}(h_2) \end{cases}$

$$[\![\varphi]\!] \triangleq \{(I, h) \mid I, h \models \varphi\} \qquad \varphi \Rightarrow \psi \text{ iff } [\![\varphi]\!] \subseteq [\![\psi]\!]$$

Transformation rules. The definitions in Table 2 imply a set of lemmas used to transform formulas in abstract values (in Sect. 5). The first set of lemmas is obtained by directing predicate definitions in both directions. For example, each definition $P(\ldots) \triangleq \vee_i \varphi_i$ introduces a set of *folding* lemmas $\varphi_i \Rightarrow P(\ldots)$ and an *unfolding* lemma $P(\ldots) \Rightarrow \vee_i \varphi_i$.

The second class of lemmas concerns list segment predicates in Table 2. The inductive definitions of these predicates satisfy the syntactic constraints defined in [12] for *compositional predicates*. Thus, every $P \in \{\mathsf{hls}, \mathsf{hlsc}, \mathsf{fls}, \mathsf{flso}\}$ satisfies the following *segment composition lemma*:

$$P(X, \vec{x}; Y, \vec{y})[W_1] * P(Y, \vec{y}; Z, \vec{z})[W_2] \wedge W = W_1.W_2 \quad \Rightarrow \quad P(X, \vec{x}; Z, \vec{z})[W] \qquad (2)$$

The reverse implication is applied to split non empty list segments. Finally, the block sub-formulas are removed, split, or folded using the following lemmas:

$$\mathsf{blk}(X; Y) \wedge X \geq Y \quad \Rightarrow \quad \mathsf{emp} \qquad (3)$$

$$\mathsf{blk}(X; Y) \wedge X < Y \quad \Rightarrow \quad \mathsf{blk}(X; Z) * \mathsf{blk}(Z; Y) \wedge X \leq Z \leq Y \qquad (4)$$

$$\mathsf{blk}(X; Y) * \mathsf{blk}(Y'; Z) \wedge X \leq Y = Y' \leq Z \quad \Rightarrow \quad \mathsf{blk}(X; Z). \qquad (5)$$

4 Abstract Domain for Hierarchical Shape Abstraction

We define in this section the join-semilattice $\langle \mathcal{A}, \sqsubseteq, \sqcup \rangle$ used in our analysis. It is parameterised by a numerical join-semilattice $\langle \mathcal{N}, \sqsubseteq^{\mathcal{N}}, \sqcup^{\mathcal{N}} \rangle$.

Concrete states. Let $\mathbb{X}$ be the set of program variables, where hli is a ghost variable of location type. Values in $\mathcal{A}$ represent sets of concrete states $M \in \mathbb{M}$ of the program. A concrete state M encloses an environment $\epsilon \in \mathbb{E} = \mathbb{X} \to \mathbb{A}$ mapping each program variable to its storing location, and a heap $h : \mathbb{A} \to \mathbb{V}^+$ mapping locations to sequences of values. For simplicity, the symbol hli is overloaded to denote the symbolic location stored by hli.

Abstract values. Values in $\mathcal{A}$ are a restricted form of logic formulas. Generally speaking, $\mathcal{A}$ is a *co-fibered product* [6] of an *extended symbolic heap domain* for the spatial part and a *data word* domain [3] for the pure part. More precisely, $\mathcal{A}$ includes a special value for $\top$ and finite mappings of the form:

$$a^\sharp ::= \{ \langle \epsilon_i^\sharp, \Sigma_i(\vec{x}, \vec{W}) \rangle \mapsto \Pi_i(\vec{x}, \vec{W} \cup \{W_H, W_F\}) \}_{i \in I} \tag{6}$$

where $\epsilon_i^\sharp : \mathbb{X} \to \mathsf{Var}$ is an abstract environment mapping program variables to symbolic location variables, Π_i includes arithmetic constraints allowed by $\mathcal{N}$, and the free variables of each formula are detailed. Furthermore, the usage of sequence variables in Σ_i and Π_i is restricted as follows:

R$_1$: A sequence variable is bound to exactly one list segment atom in Σ_i; thus Σ_i defines an injection between list segment atoms and sequence variables.
R$_2$: Π_i contains only the sequence constraints $W_H = w$ and $W_F = w'$, where W_H and W_F are special variables representing the full sequence of start addresses of chunks in the heap resp. free list levels.

In addition, the universal constraints in the pure formulas Π_i are restricted such that, in any formula $\forall X \in W \cdot A_G \Rightarrow A_U$:

R$_3$: A_G and A_U use only terms where X appears inside a field access $X.\mathtt{f}$.
R$_4$: A_G has one of the forms $X.\mathtt{size}\#i$ or $X.\mathtt{isfree} = i$.

These restrictions still permit to specify DMA policies like first-fit (see Eq. (1)) and besides enable an efficient inference of universal constraints.

Internal representation. To ease the manipulation of extended spatial formulas $\langle \epsilon^\sharp, \Sigma \rangle$, we use their Gaifman graph representation, like in Fig. 1(c): nodes represent symbolic locations variables and labeled edges represent the spatial atoms in Σ or mappings in $\epsilon^\sharp$. The universal formulas are represented by a map binding each pair (W, A_G) built from a sequence variable and some guard A_G to a numerical abstract value.

Concretisation. An abstract value of the form (6) represents a formula $\vee_i \exists \vec{x}, \vec{W} \cdot \Sigma_i \wedge \Pi_i \wedge \epsilon_i^\sharp$ where each binding $(v, x) \in \epsilon_i^\sharp$ is encoded by $v \mapsto x$ (v is the location where is stored the program variable v). The false formula represents $\bot$, which corresponds to the empty mapping. Therefore, we define the concretisation $\gamma : \mathcal{A} \to \mathbb{M}$ as the denotation of the formula represented by the abstract value, i.e., $\gamma(a^\sharp) = [\![a^\sharp]\!]$.

Ordering. The partial order $\sqsubseteq$ is defined using a sound procedure inspired by [4, 12]. For any two non trivial abstract values $a^\sharp, b^\sharp \in \mathcal{A}$, $a^\sharp \sqsubseteq b^\sharp$ if for each binding $\langle \epsilon_i^\sharp, \Sigma_i \rangle \mapsto \Pi_i \in a^\sharp$ there exists a binding $\langle \epsilon_j^\sharp, \Sigma_j \rangle \mapsto \Pi_j \in b^\sharp$ such that:

- there is a graph isomorphism between the Gaifman graphs of spatial formula at each level of abstraction from Σ_i to Σ_j; this isomorphism is defined by a bijection $\Psi : \text{img}(\epsilon_i^\sharp) \to \text{img}(\epsilon_j^\sharp)$ between symbolic location variables and a bijection Ω between sequence variables. Thus, $\Sigma_i[\Psi][\Omega] = \Sigma_j$,
- for each sequence constraint $W = w$ in $\Pi_{W,i}$, $\Omega(W) = \Omega(w)$ is a sequence constraint in $\Pi_{W,j}$,
- $\Psi(\Pi_{\exists,i}) \sqsubseteq^{\mathcal{N}} \Pi_{\exists,j}$,
- for each W defined in Σ_i and for each universal constraint $\forall X \in W \cdot A_G \Rightarrow A_U$ in $\Pi_{\forall,i}$, then $\Pi_{\forall,j}$ contains a universal constraint on $W' = \Omega(W)$ of the form $\forall X \in W' \cdot A_G \Rightarrow A_U'$ such that $\Psi(\Pi_{\exists,i} \wedge A_U) \sqsubseteq^{\mathcal{N}} A_U'$.

The following theorem is a consequence of restrictions on the syntax of formulas used in the abstract values.

Theorem 1 ($\sqsubseteq$ soundness). *If $a^\sharp \sqsubseteq b^\sharp$ then $[\![a^\sharp]\!] \subseteq [\![b^\sharp]\!]$.*

Join. Given two non-trivial abstract values, $a^\sharp$ and $b^\sharp$, their join is computed by joining the pure parts of bindings with isomorphic shape graphs [3]. Formally, for each two bindings $\langle \epsilon_i^\sharp, \Sigma_i \rangle \mapsto \Pi_i \in a^\sharp$ and $\langle \epsilon_j^\sharp, \Sigma_j \rangle \mapsto \Pi_j \in b^\sharp$ such that there is a graph isomorphism defined by Ψ and Ω between $\langle \epsilon_i^\sharp, \Sigma_i \rangle$ and $\langle \epsilon_j^\sharp, \Sigma_j \rangle$, we define their join to be the mapping $\{ \langle \epsilon_j^\sharp, \Sigma_j \rangle \mapsto \Pi \}$ where Π is defined by:

- Π includes the sequence constraints of $b^\sharp$, i.e., $\Pi_W \triangleq \Pi_{W,j}$,
- $\Pi_\exists \triangleq \Psi(\Pi_{\exists,i}) \sqcup^{\mathcal{N}} \Pi_{\exists,j}$,
- for each W sequence variable in $\text{dom}(\Omega)$ and for each type of constraint A_G, then $\Pi_\forall$ contains the formula $\forall X \in \Omega(W) \cdot A_G \Rightarrow \Psi(A_{U,i}) \sqcup^{\mathcal{N}} A_{U,j}$ where $A_{U,i}$ (resp. $A_{U,j}$) is the constraint bound to W (resp. $\Omega(W)$) in $\Pi_{\forall,i}$ (resp. $\Pi_{\forall,j}$) for guard A_G or $\top$ if no such constraint exists.

The join of two bindings with non-isomorphic spatial parts is the union of the two bindings. Then, $(a^\sharp \sqcup b^\sharp)$ computes the join of bindings in $a^\sharp$ with each binding in $b^\sharp$. Intuitively, the operator collects the disjuncts of $a^\sharp$ and $b^\sharp$ but replaces the disjuncts with isomorphic spatial parts by one disjunct which maps the spatial part to the join of the pure parts. Two universal constraints are joined when they concern the same sequence variables and guard A_G since $((\forall c \in W \cdot A_G \Rightarrow A_1) \vee (\forall c \in W \cdot A_G \Rightarrow A_2)) \Rightarrow (\forall c \in W \cdot A_G \Rightarrow (A_1 \vee A_2))$.

Theorem 2 ($\sqcup$ soundness). *For any $a^\sharp, b^\sharp \in \mathcal{A}$, $[\![a^\sharp]\!] \cup [\![b^\sharp]\!] \subseteq [\![a^\sharp \sqcup b^\sharp]\!]$.*

Cardinality of the abstract domain. The number of mappings in (6) increases during the symbolic execution by the introduction of new existential variables keeping track of the created chunks. Although the analysis stores only values with linear shape of lists (other shapes are signalled as an error state), the number of linear shapes is exponential in the number of nodes, in general. We avoid this memory explosion by eliminating existential variables using the transformation rules that replace sub-formulas by predicates, an operation classically called *predicate folding*. This operation uses lemmas (2)–(5), as discussed in Sect. 5. Thus, the domain of abstract values is bounded by an exponential on the number of pointer program variables local to DMA methods which is small in general, e.g., ≤ 3 in our benchmark. However, the domain of pure formulas used in the image of abstract values is not bounded because of integer constants. This fact requires to define widening operators for the data word domain used for the pure constraints.

5 Analysis Algorithm

We now describe the specific issues of the static analysis algorithm based on the hierarchical abstract domain presented in Sect. 4.

5.1 Main Principles

The analysis algorithm consists of the following three steps.

```
1  int main(void) {
2    minit(1024);
3    void* p = malloc(20);
4    malloc(20);
5    mfree(p); p = NULL;
6    p = malloc(20);
7    malloc(20);
8    mfree(p); p = NULL;
9    return 0;
10 }
```

Fig. 2. A client program

The first step targets on discovering the properties of the free and heap lists in order to select a suitable set of list segment predicates. It consists of an inter-procedural and non relational *symbolic execution* of a correct client program like the one in Fig. 2. The sets of reachable configurations are represented by abstract values of our domain built over the chunk and block atoms only, i.e., atoms using predicates fck, chk, chd, and blk. Thus, the heap and the free lists are completely unfolded. For example, the abstract value computed for the start location of method malloc (line 28 in Fig. 1) when executing the client program in Fig. 2 is built from four disjuncts whose shape part is given in Fig. 3. The client programs are chosen to reveal the heap list organisation (including chunk coalescing) and the shape of the free list. We don't employ the most general client or a client using an incorrect sequence of calls to the DMA methods in order to speed-up this step and avoiding configurations leading to error states.

The second step transforms the abstract values computed by the previous step to obtain an abstract value representing a pre-condition of the DMA method that constrains the global variables and the parameters of the method. For this, the variables of the client program (e.g., p in Fig. 2) are projected out and folding lemmas are applied to obtain list atoms. For example, the transformation of the abstract value in Fig. 3 leads to an abstract value with one disjunct whose spatial part is $\mathsf{hlsc}(X_0, 0; \mathsf{hli}, 0) \ni \mathsf{flso}(X_0, X_0; \mathsf{nil}, \mathsf{hli})$. The resulting pre-condition is not the weakest one, but it is bigger than (as regards $\sqsubseteq$) the abstract value computed by the symbolic execution at this control location.

The third step does forward, non-relational abstract interpretation [8] starting from the computed pre-conditions of each DMA method. The analysis follows the principles of [7, 9,10] and uses the widening operator to speed-up the convergence of the fix-point computation for program loops. The original points on abstract transformers concern the transfer of information between abstraction layers in the hierarchical unfolding, splitting, and folding of predicates, as detailed in Sects. 5.2 and 5.3. Furthermore, these operations are defined in a modular way, by extending [6] to data word numerical domains. The widening operator uses the widening of data word domain defined in [10].

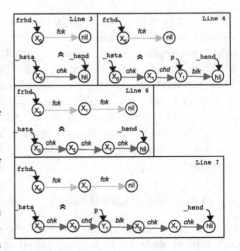

Fig. 3. Spatial formulas at line 28

5.2 Hierarchical Unfolding

Abstract transformers compute over-approximations of post-images of atomic conditions and assignments in the program. For the spatial part, the abstract value is transformed such that the program variables read or written by the program operation are constrained using predicates that may capture the effect of the program operation. This transformation is called *predicate unfolding*.

We define the following partial order between predicates blk < chd < chk < fck < hls, hlsc, fls, flso which intuitively corresponds to an increasing degree of specialisation. For each program operation s and each pointer variable x in s, an atom $P(X; \ldots)$ with $\epsilon^\sharp(x) = X$ is transformed using lemmas in Sect. 3 to obtain the atom $Q(X; \ldots)$ such that $Q \leq P$ is the maximal predicate satisfying:

- if s reads the fields of HDR, then $Q \leq$ fck,
- if s assigns x.isfree or x.fnx, then $Q \leq$ chk,
- if s mutates x using pointer arithmetics or assigns x.size, then $Q \leq$ chd.

We illustrate this procedure on the condition nxt->size > nunits at line 37 in Fig. 1(b), which reads the field size. Applied to the abstract value in Fig. 1(c), it requires to unfold the flso predicate from Y_2, to obtain the formula on top of Fig. 4. To compute the post-image of the next operation, nxt->size -= nunits, the symbolic location Y_2 shall be the root a chd predicate (third case above). Thus, Y_2 is instantiated in the heap list by (i) splitting and then unfolding the hlsc predicate using the segment composition lemma, and (ii) by unfolding chk to obtain the formula at the bottom of Fig. 4. The unfolding of chk requires to remove the fck atom from Y_2 in the free list because its definition is not more satisfied at the heap list abstraction level.

The next assignment, nxt += nxt->size, does not require to transform the predicate rooted in Y_2 because it is already $\leq$ chd. Instead, the transformer adds a new symbolic location Z_1 in the heap list level and constrain it by $Z_1 = Y_2 + Y_2.\texttt{size} \times \texttt{sizeof(HDR)}$. If Z_1 goes beyond the limit of the block of the chunk starting at Y_2 (i.e., outside the interval $[X_1, X_2)$ in Fig. 4), the analysis signals a chunk breaking. Otherwise, the blk atom from X_1 is split using lemma (4) to insert Z_1; the result is given in the top part of Fig. 5.

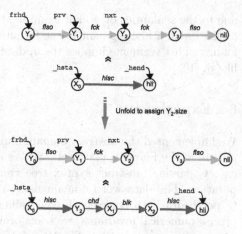

Fig. 4. Hierarchical unfolding at line 38

5.3 Hierarchical Folding

To reduce the size of abstract values, the abstract transformers finish their computation on a binding $\langle \epsilon_i^{\sharp}, \Sigma_i \rangle \mapsto \Pi_i$ by eliminating the symbolic locations which are not cut-points in Σ_i. The elimination uses predicate folding lemmas like (2) or (5) to replace sub-formulas using these variables by one predicate atom. The graph representation eases the computation of sub-formulas matching the left part of a folding lemma.

More precisely, the elimination process has the following steps. First, it searches sequences of sub-formula of the form $\mathsf{chd}(X_0; X_1) * \mathsf{blk}(X_1; X_2) \ldots * \mathsf{blk}(X_{n-1}; X_n)$ where none of X_i $(1 \leq i < n)$ is in $\mathrm{img}(\epsilon^{\sharp})$. Such sub-formulas are folded into $\mathsf{chk}(X_0; X_n)$ if the pure part of the abstract value implies $X_0.\texttt{size} \times \texttt{sizeof(HDR)} = X_n - X_0$ (see Table 2). We use the variable elimination provided by the numerical domain $\mathcal{N}$ to project out $\{X_1, \ldots, X_{n-1}\}$ from the pure part.

Furthermore, if the pure part implies $X_0.\texttt{isfree} = 1$, then the chunk atom (and its start address) is promoted as fck to the free list level.

This step is illustrated on sub-formulas $\mathsf{chd}(Y_2; X_1) * \mathsf{blk}(X_1; Z_1)$ at the top of Fig. 5. The second step folds hlsc list segments by applying their inductive definition and the composition lemma (2). The atoms $\mathsf{chk}(X_0; \ldots)$ for which the free list level contains an atom $\mathsf{fck}(X_0; \ldots)$ may be folded at the heap list level into list segments

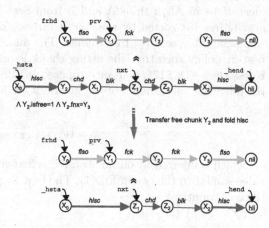

Fig. 5. Hierarchical folding after line 48

due to the semantics of $\ni$. For example, the chunk starting from location Y_2 is folded inside a hlsc segment in the formula at the bottom of Fig. 5. Notice that folding of list segments implies the update of sequence and universal constraints like in [10].

6   Experiments

We implemented the abstract domain and the analysis algorithm in Ocaml as a plug-in of the Frama-C platform [18]. We are using several modules of Frama-C, e.g., C parsing, abstract syntax tree transformations, and the fix-point computation. The data word domain uses as numerical join-lattice $\mathcal{N}$ the library of polyhedra with congruence constraints included in APRON [16]. To obtain precise numerical invariants, we transform program statements using bit-vector operations (e.g., line 16 of Fig. 1(a)) into statements allowed by the polyhedra domain which over-approximate the original effet.

Table 4. Benchmark of DMA

DMA	LOC	List Pred.	Time (s)	$|a^{\sharp}|$	$|W_H|/|W_F|$	Invariants
DKFF[19]	176	hlsc, flso	0.05	25	8/5	first-fit, MIN_SIZE-size
DKBF[19]	130	hlsc, flso	0.05	26	8/6	best-fit, MIN_SIZE-size
LA[1]	181	hlsc, flso	0.07	25	8/5	first-fit, 0-size
DKNF[19]	137	hlsc, flso	0.05	30	8/6	first-fit, MIN_SIZE-size
KR[17]	284	hlsc, flso	2.8	32	8/6	first-fit, 0-size

We applied our analysis on the benchmark of free list DMA in Table 4. (Detailed experimental results are available in [26].) DKFF and DKBF are implementations of Algorithms A and B from Sect. 2.5 of [19]. These DMA keep an acyclic free list sorted by the start addresses of chunks. The deallocation does coalescing of successive free chunks. The allocation implements a first-fit resp. best-fit policy such that the fitting chunk is not split if the remaining free part is less than MIN_SIZE (variant proposed in [19]). This property is expressed by the following sub-formula of the invariant "MIN_SIZE-size" (for MIN_SIZE=8):

$$\forall X \in W_H \cdot X.\texttt{size} \geq 8 \tag{7}$$

which is inferred by our analysis. The first-fit policy is implied by an abstract value similar to the one in Eq. (1). The best-fit policy is implied by a value using the constraint:

$$\forall X \in W_i \cdot X.\texttt{size} \geq \texttt{rsz} \Rightarrow X.\texttt{size} \geq Y.\texttt{size} \tag{8}$$

where rsz is the requested size, Y is the symbolic address of the fitting chunk, and W_i represents a list segment around the fitting chunk. LA is our running example in Fig. 1; it follows the same principles as DKFF, but get rid of the constraint for chunk splitting. For this case study, our analyser infers the "0-size" invariant, i.e., $\forall X \in W_H \cdot X.\texttt{size} \geq 4$ (=sizeof(HDR)). Notice that the code analysed fixes an obvious problem of the malloc method published in [1]. DKNF implements the next-fit policy using the "roving pointer" technique proposed in [19]: a global variable points to the chunk in the free list involved in the last allocation or deallocation; malloc searches for a fitting free chunk starting from this pointer. Thus, the next-fit policy is a first-fit from the roving pointer. DKNF is challenging because the roving pointer introduces a case splitting that increases the size (number of disjuncts) in abstract values. The KR allocator [17] keeps a circular singly linked list, circularly sorted by the chunk start addresses; the start of the free list points to the last deallocated block. The circular shape of the list requires to keep track of the free chunk with the biggest start address and this increases the size of the abstract values.

The analysis times reported in Table 4 have been obtained on a 2.53 GHz Intel Core 2 Duo laptop with 4 GB of RAM. They correspond to the total time of the three steps of the analysis starting from the client given in Fig. 2. The universally quantified invariants inferred for DMA policies are given in the last column. Columns $|a^\sharp|$ and $|W_H|/|W_F|$ provide the maximum number of disjuncts generated for an abstract value resp. the maximum number of predicate atoms in each abstraction level.

7   Related Work and Conclusion

Our analysis infers complex invariants of free list DMA implementations due to the combination of two ingredients: the hierarchical representation of the shape of the memory region managed by the DMA and an abstract domain for the numerical constraints based on universally quantified formulas. The abstract domain has a clear logical definition, which facilitates the use of the inferred invariants by other verification methods.

The proposed abstract domain extends previous works [3,5,10,11,21]. We consider the SL fragment proposed in [5] to analyse programs using pointer arithmetic. We enrich this fragment in both spatial and pure formulas to infer a richer class of invariants. E.g., we add a heap list level to track properties like chunk overlapping and universal constraints to infer first-fit policy invariants.

The split of shape abstraction on levels is inspired by work on overlaid data structures [11,21]. We consider here a specific overlapping schema based on set inclusion which is adequate for the class of DMA we consider. We propose new abstract transformers which do not require user annotations like in [21]. Another hierarchical analysis of shape and numeric properties has been proposed in [25]. They consider the analysis of linked data structures coded in arrays and track the shape of these data structures and not the organisation of the set of free chunks. Their approach is not based on logic and the invariants inferred on the content of list segments are simpler.

Our abstract domain includes a simpler version of the data word domain proposed in [3,10], since the universal constraints quantify only one position in the list. Several abstract domains have been defined to infer invariants over arrays, e.g., [13] for array sizes, [14,15] for array content. These works infer invariants of different kind on array partitions and they can not be applied directly to sequences of addresses. Recently, [22] defined an abstract domain for the analysis of array properties and applies it to the Minix 1.1 DMA, which uses chunks of fixed size. A modular combination of shape and numerical domains has been proposed in [6]. We extend their proposal to combine shape domains with domains on sequences of integers. Precise analyses exist for low level code in C [23] or for binary code [2]. They efficiently track properties about pointer alignment and memory region separations, but can not infer shape properties.

References

1. Aldridge, L.: Memory allocation in C. In: Embedded Systems Programming, pp. 35–42, August 2008
2. Balakrishnan, G., Reps, T.: Recency-abstraction for heap-allocated storage. In: Yi, K. (ed.) SAS 2006. LNCS, vol. 4134, pp. 221–239. Springer, Heidelberg (2006). doi:10.1007/11823230_15
3. Bouajjani, A., Dragoi, C., Enea, C., Sighireanu, M.: On inter-procedural analysis of programs with lists and data. In: PLDI, pp. 578–589. ACM (2011)
4. Bouajjani, A., Drăgoi, C., Enea, C., Sighireanu, M.: Accurate invariant checking for programs manipulating lists and arrays with infinite data. In: Chakraborty, S., Mukund, M. (eds.) ATVA 2012. LNCS, pp. 167–182. Springer, Heidelberg (2012). doi:10.1007/978-3-642-33386-6_14
5. Calcagno, C., Distefano, D., O'Hearn, P.W., Yang, H.: Beyond reachability: shape abstraction in the presence of pointer arithmetic. In: Yi, K. (ed.) SAS 2006. LNCS, vol. 4134, pp. 182–203. Springer, Heidelberg (2006). doi:10.1007/11823230_13
6. Chang, B.E., Rival, X.: Modular construction of shape-numeric analyzers. In: Semantics, Abstract Interpretation, and Reasoning about Programs, EPTCS, vol. 129, pp. 161–185 (2013)
7. Chang, B.-Y.E., Rival, X., Necula, G.C.: Shape analysis with structural invariant checkers. In: Nielson, H.R., Filé, G. (eds.) SAS 2007. LNCS, vol. 4634, pp. 384–401. Springer, Heidelberg (2007). doi:10.1007/978-3-540-74061-2_24
8. Cousot, P., Cousot, R.: Abstract interpretation: a unified lattice model for static analysis of programs by construction or approximation of fixpoints. In: POPL, pp. 238–252. ACM (1977)
9. Distefano, D., O'Hearn, P.W., Yang, H.: A local shape analysis based on separation logic. In: Hermanns, H., Palsberg, J. (eds.) TACAS 2006. LNCS, vol. 3920, pp. 287–302. Springer, Heidelberg (2006). doi:10.1007/11691372_19
10. Dragoi, C.: Automated verification of heap-manipulating programs with infinite data. PhD thesis, University Paris Diderot (2011)
11. Drăgoi, C., Enea, C., Sighireanu, M.: Local shape analysis for overlaid data structures. In: Logozzo, F., Fähndrich, M. (eds.) SAS 2013. LNCS, vol. 7935, pp. 150–171. Springer, Heidelberg (2013). doi:10.1007/978-3-642-38856-9_10
12. Enea, C., Sighireanu, M., Wu, Z.: On automated lemma generation for separation logic with inductive definitions. In: Finkbeiner, B., Pu, G., Zhang, L. (eds.)

ATVA 2015. LNCS, vol. 9364, pp. 80–96. Springer, Cham (2015). doi:10.1007/978-3-319-24953-7_7

13. Gulwani, S., Lev-Ami, T., Sagiv, S.: A combination framework for tracking partition sizes. In: POPL, pp. 239–251. ACM (2009)

14. Gulwani, S., McCloskey, B., Tiwari, A.: Lifting abstract interpreters to quantified logical domains. In: POPL, pp. 235–246. ACM (2008)

15. Halbwachs, N., Péron, M.: Discovering properties about arrays in simple programs. In: PLDI, pp. 339–348. ACM (2008)

16. Jeannet, B., Miné, A.: APRON: a library of numerical abstract domains for static analysis. In: Bouajjani, A., Maler, O. (eds.) CAV 2009. LNCS, vol. 5643, pp. 661–667. Springer, Heidelberg (2009). doi:10.1007/978-3-642-02658-4_52

17. Kernighan, B.W., Ritchie, D.: The C Programming Language, 2nd edn. Prentice-Hall, Englewood Cliffs (1988)

18. Kirchner, F., Kosmatov, N., Prevosto, V., Signoles, J., Yakobowski, B.: Frama-C: a software analysis perspective. FAC 27(3), 573–609 (2015)

19. Knuth, D.E.: The Art of Computer Programming, Volume I: Fundamental Algorithms, 2nd edn. Addison-Wesley, Reading (1973)

20. Lea, D.: dlmalloc (2012). ftp://gee.cs.oswego.edu/pub/misc/malloc.c

21. Lee, O., Yang, H., Petersen, R.: Program analysis for overlaid data structures. In: Gopalakrishnan, G., Qadeer, S. (eds.) CAV 2011. LNCS, vol. 6806, pp. 592–608. Springer, Heidelberg (2011). doi:10.1007/978-3-642-22110-1_48

22. Liu, J., Rival, X.: Abstraction of arrays based on non contiguous partitions. In: D'Souza, D., Lal, A., Larsen, K.G. (eds.) VMCAI 2015. LNCS, vol. 8931, pp. 282–299. Springer, Heidelberg (2015). doi:10.1007/978-3-662-46081-8_16

23. Albert, E., Arenas, P., Genaim, S., Puebla, G.: Field-sensitive value analysis by field-insensitive analysis. In: Cavalcanti, A., Dams, D.R. (eds.) FM 2009. LNCS, vol. 5850, pp. 370–386. Springer, Heidelberg (2009). doi:10.1007/978-3-642-05089-3_24

24. O'Hearn, P., Reynolds, J., Yang, H.: Local reasoning about programs that alter data structures. In: Fribourg, L. (ed.) CSL 2001. LNCS, vol. 2142, pp. 1–19. Springer, Heidelberg (2001). doi:10.1007/3-540-44802-0_1

25. Sotin, P., Rival, X.: Hierarchical shape abstraction of dynamic structures in static blocks. In: Jhala, R., Igarashi, A. (eds.) APLAS 2012. LNCS, vol. 7705, pp. 131–147. Springer, Heidelberg (2012). doi:10.1007/978-3-642-35182-2_10

26. CELIA extensions. http://www.irif.fr/~sighirea/celia/plus.html

27. Wilson, P.R., Johnstone, M.S., Neely, M., Boles, D.: Dynamic storage allocation: a survey and critical review. In: Baler, H.G. (ed.) IWMM 1995. LNCS, vol. 986, pp. 1–116. Springer, Heidelberg (1995). doi:10.1007/3-540-60368-9_19

A Productivity Checker for Logic Programming

Ekaterina Komendantskaya[1], Patricia Johann[2(✉)], and Martin Schmidt[3]

[1] Heriot-Watt University, Edinburgh, Scotland, UK
ek19@hw.ac.uk
[2] Appalachian State University, Boone, NC, USA
johannp@appstate.edu
[3] University of Osnabrück, Osnabrück, Germany

Abstract. Automated analysis of recursive derivations in logic programming is known to be a hard problem. Both termination and non-termination are undecidable problems in Turing-complete languages. However, some declarative languages offer a practical work-around for this problem, by making a clear distinction between whether a program is meant to be understood inductively or coinductively. For programs meant to be understood inductively, termination must be guaranteed, whereas for programs meant to be understood coinductively, productive non-termination (or "productivity") must be ensured. In practice, such classification helps to better understand and implement some non-terminating computations.

Logic programming was one of the first declarative languages to make this distinction: in the 1980's, Lloyd and van Emden's "computations at infinity" captured the big-step operational semantics of derivations that produce infinite terms as answers. In modern terms, computations at infinity describe "global productivity" of computations in logic programming. Most programming languages featuring coinduction also provide an observational, or small-step, notion of productivity as a computational counterpart to global productivity. This kind of productivity is ensured by checking that finite initial fragments of infinite computations can always be observed to produce finite portions of their infinite answer terms.

In this paper we introduce a notion of *observational productivity* for logic programming as an algorithmic approximation of global productivity, give an effective procedure for semi-deciding observational productivity, and offer an implemented automated observational productivity checker for logic programs.

Keywords: Logic programming · Corecursion · Coinduction · Termination · Productivity

1 Introduction

Induction is pervasive in programming and program verification. It arises in definitions of finite data (e.g., lists, trees, and other algebraic data types), in

© Springer International Publishing AG 2017
M.V. Hermenegildo and P. Lopez-Garcia (Eds.): LOPSTR 2016, LNCS 10184, pp. 168–186, 2017.
DOI: 10.1007/978-3-319-63139-4_10

program semantics (e.g., of finite iteration and recursion), and proofs (e.g., of properties of finite data and processes). Coinduction, too, is important in these arenas, arising in definitions of infinite data (e.g., lazily defined infinite streams), in program semantics (e.g., of concurrency), and in proofs (e.g., of observational equivalence, or bisimulation, of potentially infinite processes). It is thus desirable to have good support for both induction and coinduction in systems for reasoning about programs.

Given a logic program P and a term A, SLD-resolution provides a mechanism for automatically (and inductively) inferring that $P \vdash A$ holds, i.e., that P logically entails A. The "answer" for a program P and a query $? \leftarrow A$ is a substitution σ computed from P and A by SLD-resolution. Soundness of SLD-resolution ensures that $P \vdash \sigma(A)$ holds, so we also say that P *computes* $\sigma(A)$.

Example 1 (Inductive logic program). The program P_1 codes the Peano numbers:
0. nat(0) $\leftarrow$
1. nat(s(X)) $\leftarrow$ nat(X)
To answer the question *"Does $P_1 \vdash$ nat(s(X)) hold?"*, we represent it as the logic programming (LP) query $? \leftarrow$ nat(s(X)) and resolve it with P_1. It is standard in implementations of traditional LP to use a topmost clause selection strategy, which resolves goals against clauses in the order in which they appear in the program. Topmost clause selection gives the derivation nat(s(X)) $\rightarrow$ nat(X) $\rightarrow$ true for P_1 and $? \leftarrow$ nat(s(X)), which computes the answer $\{X \mapsto 0\}$ in its last step. Since P_1 computes nat(s(0)), one answer to our question is "Yes, provided X is 0."

While inductive properties of terminating computations are quite well understood [14], non-terminating LP computations are notoriously difficult to reason about, and can arise even for programs that are intended to be inductive:

Example 2 (Coinductive meaning of inductive logic program). If P_1' is obtained by reversing the order of the clauses in the program P_1 from Example 1, then the SLD-derivation for program P_1' and query $? \leftarrow$ nat(s(X)) does not terminate under standard topmost clause selection. Instead, it results in an attempt to compute the "answer" $\{X \mapsto s(s(...))\}$ by repeatedly resolving with Clause 1. Nevertheless, P_1' is still computationally meaningful, since it computes the first limit ordinal *at infinity*, in the terminology of [14].

Some programs do not admit terminating computations under *any* selection strategy:

Example 3 (Coinductive logic program). No derivation for the query $? \leftarrow$ stream(X) and the program P_2 comprising the clause
0. stream(scons(0, Y)) $\leftarrow$ stream(Y)
terminates with an answer, be it success or otherwise. Nevertheless, P_2 has computational meaning: it computes the infinite stream of 0s at infinity.

The importance of developing sufficient infrastructure to support coinduction in automated proving has been argued across several communities;

see, e.g., [13,17,21]. In LP, the ability to work with non-terminating and coinductive programs depends crucially on understanding the structural properties of non-terminating SLD-derivations. To illustrate, consider the non-terminating programs P_3, P_4, and P_5:

Program	Program definition	For query ? ← p(X), computes the answer:
P_3	p(X) ← p(X)	id
P_4	p(X) ← p(f(X))	id
P_5	p(f(X)) ← p(X)	$\{X \mapsto f(f...)\}$

Programs P_3 and P_4 each loop without producing any substitutions at all; only P_5 computes an infinite term at infinity. It is of course not a coincidence that only P_5 resembles a (co)inductive data definition by pattern matching on a constructor, as is commonly used in functional programming.

When an infinite SLD-derivation computes an infinite object, and this object can be successively approximated by applying to the initial query the substitutions computed at each step of the derivation, the derivation is said to be *globally productive*. The only derivation for program P_5 and the query ? ← p(X) is globally productive since it approximates, in the sense just described, the infinite term p(f(f...)). That is, it computes p(f(f...)) at infinity. Programs P_2 and P_1' similarly give rise to globally productive derivations. But no derivations for P_3 or P_4 are globally productive.

Since global productivity determines which non-terminating logic programs can be seen as defining coinductive data structures, we would like to identify exactly when a program is globally productive. But porting functional programming methods of ensuring productivity by static syntactic checks is hardly possible. Unlike pattern matching in functional programming, SLD-resolution is based on *unification*, which has very different operational properties—including termination and productivity properties—from pattern matching. For example, programs P_1, P_1', P_2, and P_5 are all terminating by term-matching SLD-resolution, i.e., resolution in which unifiers are restricted to matchers, as in term rewriting. We thus call this kind of derivations *rewriting derivations*.

Example 4 (Coinductive program defining an irrational infinite term). The program P_6 comprises the single clause
0. from(X, scons(X, Y)) ← from(s(X), Y)
For P_6 and the query ? ← from(0, Y), SLD-resolution computes at infinity the answer substitution $\{Y \mapsto [0, s(0), s(s(0)), ...]\}$. Here $[t_1, t_2, ...]$ abbreviates scons(t_1, scons(t_2, ...)), and similarly in the remainder of this paper. This derivation depends crucially on unification since variables occurring in the two arguments to from in the clause head overlap. If we restrict to rewriting, then there are no successful derivations (terminating or non-terminating) for this choice of program and query.

Example 4 shows that any analysis of global productivity must necessarily rely on specific properties of the operational semantics of LP, rather than on program syntax alone. It has been observed in [9,11] that one way to distinguish globally productive programs operationally is to identify those that admit infinite SLD-derivations, but whose rewriting derivations always terminate. We call this program property *observational productivity*. The programs P_1, P_1', P_2, P_5, P_6 are all observationally productive.

The key observation underlying observational productivity is that terminating rewriting derivations can be viewed as points of finite observation in infinite derivations. Consider again program P_6 and query ? $\leftarrow$ from(0, Y) from Example 4. Drawing rewriting derivations vertically and unification-based resolution steps horizontally, we see that each unification substitution applied to the original query effectively observes a further fragment of the stream computed at infinity:

$$
\begin{array}{llll}
& \{\mathtt{X} \mapsto [\mathtt{0}, \mathtt{X}']\} & \{\mathtt{X}' \mapsto [\mathtt{s}(\mathtt{0}), \mathtt{X}'']\} & \\
& \xrightarrow{\qquad} & \xrightarrow{\qquad} & \to \dots \\
\mathtt{from}(\mathtt{0}, \mathtt{X}) & \mathtt{from}(\mathtt{0}, [\mathtt{0}, \mathtt{X}']) & \mathtt{from}(\mathtt{0}, [\mathtt{0}, \mathtt{s}(\mathtt{0}), \mathtt{X}'']) & \\
& \mathtt{from}(\mathtt{s}(\mathtt{0}), \mathtt{X}') & \mathtt{from}(\mathtt{s}(\mathtt{0}), [\mathtt{s}(\mathtt{0}), \mathtt{X}'']) & \\
& & \mathtt{from}(\mathtt{s}(\mathtt{s}(\mathtt{0})), \mathtt{X}'') &
\end{array}
$$

If we compute unifiers only when rewriting derivations terminate, then the resulting derivations exhibit consumer-producer behaviour: rewriting steps consume structure (here, the constructor scons), and unification steps produce more structure (here, new sconses) for subsequent rewriting steps to consume. This style of interleaving matching and unification steps was called *structural resolution* (or S-resolution) in [9,12].

Model-theoretic properties of S-resolution relative to least and greatest Herbrand models of programs were studied in [12]. In this paper, we provide a suitable algorithm for semi-deciding observational productivity of logic programs, and present its implementation [19]; see also Appendix B online. By definition, observational productivity of a program P is in fact a conjunction of two properties of P:

1. *universal observability*: termination of *all* rewriting derivations, and
2. *existential liveness*: existence of *at least one* non-terminating S-resolution or SLD-resolution derivation.

While the former property is universal, the latter must be existential. For example, the program P_1 defining the Peano numbers can have both inductive and coinductive meaning. When determining that a program is observationally productive, we must certify that the program actually *does* admit derivations that produce infinite data, i.e., that it actually *can* be seen as a coinductive definition. Our algorithm for semi-deciding observational productivity therefore combines two checks:

1. *guardedness checks* that semi-decide universal observability: if a program is guarded, then it is universally observable. (The converse is not true in general.)
2. *liveness invariant checks* ensuring that, if a program is guarded and exhibits an invariant in its consumption-production of constructors, then it is existentially live.

This is the first work to develop productivity checks for LP. An alternative approach to coinduction in LP, known as CoLP [7,21], detects loops in derivations and closes them coinductively. However, loop detection was not intended as a tool for the study of productivity and, indeed, is insufficient for that purpose: programs P_3, P_4 and P_5, of which only the latter is productive, are all treated similarly by CoLP, and all give coinductive proofs via its loop detection mechanism.

Our approach also differs from the usual termination checking algorithms in term-rewriting systems (TRS) [1,8,22] and LP [3,15,16,18,20]. Indeed, these algorithms focus on guaranteeing termination, rather than productivity; see Sect. 5. And although the notion of productivity has been studied in TRS [4,5], the actual technical analysis of productivity is rather different there because it considers infinitary properties of rewriting, whereas observational productivity relies on termination of rewriting.

The rest of this paper is organised as follows. In Sect. 2 we introduce a *contraction ordering* on terms that extends the more common lexicographic ordering, and argue that this extension is needed for our productivity analysis. We also recall that static guardedness checks do not work for LP. In Sect. 3 we employ contraction orderings in dynamic guardedness checks and present a decidable property, called $GC2$, that characterises guardedness of a single rewriting derivation, and thus certifies existential observability. In Sect. 4 we employ $GC2$ to develop an algorithm, called $GC3$, that analyses *consumer-producer* invariants of S-resolution derivations to certify universal observability. For universally observable programs, these invariants also serve as liveness invariant checks. We also prove that $GC3$ indeed semi-decides observational productivity. In Sect. 5 we discuss related work and in Sect. 6 we discuss our implementation and applications of the productivity checker. In Sect. 7 we conclude the paper.

2   Contraction Orderings on Terms

In this section, we will introduce the contraction ordering on first-order terms, on which our productivity checks will rely. We work with the standard definition of first-order logic programs. A *signature* Σ consists of a set $\mathcal{F}$ of function symbols $f, g, \ldots$ each equipped with an arity. Nullary (0-ary) function symbols are constants. We also assume a countable set Var of variables, and a set $\mathcal{P}$ of predicate symbols each equipped with an arity. We have the following standard definition for terms, formulas and Horn clauses:

Definition 1 (Syntax of Horn clauses and programs).
  Terms Term ::= Var | $\mathcal{F}(Term, \ldots, Term)$
  Atoms At ::= $\mathcal{P}(Term, \ldots, Term)$
  (Horn) clauses CH ::= $At \leftarrow At, \ldots, At$
  Logic programs Prog ::= $CH, \ldots, CH$

In what follows, we will use letters A, B with subscripts to refer to elements of At. Given a program P, we assume all clauses are indexed by natural numbers starting from 0. When we need to refer to ith clause of program P, we will use notation $P(i)$. To refer to the head of clause $P(i)$, we will use notation $head(P(i))$.

A *substitution* is a total function $\sigma : Var \to Term$. Substitutions are extended from variables to terms as usual: if $t \in Term$ and σ is a substitution, then the *application* $\sigma(t)$ is a result of applying σ to all variables in t. A substitution σ is a *unifier* for t, u if $\sigma(t) = \sigma(u)$, and is a *matcher* for t against u if $\sigma(t) = u$. A substitution σ is a *most general unifier* (*mgu*) for t and u if it is a unifier for t and u and is more general than any other such unifier. A *most general matcher* (*mgm*) σ for t against u is defined analogously.

We can view every term and atom as a tree. Following standard definitions [2, 14], such trees can be indexed by elements of a suitably defined tree language. Let $\mathbb{N}^*$ be the set of all finite words (i.e., sequences) over the set $\mathbb{N}$ of natural numbers. A set $L \subseteq \mathbb{N}^*$ is a *(finitely branching) tree language* if the following two conditions hold: (i) for all $w \in \mathbb{N}^*$ and all $i, j \in \mathbb{N}$, if $wj \in L$ then $w \in L$ and, for all $i < j$, $wi \in L$, and (ii) for all $w \in L$, the set of all $i \in \mathbb{N}$ such that $wi \in L$ is finite. A tree language L is *finite* if it is a finite subset of $\mathbb{N}^*$, and *infinite* otherwise. Term trees (for terms and atoms over a given signature) are defined as mappings from a tree language L to that signature, see [2,9,14]. Informally speaking, every symbol occurring in a term or an atom receives an index from L.

In what follows, we will work with term tree representations of terms and atoms, and for brevity we will refer to term trees simply as *terms*. We will use notation $t(w)$ when we need to talk about the element of the term t indexed by a word $w \in L$. Note that leaf nodes are always given by variables or constants.

Example 5. Given $L = \{\epsilon, 0, 00, 01\}$, the atom `stream(scons(0, Y))` can be seen as the term tree t given by the map $t(\epsilon) = $ `stream`, $t(0) = $ `scons`, $t(00) = $ `0`, $t(01) = $ `Y`.

We can use such indexing to refer to subterms, and notation $subterm(t, w)$ will refer to the subterm of term t starting at node w. In Example 5, taking $t = $ `stream(scons(0, Y))` gives that $subterm(t, 0)$ is `scons(0, Y)`.

Two of the most popular tools for termination analysis of declarative programs are lexicographic ordering and (recursive) path ordering of terms. Informally, these can be adopted to the LP setting as follows. Suppose we have a clause $A \leftarrow B_1, \ldots, B_i, \ldots, B_n$, and want to check whether each B_i sharing the predicate with A is "smaller" than A, since this guarantees that no infinite rewriting derivation is triggered by this clause. For lexicographic ordering we will write $B_i <_l A$ and for path ordering we will write $B_i <_p A$.

Using standard orderings to prove universal observability works well for program P_2, since `stream(Y)` $<_l$ `stream(scons(0, Y))` and `stream(Y)` $<_p$ `stream(scons(0, Y))`, and so any rewriting derivation for P_2 terminates. But universal observability of P_6 cannot be shown by this method. Indeed, none of the four orderings `from(X, scons(X, Y))` $<_l$ `from(s(X), Y)`, `from(s(X), Y)` $<_l$ `from(X, scons(X, Y))`, `from(X, scons(X, Y))` $<_p$ `from(s(X), Y)`, and `from(s(X), Y)` $<_p$ `from(X, scons(X, Y))` holds because the subterms pairwise disagree on the ordering. This situation is common for LP, where some arguments hold input data and some hold output data, so that some decrease while others increase in recursive calls. Nevertheless, P_6 *is* universally observable, and we want to be able to infer this. Studying the S-resolution derivation for P_6 in Sect. 1, we note that universal observability of P_6 is guaranteed by contraction of from's second argument. It is therefore sufficient to establish that terms get smaller in only one argument. This inspires our definition of a *contraction ordering*, which takes advantage of the tree representation of terms.

Definition 2 (Contraction, recursive contraction). *If t_1 and t_2 are terms, then t_2 is a contraction of t_1 (written $t_1 \triangleright t_2$) if there is a leaf node $t_2(w)$ on a branch B in t_2, and there exists a branch B' in t_1 that is identical to B up to node w, but $t_1(w)$ is not a leaf. If, in addition, subterm(t_1, w) contains the symbol given by $t_2(w)$, then t_2 is a recursive contraction of t_1.*

We distinguish variable contractions *and* constant contractions *according as $t_2(w)$ is a variable or constant, and call subterm(t_1, w) a reducing subterm for $t_1 \triangleright t_2$ at node w. We call subterm(t_1, w) a recursive, variable, or constant reducing subterm according as $t_1 \triangleright t_2$ is a recursive, variable or constant contraction.*

Example 6 (Contraction   orderings).   We   have $\texttt{from}(\texttt{X}, \texttt{scons}(\texttt{X}, \texttt{Y})) \triangleright$
$\texttt{from}(\texttt{s}(\texttt{X}), \texttt{Y})$, since the leaf Y in the latter is "replaced" by the term $\texttt{scons}(\texttt{X}, \texttt{Y})$ in the former. Formally, $\texttt{scons}(\texttt{X}, \texttt{Y})$ is a recursive and variable reducing subterm. It can be used to certify termination of all rewriting derivations for P_6. Note that $\texttt{from}(\texttt{s}(\texttt{X}), \texttt{Y}) \triangleright \texttt{from}(\texttt{X}, \texttt{scons}(\texttt{X}, \texttt{Y}))$ also holds, with (recursive and variable) reducing subterm $\texttt{s}(\texttt{X})$.

The fact that $\triangleright$ is not well-founded makes reasoning about termination delicate. Nevertheless, contractions emerge as precisely the additional ingredient needed to formulate our productivity check for guarded (and therefore universally observable) programs.

In general, static termination checking for LP suffers serious limitations; see, e.g., [3]. The following example illustrates this phenomenon.

Example 7 (Contraction ordering on clause terms is insufficient for termination checks). The program P_7, which is not universally observable, is given by mutual recursion:

0. $\texttt{p}(\texttt{s}(\texttt{X1}), \texttt{X2}, \texttt{Y1}, \texttt{Y2}) \leftarrow \texttt{q}(\texttt{X2}, \texttt{X2}, \texttt{Y1}, \texttt{Y2})$
1. $\texttt{q}(\texttt{X1}, \texttt{X2}, \texttt{s}(\texttt{Y1}), \texttt{Y2}) \leftarrow \texttt{p}(\texttt{X1}, \texttt{X2}, \texttt{Y2}, \texttt{Y2})$

No two terms from the same clause of P_7 can be related by any contraction ordering because their head symbols differ. But recursion arises for P_7 when a derivation calls its two clauses alternately, so we would like to examine rewriting derivations for queries, such as ? $\leftarrow \texttt{p}(\texttt{s}(\texttt{X1}), \texttt{X2}, \texttt{s}(\texttt{Y1}), \texttt{Y2})$ and ? $\leftarrow \texttt{p}(\texttt{s}(\texttt{X1}), \texttt{s}(\texttt{X2}), \texttt{s}(\texttt{Y1}), \texttt{s}(\texttt{Y2}))$, that exhibit its recursive nature. Unfortunately, such queries are not given directly by P_7's syntax, and so are not available for static program analysis.

Since static checking for contraction ordering in clauses is not sufficient, we will define dynamic checks in the next section. The idea is to build a rewriting tree for each clause, and check whether the term trees featured in that derivation tree satisfy any contraction ordering.

3 Rewriting Trees: Guardedness Checks for Rewriting Derivations

To properly reason about rewriting derivations in LP, we need to take into account that (i) in LP, unlike, e.g., in TRS, we have conjuncts of terms in the bodies of clauses, and (ii) a logic program can have overlapping clauses, i.e., clauses whose heads unify. These two facts have been analysed in detail in the LP literature, usually using the notion of and-or-trees and, where optimisation has been concerned, and-or-parallel trees. We carry on this tradition and consider a variant of and-or trees for derivations. However, the trees we consider are not formed by general SLD-resolution, but rather by term matching resolution. *Rewriting trees* are so named because each of their edges represents a term matching resolution step, i.e., a matching step as in term rewriting.

Definition 3 (Rewriting tree). *Let P be a logic program with n clauses, and A be an atom. The* rewriting tree *for P and A is the possibly infinite tree T satisfying the following properties:*

- *A is the root of T*
- *Each node in T is either an and-node or an or-node*
- *Each or-node is given by $P(i)$, for some $i \in \{0, \dots, n\}$*
- *Each and-node is an atom seen as a term tree.*
- *For every and-node A' occurring in T, if there exist exactly $k > 0$ distinct clauses $P(j_1), \dots, P(j_k)$ in P (a clause $P(j_i)$ has the form $B_{j_i} \leftarrow B_1^{j_i}, \dots, B_{n_{j_i}}^{j_i}$ for some n_{j_i}), such that $A' = \theta_{j_1}(B_{j_1}) = \dots = \theta_{j_k}(B_{j_k})$, for mgms $\theta_{j_1}, \dots, \theta_{j_k}$, then A' has exactly k children given by or-nodes $P(j_1), \dots, P(j_k)$, such that every or-node $P(j_i)$ has n_{j_i} children given by and-nodes $\theta_{j_i}(B_1^{j_i}), \dots, \theta_{j_i}(B_{n_{j_i}}^{j_i})$.*

When constructing rewriting trees, we assume a suitable algorithm [9] for renaming free variables in clause bodies apart. Figure 1 gives four examples of rewriting trees. If P is a program and $t_1, \dots, t_m$ are terms, then *a rewriting reduction* is given by $[t_1, \dots, t_i, \dots, t_m] \rightarrow [t_1, \dots, t_{i-1}, \sigma(B_0), \dots \sigma(B_n), t_{i+1}, \dots, t_m]$ for $B \leftarrow B_1, \dots, B_n \in P$ and $\sigma(B) = t_i$. A sequence of rewriting reductions is a *rewriting derivation*. It is easy to see that a rewriting derivation for a term t corresponds to a subtree of a rewriting tree for t in which only one or-node is taken at every tree level.

Because mgms are unique up to variable renaming, given a program P and an atom A, the rewriting tree T for P and A is unique. Following the same principle as with definition of term trees, we use suitably defined finitely-branching tree languages for indexing rewriting trees; see [9] for precise definitions. When we need to talk about a node of a rewriting tree T indexed by a word $w \in L$, we will use notation $T(w)$.

We can now formally define our notion of universal observability.

Definition 4 (Universal observability). *A program P is* universally observable *if, for every atom A, the rewriting tree for A and P is finite.*

Programs P_1, P_1', P_2, P_5, P_6 are universally observable, whereas programs P_3, P_4 and P_7 are not. An exact analysis of why P_7 is not universally observable is given in Example 9.

We can now apply the contraction ordering we defined in the previous section to analyse termination properties of rewriting trees. A suitable notion of guardedness can be defined by checking for loops in rewriting trees whose terms fail to decrease by any contraction ordering. Note that our notion of a loop is more general than that used in CoLP [7,21] since it does not require the looping terms to be unifiable.

Definition 5 (Loop in a rewriting tree). *Given a program P and an atom A, the rewriting tree T for P and A contains a loop at nodes w and v, denoted loop(T, w, v), if w properly precedes v on some branch of T, T(w) and T(v) are and-nodes whose atoms have the same predicate, and the parent or-nodes of T(w) and T(v) are given by the same clause P(i).*

Examples of loops in rewriting trees are given (underlined) in Fig. 1.

If T has a loop at nodes w and v, and if t is a recursive reducing subterm for $T(w) \triangleright T(v)$, then $loop(T, w, v)$ is *guarded* by $(P(i), t)$, where $P(i)$ is the clause that was resolved against to obtain $T(w)$ and $T(v)$, i.e., $P(i)$ is the parent node of $T(w)$ and $T(v)$. It is *unguarded* otherwise. A rewriting tree T is *guarded* if all of its loops are guarded, and is *unguarded* otherwise. We write $GC2(T)$ when T is guarded, and say that holds for T, or simply that $GC2(T)$ holds.

Example 8. In Fig. 1, we have (underlined) loops in the third rewriting tree (for $q(s(X''), s(X''), s(Y'), Y'')$ and $q(s(X'), s(X''), Y'', Y'')$) and the fourth rewriting tree (for $q(s(X''), s(X''), s(Y'), s(Y''))$ and $q(s(X''), s(X''), s(Y''), s(Y'')))$. Neither is guarded. In the former, there is a contraction on the third argument, but because $s(Y')$ and Y'' do not share a variable, it is not recursive contraction. In the latter, there is no contraction at all.

By Definition 5, each repetition of a clause and predicate in a branch of a rewriting tree triggers a check to see if the loop is guarded by some recursive reducing subterm.

Proposition 1 ($GC2$ is decidable). $GC2$ *is a decidable property of rewriting trees.*[1]

The proof of Proposition 1 also establishes that every guarded rewriting tree is finite.

The decidable guardedness property $GC2$ is a property of individual rewriting trees. But our goal is to decide guardedness universally, i.e., for *all* of a program's rewriting trees. The next example shows that extrapolating from existential to universal guardedness is a difficult task.

---

[1] All proofs are in Appendix A, and corresponding pseudocode algorithms are in Appendix B, of the version of the paper at https://arxiv.org/abs/1608.04415.

Example 9 (Existential guardedness does not imply universal guardedness).
For program P_7, the rewriting trees constructed for the two clause heads
$p(s(X'), X'', Y', Y'')$ and $q(s(X'), X'', s(Y'), Y'')$ are both guarded since neither contains any loops at all. Nevertheless, there is a rewriting tree for P_7 (the last tree in Fig. 1) that is unguarded and infinite. The third tree is not guarded (due to the unguarded loop), but it is finite.

$$
\begin{array}{cccc}
\overset{Y'\mapsto s(Y')}{\longrightarrow} & \overset{X''\mapsto s(X'')}{\longrightarrow} & \overset{Y''\mapsto s(Y'')}{\longrightarrow} \\
p(s(X'), X'', Y', Y'') & p(s(X'), X'', s(Y'), Y'') & p(s(X'), s(X''), s(Y'), Y'') & p(s(X1), s(X''), s(Y'), s(Y'')) \\
| & | & | & | \\
P_7(0) & P_7(0) & P_7(0) & P_7(0) \\
| & | & | & | \\
q(X'', X'', Y', Y'') & q(X'', X'', s(Y'), Y'') & \underline{q(s(X''), s(X''), s(Y'), Y'')} & \underline{q(s(X''), s(X''), s(Y'), s(Y''))} \\
& | & | & | \\
& P_7(1) & P_7(1) & P_7(1) \\
& | & | & | \\
& p(X'', X'', Y'', Y'') & p(s(X''), s(X''), Y'', Y'') & p(s(X''), s(X''), s(Y''), s(Y'')) \\
& & | & | \\
& & P_7(0) & P_7(0) \\
& & | & | \\
& & \underline{q(s(X''), s(X''), Y'', Y'')} & \underline{q(s(X''), s(X''), s(Y''), s(Y''))} \\
& & & | \\
& & & P_7(1) \\
& & & | \\
& & & \cdots
\end{array}
$$

Fig. 1. An initial fragment of the derivation tree (comprising four rewriting trees) for the program P_7 of Example 7 and the atom $p(s(X'), X'', Y', Y'')$. Its third and fourth rewriting trees each contain an unguarded loop (underlined), so both are unguarded. The fourth tree is infinite.

The example above shows that checking rewriting trees generated by clause heads is insufficient to detect all cases of nonterminating rewriting. Since a similar situation can obtain for any finite set of rewriting trees, we see that universal observability, and hence observational productivity, of programs cannot be determined by guardedness of rewriting trees for program clauses alone. The next section addresses this problem.

4   Derivation Trees: Observational Productivity Checks

The key idea of this section is, given a program P, to identify a finite set S of rewriting trees for P such that checking guardedness of all rewriting trees in S is sufficient to guarantee guardedness of *all* rewriting trees for P. One way to identify such sets is to use the strategy of Example 9 and Fig. 1: for every clause $P(i)$ of P, construct a rewriting tree for the head of $P(i)$, and, if that tree is guarded, explore what kind of mgus the leaves of that tree generate and see if applications of those mgus might give an unguarded tree. As Fig. 1 shows, we may need to apply this method iteratively until we find a nonguarded rewriting tree. But we want the number of such iterations to be finite. This section shows how to do precisely this.

We start with a formal definition of rewriting tree transitions, which we have seen already in Fig. 1, and see also in Fig. 2 below.

Definition 6 (Rewriting tree transition). *Let P be a program and T be a rewriting tree for P and an atom A. If $T(w)$ is a leaf node of T given by an atom B, and B unifies with a clause $P(i)$ via mgu σ, we define a tree T_w as follows: we apply σ to every and-node of T, and extend the branches where required, according to Definition 3. Computation of T_w from T is denoted $T \to T_w$. The operation $T \to T_w$ is the* tree transition *for T and w.*

If a rewriting tree T is constructed for a program P and an atom A, a (finite or infinite) sequence $T \to T' \to T'' \to \dots$ of tree transitions is an *S-resolution derivation* for P and A. For a given rewriting tree T, several different S-resolution derivations are possible from T. This gives rise to the notion of a derivation tree.

Definition 7 (Derivation tree, guarded derivation tree). *Given a logic program P and an atom A, the* derivation tree D for P and A is *defined as follows:*

- *The root of D is given by the rewriting tree for P and A.*
- *For a rewriting tree T occurring as a node of D, if there exists a transition $T \to T_w$, for some leaf node w in T, then the node T has a child given by T_w.*

A derivation tree is guarded *if each of its nodes is a guarded rewriting tree, i.e., if $GC2(T)$ holds for each of its nodes T.*

Figure 1 shows an initial fragment of the derivation tree for P_7 and $p(s(X'), X'', Y', Y'')$.

Note that we now have three kinds of trees: term trees have signature symbols as nodes, rewriting trees have atoms (term trees) as nodes, and derivation trees have rewriting trees as nodes. For a given P and A, the derivation tree for P and A is unique up to renaming. We use our usual notation $D(w)$ to refer to the node of D at index $w \in L$.

Definition 8 (Existential liveness, observational productivity). *Let P be a universally observable program and let A be an atom. An S-resolution derivation for P and A is* live *if it constitutes an infinite branch of the derivation tree for P and A. The program P is* existentially live *if there exists a live S-resolution derivation for P and some atom A. P is* observationally productive *if it is universally observable and existentially live.*

To show that observational productivity is semi-decidable, we first show that universal observability is semi-decidable by means of a finite (i.e., decidable) guardedness check. We started this section by motivating the need to construct a finite set S of rewriting trees whose guardedness will guarantee guardedness for *any* rewriting tree for the given program. Our first logical step is to use derivation trees built for clause heads as generators of such a set S. Due to the properties of mgus used in forming branches of derivation trees, derivation trees constructed for clause heads generate the set of *most general* rewriting trees. The next lemma exposes this fact:

Lemma 1 (Guardedness of derivation trees implies universal observability). *Given a program P, if derivation trees for P and each $head(P(i))$ are guarded, then P is universally observable.*

Since derivation trees are infinite, in general, checking guardedness of *all* loops in *all* of their rewriting trees is not always feasible. It thus remains to define a method that extracts representative finite subtrees from such derivation trees; we call such subtrees *observation subtrees*. For this, we need only be able to detect an invariant property guaranteeing guardedness through tree transitions in the given derivation tree. To illustrate, let us check guardedness of the program P_6. Since it consists of just one clause, we take the head of that clause as the goal atom, and start constructing the infinite derivation tree D for P_6 and $\mathtt{from}(\mathtt{X}, \mathtt{scons}(\mathtt{X}, \mathtt{Y}))$ as shown in Fig. 2. The first rewriting tree in the derivation tree has no loops, so we cannot identify any invariants. We make a transition to the second rewriting tree which has one loop (underlined) involving the recursive reducing subterm $[\mathtt{s}(\mathtt{X}), \mathtt{Y}']$. This reducing subterm is our first candidate invariant, since it is the pattern that is *consumed* from the root of the second rewriting tree to its leaf. We now need to check this pattern is added back, or *produced*, in the next tree transition. The next mgu involves substitution $\mathtt{Y}' \mapsto [\mathtt{s}(\mathtt{s}(\mathtt{X})), \mathtt{Y}'']$. Because this derivation gradually computes an infinite irrational term (rational terms are terms that can be represented as trees that have a finite number of distinct subtrees), the two terms $[\mathtt{s}(\mathtt{X}), \mathtt{Y}']$ and $[\mathtt{s}(\mathtt{s}(\mathtt{X})), \mathtt{Y}'']$ we have identified are not unifiable. We need to be able to abstract away from their current shape and identify a common pattern, which in this case is $[\_, \_]$. Importantly, by the properties of mgus used in transitions, such most general patterns can always be extracted from clause heads themselves. Indeed, the subterm of the clause head $\mathtt{from}(\mathtt{X}, \mathtt{scons}(\mathtt{X}, \mathtt{Y}))$ has the subterm $[\mathtt{X}, \mathtt{Y}]$ that is exactly the pattern we are looking for. Thus, our current *(coinductive) assumption* is: *given a rewriting tree T in the derivation tree D, a term of the form $[\_, \_]$ will be consumed by rewriting steps from its root to its leaves, and exactly a term of the form $[\_, \_]$ will be produced (i.e., added back) in the next tree transition.* Consumption is always finite (by the loop guardedness), and production is potentially infinite.

We now need to check that this coinductive assumption will hold for the next rewriting tree of D. The third rewriting tree indeed has guarded loops with recursive reducing subterm $[\mathtt{s}(\mathtt{s}(\mathtt{X})), \mathtt{Y}'']$, and the next mgu it gives rise to is $\mathtt{Y}'' \mapsto [\mathtt{s}(\mathtt{s}(\mathtt{s}(\mathtt{X}))), \mathtt{Y}'']$. Again, to abstract away the common pattern, we look for a subterm in the clause head of $P_6(0)$ that matches with both of these terms, it is the same subterm $[\mathtt{X}, \mathtt{Y}]$. Thus, our coinductive assumption holds again, and we conclude by coinduction that the same pattern will hold for any further rewriting tree in D. When implementing this reasoning, we take the *observation subtree* of D up to the third tree shown in Fig. 2 as a sufficient set of rewriting trees to use to check guardedness of the (otherwise infinite) tree D.

The rest of this section generalises and formalises this approach. In the next definition, we introduce the notion of a *clause projection* to talk about the process of "abstracting away" a pattern from an mgu σ by matching it with a subterm

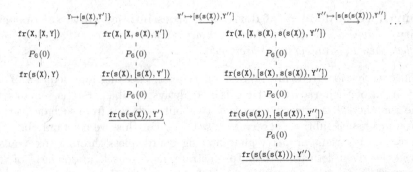

Fig. 2. An initial fragment of the infinite derivation tree D for the program P_6 from Example 4 and its clause head. It is also the observation subtree for D. We abbreviate scons by [,], and from by fr. The guarded loops in each of D's rewriting trees are underlined.

t of a clause head. When t also matches with a recursive reducing subterm of a loop in a rewriting tree, we call t a *coinductive invariant*.

Definition 9 (Clause projection and coinductive invariant). *Let P be a program and A be an atom, and let D be a derivation tree for P and A in which a tree transition from T to T' is induced by an mgu σ of $P(k)$ and an atom B given by a leaf node $T(u)$.*

The clause projection *for T', denoted $\pi(T')$, is the set of all triples $(P(k), t, v)$, where t is a subterm of $head(P(k))$ at position v, such that the following conditions hold: $\sigma(B) \triangleright B$ with variable reducing subterm t', and t' matches against t (i.e. $t' = \sigma'(t)$ for some σ').*

Additionally, the coinductive invariant *at T', denoted $\mathsf{ci}(T')$, is a subset of the* clause projection *for T' satisfying the following condition: an element $(P(k), t, v) \in \pi(T')$ is in $\mathsf{ci}(T')$ if T contains a loop in the branch leading from T's root to $T(u)$ that is guarded by $(P(k), t'')$ for some t'' such that t'' matches against t (i.e., $t'' = \theta(t)$ for some θ).*

Given a program P, an atom A, and a derivation tree D for P and A, the clause projection set *for D is $\mathsf{cproj}(D) = \bigcup_T \pi(T)$, and the* coinductive invariant set *for D is $\mathsf{cinv}(D) = \bigcup_T \mathsf{ci}(T)$, where these unions are taken over all rewriting trees T in D.*

Example 10 (Clause projections and coinductive invariants). Coming back to Fig. 2, the mgu for the first transition is $\sigma_1 = \{X' \mapsto s(X), Y \mapsto scons(s(X), Y')\}$ (renaming of variables in $P_6(0)$ with primes), that for the second is $\sigma_2 = \{X'' \mapsto s(s(X)), Y' \mapsto scons(s(s(X)), Y'')\}$ (renaming of variables in $P_6(0)$ with double primes), etc. Clause projections are given by $\pi(T) = \{(P_6(0), scons(X, Y), 1)\}$ for all trees T in this derivation, and thus $\mathsf{cproj}(D)$ is the finite set. Moreover, for the first rewriting tree T, $\mathsf{ci}(T) = \emptyset$, and $\mathsf{ci}(T') = \{(P_6(0), scons(X, Y), 1)\}$ for all trees T' except for the first one, so $\mathsf{cinv}(D) = \{(P_6(0), scons(X, Y), 1)\}$ is a finite set, too.

The clause projections for the derivation in Fig. 1 are $\pi(T') = \pi(T''') = (P(1),$ $\mathsf{s}(\mathtt{Y1}), 2)$, and $\pi(T'') = (P(0), \mathsf{s}(\mathtt{X1}), 0)$, where T', T'', T'''' refer to the second, third and fourth rewriting tree of that derivation. All coinductive invariants for that derivation are empty, since none of these rewriting trees contain guarded loops.

Generally, clause projection sets are finite, since the number of subterms in the clause heads of P is finite. This property is crucial for termination of our method.

Proposition 2 (Finiteness of clause projection sets). *Given a program* P*, an atom* A*, and a derivation tree* D *for* P *and* A*, the clause projection set* $\mathsf{cproj}(D)$ *is finite.*

In particular, this holds for derivation trees induced by clause heads.

We terminate the construction of each branch of a derivation tree when we notice a repeating coinductive invariant. A subtree we get as a result is an observation subtree. Formally, given a derivation tree D for a program P and an atom A with a branch in which nodes $D(w)$ and $D(wv)$ are defined, if $\mathsf{ci}(D(w)) = \mathsf{ci}(D(wv)) \neq \emptyset$, then D has a *guarded transition* from $D(w)$ to $D(wv)$, denoted $D(w) \implies D(wv)$. Every guarded transition thus identifies a repeated "consumer-producer" invariant in the derivation from $D(w)$ to $D(wv)$. This tells us that observation of this branch of D can be concluded. Imposing this condition on all branches of D gives us a general method to construct finite observation subtrees of potentially infinite derivation trees:

Definition 10 (Observation subtree of a derivation tree). *If* D *is a derivation tree for a program* P *and an atom* A*, the tree* D' *is the* observation subtree *of* D *if*

(1) the roots of D *and* D' *are given by the rewriting tree for* P *and* A*, and*
(2) if w *is a node in both* D *and* D'*, then the rewriting trees in* D *and* D' *at node* w *are the same and, for every child* w' *of* w *in* D*, the rewriting tree of* D' *at node* w' *exists and is the same as the rewriting tree of* D *at* w'*, unless either*
    (a) GC2 does not hold for $D(w')$*, or*
    (b) there exists a v *such that* $D(v) \implies D(w)$*.*

In either case, $D'(w)$ *is a leaf node. We say that* D' *is* unguarded *if Condition 2a holds for at least one of* D*'s nodes, and that* D' *is* guarded *otherwise.*

A branch in an observation subtree is thus truncated when it reaches an unguarded rewriting tree or its coinductive invariant repeats. The observation subtree of any derivation tree is unique. The following proposition and lemma prove the two most crucial properties of observation subtrees: that they are always finite, and that checking their guardedness is sufficient for establishing guardedness of whole derivation trees.

Proposition 3 (Finiteness of observation subtrees). *If D is a derivation tree for a program P and an atom A, then the observation subtree of D is finite.*

Lemma 2 (Guardedness of observation subtree implies guardedness of derivation tree). *If the observation subtree for a derivation tree D is guarded, then D is guarded.*

Example 11 (Finite observation subtree of an infinite derivation tree). The initial fragment D' of the infinite derivation tree D given by the three rewriting trees in Fig. 2 is D's observation subtree. The third rewriting tree T'' in D is the last node in the observation tree D' because $\mathsf{ci}(T') = \mathsf{ci}(T'') = \{(P_6(0), \mathsf{scons}(X,Y), 1)\}$ $\neq \emptyset$. Since D' is guarded, Lemma 2 above ensures that the whole infinite derivation tree D is guarded.

It now only remains to put the properties of the observation subtrees to practical use and, given a program P, to construct finite observation subtrees for each of its clauses. If none of these observation subtrees detects unguarded rewriting trees, we have guarantees that this program will never give rise to infinite rewriting trees. The next definition, lemmas, and theorem make this intuition precise.

Definition 11 (Guarded clause, guarded program). *Given a program P, its clause $P(i)$ is guarded if the observation subtree for the derivation tree for P and the atom $head(P(i))$ is guarded, and $P(i)$ is unguarded otherwise. A program P is guarded if each of its clauses $P(i)$ is guarded, and unguarded otherwise. We write $GC3(P(i))$ to indicate that $P(i)$ is guarded, and similarly for P.*

Lemma 3 uses Proposition 3 to show that $GC3$ is decidable.

Lemma 3 (GC3 is decidable). *$GC3$ is a decidable property of logic programs.*

Theorem 1 (Universal observability is semi-decidable). *If $GC3(P)$ holds, then P is universally observable.*

PROOF: If $GC3(P)$ holds, then the observation subtree for each $P(i)$ is guarded. Thus, by Lemma 2, the derivation tree for each $P(i)$ is guarded. But then, by Lemma 1, P is universally observable. Combining this with Lemma 3, we also obtain that universal observability is semi-decidable.

The converse of Theorem 1 does not hold: the program comprising the clause $\mathsf{p(a)} \leftarrow \mathsf{p(X)}$ is universally observable but not guarded, hence the above *semi-decidability* result.

From our check for universal observability we obtain the desired check for existential liveness, and thus for observational productivity:

Corollary 1 (Observational productivity is semi-decidable). *Let P be a guarded logic program. If there exists a clause $P(i)$ such that the derivation tree D for P and $P(i)$ has an observation subtree D' one of whose branches was truncated by Condition 2b of Definition 10, then P is existentially live. In this case, since P is also guarded and hence universally observable, P is observationally productive.*

5   Related Work: Termination Checking in TRS and LP

Because observational productivity is a combination of universal observability and existential liveness, and the former property amounts to termination of all rewriting trees, there is an intersection between this work and termination checking in TRS [1, 8, 22].

Termination checking via the transformation of LP into TRS has been studied in [20]. Here we consider termination of restricted form of SLD-resolution (given by rewriting derivations), and so a much simpler method for translating LP into TRS can be used for our purposes [6]: Given a logic program P and a clause $P(i) = A \leftarrow B_1, \ldots, B_n$ containing no existential variables, we define a rewrite rule $A \to f_i(B_1, \ldots, B_n)$ for some fresh function symbol f_i. Performing this translation for all clauses, we get a translation from P to a term rewriting system $\mathcal{T}_P$. Rewriting derivations for P can be shown operationally equivalent to term rewriting reductions for $\mathcal{T}_P$; see [6] for a proof. Therefore, for logic programs containing no existential variables, any termination method from TRS may be applied to check universal observability (but not existential liveness).

Algorithmically, our guardedness check compares directly with the method of dependency pairs due to Arts and Giesl [1, 8]. Consider again the TRS $\mathcal{T}_P$ obtained from a logic program P. The set R of dependency pairs contains, for each rewrite rule $A \to f_i(B_1, \ldots, B_n)$ in $\mathcal{T}_P$, a pair (A, B_j), $j = 1, \ldots, n$; see [6]. The method of dependency pairs consists of checking whether there exists an infinite chain of dependency pairs $(s_i, t_i)_{i=1,2,3,\ldots}$ such that $\sigma_i(t_i) \to^* \sigma_{i+1}(s_{i+1})$. If there is no such infinite chain, then $\mathcal{T}_P$ is terminating. Again this translation from LP to dependency pairs in TRS is simpler than in [15], since rewriting derivations are a restricted form of SLD-resolution. Due to the restricted syntax of $\mathcal{T}_P$ (compared to the general TRS syntax), generating the set of dependency pairs is equivalent to generating a set of rewriting trees for each clause of P and assuming $\sigma_i = \sigma_{i+1}$ (cf. $GC2$). To find infinite chains, a dependency graph is defined, in which dependency pairs are nodes, and arcs are defined whenever a substitution that allows a transition from one pair to another can be found. Finding such substitutions is the hardest part algorithmically. Note that every pair of neighbouring and-nodes in a rewriting tree corresponds to a node in a dependency graph. Generating arcs in a dependency graph is equivalent to using $GC3$ to find a representative set of substitutions. However, the way $GC3$ generates such substitutions via rewriting tree transitions differs completely from the methods approximating dependency graphs [1, 22], and relies on the properties of S-resolution, rather than recursive path orderings. This is because $GC3$ additionally generates coinductive invariants for checking existential liveness of programs.

Conceptually, observational productivity is a new property that does not amount to either termination or nontermination in LP or TRS. For instance, programs P_3 and P_4 are nonterminating (seen as LP or TRS), and $P_8 : p(X) \leftarrow q(Y)$ is terminating (seen as LP or TRS) but none of them is productive. This is why the existing powerful tools (such as AProVE) and methods [1, 8, 15, 20] that can check termination or nontermination in TRS or LP are not sufficient to serve as productivity checks. To check *termination* of rewriting trees, $GC3$ can be substituted by existing termination checkers for TRS, but none of the previous approaches can semi-decide existential liveness as $GC3$ does.

6   Implementation and Applications

We implemented the observational productivity checker in parallel Go (golang.org) [19], which allows experimentation with parallelisation of proof search [10]. Loading a logic program P, one runs a command line to initialise the $GC3$ check. The algorithm then certifies whether or not the program is guarded (and hence universally observable). If that is the case, it also checks whether $GC3$ found valid coinductive invariants, i.e. whether P is existentially live, and hence admits coinductive interpretations for some predicates. Appendix B (available online) gives further details.

In the context of S-resolution [9,11], observational productivity of a program is a precondition for (coinductive) soundness of S-resolution derivations. This gives the first application for the productivity checker. But the notion of global productivity (as related to *computations at infinity* [14]) was first investigated in the 1980s. A program is productive, if it admits SLD- (or S-resolution) derivations that compute (or produce) an infinite term at infinity. Thus the productivity checker has more general practical significance for Prolog. In this paper we further exposed its generality by showing that productivity can be seen as a general property of logic programs, rather than property of derivations in some special dialect of Prolog.

Based on this observation, we identify three applications for productivity checks encompassing the S-resolution framework. First, in the context of CoLP [7,21] or any other similar tool based on loop detection in SLD-derivations, one can run the observational productivity checker for a given program prior to running the usual interpreter of CoLP. If the program is certified as productive, all computations by CoLP for this program will be sound relative to computations at infinity [14]. It gives a way to characterise a subset of theorems proven by CoLP that describe the process of *production of infinite data*. For example, as explained in the introduction, CoLP will return answers for programs P_3, P_4 and P_5. But if we know that only P_5 is productive, then we also know that only CoLP's answers for P_5 will correspond to production of infinite terms at infinity. Secondly, since our productivity checker also checks *liveness* of programs, it effectively identifies which predicates may be given coinductive semantics. This knowledge can be used to type predicates as inductive or coinductive. We can use these types to mark predicates in CoLP or any other coinductive dialect of logic programming, cf. Appendix B. Finally, observational productivity is also a guarantee that a sequence of mgus approximating the infinite answer can be constructed *lazily* even if the answer is irregular. For instance, our running example of program P_6 defines an irrational term and hence cannot be handled by CoLP's loop detection. But even if we cannot form a closed-term answer for a query from(0, X), the productivity checker gives us a weaker but more general certificate that lazy approximation of our infinite answer is possible.

These three classes of applications show that the presented productivity checker can be implemented and applied in any dialect of logic programming, irrespective of the fact that it initially arose from S-resolution research [9,11].

7   Conclusions

In this paper we have introduced an observational counterpart to the classical notion of global productivity of logic programs. Using the recently introduced formalism of S-resolution, we have defined observational productivity as a combination of two program properties, namely, universal observability and existential liveness. We have introduced an algorithm for semi-deciding observational productivity for any logic program. We did not impose any restrictions on the syntax of logic programs. In particular, our algorithm handles both existential variables and non-linear recursion.

The algorithm relies on the observation that rewriting trees for productive and guarded programs must show term reduction relative to a contraction ordering from their roots to their leaves. But S-resolution derivations involving such trees can only proceed by adding term structure back in transitioning to new rewriting trees via mgus. This "producer/consumer" interaction can be formally traced by observing a derivation's coinductive invariants: these record exactly the term patterns that both reduce in the loops of rewriting trees and are added back in transitions between these trees.

References

1. Arts, T., Giesl, J.: Termination of term rewriting using dependency pairs. TCS **236**(12), 133–178 (2000)
2. Courcelle, B.: Fundamental properties of infinite trees. TCS **25**, 95–169 (1983)
3. de Schreye, D., Decorte, S.: Termination of logic programs: the never-ending story. J. Logic Program. **19–20**(Supplement 1), 199–260 (1994)
4. Endrullis, J., et al.: Productivity of stream definitions. TCS **411**(4–5), 765–782 (2010)
5. Endrullis, J., et al.: A coinductive framework for infinitary rewriting and equational reasoning. In: RTA, pp. 143–159 (2015)
6. Fu, P., Komendantskaya, E.: Operational semantics of resolution and productivity in horn clause logic. Formal Aspects of Computing (2016)
7. Gupta, G., Bansal, A., Min, R., Simon, L., Mallya, A.: Coinductive logic programming and its applications. In: Dahl, V., Niemelä, I. (eds.) ICLP 2007. LNCS, vol. 4670, pp. 27–44. Springer, Heidelberg (2007). doi:10.1007/978-3-540-74610-2_4
8. Hirokawa, N., Middeldorp, A.: Dependency pairs revisited. In: Oostrom, V. (ed.) RTA 2004. LNCS, vol. 3091, pp. 249–268. Springer, Heidelberg (2004). doi:10.1007/978-3-540-25979-4_18
9. Johann, P., et al.: Structural resolution for logic programming. In: Technical Communications of ICLP (2015)
10. Komendantskaya, E., et al.: Exploiting parallelism in coalgebraic logic programming. Electron. Notes Theor. Comput. Sci. **33**, 121–148 (2014)

11. Komendantskaya, E., et al.: Coalgebraic logic programming: from semantics to implementation. J. Logic Comput. **26**(2), 745–783 (2016)
12. Komendantskaya, E., Li, Y.: Productive corecursion in logic programming. In: Proceedings of ICLP 2017 (2017). arXiv:1707.01541. To appear in Journal of Theory and Practice of Logic Programming
13. Leino, K.R.M., Moskal, M.: Co-induction simply. In: Jones, C., Pihlajasaari, P., Sun, J. (eds.) FM 2014. LNCS, vol. 8442, pp. 382–398. Springer, Cham (2014). doi:10.1007/978-3-319-06410-9_27
14. Lloyd, J.W.: Foundations of Logic Programming, 2nd edn. Springer, Heidelberg (1988)
15. Nguyen, M.T., et al.: Termination analysis of logic programs based on dependency graphs. In: LPOSTR, pp. 8–22 (2007)
16. Pfenning, F.: Types in Logic Programming. The MIT Press, Cambridge (1992)
17. Reynolds, A., Blanchette, J.C.: A decision procedure for (co)datatypes in SMT solvers. In: Felty, A.P., Middeldorp, A. (eds.) CADE 2015. LNCS (LNAI), vol. 9195, pp. 197–213. Springer, Cham (2015). doi:10.1007/978-3-319-21401-6_13
18. Rohwedder, E., Pfenning, F.: Model and termination checking for higher-order logic programs. In: ESOP, pp. 296–310 (1996)
19. Schmidt, M.: Productivity checker for LP (2016). www.macs.hw.ac.uk/~ek19/CoALP/
20. Schneider-Kamp, P., Giesl, J., Serebrenik, A., Thiemann, R.: Automated termination analysis for logic programs by term rewriting. In: Puebla, G. (ed.) LOPSTR 2006. LNCS, vol. 4407, pp. 177–193. Springer, Heidelberg (2007). doi:10.1007/978-3-540-71410-1_13
21. Simon, L., Bansal, A., Mallya, A., Gupta, G.: Co-logic programming: extending logic programming with coinduction. In: Arge, L., Cachin, C., Jurdziński, T., Tarlecki, A. (eds.) ICALP 2007. LNCS, vol. 4596, pp. 472–483. Springer, Heidelberg (2007). doi:10.1007/978-3-540-73420-8_42
22. Terese: Term Rewriting Systems. Cambridge University Press, New York (2003)

Symbolic Abstract Contract Synthesis in a Rewriting Framework

María Alpuente, Daniel Pardo[✉], and Alicia Villanueva

DSIC, Universitat Politècnica de València,
Camino de Vera s/n, 46022 Valencia, Spain
{alpuente,daparpon,villanue}@dsic.upv.es

Abstract. We propose an automated technique for inferring software contracts from programs that are written in a non-trivial fragment of C, called KERNELC, that supports pointer-based structures and heap manipulation. Starting from the semantic definition of KERNELC in the $\mathbb{K}$ framework, we enrich the symbolic execution facilities recently provided by C with novel capabilities for assertion synthesis that are based on abstract subsumption. Roughly speaking, we define an abstract symbolic technique that explains the execution of a (modifier) C function by using other (observer) routines in the same program. We implemented our technique in the automated tool KINDSPEC 2.0, which generates logical axioms that define the precise input/output behavior of the C routines.

1 Introduction

Checking software contracts [15] is one of the most promising techniques for achieving software reliability. Contracts essentially consist of requirements that are imposed on the arguments and result values when functions are invoked. Given its interest, considerable effort has recently been invested towards giving automatic support for equipping programs with extensive contracts, yet the current contract inference tools are still often unsatisfactory in practice [7].

This paper describes a symbolic inference system that synthesizes contracts for heap-manipulating programs that are written in a non-trivial fragment of C, called KERNELC [8], which includes functions, I/O primitives, dynamically allocated structures, and pointer manipulation. By automating the tedious and time-consuming process of generating contracts, programmers can reap the benefits of assertion–based debugging and verification methods with reasonable effort.

Given a program P, the contract discovery problem is generally described as the problem of inferring a likely specification for every function m in P that uses I/O primitives and/or modifies the state. The specifications that we aim to infer consist of logical assertions that characterize the function behavior and that are expressed as method pre-conditions (imposed on the arguments) and post-conditions (relating the arguments and the result for a method).

This work has been partially supported by the EU (FEDER) and Spanish MINECO project TIN2015-69175-C4-1-R, and by Generalitat Valenciana PROMETEOII/2015/013. D. Pardo is supported by FPU-ME grant FPU14/01830.

M.V. Hermenegildo and P. Lopez-Garcia (Eds.): LOPSTR 2016, LNCS 10184, pp. 187–202, 2017.
DOI: 10.1007/978-3-319-63139-4_11

In [1,2], a preliminary specification inference technique was proposed that is based on the classification scheme for data abstractions developed in [13], where a function (method) may be either a *constructor*, a *modifier*, or an *observer*. The intended behavioral specification of any *modifier* function m of P is expressed as a set of logical assertions that characterize the pre- and post-states of the m execution by using the *observer* functions in P.

The inference technique of [1,2] is on top of the (rewriting logic) semantic framework $\mathbb{K}$ and relies on symbolic execution (SE) [12], a well-known program analysis technique that allows programs to be executed using *symbolic* input values instead of actual (concrete) data so that the program execution manipulates symbolic expressions involving the symbolic values. More precisely, for each pair (s,s') of initial and final states in the symbolic execution of m, an implicative axiom $p \implies q$ is synthesized where both the antecedent p and the consequent q are expressed in terms of the (sub-)set of program observers that *explain s* and *s'*. This is achieved by analyzing the results of symbolically executing each observer method o from initial configurations that characterize s and s'.

In this work, we improve the inference power of [1,2] by endowing $\mathbb{K}$'s symbolic execution with modern subsumption techniques based on approximation [3] and lazy initialization [11]. The fact that this symbolic infrastructure is more flexible and (potentially) language-independent allows us to define a generic, more accurate, easily maintainable and robust framework for the inference of program contracts that could be adapted to other languages defined within the $\mathbb{K}$ framework with negligible effort. We summarize our contributions as follows.

1. A symbolic algorithm that synthesizes contracts for heap-manipulating code while coping with infinite computations. This is done by
   (a) augmenting $\mathbb{K}$'s symbolic execution with lazy initialization and a widening operator based on abstract subsumption (in Sect. 4), and
   (b) synthesizing method pre- and post-conditions by means of a contract inference algorithm that explains the (initial and final) abstract symbolic execution states by using the program observers (in Sect. 5).
   Because of the abstraction, some inferred axioms for method m cannot be guaranteed to be correct and are kept apart as "candidate" (or overly general) axioms. A contract refinement algorithm is then formalized that tries to falsify them by checking whether an input call to m that satisfies the axiom antecedent ends in a final state that does not satisfy the given consequent.
2. The proposed inference technique is implemented in the KINDSPEC 2.0 system, which builds on the capabilities of the SMT solver Z3 [16] to simplify the axioms (in Sect. 6). Also, the inferred contracts are given a compact representation that abstracts the user from any implementation details.

2   Method Specification: A Running Example

By abuse, we use the standard terminology for contracts of object-oriented programming and we refer to KERNELC functions as *methods*. Like many state-of-the-art formal specification approaches, we assume to work in a contract-based setting [15], where the granularity of specification units is at the level of one method. Our inference technique relies on the classification scheme for data abstractions of [13], where a function (method) may be either a *constructor*, a *modifier*, or an *observer*. A constructor returns a new data object from scratch; a modifier alters an existing object; and an observer inspects the object and returns a value characterizing one or more of its state attributes. Since the C language does not enforce data encapsulation, we cannot assume purity of any function; thus, we do not assume the traditional premise which states that observer functions do not cause side effects. In other words, any function can potentially be a modifier and we simply define an observer as any function whose return type is different from void.

Let us introduce the leading example that we use to describe our inference methodology: a KERNELC implementation of an abstract datatype for representing sets by using linked lists. The example is composed of 7 methods: one constructor (new), one modifier (insert), and five observers (isnull, isempty, isfull, contains, and length). Note that the observers in this program do not modify any program objects, even if purity of observers is not required in our framework. As is usual in C, logical observers return value 1 (resp. 0) to represent the traditional boolean value *true* (resp. *false*).

Example 1. Consider the program fragment given in Fig. 1 (the full program code can be found in the KINDSPEC 2.0 webpage), where we define set operations over a data structure (struct set) that records the number of elements contained in the set (field size), the maximum number of elements that can be held (field capacity), and a pointer to a list that stores the set elements (field elems). Each node of the list is a record data structure (struct lnode) that contains an integer value (field value) and a pointer to the next element.

A call insert(s,x) to the insert function proceeds as follows: if the set structure has been initialized, the set is not full and it does not contain the element yet, then a new node filled with the value x is inserted at the beginning of the list and the size of the set is increased by one.

The following observers return 0 unless explicitly stated otherwise. isnull(s) returns 1 if the pointer s references to NULL memory; isempty returns 1 if s is initialized but its elems field is NULL; isfull(s) returns 1 if the size of s is greater than or equal to its capacity; and contains(s,x) returns 1 if the value x is found in s. The function length(s) incrementally counts the number of elements (nodes) in the set s and returns this number, or it returns 0 if the set s pointer is NULL.

For each modifier function m in the source program, we aim to synthesize a contract $< P, Q, \mathcal{L} >$, where P is the method precondition, Q is the method postcondition, and $\mathcal{L}$ is the set of program locations (local variables, data-structure pointers and fields, and method parameters) that are (potentially) affected by the method execution. We first compute a set of implication formulas $p \Rightarrow q$, where p and q are conjunctions of equations $l = r$. The left-hand side l of each equation can be either (1) a call to an observer function, and then r represents

```
1   #include <stdlib.h>                26   while(n != NULL) {
2                                      27    if(n->value == x)
3   struct lnode{                      28     return 0; /* x already in the set */
4    int value;                        29    end_node = n;
5    struct lnode *next;               30    n = n->next;
6   };                                 31   }
7   struct set {                       32
8    int capacity;                     33   new_node = (struct lnode*) malloc(sizeof(
9    int size;                                    struct lnode));
10   struct lnode *elems;              34   if(new_node == NULL)
11  };                                 35    return 0; /* no memory left */
12  struct set* new(int capacity) {...} 36   new_node->value = x;
13                                     37   new_node->next = s->elems;
14  int insert(struct set *s, int x) { 38
15   struct lnode *new_node;           39   s->elems = new_node;
16   struct lnode *end_node;           40   s->size += 1;
17   struct lnode *n;                  41   return 1; /* element added */
18                                     42  }
19   if(s==NULL)                       43
20    return 0; /* NULL set */         44  int isnull(struct set *s) {...}
21   if(s->size >= s->capacity)        45  int isempty(struct set *s) {...}
22    return 0; /* no space left */    46  int isfull(struct set *s) {...}
23                                     47  int contains(struct set *s, int x) {...}
24   end_node = s->elems;              48  int length(struct set *s) {...}
25   n = end_node;
```

Fig. 1. Fragment of the KERNELC implementation of a set datatype.

the return value of that call; or (2) the keyword ret, and then r represents the value returned by the modifier function m being observed. Then, given the set of implication formulas $\{p_1 \Rightarrow q_1, \ldots, p_n \Rightarrow q_n\}$, P is defined as $p_1 \vee \ldots \vee p_n$, the postcondition Q is the formula $(p_1 \Rightarrow q_1) \wedge \ldots \wedge (p_n \Rightarrow q_n)$ (similar to the idea of *named behaviors* as provided in the ACSL contract specification language for C), and the elements of $\mathcal{L}$ refer to locations whose value might be affected by the execution of m, that is, all memory locations of the pre-state that do not belong to the set $\mathcal{L}$ remain allocated and are left unchanged in the post-state.

$$(\,\text{isnull}(s) = 1\,) \Rightarrow (\,\text{isnull}(s') = 1 \wedge \text{ret} = 0\,)$$

$$(\,\text{isfull}(s) = 1\,) \Rightarrow \left(\begin{array}{l} \text{isfull}(s') = 1 \wedge \text{contains}(s',x) = \text{contains}(s,x) \wedge \\ \text{length}(s') = \text{length}(s) \wedge \text{ret} = 0 \end{array} \right)$$

$$(\,\text{contains}(s,x) = 1\,) \Rightarrow (\,\text{contains}(s',x) = 1 \wedge \text{length}(s') = \text{length}(s) \wedge \text{ret} = 0\,)$$

$$(\,\text{isempty}(s) = 1 \wedge \text{isfull}(s) = 0\,) \Rightarrow \left(\begin{array}{l} \text{isempty}(s') = 0 \wedge \text{contains}(s',x) = 1 \wedge \\ \text{length}(s') = \text{length}(s) + 1 \wedge \text{ret} = 1 \end{array} \right)$$

$$\left(\begin{array}{l} \text{isnull}(s) = 0 \wedge \text{isempty}(s) = 0 \wedge \\ \text{isfull}(s) = 0 \wedge \text{contains}(s,x) = 0 \end{array} \right) \Rightarrow \left(\begin{array}{l} \text{isnull}(s') = 0 \wedge \text{isempty}(s') = 0 \wedge \\ \text{contains}(s',x) = 1 \wedge \text{length}(s') = \text{length}(s) + 1 \wedge \\ \text{ret} = 1 \end{array} \right)$$

Fig. 2. Expected postcondition axioms for the insert method

Example 2. The intended postcondition Q for the function insert(s,x) of Example 1 contains five axioms (Fig. 2). We adopt the standard primed notation to distinguish variable values after the execution of the method from their value before the execution. The first axiom can be read as: if the outcome of isnull(s) is 1 before the call to insert(s,x), then, after execution, the set is still null and the value returned by `insert(s,x)` is 0, which means that the element was not inserted. The last axiom reads as: if the set is neither null, full nor empty and there is no node in the list with value x, then, after execution, the set remains non-null and non-empty, the value x is now in the set, the length is increased by 1, and the call to `insert(s,x)` returns 1, which denotes a successful insertion.

3   The (symbolic) $\mathbb{K}$ Framework

$\mathbb{K}$ is a rewriting-based framework for engineering language semantics [18]. Given a language definition written in $\mathbb{K}$, the system automatically generates a parser, an interpreter, and formal analysis tools such as model checkers and deductive theorem provers. Complete formal program semantics are currently available in $\mathbb{K}$ for Scheme, Java 1.4, JavaScript, Python, Verilog, and C among others [18].

A language definition in $\mathbb{K}$ consists of three parts: the BNF language syntax, the structure of program configurations, and the semantic rules. Program configurations are represented in $\mathbb{K}$ as potentially nested structures of labeled *cells* (or containers) that represent the program state. Similarly to the classic operational semantics, program configuration cells include a computation stack or continuation (named k), one or more environments (env, heap), and a call stack (stack) among others, and are represented as algebraic datatypes in $\mathbb{K}$.

The part of the $\mathbb{K}$ program configuration structure for the KERNELC semantics that is relevant to this work is $\langle\,\langle\mathsf{K}\rangle_k\langle\mathsf{Map}\rangle_{env}\langle\mathsf{Map}\rangle_{heap}\,\rangle_{cfg}$, where the env cell is a mapping of variable names to their memory positions, the heap cell binds the active memory positions to the actual values (i.e., it stores information about pointers and data structures), and the k cell represents a stack of computations waiting to be run, with the left-most element of the stack being the next computation to be undertaken. For example, the configuration $\langle\,\langle\mathsf{tv}(int,0)\rangle_k\langle\mathsf{x}\mapsto\&\mathsf{x}\rangle_{env}\langle\&\mathsf{x}\mapsto\mathsf{tv}(int,5)\rangle_{heap}\,\rangle_{cfg}$ models a final state whose return value is the integer 0 (stored in the k cell), while program variable x (stored in the env cell) has the integer value 5 (stored in the memory address given by &x in the heap cell). The symbol tv is a semantic construct aimed to encapsulate typed values. Variables representing symbolic memory addresses are written in sans-serif font preceded by the & symbol.

The semantic rules in $\mathbb{K}$ state how configurations (terms) evolve throughout the computation. A useful feature of $\mathbb{K}$ is that «rules only need to mention the minimum part of the configuration that is relevant for their operation».

For symbolic reasoning, $\mathbb{K}$ uses a particular class of first-order formulas with equality (encoded as boolean non–ground terms with constraints over them). These formulas, called *patterns*, specify those configurations that match the pattern algebraic structure and that satisfy its constraints. For instance, the pattern

$$\left\langle \begin{array}{c} \langle\mathsf{tv}(int,0)\rangle_k \\ \langle\cdots\mathsf{x}\mapsto\&\mathsf{x}, \mathsf{s}\mapsto\&\mathsf{s}\cdots\rangle_{env} \\ \langle\cdots\&\mathsf{s}\mapsto(\mathsf{size}\mapsto\mathsf{?s.size}, \mathsf{capacity}\mapsto\mathsf{?s.capacity})\cdots\rangle_{heap} \end{array} \right\rangle_{cfg}$$

$$\left\langle \&\mathsf{s}\neq\mathsf{NULL}\wedge\mathsf{?s.size}\geq\mathsf{?s.capacity} \right\rangle_{path-condition}$$

specifies the configurations satisfying that: (1) the k cell only contains the integer value 0; (2) in the env cell, program variable x (in typographic font) is associated to the memory address &x while s is bound to the pointer &s; and (3) in the heap cell, the field size of (the data structure pointed by) &s (resp. its capacity field) contains the symbolic value[1] ?s.size (resp. ?s.capacity). Additionally, &s is not null and the value of its size field is greater than or equal to its capacity.

Since patterns allow logical variables and constraints over them, by using patterns, the $\mathbb{K}$ execution principle (which is based on term rewriting) becomes *symbolic execution*. Symbolic execution in $\mathbb{K}$ relies on an automated transformation of $\mathbb{K}$ configurations and $\mathbb{K}$ rules into corresponding symbolic $\mathbb{K}$ configurations (i.e., patterns) and symbolic $\mathbb{K}$ rules that capture all required symbolic ingredients: symbolic values for data structure fields and program variables; path conditions that constrain the variables in cells; multiple branches when a condition is reached during execution, etc. [4]. The transformed, symbolic rules define how symbolic configurations are rewritten during computation. Roughly speaking, by symbolically executing a program statement, the configuration cells are updated by mapping fields and variables to new symbolic values that are represented as symbolic expressions, while the path conditions (stored in a new path-condition cell) are correspondingly updated at each branching point.

In [2], an inference procedure for KERNELC programs was defined using the $\mathbb{K}$ symbolic execution infrastructure described above. In order to avoid the exponential blow-up that is inherent to path enumeration, the symbolic procedure of [2] follows the standard approach of exploring loops up to a specified number of unfoldings. In the following, given a method call $m(args)$ and an initial path condition ϕ, and assuming an unspecified unrolling bound for loops, we denote by SE $(m(args)\{\phi\})$ the symbolic execution of method m with input arguments *args* as described in [2], which returns the set of leaves (patterns) of the symbolic execution tree for m under the constraints given by ϕ. For any function f, by $f(args)\{\phi\}$, we represent the $\mathbb{K}$ pattern $\langle\langle f(args)\rangle_k \cdots\rangle_{cfg}\langle\phi\rangle_{path-condition}$ that is built by inserting the call $f(args)$ at the top of the k cell and by initializing the path condition cell with ϕ.

4   Improving Symbolic Execution in $\mathbb{K}$

In this section, we extend $\mathbb{K}$'s symbolic execution machinery with lazy initialization techniques and abstract subsumption checking in order to support the synthesis of contracts for methods that require refined loop finitization and C pointer dereference and initialization.

Lazy initialization. Structured datatypes (struct) in C are aggregate types that define non-empty sets of sequentially allocated *member objects*[2], called fields, each of which has a name and a type. In our symbolic setting, pointer arithmetics and memory layout of C programs are abstracted by: (1) operating

---

[1] Symbolic values are preceded by a question mark.

[2] An object in C is a region of data storage in the execution environment.

with *symbolic addresses* instead of concrete addresses, and (2) mapping each structure object into a single element of the heap cell that groups all object fields (and associated values). A specific field is then accessed by combining the identifiers of both the structure object and the field name.

Symbolic execution with complex data uses lazy initialization to avoid a priori bounds on input structures [3]. We adapt the lazy initialization approach of [11] to our setting as follows: when a symbolic address (or address expression) is accessed for the first time, two cases are considered: the case in which the memory stores a null pointer; and the case in which the memory is initialized and it stores an object of its respective type. The mapping in the heap cell is correspondingly updated by assigning a new symbolic value that represents the assumptions made on the dynamic data structure. In order to deal with cyclic data structures, a third possibility is to be considered: the case in which the symbolic memory references an already existing object in the heap (*aliasing*). Since this generates a new path for *every* single object of the same type existing in the memory heap, to avoid state blow-up we enable lazy initialization to consider aliasing only when explicitly asked by the user.

To keep track of the constraints that are introduced by the lazy initialization, a new cell $\langle\rangle_{\text{init-heap}}$ is added to the configuration that represents the initialization assumptions on the heap memory at a given program point.

Symbolic subsumption. The exhaustive exploration of all program paths is in general unaffordable because the search space may be infinite and, consequently, the number of symbolic execution paths may be unbounded. A classical solution (used in [1,2]) is to establish a *bound* to the depth of the symbolic execution tree by specifying the maximum number of unfoldings for each loop and recursive function. As an alternative, the subsumption approach of [3] determines the length of the symbolic execution paths in a dynamic way. Intuitively, symbolic execution with subsumption checking proceeds as standard symbolic execution, except that before entering a loop, it is checked that the current state has not already been explored; otherwise, the execution of the loop stops. Supporting this check does not require whole execution paths to be recorded; only symbolic states that correspond to the evaluation of loop guards need to be recorded.

An algorithm for symbolic subsumption that naturally transfers to our framework is given in [3]. Let us augment symbolic program configurations C into *program states* $S = \langle C, i\rangle$ by giving the configuration pattern C a program counter i that corresponds to the line number in the source code of the subsequent instruction to be executed, or the **return** statement if the configuration C is final. Also, let us represent the conjunction of all constraints over the symbolic values of primitive-type variables and structure fields expressed[3] in the env, heap, and path-condition cells of pattern C in S, called *state constraint*, by $SC(S)$. By using the subsumption algorithm, we can decide state subsumption $S_2 \sqsubseteq S_1$ by checking that: (1) S_1 and S_2 have the same program counter; (2) the

---

[3] By abuse, we assume a logical constraint representation $x_1 = v_1 \wedge \ldots \wedge x_n = v_n$ of the symbolic heap $\{x_1 \mapsto v_1, \ldots, x_n \mapsto v_n\}$, where every x_i refers to a field of a heap data object, or to a primitive-type program variable if x_i occurs in env.

symbolic heap in S_2 is subsumed by the symbolic heap in S_1 (i.e., all possible program heaps whose concrete shape and values match the constraints in S_1 includes all concrete program heaps that satisfy the constraints in S_2); and (3) $SC(S_2) \Rightarrow SC(S_1)$.

Abstract subsumption. Symbolic execution with state subsumption is not guaranteed to terminate. In order to ensure termination and improve scalability of symbolic execution, we enhance symbolic state subsumption checking by means of abstract interpretation [3]. We abstract both primitive domains and heaps by using the abstraction function α proposed in [3]. The idea for this heap abstraction is to apply a shape transformation that collapses two or more nodes into a *summary node*. Nodes can be collapsed when they are in a sequence and can only be accessed by traversing all their predecessors.

Example 3. Node S_{27} of Fig. 3 illustrates shape abstraction for the given state. The circled nodes are abstracted into a summary node and the valuation for the field `value` of the summary node (identified by e_3) is $e_3 = ?v_0 \vee e_3 = ?v_1$.

Given the symbolic state S, we define the abstraction $S^{\sharp} = \alpha(S)$. Then, the abstract symbolic subsumption relation $S_2 \sqsubseteq^{\sharp} S_1$ is given by $S_2^{\sharp} \sqsubseteq S_1^{\sharp}$.

4.1   Symbolic Execution with Abstract Subsumption

The symbolic execution with abstract subsumption (and lazy initialization) of a given method m with arguments *args* and initial path condition ϕ, written $SE^{\sharp}(m(args)\{\phi\})$, is an approximation of the SE mechanism of [2] where, when a symbolic state S_2 is visited that corresponds to a recursive call or loop guard evaluation with the same program counter as a previously visited state S_1, abstract subsumption $S_2 \sqsubseteq^{\sharp} S_1$ is checked; if the test succeeds, the loop or recursive function stops, and the execution flow proceeds to the subsequent instruction.

Example 4. The uncontrolled symbolic execution SE of the function `insert(s,x)` from Example 1 generates an infinite state space. In contrast, $SE^{\sharp}$ terminates after three iterations of the loop. Figure 3 illustrates the fragment of the symbolic execution tree for `insert(s,x)` where the subsumption between two abstract states is exposed. The state (S_{18}) corresponds to the state where the loop guard is to be checked for the third time. This requires evaluating n, which points to an uninitialized node; hence, lazy initialization is applied. The left child S_{19} corresponds to the case when the loop guard is not satisfied and the loop is exited, whereas the right child S_{21} represents entering the loop iteration.

Program counter 29 is reached again at state S_{27} in the right branch after lazy initialization, and then the abstract subsumption check $S_{27} \sqsubseteq^{\sharp} S_{21}$ succeeds.

Let $SE^{\sharp}(f(args)\{\phi\})$ return the set of final patterns obtained from the abstract symbolic execution of the pattern $f(args)\{\phi\}$ (i.e., the leaves of the deployed abstract symbolic execution tree). We assume appropriate abstractions

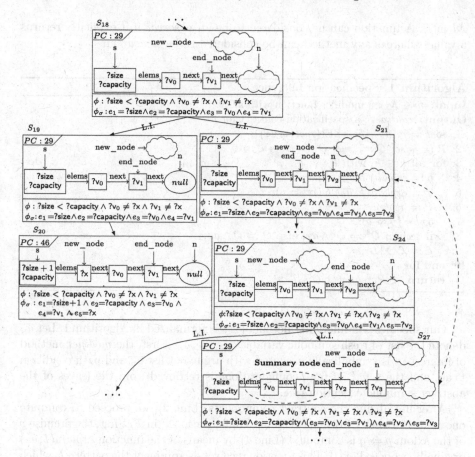

Fig. 3. Fragment of the abstract symbolic execution of `insert(s,x)`

are defined to ensure termination of $SE^\sharp$. A new (abstract subsumption) cell $\langle\rangle_{\mathsf{aSubFlag}}$ identifies with a *true* value those final abstract configurations ending any branch that was folded (at some intermediate configuration) by the application of abstract subsumption. This is used for the inference process to distinguish the inferred axioms that are ensured to hold from the *plausible*, candidate axioms that are not demonstrably correct because of the potential precision loss caused by the abstraction. Furthermore, assignable locations are easily obtained as a by-product of the SE by just adding a new cell $\langle\rangle_{\mathsf{locations}}$ that is used to record any program location whenever it is overwritten.

5   Inference Algorithm

Let us introduce the basic notions that we use in our formalization. Given an input program P, we distinguish the set of observers $\mathcal{O}$ and the set of modifiers

$\mathcal{M}$ in P. A function can be considered to be an *observer* if it explicitly returns a value, whereas any method can be considered to be a *modifier*.

Algorithm 1. Specification Inference

Input: $m \in \mathcal{M}$: a modifier function with arity n
Output: *contract* : a specification contract for m
 1: $root := m(\overline{a_n})$; $\mathcal{F} := SE^{\sharp}(root\{\mathbf{true}\})$;
 2: $P := false$; $Q := true$; $Q^{\sharp} := true$; $\mathcal{L} := \emptyset$;
 3: **for all** $F \in \mathcal{F}$, with $F = \langle \langle v \rangle_k \langle \varphi \rangle_{\text{init-heap}} \cdots \rangle_{\text{cfg}} \langle \phi \rangle_{\text{path-condition}} \langle \sharp \rangle_{\text{aSubFlag}} \langle L \rangle_{\text{locations}}$ **do**
 4:    $p := explain(I, \overline{a_n})$, where $I = \langle \langle root \rangle_k \langle \varphi \rangle_{\text{heap}} \cdots \rangle_{\text{cfg}} \langle \phi \rangle_{\text{path-condition}}$;
 5:    $q := explain(F, \overline{a_n}) \wedge (ret = v)$;
 6:    $P := P \vee p$;
 7:    $ax := (p \Rightarrow q)$;
 8:    **if** $\sharp$ **then** $Q^{\sharp} := Q^{\sharp} \wedge ax$; **else** $Q := Q \wedge ax$;
 9:    $\mathcal{L} := \mathcal{L} \cup \{L\}$;
10: **end for**
11: **return** $< P, refine(Q, Q^{\sharp}), \mathcal{L} >$;

Our specification inference methodology is formalized in Algorithm 1. Let $\overline{a_n}$ denote the list of fresh symbolic variables $a_1, \ldots, a_n$. First, the *modifier* method of interest m is symbolically executed with argument list $\overline{a_n}$ and path condition **true**, and the set $\mathcal{F}$ of final configurations is retrieved from the leaves of the abstract symbolic execution tree.

After initializing the contract components (Line 2), we proceed to compute one axiom for each (abstract) symbolic configuration F in $\mathcal{F}$. First, the premise p of the axiom $p \Rightarrow q$ is computed (Line 4) by means of the function $explain(I, as)$ originally proposed in [1]. This function receives as argument the pattern I, which expresses the initial symbolic configuration leading to F in the execution tree for m. Roughly speaking, by means of a conjunction of equations, $explain(I, \overline{a_n})$ describes what can be observed when running (under the constraints given by I) the observer functions $o \in \mathcal{O}$ over appropriate symbolic variables from $\overline{a_n}$. Each delivered equation is formed by equating each observer call to the (symbolic) value that the call returns. We require o to compute the same symbolic values at the end of all its symbolic execution branches in order to distill a (partial) observational abstraction or explanation for a given configuration in terms of o.

The consequent q of the axiom is the conjunction of $ret = v$, which specifies the return value v of the method m as recorded in the k cell of F, and the equations given by $explain(F, \overline{a_n})$, which in terms of the observers characterizes the final pattern F of the given branch.

It is important to note that, in the axioms, the different function calls in the antecedent (resp. consequent) of every implication formula are run independently of each other under the same initial configuration. This avoids making any assumptions about function purity or side-effects. Depending on the boolean value of the abstract subsumption flag $\sharp$ in F (Line 8), the synthesized axiom ax is directly added to the postcondition Q (when $\sharp$ is *false*) or to the conjunction

$Q^\sharp$ (when $\sharp$ is true) that collects all candidate axioms extracted from branches that contain at least one node that was folded by abstract subsumption. Note that, due to the under-approximation introduced by abstract subsumption [3], there may be some behaviors that are not captured by the deployed symbolic abstract traces. Therefore, axioms in $Q^\sharp$ could have spurious instances and must be double-checked. We apply a post-processing refinement $refine(Q, Q^\sharp)$ which tries to build specialized (demonstrably correct) instances of the axioms in $Q^\sharp$ that can be added to Q, while keeping in $Q^\sharp$ any axioms that remain overly general (i.e., that might have both true and false instances). A further post-processing purges the augmented Q from less general axioms.

When Algorithm 1 terminates, the generated contract is $< P, Q, \mathcal{L} >$ where the method precondition P is the disjunction of all axiom premises, the method postcondition is given by $refine(Q, Q^\sharp)$, and $\mathcal{L}$ records all program locations that are (potentially) modifiable by m. Note that we do not need to specialize the disjunction P according to the final refined postcondition Q because correctness of the contract is ensured by the specialized axiom guards of Q.

Lazy initialization is not applied when symbolically executing the observer functions. This is because we want to start from an initial configuration whose dynamic memory satisfies φ, and if any uninitialized addresses are expanded by lazy initialization, such an initial configuration (and thus the target of the observation) would be altered. This implies that some final patterns in the symbolic execution trees for the given observer may contain uninit return values, meaning that we know nothing regarding the dynamic memory from that point on. When this occurs (for all branches), the *explain* algorithm generates a conjunct where the observer call is equated to a fresh symbolic value.

Example 5. Let us use Algorithm 1 to compute a specification for insert of Example 1. We first compute $SE^\sharp$(insert(&s, ?x){true}) with &s being a symbolic address with initial value uninit and with ?x being a symbolic integer value. The abstract symbolic execution computes ten final configurations. Figure 4 represents the final state for the path where the while loop stops due to abstract subsumption (Nodes S_{18} and S_{27} of Example 4).

Roughly speaking, the execution of this path corresponds to the case when the element x (with symbolic value ?x) is effectively inserted in a non-empty list that contains three elements. The return value (k cell) of the call insert(&s, ?x) is the integer 1 (standing for success); the symbolic (initial) value ?s.size of the field size of s is increased by 1 and now the field elems of s points to an object &new_node with value ?x as the first node of the set. For the sake of simplicity, we omit any cell components that are irrelevant for comprehension.

As a side effect of applying abstract subsumption to stop the while loop, the node pointed by the field next of the last object node is not null but uninit. This implies a loss of precision: the symbolic heap is matched by any concrete heap whose first node contains the value ?x and is followed by 3 or more nodes.

The algorithm computes the explanation for the corresponding initial and final state of each of those ten configurations. Let us illustrate one of the cases.

$$
\langle tv(int, 1) \rangle_k
$$

$$
\left\langle
\begin{array}{l}
\texttt{s} \mapsto \&\texttt{s}, \texttt{x} \mapsto \texttt{?x}, \texttt{new\_node} \mapsto \&\texttt{new\_node},\\
\texttt{end\_node} \mapsto \&\texttt{s.elems.next.next}, \texttt{n} \mapsto \&\texttt{s.elems.next.next.next}
\end{array}
\right\rangle_{env}
$$

$$
\left(
\begin{array}{l}
\&\texttt{s} \mapsto (\texttt{capacity} \mapsto \texttt{?s.capacity}, \texttt{size} \mapsto \texttt{?s.size} + 1, \texttt{elems} \mapsto \&\texttt{new\_node}),\\
\quad \&\texttt{new\_node} \mapsto (\texttt{value} \mapsto \texttt{?x}, \texttt{next} \mapsto \&\texttt{s.elems}), \&\texttt{x} \mapsto \texttt{?x}\\
\quad \&\texttt{s.elems} \mapsto (\texttt{value} \mapsto \texttt{?v}_0, \texttt{next} \mapsto \&\texttt{s.elems.next}),\\
\qquad\qquad\qquad\qquad \ldots\\
\quad \&\texttt{s.elems.next.next.next} \mapsto (\texttt{value} \mapsto \texttt{?v}_3, \texttt{next} \mapsto \texttt{uninit})
\end{array}
\right)_{heap}
$$

$$
\left(
\begin{array}{l}
\&\texttt{s} \mapsto (\texttt{capacity} \mapsto \texttt{?s.capacity}, \texttt{size} \mapsto \texttt{?s.size}, \texttt{elems} \mapsto \&\texttt{s.elems}),\\
\quad \&\texttt{s.elems} \mapsto (\texttt{value} \mapsto \texttt{?v}_0, \texttt{next} \mapsto \&\texttt{s.elems.next}),\\
\qquad\qquad\qquad\qquad \ldots\\
\quad \&\texttt{s.elems.next.next.next} \mapsto (\texttt{value} \mapsto \texttt{?v}_3, \texttt{next} \mapsto \texttt{uninit})
\end{array}
\right)_{init-heap}
$$

$$
\langle \texttt{?s.size} < \texttt{?s.capacity} \wedge \texttt{?v}_0 \neq \texttt{?x} \wedge \texttt{?v}_1 \neq \texttt{?x} \wedge \texttt{?v}_2 \neq \texttt{?x} \rangle_{path-condition} \ .
$$

Fig. 4. Final configuration example

Example 6. In order to explain the final pattern F of Fig. 4, the function *explain* considers the universe of observer calls of the program, which includes the call contains (&s, ?x). The symbolic execution of contains (&s, ?x) under the constraints given by the heap and path-condition cells of F results in a single-branch tree with return value 1; hence, the equation contains(s,x)=1 is added as part of the equational explanation of F.

Example 7. In order to explain the corresponding initial pattern I, we symbolically execute the observer contains(&s, ?x) under the constraints given by I (i.e., the init-heap and path-condition cells of F); and since no element with value ?x is found in the set &s, the list is traversed until the uninit node is reached. Hence, the equation contains(s,x)=_v is generated, with _v being a symbolic value that stands for any possible value that the function may return.

Let us now illustrate how the refinement process *refine*$(Q, Q^\sharp)$ for method m works. For each candidate axiom $p \Rightarrow q$ in $Q^\sharp$, we first generate test cases (initial configurations) that satisfy the axiom antecedent p, then we run the modifier method m on the initial configurations, and finally we check whether or not the consequent q is satisfied after the method execution. Refuted candidate axioms are not automatically removed: a counterexample-guided, specialization postprocess defined in [1] is attempted first. It uses the deployed symbolic execution branches refuting the axiom as counterexample behaviors to be excluded from the symbolic execution tree. Then, by iteratively repeating the inference process on the reduced tree, new axioms that are either eventually correct (and then added to Q) or can be further specialized are distilled. Note that this process is guaranteed to terminate since the size of the tree is reduced at each iteration.

Example 8. After the for loop of Algorithm 1, one axiom for each of the (10) final patterns is synthesized. After removing duplicates, 7 axioms are kept (see Fig. 5), together with one candidate axiom (labelled as C1) that derives from the final configuration discussed in Example 5.

The refinement process is then triggered over C1 to check if it can first be falsified and then refined. Given the binary domain 0/1 of the contains(s,x) function, the axiom is straightforwardly falsified. The final state does not satisfy

$$
\text{A1} \begin{pmatrix} \texttt{isnull(s)} = 1 \wedge \texttt{isempty(s)} = 0 \wedge \\ \texttt{isfull(s)} = 0 \wedge \texttt{contains(s,x)} = 0 \wedge \\ \texttt{length(s)} = 0 \end{pmatrix} \Rightarrow \begin{pmatrix} \texttt{isnull(s')} = 1 \wedge \texttt{isempty(s')} = 0 \wedge \\ \texttt{isfull(s')} = 0 \wedge \texttt{contains(s',x)} = 0 \wedge \\ \texttt{length(s')} = 0 \wedge \texttt{ret} = 0 \end{pmatrix}
$$

$$
\text{A2} \begin{pmatrix} \texttt{isnull(s)} = 0 \wedge \texttt{isempty(s)} = \_i1 \wedge \\ \texttt{isfull(s)} = 1 \wedge \texttt{contains(s,x)} = \_i2 \wedge \\ \texttt{length(s)} = \_i3 \end{pmatrix} \Rightarrow \begin{pmatrix} \texttt{isnull(s')} = 0 \wedge \texttt{isempty(s')} = \_i1 \wedge \\ \texttt{isfull(s')} = 1 \wedge \texttt{contains(s',x)} = \_i2 \wedge \\ \texttt{length(s')} = \_i3 \wedge \texttt{ret} = 0 \end{pmatrix}
$$

$$
\text{A3} \begin{pmatrix} \texttt{isnull(s)} = 0 \wedge \texttt{isempty(s)} = 0 \wedge \\ \texttt{isfull(s)} = 0 \wedge \texttt{contains(s,x)} = 1 \wedge \\ \texttt{length(s)} = \_i1 \end{pmatrix} \Rightarrow \begin{pmatrix} \texttt{isnull(s')} = 0 \wedge \texttt{isempty(s')} = 0 \wedge \\ \texttt{isfull(s')} = 0 \wedge \texttt{contains(s',x)} = 1 \wedge \\ \texttt{length(s')} = \_i1 \wedge \texttt{ret} = 0 \end{pmatrix}
$$

$$
\text{A4} \begin{pmatrix} \texttt{isnull(s)} = 0 \wedge \texttt{isempty(s)} = 1 \wedge \\ \texttt{isfull(s)} = 0 \wedge \texttt{contains(s,x)} = 0 \wedge \\ \texttt{length(s)} = 0 \end{pmatrix} \Rightarrow \begin{pmatrix} \texttt{isnull(s')} = 0 \wedge \texttt{isempty(s')} = 0 \wedge \\ \texttt{contains(s',x)} = 1 \wedge \texttt{length(s')} = 1 \wedge \\ \texttt{ret} = 1 \end{pmatrix}
$$

$$
\text{A5} \begin{pmatrix} \texttt{isnull(s)} = 0 \wedge \texttt{isempty(s)} = 0 \wedge \\ \texttt{isfull(s)} = 0 \wedge \texttt{contains(s,x)} = 0 \wedge \\ \texttt{length(s)} = 1 \end{pmatrix} \Rightarrow \begin{pmatrix} \texttt{isnull(s')} = 0 \wedge \texttt{isempty(s')} = 0 \wedge \\ \texttt{contains(s',x)} = 1 \wedge \texttt{length(s')} = 2 \wedge \\ \texttt{ret} = 1 \end{pmatrix}
$$

$$
\text{A6} \begin{pmatrix} \texttt{isnull(s)} = 0 \wedge \texttt{isempty(s)} = 0 \wedge \\ \texttt{isfull(s)} = 0 \wedge \texttt{contains(s,x)} = 0 \wedge \\ \texttt{length(s)} = 2 \end{pmatrix} \Rightarrow \begin{pmatrix} \texttt{isnull(s')} = 0 \wedge \texttt{isempty(s')} = 0 \wedge \\ \texttt{contains(s',x)} = 1 \wedge \texttt{length(s')} = 3 \wedge \\ \texttt{ret} = 1 \end{pmatrix}
$$

$$
\text{A7} \begin{pmatrix} \texttt{isnull(s)} = 0 \wedge \texttt{isempty(s)} = 0 \wedge \\ \texttt{isfull(s)} = 0 \wedge \texttt{contains(s,x)} = 0 \wedge \\ \texttt{length(s)} = 3 \end{pmatrix} \Rightarrow \begin{pmatrix} \texttt{isnull(s')} = 0 \wedge \texttt{isempty(s')} = 0 \wedge \\ \texttt{contains(s',x)} = 1 \wedge \texttt{length(s')} = 4 \wedge \\ \texttt{ret} = 1 \end{pmatrix}
$$

$$
\text{C1} \begin{pmatrix} \texttt{isnull(s)} = 0 \wedge \texttt{isempty(s)} = 0 \wedge \\ \texttt{isfull(s)} = 0 \wedge \texttt{contains(s,x)} = \_i1 \wedge \\ \texttt{length(s)} = \_i2 \end{pmatrix} \Rightarrow \begin{pmatrix} \texttt{isnull(s')} = 0 \wedge \texttt{isempty(s')} = 0 \wedge \\ \texttt{contains(s',x)} = 1 \wedge \texttt{length(s')} = \_i2 + 1 \wedge \\ \texttt{ret} = 1 \end{pmatrix}
$$

Fig. 5. Set of axioms and candidates for Example 5.

the postcondition of axiom C1 because, since the set s already contained the desired element, insert(s,x) does not return 1 and the length is not increased.

Since the axiom has been falsified (with contains(s,x)=1), the refinement process is run with $\_i1 \mapsto 0$ and a (specialized and correct) axiom is obtained:

$$
\text{A8} \begin{pmatrix} \texttt{isnull(s)} = 0 \wedge \texttt{isempty(s)} = 0 \wedge \\ \texttt{isfull(s)} = 0 \wedge \texttt{contains(s,x)} = 0 \wedge \\ \texttt{length(s)} = \_i1 \end{pmatrix} \Rightarrow \begin{pmatrix} \texttt{isnull(s')} = 0 \wedge \texttt{isempty(s')} = 0 \wedge \\ \texttt{contains(s',x)} = 1 \wedge \texttt{length(s')} = \_i1 + 1 \wedge \\ \texttt{ret} = 1 \end{pmatrix}
$$

Note that the new axiom subsumes axioms A5, A6 and A7 of Fig. 5; hence, they are removed. After the refinement, the contract postcondition returned for insert(s,x) contains five axioms, specifically the axioms A1–4 and A8.

As for the last element of the contract, the set of assignable program locations $\mathcal{L}$ is obtained as the union of the location sets that are recorded in the $\langle\rangle_{\text{locations}}$ cells of the final symbolic execution states.

6 Implementation

We have developed a prototype implementation of the extended $\mathbb{K}$ symbolic machinery and contract inference algorithm, which we used to mechanize our running example. The KINDSPEC2 tool is publicly available together with more detailed experiments at http://safe-tools.dsic.upv.es/kindspec2.

Specification inference is notoriously expensive for accurate and strong properties. We evaluated our prototype in classical contract inference benchmark programs. Our main objective was to probe the quality of the discovered contracts as well as the viability of the method on a variety of programs with loops and recursion that are commonly used in the literature on shape analysis and program verification with automatic inference of contracts [5,9].

Our test platform was an Intel Core2 Quad CPU Q9300(2.50GHz) with 6 Gigabytes of RAM running $\mathbb{K}$ v3.4 on Maude v2.6. Table 1 summarizes the figures that we obtained for benchmark programs that contain (both cyclic and acyclic) nested data structures. The LOC column shows the number of lines of code, while the Modifiers and Observers columns list the names of the symbolically executed functions in each category. #Paths shows the number of final symbolic execution configurations reached for each program, while Extr. axioms reflects how many *different* axioms are retrieved from them. The Overly general axioms column indicates the number of candidate axioms; Discard.axioms counts how many of these candidate axioms were falsified and not specialized, so they were discarded; and Correct refined axioms are the number of axioms obtained by refining the candidate ones, as explained in Sect. 5. The Final correct axioms column shows the total number of correct axioms that are automatically distilled as a result of the whole inference process, including subsumption checking for all obtained axioms. Finally, Expected contract counts the number of axioms in a classical reference specification. Assuming an appropriate set of observer functions, we are able to infer accurate (even complete) contracts that equal the expected specification. As an exception, the inferred axioms for `merge.c` include the expected ones plus redundant axioms that are instances of the candidate one. This is because the only candidate axiom is indeed correct; hence, it cannot be falsified and then refined by our algorithm. If the candidate axiom could have been demonstrated to be correct (e.g., by using an automatic prover) and then added to the correct axiom set, the redundant axioms would get filtered out.

Table 1. Results for KINDSPEC 2.0 on programs manipulating lists and trees

Program	LOC	Modifiers	Observers	#Paths	Extr. axioms	Overly general axioms	Discard. axioms	Correct refined axioms	Final correct axioms	Expected contract
insert.c (running example)	122	insert	isnull, isempty isfull, length contains	10	8	1	0	1	5	5
delete.c (sequence of loops)	127	delete	isnull, isempty contains_node length interval_length	23	17	6	0	6	6	6
del-all-circ.c (cyclic lists)	73	delete_all	isnull, isempty length-circular	21	12	6	2	4	4	4
merge.c (two symb. lists)	134	merge	isnull, isempty length sum_sizes	124	18	1	0	0	18	6
treeinsert.c (trees and recursion)	80	insert	isnull, isempty find, depth	31	4	1	0	1	4	4

With respect to the time cost of the inference, our preliminary results are very encouraging since they show that general correct axioms can be inferred, leading to quite compact, clear, and correct specifications. The time spent in $\mathbb{K}$'s symbolic execution of methods ranges from 1 min to 5 min (depending on the quantity and complexity of the method definitions), while the time taken for actual inference of contracts (once the symbolic execution trees have been deployed) ranges from approximately 150 ms to 300 ms. The backend of $\mathbb{K}$ is currently being ported into Java, and future versions of the $\mathbb{K}$'s symbolic framework are expected to be greatly optimized.

7 Related Work and Conclusion

The wide interest in formal specifications as helpers for other analysis, validation, and verification tools has resulted in numerous approaches for (semi-) automatically computing different kinds of specifications that can take the form of contracts, snippets, summaries, properties, process models, rules, graphs, automata, interfaces, or component abstractions.

Let us briefly discuss those strands of research that have influenced our work the most. A detailed description of the related literature can be found in [1,7,9,17,20]. Our axiomatic representation is inspired by [19], which relies on a model checker for symbolic execution and generates either Spec# specifications or parameterized unit tests. Similarly to [19], we aim to infer high-level (rich) information that is easily understable by the programmer; however, we take advantage of $\mathbb{K}$ symbolic capabilities to generate simpler and more accurate formulas that avoid reasoning with the global heap. By relying on symbolic execution and abstraction, our approach is able to guarantee completeness/correctness under some conditions. This is different from testing-based approaches such as [6,10] which are limited to delivering properties that *have not been previously falsified* by a (finite) number of tests.

Another related thread of research concerns the inference of Hoare triples (and invariants) that summarize a heap manipulating program. Existing approaches usually infer low-level specifications that are intended to be used later by automated verification or optimization tools [5,14,17]. This is in contrast to our approach, which infers richer (human-readable) assertions. In addition, we handle unbounded structures by means of lazy initialization and ensure termination by using abstraction. Our experiments show that our method can infer rich summaries that advance the state of the art. For example, our tool infers contracts for challenging programs with recursive predicates, tree-like structures, and cyclic lists, which are not handled by competing tools, e.g., [5,9].

The contracts generated by our tool may be easily translated to richer (but also heavier) notations for behavioural interface C specifications such as ACSL or to the native syntax of some SMT solvers, which is planned as future work. We also plan to explore other existing abstract domains for structured data and integrate them in our tool in order to improve accuracy results and applicability.

References

1. Alpuente, M., Feliú, M.A., Villanueva, A.: Automatic inference of specifications using matching logic. In: Proceedings of PEPM 2013, pp. 127–136. ACM (2013)
2. Alpuente, M., Pardo, D., Villanueva, A.: Automatic inference of specifications in the K framework. EPTCS **200**, 1–17 (2015)
3. Anand, S., Păsăreanu, C.S., Visser, W.: Symbolic execution with abstraction. STTT **11**(1), 53–67 (2008)
4. Arusoaie, A., Lucanu, D., Rusu, V.: Symbolic execution based on language transformation. Comput. Lang. Syst. Struct. **44**(Part A), 48–71 (2015)
5. Calcagno, C., Distefano, D., O'Hearn, P.W., Yang, H.: Footprint analysis: a shape analysis that discovers preconditions. In: Nielson, H.R., Filé, G. (eds.) SAS 2007. LNCS, vol. 4634, pp. 402–418. Springer, Heidelberg (2007). doi:10.1007/978-3-540-74061-2_25
6. Claessen, K., Smallbone, N., Hughes, J.: QUICKSPEC: guessing formal specifications using testing. In: Fraser, G., Gargantini, A. (eds.) TAP 2010. LNCS, vol. 6143, pp. 6–21. Springer, Heidelberg (2010). doi:10.1007/978-3-642-13977-2_3
7. Cousot, P., Cousot, R., Fähndrich, M., Logozzo, F.: Automatic inference of necessary preconditions. In: Giacobazzi, R., Berdine, J., Mastroeni, I. (eds.) VMCAI 2013. LNCS, vol. 7737, pp. 128–148. Springer, Heidelberg (2013). doi:10.1007/978-3-642-35873-9_10
8. Ellison, C., Roşu, G.: An executable formal semantics of C with applications. In: Proceedings of POPL 2012, pp. 533–544. ACM (2012)
9. Gulavani, B.S., Chakraborty, S., Ramalingam, G., Nori, A.V.: Bottom-up shape analysis using LISF. ACM Trans. Program. Lang. Syst. **33**(5), 17 (2011)
10. Henkel, J., Diwan, A.: Discovering algebraic specifications from Java classes. In: Cardelli, L. (ed.) ECOOP 2003. LNCS, vol. 2743, pp. 431–456. Springer, Heidelberg (2003). doi:10.1007/978-3-540-45070-2_19
11. Khurshid, S., PĂsĂreanu, C.S., Visser, W.: Generalized symbolic execution for model checking and testing. In: Garavel, H., Hatcliff, J. (eds.) TACAS 2003. LNCS, vol. 2619, pp. 553–568. Springer, Heidelberg (2003). doi:10.1007/3-540-36577-X_40
12. King, J.C.: Symbolic execution and program testing. Comm. ACM **19**(7), 385–394 (1976)
13. Liskov, B., Guttag, J.: Abstraction and Specification in Program Development. MIT Press, Cambridge (1986)
14. Magill, S., Nanevski, A., Clarke, E., Lee, P.: Inferring invariants in separation logic for imperative list-processing programs. In: Proceedings of SPACE Workshop (2006)
15. Meyer, B.: Applying 'design by contract'. Computer **25**(10), 40–51 (1992)
16. Moura, L., Bjørner, N.: Z3: an efficient SMT solver. In: Ramakrishnan, C.R., Rehof, J. (eds.) TACAS 2008. LNCS, vol. 4963, pp. 337–340. Springer, Heidelberg (2008). doi:10.1007/978-3-540-78800-3_24
17. Moy, Y., Marché, C.: Modular inference of subprogram contracts for safety checking. J. Symbolic Comput. **45**(11), 1184–1211 (2010)
18. Roşu, G., Şerbănuţă, T.F.: An overview of the K semantic framework. JLAP **79**(6), 397–434 (2010)
19. Tillmann, N., Chen, F., Schulte, W.: Discovering likely method specifications. In: Liu, Z., He, J. (eds.) ICFEM 2006. LNCS, vol. 4260, pp. 717–736. Springer, Heidelberg (2006). doi:10.1007/11901433_39
20. Wei, Y., Furia, C.A., Kazmin, N., Meyer, B.: Inferring better contracts. In: Proceedings of the ICSE 2011, 191–200. ACM (2011)

Testing

On the Completeness of Selective Unification in Concolic Testing of Logic Programs

Fred Mesnard[1], Étienne Payet[1], and Germán Vidal[2(✉)]

[1] LIM - Université de la Réunion, Saint-Denis, France
{frederic.mesnard,etienne.payet}@univ-reunion.fr
[2] MiST, DSIC, Universitat Politècnica de València, Valencia, Spain
gvidal@dsic.upv.es

Abstract. Concolic testing is a popular dynamic validation technique that can be used for both model checking and automatic test case generation. We have recently introduced concolic testing in the context of logic programming. In contrast to previous approaches, the key ingredient in this setting is a technique to generate appropriate run-time goals by considering all possible ways an atom can unify with the heads of some program clauses. This is called "selective" unification. In this paper, we show that the existing algorithm is not complete and explore different alternatives in order to have a sound and complete algorithm for selective unification.

1 Introduction

A popular approach to software validation is based on so called *concolic execution* [4,11], which combines both *conc*olic and symb*olic* execution [1,3,6]. Concolic *testing* [4] is a technique based on concolic execution for finding run time errors and automatically generating test cases. In this approach, both concrete and symbolic executions are performed in parallel, so that concrete executions may help to spot (run time) errors—thus avoiding false positives—and symbolic executions are used to generate alternative input data—new test cases—so that a good coverage is obtained.

In concolic testing of imperative programs, one should augment the states with a so called *path condition* that stores the constraints on the variables of the symbolic execution. Then, after a (possibly incomplete) concolic execution, these constraints are used for producing alternative input data (e.g., by negating one of the constraints). Furthermore, and this is one of the main advantages of concolic testing over the original approach based solely on symbolic execution, if the constraints in the path condition become too complex, one can still take some values

---

This work has been partially supported by the EU (FEDER) and the Spanish *Ministerio de Economía y Competitividad* under grants TIN2013-44742-C4-1-R and TIN2016-76843-C4-1-R, and by the *Generalitat Valenciana* under grant PROMETEO-II/2015/013 (SmartLogic).

M.V. Hermenegildo and P. Lopez-Garcia (Eds.): LOPSTR 2016, LNCS 10184, pp. 205–221, 2017.
DOI: 10.1007/978-3-319-63139-4_12

from the concrete execution to simplify them. This is sound (but typically incomplete) and often allows one to explore a larger execution space than just giving up (as in the original approach based only on symbolic execution). Some successful tools that are based on concolic execution are, e.g., CUTE [11], SAGE [5], and Java Pathfinder [10].

We have recently introduced concolic testing in the context of logic programming [7]. There, a concolic state has the form $\langle S \mathbin{[\![} S' \rangle$, where S and S' are sequences of concrete and symbolic goals,[1] respectively. In logic programming, the notion of *symbolic* execution is very natural. Indeed, the structure of both S and S' is the same—the sequences of atoms have the same predicates and in the same order—and the only difference is that some atoms might be less instantiated in S' than in S.

A key ingredient of concolic testing in logic programming is the search for new concrete goals so that alternative paths can be explored, thus improving the coverage achieved so far. Let us illustrate it with an example. Consider the following (labelled) logic program:

$$
\begin{array}{lll}
(\ell_1)\ p(s(a)). & (\ell_4)\ q(a). & (\ell_6)\ r(a). \\
(\ell_2)\ p(s(W)) \leftarrow q(W). & (\ell_5)\ q(b). & (\ell_7)\ r(c). \\
(\ell_3)\ p(f(X)) \leftarrow r(X). & &
\end{array}
$$

Given the initial goal $p(f(a))$, a concolic execution would combine a concrete execution of the form

$$p(f(a)) \to_{id} r(a) \to_{id} true$$

where id denotes the empty substitution, with another one for the more general goal $p(N)$:

$$p(N) \to_{\{N/f(Y)\}} r(Y) \to_{\{Y/a\}} true$$

that only mimicks the steps of the former derivation despite being more general. The technique in [7] would basically produce the following concolic execution:

$$\langle p(f(a))_{id} \mathbin{[\![} p(N)_{id} \rangle \leadsto_{c(\{\ell_3\},\{\ell_1,\ell_2,\ell_3\})} \langle r(a)_{id} \mathbin{[\![} r(Y)_{\{N/f(Y)\}} \rangle$$
$$\leadsto_{c(\{\ell_6\},\{\ell_6,\ell_7\})} \langle true_{id} \mathbin{[\![} true_{\{N/f(a)\}} \rangle$$

where the goals are annotated with the answer computed so far. Roughly speaking, the above concolic execution is comprising the two standard SLD derivations for $p(f(a))$ and $p(N)$ above. Moreover, it also includes some further information: the labels of the clauses that unified with each concrete and symbolic goals.

For instance, the first step in the concolic execution above is labelled with $c(\{\ell_3\}, \{\ell_1, \ell_2, \ell_3\})$. This means that the concrete goal only unified with clause ℓ_3, but the symbolic goal unified with clauses ℓ_1, ℓ_2 and ℓ_3. Therefore, when looking for new run time goals that explore alternative paths, one should look

---

[1] Following the linear semantics of [12], we consider sequences of goals to represent the leaves of the SLD tree built so far.

for goals that unify with ℓ_1 but not with ℓ_2 and ℓ_3, that unify with ℓ_1 and ℓ_2 but not with ℓ_3, and so forth. In general, we should look for atoms that unify with all (and only) the feasible—i.e., those for which a solution exists—sets of clauses in $\{\{\}, \{\ell_1\}, \{\ell_1, \ell_2\}, \{\ell_1, \ell_2, \ell_3\}, \{\ell_2\}, \{\ell_2, \ell_3\}\}$. Also, some additional constraints on the groundness of some arguments are often required (e.g., to ensure that the generated goals are valid *run time* goals and, thus, will be terminating). A prototype implementation of the concolic testing scheme for pure Prolog, called contest, is publicly available from http://kaz.dsic.upv.es/contest.html.

In this paper, we focus on the so called *selective unification* problem that must be solved in order to produce the alternative goals during concolic testing. To be more precise, a selective unification problem is determined by a tuple $\langle A, \mathcal{H}^+, \mathcal{H}^-, G \rangle$ where

- A is the selected atom in a symbolic goal, e.g., $p(N)$,
- $\mathcal{H}^+$ are the atoms in the heads of the clauses we want A to unify with, e.g., for $\{\ell_1, \ell_2\}$ in the example above, we have $\mathcal{H}^+ = \{p(s(a)), p(s(W))\}$,
- $\mathcal{H}^-$ are the atoms in the heads of the clauses we do not want A to unify with, e.g., for $\{\ell_1, \ell_2\}$ in the example above, we have $\mathcal{H}^- = \{p(f(X))\}$,
- G is a set with the variables we want to be ground, e.g., $\{N\}$.

In this case, the problem is satisfiable and a solution is $\{N/s(a)\}$ since then $p(s(a))$ will unify with both atoms, $p(s(a))$ and $p(s(W))$, but it will not unify with $p(f(X))$ and, moreover, the variable N is ground.

In contrast, the case $\{\ell_1\}$ is not feasible, since there is no ground instance of $p(N)$ such that it unifies with $p(s(a))$ but not with $p(s(W))$.

In [7], we introduced a first algorithm for selective unification. Unfortunately, this algorithm was incomplete. In this paper, we further analyze this problem, identifying the potential sources of incompleteness, proving a number of properties, and introducing refined algorithms which are sound and complete under some circumstances.

2   Preliminaries

We assume some familiarity with the standard definitions and notations for logic programs as introduced in [2]. Nevertheless, in order to make the paper as self-contained as possible, we present in this section the main concepts which are needed to understand our development.

We denote by $|S|$ the cardinality of the set S. In this work, we consider a first-order language with a fixed vocabulary of predicate symbols, function symbols, and variables denoted by Π, Σ and $\mathcal{V}$, respectively. We let $\mathcal{T}(\Sigma, \mathcal{V})$ denote the set of *terms* constructed using symbols from Σ and variables from $\mathcal{V}$. Positions are used to address the nodes of a term viewed as a tree. A *position* p in a term t, in symbols $p \in \mathcal{P}os(t)$, is represented by a finite sequence of natural numbers, where ϵ denotes the root position. We let $t|_p$ denote the *subterm* of t at position p and $t[s]_p$ the result of *replacing the subterm* $t|_p$ by the term s. The depth $depth(t)$ of a term t is defined as: $depth(t) = 0$ if t is a variable and

$depth(f(t_1, \ldots, t_n)) = 1 + \max(depth(t_1), \ldots, depth(t_n))$, otherwise. We say that $t|_p$ is a subterm of t at depth k if there are k nested function symbols from the root of t to the root of $t|_p$. An *atom* has the form $p(t_1, \ldots, t_n)$ with $p/n \in \Pi$ and $t_i \in \mathcal{T}(\Sigma, \mathcal{V})$ for $i = 1, \ldots, n$. The notion of position is extended to atoms in the natural way. A *goal* is a finite sequence of atoms $A_1, \ldots, A_n$, where the *empty goal* is denoted by *true*. A *clause* has the form $H \leftarrow \mathcal{B}$ where H is an atom and $\mathcal{B}$ is a goal (note that we only consider *definite* programs). A logic *program* is a finite sequence of clauses. $Var(s)$ denotes the set of variables in the syntactic object s (i.e., s can be a term, an atom, a query, or a clause). A syntactic object s is *ground* if $Var(s) = \emptyset$. In this work, we only consider *finite* ground terms.

Substitutions and their operations are defined as usual. In particular, the set $Dom(\sigma) = \{x \in \mathcal{V} \mid \sigma(x) \neq x\}$ is called the *domain* of a substitution σ. We let *id* denote the empty substitution. The application of a substitution θ to a syntactic object s is usually denoted by juxtaposition, i.e., we write $s\theta$ rather than $\theta(s)$. The *restriction* $\theta\restriction_V$ of a substitution θ to a set of variables V is defined as follows: $x\theta\restriction_V = x\theta$ if $x \in V$ and $x\theta\restriction_V = x$ otherwise. We say that $\theta = \sigma\ [V]$ if $\theta\restriction_V = \sigma\restriction_V$. A syntactic object s_1 is *more general* than a syntactic object s_2, denoted $s_1 \leqslant s_2$, if there exists a substitution θ such that $s_2 = s_1\theta$. A *variable renaming* is a substitution that is a bijection on $\mathcal{V}$. Two syntactic objects t_1 and t_2 are *variants* (or equal up to variable renaming), denoted $t_1 \sim t_2$, if $t_1 = t_2\rho$ for some variable renaming ρ. A substitution θ is a unifier of two syntactic objects t_1 and t_2 iff $t_1\theta = t_2\theta$; furthermore, θ is the *most general unifier* of t_1 and t_2, denoted by $\mathsf{mgu}(t_1, t_2)$ if, for every other unifier σ of t_1 and t_2, we have that $\theta \leqslant \sigma$. We write $t_1 \approx t_2$ to denote that t_1 and t_2 unify for some substitution, which is not relevant here. By abuse of notation, we also use mgu to denote the most general unifier of a conjunction of equations of the form $s_1 = t_1 \wedge \ldots \wedge s_n = t_n$, i.e., $\mathsf{mgu}(s_1 = t_1 \wedge \ldots \wedge s_n = t_n) = \theta$ if $s_i\theta = t_i\theta$ for all $i = 1, \ldots, n$ and for every other unifier σ of s_i and t_i, $i = 1, \ldots, n$, we have that $\theta \leqslant \sigma$.

We say that a syntactic object o is *linear* if it does not contain multiple occurrences of the same variable. A substitution $\{X_1/t_1, \ldots, X_n/t_n\}$ is *linear* if $t_1, \ldots, t_n$ are linear and, moreover, they do not share variables.

3   The Selective Unification Problem

In this section, we first recall the unification problem from [7]. There, an algorithm for "selective unification" was proposed, and it was conjectured to be complete. Here, we prove that it is indeed incomplete and we identify two sources of incompleteness.

Definition 1 (selective unification problem). *Let A be an atom with $G \subseteq Var(A)$ a set of variables, and let $\mathcal{H}^+$ and $\mathcal{H}^-$ be finite sets of atoms such that all atoms are pairwise variable disjoint and $A \approx B$ for all $B \in \mathcal{H}^+ \cup \mathcal{H}^-$. Then, the selective unification problem for A w.r.t. $\mathcal{H}^+$, $\mathcal{H}^-$ and G is defined as follows:*

$$\mathcal{P}(A, \mathcal{H}^+, \mathcal{H}^-, G) = \left\{ \sigma\restriction_{Var(A)} \left| \begin{array}{l} \forall H \in \mathcal{H}^+ : A\sigma \approx H \\ \wedge \ \forall H \in \mathcal{H}^- : \neg(A\sigma \approx H) \\ \wedge \ G\sigma \ \text{is ground} \end{array} \right. \right\}$$

When the considered signature is finite, the following algorithm is sound and complete for solving the selective unification problem: first, bind the variables of A with terms of depth 0. If the condition above does not hold, then we try with terms of depth 1, and check it again. We keep increasing the considered term depth until a solution is found. Here, we prove that there exists a finite number n such that, if a solution has not been found when considering terms of depth n, then the problem is not satisfiable.

Theorem 1. *Let A be a linear atom with $G \subseteq Var(A)$, $\mathcal{H}^+$ be a finite set of linear atoms and $\mathcal{H}^-$ be a finite set of atoms such that all atoms are pairwise variable disjoint and $A \approx B$ for all $B \in \mathcal{H}^+ \cup \mathcal{H}^-$. Then, checking that $\mathcal{P}(A, \mathcal{H}^+, \mathcal{H}^-, G) \neq \emptyset$ is decidable.*

Proof. Here, we assume the naive algorithm sketched above. Let us first consider that all atoms in $\{A\} \cup \mathcal{H}^+ \cup \mathcal{H}^-$ are linear. Let k be the maximum depth of the atoms in $\{A\} \cup \mathcal{H}^+ \cup \mathcal{H}^-$. Consider the set

$$\Theta' = \{\theta \mid \mathcal{D}om(\theta) \subseteq \mathcal{V}ar(A), \; depth(A\theta) \leqslant k + 1\}$$

On Θ', we define the binary relation $\theta_1 \simeq \theta_2$ iff $A\theta_1 \sim A\theta_2$. The relation $\simeq$ is an equivalence relation. Let $\Theta = \Theta'/\!\simeq$. The set Θ is usually large but finite. Now, we proceed by contradiction and assume that the problem is satisfiable but there is no solution in Θ.

Let $\sigma \in \mathcal{P}(A, \mathcal{H}^+, \mathcal{H}^-, G)$ be one of such solutions with $\sigma \notin \Theta$. Let $k' \leqslant k$ be the maximum depth of the atoms in $\mathcal{H}^+$. Let $s_1, \ldots, s_n$ be the non-variable terms at depth $k' + 1$ or higher in $A\sigma$, which occur at positions $p_1, \ldots, p_n$. Trivially, all atoms in $\mathcal{H}^+$ should have a variable at depth k' or lesser in order to still unify with $A\sigma$. Therefore, replacing these terms by any term would not change the fact that it unifies with all atoms in $\mathcal{H}^+$. Formally, $(\ldots (A\sigma[t_1]_{p_1}) \ldots)[t_n]_{p_n} \approx H$ for all $H \in \mathcal{H}^+$ and for all terms $t_1, \ldots, t_n$.

Now, let us consider the negative atoms $\mathcal{H}^-$. Let us focus in the worst case, where the maximum depth of the atoms in $\mathcal{H}^-$ is $k \geq k'$. Since $\neg(A\sigma \approx H)$ for all $H \in \mathcal{H}^-$ and $(\ldots (A\sigma[t_1]_{p_1}) \ldots)[t_n]_{p_n} \approx H$ for all $H \in \mathcal{H}^+$ and for all terms $t_1, \ldots, t_n$, let us choose terms $t'_1, \ldots, t'_n$ such that $\neg((\ldots (A\sigma[t'_1]_{p_1}) \ldots)[t'_n]_{p_n} \approx H)$ for all $H \in \mathcal{H}^-$ and $(\ldots (A\sigma[t'_1]_{p_1}) \ldots)[t'_n]_{p_n}$ has depth $k + 1$. Note that this is always possible since, in the worst case, for each term in the atoms of $\mathcal{H}^-$ at depth k, we might need a term at depth $k+1$ (when the term in the atom of $\mathcal{H}^-$ is the only constant of the signature, so we need to introduce a function symbol and another constant if the argument should be ground). Let $\sigma' \subseteq \mathcal{D}om(A)$ be a subtitution such that $A\sigma' = (\ldots (A\sigma[t'_1]_{p_1}) \ldots)[t'_n]_{p_n}$. Then, $\sigma' \in \mathcal{P}(A, \mathcal{H}^+, \mathcal{H}^-, G)$ with $\sigma' \in \Theta$ and, thus, we get a contradiction.

Extending the proof to non-linear atoms is not difficult but it is tedious since we have to consider a higher depth that may depend on the multiple occurrences of the same variables. $\square$

We conjecture that the above naive algorithm would also be complete for infinite signatures (e.g., integers) since the number of symbols in the considered atoms is finite. Nonetheless, such algorithms may be so inefficient that they are impractical in the context of concolic testing.

We note that the set $\mathcal{P}(A, \mathcal{H}^+, \mathcal{H}^-, G)$ is usually infinite. Moreover, even when considering only the *most general* solutions in this set, there may still exist more than one:

Example 1. Consider $A = p(X, Y)$, $\mathcal{H}^+ = \{p(Z, Z), p(a, b)\}$, $\mathcal{H}^- = \{p(c, c)\}$ and $G = \emptyset$. Then, both substitutions $\{X/a, Y/U\}$ and $\{X/U, Y/b\}$ are most general solutions in $\mathcal{P}(A, \mathcal{H}^+, \mathcal{H}^-, G)$. In principle, any of them is equally good in our context.

In [7], we have introduced a stepwise method that, intuitively speaking, proceeds as follows:

- First, we produce some "maximal" substitutions θ for A such that $A\theta$ still unifies with the atoms in $\mathcal{H}^+$. Here, we use a special set $\mathcal{U}$ of fresh variables with $Var(\{A\} \cup \mathcal{H}^+ \cup \mathcal{H}^-) \cap \mathcal{U} = \emptyset$. The elements of $\mathcal{U}$ are denoted by U, U', U_1... Then, in θ, the variables from $\mathcal{U}$ (if any) denote positions where further binding *might* prevent $A\theta$ from unifying with some atom in $\mathcal{H}^+$.
- In a second stage, we look for another substitution η such that $\theta\eta$ is a solution of the selective unification problem, i.e., $\theta\eta \in \mathcal{P}(A, \mathcal{H}^+, \mathcal{H}^-, G)$. Here, we basically follow a generate and test algorithm (as in the naive algorithm above), but it is now much more restricted thanks to the bindings in θ and the fact that binding variables from $\mathcal{U}$ is not allowed.

In the first stage, we use the variables from the special set $\mathcal{U}$ to replace *disagreement pairs* (see [2] p. 27). Roughly speaking, given terms s and t, a subterm s' of s and a subterm t' of t form a disagreement pair if the root symbols of s' and t' are different, but the symbols from s' up to the root of s and from t' up to the root of t are the same. For instance, $X, g(a)$ and $b, h(Y)$ are disagreement pairs of the terms $f(X, g(b))$ and $f(g(a), g(h(Y)))$. A disagreement pair t, t' is called *simple* if one of the terms is a variable that does not occur in the other term and no variable of $\mathcal{U}$ occurs in t, t'. We say that the substitution $\{X/s\}$ is determined by t, t' if $\{X, s\} = \{t, t'\}$.

Definition 2 (algorithm for positive unification)

Input: *an atom A and a set of atoms $\mathcal{H}^+$ such that all atoms are pairwise variable disjoint and $A \approx B$ for all $B \in \mathcal{H}^+$.*
Output: *a substitution θ.*

1. *Let $\mathcal{B} := \{A\} \cup \mathcal{H}^+$.*
2. *While simple disagreement pairs occur in $\mathcal{B}$ do*
   (a) *nondeterministically choose a simple disagreement pair X, t (respectively, t, X) in $\mathcal{B}$;*
   (b) *set $\mathcal{B}$ to $\mathcal{B}\eta$ where $\eta = \{X/t\}$.*
3. *While $|\mathcal{B}| \neq 1$ do*
   (a) *nondeterministically choose a disagreement pair t, t' in $\mathcal{B}$;*
   (b) *replace t, t' with a fresh variable from $\mathcal{U}$.*

4. Return $\theta\gamma$, where $\mathcal{B} = \{B\}$, $A\theta = B$, $\mathcal{D}om(\theta) \subseteq \mathcal{V}ar(A)$, and γ is a variable renaming for the variables of $\mathcal{V}ar(A\theta)\backslash\mathcal{U}$ with fresh variables from $\mathcal{V}\backslash\mathcal{U}$.

We denote by $\mathcal{SU}^+(A, \mathcal{H}^+)$ the set of non-deterministic substitutions computed by the above algorithm.

Observe that the step (2a) involves two types of non-determinism:

- *Don't care* nondeterminism, when there are several disagreement pairs X, t (or t, X) for *different* variables. In this case, we can select any of them and continue with the next step. The final solution would be the same no matter the selection. This is also true for step (3a), since the order in which the non-simple disagreement pairs are selected will not affect the final result.
- *Don't know* nondeterminism, when there are several disagreement pairs X, t (or t, X) for the same variable X. In this case, we should consider all possibilities since they may give rise to different solutions.

Example 2. Let $A = p(X, Y)$ and $\mathcal{H}^+ = \{p(a, b), p(Z, Z)\}$. Therefore, we start with $\mathcal{B} := \{p(X, Y), p(a, b), p(Z, Z)\}$. The algorithm then considers the simple disagreement pairs in $\mathcal{B}$. From X, a, we get $\eta_1 := \{X/a\}$ and the action (2b) sets $\mathcal{B}$ to $\mathcal{B}\eta_1 = \{p(a, Y), p(a, b), p(Z, Z)\}$. The substitution $\eta_2 := \{Y/b\}$ is determined by Y, b and the action (2b) sets $\mathcal{B}$ to $\mathcal{B}\eta_2 = \{p(a, b), p(Z, Z)\}$. Now, we have two don't know nondeterministic possibilities:

- If we consider the disagreement pair a, Z, we have a substitution $\eta_3 := \{Z/a\}$ and action (2b) then sets $\mathcal{B}$ to $\mathcal{B}\eta_3 = \{p(a, b), p(a, a)\}$. Now, no simple disagreement pair occurs in $\mathcal{B}$, hence the algorithm jumps to the loop at line 3. Action (3b) replaces the disagreement pair b, a with a fresh variable $U \in \mathcal{U}$, hence $\mathcal{B}$ is set to $\{p(a, U)\}$. As $|\mathcal{B}| = 1$ the loop at line 3 stops and the algorithm returns the substitution $\{X/a, Y/U\}$.
- If we consider the disagreement pair b, Z instead, we have a substitution $\eta_3' := \{Z/b\}$, and action (2b) sets $\mathcal{B}$ to $\mathcal{B}\eta_3' = \{p(a, b), p(b, b)\}$. Now, by proceeding as in the previous case, the algorithm returns $\{X/U', Y/b\}$.

Therefore, $\mathcal{SU}^+(A, \mathcal{H}^+) = \{\{X/a, Y/U\}, \{X/U', Y/b\}\}$.

The soundness of the algorithm in Definition 2 can then be proved as follows (termination is straightforward, see [8]). Note that this result was incomplete in [7] since the condition on $\mathcal{R}an(\eta)$ was missing.

Theorem 2. *Let A be an atom and $\mathcal{H}^+$ be a set of atoms such that all atoms are pairwise variable disjoint and $A \approx B$ for all $B \in \mathcal{H}^+$. Then, for all $\theta \in \mathcal{SU}^+(A, \mathcal{H}^+)$, we have that $A\theta\eta \approx H$ for all $H \in \mathcal{H}^+$ and for any idempotent substitution η with $\mathcal{D}om(\eta) \subseteq \mathcal{V}ar(A\theta)\backslash\mathcal{U}$ and $\mathcal{R}an(\eta)\cap(\mathcal{V}ar(\mathcal{H}^+\cup\{A\})\cup\mathcal{U}) = \emptyset$.*

In order to prove this theorem, we first need the following results, which can be found in [8, Appendix B.2]:

Lemma 1. *Suppose that $A\theta = B\theta$ for some atoms A and B and some substitution θ. Then we have $A\theta\eta = B\eta\theta\eta$ for any substitution η with $[Dom(\eta) \cap Var(B)] \cap Dom(\theta) = \emptyset$ and $Ran(\eta) \cap Dom(\theta\eta) = \emptyset$.*

Proposition 1. *The loop at line 3 always terminates and the following statement is an invariant of this loop.*

(inv') *For each $A' \in \{A\} \cup \mathcal{H}^+$ there exists $B \in \mathcal{B}$ and a substitution θ such that $A'\theta = B\theta$, $Dom(\theta) \subseteq (Var(\mathcal{H}^+ \cup \{A\}) \cup \mathcal{U})$ and $Var(\mathcal{B}) \cap Dom(\theta) \subseteq \mathcal{U}$.*

The proof of Theorem 2 can now proceed as follows:

Proof. Upon termination of the loop at line 3 we have $|\mathcal{B}| = 1$. Let B be the element of $\mathcal{B}$ with $A\theta = B$, and let $\theta' \in \mathcal{SU}^+(A, \mathcal{H}^+)$ be a renaming of θ for the variables of $A\theta \backslash \mathcal{U}$. By Proposition 1, we have that, for all $H \in \mathcal{H}^+$, there exists a substitution μ such that $A\theta\mu = H\mu$ and the following conditions hold:

- $Dom(\mu) \subseteq (Var(\mathcal{H}^+ \cup \{A\}) \cup \mathcal{U})$ and
- $Var(A\theta) \cap Dom(\mu) \subseteq \mathcal{U}$.

Trivially, there exists a unifier μ' for $A\theta'$ and H too, and the same conditions hold: $Dom(\mu') \subseteq (Var(\mathcal{H}^+ \cup \{A\}) \cup \mathcal{U})$ and $Var(A\theta') \cap Dom(\mu') \subseteq \mathcal{U}$.

Now, in order to apply Lemma 1, we need to prove the following conditions:

- $[Dom(\eta) \cap Var(A\theta')] \cap Dom(\mu') = \emptyset$. This is trivially implied by the fact that $Dom(\eta) \subseteq Var(A\theta') \backslash \mathcal{U}$ and $Var(A\theta') \cap Dom(\mu') \subseteq \mathcal{U}$.
- $Ran(\eta) \cap Dom(\mu'\eta) = \emptyset$. First, since $Dom(\mu'\eta) \subseteq Dom(\mu') \cup Dom(\eta)$, we prove the stronger claim: $Ran(\eta) \cap Dom(\mu') = \emptyset$ and $Ran(\eta) \cap Dom(\eta) = \emptyset$. The second condition is triviallly implied by the idempotency of η. Regarding the first condition, it is implied by $Ran(\eta) \cap (Var(\mathcal{H}^+ \cup \{A\}) \cup \mathcal{U}) = \emptyset$ since $Dom(\mu') \subseteq (Var(\mathcal{H}^+ \cup \{A\}) \cup \mathcal{U})$, which is true.

Therefore, by Lemma 1, we have that $A\theta'\eta\mu'\eta = H\mu'\eta$ and, thus, $A\theta'\eta$ unifies with H. Hence, we have proved that $A\theta'\eta$ unifies with every atom in $\mathcal{H}^+$. □

Now we deal with the negative atoms and the groundness constraints by means of the following algorithm:

Definition 3 (algorithm for selective unification)

Input: *an atom A with $G \subseteq Var(A)$ a set of variables, and two finite sets $\mathcal{H}^+$ and $\mathcal{H}^-$ such that all atoms are pairwise variable disjoint and $A \approx B$ for all $B \in \mathcal{H}^+ \cup \mathcal{H}^-$.*
Output: fail *or a substitution $\theta\eta$ (restricted to the variables of A).*

1. *Generate—using a fair algorithm—pairs (θ, η) with $\theta \in \mathcal{SU}^+(A, \mathcal{H}^+)$ and η an idempotent substitution such that $G\theta\eta$ is ground, $Dom(\eta) \subseteq Var(A\theta) \backslash \mathcal{U}$ and $Ran(\eta) \cap (Var(\mathcal{H}^+ \cup \{A\}) \cup \mathcal{U}) = \emptyset$, otherwise return* fail.
2. *Check that for each $H^- \in \mathcal{H}^-$, $\neg(A\theta\eta \approx H^-)$, otherwise return* fail.

3. Return $\theta\eta\gamma$ (restricted to the variables of A), where γ is a variable renaming for $A\theta\eta$ with fresh variables from $\mathcal{V}\backslash\mathcal{U}$.

We denote by $\mathcal{SU}(A, \mathcal{H}^+, \mathcal{H}^-, G)$ the set of non-deterministic (non-failing) substitutions computed by the above algorithm.

Note that step (1) above is don't know nondeterministic and, thus, all substitutions in $\mathcal{SU}^+(A, \mathcal{H}^+)$ should in principle be considered. On the other hand, computing the first solution of the above algorithm is enough for concolic testing.

The soundness of the selective unification algorithm is a straightforward consequence of Theorem 2 and the fact that the algorithm in Definition 3 is basically a fair generate-and-test procedure.

Unfortunately, the selective unification algorithm is not complete in general, as Examples 3 and 4 below illustrate. Example 3 shows that the algorithm cannot always compute all the solutions while Example 4 shows that it may even find no solution at all for a satisfiable instance of the problem.

Example 3. Consider the atom $A = p(X_1, X_2)$ with $G = \{X_1\}$, and the sets $\mathcal{H}^+ = \{p(X, g(X)), p(Z, Z)\}$ and $\mathcal{H}^- = \{p(g(b), W)\}$. Here, we have

$$\mathcal{SU}^+(A, \mathcal{H}^+) = \{\underbrace{\{X_1/X', X_2/U\}}_{\theta_1}, \underbrace{\{X_1/U, X_2/g(X')\}}_{\theta_2}\}$$

The algorithm is able to compute the solution $\{X_1/g(a), X_2/U\}$ from θ_1, $\eta = \{X'/g(a)\}$ and $\gamma = id$. However, it cannot compute $\{X_1/g(a), X_2/g(X')\} \in \mathcal{P}(A, \mathcal{H}^+, \mathcal{H}^-, G)$.

The algorithm fails here because the instantiation of variables from $\mathcal{U}$ is not allowed. In [7], it was incorrectly assumed that *any* binding of a variable from $\mathcal{U}$ will result in a substitution θ' such that $A\theta'$ does not unify will all the atoms in $\mathcal{H}^+$ anymore. However, the universal quantification was not right. For each variable from $\mathcal{U}$, we can only ensure that *there exists some* term t such that binding this variable to t will result in a substitution that prevents A from unifying with some atom in $\mathcal{H}^+$. Therefore, since the algorithm of Definition 3 forbids the bindings of the variables in $\mathcal{U}$, completeness is lost. We will propose a solution to this problem in the next section.

Example 4. Consider $A = p(X_1, X_2)$, $\mathcal{H}^+ = \{p(X, a), p(b, Y)\}$, $\mathcal{H}^- = \{p(b, a)\}$, and $G = \emptyset$. Here, we have $\mathcal{SU}^+(A, \mathcal{H}^+) = \{\{X_1/b, X_2/a\}\}$ and, thus, the algorithm in Definition 3 fails. However, the following substitution $\{X_1/Z, X_2/Z\}$ is a solution, i.e., $\{X_1/Z, X_2/Z\} \in \mathcal{P}(A, \mathcal{H}^+, \mathcal{H}^-, G)$.

Unfortunately, we do not know how to generate such non-linear solutions except with the naive semi-algorithm mentioned at the beginning of this section, which is not generally useful in practice. Therefore, in the next section we will rule out these solutions.

4   Recovering Completeness for Linear Selective Unification

In this section, we introduce different alternatives to recover the completeness of the selective unification algorithm.

In the following, we only consider a subset of the solutions to the selective unification problem, namely those which are *linear*:

$$\mathcal{P}_{\text{lin}}(A, \mathcal{H}^+, \mathcal{H}^-, G) = \{\sigma \in \mathcal{P}(A, \mathcal{H}^+, \mathcal{H}^-, G) \mid \sigma \text{ is linear}\}$$

i.e., we rule out solutions like those in Example 4 since we do not know how such solutions can be produced using a constructive algorithm. We refer to $\mathcal{P}_{\text{lin}}(A, \mathcal{H}^+, \mathcal{H}^-, G)$ as the *linear selective unification problem*.

4.1   A Naive Extension

One of the sources of incompleteness of the algorithm in Definition 3 comes from the fact that the variables from $\mathcal{U}$ cannot be bound. Therefore, one can consider a naive extension of this algorithm as follows:

Definition 4. (extended algorithm for selective unification)

Input: *an atom A with $G \subseteq Var(A)$ a set of variables, and two finite sets $\mathcal{H}^+$ and $\mathcal{H}^-$ such that all atoms are pairwise variable disjoint and $A \approx B$ for all $B \in \mathcal{H}^+ \cup \mathcal{H}^-$.*
Output: fail *or a substitution $\theta\eta$ (restricted to the variables of A).*

1. *Generate—using a fair algorithm—pairs (θ, η) with $\theta \in \mathcal{SU}^+(A, \mathcal{H}^+)$ and η an idempotent substitution such that $G\theta\eta$ is ground, $\mathcal{D}om(\eta) \subseteq Var(A\theta)$ and $\mathcal{R}an(\eta) \cap (Var(\mathcal{H}^+ \cup \{A\}) \cup \mathcal{U}) = \emptyset$, otherwise return* fail.
2. *Check that for each $H^- \in \mathcal{H}^-$, $\neg(A\theta\eta \approx H^-)$, otherwise return* fail.
3. *Return $\theta\eta\gamma$ (restricted to the variables of A), where γ is a variable renaming for $A\theta\eta$ with fresh variables from $\mathcal{V}\backslash\mathcal{U}$.*

We denote by $\mathcal{SU}^*(A, \mathcal{H}^+, \mathcal{H}^-, G)$ the set of non-deterministic (non-failing) substitutions computed by the above algorithm.

In general, though, the above algorithm can be very inefficient since all variables in $A\theta$ can now be bound, even those in $\mathcal{U}$. Nevertheless, one can easily define a fair procedure for generating pairs (θ, η) in step (1) above which gives priority to binding the variables in $Var(A\theta)\backslash\mathcal{U}$, so that the variables from $\mathcal{U}$ are only bound when no solution can be found otherwise.

4.2   The Positive Unification Problem

Now, we introduce a more efficient instance of the algorithm for linear selective unification which is sound and complete when the atoms in A and $\mathcal{H}^+$ are linear. Formally, we are concerned with the following unification problem:

Definition 5 (positive linear unification problem). *Let A be a linear atom and let $\mathcal{H}^+$ be a finite set of linear atoms such that all atoms are pairwise variable disjoint and $A \approx B$ for all $B \in \mathcal{H}^+$. Then, the* positive linear unification problem *for A w.r.t. $\mathcal{H}^+$ is defined as follows:*

$$\mathcal{P}_{\text{lin}}^+(A, \mathcal{H}^+) = \{\sigma\vert_{\mathcal{V}ar(A)}\vert\ (\forall H \in \mathcal{H}^+ : A\sigma \approx H)\ \text{and } \sigma \text{ is linear}\}$$

Note that we do not want to find a unifier between A and *all* the atoms in $\mathcal{H}^+$, but a substitution θ such that $A\theta$ still unifies with *each* atom in $\mathcal{H}^+$ independently. So this problem is different from the usual unification problems found in the literature.

Clearly, $|\mathcal{P}_{\text{lin}}^+(A, \mathcal{H}^+)| \geq 1$ since the identity substitution is always a solution to the positive linear unification problem. In general, though, the set $\mathcal{P}_{\text{lin}}^+(A, \mathcal{H}^+)$ is infinite.

Example 5. Let us consider $A = p(X)$ and $\mathcal{H}^+ = \{p(f(Y)), p(f(g(Z)))\}$. Then, we have $\{id, \{X/f(X')\}, \{X/f(g(X'))\}, \{X/f(g(a))\}, \{X/f(g(f(X')))\}, \ldots\}\} \subseteq \mathcal{P}_{\text{lin}}^+(A, \mathcal{H}^+)$, which is clearly infinite.

Therefore, in the following, we restrict our interest to so called *maximal* solutions:

Definition 6 (maximal solution). *Let A be a linear atom and $\mathcal{H}^+$ be a finite set of linear atoms such that all atoms are pairwise variable disjoint and $A \approx B$ for all $B \in \mathcal{H}^+$. We say that a substitution $\theta \in \mathcal{P}_{\text{lin}}^+(A, \mathcal{H}^+)$ is* maximal *when the following conditions hold:*

1. *for any idempotent substitution γ with $\mathcal{D}om(\gamma) \subseteq \mathcal{V}ar(A\theta) \setminus \mathcal{U}$ and $\mathcal{R}an(\gamma) \cap (\mathcal{V}ar(\mathcal{H}^+ \cup \{A\}) \cup \mathcal{U}) = \emptyset$, $(\theta\gamma)\vert_{\mathcal{V}ar(A)}$ is still an element of $\mathcal{P}_{\text{lin}}^+(A, \mathcal{H}^+)$,*
2. *for any variable $U \in \mathcal{V}ar(A\theta) \cap \mathcal{U}$, we have that $(\theta\{U/t\})\vert_{\mathcal{V}ar(A)}$ is not an element of $\mathcal{P}_{\text{lin}}^+(A, \mathcal{H}^+)$ for all non-variable term t, and*
3. *for any $X/t \in \theta$ and for all non-variable term $t\vert_p$, replacing it by a non-variable term rooted by a different symbol will result in a substitution which is not an element of $\mathcal{P}_{\text{lin}}^+(A, \mathcal{H}^+)$ anymore.*

We let $max(A, \mathcal{H}^+)$ denote the set of maximal solutions in $\mathcal{P}_{\text{lin}}^+(A, \mathcal{H}^+)$.

Intuitively speaking, given a maximal solution θ, the first condition implies that $(\theta\gamma)\vert_{\mathcal{V}ar(A)}$ is still a solution of the positive linear unification problem as long as no variables from $\mathcal{U}$ are bound. The second and third conditions mean that the rest of the symbols in θ cannot be changed, i.e., binding a variable from $\mathcal{U}$ with a non-variable term or changing any constant or function symbol by a different one, will always result in a substitution which is not a solution of the positive linear unification problem anymore.

Example 6. Consider, e.g., $A = p(X_1, X_2)$ and $\mathcal{H}^+ = \{p(f(Y), a), p(f(g(Z)), b)\}$. Here, we have $\{X_1/X', X_2/X''\} \in \mathcal{P}_{\text{lin}}^+(A, \mathcal{H}^+)$ but it is not a maximal solution, i.e., $\{X_1/X', X_2/X''\} \notin max(A, \mathcal{H}^+)$ since binding X'' to, e.g., a, will result in a substitution which is not in $\mathcal{P}_{\text{lin}}^+(A, \mathcal{H}^+)$. In contrast,

$\{X_1/f(g(Z')), X_2/U\}$ is a maximal solution. However, any substitution of the form $\{X_1/f(g(t)), X_2/U\}$ for any non-variable term t is not a maximal solution since the third condition will not hold anymore (one can change the symbols introduced by t and still get a solution in $\mathcal{P}_{\text{lin}}^+(A, \mathcal{H}^+)$). The substitution $\{X_1/f(Y'), X_2/U\}$ is not a maximal solution as well since binding Y' to, e.g., a, will result in a substitution which is not in $\mathcal{P}_{\text{lin}}^+(A, \mathcal{H}^+)$, hence the first condition does not hold. And the same applies to $\{X_1/f(U'), X_2/U\}$, which is not a maximal solution either since we can bind U' to $g(X')$ and still get a substitution in $\mathcal{P}_{\text{lin}}^+(A, \mathcal{H}^+)$.

In contrast to $\mathcal{P}_{\text{lin}}^+(A, \mathcal{H}^+)$, the set $max(A, \mathcal{H}^+)$ is finite, since it is bounded by the depth of the terms in $\mathcal{H}^+$. Actually, for linear atoms in $\{A\} \cup \mathcal{H}^+$, there is only *one* maximal solution.

Proposition 2. *Let A be a linear atom and $\mathcal{H}^+$ be a finite set of linear atoms such that all atoms are pairwise variable disjoint and $A \approx B$ for all $B \in \mathcal{H}^+$. Then, the set $max(A, \mathcal{H}^+)$ is a singleton (up to variable renaming).*

Proof. We proceed by contradiction. Let us assume that there are two maximal solutions $\sigma, \theta \in max(A, \mathcal{H}^+)$, where $X/s \in \sigma$ and $X/t \in \theta$ for some variable $X \in Var(A)$. Let us consider that s and t differ at position p such that $s|_p$ and $t|_p$ are rooted by a different symbol. Now, we distinguish the following cases:

- If $s|_p$ and $t|_p$ are rooted by different constant or function symbols, we get a contradiction by condition (3) of maximal solution.
- If $s|_p$ is rooted by a constant or function symbol, while $t|_p$ is rooted by a variable from $\mathcal{U}$ (or viceversa), we get a contradiction by condition (2) of maximal solution.
- If $s|_p$ is rooted by a constant or function symbol, while $t|_p$ is rooted by a variable from $\mathcal{V} \backslash \mathcal{U}$ (or viceversa), we get a contradiction either by condition (1) or (3) of maximal solution.
- Finally, if $s|_p$ is rooted by a variable from $\mathcal{U}$, while $t|_p$ is rooted by a variable from $\mathcal{V} \backslash \mathcal{U}$ (or viceversa), we get a contradiction either by condition (1) or (2) of maximal solution.

Therefore, the set $max(A, \mathcal{H}^+)$ is necessarily a singleton. $\qquad \square$

Moreover, the following key property holds: a maximal solution can always be *completed* in order to get a solution to the linear unification problem when it is satisfiable. In order to prove this result, we need to recall the definition of *parallel composition* of substitutions, denoted by $\Uparrow$ in [9].

Definition 7 (parallel composition [9]). *Let θ_1 and θ_2 be two idempotent substitutions. Then, we define $\Uparrow$ as follows:*

$$\theta_1 \Uparrow \theta_2 = \begin{cases} \mathsf{mgu}(\widehat{\theta}_1 \wedge \widehat{\theta}_2) & \textit{if } \widehat{\theta}_1 \wedge \widehat{\theta}_2 \textit{ has a solution (a unifier)} \\ \textit{fail} & \textit{otherwise} \end{cases}$$

where $\widehat{\theta}$ denotes the equational representation of a substitution θ, i.e., if $\theta = \{X_1/t_1, \ldots, X_n/t_n\}$ then $\widehat{\theta} = (X_1 = t_1 \wedge \cdots \wedge X_n = t_n)$.

Proposition 3. *Let A be a linear atom and $\mathcal{H}^+$ be a finite set of linear atoms such that all atoms are pairwise variable disjoint and $A \approx B$ for all $B \in \mathcal{H}^+$. Let $\theta \in max(A, \mathcal{H}^+)$ be the maximal solution for A and $\mathcal{H}^+$. Then, if $\mathcal{P}_{\mathsf{lin}}(A, \mathcal{H}^+, \mathcal{H}^-, G)$ is satisfiable (the set contains at least one substitution), then there exists some substitution γ such that $\theta\gamma \in \mathcal{P}_{\mathsf{lin}}(A, \mathcal{H}^+, \mathcal{H}^-, G)$.*

Proof. For simplicity, we consider that $A = p(X)$, $\mathcal{H}^+ = \{p(t_1), \ldots, p(t_n)\}$ and $\mathcal{H}^- = \{p(s_1), \ldots, p(s_m)\}$. Since the atoms are linear, the claim would follow by a similar argument. Let $\theta = \{X/t\} \in max(A, \mathcal{H}^+)$ be the maximal solution. Hence, we have $t \approx t_i$ for all $i = 1, \ldots, n$. Let $\sigma \in \mathcal{P}_{\mathsf{lin}}(A, \mathcal{H}^+, \mathcal{H}^-, G)$ be a solution to the selective unification problem. By definition of maximal solution, there may be other solutions to the positive unification problem, but every introduced symbol cannot be different if we want to still unify with all terms $t_1, \ldots, t_n$ by condition (3) in the definition of maximal solution. Therefore, both substitutions must be compatible, i.e., we have $\theta \Uparrow \sigma = \delta \neq$ fail. Furthermore, taking into account the negative atoms in $\mathcal{H}^-$ as well as the groundness constraints w.r.t. G, δ can only introduce further bindings, but would never require to generalize any term introduced by θ and, thus, δ can be decomposed as $\theta\gamma$, with $\theta\gamma \in \mathcal{P}_{\mathsf{lin}}(A, \mathcal{H}^+, \mathcal{H}^-, G)$. □

Therefore, computing the maximal solution suffices to check for satisfiability. Here, we use again the algorithm in Definition 2 for computing the maximal solution, with the following differences: (i) first, both A and the atoms in $\mathcal{H}^+$ are now linear; (ii) step (2a) is now don't care nondeterministic, so the algorithm will return a single solution, which we denote by $\mathcal{SU}_{\mathsf{lin}}^+(A, \mathcal{H}^+)$.

Proposition 4. *Let A be a linear atom and $\mathcal{H}^+$ be a finite set of linear atoms such that all atoms are pairwise variable disjoint and $A \approx B$ for all $B \in \mathcal{H}^+$. Then, $\mathcal{SU}_{\mathsf{lin}}^+(A, \mathcal{H}^+) = max(A, \mathcal{H}^+)$.*

Proof (sketch). The fact that $\mathcal{SU}_{\mathsf{lin}}^+(A, \mathcal{H}^+)$ returns a singleton is trivial by definition, since the algorithm has no don't know nondeterminism and no step admits a failure.

Regarding the fact that θ is a maximal solution, let us prove that all three conditions in Definition 6 hold. The first condition of maximal solution follows by Theorem 2, which is proved for the more general case of arbitrary (possibly non-linear) atoms. The third condition holds from the fact that in step (2) of $\mathcal{SU}_{\mathsf{lin}}^+$ only symbols from the atoms A and $\mathcal{H}^+$ are introduced following a *mgu*-like algorithm; therefore they are possibly not necessary, but cannot be replaced by different symbols and still unify with all the atoms in $\mathcal{H}^+$. Finally, the second condition derives from step (3) of $\mathcal{SU}_{\mathsf{lin}}^+$ where non-simple disagreement pairs are replaced by fresh variables from $\mathcal{U}$ and, thus, any binding to a non-variable term would result in $A\theta$ not unifying with some atom of $\mathcal{H}^+$. □

4.3 Dealing with the Negative Atoms

The algorithm $\mathcal{SU}$ in Definition 3 is now redefined as follows:

Definition 8. (algorithm for linear selective unification).

Input: *a linear atom A with $G \subseteq \mathcal{V}ar(A)$ a set of variables, and two finite sets $\mathcal{H}^+$ and $\mathcal{H}^-$ such that the atoms in $\mathcal{H}^+$ are linear and all atoms are pairwise variable disjoint and $A \approx B$ for all $B \in \mathcal{H}^+ \cup \mathcal{H}^-$.*
Output: fail *or a substitution $\theta\eta$ (restricted to the variables of A).*

1. *Let $\{\theta\} = \mathcal{SU}_{\text{lin}}^+(A, \mathcal{H}^+)$. Then, generate—using a fair algorithm—linear idempotent substitutions η such that $G\theta\eta$ is ground, $\mathcal{D}om(\eta) \subseteq \mathcal{V}ar(A\theta)\backslash\mathcal{U}$ and $\mathcal{R}an(\eta) \cap (\mathcal{V}ar(\mathcal{H}^+ \cup \{A\}) \cup \mathcal{U}) = \emptyset$, otherwise return* fail.
2. *Check that for each $H^- \in \mathcal{H}^-$, $\neg(A\theta\eta \approx H^-)$, otherwise return* fail.
3. *Return $\theta\eta\gamma$ (restricted to the variables of A), where γ is a variable renaming for $A\theta\eta$ with fresh variables from $\mathcal{V}\backslash\mathcal{U}$.*

We denote by $\mathcal{SU}_{\text{lin}}(A, \mathcal{H}^+, \mathcal{H}^-, G)$ the set of non-deterministic (non-failing) substitutions computed by the above algorithm.

Example 7. Consider again $A = p(X_1, X_2)$ and $\mathcal{H}^+ = \{p(f(Y), a), p(f(g(Z)), b)\}$, together with $\mathcal{H}^- = \{p(f(g(a)), c)\}$ and $G = \{X_1\}$. The algorithm for linear positive unification returns the maximal substitution $\{X_1/f(g(Z')), X_2/U\}$. Therefore, the algorithm for linear selective unification would eventually produce a solution of the form $\theta = \{X_1/f(g(b)), X_2/X'\}$ since $A\theta = p(f(g(b)), X')$ unifies with $p(f(Y), a)$ and $p(f(g(Z)), b)$ but not with $p(f(g(a)), c)$ and, moreover, X_1 is not ground. However, if we consider a non-maximal solution, the algorithm in Definition 3 may fail, even if there exists some solution to the linear selective unification problem. This is the case, e.g., if we consider the non-maximal solution $\{X_1/f(g(a)), X_2/U\}$.

Theorem 3 (soundness). *Let A be a linear atom with $G \subseteq \mathcal{V}ar(A)$, $\mathcal{H}^+$ be a finite set of linear atoms and $\mathcal{H}^-$ be a finite set of atoms such that all atoms are pairwise variable disjoint and $A \approx B$ for all $B \in \mathcal{H}^+ \cup \mathcal{H}^-$. Then, we have $\mathcal{SU}_{\text{lin}}(A, \mathcal{H}^+, \mathcal{H}^-, G) \subseteq \mathcal{P}_{\text{lin}}(A, \mathcal{H}^+, \mathcal{H}^-, G)$.*

Proof. The claim follows from Proposition 4 by assuming that the don't know nondeterministic substitutions considered in step (1) of the algorithm of Definition 8 are obtained by a fair generate-and-test algorithm which produces substitutions systematically starting with terms of depth 0, then depth 1, etc., as in the naive algorithm described at the beginning of Sect. 3.   □

The following result states the completeness of our algorithm. In principle, we do not guarantee that all solutions are computed using our algorithms, even for the linear case. However, we can ensure that if the linear selective unification problem is satisfiable, our algorithm will find at least one solution.

Theorem 4 (completeness). *Let A be a linear atom with $G \subseteq Var(A)$, $\mathcal{H}^+$ be a finite set of linear atoms and $\mathcal{H}^-$ be a finite set of atoms such that all atoms are pairwise variable disjoint and $A \approx B$ for all $B \in \mathcal{H}^+ \cup \mathcal{H}^-$. Then, if $\mathcal{P}_{\text{lin}}(A, \mathcal{H}^+, \mathcal{H}^-, G) \neq \emptyset$ (i.e., it is satisfiable), then $\mathcal{SU}_{\text{lin}}(A, \mathcal{H}^+, \mathcal{H}^-, G) \neq \emptyset$.*

Proof. By Proposition 3, if $\mathcal{P}_{\text{lin}}(A, \mathcal{H}^+, \mathcal{H}^-, G) \neq \emptyset$ and θ is the computed maximal solution, then there exists a substitution γ such that $(\theta\gamma) \upharpoonright_{Var(A)} \in \mathcal{P}_{\text{lin}}(A, \mathcal{H}^+, \mathcal{H}^-, G)$. Moreover, such a substitution γ can be obtained by a fair generate-and-test algorithm such as that considered in Definition 8. Finally, the claim follows by Proposition 4 which ensures that the algorithm in Definition 2 will always produce the maximal solution for A and $\mathcal{H}^+$.

In general, though, we cannot ensure that all solutions are computed (which is not a drawback of the algorithm since we are only interested in finding one solution if it exists):

Example 8. Consider again $A = p(X_1, X_2)$ and $\mathcal{H}^+ = \{p(f(Y), a), p(f(g(Z)), b)\}$, together with $\mathcal{H}^- = \{p(g(W), c)\}$ and $G = \emptyset$. The algorithm for linear positive unification returns the maximal substitution $\{X_1/f(g(Z')), X_2/U\}$. Therefore, it is impossible that the algorithm in Definition 3 could produce a solution like $\{X_1/f(X'), X_2/X''\} \in \mathcal{P}_{\text{lin}}(A, \mathcal{H}^+, \mathcal{H}^-, G)$.

5 Discussion

In this paper, we have studied the soundness and completeness of selective unification, a relevant operation in the context of concolic testing of logic programs. In contrast to [7], we have provided a refined correctness result (one condition was missing in [7]), and we have also identified the main sources of incompleteness for the algorithm in [7]. Then, we have introduced several refinements so that the procedure is now sound and complete w.r.t. linear solutions. We are not aware of any other work that deals with the kind of unification problems that we consider in this paper.

Clearly, the fact that we only consider linear solutions (i.e., the relation $\mathcal{P}_{\text{lin}}$) means that our procedure can be incomplete in general. For instance, we consider the problem shown in Example 4 unsatisfiable, though a nonlinear solution exists. Nevertheless, we do not expect this restriction to have a significant impact in practice and, moreover, concolic testing algorithms are usually incomplete in order to avoid a state explosion. On the other hand, the refined algorithm in Sects. 4.2 and 4.3 only considers linear atoms. This restriction may have a more significant impact since many programs have nonlinear atoms in the heads of the clauses and/or equalities in the bodies. In such cases, we can still resort to using the algorithm of Sect. 4.1, though it may be less efficient.

As for future work, we are considering to introduce a technique to "linearize" the atoms in $A \cup \mathcal{H}^+$ by introducing some constraints which could be solved later in the algorithm (e.g., replacing $p(X, X)$ by $p(X, Y)$ and the constraint $X = Y$).

Another interesting line of research involves improving the efficiency of the selective unification algorithm. For this purpose, we plan to investigate the conditions ensuring the following property:

if $\mathcal{P}_{\mathsf{lin}}(A, \mathcal{H}^+, \mathcal{H}^-, G) = \emptyset$, then $\mathcal{P}_{\mathsf{lin}}(A\theta, \mathcal{H}^+, \mathcal{H}^-, G) = \emptyset$ for all substitution θ

If this property indeed holds, then one could check *statically* the satisfiability of all possible selective unification problems in a program, e.g., for atoms of the form $p(X_1, \ldots, X_n)$. We can then use this information during concolic testing to rule out those problems which we know are unfeasible no matter the run time values (denoted by θ). From our preliminary experience with the tool contest (http://kaz.dsic.upv.es/contest.html), this might result in significant efficiency improvements.

Finally, we are also considering the definition of a possibly approximate formulation of selective unification which could be solved using an SMT solver. This might imply a loss of completeness, but will surely improve the efficiency of the process. Moreover, it will also allow a smoother integration with the constraint solving process which is required when extending our concolic testing technique to full Prolog programs.

Acknowledgements. We would like to thank the anonymous reviewers and the participants of LOPSTR 2016 for their suggestions to improve this paper.

References

1. Anand, S., Pasareanu, C.S., Visser, W.: Symbolic execution with abstraction. STTT **11**(1), 53–67 (2009)
2. Apt, K.R.: From Logic Programming to Prolog. Prentice Hall, Englewood Cliffs (1997)
3. Clarke, L.A.: A program testing system. In: Proceedings of the 1976 Annual Conference (ACM 1976), pp. 488–491 (1976)
4. Godefroid, P., Klarlund, N., Sen, K.: DART: directed automated random testing. In: Proceedings of PLDI 2005, pp. 213–223. ACM (2005)
5. Godefroid, P., Levin, M.Y., Molnar, D.A.: Sage: whitebox fuzzing for security testing. CACM **55**(3), 40–44 (2012)
6. King, J.C.: Symbolic execution and program testing. CACM **19**(7), 385–394 (1976)
7. Mesnard, F., Payet, É., Vidal, G.: Concolic testing in logic programming. TPLP **15**(4–5), 711–725 (2015)
8. Mesnard, F., Payet, É., Vidal, G.: Concolic testing in logic programming (extended version). CoRR abs/1507.05454 (2015). http://arxiv.org/abs/1507.05454
9. Palamidessi, C.: Algebraic properties of idempotent substitutions. In: Paterson, M.S. (ed.) ICALP 1990. LNCS, vol. 443, pp. 386–399. Springer, Heidelberg (1990). doi:10.1007/BFb0032046
10. Pasareanu, C.S., Rungta, N., PathFinder, S.: symbolic execution of Java bytecode. In: Pecheur, C., Andrews, J., Nitto, E.D. (eds.) ASE, pp. 179–180. ACM (2010)

11. Sen, K., Marinov, D., Agha, G.: CUTE: a concolic unit testing engine for C. In: Proceedings of ESEC/SIGSOFT FSE 2005, pp. 263–272. ACM (2005)
12. Ströder, T., Emmes, F., Schneider-Kamp, P., Giesl, J., Fuhs, C.: A linear operational semantics for termination and complexity analysis of ISO Prolog. In: Vidal, G. (ed.) LOPSTR 2011. LNCS, vol. 7225, pp. 237–252. Springer, Heidelberg (2012). doi:10.1007/978-3-642-32211-2_16

CurryCheck: Checking Properties
of Curry Programs

Michael Hanus[(✉)]

Institut Für Informatik, CAU Kiel, 24098 Kiel, Germany
mh@informatik.uni-kiel.de

Abstract. We present CurryCheck, a tool to automate the testing of
programs written in the functional logic programming language Curry.
CurryCheck executes unit tests as well as property tests which are parameterized over one or more arguments. CurryCheck tests properties by
systematically enumerating test cases so that, for smaller finite domains,
CurryCheck can actually prove properties. Unit tests and properties can
be defined in a Curry module without being exported. Thus, they are
also useful to document the intended semantics of the source code. Furthermore, CurryCheck also supports the automated checking of specifications and contracts occurring in source programs. Hence, CurryCheck
is a useful tool that contributes to the property- and specification-based
development of reliable and well tested declarative programs.

1 Motivation

Testing is an important step to get confidence in the functionality of a program.
The advantage of testing compared to program verification is its potential for
automation. If test cases are encoded as input to test frameworks, one can automatically run and repeat them when the software is further developed, which is
also known as regression testing.

A difficulty in testing is to find appropriate inputs for the individual tests.
For this purpose, property-based testing has been proposed, well known in the
functional language Haskell with the QuickCheck tool [15]. Properties are predicates parameterized over one or more arguments. QuickCheck automates the
test execution by applying properties to randomly generated test inputs. Since
this idea is particularly reasonable for declarative languages, it is been adapted
in different forms to functional and logic programming languages. For instance,
SmallCheck [32] and GAST [26] focus on a systematic enumeration of test inputs
for functional programs, PropEr [30] adapts ideas of QuickCheck to the concurrent functional language Erlang, PrologCheck [1] transfers and extends ideas of
QuickCheck to Prolog, and EasyCheck [14] exploits functional logic programming features to property-based testing of Curry programs.

CurryCheck follows the same ideas. Actually, it is based on EasyCheck to
define properties. However, CurryCheck is intended as a comprehensive tool to
simplify the automation of test execution. To use CurryCheck, properties are
interspersed into the program as top-level definitions. Thus, properties are used

© Springer International Publishing AG 2017
M.V. Hermenegildo and P. Lopez-Garcia (Eds.): LOPSTR 2016, LNCS 10184, pp. 222–239, 2017.
DOI: 10.1007/978-3-319-63139-4_13

to document the intended semantics of the source code, which also supports test-driven program development known as "extreme programming." When CurryCheck is applied to a (set of) Curry modules, it extracts all properties, generates a program to test these properties, executes this generated program, and reports any errors. Furthermore, CurryCheck also analyzes possible contracts [7] provided in source programs and generates properties to test these contracts. Thanks to this automation, CurryCheck is a useful tool for continuous integration and deployment processes. It is used for this purpose in the Curry implementations PAKCS [22] and KiCS2 [13].

In this paper we present the ideas and usage of CurryCheck. After a review of the main features of Curry in the next section, we introduce properties in Sect. 3 and explain how they are tested in Sect. 4. The support of CurryCheck to define test inputs is presented in Sect. 5. CurryCheck's support for contract checking is described in Sect. 6. Some initial features of CurryCheck to combine testing and verification are sketched in Sect. 7. We report about our practical experience with CurryCheck in Sect. 8 before we compare CurryCheck to some related tools and conclude.

2   Functional Logic Programming and Curry

Functional logic languages [6,21] integrate the most important features of functional and logic languages in order to provide a variety of programming concepts. They support functional concepts like higher-order functions and lazy evaluation as well as logic programming concepts like non-deterministic search and computing with partial information. The declarative multi-paradigm language Curry [19] is a modern functional logic language with advanced programming concepts. In the following, we briefly review some features of Curry relevant for this paper. More details can be found in recent surveys on functional logic programming [6,21] and in the language report [23].

Curry has a Haskell-like syntax but also allows *free (logic) variables* in rules and initial expressions. Function calls with free variables are evaluated by a possibly non-deterministic instantiation of demanded arguments.

Example 1. The following simple program shows the functional and logic features of Curry. It defines the well-known list concatenation and an operation that returns some element of a list having at least two occurrences:

```
(++) :: [a] → [a] → [a]     someDup :: [a] → a
[]      ++ ys = ys          someDup xs | xs == _++ [x] ++_++ [x] ++_
(x:xs) ++ ys = x : (xs ++ ys)          = x    where x free
```

Since "++" can be called with free variables in arguments, the condition in the rule of someDup is solved by instantiating x and the anonymous free variables "_" to appropriate values before reducing the function calls. This corresponds to narrowing [31], but Curry narrows with possibly non-most-general unifiers to ensure the optimality of computations [2].

Note that `someDup` is a *non-deterministic operation* since it might deliver more than one result for a given argument, e.g., the evaluation of `someDup [1,2,2,1]` yields the values 1 and 2. Non-deterministic operations, which can formally be interpreted as mappings from values into sets of values [18], are an important feature of contemporary functional logic languages. Hence, Curry has also a predefined *choice* operation:

```
x ? _ = x
_ ? y = y
```

Thus, the expression "0 ? 1" evaluates to 0 and 1 with the value non-deterministically chosen.

Functional patterns [3] are useful to define some operations more easily. A functional pattern is a pattern occurring in an argument of the left-hand side of a rule containing defined operations (and not only data constructors and variables). Such a pattern abbreviates the set of all standard patterns to which the functional pattern can be evaluated (by narrowing). For instance, we can rewrite the definition of `someDup` as

```
someDup (_++[x]++_++[x]++_) = x
```

Functional patterns are a powerful feature to express arbitrary selections in tree structures, e.g., in XML documents [20]. Details about their semantics and a constructive implementation of functional patterns by a demand-driven unification procedure can be found in [3].

Curry has also features which are useful for application programming, like *set functions* [5] to encapsulate non-deterministic computations, *default rules* [8] to deal with partially specified operations and negation, and standard features from functional programming, like modules or monadic I/O [35]. Other features are explained when they are used in the following.

3 Properties

In this section we briefly discuss which kind of program properties to be tested are supported by CurryCheck. Since CurryCheck extends the functionality of EasyCheck [14], it supports all kinds of EasyCheck's properties which we review first.

Properties are defined top-level entities with a distinct type (see below). Thus, their syntax and type-correctness can be checked by the standard front end of any Curry system. Properties do not require a specific naming convention but CurryCheck recognizes them by their type. Moreover, the name and position of the property in the source file are used by CurryCheck to identify properties when errors are reported.

For instance, consider the list concatenation operation "++" defined in Example 1. Before discussing general properties, we define some unit tests for fixed arguments, like

```
concNull12 = []   ++ [1,2] -=- [1,2]
concCurry  = "Cu" ++ "rry" -=- "Curry"
```

The infix operator "-=-" specifies a test which is successful if both sides have single values which are identical (we will later see tests for non-deterministic operations). Since the expressions can be of any type (of course, the two arguments must be of the same type), the operator is polymorphic and has the type

```
(-=-) :: a  → a  → Prop
```

Hence, all entities defined above have type Prop.

The power of CurryCheck and similar property-based test frameworks comes from the fact that one can also test properties which are parameterized over some input data. For instance, we can check whether the concatenation operation is associative by:

```
concIsAssoc xs ys zs = (xs++ys)++zs -=- xs++(ys++zs)
```

This property is parameterized over three input values xs, ys, and zs. To test this property, CurryCheck guesses values for these parameters (see below for more details) and tests the property for these values:

```
concIsAssoc_ON_BASETYPE (module ConcDup, line 18):
 OK, passed 100 tests.
```

Indicated by the suffix _ON_BASETYPE, we see another feature of CurryCheck. If properties are polymorphic (the above property has type [a] → [a] → [a] → Prop), CurryCheck specializes the type to some base type, since there is no concrete value of a polymorphic type (and EasyCheck would fail on such properties). As a default, CurryCheck uses the predefined type Ordering having the three values LT, EQ, GT (another more involved method to instantiate polymorphic types in purely functional programs can be found in [11]). This default type can be changed to other base types, like Bool, Int, or Char, with a command-line option. One could also provide an explicit type declaration for the property. For instance, we can test the commutativity of the list concatenation on lists of integers by the property

```
concIsCommutative :: [Int]  → [Int]  → Prop
concIsCommutative xs ys = (xs ++ ys) -=- (ys ++ xs)
```

Of course, this property does not hold so that CurryCheck reports an error together with a counter-example:

```
...
concIsCommutative (module ConcDup, line 20) failed
Falsified by 8th test.
Arguments: [-1] [-3]
Results:   ([-1,-3],[-3,-1])
```

Note that the arguments of a test are ordinary expressions so that one can use any defined operation in the tests. For instance, we can (successfully) check whether the list concatenation is the addition on their lengths:

```
concAddLengths xs ys = length xs + length ys -=- length (xs++ys)
```

Since Curry covers also logic programming features, CurryCheck supports the testing of non-deterministic properties. For instance, one can check whether an expression reduces to some given value with the operator is "~>":

```
someDup1 = someDup [1,2,1,2] ~> 1
```

Another important operator is "`<~>`" which denotes the property that both arguments have the same set of values. We can write unit tests by enumerating all expected values with the choice operator "`?`":

```
someDup12 = someDup [1,2,1,2,1] <~> (1?2)
```

It should be noted that the operator "`<~>`" really compares sets and not multi-sets: Although the evaluation of `someDup [1,2,1,2,1]` returns the value `1` three times in a typical Curry system, the property `someDup12` holds. This is intended since CurryCheck tests declarative properties which are independent of specific compiler optimizations (this is in contrast to PrologCheck which tests operational properties like multiplicity of answers and modes [1]).

As another example, consider the following definition of a permutation of a list by exploiting a functional pattern to select some element in the argument list:

```
perm (xs++[x]++ys) = x : perm (xs++ys)
perm []            = []
```

An important property of a permutation is that the length of the list is not changed. Hence, we check it by the property

```
permLength xs = length (perm xs) <~> length xs
```

Since the left argument of "`<~>`" evaluates to many (identical) values, it is important to use "`<~>`" instead of "`-=-`" in this property.

We might also want to check whether our definition of `perm` computes the correct number of solutions. Since we know that a list of length n has $n!$ permutations, we write the following property, where `fac` is the factorial function and the property x `#` n is satisfied if x has n different values:

```
permCount :: [Int]  → Prop
permCount xs = perm xs # fac (length xs)
```

However, this test will be falsified with the test input `[1,1]`, since `[1,1]` has only one permuted value (actually, both computed values are identical). We can obtain a correct property if we add the condition that all elements in the input list `xs` are pairwise different. For this purpose, we use a *conditional property*: the property b `==>` p is satisfied if p is satisfied for all values where b evaluates to `True`. If the predicate `allDifferent` is satisfied iff its argument list does not contain duplicated elements, then we can reformulate our property as follows:

```
permCount xs = allDifferent xs ==> perm xs # fac (length xs)
```

Furthermore, we want to check the existence of distinguished permutations. For this purpose, consider a predicate to check whether a list is sorted:

```
sorted :: [Int]  → Bool
sorted []        = True
sorted [_]       = True
sorted (x:y:zs) = x<=y && sorted (y:zs)
```

Then we can check whether there are sorted permutations ("eventually `x`" is satisfied if some value of x is `True`):

```
permIsEventuallySorted ::  [Int]  → Prop
permIsEventuallySorted xs = eventually (sorted (perm xs))
```

Property-based testing is appropriate for declarative languages since the absence of side effects allows the execution of tests on any number of test data without influencing the individual tests. Nevertheless, real programming languages have to deal with the real world so that they support also I/O operations. Clearly, such operations should also be tested. Although there are methods to test monadic code [16], the generation of test data for I/O monadic operations (e.g., file names, socket connections) seems not reasonable. Therefore, CurryCheck supports only non-parameterized unit tests for I/O operations. For instance, the test (a `returns` x) is satisfied if the I/O action a returns the value x. For instance, we can test whether writing a file and reading it yields the same contents:

```
writeReadFile = (writeFile  "TEST"  "Hello">> readFile "TEST")
                  `returns`  "Hello"
```

Since CurryCheck executes the tests written in a source program in their textual order, one can write also several I/O tests whose side effects depend on each other. For instance, we can split the previous I/O test into two consecutive tests:

```
writeTestFile = (writeFile "TEST" "Hello") `returns` ()
readTestFile  = (readFile "TEST")               `returns` "Hello"
```

4 Testing Properties

After having seen several methods to define properties, we sketch in this section how they are actually tested. Our motivation for the development of CurryCheck is manifold:

1. Properties are an executable documentation for the intended semantics of operations.
2. Properties increase the confidence in the quality of the developed software.
3. Properties can be used for software verification by proving their validity for all possible input data.

The first point is supported by interspersing properties into the source code of the program instead of putting them into separate files. Thus, properties play the same role as comments or type annotations: they document the intended semantics. Hence, they can be extracted and put into the program documentation by automatic documentation tools [24]. In order to avoid that properties influence the interface of a module, they do not need to be exported. As an example, consider the following simple module defining the classical list reverse operation (the imported module Test.Prop contains the definitions of the property combinators introduced in Sect. 3):

```
module Rev(rev) where

import Test.Prop

rev :: [a]  → [a]
rev []      = []
rev (x:xs) = rev xs ++ [x]

revLength  xs = length (rev xs) -=- length xs
revRevIsId xs = rev (rev xs) -=- xs
```

We can run all tests of this module by invoking CurryCheck with the module name:[1]

```
> curry check Rev
Analyzing module 'Rev'...
...
Executing all tests...
revLength_ON_BASETYPE (module Rev, line 9):
 OK, passed 100 tests.
revRevIsId_ON_BASETYPE (module Rev, line 10):
 OK, passed 100 tests.
```

Although module Rev only exports the operation rev, all properties defined in the top-level of Rev are passed to the underlying EasyCheck library for testing. For this purpose, CurryCheck creates a copy of this module where all entities are exported (note that the original module cannot be modified since it might be imported to other modules to be tested). For each property a corresponding call to an operation of EasyCheck is generated which actually performs the generation of test data, runs the test, and collects all results which are passed back to CurryCheck. Furthermore, polymorphic properties are not checked but a corresponding new property on the default base type is generated which calls the polymorphic property. For instance, if the default base type is Int, CurryCheck generates the new property

```
revRevIsId_ON_BASETYPE :: [Int]  → Prop
revRevIsId_ON_BASETYPE = revRevIsId
```

which is actually checked instead of revRevIsId. Note that it might lead to a failure if the type of revRevIsId is directly specialized, since the polymorphic property revRevIsId might be used in other property definitions with a different specialized type.

After these preparations, EasyCheck tests the properties by generating test data as described in [14]. EasyCheck does not use random generators like QuickCheck or PrologCheck, but it exploits functional logic programming features to enumerate possible input values. Since logic variables are equivalent to non-deterministic generators [4], one can evaluate a logic variable of a particular type in order to get all values of this type in a non-deterministic manner. For instance, if we evaluate the Boolean variable b::Bool, we obtain the values False and True as results. Similarly, for bs::[Bool] we obtain values like [], [False], [True], [False,False], etc. In order to select a finite amount of these infinite values, one can use Curry's feature for encapsulated search to collect all non-deterministic results in a tree structure, traverse the tree with some strategy and return the result of the traversal into a list. If one selects only a finite amount of this list, the lazy evaluation strategy of Curry ensures a finite computation even if the tree is infinite. Based on these features, the EasyCheck library contains an operation

---

[1] One can also provide several module names so that they are tested at once. Furthermore, CurryCheck has various options to influence the number of test cases, default types for polymorphic properties, etc.

```
valuesOf :: a  → [a]
```
which computes the list of all values of the given argument according to a fixed strategy (in the current implementation by randomized level diagonalization [14]). Hence, we can get 20 values for a list of integers by

```
...> take 20 (valuesOf (_::[Int]))
[[],[-1],[-3],[0],[1],[-1,0],[-2],[0,0],[3],[-1,1],[-3,0],[0,1],
 [2],[-1,-1],[-5],[0,-1],[5],[-1,2],[-9],[0,2]]
```

It should be noted that valuesOf enumerates all values of the given type completely and without duplicates.[2] Hence, if the set of possible input values is finite, it is ensured that all of them are tested if sufficiently many tests are performed. In this case, the property is also verified (where QuickCheck or PrologCheck does not give such guarantees). For instance, consider the De Morgan law from Boolean algebra:

```
negOr b1 b2 = not (b1 || b2) -=- not b1 && not b2
```

This property is proved by CurryCheck after four tests with all possible input values, and the output of CurryCheck indicates that the testing was exhaustive:

```
negOr (module BoolTest, line 4):
  Passed all available tests: 4 tests.
```

5   User-Defined Test Data

Due to the use of functional logic features to generate test data, one can write properties not only on predefined data types but also on user-defined data types. For instance, consider the following definition of general polymorphic trees:

```
data Tree a = Leaf a | Node [Tree a]
```
We define operations to compute the leaves of a tree and mirroring a tree:

```
leaves (Leaf x)  = [x]
leaves (Node ts) = concatMap leaves ts

mirror (Leaf x)  = Leaf x
mirror (Node ts) = Node (reverse (map mirror ts))
```
The following properties should increase our confidence in the correctness of the implementation:

```
doubleMirrorIsId t = mirror (mirror t) -=- t

leavesOfMirrorAreReversed t = leaves t -=- reverse (leaves (mirror t))
```

CurryCheck successfully tests these properties without providing any further information about how to generate test data. However, in some cases it might be desirable to define our own test data since the generated structures are not appropriate for testing. For instance, if we test algorithms working on balanced search trees, we need correctly balanced search trees as test data. As a naive approach, we can limit the tests to correct test inputs by using conditional properties. As a simple example, consider the following operation that adds all numbers from 1 to a given limit:

---

[2] In order to get an idea of the distribution of the generated test data, CurryCheck also provides property combinators collect and classify known from QuickCheck.

```
sumUp n = if n==1 then 1 else n + sumUp (n-1)
```
Since there is also a simple formula to compute this sum, we can check it:
```
sumUpIsCorrect n = n>0 ==> sumUp n -=- n * (n+1) `div` 2
```
Note that the condition is important since sumUp diverges on non-positive numbers. As a result, CurryCheck tests this property by enumerating integers and dropping tests with non-positive numbers. While this works well, since CurryCheck performs a fairly good distribution between positive and negative numbers, this approach might have a serious drawback if the proportion of correct test data is small. In the case of balanced search trees, there are many more unbalanced trees than balanced search trees. This has the effect that CurryCheck generates many test data and drops it so that it does not make much progress. CurryCheck has an upper limit for dropping test data in the conditional operator in order to avoid spending too much work on generating unusable test data. For instance, if we want to test the above property revRevIsId on long input lists, we could define it as follows:
```
revRevIsIdLong :: [Int]  → Prop
revRevIsIdLong xs = length xs > 100 ==> rev (rev xs) -=- xs
```
Since there are a huge number of integer lists with a length smaller than 100, CurryCheck does not find any test case (with a default limit of dropping at most 10,000 incorrect test data values):
```
revRevIsIdLong (module Rev, line 13):
 Arguments exhausted after 0 test.
```
This shows that the fully automatic generation of test data is not always appropriate. Therefore, CurryCheck provides some combinators to explicitly define test data (more advanced enumeration combinators in the context of Scala are discussed in [27]).

To show the method for test data generation in more detail, we have to review Curry's methods to encapsulate non-deterministic computations. Curry defines the following structure to represent the results of a non-deterministic computation [12]:
```
data SearchTree a = Value a | Fail | Or (SearchTree a) (SearchTree a)
```
(Value v) and Fail represent a single value or a failure (i.e., no value), respectively, and (Or t1 t2) represents a non-deterministic choice between two search trees t1 and t2. Furthermore, there is a primitive search operator
```
someSearchTree :: a  → SearchTree a
```
which yields a search tree for an expression. For instance, someSearchTree (0?1) evaluates to the search tree
```
Or (Value 0) (Value 1)
```
The expression
```
someSearchTree (id $## (_::[Bool]))
```
(where "$##" is an infix application operator which evaluates the right argument to ground normal form before applying the left argument to it) yields an (infinite) search tree of all Boolean lists:
```
(Or (Value []) (Or (Or (Or (Value [False]) ...) (Or ...)) ...))
```

EasyCheck defines various strategies to traverse such search trees (see [14] for details) in order to enumerate test data. Hence, if we want to define our own test data, we have to define an operation that generates a search tree containing the test data in Value leaves. Although this is not difficult for simple data types, it could be demanding for polymorphic types where generators for polymorphic arguments must be weaved with generators for the main data structure. To simplify this task, CurryCheck offers a family of combinators genCons$n$ where each combinator takes an n-ary constructor function and n generators as arguments and produces a search tree for this constructor and all combinations of generated arguments. Hence, these combinators have the type

```
genConsn :: (a₁ → ··· → aₙ → a)  →  SearchTree a₁  →  ···
                  →  SearchTree aₙ  →  SearchTree a
```

Furthermore, there is an infix combinator "|||" to combine two search trees. For instance, consider the straightforward definition of Peano numbers:

```
data Nat = Z | S Nat
```

Then we can define a search tree generator for this type as follows:

```
genNat :: SearchTree Nat
genNat = genCons0 Z ||| genCons1 S genNat
```

Similarly, we can define a search tree generator for polymorphic trees which takes a search tree for the argument type as a parameter (where genList denotes the corresponding generator for list values):

```
genTree :: SearchTree a  → SearchTree (Tree a)
genTree ta = genCons1 Leaf ta ||| genCons1 Node (genList (genTree ta))
```

The explicit definition of value generators is reasonable when only a subset of all values should be used for testing. For instance, sumUpIsCorrect should be tested with positive numbers only. Hence, we define a generator for positive numbers:

```
genPos = genCons0 1 ||| genCons1 (+1) genPos
```

Since these numbers are slowly increasing, i.e., the search tree is actually degenerated to a list, we can also use the following definition to obtain a more balanced search tree:

```
genPos = genCons0 1 ||| genCons1 (\n  →  2*(n+1)) genPos
                    ||| genCons1 (\n  →  2*n+1)   genPos
```

To test properties with user-defined data, CurryCheck provides the property combinator

```
forAll :: [a]  → (a  → Prop)  →  Prop
```

which is satisfied if the parameterized property given as the second argument is satisfied for all values of the first argument list. Since there is also a library operation

```
valuesOfSearchTree :: SearchTree a  → [a]
```

(actually, the operation valuesOf introduced in Sect. 4 is defined via this operation) to enumerate all values of a search tree, we can redefine the property sumUpIsCorrect as follows:

```
sumUpIsCorrect = forAll (valuesOfSearchTree genPos)
                    (\n  →  sumUp n -=- n*(n+1) `div` 2)
```

Using this technique, we could also define finite tests for potentially infinite structures, e.g., one can easily define tree generators that generate all trees up to a particular depth.

6   Contract and Specification Testing

As discussed in detail in [7], the distinctive features of Curry (e.g., non-deterministic operations, demand-driven evaluation, functional patterns, set functions) support writing high-level specifications as well as efficient implementations for a given problem in the same programming language. When applying this idea, Curry can be used as a wide-spectrum language for software development. If a specification or contract is provided for some function, one can exploit this information to support run-time assertion checking with these specifications and contracts. As an additional use of this information, CurryCheck automatically generates properties to test the given specifications and contracts, which is described in the following.

According to the notation proposed in [7], a *specification* for an operation f is an operation f'spec of the same type as f. A *contract* consists of a pre- and a postcondition, where the precondition could be omitted. When provided, a *precondition* for an operation f of type $\tau \rightarrow \tau'$ is an operation

```
f'pre :: τ → Bool
```

restricting allowed argument values, whereas a *postcondition* for f is an operation

```
f'post :: τ → τ' → Bool
```

which relates input and output values (the generalization to operations with more than one argument is straightforward). A specification should precisely describe the meaning of an operation, i.e., the declarative meaning of the specification and the implementation of an operation should be equivalent. In contrast, a contract is a partial specification, e.g., all results computed by the implementation should satisfy the postcondition.

As a concrete example, consider the problem of sorting a list. The specification defines a sorted version of a given list as a permutation of the input which is sorted. Exploiting the operations introduced in Sect. 3, we define the following specification for the operation sort:

```
sort'spec :: [Int] → [Int]
sort'spec xs | ys == perm xs && sorted ys = ys   where ys free
```

A postcondition, which is easier to check, states that the input and output lists should have the same length:

```
sort'post :: [Int] → [Int] → Bool
sort'post xs ys = length xs == length ys
```

To provide a concrete implementation, we implement the quicksort algorithm as follows:

```
sort :: [Int] → [Int]
sort []     = []
sort (x:xs) = sort (filter (<x) xs) ++ [x] ++ sort (filter (>x) xs)
```

Note that specifications and contracts are optional. However, if they are included in a module processed with CurryCheck, CurryCheck automatically generates and checks properties that relate the specification and contract to the implementation. For instance, an implementation satisfies a specification if both yield the same values, and a postcondition is satisfied if each value computed for some input satisfies the postcondition relation between input and output. For our example, CurryCheck generates the following properties (if there are also preconditions for some operation, these preconditions are used to restrict the test cases via the condition operator "==>"):[3]

```
sortSatisfiesSpecification :: [Int]  → Prop
sortSatisfiesSpecification x = sort x <~> sort'spec x

sortSatisfiesPostCondition :: [Int]  → Prop
sortSatisfiesPostCondition x = always (sort'post x (sort x))
```

With CurryCheck, the framework of [7] becomes more useful since contracts are not only used as run-time assertions in concrete computations, but many possible computations are checked with various test data. For instance, CurryCheck reports that the above implementation of sort is incorrect for the example input [1,1] (as the careful reader might have already noticed). When reporting the error, the module and source code line number of the erroneous operation is shown so that the programmer can easily spot the problem.

Another kind of contracts taken into account by CurryCheck are determinism annotations [9]. An operation that yields always identical results (maybe multiple times) on identical argument values can be annotated as "deterministic" by adding DET to the result type of its type signature. For instance, the following operation tests whether a list represents a set, i.e., has no duplicate elements (the definition exploits functional patterns [3] as well as default rules [8]):

```
isSet :: [a]  → DET Bool
isSet (_++[x]++_++[x]++_) = False
isSet'default _          = True
```

The determinism annotation "→DET" has the effect that at most one result is computed for a given input, e.g., a single value False is returned for isSet [1,3,1,3,1], although the first rule can be applied multiple times to this call. Thus, after computing a first value, all attempts to compute further values are ignored. In order to ensure that this does not destroy completeness, i.e., it behaves like a "green cut" in Prolog, such operations must be deterministic from a semantical point of view. CurryCheck tests this property by generating a property for each DET-annotated operation that expresses that there is at most one value for each input. For instance, for isSet, the DET annotation is removed and the property

```
isSetIsDeterministic x1 = isSet x1 #< 2
```

is added by CurryCheck, where "e #< n" is satisfied if the set of all values of e contains less than n elements.

---

[3] The property "always x" is satisfied if all values of x are True.

7 Combining Testing and Verification

The objective of CurryCheck is to increase the confidence in the reliability of Curry programs. Testing with a lot of input data is one important step but, in case of input data types with an infinite number of values, it can only show possible errors but not the absence of them. In order to support the latter, CurryCheck has also some (preliminary) support to include the verification of program properties. For this purpose, a programmer might prove properties stated in a source program. Since there are many different possibilities to prove such properties, ranging from manual proofs to interactive proof assistants and fully automatic provers, CurryCheck does not enforce a particular proof technique. Instead, CurryCheck trusts the programmer and uses a naming convention for files containing proofs: if there is a file with name proof-t.*, CurryCheck assumes that this file contains a valid proof for property t. For instance, the following property states that sorting a list does not change its length:

```
sortlength xs = length (sort xs) <~> length xs
```

If there is a file proof-sortlength.txt containing a proof for this property, CurryCheck considers this property as valid and does not check it. Moreover, it uses this information to simplify other properties to be tested. For instance, consider the property sortSatisfiesPostCondition of the previous section. This can be simplified to always True so that it does not need to be tested. Similarly, a determinism annotation for operation f is not tested if there is a proof file fIsDeterministic.*.

Since program verification is a notoriously difficult task, a mixture of different techniques is required. Some purely functional properties can be proved in a fully automatic way. For instance, the properties

```
concLength xs = length (xs ++ ys) -=- length xs + length ys
revLength  xs = length (rev xs) -=- length xs
```

can be proved by the SMT solver Alt-Ergo. [25] discusses techniques to use the Isabelle/HOL proof assistant to verify functional properties inspired by QuickCheck. [10] describes a method to prove non-deterministic computations by translating Curry programs into the dependently typed language Agda [28]. Since these proofs can be verified by the Agda compiler, CurryCheck can test the validity of a given proof file by simply invoking the Agda compiler. For instance, assume that the file ListProps.curry contains the property concIsAssoc shown in Sect. 3. Then one can translate this property and all operations used by this property into Agda by the command

```
> curry verify --target=Agda ListProps
```

This generates the Agda program TO-PROVE-concIsAssoc.agda containing the definitions

```
++ : {a : Set} → L a → L a → L a
++ [] x = x
++ (y :: z) u = y :: (++ z u)

concIsAssoc : {a : Set} → (x : L a) → (y : L a) → (z : L a)
        → (++ (++ x y) z) ≡ (++ x (++ y z))
concIsAssoc x y z = ?
```

Since the actual proof is an easy induction on the first argument x, we use standard proof techniques of Agda [34] to complete the proof obligation in the last line to

```
concIsAssoc [] y z = refl
concIsAssoc (x :: xs) y z rewrite concIsAssoc xs y z = refl
```

Finally, we rename the complete proof file to proof-concIsAssoc.agda. Then further tests of this property are omitted by CurryCheck.

8 Practical Experience

The implementation of CurryCheck is available with the (Prolog-based) Curry implementation PAKCS [22] (since version 1.14.0) and the (Haskell-based) Curry implementation KiCS2 [13] (since version 0.5.0). The implementation exploits meta-programming features available in these systems to parse programs and transform them into new programs as described in the previous sections.

Although we could show in this paper only simple examples, we would like to remark that CurryCheck is successfully applied in a larger context. CurryCheck is regularly used for automatic regression testing during continuous integration and nightly builds of PAKCS and KiCS2. Currently, approximately 600 properties (the number is continuously growing) are regularly used to test the libraries and tools of these systems. Our practical experience is quite promising. After the development and use of CurryCheck, we found a bug in the implementation of the prelude operations quot and rem w.r.t. negative numbers and free variables which was undetected for a couple of years. Although the bug was easy to fix, the definition of a general property relating both operations and testing it with all smaller values was essential for its detection.

The run time of CurryCheck mainly depends on the specific properties to be tested. The initial translation phase, which extracts properties, contracts, and specifications from a given module and transforms them into executable tests, is a straightforward compilation process. The run time of the subsequent test execution phase depends on the number of test cases and the time needed to evaluate each property. The functional logic programming technique to generate test data described in Sect. 4 (i.e.,. collecting all non-deterministic results of evaluating a logic variable) is reasonable in practice. For instance, KiCS2 needs 0.6 seconds to test a trivial property on a list of integers with 10,000 test cases computed by the randomized level diagonalization strategy described in [14] (on a Linux machine with Intel Core i7-4790/3.60 Ghz and 8 GiB of memory).

CurryCheck has also been applied to implement *semantic versioning* in a package manager [29]. Semantic versioning aims to express semantic properties of different releases of software packages with a hierarchy of version numbers, e.g., 1.5.3, consisting of a major, minor, and patch version number. Whereas different major version numbers provide no guarantees about the compatibility of APIs, minor version numbers are incremented if new functionality is introduced, and patch version numbers are incremented if APIs are unchanged (e.g., bug fixes, code refactoring, efficiency improvements). Hence, the correct usage of this semantic versioning scheme can be tested by comparing the functionality of different versions of a software package. This is done in the Curry package manager [29] by exploiting CurryCheck. For two versions of a software package with identical major release numbers, the package manager generates a set of CurryCheck properties which test, for each operation occurring in the API of both versions, whether they compute the same sets of results. Using CurryCheck for semantic versioning increases the confidence in the correct releases of software packages.

9   Related Work

Since testing is an important part of the software development process, there is a vast literature on this topic. In the following, we compare our approach to testing, in particular, property-based testing, in declarative languages. We already mentioned QuickCheck [15] which was influential in this area and followed by other property-testing systems for functional languages, like GAST [26] or SmallCheck [32]. The same idea has also been transferred to other languages like PropEr [30] for Erlang and PrologCheck [1] for Prolog. In contrast to CurryCheck, most of these systems (except for SmallCheck) are based on randomly generating test data so that they do not provide guarantees for a complete enumeration if the sets of input values are finite, i.e., they cannot verify properties. PropEr also supports contract checking but these function contracts are limited to type specifications. PrologCheck could also check operational aspects likes modes or multiplicity of answers, whereas our properties are oriented towards declarative aspects, i.e., the input/output relation of values.

Closely related to CurryCheck is EasyCheck [14] since it can be seen as our back end. EasyCheck is the only property-based test tool covering functional and logic aspects but it is more limited than CurryCheck. EasyCheck does not support polymorphic properties, I/O properties, or combinators for user-defined generation of test data. This has been added in CurryCheck together with a full automation of the test process in order to obtain an easily usable tool. Moreover, CurryCheck expands the use of automatic testing by using it for contract and specification checking, where functional logic programming has been shown to be an appropriate framework [7], and combines it with static verification techniques.

10   Conclusion

We have presented CurryCheck, the first fully automatic tool to test functional as well as non-deterministic properties of Curry programs. CurryCheck supports unit tests and tests of I/O operations with fixed inputs as well as property tests which are parameterized over some arguments. In the latter case, they are executed with test inputs which are systematically generated for the given argument types. CurryCheck also supports specification and contract testing if such information is present in the source program.

To simplify and, thus, enhance the use property testing, properties can be interspersed in the source program and are automatically extracted by CurryCheck. Hence, CurryCheck supports test-driven program development methods like extreme programming. Properties are not only useful to obtain more reliable programs, but they can also be used by automated documentation tools to describe the intended meaning of operations, a feature which has been recently added to the CurryDoc documentation tool.[4] Moreover, properties can be interpreted as theorems about programs. If these theorems are statically proved, CurryCheck considers them to simplify the test tasks.

For future work we plan to extend the functionality of CurryCheck (e.g., generating functional values). Furthermore, we intend to integrate into CurryCheck more features that can help to improve the reliability of the source code, like abstract interpretation to approximate specific run-time properties [17,33], or program covering to show whether the test data was sufficient to reach all parts of a source program.

Acknowledgements. The author is grateful to Jan-Patrick Baye for implementing an initial version of CurryCheck and to the anonymous reviewers for their suggestions to improve this paper.

References

1. Amaral, C., Florido, M., Santos Costa, V.: PrologCheck – property-based testing in prolog. In: Codish, M., Sumii, E. (eds.) FLOPS 2014. LNCS, vol. 8475, pp. 1–17. Springer, Cham (2014). doi:10.1007/978-3-319-07151-0_1
2. Antoy, S., Echahed, R., Hanus, M.: A needed narrowing strategy. J. ACM **47**(4), 776–822 (2000)
3. Antoy, S., Hanus, M.: Declarative programming with function patterns. In: Hill, P.M. (ed.) LOPSTR 2005. LNCS, vol. 3901, pp. 6–22. Springer, Heidelberg (2006). doi:10.1007/11680093_2
4. Antoy, S., Hanus, M.: Overlapping rules and logic variables in functional logic programs. In: Etalle, S., Truszczyński, M. (eds.) ICLP 2006. LNCS, vol. 4079, pp. 87–101. Springer, Heidelberg (2006). doi:10.1007/11799573_9
5. Antoy, S., Hanus, M.: Set functions for functional logic programming. In: Proceedings of the 11th ACM SIGPLAN International Conference on Principles and Practice of Declarative Programming (PPDP 2009), pp. 73–82. ACM Press (2009)
6. Antoy, S., Hanus, M.: Functional logic programming. Commun. ACM **53**(4), 74–85 (2010)
7. Antoy, S., Hanus, M.: Contracts and specifications for functional logic programming. In: Russo, C., Zhou, N.-F. (eds.) PADL 2012. LNCS, vol. 7149, pp. 33–47. Springer, Heidelberg (2012). doi:10.1007/978-3-642-27694-1_4
8. Antoy, S., Hanus, M.: Default rules for Curry. Theory Pract. Logic Program. **17**(2), 121–147 (2017)
9. Antoy, S., Hanus, M.: Eliminating irrelevant non-determinism in functional logic programs. In: Lierler, Y., Taha, W. (eds.) PADL 2017. LNCS, vol. 10137, pp. 1–18. Springer, Cham (2017). doi:10.1007/978-3-319-51676-9_1

---

[4] See   http://www.informatik.uni-kiel.de/~pakcs/lib/Combinatorial.html   for an example.

10. Antoy, S., Hanus, M., Libby, S.: Proving non-deterministic computations in Agda. In: Proceeding of the 24th International Workshop on Functional and (Constraint) Logic Programming (WFLP 2016), vol. 234 of Electronic Proceedings in Theoretical Computer Science, pp. 180–195. Open Publishing Association (2017)

11. Bernardy, J.-P., Jansson, P., Claessen, K.: Testing polymorphic properties. In: Gordon, A.D. (ed.) ESOP 2010. LNCS, vol. 6012, pp. 125–144. Springer, Heidelberg (2010). doi:10.1007/978-3-642-11957-6_8

12. Braßel, B., Hanus, M., Huch, F.: Encapsulating non-determinism in functional logic computations. J. Funct. Logic Program. **2004**(6) (2004)

13. Braßel, B., Hanus, M., Peemöller, B., Reck, F.: KiCS2: a new compiler from Curry to Haskell. In: Kuchen, H. (ed.) WFLP 2011. LNCS, vol. 6816, pp. 1–18. Springer, Heidelberg (2011). doi:10.1007/978-3-642-22531-4_1

14. Christiansen, J., Fischer, S.: EasyCheck — test data for free. In: Garrigue, J., Hermenegildo, M.V. (eds.) FLOPS 2008. LNCS, vol. 4989, pp. 322–336. Springer, Heidelberg (2008). doi:10.1007/978-3-540-78969-7_23

15. Claessen, K., Hughes, J.: QuickCheck: a lightweight tool for random testing of Haskell programs. In: International Conference on Functional Programming (ICFP 2000), pp. 268–279. ACM Press (2000)

16. Claessen, K., Hughes, J.: Testing monadic code with QuickCheck. ACM SIGPLAN Not. **37**(12), 47–59 (2002)

17. Fähndrich, M., Logozzo, F.: Static contract checking with abstract interpretation. In: Beckert, B., Marché, C. (eds.) FoVeOOS 2010. LNCS, vol. 6528, pp. 10–30. Springer, Heidelberg (2011). doi:10.1007/978-3-642-18070-5_2

18. González-Moreno, J.C., Hortalá-González, M.T., López-Fraguas, F.J., Rodríguez-Artalejo, M.: An approach to declarative programming based on a rewriting logic. J. Logic Program. **40**, 47–87 (1999)

19. Hanus, M.: A unified computation model for functional and logic programming. In: Proceeding of the 24th ACM Symposium on Principles of Programming Languages (Paris), pp. 80–93 (1997)

20. Hanus, M.: Declarative processing of semistructured web data. In: Technical Communications of the 27th International Conference on Logic Programming, vol. 11, pp. 198–208. Leibniz International Proceedings in Informatics (LIPIcs) (2011)

21. Hanus, M.: Functional logic programming: from theory to Curry. In: Voronkov, A., Weidenbach, C. (eds.) Programming Logics. LNCS, vol. 7797, pp. 123–168. Springer, Heidelberg (2013). doi:10.1007/978-3-642-37651-1_6

22. Hanus, M., Antoy, S., Braßel, B., Engelke, M., Höppner, K., Koj, J., Niederau, P., Sadre, R., Steiner, F.: PAKCS: The Portland Aachen Kiel Curry System (2016). http://www.informatik.uni-kiel.de/pakcs/

23. M. Hanus (ed.). Curry: An Integrated Functional Logic Language (vers. 0.9.0) (2016). http://www.curry-language.org

24. Hermenegildo, M.: A documentation generator for (C)LP systems. In: Lloyd, J., Dahl, V., Furbach, U., Kerber, M., Lau, K.-K., Palamidessi, C., Pereira, L.M., Sagiv, Y., Stuckey, P.J. (eds.) CL 2000. LNCS, vol. 1861, pp. 1345–1361. Springer, Heidelberg (2000). doi:10.1007/3-540-44957-4_90

25. Johansson, M., Rosén, D., Smallbone, N., Claessen, K.: Hipster: integrating theory exploration in a proof assistant. In: Watt, S.M., Davenport, J.H., Sexton, A.P., Sojka, P., Urban, J. (eds.) CICM 2014. LNCS (LNAI), vol. 8543, pp. 108–122. Springer, Cham (2014). doi:10.1007/978-3-319-08434-3_9

26. Koopman, P., Alimarine, A., Tretmans, J., Plasmeijer, R.: GAST: generic automated software testing. In: Peña, R., Arts, T. (eds.) IFL 2002. LNCS, vol. 2670, pp. 84–100. Springer, Heidelberg (2003). doi:10.1007/3-540-44854-3_6

27. Kuraj, I., Kuncak, V., Jackson, D.: Programming with enumerable sets of structures. In: Proceeding of the 2015 ACM SIGPLAN International Conference on Object-Oriented Programming, Systems, Languages, and Applications (OOPSLA 2015), pp. 37–56. ACM (2015)

28. Norell, U.: Dependently typed programming in Agda. In: Koopman, P., Plasmeijer, R., Swierstra, D. (eds.) AFP 2008. LNCS, vol. 5832, pp. 230–266. Springer, Heidelberg (2009). doi:10.1007/978-3-642-04652-0_5

29. Oberschweiber, J.: A package manager for Curry. Master's thesis, University of Kiel (2016)

30. Papadakis, M., Sagonas, K.: A PropEr integration of types and function specifications with property-based testing. In: Proceeding of the 10th ACM SIGPLAN Workshop on Erlang, pp. 39–50 (2011)

31. Reddy, U.S.: Narrowing as the operational semantics of functional languages. In: Proceeding of IEEE International Symposium on Logic Programming, pp. 138–151, Boston (1985)

32. Runciman, C., Naylor, M., Lindblad, F.: SmallCheck and Lazy SmallCheck: automatic exhaustive testing for small values. In: Proceeding of the 1st ACM SIGPLAN Symposium on Haskell, pp. 37–48. ACM Press (2008)

33. Stulova, N., Morales, J.F., Hermenegildo, M.: Reducing the overhead of assertion run-time checks via static analysis. In: Proceeding 18th International Symposium on Principles and Practice of Declarative Programming (PPDP 2016), pp. 90–103. ACM Press (2016)

34. Stump, A.: Verified Functional Programming in Agda. ACM and Morgan & Claypool, New York (2016)

35. Wadler, P.: How to declare an imperative. ACM Comput. Surv. 29(3), 240–263 (1997)

A Hiking Trip Through the Orders of Magnitude: Deriving Efficient Generators for Closed Simply-Typed Lambda Terms and Normal Forms

Paul Tarau[(⊠)]

Department of Computer Science and Engineering,
University of North Texas, Denton, USA
paul.tarau@unt.edu

Abstract. Contrary to several other families of lambda terms, no closed formula or generating function is known and none of the sophisticated techniques devised in analytic combinatorics can currently help with counting or generating the set of *simply-typed closed lambda terms* of a given size.

Moreover, their asymptotic scarcity among the set of closed lambda terms makes counting them via brute force generation and type inference quickly intractable, with previous published work showing counts for them only up to size 10.

By taking advantage of the synergy between logic variables, unification with occurs check and efficient backtracking in today's Prolog systems, we climb 4 orders of magnitude above previously known counts by deriving progressively faster Horn Clause programs that generate and/or count the set of closed simply-typed lambda terms of sizes up to 14. A similar count for *closed simply-typed normal forms* is also derived up to size 14.

Keywords: Logic programming transformations · Type inference · Combinatorics of lambda terms · Simply-typed lambda calculus · Simply-typed normal forms

1 Introduction

Generation of lambda terms [1] has practical applications to testing compilers that rely on lambda calculus as an intermediate language, as well as in generation of random tests for user-level programs and data types. At the same time, several instances of lambda calculus are of significant theoretical interest given their correspondence with logic and proofs. Among them, simply-typed lambda terms [2,3] enjoy a number of nice properties, among which strong normalization (termination for all evaluation-orders), a cartesian closed category mapping and a set-theoretical semantics. More importantly, via the Curry-Howard correspondence lambda terms that are *inhabitants* of simple types can be seen as

© Springer International Publishing AG 2017
M.V. Hermenegildo and P. Lopez-Garcia (Eds.): LOPSTR 2016, LNCS 10184, pp. 240–255, 2017.
DOI: 10.1007/978-3-319-63139-4_14

proofs for tautologies in *minimal logic* which, in turn, correspond to the types. Extended with a fix-point operator, simply-typed lambda terms can be used as the intermediate language for compiling Turing-complete functional languages. Generation of large simply-typed lambda terms can also help with automation of testing and debugging compilers for functional programming languages [4].

Recent work on the combinatorics of lambda terms [5–8], relying on recursion equations, generating functions and techniques from analytic combinatorics [9] has provided counts for several families of lambda terms and clarified important properties like their asymptotic density. With the techniques provided by generating functions [9], it was possible to separate the *counting* of the terms of a given size for several families of lambda terms from their more computation intensive *generation*, resulting in several additions (e.g., A220894, A224345, A114851) to The On-Line Encyclopedia of Integer Sequences, [10].

On the other hand, the combinatorics of simply-typed lambda terms, given the absence of closed formulas, recurrence equations or grammar-based generators, due to the intricate interaction between type inference and the applicative structure of lambda terms, has left important problems open, including the very basic one of counting the number of closed simply-typed lambda terms of a given size. At this point, obtaining counts for simply-typed lambda terms requires going through the more computation-intensive generation process.

As a fortunate synergy, Prolog's sound unification of logic variables, backtracking and definite clause grammars have been shown to provide compact combinatorial generation algorithms for various families of lambda terms [11–14].

For the case of simply-typed lambda terms, we have pushed (in the unpublished draft [15]) the counts in sequence A220471 of [10] to cover sizes 11 and 12, each requiring about one magnitude of extra computation effort, simply by writing the generators in Prolog. In this paper we focus on going two more magnitudes higher, while also integrating the results described in [15]. Using similar techniques, we achieve the same, for the special case of simply-typed normal forms.

The paper is organized as follows. Section 2 describes our representation of lambda terms and derives a generator for closed lambda terms. Section 3 defines generators for well-formed type formulas. Section 4 introduces a type inference algorithm and then derives, step by step, efficient generators for simply-typed lambda terms and simple types inhabited by terms of a given size. Section 5 defines generators for closed lambda terms in normal form and then replicates the derivation of an efficient generator for simply-typed closed normal forms. Section 6 aggregates our experimental performance data and Sect. 7 discusses possible extensions and future improvements. Section 8 overviews related work and Sect. 9 concludes the paper.

The paper is structured as a literate Prolog program. The code has been tested with SWI-Prolog 7.3.8 and YAP 6.3.4. It is also available as a separate file at http://www.cse.unt.edu/~tarau/research/2016/lgen.pro.

2 Deriving a Generator for Lambda Terms

Lambda terms can be seen as Motzkin trees [16], also called unary-binary trees, labeled with lambda binders at their unary nodes and corresponding variables at the leaves. We will thus derive a generator for them from a generator for Motzkin trees.

2.1 A Canonical Representation with Logic Variables

We can represent lambda terms [1] in Prolog using the constructors a/2 for applications, 1/2 for lambda abstractions and v/1 for variable occurrences. Variables bound by the lambdas and their occurrences are represented as *logic variables*. As an example, the lambda term $\lambda a.(\lambda b.(a\ (b\ b))\ \lambda c.(a\ (c\ c)))$ will be represented as 1(A,a(1(B,a(v(A),a(v(B),v(B)))),1(C,a(v(A),a(v(C),v(C)))))). As variables share a unique scope (the clause containing them), this representation assumes that *distinct variables are used for distinct scopes induced by the lambda binders* in terms occurring in a given Prolog clause.

Lambda terms might contain *free variables* not associated to any binders. Such terms are called *open*. A *closed* term is such that each variable occurrence is associated to a binder.

2.2 Generating Motzkin Trees

Motzkin-trees (also called binary-unary trees) have internal nodes of arities 1 or 2. Thus they can be seen as a skeleton of lambda terms that ignores binders and variables and their leaves.

The predicate motzkin/2 generates Motzkin trees with S internal and leaf nodes.

```
motzkin(S,X):-motzkin(X,S,0).

motzkin(v)-->[].
motzkin(l(X))-->down,motzkin(X).
motzkin(a(X,Y))-->down,motzkin(X),motzkin(Y).

down(s(X),X).
```

Motzkin-trees, with leaves assumed of size 1 are counted by the sequence A001006 in [10]. Alternatively, as in our case, when leaves are assumed of size 0, we obtain binary-unary trees with S internal nodes, counted by the entry A006318 (Large Schröder Numbers) of [10].

Note the use of the predicate down/2, that assumes natural numbers in *unary notation*, with n s/1 symbols wrapped around 0 to denote $n \in \mathbb{N}$. As our combinatorial generation algorithms will usually be tractable for values of n below 15, the use of unary notation is comparable (and often slightly faster) than the call to arithmetic built-ins. Note also that this leads, after the DCG translation, to "pure" Prolog programs made exclusively of Horn Clauses, as the DCG notation can be eliminated by threading two extra arguments controlling the size of the terms.

To more conveniently call these generators with the usual natural numbers we define the converter n2s as follows.

```
n2s(0,0).
n2s(N,s(X)):-N>0,N1 is N-1,n2s(N1,X).
```

Example 1. *Motzkin trees with 2 internal nodes.*

```
?- n2s(1,S),motzkin(S,T).
S = s(0), T = l(v) ;
S = s(0), T = a(v, v) .
```

2.3   Generating Closed Lambda Terms

We derive a generator for closed lambda terms by adding logic variables as labels to their binder and variable nodes, while ensuring that the terms are closed, i.e., that the function mapping variables to their binders is total.

The predicate lambda/2 builds a list of logic variables as it generates binders. When generating a leaf variable, it picks "nondeterministically" one of the binders among the list of binders available, Vs. As in the case of Motzkin trees, the predicate down/2 controls the number of internal nodes.

```
lambda(S,X):-lambda(X,[],S,0).

lambda(v(V),Vs)-->{member(V,Vs)}.
lambda(l(V,X),Vs)-->down,lambda(X,[V|Vs]).
lambda(a(X,Y),Vs)-->down,lambda(X,Vs),lambda(Y,Vs).
```

The sequence A220471 in [10] contains counts for lambda terms of increasing sizes, with *size defined as the number of internal nodes.*

Example 2. *Closed lambda terms with 2 internal nodes.*

```
?- lambda(s(s(0)),Term).
Term = l(A, l(B, v(B))) ;
Term = l(A, l(B, v(A))) ;
Term = l(A, a(v(A), v(A))) .
```

3   A Visit to the Other Side: The Language of Types

As a result of the Curry-Howard correspondence, the language of types is isomorphic with that of *minimal logic*, with binary trees having variables at leaf positions and the implication operator ("->") at internal nodes. We will rely on the right associativity of this operator in Prolog, that matches the standard notation in type theory.

The predicate type_skel/3 generates all binary trees with given number of internal nodes and labels their leaves with unique logic variables. It also collects the variables to a list returned as its third argument.

```
type_skel(S,T,Vs):-type_skel(T,Vs,[],S,0).

type_skel(V,[V|Vs],Vs)-->[].
type_skel((X->Y),Vs1,Vs3)-->down,
  type_skel(X,Vs1,Vs2),
  type_skel(Y,Vs2,Vs3).
```

Type skeletons are counted by the Catalan numbers (sequence A000108 in [10]).

Example 3. *All type skeletons for N = 3.*

```
?- type_skel(s(s(s(0))),T,_).
T =   (A->B->C->D) ;
T =   (A-> (B->C)->D) ;
T =   ((A->B)->C->D) ;
T =   ((A->B->C)->D) ;
T =   (((A->B)->C)->D) .
```

The next step toward generating the set of all type formulas is observing that logic variables define equivalence classes that can be used to generate partitions of the set of variables, simply by selectively unifying them.

The predicate mpart_of/2 takes a list of distinct logic variables and generates partitions-as-equivalence-relations by unifying them "nondeterministically". It also collects the unique variables, defining the equivalence classes as a list given by its second argument.

```
mpart_of([],[]).
mpart_of([U|Xs],[U|Us]):-
  mcomplement_of(U,Xs,Rs),
  mpart_of(Rs,Us).
```

To implement a set-partition generator, we will split a set repeatedly in subset+complement pairs with help from the predicate mcomplement_of/2.

```
mcomplement_of(_,[],[]).
mcomplement_of(U,[X|Xs],NewZs):-
  mcomplement_of(U,Xs,Zs),
  mplace_element(U,X,Zs,NewZs).

mplace_element(U,U,Zs,Zs).
mplace_element(_,X,Zs,[X|Zs]).
```

To generate set partitions of a set of variables of a given size, we build a list of fresh variables with the equivalent of Prolog's length predicate working in unary notation, len/2.

```
partitions(S,Ps):-len(Ps,S),mpart_of(Ps,_).

len([],0).
len([_|Vs],s(L)):-len(Vs,L).
```

The count of the resulting set-partitions (Bell numbers) corresponds to the entry A000110 in [10].

Example 4. *Set partitions of size 3 expressed as variable equalities.*

```
?- partitions(s(s(s(0))),P).
P = [A, A, A] ;
P = [A, B, A] ;
P = [A, A, B] ;
P = [A, B, B] ;
P = [A, B, C].
```

We can then define the language of formulas in minimal logic, among which tautologies will correspond to simple types, as being generated by the predicate maybe_type/3.

```
maybe_type(L,T,Us):-type_skel(L,T,Vs),mpart_of(Vs,Us).
```

Example 5. *Well-formed formulas of minimal logic (possibly types) of size 2.*

```
?- maybe_type(s(s(0)),T,_).
T =   (A->A->A) ;
T =   (A->B->A) ;
T =   (A->A->B) ;
T =   (A->B->B) ;
T =   (A->B->C) ;
T =   ((A->A)->A) ;
T =   ((A->B)->A) ;
T =   ((A->A)->B) ;
T =   ((A->B)->B) ;
T =   ((A->B)->C) .
```

The sequence $2,10,75,728,8526,115764,1776060,30240210$ counting these formulas corresponds to the product of Catalan and Bell numbers.

4 Merging the Two Worlds: Generating Simply-Typable Lambda Terms

One can observe that per-size counts of both the sets of lambda terms and their potential types are very fast growing. There is an important difference, though, between computing the type of a given lambda term (if it exists) and computing an inhabitant of a type (if it exists). The first operation, called *type inference* is an efficient operation (linear in practice) while the second operation, called *the inhabitation problem* is P-space complete [17].

This brings us to design a type inference algorithm that takes advantage of operations on logic variables.

4.1 A Type Inference Algorithm

While in a functional language inferring types requires implementing unification with occurs-check, as shown for instance in [5], this operation is available in

Prolog as a built-in predicate, optimized, for instance, in SWI-Prolog [18], to proceed incrementally, only checking that no new cycles are introduced during the unification step as such.

The predicate `infer_type/3` works by using logic variables as dictionaries associating terms to their types. Each logic variable is then bound to a term of the form X:T where X will be a component of a fresh copy of the term and T will be its type. Note that we create this new term as the original term's variables end up loaded with chunks of the partial types created during the type inference process.

As logic variable bindings propagate between binders and occurrences, this ensures that types are consistently inferred.

```
infer_type((v(XT)),v(X),T):-unify_with_occurs_check(XT,X:T).
infer_type(l((X:TX),A),l(X,NewA),(TX->TA)):-infer_type(A,NewA,TA).
infer_type(a(A,B),a(X,Y),TY):-infer_type(A,X,(TX->TY)),infer_type(B,Y,TX).
```

Example 6. *illustrates typability of the term corresponding to the* S *combinator*
$\lambda x_0.\lambda x_1.\lambda x_2.((x_0\ x_2)\ (x_1\ x_2))$
and untypabilty of the term corresponding to the Y *combinator*
$\lambda x_0.(\lambda x_1.(x_0\ (x_1\ x_1))\ \lambda x_2.(x_0\ (x_2\ x_2))).$

```
?- infer_type(l(A,l(B,l(C,a(a(v(A),v(C)),a(v(B),v(C)))))),X,T),
   portray_clause((T:-X)),fail.
(A->B->C)-> (A->B)->A->C :-
      l(D,l(F,l(E, a(a(v(D), v(E)), a(v(F), v(E)))))).

?- infer_type(
     l(A,a(l(B,a(v(A),a(v(B),v(B)))),l(C,a(v(A),a(v(C),v(C)))))), X, T).
false.
```

By combining generation of lambda terms with type inference we have our first cut to an already surprisingly fast generator for simply-typable lambda terms, able to generate in a few hours counts for sizes 11 and 12 for sequence A220471 in [10].

```
lamb_with_type(S,X,T):-lambda(S,XT),infer_type(XT,X,T).
```

Example 7. *Lambda terms of size up to 3 and their types.*

```
?- lamb_with_type(s(s(s(0))),Term,Type).
Term = l(A, l(B, l(C, v(C)))), Type = (D->E->F->F) ;
Term = l(A, l(B, l(C, v(B)))), Type = (D->E->F->E) ;
Term = l(A, l(B, l(C, v(A)))), Type = (D->E->F->D) ;
Term = l(A, l(B, a(v(B), v(A)))), Type = (C-> (C->D)->D) ;
Term = l(A, l(B, a(v(A), v(B)))), Type = ((C->D)->C->D) ;
Term = l(A, a(v(A), l(B, v(B)))), Type = (((C->C)->D)->D) ;
Term = l(A, a(l(B, v(B)), v(A))), Type = (C->C) ;
Term = l(A, a(l(B, v(A)), v(A))), Type = (C->C) ;
Term = a(l(A, v(A)), l(B, v(B))), Type = (C->C).
```

Note that, for instance, when one wants to select only terms having a given type, this is quite inefficient. Next, we will show how to combine size-bound term generation, testing for closed terms and type inference into a single predicate. This will enable more efficient querying for terms inhabiting a given type, as one would expect from Prolog's multi-directional execution model, and more importantly for our purposes, to climb two orders of magnitude higher for counting simply-typed terms of size 13 and 14.

4.2   Combining Term Generation and Type Inference

We need two changes to infer_type to turn it into an efficient generator for simply-typed lambda terms. First, we need to add an argument to control the size of the terms and ensure termination, by calling down/2 for internal nodes. Second, we need to generate the mapping between binders and variables. We ensure this by borrowing the member/2-based mechanism used in the predicate lambda/4 generating closed lambda terms in Subsect. 2.3.

The predicate typed_lambda/3 does just that, with helper from DCG-expanded typed_lambda/5.

```
typed_lambda(S,X,T):-typed_lambda(_XT,X,T,[],S,0).

typed_lambda(v(V:T),v(V),T,Vs)--> {
   member(V:T0,Vs),
   unify_with_occurs_check(T0,T)
   }.
typed_lambda(l(X:TX,A),l(X,NewA),(TX->TY),Vs)-->down,
   typed_lambda(A,NewA,TY,[X:TX|Vs]).
typed_lambda(a(A,B),a(NewA,NewB),TY,Vs)-->down,
   typed_lambda(A,NewA,(TX->TY),Vs),
   typed_lambda(B,NewB,TX,Vs).
```

Like lambda/4, the predicate typed_lambda/5 relies on Prolog's DCG notation to thread together the steps controlled by the predicate down. Note also the nondeterministic use of the built-in member/2 that enumerates values for variable:type pairs ranging over the list of available pairs Vs, as well as the use of unify_with_occurs_check to ensure that unification of candidate types does not create cycles.

Example 8. *A simply-typed term of size 15 and its type.*

```
l(A,l(B,l(C,l(D,l(E,l(F,l(G,l(H,l(I,l(J,l(K,
         a(v(I),l(L,a(a(v(E),v(J)),v(J)))))))))))))))
M->N->O->P-> (Q->Q->R)->S->T->U-> ((V->R)->W)->Q->X->W
```

We will discuss exact performance data later, but let's note here that this operation brings down by an order of magnitude the computational effort to generate simply-typed terms. As expected, the number of solutions is computed as the sequence A220471 in [10]. Interestingly, by *interleaving* generation of closed terms and type inference in the predicate typed_lambda, the time to generate all the closed simply-typed terms is actually shorter than the time to generate all closed terms of the same size, e.g., 17.123 vs. 31.442 seconds for size 10 with SWI-Prolog. As, via the Curry-Howard isomorphism, closed simply typed terms correspond to proofs of tautologies in minimal logic, co-generation of terms and types corresponds to co-generation of tautologies and their proofs for proofs of given length.

4.3   One More Trim: Generating Inhabited Types

Let's first observe that the actual lambda term does not need to be built, provided that we mimic exactly the type inference operations that one would need to perform to ensure it is simply-typed. It is thus safe to remove the first argument of typed_lambda/5 as well as the building of the fresh copy performed in the second argument. To further simplify the code, we can also make the DCG-processing of the size computations explicit, in the last two arguments.

This gives the predicate inhabited_type/4 and then inhabited_type/2, that generates *all types having inhabitants of a given size*, but omits the inhabitants as such.

```
inhabited_type(X,Vs,N,N):-
  member(V,Vs),
  unify_with_occurs_check(X,V).
inhabited_type((X->Xs),Vs,s(N1),N2):-
  inhabited_type(Xs,[X|Vs],N1,N2).
inhabited_type(Xs,Vs,s(N1),N3):-
  inhabited_type((X->Xs),Vs,N1,N2),
  inhabited_type(X,Vs,N2,N3).
```

Clearly the multiset of generated types has the same count as the set of their inhabitants and this brings us an additional 1.5x speed-up.

```
inhabited_type(S,T):-inhabited_type(T,[],S,0).
```

One more (easy) step, giving a **3x** speed-up, makes reaching counts for sizes **13** and **14** achievable: using a faster Prolog, with a similar unify_with_occurs_check built-in, like YAP [19], with the last value computed in less than a day.

Example 9. *The sequence* **A220471** *completed up to N = 14*

```
first 10: 1,2,9,40,238,1564,11807,98529,904318,9006364

11:      96,709,332
12:   1,110,858,977

13:   13,581,942,434
14: 175,844,515,544
```

5 Doing It once More: Generating Closed Simply-Typed Normal Forms

We will devise similar methods for an important subclass of simply-typed lambda terms.

5.1 Generating Normal Forms

Normal forms are lambda terms that cannot be further reduced. A normal form should not be an application with a lambda as its left branch and, recursively, its subterms should also be normal forms. The predicate `normal_form/2` uses `normal_form/4` to define them inductively and generates all normal forms with S internal nodes.

```
normal_form(S,T):-normal_form(T,[],S,0).
```

```
normal_form(v(X),Vs)-->{member(X,Vs)}.
normal_form(l(X,A),Vs)-->down,normal_form(A,[X|Vs]).
normal_form(a(v(X),B),Vs)-->down,normal_form(v(X),Vs),normal_form(B,Vs).
normal_form(a(a(X,Y),B),Vs)-->down,normal_form(a(X,Y),Vs),normal_form(B,Vs).
```

Example 10. *Illustrates closed normal forms with 2 internal nodes.*

```
?- normal_form(s(s(0)),NF).
NF = l(A, l(B, v(B))) ;
NF = l(A, l(B, v(A))) ;
NF = l(A, a(v(A), v(A))) .
```

The number of solutions of our generator replicates entry A224345 in [10] that counts closed normal forms of various sizes.

The predicate `nf_with_type` applies the type inference algorithm to the generated normal forms of size S.

```
nf_with_type(S,X,T):-normal_form(S,XT),infer_type(XT,X,T).
```

5.2 Merging in Type Inference

Like in the case of the set of simply-typed lambda terms, we can define the more efficient combined generator and type inferrer predicate `typed_nf/2`.

```
typed_nf(S,X,T):-typed_nf(_XT,X,T,[],S,0).
```

It works by calling the DCG-expended `typed_nf/4` predicate, with the last two arguments enforcing the size constraints.

```
typed_nf(v(V:T),v(V),T,Vs)--> {
   member(V:T0,Vs),
   unify_with_occurs_check(T0,T)
   }.
typed_nf(l(X:TX,A),l(X,NewA),(TX->TY),Vs)-->down,
```

```
 typed_nf(A,NewA,TY,[X:TX|Vs]).
typed_nf(a(v(A),B),a(NewA,NewB),TY,Vs)-->down,
 typed_nf(v(A),NewA,(TX->TY),Vs),
 typed_nf(B,NewB,TX,Vs).
typed_nf(a(a(A1,A2),B),a(NewA,NewB),TY,Vs)-->down,
 typed_nf(a(A1,A2),NewA,(TX->TY),Vs),
 typed_nf(B,NewB,TX,Vs).
```

Example 11. *Simply-typed normal forms up to size 3.*

```
?- typed_nf(s(s(s(0))),Term,Type).
Term = l(A, l(B, l(C, v(C)))),
Type =  (D->E->F->F) ;
...
Term = l(A, a(v(A), l(B, v(B)))),
Type =  (((C->C)->D)->D) .
```

We are now able to efficiently generate counts for simply-typed normal forms of a given size.

Example 12. *Counts for closed simply-typed normal forms up to N=14.*

first 10: 1,2,6,23,108,618,4092,30413,252590,2297954

```
11:      22,640,259
12:     240,084,189
13:   2,721,455,329
14: 32,783,910,297
```

Note that if we would want to just collect the set of types having inhabitants of a given size, the *preservation of typability under β-reduction* property [3] would allow us to work with the (smaller) set of simply-typed terms in normal form.

6 Experimental Data

Figure 1 gives the number of logical inferences as counted by SWI-Prolog. This is a good measure of computational effort except for counting operations like unify_with_occurs_check as a single step, while its actual complexity depends on the size of the terms involved. Therefore, Fig. 2 gives actual timings for the same operations above N=5, where they start to be meaningful.

The "closed λ-terms" column gives logical inferences and timing for generating all closed lambda terms of size given in column 1. The column "gen, then infer" covers the algorithm that first generates lambda terms and then infers their types. The column "gen + infer" gives performance data for the significantly faster algorithm that merges generation and type inference in the same predicate. The column "inhabitants" gives data for the case when actual inhabitants are omitted in the merged generation and type inference process. The column "typed normal form" shows results for the fast, merged generation and type inference for terms in normal form.

As moving from a size to the next typically adds one order of magnitude of computational effort, computing values for N=15 and N=16 is reachable with our best algorithms for both simply typed terms and their normal form subset.

Size	closed λ-terms	gen, then infer	gen + infer	inhabitants	typed normal form
1	15	19	16	9	19
2	44	59	50	28	47
3	166	261	188	113	127
4	810	1,517	864	553	429
5	4,905	10,930	4,652	3,112	1,814
6	35,372	92,661	28,878	19,955	9,247
7	294,697	895,154	202,526	143,431	55,219
8	2,776,174	9,647,495	1,586,880	1,146,116	377,745
9	29,103,799	114,273,833	13,722,618	10,073,400	2,896,982
10	335,379,436	1,471,373,474	129,817,948	96,626,916	24,556,921

Fig. 1. Number of logical inferences used by our generators, as counted by SWI-Prolog

Size	closed λ-terms	gen, then infer	gen + infer	inhabitants	typed normal form
5	0.001	0.001	0.001	0.000	0.001
6	0.005	0.011	0.004	0.002	0.004
7	0.028	0.114	0.029	0.018	0.011
8	0.257	1.253	0.242	0.149	0.050
9	2.763	15.256	2.080	1.298	0.379
10	32.239	199.188	19.888	12.664	3.329

Fig. 2. Timings (in seconds) for our generators up to size 10 (on a 2015 MacBook, with 1.3 GHz Intel Core M processor)

7 Discussion

An interesting open problem is if this can be pushed significantly farther. We have looked into term_hash based indexing and tabling-based dynamic programming algorithms, using de Bruijn terms. Unfortunately as subterms of closed terms are not necessarily closed, even if de Bruijn terms can be used as ground keys, their associated types are incomplete and dependent on the context in which they are inferred.

While it only offers a constant factor speed-up, parallel execution is a more promising possibility. However, given the small granularity of the generation and type inference process, the most useful parallel execution mechanism would simply split the task of combined generation and inference process into a number of disjoint sets, corresponding to the number of available processors. A way to do this, is by using unranking functions (bijections originating in $\mathbb{N}$) to the sets of combinatorial objects involved, and then, for k processors, assign work on successive numbers belonging to the same equivalence class modulo k. Another way is to first generate Motzkin trees and then launch threads to "flesh them up" with logic variables, run the type inference steps and collect success counts atomically.

We have not seen any obvious way to improve these results using constraint programing systems, partly because the "inner loop" computation is unification with occurs check with computations ranging over Prolog terms rather than being objects of a constraint domain. On the other hand, for a given size, exploring grounding to propositional formulas or answer-set programming seems worth exploring as a way to take advantage of today's fast SAT-solvers.

Several concepts of size have been used in the literature, for reasons ranging from simplifying evaluation procedures, to matching the structure of the terms naturally occurring in practical programs [20]. As a byproduct, some size definitions also result in better convergence conditions of formal series in analytic combinatorics [21]. Our techniques can be easily adapted to a different size definition like the ones in [20,21] where variables in de Bruijn notation have a size proportional to the distance to their binder. We have not discussed here the use of similar techniques to improve the Boltzmann samplers described to [22], but clearly interleaving type checking with the probability-driven building of the terms would improve their performance, by excluding terms with ill-typed subterms as early as possible, during the large number of retries needed to overcome the asymptotically 0-density of simply-typed terms in the set of closed terms [6].

8   Related Work

The classic reference for lambda calculus is [1]. Various instances of typed lambda calculi are overviewed in [3].

The combinatorics and asymptotic behavior of various classes of lambda terms are extensively studied in [5,8]. Distribution and density properties of random lambda terms are described in [6].

Generation of random simply-typed lambda terms and its applications to generating functional programs from type definitions is covered in [23].

Asymptotic density properties of simple types (corresponding to tautologies in minimal logic) have been studied in [24] with the surprising result that "almost all" classical tautologies are also intuitionistic ones.

In [4] a "type-directed" mechanism for the generation of random terms is introduced, resulting in more realistic (while not uniformly random) terms, used successfully in discovering some bugs in the Glasgow Haskell Compiler (GHC). A statistical exploration of the structure of the simple types of lambda terms of a given size in [14] gives indications that some types frequent in human-written programs are among the most frequently inferred ones.

Generators for closed simply-typed lambda terms, as well as their normal forms, expressed as functional programming algorithms, are given in [5], derived from combinatorial recurrences. However, they are significantly more complex than the ones described here in Prolog, and limited to terms up to size 10.

In the unpublished draft [15] we have collected several lambda term generation algorithms written in Prolog and covering mostly de Bruijn terms and a compressed de Bruijn representation. Among them, we have covered linear, affine linear terms as well as terms of bounded unary height and in binary lambda calculus encoding. In [15] type inference algorithms are also given for SK and Rosser's X-combinator expressions. A similar (but slower) program for type inference using de Bruijn notation is also given in the unpublished draft [15], without however describing the step-by-step derivation steps leading to it, as done in this paper.

In [25] a general constraint logic programming framework is defined for size-constrained generation of data structures as well as a program-transformation mechanism. While our fine-tuned interleaving of term generation and type inference directly provides the benefits of a CLP-based scheme, the program transformation techniques described in [25] are worth exploring for possible performance improvements. In [26] a general Haskell-based framework for generating enumerable structures is introduced. While clearly useful for arbitrary free structures, the fine-grained interleaving of generation and type inference of this paper do not seem to be embeddable in it with similar performance gains.

9 Conclusion

We have derived several logic programs that have helped solve the fairly hard combinatorial counting and generation problem for simply-typed lambda terms, 4 orders of magnitude higher than previously published results.

This has put at test two simple but effective program transformation techniques naturally available in logic programming languages: (1) interleaving generators and testers by integrating them in the same predicate and (2) dropping arguments used in generators when used simply as counters of solutions, as in this case their role can be kept implicit in the recursive structure of the program. Both have turned out to be effective for speeding up computations without changing the semantics of their intended application. We have also managed (after a simple DCG translation) to work within in the minimalist framework of Horn Clauses with sound unification, showing that non-trivial combinatorics problems can be handled without any of Prolog's impure features.

Our techniques, combining unification of logic variables with Prolog's backtracking mechanism and DCG grammar notation, recommend logic programming as a convenient meta-language for the manipulation of various families of lambda terms and the study of their combinatorial and computational properties.

Acknowledgement. This research has been supported by NSF grant 1423324.

We thank the anonymous reviewers of LOPSTR'16 for their constructive suggestions and the participants of the 9th Workshop Computational Logic and Applications (https://cla.tcs.uj.edu.pl/) for enlightening discussions and for sharing various techniques clarifying the challenges one faces when having a fresh look at the emerging, interdisciplinary field of the combinatorics of lambda terms and their applications.

References

1. Barendregt, H.P.: The Lambda Calculus its Syntax and Semantics. Revised edn. vol. 103. North Holland (1984)
2. Hindley, J.R., Seldin, J.P.: Lambda-Calculus and Combinators: An Introduction. vol. 13. Cambridge University Press, Cambridge (2008)

3. Barendregt, H.P.: Lambda calculi with types. In: Handbook of Logic in Computer Science, vol. 2. Oxford University Press (1991)
4. Palka, M.H., Claessen, K., Russo, A., Hughes, J.: Testing an optimising compiler by generating random lambda terms. In: Proceedings of the 6th International Workshop on Automation of Software Test, AST 2011, pp. 91–97. ACM, New York (2011)
5. Grygiel, K., Lescanne, P.: Counting and generating lambda terms. J. Funct. Program. **23**(5), 594–628 (2013)
6. David, R., Raffalli, C., Theyssier, G., Grygiel, K., Kozik, J., Zaionc, M.: Some properties of random lambda terms. Logical Methods Comput. Sci. **9**(1) (2009)
7. Bodini, O., Gardy, D., Gittenberger, B.: Lambda-terms of bounded unary height. In: ANALCO, SIAM, pp. 23–32 (2011)
8. David, R., Grygiel, K., Kozik, J., Raffalli, C., Theyssier, G., Zaionc, M.: Asymptotically almost all λ-terms are strongly normalizing. Preprint: arXiv: math. LO/0903.5505 v3 (2010)
9. Flajolet, P., Sedgewick, R.: Analytic Combinatorics, 1st edn. Cambridge University Press, New York (2009)
10. Sloane, N.J.A.: The On-Line Encyclopedia of Integer Sequences. (2014) Published electronically at https://oeis.org/
11. Tarau, P.: On logic programming representations of lambda terms: de bruijn indices, compression, type inference, combinatorial generation, normalization. In: Pontelli, E., Son, T.C. (eds.) PADL 2015. LNCS, vol. 9131, pp. 115–131. Springer, Cham (2015). doi:10.1007/978-3-319-19686-2_9
12. Tarau, P.: Ranking/unranking of lambda terms with compressed de bruijn indices. In: Kerber, M., Carette, J., Kaliszyk, C., Rabe, F., Sorge, V. (eds.) CICM 2015. LNCS, vol. 9150, pp. 118–133. Springer, Cham (2015). doi:10.1007/978-3-319-20615-8_8
13. Tarau, P.: On a uniform representation of combinators, arithmetic, lambda terms and types. In: Albert, E. (ed.) PPDP'15: Proceedings of the 17th international ACM SIGPLAN Symposium on Principles and Practice of Declarative Programming, pp. 244–255. ACM, New York (2015)
14. Tarau, P.: On type-directed generation of lambda terms. In: De Vos, M., Eiter, T., Lierler, Y., Toni, F. (eds.) 31st International Conference on Logic Programming (ICLP 2015), Technical Communications, Cork, Ireland, CEUR available online at September 2015 http://ceur-ws.org/Vol-1433/
15. Tarau, P.: A logic programming playground for lambda terms, combinators, types and tree-based arithmetic computations. CoRR abs/1507.06944 (2015)
16. Stanley, R.P.: Enumerative Combinatorics. Wadsworth Publ. Co., Belmont (1986)
17. Statman, R.: Intuitionistic propositional logic is polynomial-space complete. Theor. Comput. Sci. **9**, 67–72 (1979)
18. Wielemaker, J., Schrijvers, T., Triska, M., Lager, T.: SWI-Prolog. Theory Pract. Logic Program. **12**, 67–96 (2012)
19. Costa, V.S., Rocha, R., Damas, L.: The YAP Prolog system. Theory and Practice of Logic Programming 12, 5–34 (2012)
20. Grygiel, K., Lescanne, P.: Counting and generating terms in the binary lambda calculus. J. Funct. Program. 25 (2015)
21. Bendkowski, M., Grygiel, K., Lescanne, P., Zaionc, M.: A natural counting of lambda terms. In: Freivalds, R.M., Engels, G., Catania, B. (eds.) SOFSEM 2016. LNCS, vol. 9587, pp. 183–194. Springer, Heidelberg (2016). doi:10.1007/978-3-662-49192-8_15

22. Lescanne, P.: Boltzmann samplers for random generation of lambda terms. CoRR abs/1404.3875 (2014)
23. Fetscher, B., Claessen, K., Pałka, M., Hughes, J., Findler, R.B.: Making random judgments: automatically generating well-typed terms from the definition of a type-system. In: Vitek, J. (ed.) ESOP 2015. LNCS, vol. 9032, pp. 383–405. Springer, Heidelberg (2015). doi:10.1007/978-3-662-46669-8_16
24. Genitrini, A., Kozik, J., Zaionc, M.: Intuitionistic vs. classical tautologies, quantitative comparison. In: Miculan, M., Scagnetto, I., Honsell, F. (eds.) TYPES 2007. LNCS, vol. 4941, pp. 100–109. Springer, Heidelberg (2008). doi:10.1007/978-3-540-68103-8_7
25. Fioravanti, F., Proietti, M., Senni, V.: Efficient generation of test data structures using constraint logic programming and program transformation. J. Logic Comput. 25(6), 1263–1283 (2015)
26. Kuraj, I., Kuncak, V., Jackson, D.: Programming with enumerable sets of structures. In: Proceedings of the 2015 ACM SIGPLAN International Conference on Object-Oriented Programming, Systems, Languages, and Applications, OOPSLA 2015, pp. 37–56. ACM, New York (2015)

Semantics and Model Checking

A Reversible Semantics for Erlang

Naoki Nishida[1], Adrián Palacios[2], and Germán Vidal[2(⊠)]

[1] Graduate School of Informatics, Nagoya University,
Furo-cho, Chikusa-ku, Nagoya 4648603, Japan
nishida@i.nagoya-u.ac.jp
[2] MiST, DSIC, Universitat Politècnica de València,
Camino de Vera, s/n, 46022 Valencia, Spain
{apalacios,gvidal}@dsic.upv.es

Abstract. In a reversible language, any forward computation can be undone by a finite sequence of backward steps. Reversible computing has been studied in the context of different programming languages and formalisms, where it has been used for debugging and for enforcing fault-tolerance, among others. In this paper, we consider a subset of Erlang, a concurrent language based on the actor model, and formally introduce a semantics for reversible computation. To the best of our knowledge, this is the first attempt to define a reversible semantics for Erlang.

1 Introduction

Let us consider that the operational semantics of a programming language is specified by a state transition relation R such that $R(s, s')$ holds if the state s' is reachable—in one step—from state s. As it is common practice, we let R^* denote the reflexive and transitive closure of R. Then, we say that a programming language (or formalism) is *reversible* if there exists a constructive algorithm that can be used to, given a computation from state s to state s', in symbols $R^*(s, s')$, obtain the state s from s'. In general, such a property does not hold for most programming languages and formalisms. We refer the interested reader to, e.g., [3,10,24,25] for a high level account of the principles of reversible computation.

The notion of *reversible computation* was first introduced in Landauer's seminal work [14] and, then, further improved by Bennett [2] in order to avoid the generation of "garbage" data. The idea underlying these works is that any programming language or formalism can be made reversible by adding the *history* of

This work has been partially supported by the EU (FEDER) and the Spanish *Ministerio de Economía y Competitividad* (MINECO) under grants TIN2013-44742-C4-1-R and TIN2016-76843-C4-1-R, by the *Generalitat Valenciana* under grant PROMETEO-II/2015/013 (SmartLogic), and by COST Action IC1405 on Reversible Computation - extending horizons of computing.
Partially supported by the EU (FEDER) and the Spanish programs *Ayudas para contratos predoctorales para la formación de doctores* and *Ayudas a la movilidad predoctoral para la realización de estancias breves en centros de I+D*, MINECO (SEIDI), under FPI grants BES-2014-069749 and EEBB-I-16-11469.

© Springer International Publishing AG 2017
M.V. Hermenegildo and P. Lopez-Garcia (Eds.): LOPSTR 2016, LNCS 10184, pp. 259–274, 2017.
DOI: 10.1007/978-3-319-63139-4_15

the computation to each state, which is usually called a *Landauer's embedding*. Although carrying the history of a computation might seem infeasible because of its size, there are several successful proposals that are based on this idea. In particular, one can restrict the original language or apply a number of analysis in order to restrict the required information in the history as much as possible, as in, e.g., [18,19,22] in the context of a functional language.

In this paper, we aim at introducing a form of reversibility in the context of a programming language that follows the actor model (concurrency based on message passing), and that can be considered as a subset of the concurrent and functional language Erlang [1]. Previous approaches have mainly considered reversibility in—mostly synchronous—concurrent calculi like CCS [7,8], a general framework for reversibility of algebraic process calculi [20], or the recent approach to reversible *session-based* π-calculus [23]. However, we can only find a few approaches that considered the reversibility of *asynchronous* calculi, e.g., Cardelli and Laneve's reversible structures [5] or the approach based on a rollback construct of [11,15,16] (for a higher-order asynchronous π-calculus), [12] (for μKlaim) and [17] (for μOz).

To the best of our knowledge, our work is the first one that considers reversibility in the context of the functional, concurrent, and distributed language Erlang. Here, given a running Erlang system consisting of a pool of interacting processes, possibly distributed in several computers, we aim at allowing a *single* process to undo its actions in a stepwise manner, including the interactions with other processes, following a rollback fashion. In this context, we must ensure *causal consistency* [7], i.e., an action cannot be undone until all the actions that depend on it have already been undone. E.g., if a process spawns another process, we cannot undo this process spawning until all the actions performed by the new process are undone too. This is particularly challenging in our asynchronous and distributed setting since there is no *global* order for the language events. In this paper, we introduce a rollback operator that undoes the actions of a process until a given *checkpoint* is reached.

In this paper, we consider a simple Erlang-like language that can be considered a subset of *Core Erlang* [6]. We present the following contributions: First, we introduce an appropriate standard semantics for the language. In contrast to monolothic previous semantics like that in [4], our semantics is more modular, which simplifies the definition of a reversible extension. In contrast to [21], although we follow some of the ideas in this approach (e.g., the use of a global mailbox), we include the evaluation of expressions and, moreover, our treatment of messages is more deterministic.[1] We then introduce a reversible extension of the standard semantics (basically, a Landauer's embedding) where forward and backward computations are done stepwise. Here, we focus only on the concurrent actions (namely, process spawning, message sending and receiving) and, thus, do not consider the reversibilization of the functional component of the

---

[1] E.g., in the semantics of [21], at the expression level, the semantics of an expression containing a receive statement is, in principle, infinitely branching, since their formulation allows for an infinite number of possible queues and selected messages.

$$
\begin{aligned}
Module &::= \text{module } Atom = fun_1, \ldots, fun_n \\
fun &::= fname = \text{fun } (X_1, \ldots, X_n) \rightarrow expr \\
fname &::= Atom/Integer \\
lit &::= Atom \mid Integer \mid Float \mid [\,] \\
expr &::= Var \mid lit \mid fname \mid [expr_1|expr_2] \mid \{expr_1, \ldots, expr_n\} \\
&\mid \text{ call } expr\ (expr_1, \ldots, expr_n) \mid \text{apply } expr\ (expr_1, \ldots, expr_n) \\
&\mid \text{ case } expr \text{ of } clause_1; \ldots; clause_m \text{ end} \\
&\mid \text{ let } Var = expr_1 \text{ in } expr_2 \mid \text{receive } clause_1; \ldots; clause_n \text{ end} \\
&\mid \text{ spawn}(expr, [expr_1, \ldots, expr_n]) \mid expr_1\ !\ expr_2 \mid \text{self}() \\
clause &::= pat \text{ when } expr_1 \rightarrow expr_2 \\
pat &::= Var \mid lit \mid [pat_1|pat_2] \mid \{pat_1, \ldots, pat_n\}
\end{aligned}
$$

Fig. 1. Language syntax rules

language; rather, we assume that the state of the process—the current expression and its environment—is stored in the history after each execution step. This approach could be improved following, e.g., the approaches from [18,19,22]. Finally, we introduce a backward semantics that can be used to undo the actions of a given process, in a rollback fashion, until a checkpoint—introduced by the programmer—is reached. Here, ensuring causal consistency is essential and might propagate the rollback action to other, dependent processes.

2 Language Syntax

In this section, we present the syntax of a first-order concurrent and distributed functional language that follows the actor model. Our language is basically equivalent to a subset of Core Erlang [6].

The syntax of the language can be found in Fig. 1. Here, a module is a sequence of function definitions, where each function name f/n (atom/arity) has an associated definition of the form fun $(X_1, \ldots, X_n) \rightarrow e$. We consider that a program consists of a single module for simplicity. The body of a function is an *expression*, which can include variables, literals, function names, lists, tuples, calls to built-in functions—mainly arithmetic and relational operators—, function applications, case expressions, let bindings, and receive expressions; furthermore, we also consider the functions spawn, "!" (for sending a message), and self() that are usually considered built-ins in the Erlang language.

Despite the general syntax in Fig. 1, as mentioned before, we only consider first-order expressions. Therefore, the first expression in calls, applications and spawns can only be function names (instead of arbitrary expressions or closures).

In this language, we distinguish expressions, patterns, and values. As mentioned before, expressions can include all constructs of the language. In contrast, *patterns* are built from variables, literals, lists, and tuples. Finally, *values* are built from literals, lists, and tuples, i.e., they are *ground*—without variables—patterns. Expressions are denoted by $e, e', e_1, e_2, \ldots$, patterns by $p, p', p_1, p_2, \ldots$ and values by $v, v', v_1, v_2, \ldots$ As it is common practice, a *substitution* θ is a mapping from variables to expressions such that $\mathcal{D}om(\theta) = \{X \in Var \mid X \neq \theta(X)\}$ is its domain. Substitutions are usually denoted by sets of mappings like, e.g., $\{X_1 \mapsto v_1, \ldots, X_n \mapsto v_n\}$. Substitutions are extended to morphisms from expressions to expressions in the natural way. The identity substitution is denoted by id. Composition of substitutions is denoted by juxtaposition, i.e., $\theta\theta'$ denotes a substitution θ'' such that $\theta''(X) = \theta'(\theta(X))$ for all $X \in Var$. Also, we denote by $\theta[X_1 \mapsto v_1, \ldots, X_n \mapsto v_n]$ the *update* of θ with the mapping $X_1 \mapsto v_1, \ldots, X_n \mapsto v_n$, i.e., it denotes a new substitution θ' such that $\theta'(X) = v_i$ if $X = X_i$, for some $i \in \{1, \ldots, n\}$, and $\theta'(X) = \theta(X)$ otherwise.

In a case expression "case e of p_1 when $e_1 \rightarrow e_1'$; $\ldots$; p_n when $e_n \rightarrow e_n'$ end", we first evaluate e to a value, say v; then, we should find (if any) the first clause p_i when $e_i \rightarrow e_i'$ such that v matches p_i (i.e., there exists a substitution σ for the variables of p_i such that $v = p_i\sigma$) and $e_i\sigma$—the *guard*—reduces to *true*; then, the case expression reduces to $e_i'\sigma$. Note that guards can only contain calls to built-in functions (typically, arithmetic and relational operators).

As for the concurrent features of the language, we consider that a *system* is of a pool of processes that can only interact through message sending and receiving (i.e., there is no shared memory). Each process has an associated *pid* (process identifier), which is unique in a system. For clarity, we often denote pids with roman letters $p, p', p_1, \ldots$, though they are considered values in our language (i.e., atoms). By abuse of notation, when no confusion can arise, we refer to a process with its pid.

An expression of the form $\mathsf{spawn}(f/n, [e_1, \ldots, e_n])$ has, as a *side effect*, the creation of a new process with a fresh pid p which is initialized with the expression $\mathsf{apply}\ f/n\ (e_1, \ldots, e_n)$; the expression $\mathsf{spawn}(f/n, [e_1, \ldots, e_n])$ itself evaluates to the new pid p. The function $\mathsf{self}()$ just returns the pid of the current process. An expression of the form $p\ !\ v$ evaluates to the value v and, as a side effect, stores the value v—the *message*—in the queue or *mailbox* of process p.

Finally, an expression "receive p_1 when $e_1 \rightarrow e_1'$; $\ldots$; p_n when $e_n \rightarrow e_n'$ end" traverses the messages in the process' queue until one of them matches a branch in the receive statement; i.e., it should find the *first* message v in the process' queue (if any) such that case v of p_1 when $e_1 \rightarrow e_1'$; $\ldots$; p_n when $e_n \rightarrow e_n'$ end can be reduced; then, the receive expression evaluates to the same expression to which the above case expression would be evaluated, with the additional side effect of deleting the message v from the process' queue. If there is no matching message in the queue, the process suspends its execution until a matching message arrives.

Example 1. Consider the program shown in Fig. 2, where the symbol "_" is used to denote an *anonymous* variable, i.e., a variable whose name is not relevant. The computation starts with "apply $main/0$ ()." Then, this process, say $P1$, spawns two new processes, say $P2$ and $P3$, and then sends the message "*world*" to process $P3$ and the message $\{P3, hello\}$ to process $P2$, which then resends "*hello*" to $P3$. In our language, there is no guarantee regarding which message arrives first to $P3$, i.e., "apply $main/0$ ()" can evaluate nondeterministically to either $\{hello, world\}$ or $\{world, hello\}$. This is coherent with the semantics of

```
main/0 = fun () → let P2 = spawn(echo/0, [])
              in let P3 = spawn(target/0, [])
              in let _ = P3 ! world
              in let P2 ! {P3, hello}
```

```
target/0 = fun () → receive
                 A → receive                echo/0 = fun () → receive
                      B → {A, B}                              {P, M} → P ! M
                    end                                     end
               end
```

Fig. 2. A simple concurrent program

Erlang, where the only guarantee is that if two messages are sent from process p to process p′ and both are delivered, then the order of these messages is kept.

3   The Language Semantics

In order to set precisely the framework for our proposal, in this section we formalize the semantics of the considered language.

Definition 1 (process). *A process is denoted by a tuple of the form* $\langle p, (\theta, e), q \rangle$ *where* p *is the pid of the process,* (θ, e) *is the control of the state—which consists of an environment (a substitution) and an expression to be evaluated—, and* q *is the process' mailbox, a FIFO queue with the sequence of messages that have been sent to the process.*

A running *system* is then a pool of processes, which is formally defined as follows:

Definition 2 (system). *A system is denoted by* $\Gamma; \Pi$*, where* Γ *is a global mailbox of the system (see below) and* Π *is a pool of processes, denoted by an expression of the form* $\langle p_1, (\theta_1, e_1), q_1 \rangle \,\&\, \cdots \,\&\, \langle p_n, (\theta_n, e_n), q_n \rangle$*, where "&" is an associative and commutative operator. We typically denote a system by an expression of the form* $\Gamma; \langle p, (\theta, e), q \rangle \& \Pi$ *to point out that* $\langle p, (\theta, e), q \rangle$ *is an arbitrary process of the pool (thanks to the fact that "&" is associative and commutative).*

The role of Γ (which is similar to the "ether" in [21]) will be clarified later, but it is essential to guarantee that all admissible interleavings can be modelled with the semantics. Here, we define Γ as a set of FIFO queues among all (non-necessarily different) pids, i.e., Γ is made of elements of the form $(p, q, [v_1, \ldots, v_n])$, where p, q are (not necessarily different) pids and $[v_1, \ldots, v_n]$ is a (possibly empty) ordered list of messages such that v_1 is the oldest message and v_n is the most recent one. For simplicity, we assume that Γ is initialized as follows: $\{(p, q, []) \mid p, q \text{ are pids}\}$. Then, we use the following notation: $\Gamma \cup (p, q, v)$ denotes $\Gamma \setminus \{(p, q, vs)\} \cup \{(p, q, vs{+}{+}[v])\}$, while $\Gamma \setminus (p, q, v)$ denotes $\Gamma \setminus \{(p, q, v : vs)\} \cup \{(p, q, vs)\}$, where ++ is the list concatenation operator.

In the following, we denote by $\overline{o_n}$ the sequence of syntactic objects $o_1, \ldots, o_n$ for some n. We also write $\overline{o_{i,j}}$ for the sequence $o_i, \ldots, o_j$ when $i \leq j$ (and the

$$(Var) \; \frac{}{\theta, X \xrightarrow{\tau} \theta, \theta(X)} \qquad (Tuple) \; \frac{\theta, e_i \xrightarrow{\ell} \theta', e_i' \quad i \in \{1, \dots, n\}}{\theta, \{e_1, \dots, e_n\} \xrightarrow{\ell} \theta', \{\overline{e_{1,i-1}}, e_i', \overline{e_{i+1,n}}\}}$$

$$(List1) \; \frac{\theta, e_1 \xrightarrow{\ell} \theta', e_1'}{\theta, [e_1 | e_2] \xrightarrow{\ell} \theta', [e_1' | e_2]} \qquad (List2) \; \frac{\theta, e_2 \xrightarrow{\ell} \theta', e_2'}{\theta, [e_1 | e_2] \xrightarrow{\ell} \theta', [e_1 | e_2']}$$

$$(Let1) \; \frac{\theta, e_1 \xrightarrow{\ell} \theta', e_1'}{\theta, \mathsf{let}\ X = e_1\ \mathsf{in}\ e_2 \xrightarrow{\ell} \theta', \mathsf{let}\ X = e_1'\ \mathsf{in}\ e_2} \qquad (Let2) \; \frac{}{\theta, \mathsf{let}\ X = v\ \mathsf{in}\ e \xrightarrow{\tau} \theta[X \mapsto v], e}$$

$$(Case1) \; \frac{\theta, e \xrightarrow{\ell} \theta', e'}{\theta, \mathsf{case}\ e\ \mathsf{of}\ cl_1; \dots; cl_n\ \mathsf{end}} \qquad (Case2) \; \frac{\mathsf{match}(v, cl_1, \dots, cl_n) = \langle \theta_i, e_i \rangle}{\theta, \mathsf{case}\ v\ \mathsf{of}\ cl_1; \dots; cl_n\ \mathsf{end} \xrightarrow{\tau} \theta\theta_i, e_i}$$
$$\xrightarrow{\ell} \theta', \mathsf{case}\ e'\ \mathsf{of}\ cl_1; \dots; cl_n\ \mathsf{end}$$

$$(Call1) \; \frac{\theta, e_i \xrightarrow{\ell} \theta', e_i' \quad i \in \{1, \dots, n\}}{\theta, \mathsf{call}\ op\ (\overline{e_n}) \xrightarrow{\ell} \theta', \mathsf{call}\ op\ (\overline{e_{1,i-1}}, e_i', \overline{e_{i+1,n}})} \qquad (Call2) \; \frac{\mathsf{eval}(op, v_1, \dots, v_n) = v}{\theta, \mathsf{call}\ op\ (v_1, \dots, v_n) \xrightarrow{\tau} \theta, v}$$

$$(Apply1) \; \frac{\theta, e_i \xrightarrow{\ell} \theta', e_i' \quad i \in \{1, \dots, n\}}{\theta, \mathsf{apply}\ a/n\ (\overline{e_n}) \xrightarrow{\ell} \theta', \mathsf{apply}\ a/n\ (\overline{e_{1,i-1}}, e_i', \overline{e_{i+1,n}})}$$

$$(Apply2) \; \frac{\mu(a/n) = \mathsf{fun}\ (X_1, \dots, X_n) \to e}{\theta, \mathsf{apply}\ a/n\ (v_1, \dots, v_n) \xrightarrow{\tau} \{X_1 \mapsto v_1, \dots, X_n \mapsto v_n\}, e}$$

Fig. 3. Standard semantics: evaluation of sequential expressions

empty sequence otherwise). We write $\bar{o}$ when the number of elements is not relevant.

The semantics is defined by means of two transition relations: $\longrightarrow$ for expressions and $\longmapsto$ for systems. Let us first consider the labelled transition relation

$$\longrightarrow : (Env, Exp) \times Label \times (Env, Exp)$$

where Env and Exp are the domains of environments (i.e., substitutions) and expressions, respectively, and $Label$ denotes an element of the set

$$\{\tau, \mathsf{send}(v_1, v_2), \mathsf{rec}(y, \overline{cl_n}), \mathsf{spawn}(y, a/n, [\overline{e_n}]), \mathsf{self}(y)\}$$

whose meaning will be explained below. For clarity, we divide the transition rules of the semantics for expressions in two sets, depicted in Figs. 3 and 4 for sequential and concurrent expressions, respectively.

Most of the rules are self-explanatory. In the following, we only discuss some subtle or complex issues. In principle, the transitions are labelled either with τ (a sequential expression) or with a label that identifies a concurrent action. Labels are used in the system rules (Fig. 5) to perform the associated side effects.

In some of the rules (e.g., for evaluating tuples, lists, etc.) we consider for simplicity that elements are evaluated in a non-deterministic way. In an actual programming language the order of evaluation of the arguments in the tuple or list is usually fixed. E.g., in Erlang, reduction takes place from left to right.

$$(Send1) \quad \frac{\theta, e_1 \xrightarrow{\ell} \theta', e_1'}{\theta, e_1 \,!\, e_2 \xrightarrow{\ell} \theta', e_1' \,!\, e_2} \qquad \frac{\theta, e_2 \xrightarrow{\ell} \theta', e_2'}{\theta, e_1 \,!\, e_2 \xrightarrow{\ell} \theta', e_1 \,!\, e_2'}$$

$$(Send2) \quad \frac{}{\theta, v_1 \,!\, v_2 \xrightarrow{send(v_1, v_2)} \theta, v_2}$$

$$(Receive) \quad \frac{}{\theta, \mathsf{receive}\ cl_1; \ldots; cl_n\ \mathsf{end} \xrightarrow{rec(y, \overline{cl_n})} \theta, y}$$

$$(Spawn) \quad \frac{}{\theta, \mathsf{spawn}(a/n, [e_1, \ldots, e_n]) \xrightarrow{spawn(y, a/n, [\overline{e_n}])} \theta, y}$$

$$(Self) \quad \frac{}{\theta, \mathsf{self}() \xrightarrow{self(y)} \theta, y}$$

Fig. 4. Standard semantics: evaluation of concurrent expressions

For case evaluation, we assume an auxiliary function match which selects the first clause, $cl_i = (p_i \ \mathsf{when}\ e_i' \to e_i)$, such that v matches p_i, i.e., $v = \theta_i(p_i)$, and the guard holds, i.e., $\theta\theta_i, e_i' \longrightarrow^* \theta', true$. Note that, for simplicity, we do not consider here the case in which the argument v matches no clause.

Function calls can either be defined in the program (apply) or be a built-in (call). In the latter case, they are evaluated using the auxiliary function eval. In rule *Apply2*, we consider that the mapping μ stores all function definitions, i.e., it maps every function name a/n to its definition $\mathsf{fun}\ (X_1, \ldots, X_n) \to e$ in the program. As for the applications, note that we only consider first-order functions. In order to extend our semantics to also consider higher-order functions, one should reduce the function name to a *closure* of the form $(\theta', \mathsf{fun}\ (X_1, \ldots, X_n) \to e)$ and, then, reduce e in the environment $\theta'[X_1 \mapsto v_1, \ldots, X_n \mapsto v_n]$. We skip this extension since it is orthogonal to our approach.

Let us now consider the evaluation of concurrent expressions that produce some side effect (Fig. 4). Here, we can distinguish two kinds of rules. On the one hand, we have the rules for "!", *Send1* and *Send2*. In this case, we know *locally* what the expression should be reduced to (i.e., v_2 in rule *Send2*). For the remaining rules, this is not known locally and, thus, we return a fresh distinguished symbol, $y \notin Var$ (by abuse, y is dealt with as a variable), so that the system rules will eventually bind y to its correct value. This *trick* allows us to keep the rules for expressions and systems separated (i.e., the semantics shown in Figs. 3 and 4 is mostly independent from the rules in Fig. 5), in contrast to other calculi, e.g., [4], where they are combined into a single transition relation.

Let us finally consider the system rules, which are depicted in Fig. 5. In most of the rules, we consider an arbitrary system of the form $\Gamma; \langle p, (\theta, e), q \rangle \& \Pi$, where Γ is the global mailbox and $\langle p, (\theta, e), q \rangle \& \Pi$ is a pool of process that contains at least one process $\langle p, (\theta, e), q \rangle$.

Note that, in rule *Send*, we add the triple (p, p'', v) to Γ instead of adding it to the queue of process p''. This is necessary to ensure that all possible non-deterministic results can be obtained (as discussed in Example 1). Observe that

(Exp)
$$\frac{\theta, e \xrightarrow{\tau} \theta', e'}{\Gamma; \langle p, (\theta, e), q \rangle \& \Pi \longmapsto \Gamma; \langle p, (\theta', e'), q \rangle \& \Pi}$$

$(Send)$
$$\frac{\theta, e \xrightarrow{\mathsf{send}(p'', v)} \theta', e'}{\Gamma; \langle p, (\theta, e), q \rangle \& \Pi \longmapsto \Gamma \cup (p, p'', v); \langle p, (\theta', e'), q \rangle \& \Pi}$$

$(Receive)$
$$\frac{\theta, e \xrightarrow{\mathsf{rec}(y, \overline{cl_n})} \theta', e' \quad \mathsf{matchrec}(\overline{cl_n}, q) = (\theta_i, e_i, q')}{\Gamma; \langle p, (\theta, e), q \rangle \& \Pi \longmapsto \Gamma; \langle p, (\theta' \theta_i, e'\{y \mapsto e_i\}), q' \rangle \& \Pi}$$

$(Spawn)$
$$\frac{\theta, e \xrightarrow{\mathsf{spawn}(y, a/n, [\overline{e_n}])} \theta', e' \quad p' \text{ is a fresh pid}}{\Gamma; \langle p, (\theta, e), q \rangle \& \Pi \longmapsto \Gamma; \langle p, (\theta', e'\{y \mapsto p'\}), q \rangle \& \langle p', (\theta', \mathsf{apply}\ a/n\ (\overline{e_n})), [] \rangle \& \Pi}$$

$(Self)$
$$\frac{\theta, e \xrightarrow{\mathsf{self}(y)} \theta', e'}{\Gamma; \langle p, (\theta, e), q \rangle \& \Pi \longmapsto \Gamma; \langle p, (\theta', e'\{y \mapsto p\}), q \rangle \& \Pi}$$

$(Sched)$
$$\frac{\alpha(\Gamma) = (p', p) \quad \Pi = \langle p, (\theta, e), q \rangle \& \Pi'}{\Gamma; \Pi \longmapsto \Gamma \setminus \{(p', p, v)\}; \langle p, (\theta, e), v:q \rangle \& \Pi'}$$

Fig. 5. Standard semantics: system rules

e' is usually different from v since e may have different nested operators. E.g., if e has the form "case $p\,!\,v$ of $\{\ldots\}$," then e' will be "case v of $\{\ldots\}$" with label send(p, v).

In rule *Receive*, we use the auxiliary function matchrec to evaluate a receive expression. The main difference with match is that matchrec also takes a queue q and returns the modified queue q'. Then, the distinguished variable y is bound to the expression in the selected clause, e_i, and the environment is extended with the matching substitution. If no message in the queue q matches any clause, then the rule is not applicable and the selected process cannot be reduced (i.e., it suspends).

With the rules presented so far, any system will soon reach a state in which no reduction can be performed, since messages are stored in the global mailbox, but they are not dispatched to the queues of the processes. This is precisely the task of the scheduler, which is modelled by rule *Sched*. The rule is non-deterministic, so any scheduling policy can be modelled by the semantics. A message is selected from the list of messages by the auxiliary function α, which can select any arbitrary pair of (non-necessarily different) pids (p', p). Note that we take the oldest message in the queue—the first one in the list—, which is necessary to ensure that "the messages sent—directly—between two given processes arrive in the same order they were sent", as mentioned in the previous section.

Example 2. Let us consider the program shown in Fig. 6 and a possible execution trace. This trace is modelled by our semantics. For clarity, we only show in Fig. 7 the transition steps that correspond to the last two messages sent between *client1* and *server*.

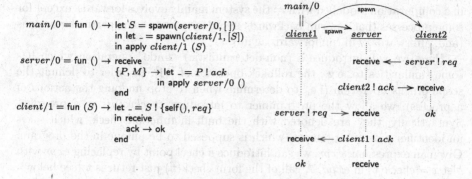

$main/0 = $ fun $() \rightarrow$ let $S = $ spawn$(server/0, [\,])$
            in let $_ = $ spawn$(client/1, [S])$
            in apply $client/1$ (S)

$server/0 = $ fun $() \rightarrow$ receive
            $\{P, M\} \rightarrow$ let $\_ = P\,!\,ack$
                         in apply $server/0$ $()$
            end

$client/1 = $ fun $(S) \rightarrow$ let $\_ = S\,!\,\{$self$(), req\}$
            in receive
            $ack \rightarrow ok$
            end

Fig. 6. A simple client-server

$[\,]; \quad \langle$c1$, (id, $apply $main/0$ $()), [\,]\rangle$

$\longmapsto \quad \ldots$

$\longmapsto \quad [\,]; \quad \langle$c1$, (\sigma, $let $\_ = S\,!\,v_2$ in $\ldots), [\,]\rangle$ & $\langle$s$, (id, $receive $\{P, M\} \rightarrow \ldots), [\,]\rangle$ &
            $\langle$c2$, (\sigma, ok), [\,]\rangle$

$\longmapsto \quad [($c1$, s, [v_2])]; \quad \langle$c1$, (\sigma, $let $\_ = v_2$ in $\ldots), [\,]\rangle$ & $\langle$s$, (id, $receive $\{P, M\} \rightarrow \ldots), [\,]\rangle$ &
            $\langle$c2$, (\sigma, ok), [\,]\rangle$

$\longmapsto \quad [($c1$, s, [v_2])]; \quad \langle$c1$, (\sigma, $receive $ack \rightarrow \ldots), [\,]\rangle$ & $\langle$s$, (id, $receive $\{P, M\} \rightarrow \ldots), [\,]\rangle$ &
            $\langle$c2$, (\sigma, ok), [\,]\rangle$

$\longmapsto \quad [\,]; \quad \langle$c1$, (\sigma, $receive $ack \rightarrow \ldots), [\,]\rangle$ & $\langle$s$, (id, $receive $\{P, M\} \rightarrow \ldots), [v_2]\rangle$ &
            $\langle$c2$, (\sigma, ok), [\,]\rangle$

$\longmapsto \quad [\,]; \quad \langle$c1$, (\sigma, $receive $ack \rightarrow \ldots), [\,]\rangle$ & $\langle$s$, (\theta_2, $let $\_ = P\,!\,ack$ in $\ldots), [\,]\rangle$ &
            $\langle$c2$, (\sigma, ok), [\,]\rangle$

$\longmapsto \quad [($s$, $c1$, [ack])]; \quad \langle$c1$, (\sigma, $receive $ack \rightarrow \ldots), [\,]\rangle$ & $\langle$s$, (\theta_2, $let $\_ = ack$ in $\ldots), [\,]\rangle$ &
            $\langle$c2$, (\sigma, ok), [\,]\rangle$

$\longmapsto \quad [($s$, $c1$, [ack])]; \quad \langle$c1$, (\sigma, $receive $ack \rightarrow \ldots), [\,]\rangle$ & $\langle$s$, (\theta_2, $apply $server/0$ $()), [\,]\rangle$ &
            $\langle$c2$, (\sigma, ok), [\,]\rangle$

$\longmapsto \quad [($s$, $c1$, [ack])]; \quad \langle$c1$, (\sigma, $receive $ack \rightarrow \ldots), [\,]\rangle$ & $\langle$s$, (id, $receive $\{P, M\} \rightarrow \ldots), [\,]\rangle$ &
            $\langle$c2$, (\sigma, ok), [\,]\rangle$

$\longmapsto \quad [\,]; \quad \langle$c1$, (\sigma, $receive $ack \rightarrow \ldots), [ack]\rangle$ & $\langle$s$, (id, $receive $\{P, M\} \rightarrow \ldots), [\,]\rangle$ &
            $\langle$c2$, (\sigma, ok), [\,]\rangle$

$\longmapsto \quad [\,]; \quad \langle$c1$, (\sigma, ok), [\,]\rangle$ & $\langle$s$, (id, $receive $\{P, M\} \rightarrow \ldots), [\,]\rangle$ &
            $\langle$c2$, (\sigma, ok), [\,]\rangle$

Fig. 7. A trace with $\sigma = \{S \mapsto s\}$, $\theta_2 = \{P \mapsto $c1$, M \mapsto req\}$, and $v_2 = \{$c1$, req\}$.

4   Reversible Semantics

In this section, we introduce a reversible extension of the semantics defined so far. Moreover, thanks to our modular design, the semantics for the language expressions needs not be changed.

To be precise, in this section we introduce two transition relations: $\rightharpoonup$ and $\leftharpoonup$. The first relation, $\rightharpoonup$, is a conservative extension of the standard semantics $\longmapsto$ (Fig. 5) to also include some additional information in the states, following a typical Landauer's embedding. We refer to $\rightharpoonup$ as the *forward* reversible semantics (or simply the forward semantics). In contrast, the second relation, $\leftharpoonup$, proceeds in the backwards direction, "undoing" the actions of a single process step by step (and, by causal consistency, possibly propagating it to other processes). We refer to $\leftharpoonup$ as the backward (reversible) semantics. We denote the union $\rightharpoonup \cup \leftharpoonup$ by $\rightleftharpoons$. Then, in a computation modelled with $\rightleftharpoons$ the system mainly evolves forwards, except for some processes that can run backwards in order to undo some particular actions (and, afterwards, will run forwards again).

Here, we will introduce a (non-deterministic) "undo" operation which has some similarities to, e.g., the rollback operator of [11]. In order to delimit the scope of this operation (i.e., to determine when to stop undoing the actions of a process), we allow the programmer to introduce *checkpoints* in a program. Syntactically, they are denoted with the built-in function check, which takes an identifier t as an argument, which is supposed to be unique in the program. Given an expression, *expr*, we can introduce a checkpoint by replacing *expr* with "let $x = $ check(t) in *expr*". A call of the form check(t) just returns t (see below). In the following, we consider that the rules to evaluate the language expressions (Figs. 3 and 4) are extended with the following rule:

$$(Check) \quad \frac{}{\theta, \text{check}(t) \xrightarrow{\text{check}(t)} \theta, t}$$

In the next section, we will see that the only effect of a call to function check is to add a checkpoint to the trace of a given process.

4.1   Forward Semantics

First, we introduce the forward (reversible) semantics. Since the expression rules are the same (except for the additional rule for check mentioned above), we will only introduce the reversible system rules, which are shown in Fig. 8. Processes now include a memory (or *trace*) π that records the intermediate states of a process. Here, we use terms headed by constructors τ, check, send, rec, spawn, self, and sched to record the steps given with the forward semantics. Note that we could optimize the information stored in these terms by following a strategy similar to that in [18, 19, 22] for the reversibility of functional expressions, but this is orthogonal to our purpose in this paper, so we focus only on the concurrent actions.

The rules are mostly self-explanatory. Checkpoints introduced by the programmer, of the form check(θ, e, t), represent a *safe* point in the program execution. Rollback operations and checkpoints introduced by the programmer lay the ground for defining *safe* sessions whose actions can be undone if, e.g., an exception occurs before they are completed. Besides these checkpoints, we also consider checkpoints associated to receiving a message, denoted by sched(p, p', v), and spawning a process (empty trace). These checkpoints are internal and only used to ensure causal consistency.

Example 3. Consider again the program shown in Fig. 6, where the function *client*/1 is now defined as follows:

$$client/1 = \text{fun } (S) \rightarrow \text{let } \_ = \text{check}(t) \text{ in let } \_ = S \,!\, \{\text{self}(), req\}$$
$$\text{in receive ack} \rightarrow \text{ok end}$$

and the execution trace shown in Fig. 7. The corresponding forward (reversible) computation is shown in Fig. 9.

$(Internal)$
$$\frac{\theta, e \xrightarrow{\tau} \theta', e'}{\Gamma; \langle \pi, p, (\theta, e), q\rangle \& \Pi \rightarrow \Gamma; \langle \tau(\theta, e):\pi, p, (\theta', e'), q\rangle \& \Pi}$$

$(Check)$
$$\frac{\theta, e \xrightarrow{\mathsf{check(t)}} \theta', e'}{\Gamma; \langle \pi, p, (\theta, e), q\rangle \& \Pi \rightarrow \Gamma; \langle \mathsf{check}(\theta, e, \mathsf{t}):\pi, p, (\theta', e'), q\rangle \& \Pi}$$

$(Send)$
$$\frac{\theta, e \xrightarrow{\mathsf{send}(p'',v)} \theta', e'}{\Gamma; \langle \pi, p, (\theta, e), q\rangle \& \Pi \rightarrow \Gamma \cup (p, p'', v); \langle \mathsf{send}(\theta, e, p, p'', v):\pi, p, (\theta', e'), q\rangle \& \Pi}$$

$(Receive)$
$$\frac{\theta, e \xrightarrow{\mathsf{rec}(y, \overline{cl_n})} \theta', e' \quad matchrec(\overline{cl_n}, q) = (\theta_i, e_i, q')}{\Gamma; \langle \pi, p, (\theta, e), q\rangle \& \Pi \rightarrow \Gamma; \langle \mathsf{rec}(\theta, e, q):\pi, p, (\theta'\theta_i, e'\{y \mapsto e_i\}), q'\rangle \& \Pi}$$

$(Spawn)$
$$\frac{\theta, e \xrightarrow{\mathsf{spawn}(y, a/n, [e_1, \ldots, e_n])} \theta', e' \quad p' \text{ is a fresh pid}}{\Gamma; \langle \pi, p, (\theta, e), q\rangle \& \Pi \rightarrow \Gamma; \langle \mathsf{spawn}(\theta, e, p'):\pi, p, (\theta', e'\{y \mapsto p'\}), q\rangle \\ \& \langle [\,], p', (\theta, \mathsf{apply}\ a/n\ (e_1, \ldots, e_n)), [\,]\rangle \& \Pi}$$

$(Self)$
$$\frac{\theta, e \xrightarrow{\mathsf{self}(y)} \theta', e'}{\Gamma; \langle \pi, p, (\theta, e), q\rangle \& \Pi \rightarrow \Gamma; \langle \mathsf{self}(\theta, e):\pi, p, (\theta', e'\{y \mapsto p\}), q\rangle \& \Pi}$$

$(Sched)$
$$\frac{\alpha(\Gamma) = (p', p) \quad \Pi = \langle \pi, p, (\theta, e), q\rangle \& \Pi'}{\Gamma; \Pi \rightarrow \Gamma \setminus (p', p, v); \langle \mathsf{sched}(p', p, v):\pi, p, (\theta, e), v:q\rangle \& \Pi'}$$

Fig. 8. Reversible semantics: system rules

$\quad\quad$ $[\,]; \langle [\,], \mathsf{c1}, (id, \underline{\mathsf{apply}\ main/0\ ()}), [\,]\rangle$

$\rightarrow$ $\quad \ldots$

$\rightarrow$ $\quad [\,]; \langle \pi_i, \mathsf{c1}, (\sigma, \mathsf{let}\ \_ = \underline{\mathsf{check(t)}}\ \mathsf{in} \ldots), [\,]\rangle\ \&\ \langle \pi'_i, \mathsf{s}, (id, \underline{\mathsf{receive}\ \{P, M\} \rightarrow \ldots}), [\,]\rangle\ \&$
$\quad\quad \langle \pi''_i, \mathsf{c2}, (\sigma, \underline{ok}), [\,]\rangle$

$\rightarrow$ $\quad [\,]; \langle \mathsf{check}(\sigma, \mathsf{let}\ \_ = \mathsf{check(t)}\ \mathsf{in} \ldots, \mathsf{t}):\pi_i, \mathsf{c1}, (\sigma, \underline{\mathsf{let}\ \_ = \mathsf{t}\ \mathsf{in} \ldots}), [\,])\ \&$
$\quad\quad \langle \pi'_i, \mathsf{s}, (id, \mathsf{receive}\ \{P, M\} \rightarrow \ldots), [\,]\rangle\ \&\ \langle \pi''_i, \mathsf{c2}, (\sigma, ok), [\,]\rangle$

$\rightarrow$ $\quad [\,]; \langle \tau(\sigma, \mathsf{let}\ \_ = \mathsf{t}\ \mathsf{in} \ldots):\mathsf{check}(\sigma, \mathsf{let}\ \_ = \mathsf{check(t)}\ \mathsf{in} \ldots, \mathsf{t}):\pi_i,$
$\quad\quad \mathsf{c1}, (\sigma, \underline{\mathsf{let}\ \_ = S\,!\,v_2\ \mathsf{in} \ldots}), [\,])\ \&$
$\quad\quad \langle \pi'_i, \mathsf{s}, (id, \mathsf{receive}\ \{P, M\} \rightarrow \ldots), [\,]\rangle\ \&\ \langle \pi''_i, \mathsf{c2}, (\sigma, ok), [\,]\rangle$

$\rightarrow [(\mathsf{c1}, \mathsf{s}, [v_2])];$ $\langle \mathsf{send}(\sigma, \mathsf{let}\ \_ = S\,!\,v_2\ \mathsf{in} \ldots, \mathsf{c1}, \mathsf{s}, v_2):\tau(\sigma, \mathsf{let}\ \_ = \mathsf{t}\ \mathsf{in} \ldots)$
$\quad\quad :\mathsf{check}(\sigma, \mathsf{let}\ \_ = \mathsf{check(t)}\ \mathsf{in} \ldots, \mathsf{t}):\pi_i, \mathsf{c1}, (\sigma, \underline{\mathsf{let}\ \_ = v_2\ \mathsf{in} \ldots}), [\,])\ \&$
$\quad\quad \langle \pi'_i, \mathsf{s}, (id, \mathsf{receive}\ \{P, M\} \rightarrow \ldots), [\,]\rangle\ \&\ \langle \pi''_i, \mathsf{c2}, (\sigma, ok), [\,]\rangle$

$\rightarrow [\underline{(\mathsf{c1}, \mathsf{s}, [v_2])}];$ $\langle \tau(\sigma, \mathsf{let}\ \_ = v_2\ \mathsf{in} \ldots):\mathsf{send}(\sigma, \mathsf{let}\ \_ = S\,!\,v_2\ \mathsf{in} \ldots, \mathsf{c1}, \mathsf{s}, v_2):\tau(\sigma, \mathsf{let}\ \_ = \mathsf{t}\ \mathsf{in} \ldots)$
$\quad\quad :\mathsf{check}(\sigma, \mathsf{let}\ \_ = \mathsf{check(t)}\ \mathsf{in} \ldots, \mathsf{t}):\pi_i, \mathsf{c1}, (\sigma, \mathsf{receive}\ ack \rightarrow \ldots), [\,])\ \&$
$\quad\quad \langle \pi'_i, \mathsf{s}, (id, \mathsf{receive}\ \{P, M\} \rightarrow \ldots), [\,]\rangle\ \&\ \langle \pi''_i, \mathsf{c2}, (\sigma, ok), [\,]\rangle$

$\rightarrow$ $\quad [\,]; \langle \tau(\sigma, \mathsf{let}\ \_ = v_2\ \mathsf{in} \ldots):\mathsf{send}(\sigma, \mathsf{let}\ \_ = S\,!\,v_2\ \mathsf{in} \ldots, \mathsf{c1}, \mathsf{s}, v_2):\tau(\sigma, \mathsf{let}\ \_ = \mathsf{t}\ \mathsf{in} \ldots)$
$\quad\quad :\mathsf{check}(\sigma, \mathsf{let}\ \_ = \mathsf{check(t)}\ \mathsf{in} \ldots, \mathsf{t}):\pi_i, \mathsf{c1}, (\sigma, \mathsf{receive}\ ack \rightarrow \ldots); [\,])\ \&$
$\quad\quad \langle \mathsf{sched}(\mathsf{c1}, \mathsf{s}, v_2):\pi'_i, \mathsf{s}, (id, \underline{\mathsf{receive}\ \{P, M\} \rightarrow \ldots}), [v_2]\rangle\ \&$
$\quad\quad \langle \pi''_i, \mathsf{c2}, (\sigma, ok), [\,]\rangle$

$\rightarrow$ $\quad [\,]; \langle \tau(\sigma, \mathsf{let}\ \_ = v_2\ \mathsf{in} \ldots):\mathsf{send}(\sigma, \mathsf{let}\ \_ = S\,!\,v_2\ \mathsf{in} \ldots, \mathsf{c1}, \mathsf{s}, v_2):\tau(\sigma, \mathsf{let}\ \_ = \mathsf{t}\ \mathsf{in} \ldots)$
$\quad\quad :\mathsf{check}(\sigma, \mathsf{let}\ \_ = \mathsf{check(t)}\ \mathsf{in} \ldots, \mathsf{t}):\pi_i, \mathsf{c1}, (\sigma, \mathsf{receive}\ ack \rightarrow \ldots), [\,])\ \&$
$\quad\quad \langle \mathsf{rec}(id, \mathsf{receive}\ \{P, M\} \rightarrow \ldots, [v_2]):\mathsf{sched}(\mathsf{c1}, \mathsf{s}, v_2):\pi'_i,$
$\quad\quad \mathsf{s}, (\theta_2, \mathsf{let}\ \_ = \underline{P\,!\,ack}\ \mathsf{in} \ldots), [\,])\ \&\ \langle \pi''_i, \mathsf{c2}, (\sigma, ok), [\,]\rangle$

$\rightarrow$ $\quad \ldots$

Fig. 9. A (partial) trace with the forward reversible semantics, where $\sigma = \{S \mapsto \mathsf{s}\}$, $\theta_2 = \{P \mapsto \mathsf{c1}, M \mapsto req\}$, and $v_2 = \{\mathsf{c1}, req\}$

In the following, we let $s_1, s_2, \ldots$ denote systems of the standard semantics (Fig. 5) and $rs_1, rs_2, \ldots$ denote systems of the instrumented reversible semantics (Fig. 8). Here, we denote by $\overline{rs}$ the system that results from rs by removing the traces of the processes; formally, $\overline{\Gamma; \langle \pi_1, p_1, (\theta_1, e_2), q_1 \rangle \& \ldots \& \langle \pi_n, p_n, (\theta_n, e_n), q_n \rangle} = \Gamma; \langle p_1, (\theta_1, e_2), q_1 \rangle \& \ldots \& \langle p_n, (\theta_n, e_n), q_n \rangle$. The following result states that $\rightarrowtail$ is indeed a conservative extension of the standard semantics $\longmapsto$:

Theorem 1. *Let $\mathcal{P}$ be a program without occurrences of "check". Let s_1 be a system of the standard semantics and rs_1 a system of the reversible semantics with $\overline{rs_1} = s_1$. Then, $s_1 \longmapsto^* s_2$ iff $rs_1 \rightarrowtail^* rs_2$ and $\overline{rs_2} = s_2$.*

4.2 Backward Semantics

In the following, we denote a process running backwards with $\lfloor proc \rfloor_\#$, where $\#$ is a rollback label that refers to the checkpoint that the backward computation of *proc* has to go through before resuming its forward computation. For instance, a process of the form $\lfloor proc \rfloor_{\#_{\mathsf{ch}}^t}$ should go backwards until a checkpoint $\mathsf{check}(\theta, e, t)$ is found in its trace, a process $\lfloor proc \rfloor_{\#_{\mathsf{sch}}^{p,v}}$ should go backwards until an event of the form $\mathsf{sched}(p, p', v)$ is found in its trace, and a process $\lfloor proc \rfloor_{\#_{\mathsf{sp}}}$ should go backwards until its initial state is reached (i.e., it should be completely undone).

In order to introduce a rollback operator (e.g., when a process crashes or some undesired situation occurs), we fire the following rule:

$$(Undo) \quad \Gamma; \langle \pi, p, (\theta, e), q \rangle \& \Pi \leftharpoondown \Gamma; \lfloor \langle \pi, p, (\theta, e), q \rangle \rfloor_{\#_{\mathsf{ch}}^t} \& \Pi$$

for some checkpoint identifier t.

Let us now discuss the rules for performing backward computations, which are shown in Fig. 10, where $\#$ denotes an arbitrary rollback label. In general, all rules restore the control (and sometimes also the queue) of a process.

Rule $\overline{Check1}$ resumes the forward computation of a process rolling back with $\#_{\mathsf{ch}}^t$ when we reach a term of the form $\mathsf{check}(\ldots, t)$ in the trace. When the label is different (i.e., $\#_{\mathsf{sp}}$ or $\#_{\mathsf{sch}}^{p,v}$) or it is a label $\#_{\mathsf{ch}}^{t'}$ with $t \neq t'$, then rule $\overline{Check2}$ just removes the $\mathsf{check}(\ldots)$ from the trace.

In order to undo the sending of a message, rule $\overline{Send1}$ removes a message from Γ when the message has not been delivered yet (using rule $Sched$). Here, we use the operator "$\backslash\backslash$" to denote the removal of the last (newest) message between two given processes—in contrast to "$\backslash$", which always removes the oldest one. Otherwise, i.e., when the message has already been delivered, rule $\overline{Send2}$ *freezes* the process,[2] denoted with $\lceil \ldots \rceil_\#$, and applies a rollback operator to the receiver labelled with $\#_{\mathsf{sch}}^{p,v}$. This will cause the receiver process to undo all the actions that it has performed since it received the message, thus ensuring *causal consistency*. Once all these actions have been undone, rule $\overline{Send3}$ applies, resuming the forward computation for the receiver and the backward computation for the sender.

Analogously, for undoing the creation of a process, rule $\overline{Spawn1}$ freezes the process and marks the child process with label $\#_{\mathsf{sp}}$. The child process will then

---

[2] Note that we use the notation $\lceil \ldots \rceil$ to explicitly denote that a process is frozen, though it is not really necessary since no transition rule would be applicable anyway.

$(\overline{Internal})$ $\qquad \Gamma; \lfloor \langle \tau(\theta, e) : \pi, p, (\theta', e'), q \rangle \rfloor_{\#} \,\&\, \Pi \,\leftharpoonup\, \Gamma; \lfloor \langle \pi, p, (\theta, e), q \rangle \rfloor_{\#} \,\&\, \Pi$

$(\overline{Check1})$ $\qquad \Gamma; \lfloor \langle \mathsf{check}(\theta, e, \mathsf{t}) : \pi, p, (\theta', e'), q \rangle \rfloor_{\#^t_{\mathsf{ch}}} \,\&\, \Pi \,\leftharpoonup\, \Gamma; \langle \pi, p, (\theta, e), q \rangle \,\&\, \Pi$

$(\overline{Check2})$ $\qquad \Gamma; \lfloor \langle \mathsf{check}(\theta, e, \mathsf{t}) : \pi, p, (\theta', e'), q \rangle \rfloor_{\#} \,\&\, \Pi \,\leftharpoonup\, \Gamma; \lfloor \langle \pi, p, (\theta', e'), q \rangle \rfloor_{\#} \,\&\, \Pi$ if $\# \neq \#^t_{\mathsf{ch}}$

$(\overline{Send1})$ $\qquad \Gamma; \lfloor \langle \mathsf{send}(\theta, e, p, p', v) : \pi, p, (\theta', e'), q \rangle \rfloor_{\#} \,\&\, \Pi \,\leftharpoonup\, \Gamma'; \lfloor \langle \pi, p, (\theta, e), q \rangle \rfloor_{\#} \,\&\, \Pi$
$\qquad\qquad$ if (p, p', v) occurs in Γ, with $\Gamma' = \Gamma \setminus\!\setminus (p, p', v)$

$(\overline{Send2})$
$\qquad \Gamma; \lfloor \langle \mathsf{send}(\theta, e, p, p'', v) : \pi, p, (\theta', e'), q \rangle \rfloor_{\#} \,\&\, \langle \pi'', p'', (\theta'', e''), q'' \rangle \,\&\, \Pi$
$\qquad\quad \leftharpoonup\, \Gamma; \lceil \langle \mathsf{send}(\theta, e, p, p'', v) : \pi, p, (\theta, e), q \rangle \rceil_{\#} \,\&\, \lfloor \langle \pi'', p'', (\theta'', e''), q'' \rangle \rfloor_{\#^{p,v}_{\mathsf{sch}}} \,\&\, \Pi$
$\qquad\qquad$ if (p, p'', v) does not occur in Γ

$(\overline{Send3})$
$\qquad \Gamma; \lceil \langle \mathsf{send}(\theta, e, p, p'', v) : \pi, p, (\theta, e), q \rangle \rceil_{\#} \,\&\, \lfloor \langle \mathsf{sched}(p, p'', v) : \pi'', p'', (\theta'', e''), v : q'' \rangle \rfloor_{\#^{p,v}_{\mathsf{sch}}} \,\&\, \Pi$
$\qquad\quad \leftharpoonup\, \Gamma; \lfloor \langle \pi, p, (\theta, e), q \rangle \rfloor_{\#} \,\&\, \langle \pi'', p'', (\theta'', e''), q'' \rangle \,\&\, \Pi$

$(\overline{Receive})$ $\qquad \Gamma; \lfloor \langle \mathsf{rec}(\theta, e, q) : \pi, p, (\theta', e'), q' \rangle \rfloor_{\#} \,\&\, \Pi \,\leftharpoonup\, \Gamma; \lfloor \langle \pi, p, (\theta, e), q \rangle \rfloor_{\#} \,\&\, \Pi$

$(\overline{Spawn1})$
$\qquad \Gamma; \lfloor \langle \mathsf{spawn}(\theta, e, p'') : \pi, p, (\theta', e'), q \rangle \rfloor_{\#} \,\&\, \langle \pi'', p'', (\theta'', e''), q'' \rangle \,\&\, \Pi$
$\qquad\quad \leftharpoonup\, \Gamma; \lceil \langle \mathsf{spawn}(\theta, e, p'') : \pi, p, (\theta, e), q \rangle \rceil_{\#} \,\&\, \lfloor \langle \pi'', p'', (\theta'', e''), q'' \rangle \rfloor_{\#_{\mathsf{sp}}} \,\&\, \Pi$

$(\overline{Spawn2})$
$\qquad \Gamma; \lceil \langle \mathsf{spawn}(\theta, e, p'') : \pi, p, (\theta, e), q \rangle \rceil_{\#} \,\&\, \lfloor \langle [\,], p'', (\theta'', e''), q'' \rangle \rfloor_{\#_{\mathsf{sp}}} \,\&\, \Pi$
$\qquad\quad \leftharpoonup\, \Gamma; \lfloor \langle \pi, p, (\theta, e), q \rangle \rfloor_{\#} \,\&\, \Pi$

$(\overline{Self})$ $\qquad \Gamma; \lfloor \langle \mathsf{self}(\theta, e) : \pi, p, (\theta', e'), q \rangle \rfloor_{\#} \,\&\, \Pi \,\leftharpoonup\, \Gamma; \lfloor \langle \pi, p, (\theta, e), q \rangle \rfloor_{\#} \,\&\, \Pi$

$(\overline{Sched})$
$\qquad \Gamma; \lfloor \langle \mathsf{sched}(p'', p, v) : \pi, p, (\theta, e), v : q \rangle \rfloor_{\#} \,\&\, \Pi$
$\qquad\quad \leftharpoonup\, \Gamma \uplus (p'', p, v); \lfloor \langle \pi, p, (\theta, e), q \rangle \rfloor_{\#} \,\&\, \Pi$ if $\# \neq \#^{p'',v}_{\mathsf{sch}}$

Fig. 10. Backward semantics: Rules for backward computation.

run backwards until, eventually, its trace is empty and rule $\overline{Spawn2}$ removes it from the system, resuming the backward computation for the spawning process.

Observe that, at first glance, one may think rule $\overline{Receive}$ should also introduce some new rollback operation for causal consistency. However, if we take a closer look, we will realize that receiving a message in our context is just about processing the message, and not actually receiving it. In fact, the processed message could have been delivered to the process mailbox a long time ago, and triggering a backward computation on the sending process would be unnecessary.

Finally, rule $\overline{Sched}$ applies when we find a term of the form $\mathsf{sched}(p, p'', v)$ in a trace and the rollback is not labelled with $\#^{p'',v}_{\mathsf{sch}}$ (since, in this case, rule $\overline{Send3}$ should be applied). Here, we just move the message back to the global mailbox Γ and continue undoing the remaining actions. The operator $\uplus$ is used to add messages to the head of the corresponding list instead of to its end, i.e., $\Gamma \uplus (\mathsf{p}, \mathsf{q}, \{\mathsf{t}, v\})$ denotes $\Gamma \setminus \{(\mathsf{p}, \mathsf{q}, vs)\} \cup \{(\mathsf{p}, \mathsf{q}, \{\mathsf{t}, v\} : vs)\}$.

Example 4. Consider the forward execution trace shown in Fig. 9. A corresponding backward computation is shown in Fig. 11.

Correctness. The rules of the backward semantics in Fig. 10 basically *sequentialize* the backward computations for a given process. When a rollback operator is applied to a process p, we start undoing the actions in its trace until we find a concurrent action that may affect to other processes, like spawning a process or

$[\,]; \ \lfloor\langle\tau(\sigma,\mathsf{let}\ \_=v_2\ \mathsf{in}\ldots):\mathsf{send}(\sigma,\mathsf{let}\ \_=S\,!\,v_2\ \mathsf{in}\ldots,c_1,\mathsf{s},v_2):\tau(\sigma,\mathsf{let}\ \_=\mathsf{t}\ \mathsf{in}\ldots)$
$\quad:\mathsf{check}(\sigma,\mathsf{let}\ \_=\mathsf{check}(\mathsf{t})\ \mathsf{in}\ldots,\mathsf{t}):\pi_i,\mathsf{c1},(\sigma,\mathsf{receive}\ ack\to\ldots),[\,])\rfloor_{\#^t_{ch}}\ \&$
$\quad\langle rec(id,\mathsf{receive}\ \{P,M\}\to\ldots,[v_2]):\mathsf{sched}(\mathsf{c1},\mathsf{s},v_2):\pi'_i,$
$\quad\mathsf{s},(\theta_2,\mathsf{let}\ \_=P\,!\,ack\ \mathsf{in}\ \ldots),[\,])\ \&\ \langle\pi''_i,\mathsf{c2},(\sigma,ok),[\,]\rangle$
$\leftarrow[\,]; \ \lfloor\langle\mathsf{send}(\sigma,\mathsf{let}\ \_=S\,!\,v_2\ \mathsf{in}\ldots,c_1,\mathsf{s},v_2):\tau(\sigma,\mathsf{let}\ \_=\mathsf{t}\ \mathsf{in}\ldots)$
$\quad:\mathsf{check}(\sigma,\mathsf{let}\ \_=\mathsf{check}(\mathsf{t})\ \mathsf{in}\ldots,\mathsf{t}):\pi_i,\mathsf{c1},(\sigma,\mathsf{let}\ \_=v_2\ \mathsf{in}\ldots),[\,])\rfloor_{\#^t_{ch}}\ \&$
$\quad\langle rec(id,\mathsf{receive}\ \{P,M\}\to\ldots,[v_2]):\mathsf{sched}(\mathsf{c1},\mathsf{s},v_2):\pi'_i,$
$\quad\mathsf{s},(\theta_2,\mathsf{let}\ \_=P\,!\,ack\ \mathsf{in}\ \ldots),[\,])\ \&\ \langle\pi''_i,\mathsf{c2},(\sigma,ok),[\,]\rangle$
$\leftarrow[\,]; \ \lceil\langle\mathsf{send}(\sigma,\mathsf{let}\ \_=S\,!\,v_2\ \mathsf{in}\ldots,c_1,\mathsf{s},v_2):\tau(\sigma,\mathsf{let}\ \_=\mathsf{t}\ \mathsf{in}\ldots)$
$\quad:\mathsf{check}(\sigma,\mathsf{let}\ \_=\mathsf{check}(\mathsf{t})\ \mathsf{in}\ldots,\mathsf{t}):\pi_i,\mathsf{c1},(\sigma,\mathsf{let}\ \_=S\,!\,v_2\ \mathsf{in}\ldots),[\,])\rceil_{\#^t_{ch}}\ \&$
$\quad\lfloor\langle rec(id,\mathsf{receive}\ \{P,M\}\to\ldots,[v_2]):\mathsf{sched}(\mathsf{c1},\mathsf{s},v_2):\pi'_i,$
$\quad\mathsf{s},(\theta_2,\mathsf{let}\ \_=P\,!\,ack\ \mathsf{in}\ \ldots),[\,])\rfloor_{\#_{sch}}\ \&\ \langle\pi''_i,\mathsf{c2},(\sigma,ok),[\,]\rangle$
$\leftarrow[\,]; \ \lceil\langle\mathsf{send}(\sigma,\mathsf{let}\ \_=S\,!\,v_2\ \mathsf{in}\ldots,c_1,\mathsf{s},v_2):\tau(\sigma,\mathsf{let}\ \_=\mathsf{t}\ \mathsf{in}\ldots)$
$\quad:\mathsf{check}(\sigma,\mathsf{let}\ \_=\mathsf{check}(\mathsf{t})\ \mathsf{in}\ldots,\mathsf{t}):\pi_i,\mathsf{c1},(\sigma,\mathsf{let}\ \_=S\,!\,v_2\ \mathsf{in}\ldots),[\,])\rceil_{\#^t_{ch}}\ \&$
$\quad\lfloor\langle\mathsf{sched}(\mathsf{c1},\mathsf{s},v_2):\pi'_i,$
$\quad\mathsf{s},(id,\mathsf{receive}\ \{P,M\}\to\ldots),[v_2])\rfloor_{\#_{sch}}\ \&\ \langle\pi''_i,\mathsf{c2},(\sigma,ok),[\,]\rangle$
$\leftarrow[\,]; \ \lfloor\langle\tau(\sigma,\mathsf{let}\ \_=\mathsf{t}\ \mathsf{in}\ldots)$
$\quad:\mathsf{check}(\sigma,\mathsf{let}\ \_=\mathsf{check}(\mathsf{t})\ \mathsf{in}\ldots,\mathsf{t}):\pi_i,\mathsf{c1},(\sigma,\mathsf{let}\ \_=S\,!\,v_2\ \mathsf{in}\ldots),[\,])\rfloor_{\#^t_{ch}}\ \&$
$\quad\langle\pi'_i,\mathsf{s},(id,\mathsf{receive}\ \{P,M\}\to\ldots),[\,])\ \&\ \langle\pi''_i,\mathsf{c2},(\sigma,ok),[\,]\rangle$
$\leftarrow[\,]; \ \lfloor\langle\mathsf{check}(\sigma,\mathsf{let}\ \_=\mathsf{check}(\mathsf{t})\ \mathsf{in}\ldots,\mathsf{t}):\pi_i,\mathsf{c1},(\sigma,\mathsf{let}\ \_=\mathsf{t}\ \mathsf{in}\ldots),[\,])\rfloor_{\#^t_{ch}}\ \&$
$\quad\langle\pi'_i,\mathsf{s},(id,\mathsf{receive}\ \{P,M\}\to\ldots),[\,])\ \&\ \langle\pi''_i,\mathsf{c2},(\sigma,ok),[\,]\rangle$
$\leftarrow[\,]; \ \langle\pi_i,\mathsf{c1},(\sigma,\mathsf{let}\ \_=\mathsf{check}(\mathsf{t})\ \mathsf{in}\ldots,\mathsf{t}),[\,])\ \&$
$\quad\langle\pi'_i,\mathsf{s},(id,\mathsf{receive}\ \{P,M\}\to\ldots),[\,])\ \&\ \langle\pi''_i,\mathsf{c2},(\sigma,ok),[\,]\rangle$

Fig. 11. A (partial) trace with the backward reversible semantics, where $\sigma=\{S\mapsto\mathsf{s}\}$, $\theta_2=\{P\mapsto\mathsf{c1},M\mapsto req\}$, and $v_2=\{\mathsf{c1},req\}$.

sending a message. In these cases, we freeze the backward computation of process p and propagate the rollback operator to the spawned process or to the receiver of a message, respectively. In particular, for a term of the form $\mathsf{spawn}(\theta,e,\mathsf{p}'')$, we freeze the process p and put a rollback operator on the spawned process p''. Only when all the actions of process p'' are undone and its trace is empty, we remove process p'' and resume the backward computation of process p. A similar behavior occurs when we find a term of the form $\mathsf{send}(\theta,e,\mathsf{p},\mathsf{p}'',v)$. Therefore, causal consistency is ensured since no action can be undone until all the consequences of such an action are undone first.

Note that for undoing the delivery of a message, we do not propagate the rollback to the sender but just move the message back to the global mailbox. This is enough to ensure the correctness of the approach while minimizing the effects of the backward computation. Moreover, it can help to avoid a (possibly cyclic) *cascade* of rollback operators.

The correctness of our rollback operator is now stated as follows. Here, we consider a limited scenario for simplicity. Extending the proof to a more general case is not difficult but would require a longer proof scheme.

Lemma 1. *Let $\mathcal{P}$ be a program, and consider the following forward derivation:*

$$\Gamma;\langle\pi,\mathsf{p},(\theta,\mathsf{let}\ \_=\mathsf{check}(\mathsf{t})\ \mathsf{in}\ e),q\rangle\&\Pi$$
$$\to\Gamma;\langle\mathsf{check}(\theta,\mathsf{let}\ \_=\mathsf{check}(\mathsf{t})\ \mathsf{in}\ e,\mathsf{t}):\pi,\mathsf{p},(\theta,\mathsf{let}\ \_=\mathsf{t}\ \mathsf{in}\ e),q\rangle\&\Pi$$
$$\to^*\Gamma';\langle\pi',\mathsf{p},(\theta',e'),q'\rangle\&\Pi'$$

where the processes of Π do not send messages to process p. *Then, we have*

$$\Gamma'; \lfloor \langle \pi', \mathsf{p}, (\theta', e'), q' \rangle \rfloor_{\#_{ch}^t} \& \Pi' \rightharpoonup^* \Gamma; \langle \pi, \mathsf{p}, (\theta, \mathsf{let}\ \_ = \mathsf{check}(\mathsf{t})\ \mathsf{in}\ e), q \rangle \& \Pi$$

5 Discussion

We have defined a reversible semantics for a first-order subset of Erlang that undoes the actions of a process step by step in a sequential way. To the best of our knowledge, this is the first attempt to define a reversible semantics for Erlang. As mentioned in the introduction, the closest to our work is the debugging approach based on a rollback construct of [11,12,15–17], but it is defined in the context of a different language or formalism. Also, we share some similarities with the checkpointing technique for fault-tolerant distributed computing of [9,13], although the aim is different (they aim at defining a new language rather than extending an existing one).

As future work, we consider the definition of mechanisms to control reversibility to avoid storing history information at any time. This could be essential to extend Erlang with a new construct for *safe sessions*, where all the actions in a session can be undone if the session aborts. Such a construct could have a great potential to automate the fault-tolerance capabilities of the language Erlang.

Acknowledgements. We would like to thank Ivan Lanese and the anonymous reviewers for many useful suggestions to improve this paper.

References

1. Armstrong, J., Virding, R., Williams, M.: Concurrent Programming in Erlang, 2nd edn. Prentice Hall, Englewood Cliffs (1996)
2. Bennett, C.: Logical reversibility of computation. IBM J. Res. Dev. **17**, 525–532 (1973)
3. Bennett, C.: Notes on the history of reversible computation. IBM J. Res. Dev. **44**(1), 270–278 (2000)
4. Caballero, R., Martn-Martn, E., Riesco, A., Tamarit, S.: A declarative debugger for concurrent Erlang programs (extended version). Technical report SIC-15/13, UCM (2013). http://maude.sip.ucm.es/~adrian/files/conc_cal_tr.pdf
5. Cardelli, L., Laneve, C.: Reversible structures. In: Proceedings of CMSB 2011, pp. 131–140. ACM (2011)
6. Carlsson, R., Gustavsson, B., Johansson, E., et al.: Core Erlang 1.0.3. language specification (2004). https://www.it.uu.se/research/group/hipe/cerl/doc/core_erlang-1.0.3.pdf
7. Danos, V., Krivine, J.: Reversible communicating systems. In: Gardner, P., Yoshida, N. (eds.) CONCUR 2004. LNCS, vol. 3170, pp. 292–307. Springer, Heidelberg (2004). doi:10.1007/978-3-540-28644-8_19
8. Danos, V., Krivine, J.: Transactions in RCCS. In: Abadi, M., Alfaro, L. (eds.) CONCUR 2005. LNCS, vol. 3653, pp. 398–412. Springer, Heidelberg (2005). doi:10.1007/11539452_31

9. Field, J., Varela, C.A.: Transactors: a programming model for maintaining globally consistent distributed state in unreliable environments. In: Proceedings of POPL 2005, pp. 195–208. ACM (2005)
10. Frank, M.P.: Introduction to reversible computing: motivation, progress, and challenges. In: Proceedings of 2nd Conference on Computing Frontiers, pp. 385–390. ACM (2005)
11. Giachino, E., Lanese, I., Mezzina, C.A.: Causal-consistent reversible debugging. In: Gnesi, S., Rensink, A. (eds.) FASE 2014. LNCS, vol. 8411, pp. 370–384. Springer, Heidelberg (2014). doi:10.1007/978-3-642-54804-8_26
12. Giachino, E., Lanese, I., Mezzina, C.A., Tiezzi, F.: Causal-consistent Reversibility in a Tuple Based Language. In: Proceedings of PDP 2015, pp. 467–475. IEEE Computer Society (2015)
13. Kuang, P., Field, J., Varela, C.A.: Fault tolerant distributed computing using asynchronous local checkpointing. In: Proceedings of AGERE! 2014, pp. 81–93. ACM (2014)
14. Landauer, R.: Irreversibility and heat generation in the computing process. IBM J. Res. Dev. 5, 183–191 (1961)
15. Lanese, I., Mezzina, C.A., Schmitt, A., Stefani, J.-B.: Controlling reversibility in higher-order Pi. In: Katoen, J.-P., König, B. (eds.) CONCUR 2011. LNCS, vol. 6901, pp. 297–311. Springer, Heidelberg (2011). doi:10.1007/978-3-642-23217-6_20
16. Lanese, I., Mezzina, C.A., Stefani, J.: Reversibility in the higher-order π-calculus. Theor. Comput. Sci. 625, 25–84 (2016)
17. Lienhardt, M., Lanese, I., Mezzina, C.A., Stefani, J.-B.: A reversible abstract machine and its space overhead. In: Giese, H., Rosu, G. (eds.) FMOODS/FORTE -2012. LNCS, vol. 7273, pp. 1–17. Springer, Heidelberg (2012). doi:10.1007/978-3-642-30793-5_1
18. Matsuda, K., Hu, Z., Nakano, K., Hamana, M., Takeichi, M.: Bidirectionalization transformation based on automatic derivation of view complement functions. In Proceedings of ICFP 2007, pp. 47–58. ACM (2007)
19. Nishida, N., Palacios, A., Vidal, G.: Reversible term rewriting. In: Proceedings of FSCD 2016. Leibniz International Proceedings in Informatics (2016)
20. Phillips, I., Ulidowski, I.: Reversing algebraic process calculi. J. Log. Algebr. Program. 73(1–2), 70–96 (2007)
21. Svensson, H., Fredlund, L.A., Earle, C.B.: A unified semantics for future Erlang. In: Proceedings of the 9th ACM SIGPLAN workshop on Erlang, pp. 23–32. ACM (2010)
22. Thomsen, M.K., Axelsen, H.B.: Interpretation and programming of the reversible functional language RFUN. In: Proceedings of IFL 2015, p. 8:1–8:13. ACM (2016)
23. Tiezzi, F., Yoshida, N.: Reversible session-based pi-calculus. J. Log. Algebr. Meth. Program. 84(5), 684–707 (2015)
24. Yokoyama, T.: Reversible computation and reversible programming languages. Electron. Notes Theor. Comput. Sci. 253(6), 71–81 (2010). Proceedings of the Workshop on Reversible Computation (RC 2009)
25. Yokoyama, T., Axelsen, H.B., Glück, R.: Principles of a reversible programming language. In: Proceedings of the 5th Conference on Computing Frontiers, pp. 43–54. ACM (2008)

Scaling Bounded Model Checking
by Transforming Programs with Arrays

Anushri Jana[1]([✉]), Uday P. Khedker[2], Advaita Datar[1],
R. Venkatesh[1], and Niyas C.[1]

[1] Tata Research Development and Design Centre, Pune, India
{anushri.jana,advaita.datar,r.venky,niyas.c}@tcs.com
[2] Indian Institute of Technology Bombay, Mumbai, India
uday@cse.iitb.ac.in

Abstract. Bounded Model Checking is one the most successful techniques for finding bugs in program. However, model checkers are resource hungry and are often unable to verify programs with loops iterating over large arrays. We present a transformation that enables bounded model checkers to verify a certain class of array properties. Our technique transforms an array-manipulating (ANSI-C) program to an array-free and loop-free (ANSI-C) program thereby reducing the resource requirements of a model checker significantly. Model checking of the transformed program using an off-the-shelf bounded model checker simulates the loop iterations efficiently. Thus, our transformed program is a sound abstraction of the original program and is also precise in a large number of cases—we formally characterize the class of programs for which it is guaranteed to be precise. We demonstrate the applicability and usefulness of our technique on both industry code as well as academic benchmarks.

Keywords: Program transformation · Bounded model checking · Array · Verification

1 Introduction

Bounded Model Checking is one of the most successful techniques for finding bugs [11] as evidenced by success achieved by the tools implementing this technique in verification competitions [1,2]. Given a program P and a property φ, Bounded Model Checkers (BMCs) unroll the loops in P, a fixed number of times and search for violations to φ in the unrolled program. However, for programs with loops of large or unknown bounds, bounded model checking instances often exceed the limits of resources available. In our experience, programs manipulating large arrays invariably have such loops iterating over indices of the array. Consequently, BMCs routinely face the issue of scalability in proving properties on arrays. The situation is no different even when the property is an *array invariant* i.e., it holds for every element of the array—a characteristic which can potentially be exploited for efficient bounded model checking.

© Springer International Publishing AG 2017
M.V. Hermenegildo and P. Lopez-Garcia (Eds.): LOPSTR 2016, LNCS 10184, pp. 275–292, 2017.
DOI: 10.1007/978-3-319-63139-4_16

```
1. struct S {
2.     unsigned int p;
3.     unsigned int q;
4. } a[100000];
5. int i,k;

06. main()
07. {
08.   for(i=0; i<100000; i++)
09.   {
10.     k = i;
11.     a[i].p = k;
12.     a[i].q = k * k ;
13.   }

14.   for (i=0; i<100000; i++)
15.   {
16.     assert(a[i].q ==
               a[i].p * a[i].p);
17.   }
18. }
```

```
1. struct S{
2.     unsigned int p;
3.     unsigned int q;
4. }x_a;
5. int i_a;
6. int i,k;
7. main()
8. {
9.   i_a = nd(0,99999);

//first loop body
10.   k = nd(0,100000);
11.   i = i_a;
12.   k = i;
13.   (i == i_a)? x_a.p = k : k;
14.   (i == i_a)? x_a.q = k * k : k*k ;
15.   k = nd(0,100000);

//second loop body
16.   i = i_a;
17.   assert(((i==i_a)?x_a.q:nd())
             ==((i==i_a)?x_a.p:nd())
             *((i==i_a)?x_a.p:nd()));
18. }
```

Fig. 1. Motivating example   **Fig. 2.** Transformed code

Consider the example in Fig. 1 manipulating an array of structures a. The structure has two fields, p and q, whose values are assigned in the first *for* loop (lines 8–13) such that $a[i].q$ is the square of $a[i].p$ for every index i. The second *for* loop (lines 14–17) asserts that this property indeed holds for each element in a. This is a *safe* program i.e., the assertion does not admit a counterexample. CBMC [9], a bounded model checker for C, tries to unwind the first loop 100000 times and runs out of memory before reaching the loop with the assertion. We tried this example with several model checkers[1] and none of them was able to prove this property because of a large loop bound.

One of the ways of proving this example safe is to show that the property holds for any arbitrary element of the array, say at index i_c. This allows us to get rid of those parts of the program that do not update $a[i_c]$ which, in turn, eliminates the loop iterating over all the array indices. This enables CBMC to verify the assertion without getting stuck in the loop unrolling. Moreover, since i_c is chosen nondeterministically from the indices of a, the property holds for every array element without loss of generality.

This paper presents the transformation sketched above with the aim that the transformed program is easier for a BMC to verify as compared to the original program. The transformation is over-approximative i.e., it give more values than that by the original program. This ensures that if the original program is safe with respect to the chosen property, so is the transformed program. However,

---

[1] Result for *motivatingExample.c* at
https://sites.google.com/site/datastructureabstraction/.

the over-approximation raises two important questions spanning practical and intellectual considerations:

(1) *Is the proposed approach practically useful? Does the transformation enable a BMC to verify real-world programs or academic benchmarks fairly often?* We answer this through an extensive experimental evaluation over industry code as well as examples in the array category of SV-COMP 2016 benchmarks. Our approach helps CBMC to scale in each case. We further demonstrate the applicability of our technique to successfully identify a large number of false warnings (on an average 73%) reported by a static analyzer on arrays in large programs.

(2) *Is it possible to characterize a class of properties for which it is precise?* In order to address this we provide a formal characterization of properties for which the transformation is precise i.e., we state criteria under which the transformed program is unsafe only when the original program is unsafe (Sect. 6).

To summarize, this paper makes the following contributions:

- A new technique combining static analysis and model checking enabling verification of array invariant properties in programs with loops iterating over large arrays.
- A novel concept of using pair of a *witness variable* and a *witness index* which allows us to remove the loops and arrays from programs and simulate the iterations accessing different elements of arrays during model checking.
- A formal characterization of properties for which the transformation is precise.
- A transformation engine implementing the technique.
- An extensive experimental evaluation showing the applicability of our technique to real-world programs as well as academic benchmarks.

The rest of the paper starts with an informal description of the transformation (Sect. 2) before we define the semantics (Sect. 3) and formally state the transformations rules (Sect. 4). Sections 5 and 6, respectively, describe the soundness and precision of our approach. Section 7 presents the experimental setup and results. We discuss the related work in Sect. 8 before concluding in Sect. 9.

2   Informal Description

Given a program P containing loops iterating over an array a, we transform it to a program P' that has a pair $\langle x_a, i_a \rangle$ of a *witness variable* and a *witness index* for the array and its index such that x_a represents the element $a[i_a]$ of the original program. Further, loops are replaced by their customized bodies that operate only on the witness variable x_a instead of all elements of the array a.

To understand the intuition behind our transformation, consider a trace t of P ending on the assertion A_n. Consider the last occurrence of a statement $s : a[e_1] = e_2$ in t. We wish to transform P such that there exists a trace t' of

P' ending on A_n in which the value of i_a is equal to that of e_1 and the value of x_a is equal to that of e_2. We achieve this by generating a transformed program such that:

- i_a gets a non-deterministically chosen value at the start of the program (this facilitates an arbitrary choice of array element $a[i_a]$).
- array writes and reads for $a[i_a]$ are replaced by the witness variable x_a.
- array writes other than $a[i_a]$ are eliminated and reads are replaced by a non-deterministically chosen value.
- loop body is executed only once either unconditionally or non-deterministically; based on loop characteristics. During the execution of the transformed loop body,
    - the loop iterator variable either gets the value of i_a or a non-deterministically chosen value (depending on loop characteristics), and
    - all other scalar variables whose values may be different in different iterations gets non-deterministically chosen values.

Figure 2 shows the transformed program P' for the program P of Fig. 1. Function nd(l,u) returns a non-deterministically chosen value in the range $[l..u]$. In P', the witness index i_a for array a is globally assigned a non-deterministically chosen value within the range of array size (at line 9). In a run of BMC, the assertion is checked for this non-deterministically chosen element $a[i_a]$. To ensure that the values for the same index $a[i_a]$ are written and read, we replace the array accesses by the witness variable x_a only when the value of the index i matches with that of i_a (lines 13, 14 and 17). We remove the loop header but retain the loop body. To over-approximate the effect of the removal of loop iterations, we add non-deterministic assignments to all variables modified in the loop body, at the start of the transformed loop body and also after the transformed loop body (lines 11 and 15). Note that we retain the original assignment statements too (line 12). Since the loops at line 8 and line 14 in the original program iterate over the entire array, we equate loop iterator variable i to i_a (line 11 and 16) and the transformed loop bodies (lines 10–14 and lines 16–17) are executed unconditionally.

We are using a single variable, x_a, to represent the array a. However, x_a takes different values in different runs of the BMC based on an arbitrarily chosen value of i_a and k. Our technique is able to verify the program in Fig. 1 because we do not conflate the values of expressions across different runs as is done in any static analysis. In a sense, we go beyond a static analysis and use a dynamic analysis through a BMC to verify the property.

We explain the transformation rules formally in Sect. 4. The transformed program can be verified by an off-the-shelf BMC. Note that each index will be considered in some run of the BMC since i_a is chosen non-deterministically. Hence, if an assertion fails for any index in the original program, it fails in the transformed program too.

3   Semantics

In this section we formalize our technique by explaining the language and defining a representation of states.

3.1   Language

We formulate our analysis over a language modelled on C. For simplicity of exposition we restrict our description to a subset of C which includes structures and 1-dimensional arrays. For a given program, let $\mathbb{C}$, $\mathbb{V}$, and $\mathbb{E}$ be the sets of values computed by the program, the variables appearing in the program, and the expressions appearing in the program, respectively. A value $c \in \mathbb{C}$ can be an integer, a floating-point or a boolean value. A variable $v \in \mathbb{V}$ can be a scalar variable, a structure variable, or an array variable. We define our program to have only one array variable denoted as a. However, our implementation handles multiple arrays as explained in our technical report [24]. We also define $\mathbb{E}_A \subseteq \mathbb{E}$ as the set of array expressions of the form $a\,[E\,]$. An lval L can be an array access expression or a variable. Let $c \in \mathbb{C}$, $x, i \in (\mathbb{V} - \{a\})$. We consider assignment statements, conditional statements, loop statements, and assertion statements defined by the following grammar. We define the grammar of our language using the following non-terminals: Program P consists of statements S which may use lvalues L and expressions E. We assume that programs are type correct as per C typing rules.

$$
\begin{aligned}
P &\rightarrow\ S \\
S &\rightarrow\ \textbf{if } (E)\ S\ \textbf{else}\ S \ \mid\ \textbf{if } (E)\ S \ \mid\ \textbf{for } (i = E;\ E;\ E)\ S \ \mid \\
  &\quad\ S\,;\ S \ \mid\ L = E \ \mid\ \textbf{assert}(E) \\
L &\rightarrow\ a[E] \ \mid\ x \\
E &\rightarrow\ E \oplus E \ \mid\ L \ \mid\ c
\end{aligned}
\tag{1}
$$

In practice, we analyze ANSI-C language programs that include functions, pointers, composite data-structures, all kinds of definitions, and all control structures except multi-dimensional arrays.

3.2   Representing Program States

We define program states in terms of memory locations and the values stored in memory locations. We distinguish between *atomic* variables (such as scalar and structure variables) whose values can be copied atomically using a single assignment operation, from non-atomic variables such as arrays. Since we are considering 1-dimensional arrays, the array elements are atomic locations.

Function $\ell(a[i])$ returns the memory location corresponding to the ith index of array a. The memory of an input program consists of all atomic locations:

$$
\mathbb{M} = (\mathbb{V} - \{a\}) \cup \big\{\ell(a[i]) \mid 0 \le i \le \mathit{lastof}(a)\big\}
\tag{2}
$$

The function $\mathit{lastof}(a)$ returns the highest index value for array a.

A *program state* is a map $\sigma : \mathbb{M} \to \mathbb{C}$. $\llbracket e \rrbracket_\sigma$ denotes the value of expression e in the program state σ.

We transform a program by creating a pair $\langle i_a, x_a \rangle$ for array a where i_a is the witness index and x_a is the witness variable. The memory of a transformed program with additional variables is:

$$\mathbb{M}' = (\mathbb{V} - \{a\}) \cup \{x_a\} \cup \{i_a\} \tag{3}$$

For a transformed program, a program state is denoted by σ' and is defined over $\mathbb{M}'$. A set of states is denoted by Σ' and set of states at program point l as Σ'_l. $\llbracket e \rrbracket_{\Sigma'}$ denotes the set of value of expression e in the set of program states Σ'.

We illustrate the states in the original and the transformed program through an example. Let a program P have an array variable a and a variable k holding the size of the array a. Let the array contain the values $c_i \in \mathbb{C}$, $0 \le i < n$, where $n \in \mathbb{C}$ is the value of size of the array.

Then, a program state, σ at any program point l can be:

$$\sigma = \left\{ (k, n), \left(\ell\left(a[0]\right), c_0 \right), \left(\ell\left(a[1]\right), c_1 \right), \ldots, \left(\ell\left(a[n-1]\right), c_{n-1} \right) \right\} \tag{4}$$

In the transformed program P', let x_a and i_a be the witness variable and witness index respectively. Let l' be the program point in P' that corresponds to l in P. Then, all possible states in the transformed program at l' are,

$$\sigma'_0 = \{(k, n), (i_a, 0), (x_a, c_0)\}$$
$$\sigma'_1 = \{(k, n), (i_a, 1), (x_a, c_1)\}$$
$$\ldots$$
$$\sigma'_{n-1} = \{(k, n), (i_a, n-1), (x_a, c_{n-1})\}$$
$$\Sigma' = \{\sigma'_0, \sigma'_1 \ldots \sigma'_{n-1}\}$$

We now formally define how the states at a program point in the transformed program represents a state at the corresponding program point in the original program.

Definition 1. *Let σ be a state at a program point in P and let σ' be a state at the corresponding program point in P'. Then, for any index c_1 under consideration, σ' represents σ, denoted as $\sigma' \rightsquigarrow \sigma$, if*

$$(\ell(a[c_1]), c_2) \in \sigma \implies \sigma' = \{(i_a, c_1), (x_a, c_2)\} \cup \{(y, c) \mid (y, c) \in \sigma, y \in (\mathbb{V} - \{a\})\}$$

Definition 2. *Let σ be a state at a program point in P and let Σ' be set of states at the corresponding program point in P'. Then, Σ' represents σ, denoted as $\Sigma' \rightsquigarrow \sigma$, if*

$\forall c_i$ *such that* $(\ell(a[c_i]), c_j) \in \sigma$, $\exists \sigma' \in \Sigma'$ *such that* $\sigma' \rightsquigarrow \sigma$.

Let A_n be the assertion at line n in program P. Let σ be a state reaching A_n in the original program with pair $(\ell(a(\llbracket e_1 \rrbracket_\sigma)), \llbracket e_2 \rrbracket_\sigma)$. Let σ' be the state in transformed program, σ' represents σ. Thus, σ' has two pairs, $(i_a, \llbracket e_3 \rrbracket_{\sigma'})$ and $(x_a, \llbracket e_4 \rrbracket_{\sigma'})$ such that $\llbracket e_3 \rrbracket_{\sigma'} = \llbracket e_1 \rrbracket_\sigma$ and $\llbracket e_4 \rrbracket_{\sigma'} = \llbracket e_2 \rrbracket_\sigma$. Hence, if the assertion A_n holds in transformed program, it holds in the original program too.

4   Transformation

The transformation rules are given in Fig. 3. A transformed program satisfies the following grammar derived from that of the original program (Grammar 1). Let $x, x_a, i_a \in \mathbb{V}$ denote a scalar variable, the witness variable, and the witness index, respectively. Let $c, l, u \in \mathbb{C}$ denote the values. Then,

$$
\begin{aligned}
P &\rightarrow I;\ S \\
I &\rightarrow i_a = nd(l, u) \\
S &\rightarrow \textbf{if } (E)\ S \textbf{ else } S \mid \textbf{if } (E)\ S \mid S;\ S \mid L = E \mid \textbf{assert}(E) \qquad (5) \\
L &\rightarrow x \mid x_a \mid i_a \\
E &\rightarrow E \oplus E \mid L \mid c \mid nd() \mid nd(l, u)
\end{aligned}
$$

The non-terminal I represents the initialization statements for witness index. Witness variable is initialized in the same scope as that in the original program.

Following are the functions used in the transformation rules.

- Function $nd(l, u)$ returns a non-deterministically chosen value between the lower limit l and the upper limit u. When a range is not provided, nd returns a non-deterministically chosen value based on the type of L.
- Function *transform* transforms the code represented by its argument non-terminal. Function *emit* shows the actual code that would be emitted. We assume that it takes the code emitted by *transform* and possibly some additional statements and outputs the combined code. It has been used only to distinguish the transformation time activity and run time activity. For example, the boolean conditions in cases $3.E_2$ and $3S_1$ are not evaluated by the body of function *transform* but is a part of the transformed code and is evaluated at run time when the transformed program is executed. Similar remarks apply to the **if** statements and other operations inside the parenthesis of *emit* function.
- Function *fullarrayaccess*(S) analyzes[2] the characteristics of the loop S.
  - When the loop S accesses array a completely, *fullarrayaccess*(S) returns true. This means that loop either reads from or writes to all the indices of the array; this could well be under different conditions in the code.
  - When the loop S accesses array a partially, *fullarrayaccess*(S) returns false. This means that the loop may not access all the indices or some indices are being read while some other indices are being written.
  - When loop S does not access an array, *fullarrayaccess*(S) returns false.
- Function *loopdefs*(S) returns a possibly over-approximated set of variables modified in loop S.
  - Scalar variables are included in this set if they appear on the left hand side of an assignment statement in S (except when the RHS is a constant).
  - Loop iterator variable i of loop S is not included in this set.
  - Array variable a is included in this set when the array access expression appears on the left hand side of an assignment and the value of index expression is different from the current value of the loop iterator i.

---

[2] Results of analysis may be over-approximated.

$$transform(E) =$$

$E \equiv (E_1 \oplus E_2)$	$\Rightarrow$ $emit(transform(E_1) \oplus transform(E_2))$	$(3.E_1)$
$E \in \mathbb{E}_A,\ E \equiv a[E_1]$	$\Rightarrow$ $emit((E_1 == i_a)\,?\,x_a : nd())$	$(3.E_2)$
otherwise	$\Rightarrow$ $emit(E)$	$(3.E_3)$

$$transform(S) =$$

$S \equiv (L = E),\ L \equiv a[E_1] \quad \Rightarrow \quad emit\big((E_1 == i_a)\,?$
$$x_a = transform(E) : transform(E)\big) \quad (3.S_1)$$

$S \equiv (L = E), L \not\equiv a[E_1] \quad \Rightarrow \quad emit(L = transform(E)) \quad (3.S_2)$

$S \equiv (\textbf{for}(i = E_1;\ E_2;\ E_3)\ S_1), \Rightarrow\ emit\big(u = nd();\qquad //\forall u \in loopdefs(S_1) \quad (3.S_3)$
$\qquad fullarrayaccess(S),$
$\qquad u \in loopdefs(S_1)$
$$i = i_a;$$
$$transform(S_1);$$
$$u = nd();\qquad //\forall u \in loopdefs(S_1)$$
$$\big)$$

$S \equiv (\textbf{for}(i = E_1;\ E_2;\ E_3)\ S_1), \Rightarrow\ emit\big(\textbf{if}(nd(0,1)) \qquad\qquad\qquad (3.S_4)$
$\qquad \neg fullarrayaccess(S),$
$\qquad u \in loopdefs(S_1)$
$$\{\ u = nd();\qquad //\forall u \in loopdefs(S_1)$$
$$i = nd(loopbound(S));$$
$$transform(S_1);$$
$$\}$$
$$u = nd();\qquad //\forall u \in loopdefs(S_1)$$
$$\big)$$

$S \equiv (\textbf{if}(E)\ S_1\ \textbf{else}\ S_2) \quad \Rightarrow \quad emit\big(\textbf{if}(transform(E))$
$$transform(S_1)\ \textbf{else}\ transform(S_2)\big) \quad (3.S_5)$$

$S \equiv (\textbf{if}(E)\ S_1)$	$\Rightarrow$ $emit(\textbf{if}(transform(E))\ transform(S_1))$	$(3.S_6)$
$S \equiv (S_1; S_2)$	$\Rightarrow$ $emit(transform(S_1); transform(S_2))$	$(3.S_7)$
$S \equiv (\textbf{assert}(E))$	$\Rightarrow$ $emit(\textbf{assert}(transform(E)))$	$(3.S_8)$
otherwise	$\Rightarrow$ $emit(S)$	$(3.S_9)$

$$transform(P) =$$

$P \equiv S \qquad\qquad \Rightarrow \quad emit\big(i_a = nd(lastof(a)); \qquad\qquad (3.P)$
$$transform(S)$$
$$\big)$$

Fig. 3. Program transformation rules. Non-terminals P, S, E, L represent the code fragment in the input program derivable from them.

- Function $lastof(a)$ returns the highest index value for array a.

With the above functions, the transformation rules are easy to understand. Here we explain non-trivial transformations.

- To choose an array index for a run, witness index (i_a) is initialized at the start of the program to a non-deterministically chosen value from the range of the indices of the array (case $3.P$). This value determines the array element $(a[i_a])$ represented by the witness variable (x_a).
- An array access expression in LHS or RHS is replaced by the witness variable (x_a) only when the values of the witness index and index expression of the

array access expression match. When the values do not match, it implies that an element other than i_a is being accessed. Hence for any other index the assignment does not happen (case $3.S_1$). However RHS of such assignment statement is retained to handle side-effects of expressions (not included in the grammar). Similarly, when an index other than i_a is read, it is replaced by a non-deterministically chosen value (case $3.E_2$).

– Loop iterations are eliminated by removing the loop header containing initialization, test, and increment expression for the loop iterator variable. The loop bodies are transformed as follows:
  - Each variable in the set returned by *loopdefs*(S) is assigned a non-deterministically chosen value at the start of the loop body and also after the loop body. These assignments ensure that values dependent on loop iterations are over-approximated when used inside or outside the loop body.
  - The loop iterator i is a special scalar variable. A loop S where *fullarrayaccess*(S) holds (case $3.S_3$) essentially means that loop bound is same as the array size and array is accessed using loop iterator as index. Hence it is safe to replace array access with x_a where the values of loop iterator and index expression match. To ensure this we equate loop iterator with i_a. This models the behaviour of the original program precisely. However, when *fullarrayaccess*(S) does not hold (case $3.S_4$), we assign loop iterator i to a non-deterministically chosen value from the loop bound.
  - Each statement in the loop body is transformed as per the transformation rules.
  - Finally, the entire loop body is made conditional using a non-deterministically chosen true/false value when *fullarrayaccess*(S) does not hold. This models the partial accesses of array indices which imply that some of the values defined before the loop may reach after the loop. However, the transformed loop body is unconditionally executed when *fullarrayaccess*(S) holds.

5 Soundness

This section outlines our soundness claim: if the transformed program is safe, then so is the original program. As discussed in Sect. 3, the soundness is immediate if the abstract states "represent" the original states. We therefore, prove that the proposed transformations ensure that the *represents* relation, $\rightsquigarrow$, holds between abstract and original states. For the base case, we prove that $\rightsquigarrow$ holds in the beginning before applying any transformation (Lemma 1). In the inductive step, we prove that if $\rightsquigarrow$ holds at some stage during the transformation, then the subsequent transformation continues to preserve $\rightsquigarrow$ (Lemma 3). We prove this by structural induction on program transformations. We prove that each transformed expression is over-approximated when $\rightsquigarrow$ holds (Lemma 2). A detailed proof is provided in our technical report [24].

Lemma 1. *Let the start of the original program (i.e. the program point just before the code derivable from non-terminal S in production $P \to S$ in grammar defined in Eq. (1) be denoted by l. The corresponding program point in the transformed program P', denoted by l', is just after l and just before the non-terminal S in production $P \to l$; S (Grammar in Eq. 5). Let σ be the state at l and Σ' be the set of states at l' in P and P' respectively. Then, $\Sigma'_{l'} \rightsquigarrow \sigma_l$.*

Proof Outline. Since the initial values of non-array variables are preserved, the initial value of $a[i_a]$ is assigned to x_a, and i_a is non-deterministically chosen, the lemma holds.

Lemma 2. *Let σ_l be a state at a program point l in P and $\Sigma'_{l'}$ be set of states at the corresponding program point l' in transformed program P'. Consider an arbitrary expression $e \in \mathbb{E}$ just after l in original program P. Then,*

$$\Sigma'_{l'} \rightsquigarrow \sigma_l \Rightarrow [\![transform(e)]\!]_{\Sigma'_{l'}} \supseteq \{[\![e]\!]_{\sigma_l}\}.$$

Proof Outline. Since e is derived from E (Grammar 1), the over-approximation of values can be proved by structural induction on the productions for E.

Lemma 3. *Let l and m be the program points just before and after a statement s in P and let σ_l and σ_m be the states at l and m respectively. Let l' and m' be the program points just before and after the corresponding transformed statement transform(s) in P'. Let $\Sigma'_{l'}$ and $\Sigma'_{m'}$ be the set of states at l' and m' respectively. Then, $\Sigma'_{l'} \rightsquigarrow \sigma_l \Rightarrow \Sigma'_{m'} \rightsquigarrow \sigma_m$.*

Proof Outline. Since statement s is derived from non-terminal S in the Grammar 1 the lemma can be proved by structural induction on S.

Theorem 1. *If the assertion A_n is violated in the original program P, then it will be violated in transformed program P' also.*

Proof. Let the assert get violated for some $a[c]$. Since i_a is initialized non-deterministically it can take the value c and we have shown in Lemma 2 that all expressions in P' are over-approximated. Lemmas 1 and 3 ensure the premise for Lemma 2. Hence the theorem follows.

6   Precision

We characterize the assertions for which our transformation is precise – an assertion will fail in P' if and only if it does so in P. We denote such an assertion as A_n^{inv}. We focus on A_n^{inv} in a loop. In case of array accesses outside loops, we do not claim precision. Our experience shows that such situations are rare in programs with large arrays.

The transformed program is over-approximative because our transformation rules ($3.S_3$, $3.S_4$, $3.E_2$) introduce non-deterministically chosen values. In this section we show that if assertion is of the form A_n^{inv} then none of these transformation rules introduce non-deterministically chosen values in the transformed program.

Our transformations replace array access expressions and loop statements while the statements involving scalars alone outside the loop remain unmodified. Hence precision criteria need to focus on the statements within loops and not outside it.

Let assertion A_n^{inv} appear in a loop statement $S_{A_n}^{inv}$. Let $\mathbb{V}_{imp}$ be the set of variables and $\mathbb{E}_{imp}$ be the set of array access expressions on which A_n^{inv} is data or control dependent within the loop $S_{A_n}^{inv}$. Let the set of loop statements from where definitions reach A_n^{inv} be denoted by $\mathbb{S}_{def}$, note that this set is a transitive closure for data dependence. Our technique is precise when:

- *fullarrayaccess*(S) holds for each $S \in \{S_{A_n}^{inv}\} \cup \mathbb{S}_{def}$ (rule l_1)
- If $a[e] \in \mathbb{E}_{imp}$ then
  - the index expression $e = i$ where i is the loop iterator of loop $S_{A_n}^{inv}$ (rule a_2)
  - $a \notin$ *loopdefs*(S) where $S \in \{S_{A_n}^{inv}\} \cup \mathbb{S}_{def}$ (rule a_3)
- If $x \in \mathbb{V}_{imp}$ then $x \notin$ *loopdefs*(S) where $S \in \{S_{A_n}^{inv}\} \cup \mathbb{S}_{def}$ (rule s_4)
- For an assignment statement of the form $a[e_1] = e_2$ in loop S where $S \in \mathbb{S}_{def}$,
  - if e_2 is an array access expression then it must be of the form $a[i]$ where i is the loop iterator of loop S (rule d_5)
  - if e_2 is x then $x \notin$ *loopdefs*(S) where $S \in \mathbb{S}_{def}$ (rule d_6)

Theorem 2. *If an assertion A_n^{inv} that satisfies above rules holds in the original program P, then it will hold in the transformed program P' also.*

Proof. We show that when all of above rules hold, non-deterministically chosen values are not introduced in transformed program.

- Since rule l_1 holds unconditionally, loops will be transformed as per $3.S_3$ and not $3.S_4$ and extra paths are not added. Also, the assignment $i = i_a$ at the start of the loop ensures that the condition is true for each transformed array access expression.
- When rule a_2 holds, rule l_1 also holds and $a[e]$ is always replaced by x_a (case $3.E_2$).
- When rule a_3 holds, assignment $x_a = nd()$ is not added (case $3.S_3$).
- When rule s_4 holds, assignment $x = nd()$ is not added (case $3.S_3$).
- When rule d_5 holds, rule l_1 holds and $a[e]$ in RHS is replaced by x_a (case $3.E_2$).
- When rule d_6 holds, scalars used in RHS are not assigned a non-deterministically chosen values.

Rules s_4 and d_6 are strong requirements for ensuring that non-deterministically chosen values do not reach A_n^{inv}. We can relax these rules when $x \in$ *loopdefs*$(S_{A_n}^{inv})$ when:

Table 1. Results on SV-COMP benchmark programs.

#programs = 118	#correct true	#correct false	#incorrect true	#incorrect false	#no result
Expected results	84	34	–	–	0
$CBMC_\alpha$	47	6	6	0	59
$CBMC_\beta$	9	5	0	0	104
Transformation + $CBMC_\beta$	25	34	0	59	0

$CBMC_\alpha$ - SV-COMP2016 (unsound) CBMC, $CBMC_\beta$ - sound CBMC 5.4.

- A definition of x appears before the use of x in RHS in the loop. (rule $d_{6.1}$)
- Variable x is defined with a constant value or using loop iterator i only. (rule $d_{6.2}$)

Since the original assignments to x are retained in the transformed loop body, assignment of x to non-deterministically chosen value ($x = nd()$) gets re-defined. Also, when x is defined with a constant or i ($i = i_a$ is added for S_{An}^{inv}), its value is not over-approximated.

The assertion in Fig. 1 is A_n^{inv} since it satisfies all the rules:

- S_{An}^{inv} is the loop at line 14 containing the assertion. $\mathbb{S}_{def}$ contains the loop at line 8. For both these loops, rule l_1 holds.
- $\mathbb{E}_{imp}$ consists of the three array access expressions at line 16. Rules a_2 and a_3 hold for all the three expressions.
- $\mathbb{V}_{imp}$ consist of the loop iterator i hence rule s_4 holds.
- For assignments at line 11 and 12 of the lone loop in $\mathbb{S}_{def}$,
  - rule d_5 holds.
  - x is k which is in *loopdefs(S)*. However, k is defined using loop iterator i at line 10. Hence rule $d_{6.2}$ hold.

The transformed program in Fig. 2 is not over-approximated and hence BMC is able to prove the assertion.

7 Experimental Evaluation

We have implemented our transformation engine using a static analysis framework called PRISM developed at TRDDC, Pune [10,25]. Our implementation supports ANSI-C programs with 1-dimensional arrays. The experiments are performed on a 64-bit Linux machine with 16 Intel Xeon processors running at 2.4 GHz, and 20 GB of RAM. More details of optimization and implementation, including handling of multiple arrays, are provided in our technical report [24].

Our transformation engine outputs C programs. Although we could take any off-the-shelf BMC for C program to verify the transformed code, we use CBMC in our experiments as it is known to handle all the constructs of ANSI-C. We discuss the results of our experiments on academic benchmarks and industry codes. For want of space, we omit the results of various BMCs on patterns from industry code; those results are shared in our technical report [24].

7.1   Experiment 1: SV-COMP Benchmarks

SV-COMP benchmarks [29] contain an established set of programs under various categories intended for comparing software verifiers. Results for $ArraysReach$[3] from the $array$ category for CBMC used in SV-COMP 2016 ($CBMC_\alpha$), CBMC 5.4 ($CBMC_\beta$) and CBMC 5.4 on transformed programs (Transformation + $CBMC_\beta$) are consolidated[4] in Table 1. $ArraysReach$ has 118 programs. $CBMC_\alpha$, an unsound version of CBMC, gave correct results for 53 programs. However, $CBMC_\beta$ gave correct results for 14 programs. We compare the results of Transformation + $CBMC_\beta$ on three criteria:

- Scalability: it scaled up for all 118 programs.
- Soundness: it gave sound results for all 118 programs. For the 6 programs for which $CBMC_\alpha$ gave unsound results, our results are not only sound but are also precise.
- Precision: it gave precise results for 59 programs. Out of these $CBMC_\alpha$ ran out of memory for 45 programs ($CBMC_\alpha$ ran out of memory for 14 additional programs). On the other hand, 22 true programs reported correctly by $CBMC_\alpha$ were verified as false by Transformation + $CBMC_\beta$. Transformation + $CBMC_\beta$ verified 25 programs as true which did not include 8 of the programs reported correctly as true by $CBMC_\beta$.

Our technique is imprecise for the other 59 of 118 programs as they do not comply with the characterization of precision provided in Sect. 6. As can be seen, there is a trade-off between scalability and precision. From the view point of reliability of results, soundness is the most desirable property of a verifier. Our technique satisfies this requirement. Further, it not only scales up but is also precise in many situations implying its practical usefulness.

7.2   Experiment 2: Real-Life Applications

We applied our technique on 3 real-life applications - $navi1$ and $navi2$ are industry codes implementing the navigation system of an automobile and icecast_2.3.1 is an open source project for streaming media [23]. To verify a meaningful property, we used $Null$ $Pointer$ $Dereference$ (NPD) warnings generated by a sound static analysis tool build using PRISM[5]. PRISM performs weak updates for arrays (similar to array smashing) and hence generates a large number of warnings on arrays, most of which are false. We appended assertions as follows. Lets say the dereference expression is $*a[i].p$. A statement $assert(a[i].p! = null)$ is

---

[3] Programs in $ArrayMemSafety$ access arrays without using index and cannot be transformed.

[4] Case by case results available at https://sites.google.com/site/datastructureabstr action/home/sv-comp-benchmark-evaluation-1.

[5] TCS Embedded Code Analyzer (TCS ECA) http://www.tcs.com/offerings/ engineering_services/Pages/TCS-Embedded-Code-Analyzer.aspx.

Table 2. Real-life application evaluation

Application details				Sliced + CBMC			Sliced + Transformation + CBMC			% False positive reduction
Name	Size (LoC)	$\%loop^{full}$	#Asserts	#P	#F	#T	#P	#F	#T	
navi1	1.54 M	100	63	0	0	63	52	1	10	82.5
navi2	3.3 M	93.4	103	0	0	103	95	1	7	92.2
icecast_2.3.1	336 K	59.1	114	0	0	114	53	61	0	46.5

$loop^{full}$ - loop S where $fullarrayaccess(S)$ holds, P - Assertion Proved, F - Assertion Failed, T - Timeout.

added in the code just before the statement containing dereference expression. We then slice[6] these programs as per assertion.

Table 2 shows the consolidated results of our experiments. CBMC did not scale on the sliced programs. However, after transformation (sliced + transformation + CBMC) CBMC proved 200 out of 280 assertions, taking 12 min on average for transformation + verification. This is much less in comparison to the time given to CBMC for sliced programs (sliced+CBMC), which was 30 min.

To verify the correctness of our implementation, we analyzed the warnings manually. We found that all 280 warnings were false, implying that all the assertions should have been proved successfully.

- Scalability: CBMC could scale up for such large applications because there are no loops in transformed programs. However, CBMC could not scale for 17 cases even after transformation because of long recursive call chain through function pointers.
- Precision: Our technique proved 200 assertions, where all the conditions for precision mentioned in Sect. 6 get fulfilled. In all these cases since $fullarrayaccess(S)$ hold, the witness variable gets precise value in each run of BMC for each value of witness index. 63 of the assertions could not be proved since array definitions reaching at the assertion were from the loops where $fullarrayaccess(S)$ did not hold and values received by witness variable is over-approximative.

Replacing array expressions with witness variable enables elimination of loops. However, by using witness index BMC simulates loop iterations with providing run-based value to witness variable. Note that the number of false warnings eliminated in an application is proportional to the number of loops for which $fullarrayaccess(S)$ hold. Over a diverse set of applications, we found that our technique could eliminate 40–90% of false warnings. This is a significant value addition to static analysis tools that try to find defects and end up generating a large number of warnings.

8   Related Work

There is a sizeable body of work on reasoning about values of array elements. We give a brief overview of the relevant literature here.

---

[6] PRISM implements [22] for slicing.

Blanchet et al. proposed the use of abstract elements for array indices [8]. Though of limited practicability, they suggested two approaches - one that uses an abstract element for each index in the array i.e. *array expansion*, and another where a single abstract element is used for the entire array i.e. *array smashing*. Array expansion is precise but it cannot be used effectively for large arrays. Array smashing, on the other hand, allows handling arbitrary arrays efficiently, but suffers significant precision losses due to its inability to perform strong updates. As a result, it cannot be applied to prove the correctness of our example in Fig. 1.

While expansion and smashing are at two extremes in their use of abstract elements, there are several "midway" approaches that are aimed at combining the benefits of both. Gopan et al. [19] proposed that those elements that are read or written could be dynamically expanded to incorporate strong updates, while the remaining elements could be smashed. This was extended to partitioning arrays into symbolic intervals spanning the entire array, and using an abstract variable to represent each such interval [21]. To avoid the exponential multiplication of array slices that prevented these techniques from scaling, Cousot et al. proposed an improvement [13] that automatically, semantically divides arrays into consecutive non-overlapping segments. Clousot [17], a tool that implements this improvement, indeed scales better than [19,21] but still runs out of resources while verifying our example in Fig. 1.

Another way of partitioning an array is to exploit its semantic properties and split the elements into groups. Grouping array cells of similar properties, e.g. [27], has the advantage that it allows partitions to be non-contiguous. This is orthogonal to the work of Dillig et al. [16] where they introduce fluid updates of arrays using indexed locations along with bracketing constraints, to specify the concrete elements being updated. Cornish et al. [12] apply a program-to-program translation over the LLVM intermediate representation, followed by a scalar analysis. Although the abstraction in these approaches is expressible as a composition of our abstraction followed by further abstraction, our implementation of *fullarrayaccess(S)* guarantees an array-free and loop-free programs whenever possible. Moreover, we exploit the power of model checking to obtain a precise path-sensitive analysis.

In a recent work [28], Monniaux et al. proposed to convert array programs into array-less non-linear Horn clauses. The precision of this transformation is adjustable through a Galois connection parameterized by the number of distinguished cells, which, however, needs to be decided manually. An analogous technique, based on Horn clauses over array variables that requires user inputs in form of pre- and post-conditions, is that of [15] proposed by De Angelis et al. This is practically infeasible for real-life programs, and therefore affects scalability. Another limitation of these approaches is their back-end solvers which cannot handle non-linear arithmetic. This reflects in their inability to work for our motivating example of Fig. 1. Besides, unlike these approaches, our technique needs no manual input and successfully scales to large industry code.

Template-based methods [7,20] have been very useful in synthesizing invariants but these techniques are ultimately limited by the space of possible templates that must be searched for a good candidate. This has led to semi-automatic approaches, such as [18], where the predicates are usually suggested by the user. Our approach, in contrast, is fully automatic and proves safety by solving a bounded model checking instance instead of computing an invariant explicitly.

Verification tools based on CEGAR have been applied successfully to certain classes of programs, e.g. device drivers [6]. However, this technique is orthogonal to ours. In fact, a refinement framework in addition to our abstraction would make our technique complete too. Several other techniques have been used to scale bounded model checkers to tackle complex, real-world programs such as acceleration [26] and loop-abstraction [14]. But these techniques are not shown to be beneficial in abstracting complex data structures. Booster [4] integrates acceleration and lazy abstraction with interpolants for arrays. However, there are syntactic restrictions that limit the applicability of acceleration in general for programs handling arrays. Also, interpolation over array properties is difficult, especially since the goal is not to provide any interpolant, but one that generalizes well to an invariant [3,5].

9   Conclusions and Future Work

Verification of programs with loops iterating over arrays is a challenging problem because of large sizes of arrays. We have explored a middle ground between the two extremes of relying completely on dynamic approaches of using model checkers on the one hand and using completely static analysis involving complex domains and fix point computations on the other hand. Our experience shows that using static analysis to transform the program and letting the model checkers do the rest is a sweet spot that enables verification of properties of arrays using an automatic technique that is generic, sound, scalable, and reasonably precise.

Our experiments show that the effectiveness of our technique depends on the characteristics of programs We are able to eliminate 40–90% of false warnings from diverse applications. This is a significant value addition to static analysis that try to find defects and end up generating a large number of warnings which need to be resolved manually.

We plan to make our technique more precise and extend it for other data structures.

References

1. 2015 4th International Competition on Software Verification. http://sv-comp.sosy-lab.org/2015/results/. Accessed 12 Feb 2017
2. 2016 5th International Competition on Software Verification. http://sv-comp.sosy-lab.org/2016/results/results-verified/. Accessed 12 Feb 2017
3. Alberti, F., Bruttomesso, R., Ghilardi, S., Ranise, S., Sharygina, N.: An extension of lazy abstraction with interpolation for programs with arrays. In: Formal Methods in System Design (2014)

4. Alberti, F., Ghilardi, S., Sharygina, N.: Booster: an acceleration-based verification framework for array programs. In: Cassez, F., Raskin, J.-F. (eds.) ATVA 2014. LNCS, vol. 8837, pp. 18–23. Springer, Cham (2014). doi:10.1007/978-3-319-11936-6_2
5. Alberti, F., Monniaux, D.: Polyhedra to the rescue of array interpolants. In: Annual ACM Symposium on Applied Computing (2015)
6. Ball, T., Rajamani, S.K.: The slam project: debugging system software via static analysis. In: ACM SIGPLAN Notices, vol. 37 (2002)
7. Beyer, D., Henzinger, T.A., Majumdar, R., Rybalchenko, A.: Invariant synthesis for combined theories. In: Cook, B., Podelski, A. (eds.) VMCAI 2007. LNCS, vol. 4349, pp. 378–394. Springer, Heidelberg (2007). doi:10.1007/978-3-540-69738-1_27
8. Blanchet, B., Cousot, P., Cousot, R., Feret, J., Mauborgne, L., Miné, A., Monniaux, D., Rival, X.: Design and implementation of a special-purpose static program analyzer for safety-critical real-time embedded software. In: Mogensen, T.Æ., Schmidt, D.A., Sudborough, I.H. (eds.) The Essence of Computation. LNCS, vol. 2566, pp. 85–108. Springer, Heidelberg (2002). doi:10.1007/3-540-36377-7_5
9. CBMC. http://www.cprover.org/cbmc/. Accessed 12 Feb 2017
10. Chimdyalwar, B., Kumar, S.: Effective false positive filtering for evolving software. In: ISEC (2011)
11. Copty, F., Fix, L., Fraer, R., Giunchiglia, E., Kamhi, G., Tacchella, A., Vardi, M.Y.: Benefits of bounded model checking at an industrial setting. In: Berry, G., Comon, H., Finkel, A. (eds.) CAV 2001. LNCS, vol. 2102, pp. 436–453. Springer, Heidelberg (2001). doi:10.1007/3-540-44585-4_43
12. Cornish, J.R.M., Gange, G., Navas, J.A., Schachte, P., Søndergaard, H., Stuckey, P.J.: Analyzing array manipulating programs by program transformation. In: Proietti, M., Seki, H. (eds.) LOPSTR 2014. LNCS, vol. 8981, pp. 3–20. Springer, Cham (2015). doi:10.1007/978-3-319-17822-6_1
13. Cousot, P., Cousot, R., Logozzo, F.: A parametric segmentation functor for fully automatic and scalable array content analysis. In: ACM SIGPLAN Notices, vol. 46 (2011)
14. Darke, P., Chimdyalwar, B., Venkatesh, R., Shrotri, U., Metta, R.: Over-approximating loops to prove properties using bounded model checking. In: DATE (2015)
15. De Angelis, E., Fioravanti, F., Pettorossi, A., Proietti, M.: A rule-based verification strategy for array manipulating programs. Fundamenta Informaticae **140**, 329–355 (2015)
16. Dillig, I., Dillig, T., Aiken, A.: Fluid updates: beyond strong vs. weak updates. In: Gordon, A.D. (ed.) ESOP 2010. LNCS, vol. 6012, pp. 246–266. Springer, Heidelberg (2010). doi:10.1007/978-3-642-11957-6_14
17. Fähndrich, M., Logozzo, F.: Static contract checking with abstract interpretation. In: Beckert, B., Marché, C. (eds.) FoVeOOS 2010. LNCS, vol. 6528, pp. 10–30. Springer, Heidelberg (2011). doi:10.1007/978-3-642-18070-5_2
18. Flanagan, C., Qadeer, S.: Predicate abstraction for software verification. ACM SIGPLAN Not. **37**, 191–202 (2002)
19. Gopan, D., Reps, T., Sagiv, M.: A framework for numeric analysis of array operations. ACM SIGPLAN Not. **40**(1), 338–350 (2005)
20. Gulwani, S., McCloskey, B., Tiwari, A.: Lifting abstract interpreters to quantified logical domains. In: POPL (2008)
21. Halbwachs, N., Péron, M.: Discovering properties about arrays in simple programs. ACM SIGPLAN Not. **43**, 339–348 (2008)
22. Horwitz, S., Reps, T., Binkley, D.: Interprocedural slicing using dependence graphs. ACM Trans. Program. Lang. Syst. **12**, 26–60 (1990)

23. Ice Cast. http://icecast.org/. Accessed 12 Feb 2017
24. Jana, A., Khedker, U.P., Datar, A., Venkatesh, R.: Scaling bounded model checking by transforming programs with arrays. CoRR, arXiv:1606.06974 (2016)
25. Khare, S., Saraswat, S., Kumar, S.: Static program analysis of large embedded code base: an experience. In: ISEC (2011)
26. Kroening, D., Lewis, M., Weissenbacher, G.: Under-approximating loops in C programs for fast counterexample detection. In: Sharygina, N., Veith, H. (eds.) CAV 2013. LNCS, vol. 8044, pp. 381–396. Springer, Heidelberg (2013). doi:10.1007/978-3-642-39799-8_26
27. Liu, J., Rival, X.: Abstraction of arrays based on non contiguous partitions. In: D'Souza, D., Lal, A., Larsen, K.G. (eds.) VMCAI 2015. LNCS, vol. 8931, pp. 282–299. Springer, Heidelberg (2015). doi:10.1007/978-3-662-46081-8_16
28. Monniaux, D., Gonnord, L.: Cell morphing: from array programs to array-free horn clauses. In: Rival, X. (ed.) SAS 2016. LNCS, vol. 9837, pp. 361–382. Springer, Heidelberg (2016). doi:10.1007/978-3-662-53413-7_18
29. SV-COMP 2016 Benchmarks. https://sv-comp.sosy-lab.org/2016/benchmarks.php. Accessed 12 Feb 2017

Intuitionistic Logic Programming for SQL

Fernando Sáenz-Pérez[⊠] (iD)

Declarative Programming Group, Dept. Ingeniería del Software e Inteligencia
Artificial, Universidad Complutense de Madrid, Madrid, Spain
fernan@sip.ucm.es

Abstract. Intuitionistic logic programming provides the notion of
embedded implication in rule bodies, which can be used to reason about
a current database modified by the antecedent. This can be applied to
a system that translates SQL to Datalog to solve SQL WITH queries, for
which relations are locally defined and can therefore be understood as
locally added to the current database. In addition, assumptions in SQL
queries as either adding or removing data can be modelled in this way as
well, which is an interesting feature for decision-support scenarios. This
work suggests a way to apply intuitionistic logic programming to SQL,
and provides a pointer to a working system implementing this idea.

Keywords: Intuitionistic logic programming · SQL · Datalog ·
Extended relational algebra

1 Introduction

SQL is the *de facto* relational database query language that stands still [2] despite
the advent of new trends as Big Data, NoSQL, RDF stores and others. It builds
upon the Codd's [8,9] seminal relational data model accompanied by an algebra
and calculus to operate on data. Further proposals such as [12] better provide
a formal framework for current SQL implementations. As a query language,
SQL can be well understood from Codd's tuple relational calculus but also from
logic programming (in particular, [23] includes equivalences between relational
operations and logic rules). However, among other features beyond the original
relational model, SQL provides the notion of temporary view as defined in a
WITH clause (described in Sect. 2), whose definition is available only to the query
in which it occurs [21]. This is no longer representable either in relational formal
languages or directly in logic programming.

Here is when intuitionistic logic programming may help to providing first-
class citizen semantics: Approaches as [4,10,13–15] fit into this logic, an extension of logic programming including in particular embedded implications. Adding
negation to intuitionistic logic programming might develop paradoxes which are
circumvented in [5] by dealing with two kind of implications: for rules ($\leftarrow$) and
for goals ($\Leftarrow$, i.e., an embedded implication). Intuitively, whereas in the formula $A \leftarrow B$, the atom B is "executed" for proving A, in the formula $A \Leftarrow B$,
the atom B is "assumed" to be true for proving A. The work of Bonner about

© Springer International Publishing AG 2017
M.V. Hermenegildo and P. Lopez-Garcia (Eds.): LOPSTR 2016, LNCS 10184, pp. 293–308, 2017.
DOI: 10.1007/978-3-319-63139-4_17

Hypothetical Datalog incorporated this logic and has been a proposal thoroughly studied from semantic [3,5,6] and complexity point-of-views [4]. The work [17] (recalled and adapted in Sect. 3) presented an extended (with respect to [3,5,6]) intuitionistic setting along with an implementation in the deductive system DES [20], in several points: First, a rule is accepted in the antecedent of an embedded implication, and not only facts as in [5], second, duplicates are allowed, and third, strong constraints are included.

Driven from the need for supporting a broader subset of SQL in this system, we show how to take advantage of the intuitionistic embedded implication to model SQL WITH queries in a logic setting, an application which has not been proposed to the best of our knowledge so far. Thus, it is possible to have such SQL queries translated into Hypothetical Datalog, and can be therefore processed by a deductive engine. To ensure correct results, on the one hand, we provide a translation from SQL to extended relational algebra (ERA) and its semantics in Sect. 2, and, on the other hand, a translation from SQL to Hypothetical Datalog in Sect. 4, relying on an extended semantics (Sect. 3), and finally proving the semantic equivalence between both translations (Sect. 4).

Hypothetical Datalog is powerful enough to even apply the same technique to model assumptions in SQL queries, with the (non-standard) clause ASSUME. This clause enables both positive and negative assumptions on data, as shown in Sect. 5, which are useful for modelling "what-if" scenarios in typical decision-support systems. Finally, we present the deductive system DES at work with examples of WITH and ASSUME queries in Sect. 6. Our approach is also useful for connecting with external relational database systems which cannot process these clauses. DES then behaves as a front-end capable of processing either novel (assumptions) or unsupported features (temporary views) in such systems. In particular, this makes it easier to develop decision-support systems such as those based on (either real or finite domain) constraints defined by relational database tables (as in IBM ILOG OPL Studio), letting the user play with assumptions in a layer between the constraint system and the relational database.

2   The SQL WITH Clause

Typically, complex SQL queries are broken-down for applying the *divide-and-conquer* principle as well as for enhancing readability and maintenance. Introducing intermediate views with CREATE VIEW statements is in the order of the day, but this might neither be recommendable (making these views observable for other users) nor possible (only certain users with permissions granted by an administrator are allowed to create views). The WITH clause provides a form of encapsulation in SQL by locally defining those broken-down views, making their realms pertain to the context of a given query. The syntax of a query Q including this clause is WITH R_1 AS SQL_1, ..., R_n AS SQL_n SQL, where each R_1 is a temporary view name defined by the SQL statement SQL_i, and which can be referenced only in SQL, the ultimate query that builds the outcome of the query Q. This query can be understood as a relation with name R and defined with the DDL statement CREATE VIEW R AS Q.

$$
\begin{aligned}
q &\;::=\; \texttt{SELECT e,...,e [FROM r,...,r [WHERE c]] } | \\
&\quad\;\; \texttt{q sop q } | \\
&\quad\;\; \texttt{WITH R AS q q} \\
e &\;::=\; \texttt{C } | \texttt{ r.a} \\
r &\;::=\; \texttt{R } | \texttt{ q} \\
c &\;::=\; \texttt{e cop e } | \texttt{ NOT c } | \texttt{ c lop c } | \texttt{ TRUE } | \texttt{ FALSE} \\
cop &\;::=\; \texttt{> } | \texttt{ < } | \texttt{ = } | \texttt{ <> } | \texttt{ >= } | \texttt{ <=} \\
sop &\;::=\; \texttt{UNION } | \texttt{ EXCEPT } | \texttt{ INTERSECT} \\
lop &\;::=\; \texttt{AND } | \texttt{ OR}
\end{aligned}
$$

Where `true-typed` words stand for terminal symbols, C for constants, and R for relations (either tables or views). Set operators keep duplicates and the keyword `ALL` is omitted for simplicity.

Fig. 1. A grammar for a simple subset of SQL

In this work we consider standard SQL as found in many textbooks (e.g., [21]), but also allowing `FROM`-less statements, i.e., providing a single-row output constructed with the comma-separated expressions after the `SELECT` keyword (Oracle, for instance, resorts to feed the single row from the `dual` table to express the same feature). Figure 1 includes a grammar for a simple subset of SQL.

A series of local definitions `WITH` R_1 `AS` q_1, ..., R_n `AS` q_n q is rewritten as a nested query `WITH` R_1 `AS` q_1 (`WITH` R_2 `AS` q_2 (...(`WITH` R_n `AS` q_n q)...). A table (extensional relation) with name T is defined as `CREATE TABLE T`$(\overline{S})$, with $\overline{S}$ being a comma-separated sequence of A D, where A is an attribute name and D its type (referred to as domain in SQL). A view (intensional relation) with name V is defined as `CREATE VIEW V AS q`. View types are inherited from tables. As syntax sugar we allow the symbol * in the projection list referring to all the arguments of the relations in the `FROM` list.

With respect to the semantics of an SQL query, we recall and adapt the notation in [7] which in turn is based on [12]. A database Δ is composed of relation instances and relation definitions. A *relation instance* of a relation R are the atoms (following logic programming instead of relational databases) of the form $R\overline{T}$, where $\overline{T}$ is a ground tuple. The notation $\Delta(R)$ represents the instance of a relation R in Δ. Φ_R represents the ERA (Extended Relational Algebra) expression associated to an SQL query or view R, as explained in [11] and formalized later (Definition 3). Figure 2 shows the grammar of ERA expressions, which includes extended relational operations: π (generalized projection), σ (selection), $\times$ (Cartesian product), $\cup$ (multiset union), $\cap$ (intersection), $-$ (multiset difference), duplicate elimination (δ), and $\leftarrow$ (assignment). A set operation is built with the operation δ applied to a multiset (e.g., the set union of r_1 and r_2 becomes $\delta(r_1 \cup r_2)$). Operators in conditions include: $\neg$ (negation), $\wedge$ (conjunction), $\vee$ (disjunction), and comparison operators ($<$, $>$, $=$, $\leq$, and $\geq$). The truth constants *true* and *false* are included in the signature. A *relation definition* is the relational assignment $R \leftarrow \Phi$ for a relation R and ERA expression Φ. An *extensional database* is a database with no relation definitions (i.e., a set

$$q \quad ::= \pi_{e,\ldots,e}(q) \mid \sigma_c(q) \mid \delta(q) \mid q \text{ sop } q$$
$$e \quad ::= C \mid r.a$$
$$r \quad ::= R \mid q$$
$$c \quad ::= e \text{ cop } e \mid \neg c \mid c \text{ lop } c \mid true \mid false$$
$$\text{cop} ::= > \mid < \mid = \mid \neq \mid \geq \mid \leq$$
$$\text{sop} ::= \cup \mid - \mid \cap$$
$$\text{lop} ::= \wedge \mid \vee$$

Where *italic* words stand for terminal symbols, C for constants, and R for relations.

Fig. 2. A grammar for ERA

of atoms). Finally, $\mathcal{C}$ represents the constants in the database, including those occurring in queries.

An intensional relation usually depends on previously defined relations, and sometimes it will be useful to write $\Phi_R(R_1, \ldots, R_n)$ indicating that R depends on $R_1, \ldots, R_n$. Here, we assume that each extensional relation in a database has attached type information for each one of its named arguments. As well, each intensional relation argument receives its type via inferencing and arbitrary names if not provided in its definition. Tables are denoted by their names, that is, $\Phi_T = T$ if T is a table.

Definition 1. The *computed answer* of an ERA expression Φ_R with respect to some database Δ is denoted by $\|\Phi_R\|_\Delta$, where:

- If R is an extensional relation, $\|\Phi_R\|_\Delta = \Delta(R)$.
- If R is an intensional relation and $R_1, \ldots, R_n$ the relations defined in R, then
$\|\Phi_R\|_\Delta = \Phi_R(\|\Phi_{R_1}\|_\Delta, \ldots, \|\Phi_{R_n}\|_\Delta)$. □

Queries are executed by SQL systems. The answer for a query Q and a database Δ in an implementation is represented by $\mathcal{SQL}_\Delta(Q)$. The notation $\mathcal{SQL}_\Delta(R)$ abbreviates $\mathcal{SQL}_\Delta(\text{SELECT } * \text{ FROM } R)$. In particular, we assume the existence of *correct* SQL implementations.

Definition 2. A *correct* SQL implementation verifies that $\mathcal{SQL}_\Delta(Q) = \|\Phi_Q\|_\Delta$ for every query Q. □

Here, we define a translation function SQL_to_ERA that delivers a single choice of the possible execution plans as ERA operator compositions, extending the informal presentation in [11] and including WITH clauses. This function takes as input an SQL query and a database, and returns an ERA expression. A condition-less statement is equivalent to the same statement including WHERE TRUE. We also assume the void relation DUAL with a single tuple in any database (columns in this table are irrelevant and are not retrieved with functions as *). Thus, a from-less statement is equivalent to the same statement including FROM DUAL. Given these considerations we can simplify the cases of the function SQL_to_ERA to the ones in next Definition 3. From here on, $A[B/C]$ represents the syntactic substitution C by B in A.

Definition 3. The function SQL_to_ERA takes an SQL statement and database Δ as input and returns an ERA expression as defined by cases as follows:

$$SQL\_to\_ERA(\text{SELECT } SelectList \ \text{ FROM } R_1, \ldots, R_n \ \text{ WHERE } SCond, \Delta) =$$
$$\pi_{SelectList}(\sigma_{ECond}(R_1 \times \cdots \times R_n))$$

where each R_i is a relation name and $ECond$ is the corresponding ERA condition to the SQL condition $SCond$, i.e., with the following syntactical replacements:
$$EC = ((((((SC[\leq /\texttt{<=}])[\neq /\texttt{<>}])[\geq /\texttt{>=}])[\neg/\texttt{NOT}])[\wedge/\texttt{AND}])[\vee/\texttt{OR}]$$

$$SQL\_to\_ERA(\text{SELECT } SelectList \text{ FROM } FromList \text{ WHERE } Cond, \ \Delta) =$$
$$SQL\_to\_ERA(\text{WITH } R_i \text{ AS } SQL_i \text{ SELECT } SelectList\text{FROM } FromList' \text{ WHERE } Cond, \ \Delta)$$

where the query SQL_i occurs in $SelectList$, R_i is a fresh new relation name, and $FromList' = FromList[R_i/SQL_i]$.

$$SQL\_to\_ERA(SQL_1 \ SQLSetOp \ SQL_2, \Delta) =$$
$$SQL\_to\_ERA(SQL_1, \Delta) \ ERASetOp \ SQL\_to\_ERA(SQL_2, \Delta)$$

where $(SQLSetOp, ERASetOp) \in \{(\texttt{UNION},\cup), (\texttt{EXCEPT},-), (\texttt{INTERSECT},\cap)\}$

$$SQL\_to\_ERA(\text{WITH } R \text{ AS } SQL_1 \ SQL_2, \Delta) =$$
$$SQL\_to\_ERA(SQL_2, \Delta \cup \{R \leftarrow SQL\_to\_ERA(SQL_1, \Delta)\}) \qquad \square$$

The first case covers SELECT statements with only relations in the FROM list, whereas the second one rewrites a SELECT statement with a query in its FROM clause into a WITH statement, by replacing the query with a relation name defining the query. The third case covers multiset operations. Finally, the fourth case deals with WITH statements by augmenting the database for sec4 SQL_2 with a new relation definition R as the translation of SQL_1 to ERA for the current database.

3   Hypothetical Datalog

Hypothetical Datalog is an extension of function-free Horn logic [5]. Following [17], the syntax of the logic is first order and includes a universe of constant symbols, a set of variables and a set of predicate symbols. Following Prolog syntax, we write variables starting with either an upper-case letter or an underscore, and the rest of symbols either starting with lower-case or delimited by single quotes. Removing function symbols from the logic is a condition for finiteness of answers, a natural requirement of relational database users. As in Horn-logic, a rule has the form $A \leftarrow \phi$, where A is an atom and ϕ is a conjunction of goals. Since we consider a hypothetical system, a goal can also take the form $R_1 \wedge \ldots \wedge R_n \Rightarrow G$, a construction known as an *embedded implication*. The following definition captures the syntax of the language, where $vars(T)$ is the set of variables occurring in T:

Definition 4. $R := A \mid A \leftarrow G_1 \wedge \ldots \wedge G_n$
$G := A \mid \neg A \mid \delta(A) \mid G_1 \vee G_2 \mid R_1 \wedge \ldots \wedge R_n \Rightarrow G$
where R and R_i stand for rules, G and G_i for goals, A for an atom (possibly containing variables and constants, but no compound terms), and $vars(R_i)$ do not occur out of R_i.   □

The condition on variables of each assumed rule R_i ensures that R_i is not specialized by any substitution out of it along inferencing, so R_i can be assumed "as is" for any inference step. The next section recalls this requirement as adequate for modelling local definitions in SQL WITH statements.

A Datalog database can contain facts (atoms, as in SQL), and rules instead of relation definitions. Here, a database is also referred to as a program. Each rule $A \leftarrow G_1 \vee G_2$ in a database is rewritten as two rules $A \leftarrow G_1$ and $A \leftarrow G_2$.

For dealing with negation, predicates are collected into strata, which are built using a predicate dependency graph (PDG) [24], showing both the positive and negative dependencies between predicates in the database. Each node in this graph is a predicate (relation) symbol and there are as many nodes as such symbols in the database. Arcs come from each predicate in a rule body (antecedent) to its rule predicate. Arcs are labelled as either negative ($\overset{\leftharpoonup}{\leftarrow}$), if the antecedent node occurs negated, or positive otherwise ($\leftarrow$). A stratification collects predicates into numbered strata so that, given the function $str(\Delta, \mathbf{p})$ which assigns a stratum number to predicate $\mathbf{p}$ in the database Δ, then for a positive arc $\mathbf{p} \leftarrow \mathbf{q}$, $str(\Delta, \mathbf{p}) \leq str(\Delta, \mathbf{q})$, and for a negative arc $p \overset{\leftharpoonup}{\leftarrow} \mathbf{q}$, $str(\Delta, \mathbf{p}) < str(\Delta, \mathbf{q})$. Predicates in lower strata are solved before those in upper strata to avoid non-monotonicity in fixpoint iterations [23].

Semantics is built with the stratified inference system defined in [17]. This system is adapted next for dealing with SQL duplicates (identifiers for axioms are constructed as identifier compositions), and extended with duplicate elimination (strong constraints are omitted as they are out of the scope of this paper). As in [17], $\Delta \vdash \psi$ is an *inference expression*, where Δ is a database, ψ can be either an identified ground atom $id : A$, or $\bot$. A *negative inference expression* is of the form $\Delta \vdash id : -A$.

Definition 5. Given a database Δ and a set of input inference expressions $\mathcal{E}$, the inference system associated to the s-th stratum is defined as follows, where $d_s(\mathcal{E})$ is a closure operator that denotes the set of inference expressions derivable in this system
Axioms:

- $\Delta \vdash id : A$ is an axiom for each (ground) atomic formula $id : A$ in Δ, where $str(\Delta, pred(A)) = s$
- Each expression in $\mathcal{E}$ is an axiom.

Inference Rules:

- For any rule $A \leftarrow \phi_1 \wedge \ldots \wedge \phi_n$ with identifier id in Δ, where $str(\Delta, pred(A)) = s$ and for any ground substitution θ:

$$\frac{\Delta \vdash id_i : \phi_i\theta \text{ for each } i}{\Delta \vdash id' : A\theta} \qquad\qquad (Clause)$$

where id' is the composition of identifiers $id \cdot id_1 \cdots id_n$
- For any atom A:

$$\frac{\Delta \vdash id : A}{\Delta \vdash \alpha : \delta(A)} \qquad\qquad (Duplicates)$$

where α is a single, unique identifier.
- For any goal ϕ:

$$\frac{\Delta \cup \{R_1, \ldots, R_n\} \vdash \phi}{\Delta \vdash R_1 \wedge \ldots \wedge R_n \Rightarrow \phi} \qquad\qquad (Assumption)$$

Each rule in this inference system is read as: If the formulas above the line can be inferred, then those below the line can also be inferred. We recall the intuition behind the inference rule for the embedded implication: For proving the conclusion ϕ, rules R_i, together with the current database Δ can be used in subsequent inference steps. So, this inference rule captures what SQL WITH statements need if translated to Hypothetical Datalog, because each R_i can represent each temporary view definition, as will be shown in the next section. The inference rule (*Duplicates*) performs duplicate elimination by grouping all inferred atoms with a single identifier α (recall that $\mathcal{E}$ is a set).

Negative information is deduced by applying the closed world assumption to a set of inference expressions $\mathcal{E}$ (written as $cwa(\mathcal{E})$) as the union of $\mathcal{E}$ and the negative inference expression for $\Delta \vdash \phi$ such that $\Delta \vdash \phi \notin \mathcal{E}$.

Thus, a stratified bottom-up construction of the *unified stratified semantics* can be specified by:

- $\mathcal{E}^0 = \emptyset$
- $\mathcal{E}^{s+1} = cwa(d_{s+1}(\mathcal{E}^s))$ for $s \geq 0$.

which builds a set of axioms $\mathcal{E}$ that provides a means to assign a meaning to a goal as: $solve(\phi, \mathcal{E}) = \{\Delta \vdash id : \psi \in \mathcal{E}$ such that $\phi\theta = \psi\}$, where θ is a substitution and each axiom in $\mathcal{E}$ is mapped to the database Δ it was deduced for, and the inferred fact ψ is labelled with its data source (for supporting duplicates). We use $\Delta(\mathcal{E})$ to denote the multiset of facts ψ so that $\Delta \vdash id : \psi \in \mathcal{E}$ for any id.

4   Translating SQL into Datalog

Here, we define the function *SQL_to_DL* which takes a relation name and an SQL statement as input and returns a multiset of Datalog rules providing the same meaning as the SQL relation for a corresponding predicate with the same name as the relation. From here on, set-related operators and symbols refer to multisets, as SQL relations can contain duplicates.

Definition 6. The function *SQL_to_DL* takes a relation name and an SQL statement as input and returns a Datalog program as defined by cases as follows:

% Basic SELECT statement
$SQL\_to\_DL\,(r,\ \text{SELECT A}_1, \ldots, \text{A}_n\ \text{FROM}\ Rel\ \text{WHERE}\ Cond) =$
$\quad \{r(\overline{X}) \leftarrow DLRel(\overline{Y}) \wedge DLCond(\overline{Z})\} \bigcup RelRules \bigcup CondRules,$
where $SQLREL\_to\_DL\,(Rel) = (DLRel(\overline{Y}), RelRules)$, and
$\quad SQLCOND\_to\_DL\,(Cond) = (DLCond(\overline{Z}), CondRules)$

Here, each A_i is either a constant or an argument name present in the relation
Rel with corresponding logic variable $X_i \in \overline{X}$. Rel is either a single defined
relation (table or view), or a join of relations, or an SQL statement. Function $SQLREL\_to\_DL$ (respectively, $SQLCOND\_to\_DL$) takes an SQL relation (respectively, condition) and returns a goal with as many variables $\overline{Y}$ as arguments of
Rel and, possibly, additional rules which result from the translation. Variables
$\overline{Z} \subseteq \overline{Y}$ come as a result of the translation of the condition $DLCond$ to a goal.

% Union
$SQL\_to\_DL\,(r,\ SQL_1\ \text{UNION}\ SQL_2) =$
$\quad SQL\_to\_DL\,(r,\ SQL_1) \bigcup SQL\_to\_DL(r,\ SQL_2)$

% Difference
$SQL\_to\_DL\,(r,\ SQL_1\ \text{EXCEPT}\ SQL_2) =$
$\quad \{r(\overline{X}) \leftarrow s(\overline{X}) \wedge \neg t(\overline{X})\} \bigcup SQL\_to\_DL\,(s,\ SQL_1) \bigcup SQL\_to\_DL\,(t,\ SQL_2)$

% Intersection
$SQL\_to\_DL\,(r,\ SQL_1\ \text{INTERSECT}\ SQL_2) =$
$\quad \{r(\overline{X}) \leftarrow s(\overline{X}) \wedge t(\overline{X})\} \bigcup SQL\_to\_DL\,(s,\ SQL_1) \bigcup SQL\_to\_DL\,(t,\ SQL_2)$ □

Definition 7. The function $SQLREL\_to\_DL$ takes an SQL relation (either a relation name or statement) as input and returns both a Datalog goal and program
as defined by cases as follows:

% Extensional/Intensional relation name
$SQLREL\_to\_DL\,(RelName) = (RelName(\overline{X}), \{\})$
where $\overline{X}$ are the n variables corresponding to the n-degree relation $RelName$.

% Join of relations
$SQLREL\_to\_DL\,((Rel_1, \ldots, Rel_n)) = (DLRel(\overline{X_1}) \wedge \cdots \wedge DLRel(\overline{X_n}), RelRules_1 \cup$
$\cdots \cup RelRules_n)$
where $SQLREL\_to\_DL\,(Rel_i) = (DLRel(\overline{X_i}), RelRules_i)$

% SQL statement
$SQLREL\_to\_DL\,(SQL) = (RelName(\overline{X}), SQL\_to\_DL\,(RelName, SQL))$
where $\overline{X}$ are the n variables corresponding to the n-degree statement SQL, and
$RelName$ is an arbitrary, fresh new relation name.   □

Definition 8. The function $SQLCOND\_to\_DL$ takes an SQL condition as input
and returns both a Datalog goal and program as defined by cases as follows:

% Basic condition
$SQLCOND\_to\_DL\,(\text{A}_1\ cop\ \text{A}_2) = (X_1\ cop'\ X_2, \emptyset)$

where each X_i is either the constant or the variable corresponding to the attribute name A_1, and cop' is the Datalog corresponding comparison operator to cop.

% Conjunction
$SQLCOND\_to\_DL\,(C_1 \text{ AND } C_2) = (C_1' \;\wedge\; C_2', CRules_1 \cup CRules_2)$
where C_i are conditions and $SQLCOND\_to\_DL\,(C_i)=(C_i', CRules_i)$.

% Disjunction
$SQLCOND\_to\_DL\,(C_1 \text{ OR } C_2) = (\delta(d), \{d \leftarrow C_1', d \leftarrow C_2'\} \cup CRules_1 \cup CRules_2)$
where C_i are conditions, $SQLCOND\_to\_DL\,(C_i) = (C_i', CRules_i)$, and d is a fresh atom.

% Negated condition
$SQLCOND\_to\_DL\,(\text{NOT } C) = (C', CRules)$
where $C' = SQLCOND\_to\_DL\,(\overline{C}) = (C', CRules)$, and $\overline{C}$ represents the logical complement of C $(\overline{X < Y} = X \geq Y,\ \overline{C_1 \wedge C_2} = \overline{C_1} \vee \overline{C_2}$, and so on). □

Note that disjunction requires duplicate elimination because, otherwise, there can be more tuples in the result as a disjunction in a rule is rewritten as two rules (cf. Sect. 3).

Completing the function SQL_to_DL in Definition 6 by including the WITH statement is straightforward because every temporary view can be represented by a predicate resulting from the translation of the temporary view definition into Datalog rules. Assuming such predicates as the antecedent of an embedded implication can be used to augment the (local, temporary) database for interpreting the meaning of the translated SQL outcome query, as follows:

$$SQL\_to\_DL\,(r, \text{WITH } r_1 \text{ AS } SQL_1\ SQL\,) =$$
$$\{r(\overline{X}) \leftarrow \bigwedge(SQL\_to\_DL\,(r_1,\ SQL_1)) \Rightarrow s(\overline{X})\} \bigcup SQL\_to\_DL\,(s,\ SQL)$$

where $\bigwedge(Bag)$ denotes $B_1 \wedge \cdots \wedge B_m$ $(B_i \in Bag)$. Note that variables in the antecedent of the embedded implication are not in $\overline{X}$ (cf. Definition 4), which is adequate because SQL_1 and SQL are independent sentences.

The following theorem establishes the semantic equivalence of an SQL relation and its counterpart Datalog translation.

Theorem 1. The semantics of an SQL n-degree relation r defined by the query Q on an extensional database Δ coincides with the meaning of a goal $r(\overline{X_i})$, $1 \leq i \leq n$, for $\Delta' = \Delta \bigcup SQL\_to\_DL\,(r, Q)$, that is: $\mathcal{SQL}_\Delta(Q) = \Delta(solve(r(\overline{X_i}), \mathcal{E}))$, where $\mathcal{E}$ is the unified stratified semantics for Δ'. □

Proof. To prove $\mathcal{SQL}_\Delta(Q) = \Delta(solve(r(\overline{X_i}), \mathcal{E}))$, on the one hand, as stated in Definition 2, we assume a correct implementation such that $\mathcal{SQL}_\Delta(Q) = \|\Phi_Q\|_\Delta$ for every query Q. Definition 3 provides a translation from an SQL query to an ERA expression Φ, and Definition 1 provides an interpretation for a computed answer in terms of the ERA operators. On the other hand, Definition 6 provides a Datalog program with a predicate r representing the relation r defined by query Q. This Datalog program is interpreted with the unified stratified semantics in

Sect. 3, which provides the set of axioms $\mathcal{E}$ for the original database Δ augmented with the translation of the query Q to this Datalog program. So, the proof proceeds by cases showing the semantic equivalence of the translation from the SQL query Q into an ERA expression ϕ for a relation r (with *SQL_to_ERA*), and the translation of Q into a Datalog program (with *SQL_to_DL*).

5   Beyond the with Clause: Expressing Assumptions

As a novel feature and inspired in [16], hypothetical SQL queries were introduced for the first time in DES version 2.6 in order to solve "what-if" scenarios for decision-support systems. Syntax for such queries is:

$$\text{ASSUME } SQL_1 \text{ IN } Rel_1, \ \ldots, \ SQL_n \text{ IN } Rel_n \ SQL;$$

which makes to *assume* the result of SQL_i in Rel_i (either a relation name or a complete schema, i.e., with attribute names) when processing *SQL*. This means that the semantics of each Rel_i is either overloaded (if the relation already exists) or otherwise defined with the facts of SQL_i.

For including this new statement in the SQL syntax, the case ASSUME q IN R q is added to the definition of q in Fig. 1. Similar to WITH, a series of assumptions ASSUME q_1 IN R_1, ..., q_n IN R_n q is rewritten as a nested query ASSUME q_1 AS R_1 (ASSUME q_2 AS R_2 (... (ASSUME q_n AS R_n q)...)).

Its semantics can be understood by adding the following case to the function *SQL_to_ERA* in Definition 3:

$$SQL\_to\_ERA(\text{ASSUME} SQL_1 \text{IN} R SQL_2, \Delta) =$$
$$SQL\_to\_ERA(SQL_2, (\Delta - \{R \leftarrow ERA\}) \cup$$
$$\{R \leftarrow ERA \cup SQL\_to\_ERA(SQL_1, \Delta)\})$$

Note that if R is an extensional relation, it can be intensionally represented in a database as a union of from-less select statements (SELECT*tuple*$_1$ UNION ... SELECT *tuple*$_n$).

Assumptions in DES 2.6 were un-nested and restricted to the top-level (i.e., at the system prompt) and its implementation resorted to *globally* define each Rel_i. Before solving an ASSUME query, each Rel_i was overloaded by inserting into it the required tuples from its assumption, and after solving, each Rel_i was restored by deleting the same tuples that were inserted. Nested assumptions were precluded because select statements in outer assumptions could not safely include inner assumptions, as in:

```
ASSUME SELECT 1 IN r(a),
(ASSUME SELECT 2 IN r(a) SELECT * FROM r) IN s(a)
  SELECT * FROM r,s;
```

because the meaning of r in the context of SELECT * FROM r,s would be overloaded with both $\{(1)\}$ and $\{(2)\}$, instead of just $\{(1)\}$.

Such statements were restricted to the top-level because, otherwise they could form part of a relation definition and the same problem might arise, as in:

```
CREATE VIEW v(a) AS ASSUME SELECT 2 IN r(a) SELECT * FROM r;
ASSUME SELECT 1 IN r(a), SELECT * FROM v IN s(a)
  SELECT * FROM r,s;
```

which is an equivalent formulation to the last example query, replacing the in-line inner-assumption statement by a reference to a relation v.

Applying hypothetical reasoning solves these issues in the (Hypothetical Datalog) setting of DES. In particular, the function SQL_to_DL in Definition 6 is augmented with the following case for supporting single assumptions:

$$SQL\_to\_DL\,(r, \text{ASSUME } SQL_1 \text{ IN } r_1 \; SQL\,) =$$
$$\{r(\overline{X}) \leftarrow \bigwedge(SQL\_to\_DL\,(r_1, \; SQL_1)) \Rightarrow s(\overline{X})\} \cup SQL\_to\_DL\,(s, \; SQL\,)$$

Here, the antecedent of the embedded implication includes all the clauses resulting from transforming SQL_1 into Datalog, which are (most likely) used in solving $s(\overline{X_i})$, the goal corresponding to SELECT * FROM s, where $s \leftarrow SQL$.

Intuitionistic logic programming allows us not only to deal with the issues above, but also to take advantage of negative assumptions [5,19]. A negative assumption allows to *remove* facts from the meaning of a relation, which broadens the applicability of queries in decision-support scenarios. To specify negative assumptions, NOT IN is used instead of just IN so that the SQL syntax (Definition 2) is enlarged with negative assumptions ASSUME q NOT IN R q. Its semantics can be understood with the following case added to Definition 3:

$$SQL\_to\_ERA(\text{ASSUME } SQL_1 \text{ NOT IN } R \; SQL_2, \; \Delta) =$$
$$SQL\_to\_ERA(SQL_2, (\Delta - \{R \leftarrow ERA\}) \cup$$
$$\{R \leftarrow ERA - SQL\_to\_ERA(SQL_1, \Delta)\})$$

So, instead of adding the semantics of SQL_1 to R in a (positive) assumption with a union operator, a negative assumption removes this semantics from R with a set difference operator.

Hypothetical Datalog in [19] introduces the notion of *restricted predicate* to handle negative assumptions in embedded implications. A restricted predicate includes at least a *restricting* rule, which is a regular rule whose head is an atom preceded by a minus sign. (We use the term *regular rule* for a usual Datalog rule, i.e., a rule whose head is an atom with non-structured arguments). Restricting rules are intended to prune the semantics of predicates, so that the meaning of a restricted predicate is the set of facts deduced from regular rules minus the set of facts deduced from restricting rules. Semantics in [19] formalizes this in the definition of the closed world assumption of a set of inference expressions $\mathcal{A}$, in which any restricting axiom $\Delta \vdash id : -\phi$ occurs as a negative inference expression. Similar to handling negation, the inclusion of restricted predicates involves adding negative dependencies between each restricted predicate p and all the predicates depending on p [19]. This way, any predicate using a restricted predicate p is located at a higher stratum and therefore its meaning is safely computed.

An SQL negative assumption can therefore be modelled with a restricting rule in the antecedent of an embedded implication, so that the translation from SQL to Hypothetical Datalog for ASSUME statements becomes:

$$SQL\_to\_DL(r, \ \text{ASSUME} \ SQL_1 \ \text{NOT} \ \text{IN} \ r_1 \ SQL) =$$
$$\{r(\overline{X}) \ \leftarrow \ \bigwedge(SQL\_to\_DL(r_1, SQL_1)[-r_n/r_n]) \ \Rightarrow \ s(\overline{X})\} \ \cup$$
$$SQL\_to\_DL(s, \ SQL)$$

Here, translating the SQL negative assumption for a relation r_1 into Datalog rules requires replacing every occurrence of the predicate r_1 by $-r_1$, in particular making it a restricted predicate as rule heads for r_1 become restricting atoms.

6 Playing with the System

The formal setting described in this paper has been implemented in the deductive system DES [20], which in particular supports such features and inputs from several query languages, including (hypothetical) Datalog and SQL. This interactive system supports a dynamic database allowing users to add, modify, remove and query relations, which can be either in-memory or persistent. Solving a query in any of the supported languages resorts to a translation from the input language to a Datalog core language. The translated query is then solved by the deductive engine, which may redirect some computations to an external database system if there are persistent predicates involved. Another possibility for external computations is opening an external database and making DES its front-end for submitting SQL queries. In this scenario, queries in other languages (Datalog, ERA, TRC and DRC) are solved by the deductive engine and references to external relations are solved by the external database engine. Next, we introduce a couple of examples to show the translation from SQL to Datalog, its solving and the connection to external databases. Concrete, textual syntax in DES for Datalog follows the syntax of Prolog.

Let us consider a database Δ containing the relations `student(name)` and `take(name, title)`. The first one states names of students and the second one the course (`title`) each student (`name`) is enrolled in. Types can be specified either with a Datalog assertion (as

student	take
(adam)	(adam,db)
(bob)	(pete,db)
(pete)	(pete,lp)
(scott)	(scott,lp)

`:-type(student(name:string))` for the first relation) or a DDL SQL statement (as `create table take(name string, title string)` for the second one, where a foreign key `take.name` $\rightarrow$ `student.name` could be stated as well). We consider the database instance depicted in the tables above.

The next SQL statement (looking for students that have not been already enrolled in a course) is translated as follows in a system session with DES 4.0 (issuing the command "`/show_compilations on`" makes translations to be displayed):

```
DES> SELECT * FROM student EXCEPT SELECT name FROM take
Info: SQL statement compiled to:
   answer(A) :- student(A), not take(A,_B).
answer(student.name:string) ->
{ answer(bob) }
Info: 1 tuple computed.
```

This example shows a few of things. First, as a query Q is allowed at the system prompt, the call to the translation function becomes SQL_to_DL (answer, Q), i.e., the outcome relation is automatically renamed to the reserved keyword answer. Second, the outcome schema answer(student.name:string) shows that the single output argument comes from the argument name of the relation student, with type string. Third, following the definition of the translation function, this query should be translated into:

```
answer(A) :- '$r_1'(A), not '$r_2'(A).
'$r_1'(A) :- student(A).          '$r_2'(A) :- take(A,_B).
```

However, a folding/unfolding [22] stage simplifies this by removing the dependent relations '$r_1' and '$r_2' as it was displayed in the system session. Since DES implements a tabling mechanism [17], the meaning of each dependent relation (either complete or restricted to a given call) is stored in the answer table, so that reducing the number of these dependent relations also reduces the space and time requirements.

Finally, this example also shows that non-relevant variables to a rule outcome are underscored (otherwise, they would be signalled as singletons). This is important in this case to identify as safe the rule in which this underscored variable occurs. Classical safety [23] would tag the rule answer(A) :- student(A), not take(A,_B) as unsafe because _B does not occur in a positive goal in the same rule. However, there exists an equivalent set of safe rules (as listed above before applying folding/unfolding). Therefore, taking this fact into account, underscored variables are used as a means to encapsulate this form of safety, which is identified by the system and processed correspondingly with no safety errors.

As an example of a WITH query, the following statement defines the relation grad intended to retrieve the eligible students for graduation (those that took both db and lp in this tiny example):

```
DES> WITH grad(name) AS
   (SELECT student.name
    FROM student, take t1, take t2
    WHERE student.name=t1.name AND t1.name=t2.name AND
          t1.title='db' AND t2.title='lp')
   SELECT * FROM grad;
Info: SQL statement compiled to:
   answer(A) :-
   (grad(B) :- student(B), take(B,db), take(B,lp)) => grad(A).
answer(grad.name:string) ->
{ answer(pete) }
Info: 1 tuple computed.
```

Solving this query amounts to solve grad(A) in the database Δ augmented with the single rule in the antecedent of =>.

As an example of an ASSUME query, we reuse the grad definition above, assume that adam is not an eligible student, and that adam and scott took lp and db respectively:

```
DES> ASSUME
        (SELECT 'adam') NOT IN student,
        (SELECT 'adam','lp' UNION ALL SELECT 'scott','db')
          in take,
        (SELECT student.name FROM student, take t1, take t2
          WHERE student.name=t1.name AND t1.name=t2.name AND
                  t1.title='lp' AND t2.title='db') IN grad(name)
      SELECT * FROM grad;
Info: SQL statement compiled to:
  answer(A) :-
  -student(adam) /\ take(adam,lp) /\  take(scott,db) /\
  (grad(B) :- student(B), take(B,lp), take(B,db)) => grad(A).
answer(grad.name:string) ->
{ answer(pete), answer(scott) }
Info: 2 tuples computed.
```

Here, the assumption on **student** is negative and is compiled to a restricting fact. The second one is compiled to a couple of facts because of the union. The last one is the same as the previous example. The SQL statement after the assumptions simply leads to the goal **grad(A)**, for which even when **adam** took the courses to graduate, he was removed as an eligible student and therefore from the answer.

If the extensional relations **student** and **take** are already defined in an external relational database (as, e.g., MySQL or PostgreSQL), they can be made available to DES via an ODBC connection (with the command /open_db), and queried as if they were local [18]. This way, DES behaves as a front-end for both straight calls to native (i.e., supported by the external relational system) SQL queries and non-native queries (as those including **ASSUME**). For non-native queries, prepending the command /des to the query makes DES to handle them. In the next example, we consider MySQL (which does not provide support for the **WITH** clause) with the relations **student** and **take** already available.

```
DES> /open_db mysql
DES> /des WITH grad(name) AS ...
```

After opening the ODBC connection, the former example query (omitted here in the ellipses) can be solved by the deductive engine with the Datalog translation and obtaining the same answer as before. Note that references to the relations **student** and **take** are solved by the external MySQL engine.

Finally, we highlight that even when the **WITH** clause is supported in several relational database systems (as PostgreSQL), they are somewhat restricted because, referring to the syntax in Sect. 2, *SQL* cannot contain a **WITH** clause, whereas we do allow for it.

7   Conclusions

This work has presented a proposal to take advantage of intuitionistic logic programming to model both temporary definitions (with the **WITH** clause) and assumptions (with the ASSUME clause) in SQL. Its motivation lies in providing support for these clauses in a deductive system which translates SQL to Datalog, additionally providing a clean semantics that makes assumptions to behave as first-class citizen in the object language. The deductive database system DES was used as a test bed to experiment with assumptions and local definitions in SQL. Further, this system can be used first as a front-end to relational systems either lacking support for the WITH clause or providing restricted uses of this clause, and second, to submit out-of-the-standard ASSUME clauses to external database systems. In particular, this is interesting as a middle-ware between a constraint system and a relational database to experiment in decision-support scenarios. The most related work is [1], which includes assumptions in SQL with a tailored semantics, and generates SQL scripts implementing fixpoint computations. With respect to the intuitionistic formal framework, our work is based on [3–6] and adapted to assume rules and deal with duplicates in [17,19]. However, it is not powerful enough to include embedded universal quantifiers in premises as in [6], which provides the ability to create new constant symbols hypothetically along inference. Though this is not directly applicable to the current work, it is indeed an interesting subject to explore by considering that domains can be finitely constrained in practical applications, as with foreign keys.

Acknowledgements. Thanks to the anonymous referees for their suggestions to improve this work, which has been partially supported by the Spanish MINECO project CAVI-ART (TIN2013-44742-C4-3-R), Madrid regional project N-GREENS Software-CM (S2013/ICE-2731) and UCM grant GR3/14-910502.

References

1. Aranda-López, G., Nieva, S., Sáenz-Pérez, F., Sánchez-Hernández, J.: Incorporating hypothetical views and extended recursion into SQL database systems. In: Mcmillan, K., Middeldorp, A., Sutcliffe, G., Voronkov, A. (eds.) International Conference on Logic for Programming, Artificial Intelligence and Reasoning (LPAR-19). EPiC Series in Computing, vol. 26, pp. 9–22. EasyChair (2014)
2. Atzeni, P., Jensen, C.S., Orsi, G., Ram, S., Tanca, L., Torlone, R.: The relational model is dead, SQL is dead, and i don't feel so good myself. SIGMOD Rec. **42**(2), 64–68 (2013)
3. Bonner, A.J., Datalog, H.: Negation and linear recursion. In: Proceedings of the ACM Symposium on Principles of Database Systems (PODS), pp. 286–300 (1989)
4. Bonner, A.J.: Hypothetical datalog: complexity and expressibility. Theor. Comput. Sci. **76**, 3–51 (1990)
5. Bonner, A.J., McCarty, L.T.: Adding negation-as-failure to intuitionistic logic programming. In: Lusk, E.L., Overbeek, R.A. (eds.) Proceedings of the North American Conference on Logic Programming (NACLP), pp. 681–703. The MIT Press (1990)
6. Bonner, A.J., McCarty, L.T., Vadaparty, K.: Expressing database queries with intuitionistic logic. In: Lusk, E.L., Overbeek, R.A. (eds.) Proceedings of the North American Conference on Logic Programming (NACLP), pp. 831–850 (1989)

7. Caballero, R., García-Ruiz, Y., Sáenz-Pérez, F.: Declarative debugging of wrong and missing answers for SQL views. In: Schrijvers, T., Thiemann, P. (eds.) FLOPS 2012. LNCS, vol. 7294, pp. 73–87. Springer, Heidelberg (2012). doi:10. 1007/978-3-642-29822-6_9

8. Codd, E.: A relational model for large shared databanks. Commun. ACM **13**(6), 377–390 (1970)

9. Codd, E.: Relational completeness of data base sublanguages. In: Rustin, R. (ed.) Data Base Systems, Courant Computer Science Symposia Series, vol. 6. Prentice-Hall, Englewood Cliffs (1972)

10. Gabbay, D.M.: N-prolog: an extension of prolog with hypothetical implication II - logical foundations, and negation as failure. J. Log. Program. **2**(4), 251–283 (1985)

11. Garcia-Molina, H., Ullman, J.D., Widom, J.: Database Systems: The Complete Book. Prentice Hall PTR, Upper Saddle River (2008)

12. Grefen, P.W., de By, R.A.: A multi-set extended relational algebra.: a formal approach to a practical issue. In: Proceedings of the Tenth International Conference on Data Engineering (ICDE), pp. 80–88. IEEE (1994)

13. Hodas, J., Miller, D.: Logic programming in a fragment of intuitionistic linear logic. Inf. Comput. **110**(2), 327–365 (1994)

14. McCarty, L.T.: Clausal intuitionistic logic I - fixed-point semantics. J. Log. Program. **5**(1), 1–31 (1988)

15. Miller, D.: A logical analysis of modules in logic programming. J. Log. Program. **6**(1), 79–108 (1989)

16. Nieva, S., Sánchez-Hernández, J., Sáenz-Pérez, F.: Formalizing a constraint deductive database language based on hereditary Harrop formulas with negation. In: Garrigue, J., Hermenegildo, M.V. (eds.) FLOPS 2008. LNCS, vol. 4989, pp. 289–304. Springer, Heidelberg (2008). doi:10.1007/978-3-540-78969-7_21

17. Sáenz-Pérez, F.: Implementing tabled hypothetical datalog. In: Proceedings of the 25th IEEE International Conference on Tools with Artificial Intelligence (ICTAI), pp. 596–601, November 2013

18. Sáenz-Pérez, F.: Towards bridging the expressiveness gap between relational and deductive databases. Electron. Commun. EASST **64**, 1–22 (2014)

19. Sáenz-Pérez, F.: Restricted predicates for hypothetical datalog. Electron. Proc. Theor. Comput. Sci. **200**, 64–79 (2015)

20. Sáenz-Pérez, F.: Datalog educational system (2016). http://des.sourceforge.net/

21. Silberschatz, A., Korth, H., Sudarshan, S.: Database Systems Concepts, 6th edn. McGraw-Hill Inc., New York (2010)

22. Sterling, L., Shapiro, E.: The Art of Prolog: Advanced Programming Techniques. MIT Press, Cambridge (1986)

23. Ullman, J.D.: Database and Knowledge-Base Systems, vols. I (Classical Database Systems) and II (The New Technologies). Computer Science Press (1988)

24. Zaniolo, C., Ceri, S., Faloutsos, C., Snodgrass, R.T., Subrahmanian, V.S., Zicari, R.: Advanced Database Systems. Morgan Kaufmann, San Francisco (1997)

Types, Unification, and Logic

Coinductive Soundness of Corecursive Type Class Resolution

František Farka[1,2]([⊠]), Ekaterina Komendantskaya[2], and Kevin Hammond[1]

[1] University of St Andrews, St Andrews, Scotland
{ff32,kh8}@st-andrews.ac.uk
[2] Heriot-Watt University, Edinburgh, Scotland
ek19@hw.ac.uk

Abstract. Horn clauses and first-order resolution are commonly used to implement *type classes* in Haskell. Several corecursive extensions to type class resolution have recently been proposed, with the goal of allowing (co)recursive dictionary construction where resolution does not terminate. This paper shows, for the first time, that corecursive type class resolution and its extensions are *coinductively sound* with respect to the greatest Herbrand models of logic programs and that they are *inductively unsound* with respect to the least Herbrand models. We establish incompleteness results for various fragments of the proof system.

Keywords: Resolution · Coinduction · Herbrand models · Type classes · Haskell · Horn clauses

1 Introduction

Type classes can be used to implement ad-hoc polymorphism and overloading in functional languages. The approach originated in Haskell [7,16] and has been further developed in dependently typed languages [3,6]. For example, it is convenient to define equality for all data structures in a uniform way. In Haskell, this is achieved by introducing the equality class Eq:

```
class Eq x where
  eq :: Eq x ⇒ x → x → Bool
```

and then declaring any necessary instances of the class, e.g. for pairs and integers:

```
instance (Eq x, Eq y) ⇒ Eq (x, y) where
  eq (x1, y1) (x2, y2) = eq x1 x2 && eq y1 y2
instance Eq Int where
  eq x y = primtiveIntEq x y
```

Type class resolution is performed by the Haskell compiler and involves checking whether all the instance declarations are valid. For example, the following function triggers a check that Eq (Int, Int) is a valid instance of type class Eq:

```
test :: Eq (Int, Int) ⇒ Bool
test = eq (1,2) (1,2)
```

© Springer International Publishing AG 2017
M.V. Hermenegildo and P. Lopez-Garcia (Eds.): LOPSTR 2016, LNCS 10184, pp. 311–327, 2017.
DOI: 10.1007/978-3-319-63139-4_18

It is folklore that type class instance resolution resembles SLD-resolution from logic programming. The type class instance declarations above could, for example, be viewed as the following two Horn clauses:

Example 1 (Logic program P_{Pair}).

$$\kappa_1 : \quad eq(x),\ eq(y) \Rightarrow eq(pair(x,y))$$
$$\kappa_2 : \qquad\qquad\qquad \Rightarrow eq(int)$$

Then, given the query ? $eq(pair(int, int))$, SLD-resolution terminates successfully with the following sequence of inference steps:

$$eq(pair(int, int)) \rightarrow_{\kappa_1} eq(int), eq(int) \rightarrow_{\kappa_2} eq(int) \rightarrow_{\kappa_2} \emptyset$$

The proof witness $\kappa_1\kappa_2\kappa_2$ (called a "dictionary" in Haskell) is constructed by the Haskell compiler. This is treated internally as an executable function.

Despite the apparent similarity of type class syntax and type class resolution to Horn clauses and SLD-resolution they are not, however, identical. At a syntactic level, type class instance declarations correspond to a restricted form of Horn clauses, namely ones that: (i) do not *overlap* (*i.e.* whose heads do not unify); and that (ii) do not contain existential variables (*i.e.* variables that occur in the bodies but not in the heads of the clauses). At an algorithmic level, (iii) type class resolution corresponds to SLD-resolution in which unification is restricted to term-matching. Assuming there is a clause $B_1, \ldots B_n \Rightarrow A'$, then a query ? A' can be resolved with this clause only if A can be matched against A', *i.e.* if a substitution σ exists such that $A = \sigma A'$. In comparison, SLD-resolution incorporates *unifiers*, as well as *matchers*, *i.e.* it also proceeds to resolve the above query and clause in all the cases where $\sigma A = \sigma A'$ holds.

These restrictions guarantee that type class inference computes the *principal* (most general) type. Restrictions (i) and (ii) amount to deterministic inference by resolution, in which only one derivation is possible for every query. Restriction (iii) means that no substitution is applied to a query during inference, *i.e.* we prove the query in an implicitly universally quantified form. It is common knowledge that (as with SLD-resolution) type class resolution is *inductively sound*, *i.e.* that it is sound relative to the least Herbrand models of logic programs [12]. Moreover, in Sect. 3 we establish, for the first time, that it is also *universally inductively sound*, *i.e.* that if a formula A is proved by type class resolution, every ground instance of A is in the least Herbrand model of the given program. In contrast to SLD-resolution, however, type class resolution is *inductively incomplete*, *i.e.* it is incomplete relative to least Herbrand models, even for the class of Horn clauses that is restricted by conditions (i) and (ii). For example, given a clause $\Rightarrow q(f(x))$ and a query ? $q(x)$, SLD-resolution is able to find a proof (by instantiating x with $f(x)$), but type class resolution fails. Lämmel and Peyton Jones have suggested [11] an extension to type class resolution that accounts for some non-terminating cases of type class resolution. Consider, for example, the following mutually defined data structures:

```
data OddList a  =  OCons a (EvenList a)
data EvenList a  =  Nil | ECons a (OddList a)
```

which give rise to the following instance declarations for the Eq class:

```
instance (Eq a, Eq (EvenList a)) ⇒ Eq (OddList a) where
    eq (OCons x xs) (OCons y ys) =  eq x y && ·eq xs ys

instance (Eq a, Eq (OddList a)) ⇒ Eq (EvenList a) where
    eq Nil          Nil          =  True
    eq (ECons x xs) (ECons y ys) =  eq x y && eq xs ys
    eq _            _            =  False
```

The test function below triggers type class resolution in the Haskell compiler:

```
test :: Eq (EvenList Int) ⇒ Bool
test = eq Nil Nil
```

However, inference by resolution does not terminate in this case. Consider the Horn clause representation of the type class instance declarations:

Example 2 (Logic program $P_{EvenOdd}$).

$$\kappa_1 : \; \mathsf{eq}(x),\; \mathsf{eq}(\mathsf{evenList}(x)) \;\Rightarrow \mathsf{eq}(\mathsf{oddList}(x))$$
$$\kappa_2 : \; \mathsf{eq}(x),\; \mathsf{eq}(\mathsf{oddList}(x)) \;\Rightarrow \mathsf{eq}(\mathsf{evenList}(x))$$
$$\kappa_3 : \hspace{4.2cm} \Rightarrow \mathsf{eq}(\mathsf{int})$$

The non-terminating resolution trace is given by:

$$\underline{\mathsf{eq}(\mathsf{evenList}(\mathsf{int}))} \to_{\kappa_2} \mathsf{eq}(\mathsf{int}), \mathsf{eq}(\mathsf{oddList}(\mathsf{int})) \to_{\kappa_3} \mathsf{eq}(\mathsf{oddList}(\mathsf{int}))$$
$$\to_{\kappa_1} \mathsf{eq}(\mathsf{int}), \mathsf{eq}(\mathsf{evenList}(\mathsf{int})) \to_{\kappa_3} \underline{\mathsf{eq}(\mathsf{evenList}(\mathsf{int}))} \to_{\kappa_2} \dots$$

A goal $\mathsf{eq}(\mathsf{evenList}(\mathsf{int}))$ is simplified using the clause κ_2 to goals $\mathsf{eq}(\mathsf{int})$ and $\mathsf{eq}(\mathsf{oddList}(\mathsf{int}))$. The first of these is discarded using the clause κ_3. Resolution continues using κ_1 and κ_3, resulting in the original goal $\mathsf{eq}(\mathsf{evenList}(\mathsf{int}))$. It is easy to see that such a process could continue infinitely and that this goal constitutes a *cycle* (underlined above).

As suggested by Lämmel and Peyton Jones [11], the compiler can obviously terminate the infinite inference process as soon as it detects the underlined cycle. Moreover, it can also construct the corresponding proof witness in a form of a recursive function. For the example above, such a function is given by the fixed point term $\nu\alpha.\kappa_2\kappa_3(\kappa_1\kappa_3\alpha)$, where ν is a fixed point operator. The intuitive reading of such a proof is that an infinite proof of the query ? eq (evenList(int)) exists, and that its shape is fully specified by the recursive proof witness function above. We say that the proof is given by *corecursive type class resolution*.

Corecursive type class resolution is not inductively sound. For example, the formula $\mathsf{eq}(\mathsf{evenList}(\mathsf{int}))$ is not in the least Herbrand model of the corresponding logic program. However, as we prove in Sect. 4, it is *(universally) coinductively sound*, *i.e.* it is sound relative to the greatest Herbrand models. For example, eq(evenList(int)) is in the greatest Herbrand model of the program $P_{EvenOdd}$. Similarly to the inductive case, corecursive type class resolution is coinductively incomplete. Consider the clause $\kappa_{inf} : p(x) \Rightarrow p(f(x))$. This clause may be given an interpretation by the greatest (complete) Herbrand models. However, corecursive type class resolution does not yield infinite proofs.

Unfortunately, this simple method of cycle detection does not work for all non-terminating programs. Consider the following example, which defines a data type Bush (for bush trees), and its corresponding instance for Eq:

```
data Bush a = Nil | Cons a (Bush (Bush a))
instance Eq a, Eq (Bush (Bush a)) ⇒ Eq (Bush a) where { ... }
```

Here, type class resolution does not terminate. However, it does not exhibit cycles either. Consider the Horn clause translation of the problem:

Example 3 (Logic program P_{Bush}).

$$\kappa_1 : \qquad\qquad\qquad\qquad\qquad \Rightarrow eq(int)$$
$$\kappa_2 : eq(x), eq(bush(bush(x))) \qquad\qquad \Rightarrow eq(bush(x))$$

The derivation below shows that no cycles arise when we resolve the query ? eq(bush(int)) against the program P_{Bush}:

$$eq(bush(int)) \to_{\kappa_2} eq(int), eq(bush(bush(int))) \to_{\kappa_1} \cdots \to_{\kappa_2}$$
$$eq(bush(int)), eq(bush(bush(bush(int)))) \to_{\kappa_1} \cdots$$

Fu *et al.* [5] have recently introduced an extension to corecursive type class resolution that allows implicative queries to be proved by corecursion and uses the recursive proof witness construction. Implicative queries require the language of proof terms to be extended with λ-abstraction. For example, in the above program the Horn formula $eq(x) \Rightarrow eq(bush(x))$ can be (coinductively) proven with the recursive proof witness $\kappa_3 = \nu\alpha.\lambda\beta.\kappa_2\beta(\alpha(\alpha\beta))$. If we add this Horn clause as a third clause to our program, we obtain a proof of eq(bush(int)) by applying κ_3 to κ_1. In this case, it is even more challenging to understand whether the proof $\kappa_3\kappa_1$ of eq(bush(int)) is indeed sound: whether inductively, coinductively or in any other sense. In Sect. 5, we establish, for the first time, *coinductive soundness* for proofs of such implicative queries, relative to the greatest Herbrand models of logic programs. Namely, we determine that proofs that are obtained by extending the proof context with coinductively proven Horn clauses (such as κ_3 above) are coinductively sound but inductively unsound. This result completes our study of the semantic properties of corecursive type class resolution. Sections 3 and 5 summarise our arguments concerning the inductive and coinductive incompleteness of corecursive type class resolution.

Contributions. By presenting the described results, we answer three research questions:

(1) whether type class resolution and its two recent corecursive extensions [5, 11] are sound relative to the standard (Herbrand model) semantics of logic programming;

(2) whether these new extensions are indeed "corecursive", i.e. whether they are better modelled by the greatest Herbrand model semantics rather than by the least Herbrand model semantics; and

(3) whether the context update technique given in [5] can be reapplied to logic programming and can be re-used in its corecursive dialects such as CoLP [14] and CoALP [10] or, even broader, can be incorporated into program transformation techniques [2].

We answer questions (1) and (2) in the affirmative. The answer to question (3) is less straightforward. The way the implicative coinductive lemmata are used in proofs alongside all other Horn clauses in [5] indeed resembles a program transformation method when considered from the logic programming point of view. In reality, however, different fragments of the calculus given in [5] allow proofs for Horn formulae which, when added to the initial program, may lead to inductively or coinductively unsound extensions. We analyse this situation carefully, throughout the technical sections that follow. In this way, we highlight which program transformation methods can be soundly borrowed from existing work on corecursive resolution. We will use the formulation of corecursive type class resolution given by Fu *et al.* [5]. This extends Howard's simply-typed λ-calculus [4,8] with a resolution rule and a ν-rule. The resulting calculus is general and accounts for all previously suggested kinds of type class resolution.

2   Preliminaries

This section describes our notation and defines the models that we will use in the rest of the paper. As is standard, a first-order signature Σ consists of the set $\mathcal{F}$ of function symbols and the set $\mathcal{P}$ of predicate symbols, all of which possess an *arity*. Constants are function symbols of arity 0. We also assume a countable set $\mathcal{V}$ of variables. Given Σ and $\mathcal{V}$, we have the following standard definitions:

Definition 1 (Syntax of Horn formuale and logic programs).

First-order term	$Term ::= \mathcal{V} \mid \mathcal{F}(Term, \ldots, Term)$
Horn formula (clause)	$CH ::= At, \ldots, At \Rightarrow At$
Atomic formula	$At ::= \mathcal{P}(Term, \ldots, Term)$
Logic program	$Prog ::= CH, \ldots, CH$

We use identifiers t and u to denote terms and A, B, C to denote atomic formulae. We use P with indicies to refer to elements of *Prog*. We say that a term or an atomic formula is *ground* if it contains no variables. We assume that all variables in Horn formulae are implicitly universally quantified. Moreover, restriction (ii) from Sect. 1 requires that there are no *existential variables*, *i.e.* given a clause $B_1, \ldots, B_n \Rightarrow A$, if a variable occurs in B_i, then it also occurs in A. We use the common term *formula* to refer to both atomic formulae and to Horn formulae. A *substitution* and the *application* of a substitution to a term or a formula are defined in the usual way. We denote application of a substitution σ to a term t or to an atomic formula A by σt and σA respectively. We denote composition of substitutions σ and τ by $\sigma \circ \tau$. A substitution σ is a *grounding* substitution for a term t if σt is a ground term, and similarly for an atomic formula.

2.1 Models of Logic Programs

Throughout this paper, we use the standard definitions of the least and greatest Herbrand models. Given a signature Σ, the *Herbrand universe* $\mathbf{U}_\Sigma$ is the set of all ground terms over Σ. Given a Herbrand universe $\mathbf{U}_\Sigma$ we define the *Herbrand base* $\mathbf{B}_\Sigma$ as the set of all atoms consisting only of ground terms in $\mathbf{U}_\Sigma$.

Definition 2 (Semantic operator). *Let P be a logic program over signature Σ. The mapping $\mathcal{T}_P : 2^{\mathbf{B}_\Sigma} \to 2^{\mathbf{B}_\Sigma}$ is defined as follows. Let I be a subset of $\mathbf{B}_\Sigma$.*

$$\mathcal{T}_P(I) = \{A \in \mathbf{B}_\Sigma \mid B_1, \ldots B_n \Rightarrow A \; is\,a\,ground\,instance\,of\,a\,clause\,in\,P,$$
$$and\ \{B_1, \ldots, B_n\} \subseteq I\}$$

The operator gives inductive and coinductive interpretation to a logic program.

Definition 3. *Let P be a logic program.*

- *The* least Herbrand model *is the least set $\mathcal{M}_P \in \mathbf{B}_\Sigma$ such that $\mathcal{M}_P$ is a fixed point of $\mathcal{T}_P$.*
- *The* greatest Herbrand model *is the greatest set $\mathcal{M}'_P \in \mathbf{B}_\Sigma$ such that $\mathcal{M}'_P$ is a fixed point of $\mathcal{T}_P$.*

Lloyd [12] introduces the operators $\downarrow$ and $\uparrow$ and proves that $\mathcal{T}_P \downarrow \omega$ gives the greatest Herbrand model of P, and that $\mathcal{T}_P \uparrow \omega$ gives the least Herbrand model of P. We will use these constructions in our own proofs. The validity of a formula in a model is defined as usual. An atomic formula is *valid* in a model I if and only if for any grounding substitution σ, we have $\sigma F \in I$. A Horn formula $B_1, \ldots, B_n \Rightarrow A$ is valid in I if for any substitution σ, if $\sigma B_1, \ldots, \sigma B_n$ are valid in I then σA is valid in I. We use the notation $P \vDash_{ind} F$ to denote that a formula F is valid in $\mathcal{M}_P$ and $P \vDash_{coind} F$ to denote that a formula F is valid in $\mathcal{M}'_P$.

Lemma 1. *Let P be a logic program and let σ be a substitution. The following holds:*

(a) If $(\Rightarrow A) \in P$ then both $P \vDash_{ind} \sigma A$ and $P \vDash_{coind} \sigma A$
(b) If, for all i, $P \vDash_{ind} \sigma B_i$ and $(B_1, \ldots, B_n \Rightarrow A) \in P$ then $P \vDash_{ind} \sigma A$
(c) If, for all i, $P \vDash_{coind} \sigma B_i$ and $(B_1, \ldots, B_n \Rightarrow A) \in P$ then $P \vDash_{coind} \sigma A$

The proof of the lemma can be found in the existing literature [12] and follows from the fact that both $\mathcal{M}_P$ and $\mathcal{M}'_P$ are fixed points of the operator $\mathcal{T}_P$.

2.2 Proof Relevant Resolution

In [5], the usual syntax of Horn formulae was embedded into a type-theoretic framework, with Horn formulae seen as types inhabited by proof terms. In this setting, a judgement has the form $\Phi \vdash e : F$, where e is a proof term inhabiting formula F, and Φ is an *axiom environment* containing annotated Horn formulae that correspond to the given logic program. This gives rise to the following syntax, in addition to that of Definition 1. We assume a set of proof term symbols K, and a set of proof term variables U.

Definition 4 (Syntax of proof terms and axiom environments).

$$Proof\ term \quad E ::= K \mid U \mid EE \mid \lambda U.E \mid \nu U.E$$
$$Axiom\ environment \quad Ax ::= \cdot \mid Ax, (E : CH)$$

We use the notation κ with indices to refer to elements of K, α and β with indices to refer to elements of U, e to refer to proof terms in E, and Φ to refer to axiom environments in Ax. Given a judgement $\Phi \vdash e : F$, we call F an *axiom* if $e \in K$, and we call F a *lemma* if $e \notin K$ is a closed term, *i.e.* it contains no free variables. A proof term e is in *guarded head normal form* (denoted gHNF(e)), if $e = \lambda \underline{\alpha}.\kappa \underline{e}$ where $\underline{\alpha}$ and $\underline{e}$ denote (possibly empty) sequences of variables $\alpha_1, \ldots, \alpha_n$ and proof terms $e_1 \ldots e_m$ respectively where n and m are known from the context or are unimportant. The intention of the above definition is to interpret logic programs, seen as sets of Horn formulae, as types. Example 1 shows how the proof term symbols κ_1 and κ_2 can be used to annotate clauses in the given logic program. We capture this intuition in the following formal definition:

Definition 5. *Given a logic program P_A consisting of Horn clauses $H_1, \ldots, H_n$, with each H_i having the shape $B_1^i, \ldots, B_k^i \Rightarrow A^i$, the axiom environment Φ_A is defined as follows. We assume proof term symbols $\kappa_1, \ldots, \kappa_n$, and define, for each H_i, $\kappa_i : B_1^i, \ldots, B_k^i \Rightarrow A^i$.*

Revisiting Example 1, we can say that it shows the result of translation of the program P_{Pair} into Φ_{Pair} and Φ_{Pair} is an axiom environment for the logic program P_{Pair}. In general, we say that Φ_A is an axiom environment for a logic program P_A if and only if there is a translation of P_A into Φ_A. We drop the index A where it is known or unimportant. Restriction (i) from Sect. 1 requires that axioms in an axiom environment do not overlap. However, a lemma may overlap with other axioms and lemmata—only axioms are subject to restriction (i). We refer the reader to [5] for complete exposition of proof-relevant resolution. In the following sections, we will use this syntax to gradually introduce inference rules for proof-relevant corecursive resolution. We start with its "inductive" fragment, *i.e.* the fragment that is sound relative to the least Herbrand models, and then in subsequent sections consider its two coinductive extensions (which are both sound with respect to the greatest Herbrand models).

3   Inductive Soundness of Type Class Resolution

This section describes the inductive fragment of the calculus for the extended type class resolution that was introduced by Fu *et al.* [5]. We reconstruct the standard theorem of universal inductive soundness for the resolution rule. We consider an extended version of type class resolution, working with queries given by Horn formulae, rather than just atomic formulae. We show that the resulting proof system is inductively sound, but coinductively unsound; we also show that it is incomplete. Based on these results, we discuss the program transformation methods that can arise.

Definition 6 (Type class resolution).

$$if(e : B_1, \ldots, B_n \Rightarrow A) \in \Phi \frac{\Phi \vdash e_1 : \sigma B_1 \quad \cdots \quad \Phi \vdash e_n : \sigma B_n}{\Phi \vdash ee_1 \cdots e_n : \sigma A} \qquad \text{(LP-M)}$$

If, for a given atomic formula A, and a given environment Φ, $\Phi \vdash e : A$ is derived using the LP-M rule we say that A is entailed by Φ and that the proof term e witnesses this entailment. We define derivations and derivation trees resulting from applications of the above rule in the standard way (*cf.* Fu *et al.* [5]).

Example 4. Recall the logic program P_{Pair} in Example 1. The inference steps for eq(pair(int, int)) correspond to the following derivation tree:

$$\frac{\Phi_{Pair} \vdash \kappa_2 : \text{eq(int)} \qquad \Phi_{Pair} \vdash \kappa_2 : \text{eq(int)}}{\Phi_{Pair} \vdash \kappa_1 \kappa_2 \kappa_2 : \text{eq(pair(int, int))}}$$

The above entailment is inductively sound, *i.e.* it is sound with respect to the least Herbrand model of P_{Pair}:

Theorem 1. *Let Φ be an axiom environment for a logic program P, and let $\Phi \vdash e : A$ hold. Then $P \vDash_{ind} A$.*

Proof. By structural induction on the derivation tree and construction of the least Herbrand model, using Lemma 1.   □

The rule LP-M also plays a crucial role in the coinductive fragment of type class resolution, as will be discussed in Sects. 4 and 5. We now discuss the other rule that is present in the work of Fu *et al.* [5], i.e. the rule that allows us to prove Horn formulae:

Definition 7.

$$\frac{\Phi, (\beta_1 : \Rightarrow B_1), \ldots, (\beta_n : \Rightarrow B_n) \vdash e : A}{\Phi \vdash \lambda \beta_1, \ldots, \beta_n.e : B_1, \ldots, B_n \Rightarrow A} \qquad \text{(LAM)}$$

Example 5. To illustrate the use of the LAM rule, consider the following program: Let P consist of two clauses: $A \Rightarrow B$ and $B \Rightarrow C$. Both the least and the greatest Herbrand model of P are empty. Equally, no formulae can be derived from the corresponding axiom environment by the LP-M rule. However, we can derive $A \Rightarrow C$ by using a combination of the LAM and LP-M rules. Let $\Phi = (\kappa_1 : A \Rightarrow B), (\kappa_2 : B \Rightarrow C)$. The following is then a derivation tree for a formula $A \Rightarrow C$:

$$\cfrac{\cfrac{\cfrac{\Phi, (\alpha : \Rightarrow A) \vdash \alpha : A}{\Phi, (\alpha : \Rightarrow A) \vdash \kappa_1 \alpha : B}}{\Phi, (\alpha : \Rightarrow A) \vdash \kappa_2(\kappa_1 \alpha) : C}}{\Phi \vdash \lambda\alpha.\kappa_2(\kappa_1 \alpha) : A \Rightarrow C} \text{ LAM}$$

When there is no label on the right-hand side of an inference step, inference uses the LP-M rule. We follow this convention throughout the paper.

We can show that the calculus comprising the rules LP-M and LAM is again (universally) inductively sound.

Lemma 2. *Let P be a logic program and let $A, B_1, \ldots, B_n$ be atomic formulae. If $P, (\Rightarrow B_1), \ldots, (\Rightarrow B_n) \vDash_{ind} A$ then $P \vDash_{ind} B_1, \ldots, B_n \Rightarrow A$.*

Proof. By induction on construction of $\mathcal{M}_P$. □

Theorem 2. *Let Φ be an axiom environment for a logic program P and F a formula. Let $\Phi \vdash e : F$ be by the LP-M and LAM rules. Then $P \vDash_{ind} F$.*

Proof. By structural induction on the derivation tree using Lemmas 1 and 2. □

Inductive Completeness and Incompleteness of the Proof System LP-M + LAM. In principle, one can consider two different variants. Extending the standard results of [12], our first formulation is:

Inductive Completeness-1: *if a ground atomic formula F is in $\mathcal{M}_P$, then $\Phi_P \vdash e : F$ is in the LP-M + LAM proof system.*

Such a result can be proved, as in [12], by straightforward induction on the construction of $\mathcal{M}_P$. Such a proof will be based solely on the properties of the rule LP-M and on the properties of the semantic operator $\mathcal{T}_P$ that is used to construct the least Herbrand models. An alternative formulation of the completeness result, this time involving implicative formulae and hence the rule LAM in the proof, would be:

Inductive Completeness-2: *if $\mathcal{M}_P \vDash_{ind} F$ then $\Phi_P \vdash e : F$ is in the LP-M + LAM proof system.*

However, this result would not hold for either system LP-M or LP-M + LAM. Consider the following examples.

Example 6. Let Σ be a signature consisting of a unary predicate symbol A, a unary function symbol f and a constant function symbol g. Let P_6 be a program given by the following axiom environment:

$$\kappa_1 : \Rightarrow A(f(x))$$
$$\kappa_2 : \Rightarrow A(g)$$

The least Herbrand model of P_6 is $\mathcal{M}_{P_6} = \{A(g), A(f(g)), A(f(f(g))), \ldots\}$. Therefore, $P \vDash_{ind} A(x)$. However, neither κ_1 nor κ_2 matches $A(x)$ and there is thus no way to construct a proof term e satisfying:

$$\frac{\cdots}{P \vdash e : A(x)}\text{Lp-m}$$

We demonstrate the incompleteness of the proof system Lp-m + Lam through the following example:

Example 7. Let Σ be a signature consisting of the unary predicate symbols A and B, and a constant function symbol f. Consider a program P_7 given by the following axiom environment:

$$\kappa_1 : \Rightarrow A(f)$$
$$\kappa_2 : \Rightarrow B(f)$$

The least Herbrand model is $\mathcal{M}_{P_7} = \{A(f), B(f)\}$. Therefore $P \vDash_{ind} B(x) \Rightarrow A(x)$. However, any proof of $B(x) \Rightarrow A(x)$ needs to show that:

$$\frac{\cdots}{\frac{(P, \alpha : \Rightarrow B(x)) \vdash e : A(x)}{P \vdash \lambda\alpha.e : B(x) \Rightarrow A(x)}}\text{Lam}$$

where e is a proof term. This proof will not succeed since no axiom or hypothesis matches $A(x)$.

Related Program Transformation Methods. For Fu *et al.* [5], the main purpose of introducing the rule Lam was to increase expressivity of the proof system. In particular, obtaining an entailment $\Phi \vdash e : H$ of a Horn formula H enabled the environment Φ to be extended with $e : H$, which could be used in future proofs. We show that transforming (the standard, untyped) logic programs in this way is inductively sound. The following theorem follows from Lemma 2:

Theorem 3. *Let Φ be an axiom environment for a logic program P, and let $\Phi \vdash e : F$ for a formula F by the Lp-m and Lam rules. Given a formula F', $P \vDash_{ind} F'$ iff $P, F \vDash_{ind} F'$.*

Note, however, that the above theorem is not as trivial as it looks, in particular, it would not hold coinductively, *i.e.* if we changed $\vDash_{ind}$ to $\vDash_{coind}$ in the statement above. Consider the following proof of the formula $A \Rightarrow A$:

Example 8. Using the LAM rule, one can prove $\emptyset \vdash \lambda\alpha.\alpha : A \Rightarrow A$:

$$\frac{(\alpha : \Rightarrow A) \vdash \alpha : A}{\emptyset \vdash \lambda\alpha.\alpha : A \Rightarrow A} \text{ LAM}$$

Assume a program consisting of a single formula $A \Rightarrow B$. Both the least and the greatest Herbrand model of this program are empty. However, adding the formula $A \Rightarrow A$ to the program results in the greatest Herbrand model $\{A, B\}$. Thus, $\mathcal{M}'_P \neq \mathcal{M}'_{P,(A\Rightarrow A)}$.

4 Coinductive Soundness of Corecursive Type Class Resolution

The LP-M rule may result in non-terminating resolution. This can be demonstrated by the program $P_{EvenOdd}$ and the query ? eq(evenList(Int)) from Sect. 1. Lämmel and Peyton Jones observed [11] that in such cases there may be a cycle in the inference that can be detected. This treatment of cycles amounts to coinductive reasoning and results in building a corecursive proof witness—*i.e.* a *(co-)recursive dictionary*.

Definition 8 (Coinductive type class resolution).

$$if \ gHNF(e)\frac{\Phi,(\alpha: \Rightarrow A) \vdash e : A}{\Phi \vdash \nu\alpha.e : A} \qquad (\text{Nu'})$$

The side condition of Nu' requires the proof witness to be in guarded head normal form. Since, in this section, we are working with a calculus consisting of the rules LP-M and Nu, there is no way to introduce a λ-abstraction into a proof witness. Therefore, in this section, we restrict ourselves to guarded head normal form terms of the form $\kappa \ \underline{e}$.

Example 9. Recall the program $P_{EvenOdd}$ in Example 2. The originally non-terminating resolution trace for the query ? eq(evenList(int)) is resolved using the Nu' rule as follows:

$$\frac{\dfrac{\kappa_3 : \text{eq(int)}}{\vdash \kappa_3 : \text{eq(int)}} \quad \dfrac{\dfrac{\kappa_3 : \text{eq(int)}}{\vdash \kappa_3 : \text{eq(int)}} \quad \dfrac{\alpha: \ \Rightarrow \text{eq(evenList(int))}}{\vdash \alpha : \text{eq(evenList(int))}}}{\dfrac{\Phi_{EvenOdd}, \alpha : \_ \vdash \kappa_1\kappa_3\alpha : \text{eq(oddList(int))}}{\Phi_{EvenOdd}, \alpha : \_ \vdash \kappa_2\kappa_3(\kappa_1\kappa_3\alpha) : \text{eq(evenList(int))}}}}{\Phi_{EvenOdd} \vdash \nu\alpha.\kappa_2\kappa_3(\kappa_1\kappa_3\alpha) : \text{eq(evenList(int))}} \text{ Nu'}$$

Note that we abbreviate repeated formulae in the environment using an underscore. We will use this notation in the rest of the paper.

We can now discuss the coinductive soundness of the Nu' rule, *i.e.* its soundness relative to the greatest Herbrand models. We note that, not surprisingly (*cf.* [13]), the Nu' rule is inductively unsound. Given a program consisting of just one clause: $\kappa : A \Rightarrow A$, we are able to use the rule Nu' to entail A (the derivation of this will be similar to, albeit a lot simpler than, that in the above example). However, A is not in the least Herbrand model of this program. Similarly, the formula eq(oddList(int)) that was proved above is also not inductively sound. Thus, the coinductive fragment of the extended corecursive resolution is only coinductively sound. When proving the coinductive soundness of the Nu' rule, we must carefully choose the proof method by which we proceed. Inductive soundness of the LP-M rule was proven by induction on the derivation tree and through the construction of the least Herbrand models by iterations of $\mathcal{T}_P$. Here, we give an analogous result, where coinductive soundness is proved by structural coinduction on the iterations of the semantic operator $\mathcal{T}_P$.

In order for the principle of structural coinduction to be applicable in our proof, we must ensure that the construction of the greatest Herbrand model is completed within ω steps of iteration of $\mathcal{T}_P$. This does not hold in general for the greatest Herbrand model construction, as was shown e.g. in [12]. However, it does hold for the restricted shape of Horn clauses we are working with. It was noticed by Lloyd [12] that Restriction (ii) from Sect. 1 implies that the $\mathcal{T}_P$ operator converges in at most ω steps. We will capitalise on this fact. The essence of the coinductive soundness of Nu' is captured by the following lemma:

Lemma 3. *Let P be a logic program, let σ be a substitution, and let A, B_1, ..., B_n be atomic formulae. If, $\forall i \in \{1,\dots,n\}$, $P,(\Rightarrow \sigma A) \vDash_{coind} \sigma B_i$ and $(B_1,\dots,B_n \Rightarrow A) \in P$ then $P \vDash_{coind} \sigma A$.*

The proof of the lemma is similar to the proof of the Lemma 4 in the next section and we do not state it here. Finally, Theorem 4 states universal coinductive soundness of the coinductive type class resolution:

Theorem 4. *Let Φ be an axiom environment for a logic program P and F a formula. Let $\Phi \vdash e : F$ be by the LP-M and Nu' rules. Then $\Phi \vDash_{coind} F$.*

Proof. By structural induction on the derivation tree using Lemmas 1 and 3. □

Choice of Coinductive Models. Perhaps the most unusual feature of the semantics given in this section is the use of the greatest Herbrand models rather than the greatest *complete* Herbrand models. The latter is more common in the literature on coinduction in logic programming [10,12,14]. *The greatest complete Herbrand models* are obtained as the greatest fixed point of the semantic operator $\mathcal{T}_P'$ on the *complete Herbrand base*, *i.e.* the set of all finite and *infinite* ground atomic formulae formed by the signature of the given program. This construction is preferred in the literature for two reasons. Firstly, $\mathcal{T}_P'$ reaches its greatest fixed point in at most ω steps, whereas $\mathcal{T}_P$ may take more than ω steps in the general case. This is due to compactness of the complete Herbrand base. Moreover, greatest complete Herbrand models give a more natural characterisation for programs like the one given by the clause $\kappa_{inf} : \mathtt{p}(x) \Rightarrow \mathtt{p}(\mathtt{f}(x))$. The greatest Herbrand model of that program is empty. However, its greatest complete Herbrand model contains the infinite formula $p(f(f(...)))$. Restrictions (i)–(iii), imposed by type class resolution, mean that the greatest Herbrand models regain those same advantages as complete Herbrand models. It was noticed by Lloyd [12] that restriction (ii) implies that the semantic operator converges in at most ω steps. Restrictions (i) and (iii) imply that proofs by type class resolution have a universal interpretation, *i.e.* that they hold for all finite instances of queries. Therefore, we never need to talk about programs for which only one infinite instance of a query is valid.

5   Coinductive Soundness of Extended Corecursive Type Class Resolution

The class of problems that can be resolved by coinductive type class resolution is limited to problems where a coinductive hypothesis is in atomic form. Fu *et al.* [5] extended coinductive type class resolution with implicative reasoning and adjusted the rule Nu' such that this restriction of coinductive type class resolution is relaxed:

Definition 9 (Extended coinductive type class resolution).

$$if\ gHNF(e)\frac{\Phi,(\alpha:B_1,\ldots,B_n\Rightarrow A)\vdash e:B_1,\ldots,B_n\Rightarrow A}{\Phi\vdash \nu\alpha.e:B_1,\ldots,B_n\Rightarrow A}\qquad\text{(Nu)}$$

The side condition of the Nu rule requires the proof witness to be in guarded head normal form. However, unlike coinductive type class resolution, extended coinductive type class resolution also uses the Lam rule and a guarded head normal term is of the more general form $\lambda\underline{\alpha}.\kappa\underline{e}$ for a possibly non-empty sequence of proof term variables $\underline{\alpha}$. First, let us note that extended coinductive type class resolution indeed extends the calculus of Sect. 4:

Proposition 1. *The inference rule* Nu' *is admissible in the extended coinductive type class resolution.*

Furthermore, this is a proper extension. The Nu' rule allows queries to be entailed that were beyond the scope of coinductive type class resolution. In Sect. 1, we demonstrated a derivation for query ? $eq(bush(int))$ where no cycles arise and thus the query cannot be resolved by coinductive type class resolution.

Example 10. Recall the program P_{Bush} we defined in the Example 3. The query ? $eq(bush(int))$ is resolved as follows:

$$\cfrac{\Phi_{Bush}\vdash}{\kappa_1:eq(int)}\quad\cfrac{\cfrac{\cfrac{(\beta:\ \Rightarrow eq(x))}{\vdash\beta:eq(x)}\quad\cfrac{\cfrac{\cfrac{(\beta:\ \Rightarrow eq(x))\vdash\beta:eq(x)}{(\alpha:eq(x)\Rightarrow eq(bush(x))),(\beta:\_)\vdash}{\alpha\beta:eq(bush(x))}}{(\alpha:\_),(\beta:\_)\vdash\alpha(\alpha\beta):eq(bush(bush(x)))}}{\Phi_{Bush},(\alpha:\_),(\beta:\_)\vdash\kappa_2\beta(\alpha(\alpha\beta)):eq(bush(x))}}{\cfrac{\Phi_{Bush},(\alpha:\_)\vdash\lambda\beta.\kappa_2\beta(\alpha(\alpha\beta)):eq(x)\Rightarrow eq(bush(x))}{\Phi_{Bush}\vdash\nu\alpha.\lambda\beta.\kappa_2\beta(\alpha(\alpha\beta)):eq(x)\Rightarrow eq(bush(x))}}\ \text{Lam}\ \text{Nu}}{\Phi_{Bush}\vdash(\nu\alpha.\lambda\beta.\kappa_2\beta(\alpha(\alpha\beta)))\kappa_1:eq(bush(int))}$$

Before proceeding with the proof of soundness of extended type class resolution we need to show two intermediate lemmata. The first lemma states that inference by the NU' rule preserves coinductive soundness:

Lemma 4. *Let P be a logic program, let σ be a substitution, and let A, $B_1,\ldots$, B_n, C_1, ..., C_m be atomic formulae. If, for all i, $P, B_1, \ldots, B_n, (B_1, \ldots, B_n \Rightarrow \sigma A) \vDash_{coind} \sigma C_i$ and $(C_1, \ldots, C_m \Rightarrow A) \in P$ then $P \vDash_{coind} B_1 \ldots B_n \Rightarrow \sigma A$.*

Proof. Consider the construction of the greatest Herbrand model of the program P and proceed by coinduction with coinductive hypothesis: for all n, $B_1, \ldots, B_n => \sigma A$ is valid in $T_P \downarrow n$. Assume that, for a grounding substitution τ, for all i, $\tau B_i \in T_P \downarrow n$. Then also $(\tau \circ \sigma)A \in T_P \downarrow n$. For the definition of the semantic operator, it follows from the monotonicity of the operator itself, and from the assumptions made by the lemma that $(\tau \circ \sigma)C_i \in T_P \downarrow n$. Since $C_1, \ldots, C_n => A \in P$ also $(\tau \circ \sigma)A \in T_P \downarrow (n+1)$. If the assumption does not hold then from the monotonicity of T_P it follows that, for all i, $\tau B_i \notin T_P \downarrow (n+1)$. Therefore, $B_1, \ldots, B_n => \sigma A$ is valid in $T_P \downarrow (n+1)$. We apply the coinductive hypothesis to conclude that the same holds for all subsequent iterations of T_P. Hence whenever, for a substitution τ, all instances of τB_1 to τB_n are in the greatest Herbrand model then also all instances of $(\tau \circ \sigma)A$ are in the greatest Herbrand model. Hence $P \vDash_{coind} B_1, \ldots, B_n \Rightarrow \sigma A$.   □

The other lemma that we need in order to prove coinductive soundness of extended type class resolution states that inference using LAM preserves coinductive soundness, *i.e.* we need to show the coinductive counterpart to Lemma 2:

Lemma 5. *Let P be a logic program and A, B_1, ..., B_n atomic formulae. If $P, (\Rightarrow B_1), \ldots (\Rightarrow B_n) \vDash_{coind} A$ then $P \vDash_{coind} B_1, \ldots, B_n \Rightarrow A$.*

Now, the universal coinductive soundness of extended coinductive type class resolution follows straightforwardly:

Theorem 5. *Let Φ be an axiom environment for a logic program P, and let be $\Phi \vdash e : F$ for a formula F by the LP-M, LAM, and NU' rules. Then $P \vDash_{coind} F$.*

Proof. By induction on the derivation tree using Lemmas 1, 4, and 5.   □

Coinductive Incompleteness of the Proof System LP-M + LAM + NU.

In Sect. 3, we considered two ways of stating inductive completeness of type class resolution. We state the corresponding result for the coinductive case here. As both the notions of completeness are shown not to hold we discuss them in the reversed order than the inductive completeness, first the more general case and then the more restricted one:

Coinductive Completeness-2: *if $\mathcal{M}'_P \vDash_{coind} F$ then $\Phi_P \vdash e : F$ in the LP-M + LAM + NU proof system.*

Recall Examples 6 and 7, and the programs P_6 and P_7. We demonstrated that, in general, there are formulae that are valid in $\mathcal{M}_P$ but do not have a proof in P. The same two examples will serve our purpose here. For example, the greatest Herbrand model of the program P_6 is $\mathcal{M}'_P = \mathcal{M}_P = \{A(g), A(f(g)), A(f(f(g))), \dots\}$. Therefore, for an atomic formula $A(x)$, $P \vDash_{coind} A(x)$. However, it is impossible to construct a proof:

$$\frac{\dots}{P \vdash e : A(x)}\text{Lp-m}$$

The rules Lp-m and Lam are not applicable for the same reasons as in the inductive case and the rule Nu' is not applicable since $A(x)$ is not a Horn formula.

Moreover, a more restricted formulation in the traditional style of Lloyd [12] does not improve the situation:

Coinductive Completeness-1: *if a ground atomic formula F is in $\mathcal{M}'_P$, then* $\Phi_P \vdash e : F$ *in the* Lp-m $+$ Lam $+$ Nu *proof system.* Such a result does not hold, since there exist coinductive logic programs that define corecursive schemes that cannot be captured in this proof system. Consider the following example [5]:

Example 11. Let Σ be a signature with a binary predicate symbol D, a unary function symbol s and a constant function symbol z. Consider a program P_{11} with the signature Σ given by the following axiom environment:

$$\kappa_1 : \quad D(x, s(y)) \Rightarrow D(s(x), y)$$
$$\kappa_2 : \quad D(s(x), z) \Rightarrow D(z, x)$$

Let us denote a term $s(s(\dots s(x) \dots))$ where the symbol s is applied i-times as $s^i(x)$. By observing the construction of $\mathcal{M}'_P$ we can see that, for all i, if $D(z, s^i(x))$ then $D(s^i(x), z) \in \mathcal{M}'_P$ and also $D(z, s^{i-1}(x)) \in \mathcal{M}'_P$. Therefore $D(z, z) \in \mathcal{M}'_P$. However, there is no proof of $D(z, z)$ since any number of proof steps resulting from the use of Lp-m generates yet another ground premise that is different from all previous premises. Consequently, the proof cannot be closed by Nu'. Also, no lemma that would allow for a proof can be formulated; an example of such a lemma would be the above $D(z, s^i(x)) \Rightarrow D(z, s^{i-1}(x))$. This is a higher order formula and cannot be expressed in a first order Horn clause logic.

Related Program Transformation Methods. We conclude this section with a discussion of program transformation with Horn formulae that are entailed by the rules Lam and Nu. From the fact that the Nu rule is inductively unsound, it is clear that using program transformation techniques based on the lemmata that were proved by the Lam and Nu rules would also be inductively unsound.

However, a more interesting result is that adding such program clauses will not change the coinductive soundness of the initial program:

Theorem 6. *Let Φ be an axiom environment for a logic program P, and let $\Phi \vdash e : F$ for a formula F by the* Lp-m, Lam *and* Nu' *rules such that* $\mathrm{gHNF}(e)$. *Given a formula F', $P \vDash_{coind} F'$ iff $(P, F) \vDash_{coind} F'$.*

The above result is possible thanks to the guarded head normal form condition, since it is then impossible to use a clause $A \Rightarrow A$ that was derived from an empty context by the rule LAM. It is also impossible to make such a derivation within the proof term e itself and to then derive A by the NU' rule from $A \Rightarrow A$. The resulting proof term will fail to satisfy the guarded head normal form condition that is required by NU'. Since this condition guards against any such cases, we can be sure that this program transformation method is coinductively sound and hence that it is safe to use with any coinductive dialect of logic programming, e.g. with CoLP [14].

6   Related Work

The standard approach to type inference for type classes, corresponding to type class resolution as studied in this paper, was described by Stuckey and Sulzman [15]. Type class resolution was further studied by Lämmel and Peyton Jones [11], who described what we here call *coinductive type class resolution*. The description of the extended calculus of Sect. 5 was first presented by Fu *et al.* [5]. Generally, there is a body of work that focuses on allowing for infinite data structures in logic programming. Logic programming with rational trees [1,9] was studied from both an operational semantics and a declarative semantics point of view. Simon *et al.* [14] introduced *co-logic programming* (co-LP) that also allows for terms that are rational infinite trees and hence that have infinite proofs. Corecursive resolution, as studied in this paper, is more expressive than co-LP: while also allowing infinite proofs, and closing of coinductive hypotheses is less constrained in our approach.

7   Conclusions and Future Work

In this paper, we have addressed three research questions. First, we provided a uniform analysis of type class resolution in both inductive and coinductive settings and proved its soundness relative to (standard) least and greatest Herbrand models. Secondly, we demonstrated, through several examples, that coinductive resolution is indeed coinductive—that is, it is not sound relative to least Herbrand models. Finally, we addressed the question of whether the methods listed in this paper can be reapplied to coinductive dialects of logic programming *via* soundness preserving program transformations.

As future work, we intend to extend our analysis of Horn-clause resolution to Horn clauses with existential variables and existentially quantified goals. We believe that such resolution accounts to type inference for other language constructs than type classes, namely type families and algebraic data types.

Acknowledgements. This work has been supported by the EPSRC grant "Coalgebraic Logic Programming for Type Inference" EP/K031864/1-2, EU Horizon 2020 grant "RePhrase: Refactoring Parallel Heterogeneous Resource-Aware Applications - a Software Engineering Approach" (ICT-644235), and by COST Action IC1202 (TACLe), supported by COST (European Cooperation in Science and Technology).

References

1. Colmerauer, A.: Equations and inequations on finite and infinite trees. In: FGCS, pp. 85–99 (1984)
2. De Angelis, E., Fioravanti, F., Pettorossi, A., Proietti, M.: Proving correctness of imperative programs by linearizing constrained horn clauses. TPLP **15**(4–5), 635–650 (2015)
3. Devriese, D., Piessens, F.: On the bright side of type classes: instance arguments in Agda. In: Proceedings of ICFP 2011, Tokyo, 19–21 September 2011, pp. 143–155 (2011)
4. Fu, P., Komendantskaya, E.: Operational semantics of resolution and productivity in Horn clause logic. Form. Asp. Comput. **29**, 453–474 (2017). doi:10.1007/s00165-016-0403-1
5. Fu, P., Komendantskaya, E., Schrijvers, T., Pond, A.: Proof relevant corecursive resolution. In: Kiselyov, O., King, A. (eds.) FLOPS 2016. LNCS, vol. 9613, pp. 126–143. Springer, Cham (2016). doi:10.1007/978-3-319-29604-3_9
6. Gonthier, G., Ziliani, B., Nanevski, A., Dreyer, D.: How to make ad hoc proof automation less ad hoc. In: Proceedings of ICFP 2011, Tokyo, 19–21 September 2011, pp. 163–175 (2011)
7. Hall, C.V., Hammond, K., Jones, S.L.P., Wadler, P.: Type classes in Haskell. ACM Trans. Program. Lang. Syst. **18**(2), 109–138 (1996)
8. Howard, W.: The formulae-as-types notion of construction. In: Seldin, J.P., Hindley, J.R. (eds.) To H.B. Curry: Essays on Combinatory Logic, Lambda-Calculus, and Formalism, pp. 479–490. Academic Press, New York (1980)
9. Jaffar, J., Stuckey, P.J.: Semantics of infinite tree logic programming. Theor. Comput. Sci. **46**(3), 141–158 (1986)
10. Komendantskaya, E., Li T.: Productive corecursion in logic programming. In: Proceedings of ICLP 2017. TPLP (to appear, 2017)
11. Lämmel, R., Peyton Jones, S.L.: Scrap your boilerplate with class: extensible generic functions. In: Proceedings of ICFP 2005, Tallinn, 26–28 September 2005, pp. 204–215 (2005)
12. Lloyd, J.W.: Foundations of Logic Programming, 2nd edn. Springer, Heidelberg (1987)
13. Sangiorgi, D.: On the origins of bisimulation and coinduction. ACM Trans. Program. Lang. Syst. **31**(4), 15:1–15:41 (2009)
14. Simon, L., Bansal, A., Mallya, A., Gupta, G.: Co-logic programming: extending logic programming with coinduction. In: Arge, L., Cachin, C., Jurdziński, T., Tarlecki, A. (eds.) ICALP 2007. LNCS, vol. 4596, pp. 472–483. Springer, Heidelberg (2007). doi:10.1007/978-3-540-73420-8_42
15. Stuckey, P.J., Sulzmann, M.: A theory of overloading. ACM Trans. Program. Lang. Syst. **27**(6), 1216–1269 (2005)
16. Wadler, P., Blott, S.: How to make ad-hoc polymorphism less ad hoc. In: Proceedings of POPL 1989, pp. 60–76. ACM, New York (1989)

Nominal Unification of Higher Order Expressions with Recursive Let

Manfred Schmidt-Schauß[1]([⊠]), Temur Kutsia[2], Jordi Levy[3],
and Mateu Villaret[4]

[1] GU Frankfurt, Frankfurt, Germany
schauss@ki.cs.uni-frankfurt.de
[2] RISC, JKU Linz, Linz, Austria
kutsia@risc.jku.at
[3] IIIA - CSIC, Barcelona, Spain
levy@iiia.scic.es
[4] IMA, Universitat de Girona, Girona, Spain
villaret@ima.udg.edu

Abstract. A sound and complete algorithm for nominal unification of higher-order expressions with a recursive let is described, and shown to run in non-deterministic polynomial time. We also explore specializations like nominal letrec-matching for plain expressions and for DAGs and determine their complexity.

Keywords: Nominal unification · Lambda calculus · Higher-order expressions · Recursive let · Operational semantics

1   Introduction

Unification [7] is an operation to make two logical expressions equal by finding substitutions into variables. There are numerous applications in computer science, in particular of (efficient) first-order unification, for example in automated reasoning, type checking and verification. Unification algorithms are also extended to higher-order calculi with various equivalence relations. If equality includes α-conversion and β-reduction and perhaps also η-conversion of a (typed or untyped) lambda-calculus, then unification procedures are known (see e.g. [18]), however, the problem is undecidable [17,20].

Our motivation comes from syntactical reasoning on higher-order expressions, with equality being alpha-equivalence of expressions, and where a unification algorithm is demanded as a basic service. Nominal unification is the extension of first-order unification with abstractions. It unifies expressions w.r.t. alpha-equivalence, and employs permutations as a clean treatment of renamings.

This research has been partially founded by the MINECO/FEDER projects RASO (TIN2015-71799-C2-1-P) and LoCoS (TIN2015-66293-R) and the UdG project MPCUdG2016/055.

M.V. Hermenegildo and P. Lopez-Garcia (Eds.): LOPSTR 2016, LNCS 10184, pp. 328–344, 2017.
DOI: 10.1007/978-3-319-63139-4_19

It is known that nominal unification is decidable [35,36], where the complexity of the decision problem is polynomial time [9]. It can be seen also from a higher-order perspective [12,22], as equivalent to Miller's higher-order pattern unification [26]. There are efficient algorithms [9,21], formalizations of nominal unification [6], formalizations with extensions to commutation properties within expressions [4], and generalizations of nominal unification to narrowing [5]. Equivariant (nominal) unification [1,10,11,14] extends nominal unification by permutation-variables, but it can also be seen as a generalization of nominal unification by permitting abstract names for variables.

We are interested in unification w.r.t. an additional extension with cyclic let. To the best of our knowledge, there is no nominal unification algorithm for higher-order expressions permitting general binding structures like a cyclic let.

The motivation and intended application scenario is as follows: constructing syntactic reasoning algorithms for showing properties of program transformations on higher-order expressions in call-by-need functional languages (see for example [27,31]) that have a letrec-construct (also called cyclic let) [3] as in Haskell [24], (see e.g. [13] for a discussion on reasoning with more general name binders, and [34] for a formalization of general binders in Isabelle). There may be applications also to coinductive extensions of logic programming [33] and strict functional languages [19]. Basically, overlaps of expressions have to be computed (a variant of critical pairs) and reduction steps (under some strategy) have to be performed. To this end, first an expressive higher-order language is required to represent the meta-notation of expressions. For example, the meta-notation $((\lambda x.e_1)\ e_2)$ for a beta-reduction is made operational by using unification variables X_1, X_2 for e_1, e_2. The scoping of X_1 and X_2 is different, which can be dealt with by nominal techniques. In fact, a more powerful unification algorithm is required for meta-terms employing recursive letrec-environments.

Our main algorithm LETRECUNIFY is derived from first-order unification and nominal unification: From first-order unification we borrowed the decomposition rules, and the sharing method from Martelli-Montanari-style unification algorithms [25]. The adaptations of decomposition for abstractions and the advantageous use of permutations of atoms is derived from nominal unification algorithms. Decomposing letrec-expression requires an extension by a permutation of the bindings in the environment, where, however, one has to take care of scoping. Since in contrast to the basic nominal unification, there are nontrivial fixpoints of permutations (see Example 2.2), novel techniques are required and lead to a surprisingly moderate complexity: a fixed-point shifting rule (FPS) and a redundancy removing rule (ElimFP) together bound the number of fixpoint equations $X \doteq \pi{\cdot}X$ (where π is a permutation) using techniques and results from computations in permutation groups. The application of these techniques is indispensable (see Example 3.6) for obtaining efficiency.

Results: The nominal letrec unification algorithm LETRECUNIFY is complete and runs in nondeterministic polynomial time (Theorems 4.1, 4.3). The nominal letrec matching is NP-complete (Theorems 5.2, 6.1), as well as the nominal unification problem (Theorems 4.3, 6.1).

Nominal letrec matching for dags is in NP and outputs substitutions only (Theorem 5.4), and a very restricted nominal letrec matching problem is graph-isomorphism hard (Theorem 6.3). Nominal matching including letrec-environment variables is in NP (Theorem 7.4).

2   The Ground Language of Expressions

The very first idea of nominal techniques [35] is to use concrete variable names in lambda-calculi (also in extensions), in order to avoid implicit α-renamings, and instead uses operations for explicitly applying α-renaming operations. Suppose $s = \lambda xx.xx$ and $t = \lambda yy.yy$ are concrete (syntactically different) lambda-expressions. The nominal technique provides explicit name-changes using permutations. These permutations are applied irrespective of binders. For example $(xx\ yy)(\lambda xx.\lambda xx.a)$ results in $\lambda yy.\lambda yy.a$. Syntactic reasoning on higher-order expressions, for example unification of higher-order expressions modulo α-equivalence will be done by nominal techniques on a language with concrete names, where the algorithms require certain extra constraints and operations. The gain is that all conditions and substitutions etc. can be computed and thus more reasoning tasks can be automated, whereas the implicit name conditions under implicit α-equivalence has a tendency to complicate (unification-) algorithms and to hide the required conditions on equality/disequality/occurrence/non-occurrence of names.

2.1   Preliminaries

We define the language LRL (**LetRec Language**) of (ground-)expressions, which is a lambda calculus extended with a recursive let construct. The notation is consistent with [35]. The (infinite) set of atoms $\mathbb{A}$ is a set of (concrete) symbols a, b which we usually denote in a meta-fashion; so we can use symbols a, b also with indices (the variables in lambda-calculus). There is a set $\mathcal{F}$ of function symbols with arity $ar(\cdot)$. The syntax of the expressions e of LRL is:

$$e ::= a \mid \lambda a.e \mid (f\ e_1\ \dots\ e_{ar(f)}) \mid (\texttt{letrec}\ a_1.e_1; \dots; a_n.e_n\ \texttt{in}\ e)$$

We also use tuples, which are written as $(e_1, \dots, e_n)$, and which are treated as functional expressions in the language. We assume that binding atoms $a_1, \dots, a_n$ in a letrec-expression ($\texttt{letrec}\ a_1.e_1; \dots; a_n.e_n\ \texttt{in}\ e$) are pairwise distinct. Sequences of bindings $a_1.e_1; \dots; a_n.e_n$ are abbreviated as env.

The *scope* of atom a in $\lambda a.e$ is standard: a has scope e. The $\texttt{letrec}$-construct has a special scoping rule: in ($\texttt{letrec}\ a_1.s_1; \dots; a_n.s_n\ \texttt{in}\ r$), every free atom a_i in some s_j or r is bound by the environment $a_1.s_1; \dots; a_n.s_n$. This defines the notion of free atoms $FA(e)$, bound atoms $BA(e)$ in expression e, and all atoms $AT(e)$ in e. For an environment $env = \{a_1.e_1, \dots, a_n.e_n\}$, we define the set of letrec-atoms as $LA(env) = \{a_1, \dots, a_n\}$. We say a *is fresh for* e iff $a \notin FA(e)$ (also denoted as $a\#e$). As an example, the expression ($\texttt{letrec}\ f = cons\ s_1\ g; g = cons\ s_2\ f\ \texttt{in}\ f$)

represents an infinite list $(cons\ s_1\ (cons\ s_2\ (cons\ s_1\ (cons\ s_2\ \ldots))))$, where s_1, s_2 are expressions. However, since our language LRL is only a fragment of core calculi [27,31], the reader may find more programming examples there.

We will use mappings on atoms from $\mathbb{A}$. A *swapping* $(a\ b)$ is a function that maps an atom a to atom b, atom b to a, and is the identity on other atoms. We will also use finite permutations on atoms from $\mathbb{A}$, which are represented as a composition of swappings in the algorithms below. Let $dom(\pi) = \{a \in \mathbb{A} \mid \pi(a) \neq a\}$. Then every finite permutation can be represented by a composition of at most $(|dom(\pi)| - 1)$ swappings. Composition $\pi_1 \circ \pi_2$ and inverse π^{-1} can be immediately computed. Permutations π operate on expressions simply by recursing on the structure. For a letrec-expression this is $\pi \cdot (\texttt{letrec}\ a_1.s_1; \ldots; a_n.s_n\ \texttt{in}\ e)$ $= (\texttt{letrec}\ \pi \cdot a_1.\pi \cdot s_1; \ldots; \pi \cdot a_n.\pi \cdot s_n;\ \texttt{in}\ \pi \cdot e)$. Note that permutations also change names of bound atoms.

We will use the following definition of α-equivalence:

Definition 2.1. *The equivalence $\sim$ on expressions $e \in LRL$ is defined as follows:*

- $a \sim a$.
- *if $e_i \sim e_i'$ for all i, then $f e_1 \ldots e_n \sim f e_1' \ldots e_n'$ for an n-ary $f \in \mathcal{F}$.*
- *If $e \sim e'$, then $\lambda a.e \sim \lambda a.e'$.*
- *If $a \# e'$, $e \sim (a\ b) \cdot e'$, then $\lambda a.e \sim \lambda b.e'$.*
- $\texttt{letrec}\ a_1.e_1; \ldots; a_n.e_n\ \texttt{in}\ e_0 \sim \texttt{letrec}\ a_1'.e_1'; \ldots; a_n'.e_n'\ \texttt{in}\ e_0'$ *iff there is some permutation ρ on $\{1, \ldots, n\}$, such that $\lambda a_1. \ldots .\lambda a_n.(e_1, \ldots, e_n, e_0) \sim \lambda a_{\rho(1)}'. \ldots .\lambda a_{\rho(n)}'.(e_{\rho(1)}', \ldots, e_{\rho(n)}', e_0')$.* $\square$

Note that $\sim$ is identical to the equivalence relation generated by α-equivalence of binding constructs and permutation of bindings in a letrec.

Note also that $e_1 \sim e_2$ is equivalent to $\pi \cdot e_1 \sim \pi \cdot e_2$, which will be implicitly used in the arguments below.

We need fixpoint sets of permutations π: We define $Fix(\pi) = \{e \mid \pi \cdot e \sim e\}$. In usual nominal unification, these sets can be characterized by using freshness constraints [35]. Clearly, all these sets and also all finite intersections are non-empty, since at least fresh atoms are elements and since $\mathbb{A}$ is infinite. However, in our setting, these sets are nontrivial:

Example 2.2. The α-equivalence $(a\ b) \cdot (\texttt{letrec}\ c.a; d.b\ \texttt{in}\ True) \sim (\texttt{letrec}\ c.a; d.b\ \texttt{in}\ True)$ holds, which means that there are expressions t in LRL with $t \sim (a\ b) \cdot t$ and $FA(t) = \{a, b\}$. This is in contrast to usual nominal unification.

In the following we will use the results on complexity of operations in permutation groups, see [15,23]. We consider a set $\{a_1, \ldots, a_n\}$ of distinct objects (in our case the atoms), the symmetric group $\Sigma(\{a_1, \ldots, a_n\})$ (of size $n!$) of permutations of the objects, and consider its elements, subsets and subgroups. Subgroups are always represented by a set of generators (represented as permutations on $\{a_1, \ldots, a_n\}$). If H is a set of elements (or generators), then $\langle H \rangle$ denotes the generated subgroup. Some facts are:

- A permutation can be represented in space linear in n.
- Every subgroup of $\Sigma(\{a_1, \ldots, a_n\})$ can be represented by $\leq n^2$ generators.

However, elements in a subgroup may not be representable as a product of polynomially many generators.

The following questions can be answered in polynomial time:

- The element-question: $\pi \in G$?,
- The subgroup question: $G_1 \subseteq G_2$.

However, intersection of groups and set-stabilizer (i.e. $\{\pi \in G \mid \pi(M) = M\}$) are not known to be computable in polynomial time, since those problems are as hard as graph-isomorphism (see [23]).

3   A Nominal Letrec Unification Algorithm

As an extension of LRL, there is also a countably infinite set of (unification) variables X, Y also denoted perhaps using indices.

The syntax of the language $LRLX$ (**LetRec L**anguage e**X**tended) is

$$e ::= a \mid X \mid \pi \cdot X \mid \lambda a.e \mid (f\ e_1\ \ldots e_{ar(c)}) \mid (\texttt{letrec}\ a_1.e_1; \ldots; a_n.e_n\ \texttt{in}\ e)$$

Var is the set of variables and $Var(e)$ is the set of variables X occurring in e.

The expression $\pi \cdot e$ for a non-variable e means an operation, which is performed by shifting π down, using the simplification $\pi_1 \cdot (\pi_2 \cdot X) \to (\pi_1 \circ \pi_2) \cdot X$, apply it to atoms, where only expressions $\pi \cdot X$ remain, which are called *suspensions*.

A *freshness constraint* in our unification algorithm is of the form $a \# e$, where e is an $LRLX$-expression, and an *atomic* freshness constraint is of the form $a \# X$.

Definition 3.1 (Simplification of Freshness Constraints).

$$\frac{\{a\#b\} \cup \nabla}{\nabla} \qquad \frac{\{a\#(f\ s_1 \ldots s_n)\} \cup \nabla}{\{a\#s_1, \ldots, a\#s_n\} \cup \nabla} \qquad \frac{\{a\#(\lambda a.s)\} \cup \nabla}{\nabla} \qquad \frac{\{a\#(\lambda b.s)\} \cup \nabla}{\{a\#s\} \cup \nabla}$$

$$\frac{\{a\#(\texttt{letrec}\ a_1.s_1; \ldots; a_n.s_n\ \texttt{in}\ r)\} \cup \nabla}{\nabla} \quad \text{if } a \in \{a_1, \ldots, a_n\}$$

$$\frac{\{a\#(\texttt{letrec}\ a_1.s_1; \ldots; a_n.s_n\ \texttt{in}\ r)\} \cup \nabla}{\{a\#s_1, \ldots a\#s_n, a\#r\} \cup \nabla} \quad \text{if } a \notin \{a_1, \ldots, a_n\} \qquad \frac{\{a\#(\pi \cdot X)\} \cup \nabla}{\{\pi^{-1}(a)\#X\} \cup \nabla}$$

Definition 3.2. *An $LRLX$-unification problem is a pair (Γ, ∇), where Γ is a set of equations $s_1 \doteq t_1, \ldots, s_n \doteq t_n$, and ∇ is a set of freshness constraints, permitting $LRLX$-expressions. A (ground) solution of (Γ, ∇) is a substitution ρ (mapping variables in $Var(\Gamma, \nabla)$ to ground expressions), such that $s_i\rho \sim t_i\rho$ for $i = 1, \ldots, n$ and for all $a\#e \in \nabla$: $a \notin FA(e\rho)$ holds.*

The decision problem is whether there is a solution for given (Γ, ∇).

Definition 3.3. *Let (Γ, ∇) be an $LRLX$-unification problem. We consider triples $(\sigma, \nabla', \mathcal{X})$, where σ is a substitution (compressed as a dag) mapping variables to $LRLX$-expressions, ∇' is a set of freshness constraints, and $\mathcal{X}$ is a set of fixpoint constraints of the form $X \in Fix(\pi)$, where $X \notin dom(\sigma)$. A triple $(\sigma, \nabla', \mathcal{X})$ is a* unifier of (Γ, ∇), if (i) there exists a ground substitution ρ that solves $(\nabla'\sigma, \mathcal{X})$, i.e., for every $a\#e$ in ∇', $a\#e\sigma\rho$ is valid, and for every constraint $X \in Fix(\pi)$ in $\mathcal{X}$, $X\rho \in Fix(\pi)$; and (ii) for every ground substitution ρ that instantiates all variables in $Var(\Gamma, \nabla)$ which solves $(\nabla'\sigma, \mathcal{X})$, the ground substitution $\sigma\rho$ is a solution of (Γ, ∇). A set M of unifiers is complete, if every solution μ is covered by at least one unifier, i.e. there is some unifier $(\sigma, \nabla', \mathcal{X})$ in M, and a ground substitution ρ, such that $X\mu \sim X\sigma\rho$ for all $X \in Var(\Gamma, \nabla)$. □

We will employ nondeterministic rule-based algorithms computing unifiers: There is a clearly indicated disjunctive (don't know non-deterministic) rule, all other rules are don't care non-deterministic. The *collecting variant* of the algorithm runs and collects all solutions from all alternatives of the disjunctive rule(s). The *decision variant* guesses one possibility and tries to compute a single unifier.

Since we want to avoid the exponential size explosion of the Robinson-style unification algorithms, keeping the good properties of Martelli Montanari-style unification algorithms [25], but not their notational overhead, we stick to a set of equations as data structure. As a preparation for the algorithm, all expressions in equations are exhaustively flattened as follows: $(f\ t_1 \ldots t_n) \to (f\ X_1 \ldots X_n)$ plus the equations $X_1 \doteq t_1, \ldots, X_n \doteq t_n$. Also $\lambda a.s$ is replaced by $\lambda a.X$ with equation $X \doteq s$, and $(\mathtt{letrec}\ a_1.s_1; \ldots; a_n.s_n\ \mathtt{in}\ r)$ is replaced by $(\mathtt{letrec}\ a_1.X_1; \ldots; a_n.X_n\ \mathtt{in}\ X)$ with the additional equations $X_1 \doteq s_1; \ldots; X_n \doteq s_n; X \doteq r$. The introduced variables are always fresh ones. We may denote the resulting set of equations of flattening an equation eq as $flat(eq)$. Thus, all expressions in equations are of depth at most 1, where we do not count the permutation applications in the suspensions.

A dependency ordering on $Var(\Gamma)$ is required: If $X \doteq e$ is in Γ, and e is not a variable nor a suspension and $X \neq Y \in Var(e)$, then $X \succ_{vd} Y$. Let $>_{vd}$ be the transitive closure of $\succ_{vd}$. This ordering is only used, if no standard rules and no failure rules (see Definition 3.4) apply, hence if $>_{vd}$ is used in rule, there are no cycles.

3.1 Rules of the Algorithm LETRECUNIFY

LETRECUNIFY operates on a tuple (Γ, ∇, θ), where Γ is a set of flattened equations $e_1 \doteq e_2$, where we assume that $\doteq$ is symmetric, ∇ contains freshness constraints, θ represents the already computed substitution as a list of replacements of the form $X \mapsto e$. Initially θ is empty. The final state will be reached, i.e. the output, when Γ only contains fixpoint equations of the form $X \doteq \pi \cdot X$ that are non-redundant, and the rule (Output) fires.

In the notation of the rules, we use $[e/X]$ as substitution that replaces X by e. In the rules, we may omit ∇ or θ if they are not changed. We will use a notation "|" in the consequence part of one rule, perhaps with a set of possibilities, to denote disjunctive (i.e. don't know) nondeterminism. The only nondeterministic rule that requires exploring all alternatives is rule (7) below. The other rules can be applied in any order, where it is not necessary to explore alternatives.

Standard (1, 2, 3, 3') and decomposition rules (4,5,6,7):

$$(1) \quad \frac{\Gamma \cup \{e \doteq e\}}{\Gamma} \qquad (2) \quad \frac{\Gamma \cup \{\pi \cdot X \doteq s\} \quad s \notin Var}{\Gamma \cup \{X \doteq \pi^{-1} \cdot s\}}$$

$$(3) \quad \frac{\Gamma \cup \{X \doteq \pi \cdot Y\}, \nabla, \theta \quad X \neq Y}{\Gamma[\pi \cdot Y/X], \nabla[\pi \cdot Y/X], \theta \cup \{X \mapsto \pi \cdot Y\}} \qquad (3') \quad \frac{\Gamma \cup \{X \doteq Y\}, \nabla, \theta \quad X \neq Y}{\Gamma[Y/X], \nabla[Y/X], \theta \cup \{X \mapsto Y\}}$$

$$(4) \quad \frac{\Gamma \cup \{(f \ s_1 \ldots s_n) \doteq (f \ s_1' \ldots s_n')\}}{\Gamma \cup \{s_1 \doteq s_1', \ldots, s_n \doteq s_n'\}}$$

$$(5) \quad \frac{\Gamma \cup (\lambda a.s \doteq \lambda a.t)}{\Gamma \cup \{s \doteq t\}} \qquad (6) \quad \frac{\Gamma \cup (\lambda a.s \doteq \lambda b.t), \nabla}{\Gamma \cup \{s \doteq (a \ b) \cdot t\}, \nabla \cup \{a \# t\}}$$

$$(7) \quad \frac{\Gamma \cup \{\texttt{letrec} \ a_1.s_1; \ldots, a_n.s_n \ \texttt{in} \ r \doteq \texttt{letrec} \ b_1.t_1; \ldots, b_n.t_n \ \texttt{in} \ r'\}}{\underset{\forall \rho}{\big|} \ \Gamma \cup flat(\lambda a_1. \ldots \lambda a_n.(s_1, \ldots, s_n, r) \doteq \lambda b_{\rho(1)}. \ldots \lambda b_{\rho(n)}.(t_{\rho(1)}, \ldots, t_{\rho(n)}, r'))}$$

where ρ is a permutation on $\{1, \ldots, n\}$.

Main Rules: The following rules (MMS) (Martelli-Montanari-Simulation) and (FPS) (Fixpoint-Shift) will always be immediately applied followed by a decomposition of the resulting set of equations.

$$(\text{MMS}) \quad \frac{\Gamma \cup \{X \doteq e_1, X \doteq e_2\}, \nabla}{\Gamma \cup \{X \doteq e_1, e_1 \doteq e_2\}, \nabla}, \qquad \begin{array}{l} \text{if } e_1, e_2 \text{ are neither variables} \\ \text{nor suspensions.} \end{array}$$

$$(\text{FPS}) \quad \frac{\Gamma \cup \{X \doteq \pi_1 \cdot X, \ldots, X \doteq \pi_n \cdot X, X \doteq e\}, \theta}{\Gamma \cup \{e \doteq \pi_1 \cdot e, \ldots, e \doteq \pi_n \cdot e\}, \theta \cup \{X \mapsto e\}}, \qquad \begin{array}{l} \text{if } X \text{ is maximal w.r.t. } >_{vd}, \\ X \notin Var(\Gamma), \text{ and } e \text{ is neither} \\ \text{a variable nor a suspension,} \\ \text{and no failure rule (see below)} \\ \text{is applicable} \end{array}$$

$$(\text{ElimFP}) \quad \frac{\Gamma \cup \{X \doteq \pi_1 \cdot X, \ldots, X \doteq \pi_n \cdot X, X \doteq \pi \cdot X\}, \theta}{\Gamma \cup \{X \doteq \pi_1 \cdot X, \ldots, X \doteq \pi_n \cdot X\}, \theta}, \text{ if } \pi \in \langle \pi_1, \ldots, \pi_n \rangle.$$

$$(\text{Output}) \quad \frac{\Gamma, \nabla, \theta}{\theta, \nabla, \{\text{``} X \in Fix(\pi) \text{''} \mid X \doteq \pi \cdot X \in \Gamma\}} \qquad \begin{array}{l} \text{if } \Gamma \text{ only consists of} \\ \text{fixpoint-equations.} \end{array}$$

We assume that the rule (ElimFP) will be applied whenever possible.

Note that the two rules (MMS) and (FPS), without further precaution, may cause an exponential blow-up in the number of fixpoint-equations (see Example 3.6).

The rule (ElimFP) will limit the number of fixpoint equations by exploiting knowledge on operations on permutation groups.

The rule (Output) terminates an execution on Γ_0 by outputting a unifier $(\theta, \nabla', \mathcal{X})$. Note that in any case at least one solution is represented.

The top symbol of an expression is defined as $tops(X) = X$, $tops(\pi \cdot X) = X$, $tops(f\ s_1 \ldots s_n) = f$, $tops(a) = a$, $tops(\lambda a.s) = \lambda$, $tops(\texttt{letrec } env \texttt{ in } s) = \texttt{letrec}$. Let $\mathcal{F}^x := \mathcal{F} \cup \mathbb{A} \cup \{\texttt{letrec}, \lambda\}$.

Definition 3.4. Failure Rules of LETRECUNIFY

Clash Failure: *If* $s \doteq t \in \Gamma$, $tops(s) \in \mathcal{F}^x$, $tops(t) \in \mathcal{F}^x$, *but* $tops(s) \neq tops(t)$.
Cycle Detection: *If there are equations* $X_1 \doteq s_1, \ldots, X_n \doteq s_n$ *where* $tops(s_i) \in \mathcal{F}^x$, *and* X_{i+1} *occurs in* s_i *for* $i = 1, \ldots, n-1$ *and* X_1 *occurs in* s_n.
Freshness Fail: *If there is a freshness constraint* $a\#a$.
Freshness Solution Fail: *If there is a freshness constraint* $a\#X \in \nabla$, *and* $a \in FA((X)\theta)$.

The computation of $FA((X)\theta)$ can be done in polynomial time by iterating over the solution components.

Example 3.5. We illustrate the letrec-rule by a ground example without flattening. Let the equation be: $\texttt{letrec } a.(a, b), b.(a, b) \texttt{ in } b \doteq \texttt{letrec } b.(b, c)$, $c.(b, c) \texttt{ in } c$. Select the identity permutation ρ, which results in:

$$\lambda a.\lambda b.((a, b), (a, b), b) \doteq \lambda b.\lambda c.((b, c), (b, c), c). \quad \text{Then:}$$
$$\lambda b.((a, b), (a, b), b) \doteq (a\ b) \cdot \lambda c.((b, c), (b, c), c) = \lambda c.((a, c), (a, c), c).$$

(The freshness constraint $a\# \ldots$ holds). Then the application of the λ-rule gives $((a, b), (a, b), b) \doteq (b\ c) \cdot ((a, c), (a, c), c)$ (the freshness constraint $b\# \ldots$ holds). The resulting equation is $((a, b), (a, b), b) \doteq ((a, b), (a, b), b)$, which is valid.

Example 3.6. This example shows that FPS (together with the standard and decomposition rules) may give rise to an exponential number of equations in the size of the original problem. Let there be variables $X_i, i = 0, \ldots, n$ and the equations $\Gamma = \{X_n \doteq \pi \cdot X_n, X_n \doteq (f\ X_{n-1}\ \rho_n \cdot X_{n-1}), \ldots, X_2 \doteq (f\ X_1\ \rho_2 \cdot X_1)\}$ where $\pi, \rho_1, \ldots, \rho_n$ are permutations.

We prove that this unification problem may give rise to 2^{n-1} equations, if the redundancy rule (ElimFP) is not there.

The first step is by (FPS): $\left\{ \begin{array}{r} f\ X_{n-1}\ \rho_n \cdot X_{n-1} \doteq \pi \cdot (f\ X_{n-1}\ \rho_n \cdot X_{n-1}), \\ X_{n-1} \doteq (f\ X_{n-2}\ \rho_{n-1} \cdot X_{n-2}), \ldots \end{array} \right\}$

Using decomposition and inversion: $\left\{ \begin{array}{l} X_{n-1} \doteq \pi \cdot X_{n-1}, \\ X_{n-1} \doteq \rho_n^{-1} \cdot \pi \cdot \rho_n \cdot X_{n-1}, \\ X_{n-1} \doteq (f\ X_{n-2}\ \rho_{n-1} \cdot X_{n-2}), \ldots \end{array} \right\}$

After (FPS): $\left\{ \begin{array}{r} (f\ X_{n-2}\ \rho_{n-1} \cdot X_{n-2}) \doteq \pi \cdot (f\ X_{n-2}\ \rho_{n-1} \cdot X_{n-2}), \\ (f\ X_{n-2}\ \rho_{n-1} \cdot X_{n-2}) \doteq \rho_n^{-1} \cdot \pi \cdot \rho_n \cdot (f\ X_{n-2}\ \rho_{n-1} \cdot X_{n-2}), \\ X_{n-2} \doteq (f\ X_{n-3}\ \rho_{n-2} \cdot X_{n-3}), \ldots \end{array} \right\}$

decomposition and inversion:
$$\left\{ \begin{array}{l} X_{n-2} \doteq \pi \cdot X_{n-2}, \\ X_{n-2} \doteq \rho_{n-1}^{-1} \cdot \pi \cdot \rho_{n-1} \cdot X_{n-2}, \\ X_{n-2} \doteq \rho_n^{-1} \cdot \pi \cdot \rho_n \cdot X_{n-2}, \\ X_{n-2} \doteq \rho_{n-1}^{-1} \cdot \rho_n^{-1} \cdot \pi \cdot \rho_n \cdot \rho_{n-1} \cdot X_{n-2}, \\ X_{n-2} \doteq (f \ X_{n-3} \ \rho_{n-2} \cdot X_{n-3}), \ldots \end{array} \right\}$$

Now it is easy to see that all equations $X_1 \doteq \pi' \cdot X_1$ are generated, with $\pi' \in \{\rho^{-1} \pi \rho$ where ρ is a composition of a subsequence of $\rho_n, \rho_{n-1}, \ldots, \rho_2\}$, which makes 2^{n-1} equations. The permutations are pairwise different using an appropriate choice of ρ_i and π. The starting equations can be constructed using the decomposition rule of abstractions.

4 Soundness, Completeness, and Complexity of LETRECUNIFY

Theorem 4.1. *The decision variant of the algorithm* LETRECUNIFY *runs in nondeterministic polynomial time. Its collecting version returns a complete set of at most exponentially many unifiers, every one represented in polynomial space.*

Proof. Note that we assume that the input equations are flattened before applying the rules, which can be performed in polynomial time.

Let Γ_0, ∇_0 be the input, and let $S = size(\Gamma_0, \nabla_0)$. The execution of a single rule can be done in polynomial time depending on the size of the intermediate state, thus we have to show that the size of the intermediate states remains polynomial and that the number of rule applications is at most polynomial.

The termination measure $(\mu_1, \mu_2, \mu_3, \mu_4, \mu_5, \mu_6)$, which is ordered lexicographically, is as follows: μ_1 is the number of letrec expressions in Γ, μ_2 is the number of letrec-, λ-symbols, function-symbols and atoms in Γ, μ_3 is the number of different variables in Γ, μ_4 is the number of occurrences of variables in Γ, μ_5 is the number of equations not of the form $X \doteq e$, and μ_6 is the number of equations.

Since shifting permutations down and simplification of freshness constraints both terminate and do not increase the measures, we only compare states which are normal forms for shifting down permutations and simplifying freshness constraints. We assume that the algorithm stops if a failure rule is applicable, and that the rules (MMS) and (FPS) are immediately followed by a full decomposition of the results (or failure).

Now it is easy to check that the rule applications strictly decrease μ: The rules (MMS) and (FPS) together with the subsequent decomposition strictly decrease (μ_1, μ_2). Since expressions in equations are flat, (MMS) does not increase the size: $X \doteq s_1, X \doteq s_2$ is first replaced by $X \doteq s_1, s_1 \doteq s_2$, and the latter is decomposed, which due to flattening results only in equations containing variables and suspensions. Thus μ_2 is reduced by the size of s_2. In the same way (FPS) strictly decreases (μ_1, μ_2). In addition μ_2 is at most S^2, since only the letrec-decomposition rule can add $\lambda a.$-constructs.

The number of fixpoint-equations for every variable X is at most $c_1 * S * log(S))$ for some (fixed) c_1, since the number of atoms is never increased, and since we assume that (ElimFP) is applied whenever possible. The size of the permutation group is at most $S!$, and so the length of proper subset-chains and hence the maximal number of generators of a subgroup is at most $log(S!) = O(S * log(S))$. Note that the redundancy of generators can be tested in polynomial time depending on the number of atoms.

Now we prove a (global) upper bound on the number μ_3 of variables: An application of (7) may increase μ_3 at most by S. An application of (FPS) may increase this number at most by $c_1 * S \log(S) * S$, where the worst case occurs when e is a letrec-expression. Since (MMS) and (FPS) can be applied at most S times, the number of variables is smaller than $c_1 * S^3 \log(S)$.

The other rules strictly decrease (μ_1, μ_2), or they do not increase (μ_1, μ_2), and strictly decrease $(\mu_3, \mu_4, \mu_5, \mu_6)$ and can be performed in polynomial time.   □

The problematic rule for complexity is (FPS), which does not increase μ_1 and μ_2, but may increase μ_3, μ_4 and μ_6 (see Example 3.6). This increase is defeated by the rule (ElimFP), which helps to keep the numbers μ_4 and μ_6 low.

Theorem 4.2. *The algorithm* LETRECUNIFY *is sound and complete.*

Proof. Soundness of the algorithm holds, by easy arguments for every rule, similar as in [35], and since the letrec-rule follows the definition of $\sim$ in Definition 2.1. A further argument is that the failure rules are sufficient to detect final states without solutions.

Completeness requires more arguments. The decomposition and standard rules (with the exception of rule (7)), retain the set of solutions. The same for (MMS), (FPS), and (ElimFP). The nondeterministic Rule (7) provides all possibilities for potential ground solutions. Moreover, the failure rules are not applicable to states that are solvable.

A final output of LETRECUNIFY has at least one ground solution as instance: we can instantiate all variables that remain in Γ_{out} by a fresh atom. Then all fixpoint equations are satisfied, since the permutations cannot change this atom, and since the (atomic) freshness constraints hold. This ground solution can be represented in polynomial space by using θ, plus an instance $X \mapsto a$ for all remaining variables X and a fresh atom a, and removing all fixpoint equations and freshness constraints.   □

Theorem 4.3. *The nominal letrec-unification problem is in NP.*

Proof. This follows from Theorems 4.1 and 4.2.

5 Nominal Matching with Letrec: LETRECMATCH

Reductions in higher order calculi with letrec, in particular on a meta-notation, require a matching algorithm, matching its left hand side to an expression.

Example 5.1. Consider the (lbeta)-rule, which is the version of (beta) used in call-by-need calculi with sharing [2,27,31]. Note that only the sharing power of the recursive environment is used here.

$$(lbeta) \quad (\lambda x.e_1)\, e_2 \rightarrow \texttt{letrec } x.e_2 \texttt{ in } e_1.$$

An (lbeta) step, for example, on $(\lambda x.x)\,(\lambda y.y)$ is performed by switching to the language LRL and then matching $(app\ (\lambda c.X_1)\ X_2) \trianglelefteq (app\ (\lambda a.a)\ (\lambda b.b))$, where app is the explicit representation of the binary application operator. This results in $\sigma := \{X_1 \mapsto c; X_2 \mapsto (\lambda b.b)\}$, and the reduction result is the σ-instance of $(\texttt{letrec } c.X_2 \texttt{ in } X_1)$, which is $(\texttt{letrec } c.(\lambda b.b) \texttt{ in } c)$. Note that this form of reduction implicitly uses α-equivalence.

We derive a nominal matching algorithm as a specialization of LETRECU-NIFY. We use nonsymmetric equations written $s \trianglelefteq t$, where s is an $LRLX$-expression, and t does not contain variables. Note that neither freshness constraints nor suspensions are necessary (and hence no fixpoint equations) in the solution. We assume that the input is a set of equations of (plain) expressions.

The rules of the algorithm LETRECMATCH are:

$$\frac{\Gamma \cup \{e \trianglelefteq e\}}{\Gamma} \qquad \frac{\Gamma \cup \{(f\ s_1 \ldots s_n) \trianglelefteq (f\ s_1' \ldots s_n')\}}{\Gamma \cup \{s_1 \trianglelefteq s_1', \ldots, s_n \trianglelefteq s_n'\}} \qquad \frac{\Gamma \cup \{\lambda a.s \trianglelefteq \lambda a.t\}}{\Gamma \cup \{s \trianglelefteq t\}}$$

$$\frac{\Gamma \cup \{\lambda a.s \trianglelefteq \lambda b.t\}}{\Gamma \cup \{s \trianglelefteq (a\ b)\cdot t\}} \quad if\, a \,\#\, t, otherwise Fail. \qquad \frac{\Gamma \cup \{\pi \cdot X \trianglelefteq e\}}{\Gamma \cup \{X \trianglelefteq \pi^{-1}\cdot e\}}$$

$$\frac{\Gamma \cup \{\texttt{letrec } a_1.s_1; \ldots; a_n.s_n \texttt{ in } r \trianglelefteq \texttt{letrec } b_1.t_1; \ldots; b_n.t_n \texttt{ in } r'\}}{\underset{\forall \rho}{\mid}\ \Gamma \cup \{\lambda a_1. \ldots . \lambda a_n.(s_1, \ldots, s_n, r) \trianglelefteq \lambda a_{\rho(1)}. \ldots . \lambda a_{\rho(n)}.(t_{\rho(1)}, \ldots, t_{\rho(n)}, r')\}}$$

where ρ is a (mathematical) permutation on $\{1, \ldots, n\}$

$$\frac{\Gamma \cup \{X \trianglelefteq e_1, X \trianglelefteq e_2\}}{\Gamma \cup \{X \trianglelefteq e_1\}} \text{ if } e_1 \sim e_2, \text{ otherwise Fail}$$

The test $e_1 \sim e_2$ will be performed as a subroutine call to this (nondeterministic) matching procedure in the collecting version, i.e. the test succeeds if there is a nondeterministic execution with success as result.

Clash Failure: if $s \doteq t \in \Gamma$, $tops(s) \in \mathcal{F}^x$, $tops(t) \in \mathcal{F}^x$, but $tops(s) \neq tops(t)$.

Theorem 5.2. LETRECMATCH *is sound and complete for nominal letrec matching. It decides nominal letrec matching in nondeterministic polynomial time. Its collecting version returns a finite complete set of an at most exponential number of matching substitutions, which are of at most polynomial size.*

Proof. This follows by standard arguments.

Theorem 5.3. *Nominal letrec matching is NP-complete.*

Proof. The problem is in NP, which follows from Theorem 5.2. It is also NP-hard, which follows from the (independent) Theorem 6.1.

A slightly more general situation for nominal matching occurs, when the matching equations Γ_0 are compressed using a dag. We construct a practically more efficient algorithm LETRECDAGMATCH from LETRECUNIFY as follows. First we generate Γ_1 from Γ_0, which only contains (plain) flattened expressions by encoding the dag-nodes as variables together with an equation. An expression is said Γ_0-ground, if it does not reference variables from Γ_0 (also via equations). In order to avoid suspension (i.e. to have nicer results), the decomposition rule for λ-expressions with different binder names is modified as follows:

$$\frac{\Gamma \cup (\lambda a.s \doteq \lambda b.t\}, \nabla}{\Gamma \cup \{s \doteq (a\ b)\cdot t\}, \nabla \cup \{a\#t\}} \quad \lambda b.t \text{ is } \Gamma_0\text{-ground}$$

The extra conditions $a\#t$ and Γ_0-ground can be tested in polynomial time. The equations Γ_1 are processed applying LETRECUNIFY (with the mentioned modification) with the guidance that the right-hand sides of match-equations are also right-hand sides of equations in the decomposition rules. The resulting matching substitutions can be interpreted as the instantiations into the variables of Γ_0. Since Γ_0 is a matching problem, the result will be free of fixpoint equations, and there will be no freshness constraints in the solution. Thus we have:

Theorem 5.4. *The collecting variant of* LETRECDAGMATCH *outputs an at most exponential set of dag-compressed substitutions that is complete and where every unifier is represented in polynomial space.*

6   Hardness of Nominal Letrec Matching and Unification

Theorem 6.1. *Nominal letrec matching (hence also unification) is NP-hard, for two letrec expressions, where subexpressions are free of letrec.*

Proof. We encode the NP-hard problem of finding a Hamiltonian cycle in a regular graph [16,28], which are graphs where all nodes have the same degree $k \geq 3$. Let $a_1, \ldots, a_n$ be the vertexes of the graph, and E be the set of edges. The first environment part is $env_1 = a_1.(node\ a_1); \ldots; a_n.(node\ a_n)$, and a second environment part env_2 consists of bindings $b.(f\ a\ a')$ and $b'.(f\ a'\ a)$ for every edge $(a, a') \in E$ for fresh names b, b'. Then let $s := (\texttt{letrec}\ env_1; env_2\ \texttt{in}\ 0)$ representing the graph. Let the second expression encode the question whether there is a Hamiltonian cycle in a regular graph as follows. The first part of the environment is $env'_1 = a_1.(node\ X_1), \ldots, a_n.(node\ X_n)$. The second part is env'_2 consisting of $b_1.f\ X_1\ X_2; b_2.f\ X_2\ X_3; \ldots b_n.f\ X_n\ X_1$, and the third part consisting of a number of (dummy) entries of the form $b.f\ Z\ Z'$, where b is always a fresh atom for every binding, and Z, Z' are fresh variables for every entry. The number of these dummy entries is $k * n - n$. Then the matching problem is solvable iff the graph has a Hamiltonian cycle.

Theorem 6.2. *The nominal letrec-unification problem is NP-complete.*

Proof. This follows from Theorems 4.3 and 6.1.

We say that an expression t *contains garbage*, iff there is a subexpression ($\texttt{letrec}\ env\ \texttt{in}\ r$), and the environment env can be split into two environments $env = env_1; env_2$, such that env_1 is not trivial, and the atoms from $LA(env_1)$ do not occur in env_2 nor in r. Otherwise, the expression is *free of garbage*. Since α-equivalence of *LRL*-expressions is Graph-Isomorphism-complete [29], but α-equivalence of garbage-free *LRL*-expressions is polynomial, it is useful to look for improvements of unification and matching for garbage-free expressions. As a remark: Graph-Isomorphism is known to have complexity between *PTIME* and *NP*; there are arguments that it is weaker than the class of NP-complete problems [32]. There is also a claim that it is quasi-polynomial [8], which means that it requires less than exponential time.

Theorem 6.3. *Nominal letrec matching with one occurrence of a single variable and a garbage-free target expression is Graph-Isomorphism-hard.*

Proof. Let G_1, G_2 be two graphs. Let s be ($\texttt{letrec}\ env_1\ \texttt{in}\ g\ b_1 \ldots, b_m$) the encoding of a arbitrary graph G_1 where env_1 is the encoding as in the proof of Theorem 6.1 and, nodes are encoded as $a_1 \ldots a_n$, and the edge-binders are b_i. Then the expression s is free of garbage. Let the environment env_2 be the encoding of G_2 in the expression $t = \texttt{letrec}\ env_2\ \texttt{in}\ X$. Then t matches s iff the graphs G_1, G_2 are isomorphic. Hence we have *GI*-hardness. If there is an isomorphism of G_1 and G_2, then it is easy to see that this bijection leads to an equivalence of the environments, and we can instantiate X with ($g\ b_1 \ldots, b_m$). $\square$

7   Nominal Letrec Matching with Environment Variables

We extend the language LRLX by variables E that may encode partial letrec-environments, which leads to a larger coverage of unification problems in reasoning about the semantics of programming languages.

Example 7.1. Consider as an example a rule (llet-e) of the operational semantics, that merges $\texttt{letrec}$-environments (see [31]):
($\texttt{letrec}\ E_1\ \texttt{in}\ (\texttt{letrec}\ E_2\ \texttt{in}\ X)$) $\rightarrow$ ($\texttt{letrec}\ E_1; E_2\ \texttt{in}\ X$).
It can be applied to an expression ($\texttt{letrec}\ a.0; b.1\ \texttt{in}\ \texttt{letrec}\ c.(a, b, c)\ \texttt{in}\ c$) as follows: The left-hand side ($\texttt{letrec}\ E_1\ \texttt{in}\ (\texttt{letrec}\ E_2\ \texttt{in}\ X)$) of the reduction rule matches ($\texttt{letrec}\ a.0; b.1\ \texttt{in}\ (\texttt{letrec}\ c.(a, b, c)\ \texttt{in}\ c$)) with the match: $\{E_1 \mapsto \{a.0; b.1\}; E_2 \mapsto \{c.(a, b, c)\}; X \mapsto c\}$, producing the next expression as an instance of the right hand side ($\texttt{letrec}\ E_1; E_2\ \texttt{in}\ X$), which is: ($\texttt{letrec}\ a.0; b.1; c.(a, b, c)\ \texttt{in}\ c$). Note that for application to extended lambda calculi, more care is needed w.r.t. scoping in order to get valid reduction results in all cases. The restriction that a single letrec environment binds different variables becomes more important. The reduction (llet-e) is correctly applicable, if the target expression satisfies the so-called distinct variable convention, which means that all bound variables are different and that all free variables in the expression are different from all bound variables.

An alternative that is used for a similar unification task in [30] requires an additional construct of non-capture constraints: $NCC(env_1, env_2)$, which means that for every valid instantiation ρ: variables occurring free in $env_1\rho$ are not captured by the top letrec-binders in $env_2\rho$. In this paper we focus on matching, and leave the combination with reduction rules for further work.

Definition 7.2. *The grammar for the extended language LRLXE (**L**et**R**ec **L**anguage e**X**tended with **E**nvironments) is:*

$$env ::= E \mid \pi \cdot E \mid a.e \mid env; env$$
$$e \quad ::= a \mid X \mid \pi \cdot X \mid \lambda a.e \mid (f\ e_1 \ldots e_{ar(c)}) \mid (\texttt{letrec}\ env\ \texttt{in}\ e)$$

We define a matching algorithm, where environment variables may occur in left hand sides. This algorithm needs a more expressive data structure in equations. The variant $\texttt{letr*}$ of $\texttt{letrec}$ is used with two environment-components, (i) a list of bindings that are already fixed in the correspondence to the bindings of the other environment, and (ii) an environment that is not yet fixed. We denote the fixed bindings as a list, which is the first component. The scoping is the same. In the notation we assume that the (non-fixed) letrec-environment part on the right hand side may be arbitrarily permuted before the rules are applied. The justification for this special data structure is the scoping in letrec expressions. The usual letrec is the extended letrec with an empty list as first component. Note that suspensions ($\pi \cdot E$, $\pi \cdot X$) are not generated nor a part of the result of this matching algorithm (but may be in the input).

Definition 7.3. *The matching algorithm* LETRECENVMATCH *for expressions where environment variables E and expression variables X may occur only in the left hand sides of match equations is described below. Initially, every* $(\texttt{letrec}\ env\ \texttt{in}\ e)$ *is modified to* $(\texttt{letr*}\ \emptyset; env\ \texttt{in}\ e)$. *The rules are:*

$$\frac{\Gamma \cup \{e \trianglelefteq e\}}{\Gamma} \qquad \frac{\Gamma \cup \{(f\ s_1 \ldots s_n) \trianglelefteq (f\ s_1' \ldots s_n')\}}{\Gamma \cup \{s_1 \trianglelefteq s_1', \ldots, s_n \trianglelefteq s_n'\}} \qquad \frac{\Gamma \cup \{\lambda a.s \trianglelefteq \lambda a.t\}}{\Gamma \cup \{s \trianglelefteq t\}}$$

$$\frac{\Gamma \cup \{\lambda a.s \trianglelefteq \lambda b.t\}}{\Gamma \cup \{s \trianglelefteq (a\ b) \cdot t\}} \qquad \textit{if, } a \# t \quad \textit{otherwise Fail}$$

$$\frac{\Gamma \cup \{(\texttt{letr*}\ ls; a.s; env\ \texttt{in}\ r) \trianglelefteq (\texttt{letr*}\ ls'; b.t; env'\ \texttt{in}\ r')\}}{\forall (b.t) \quad \Gamma \cup \{(\texttt{letr*}\ ((a.s) : ls); env\ \texttt{in}\ r) \trianglelefteq (a\ b)(\texttt{letr*}\ ((b.t) : ls';\ env'\ \texttt{in}\ r')\}}$$

if $a \# (\texttt{letr*}\ ls'; b.t; env'\ \texttt{in}\ r')$, *otherwise Fail.*

$$\frac{\Gamma \cup \{(\texttt{letr*}\ ls; \pi \cdot E; env\ \texttt{in}\ r) \trianglelefteq (\texttt{letr*}\ ls'; env_1'; env_2'\ \texttt{in}\ r')\}}{\begin{array}{c} \mid \quad \Gamma \cup \{(\texttt{letr*}\ (E : ls); env\ \texttt{in}\ r) \trianglelefteq (\texttt{letr*}\ (\pi^{-1} \cdot (env_1') : ls');\ env_2'\ \texttt{in}\ r')\} \\ env_1' \end{array}}$$

$$\frac{\Gamma \cup \left\{ \begin{array}{l} (\texttt{letr*}\ ls; \emptyset\ \texttt{in}\ r) \\ \trianglelefteq (\texttt{letr*}\ ls'; \emptyset\ \texttt{in}\ r') \end{array} \right\}}{\Gamma \cup \{ls \trianglelefteq ls'; r \trianglelefteq r'\}} \qquad \frac{\Gamma \cup \{[e_1; \ldots; e_n] \trianglelefteq [e_1'; \ldots; e_n']\}}{\Gamma \cup \{e_1 \trianglelefteq e_1'; \ldots; e_n \trianglelefteq e_n'\}}$$

$$\frac{\Gamma \cup \{\pi \cdot X \trianglelefteq e\}}{\Gamma \cup \{X \trianglelefteq \pi^{-1} e\}} \qquad \frac{\Gamma \cup \{X \trianglelefteq e_1, X \trianglelefteq e_2\}}{\Gamma \cup \{X \trianglelefteq e_1, e_1 \doteq e_2\}} \qquad \frac{\Gamma \cup \{E \trianglelefteq env_1, E \trianglelefteq env_2\}}{\Gamma \cup \{E \trianglelefteq env_1, env_1 \doteq env_2\}}$$

Testing $e_1 \doteq e_2$ and $env_1 \doteq env_2$ is done with high priority using the (nondeterministic) matching rules in Sect. 5, where for testing $env_1 \doteq env_2$ all permutations of the bindings are checked. Fail, if the equations does not hold.

Clash Failure: *If $s \doteq t \in \Gamma$, $tops(s) \in \mathcal{F}^x$, $tops(t) \in \mathcal{F}^x$, but $tops(s) \neq tops(t)$.*

After successful execution, the result will be a set of match equations with components $X \trianglelefteq e$, and $E \trianglelefteq env$, which represents a matching substitution, where the letr*-expressions are retranslated to letrec-expressions.

Theorem 7.4. *The algorithm Definition 7.3 (LETRECENVMATCH) is sound and complete. It runs in non-deterministic polynomial time. The corresponding decision problem is NP-complete.*

The collecting version of LETRECENVMATCH returns an at most exponentially large, complete set of representations of matching substitutions, where the representations are of at most polynomial size.

Proof. The reasoning for soundness, completeness and termination in polynomial time is a variation of previous arguments. The nonstandard part is fixing the correspondence of environment parts step-by-step and keeping the scoping.

8   Conclusion and Future Research

We constructed a nominal letrec unification algorithm, several nominal letrec matching algorithms for variants, which all run in nondeterministic polynomial time. Future research is to investigate extensions of unification with environment variables E, with abstract variables for (concrete) variables, (or alternatively extending equivariant nominal unification [1,10,11,14] to letrec,) and to investigate nominal matching together with equational theories. Also applications of nominal techniques to reduction steps in operational semantics and transformations should be investigated.

References

1. Aoto, T., Kikuchi, K.: A rule-based procedure for equivariant nominal unification. In: Informal Proceedings HOR, p. 5 (2016)
2. Ariola, Z.M., Felleisen, M., Maraist, J., Odersky, M., Wadler, P.: A call-by-need lambda calculus. In: POPL 1995, pp. 233–246. ACM Press, San Francisco (1995)
3. Ariola, Z.M., Klop, J.W.: Cyclic lambda graph rewriting. In: Proceedings of IEEE LICS, pp. 416–425. IEEE Press (1994)
4. Ayala-Rincón, M., de Carvalho-Segundo, W., Fernández, M., Nantes-Sobrinho, D.: A formalisation of nominal alpha-equivalence with A and AC function symbols. In: Proceedings of LSFA 2016, pp. 78–93 (2016)
5. Ayala-Rincón, M., Fernández, M., Nantes-Sobrinho, D.: Nominal narrowing. In: Pientka, B., Kesner, D. (eds.) Proceedings of First FSCD, pp. 11:1–11:17. LIPIcs (2016)

6. Ayala-Rincón, M., Fernández, M., Rocha-Oliveira, A.C.: Completeness in PVS of a nominal unification algorithm. ENTCS **323**(3), 57–74 (2016)
7. Baader, F., Snyder, W.: Unification theory. In: Robinson, J.A., Voronkov, A. (eds.) Handbook of Automated Reasoning, pp. 445–532. Elsevier, MIT Press, New York, Cambridge (2001)
8. Babai, L.: Graph isomorphism in quasipolynomial time (2016). http://arxiv.org/abs/1512.03547v2
9. Calvès, C., Fernández, M.: A polynomial nominal unification algorithm. Theor. Comput. Sci. **403**(2–3), 285–306 (2008)
10. Cheney, J.: Nominal Logic Programming. Ph.D. thesis, Cornell University, Ithaca (2004)
11. Cheney, J.: Equivariant unification. In: Giesl, J. (ed.) RTA 2005. LNCS, vol. 3467, pp. 74–89. Springer, Heidelberg (2005). doi:10.1007/978-3-540-32033-3_7
12. Cheney, J.: Relating higher-order pattern unification and nominal unification. In: Proceedings of 19th International Workshop on Unification (UNIF 2005), pp. 104–119 (2005)
13. Cheney, J.: Toward a general theory of names: binding and scope. In: MERLIN 2005, pp. 33–40. ACM (2005)
14. Cheney, J.: Equivariant unification. J. Autom. Reasoning **45**(3), 267–300 (2010). http://dx.doi.org/10.1007/s10817-009-9164-3
15. Furst, M.L., Hopcroft, J.E., Luks, E.M.: Polynomial-time algorithms for permutation groups. In: 21st FoCS, pp. 36–41. IEEE Computer Society (1980)
16. Garey, M.R., Johnson, D.S., Tarjan, R.E.: The planar Hamiltonian circuit problem is NP-complete. SIAM J. Comput. **5**(4), 704–714 (1976)
17. Goldfarb, W.D.: The undecidability of the second-order unification problem. Theor. Comput. Sci. **13**, 225–230 (1981)
18. Huet, G.P.: A unification algorithm for typed lambda-calculus. Theor. Comput. Sci. **1**(1), 27–57 (1975)
19. Jeannin, J.B., Kozen, D., Silva, A.: CoCaml: programming with coinductive types. Technical report Computing and Information Science, Cornell University, fundamenta Informaticae (2012). http://hdl.handle.net/1813/30798
20. Levy, J., Veanes, M.: On the undecidability of second-order unification. Inf. Comput. **159**(1–2), 125–150 (2000)
21. Levy, J., Villaret, M.: An efficient nominal unification algorithm. In: Lynch, C. (ed.) Proceedings of 21st RTA, LIPIcs, vol. 6, pp. 209–226. Schloss Dagstuhl (2010)
22. Levy, J., Villaret, M.: Nominal unification from a higher-order perspective. ACM Trans. Comput. Log. **13**(2), 10 (2012)
23. Luks, E.M.: Permutation groups and polynomial-time computation. In: Finkelstein, L., Kantor, W.M. (eds.) Groups And Computation, Proceedings of a DIMACS Workshop (DIMACS), vol. 11, pp. 139–176. DIMACS/AMS (1991)
24. Marlow, S. (ed.): Haskell 2010 - Language Report (2010)
25. Martelli, A., Montanari, U.: An efficient unification algorithm. ACM Trans. Program. Lang. Syst. **4**(2), 258–282 (1982)
26. Miller, D.: A logic programming language with lambda-abstraction, function variables, and simple unification. J. Log. Comput. **1**(4), 497–536 (1991)
27. Moran, A., Sands, D., Carlsson, M.: Erratic fudgets: a semantic theory for an embedded coordination language. In: Ciancarini, P., Wolf, A.L. (eds.) COORDINATION 1999. LNCS, vol. 1594, pp. 85–102. Springer, Heidelberg (1999). doi:10.1007/3-540-48919-3_8
28. Picouleau, C.: Complexity of the Hamiltonian cycle in regular graph problem. Theor. Comput. Sci. **131**(2), 463–473 (1994)

29. Schmidt-SchauSS, M., Rau, C., Sabel, D.: Algorithms for extended alpha-equivalence and complexity. In: van Raamsdonk, F. (ed.) 24th RTA 2013. LIPIcs, vol. 21, pp. 255–270. Schloss Dagstuhl (2013)
30. Schmidt-Schauß, M., Sabel, D.: Unification of program expressions with recursive bindings. In: Cheney, J., Vidal, G. (eds.) 18th PPDP, pp. 160–173. ACM (2016). http://doi.acm.org/10.1145/2967973.2968603
31. Schmidt-Schauß, M., Schütz, M., Sabel, D.: Safety of Nöcker's strictness analysis. J. Funct. Program. **18**(04), 503–551 (2008)
32. Schöning, U.: Graph isomorphism is in the low hierarchy. J. Comput. Syst. Sci. **37**(3), 312–323 (1988)
33. Simon, L., Mallya, A., Bansal, A., Gupta, G.: Coinductive logic programming. In: Etalle, S., Truszczyński, M. (eds.) ICLP 2006. LNCS, vol. 4079, pp. 330–345. Springer, Heidelberg (2006). doi:10.1007/11799573_25
34. Urban, C., Kaliszyk, C.: General bindings and alpha-equivalence in nominal Isabelle. Log. Methods Comput. Sci. **8**(2:14), 1–35 (2012). www.lmcs-online.org
35. Urban, C., Pitts, A., Gabbay, M.: Nominal unification. In: Baaz, M., Makowsky, J.A. (eds.) CSL 2003. LNCS, vol. 2803, pp. 513–527. Springer, Heidelberg (2003). doi:10.1007/978-3-540-45220-1_41
36. Urban, C., Pitts, A.M., Gabbay, M.J.: Nominal unification. Theor. Comput. Sci. **323**(1–3), 473–497 (2004)

Automata Theory Approach
to Predicate Intuitionistic Logic

Maciej Zielenkiewicz$^{(\boxtimes)}$ and Aleksy Schubert

Institute of Informatics, University of Warsaw, Warsaw, Poland
{maciekz,alx}@mimuw.edu.pl

Abstract. Predicate intuitionistic logic is a well established fragment of dependent types. According to the Curry-Howard isomorphism proof construction in the logic corresponds well to synthesis of a program the type of which is a given formula. We present a model of automata that can handle proof construction in full intuitionistic first-order logic. The automata are constructed in such a way that any successful run corresponds directly to a normal proof in the logic. This makes it possible to discuss formal languages of proofs or programs, the closure properties of the automata and their connections with the traditional logical connectives.

1 Introduction

Investigations in automata theory lead to abstraction of algorithmic processes of various kinds. This enables analysis of their strength both in terms of their expressibility (i.e. which problems can be solved with them) and in terms of resources they consume (e.g. time or space). They also make it possible to shed a different light on the original problem (e.g. the linguistic problem of languages generated by grammars can be reduced to the analysis of pushdown automata) which makes it possible to conduct analysis that was not possible before. In addition, the automata become a particular compact data structure that can in itself, when defined formally, be subject to further investigation, as finite or pushdown automata are in automata theory.

Typically, design of automata requires one to select a finite control over the process of interest. This is not always immediate when λ-calculi come into play as λ-terms can contain bound variables from an infinite set. One possibility consists of restricting the programming language so that there is no need to introduce binders. This method was used in the work of Düdder et al. [3], which was powerful enough to synthesise λ-terms that were programs in a simple but expressive functional language.

Another approach would be to restrict the program search to programs in *total discharge form*. In programs of this form, it is needed to keep track of types of available library calls, but not of the call names themselves. This idea was explored by Takahashi et al. [11] who defined context-free grammars that can be used for proof search in propositional intuitionistic logic, which is, by

M.V. Hermenegildo and P. Lopez-Garcia (Eds.): LOPSTR 2016, LNCS 10184, pp. 345–360, 2017.
DOI: 10.1007/978-3-319-63139-4_20

Curry-Howard isomorphism, equivalent to program search in the simply typed λ-calculus. Actually, the grammars can be viewed as performing program search using tree automata by means of the known correspondence between grammars and tree automata. However, the limitation to the total discharge form can be avoided by means of techniques developed by Schubert, Dekkers and Barendregt [8].

A different approach to abstract machinery behind program search process was proposed by Broda and Damas [2] who developed a formula-tree proof method. This technique provides a realisation of the proof search procedure for a particular propositional formula as a data structure, which can be further subject to algorithmic manipulation.

In addition to these investigations for intuitionistic propositional logic there was a proposal of applying automata theoretic notions to proof search in first-order logic [6]. In this paper, Hetzl characterises a class of proofs in intuitionistic first-order logic recognisable by *tree automata with global equalities and disequalities* (TAGED) [4]. The characterisation makes it possible to recognise proofs that are not necessarily in normal form, but is also limited to certain class of tautologies as the emptiness problem for the automata is decidable.

In this paper we propose an automata-theoretical abstraction of the proving process in full intuitionistic first-order logic. Its advantages can be best expressed by stating in which implicit but crucial features of the proof search process become explicit. In our automata the following elements of the proving process are exposed.

- The finite control of the proving process is made explicit.
- A binary internal structure of the control is explicated where one component corresponds to a subformula of the original formula and one to the internal operations that should be done to handle the proof part relevant for the subformula. As a by-product of this formulation it becomes apparent how crucial a role the subformula property plays in the proving process.
- The resource that serves to represent eigenvariables which occur in the process is distinguished. This abstraction is important as the variables play a crucial role in complexity results concerning the logic [9,10].
- The automata enable the possibility of getting rid of the particular syntactical form of formulas and instead work on more abstract structures.
- The definition of automaton distils the basic instructions necessary to conduct the proof process, which brings into the view more elementary operations the proving process depends on.

Although the work is formulated in terms of logic, it can be viewed as synthesis of programs in a restricted class of dependently typed functional programs.

Organisation of the paper. We fix the notation and present intuitionistic first-order logic in Sect. 2. Next, we define our automata in Sect. 3. We summarise the account in Sect. 4.

2   Preliminaries

We present the notation and the basic facts about intuitionistic first-order logic. The notation $A \rightharpoonup B$ is used to denote the type of partial functions from A to B. We write $\mathrm{dom}(f)$ for the domain of the function $f : A \rightharpoonup B$. For two partial functions f, g we define $f \ll g = f \cup \{\langle x, y \rangle \in g \mid x \notin \mathrm{dom}(f)\}$. The set of all subsets of a set A is $P(A)$.

A prefix closed set of strings $\mathbb{N}^*$ over $\mathbb{N}$ is called a *carrier of a tree*. A tree is a tuple $\langle A, \leq, L, l \rangle$ where A is a carrier of the tree, $\leq$ is the prefix order on $\mathbb{N}^*$, L is the set of labels and $l : A \to L$ is the *labelling function*. Whenever the set of labels and the labelling function are clear from the context, we abbreviate the quadruple to the tuple $\langle A, \leq \rangle$. Since the formula notation makes it easy, we sometimes use a subtree φ of A to actually denote a node in A at which φ starts.

2.1   Intuitionistic First-Order Logic

The basis for our study is the first-order intuitionistic logic (for more details see e.g. the work of Urzyczyn [12]). We assume that we have a set of predicates $\mathcal{P}$ that can be used to form atomic formulae and an infinite set $\mathcal{X}_1$ of first-order variables, usually noted as X, Y, Z etc. with possible annotations. Each element P of $\mathcal{P}$ has an arity, denoted $\mathrm{arity}(\mathrm{P})$. The formulae of the system are:

$$\varphi, \psi ::= \mathrm{P}(X_1, \ldots, X_n) \mid \varphi_1 \wedge \varphi_2 \mid \varphi_1 \vee \varphi_2 \mid \varphi_1 \to \varphi_2 \mid \forall X.\varphi \mid \exists X.\varphi \mid \bot$$

where P is an n-ary predicate and $X, X_1, \ldots, X_n \in \mathcal{X}_1$. We follow Prawitz and introduce negation as a notation defined $\neg\varphi ::= \varphi \to \bot$. A formula of the form $\mathrm{P}(X_1, \ldots, X_n)$ is called an *atom*. A *pseudo-atom formula* is a formula of one of the three forms: atom formula, a formula of the form $\exists X.\varphi$, or a formula of the form $\varphi_1 \vee \varphi_2$. We do not include parentheses in the grammar since we actually understand the formulas as abstract syntax trees instead of strings. The tree is traditionally labelled with the cases of the above mentioned grammar. We assume that, for a given case in the grammar, the corresponding node of the tree has as many sons as there are non-terminal symbols in the case. In addition, we use in writing traditional disambiguation conventions for $\wedge, \vee$ and insert parentheses to further disambiguate whenever this is necessary. The connective $\to$ is understood as right-associative so that $\varphi_1 \to \varphi_2 \to \varphi_3$ is equivalent to $\varphi_1 \to (\varphi_2 \to \varphi_3)$. In a formula $\varphi = \varphi_1 \to \cdots \to \varphi_n \to \varphi'$, where φ' is a pseudo-atom, the formula φ' is called the *target of* φ.

Each time we use the term *subformula* ψ of φ, we implicitly mean a particular occurrence of ψ in φ. This occurrence is in our text either unimportant or obvious from the context.

We define the set of *free first-order variables* in a formula φ:

- $\mathrm{FV}_1(\mathrm{P}(X_1, \ldots, X_n)) = \{X_1, \ldots, X_n\}$,
- $\mathrm{FV}_1(\varphi_1 * \varphi_2) = \mathrm{FV}_1(\varphi_1) \cup \mathrm{FV}_1(\varphi_2)$ where $* \in \{\wedge, \vee, \to\}$,
- $\mathrm{FV}_1(\nabla X.\varphi) = \mathrm{FV}_1(\varphi)\backslash\{X\}$ where $\nabla \in \{\exists, \forall\}$,
- $\mathrm{FV}_1(\bot) = \emptyset$.

Other variables that occur in a formula are bound. Terms that differ only in renaming of bound variables are α-equivalent and we do not distinguish between them. To describe the binding structure of a formula we use a special bind function. Let us assume that a formula φ has no free variables (i.e. $FV_1(\varphi) = \emptyset$) and let ψ be its subformula together with a variable X free in ψ. We define $\text{bind}_\varphi(\psi, X)$ as the subformula of φ that binds the free occurrences of X in ψ, i.e. the least subformula φ' of φ such that, for each its proper subformula ψ'' that contains ψ as a subformula, $X \in FV(\psi'')$. For instance $\text{bind}_{\perp \rightarrow \exists X. \perp \rightarrow P(X)}(P(X), X) = \exists X. \perp \rightarrow P(X)$.

$$\frac{}{\Gamma, x{:}\varphi \vdash x : \varphi} \ (var)$$

$$\frac{\Gamma \vdash M_1 : \varphi_1 \quad \Gamma \vdash M_2 : \varphi_2}{\Gamma \vdash \langle M_1, M_2 \rangle : \varphi_1 \wedge \varphi_2} \ (\wedge I)$$

$$\frac{\Gamma \vdash M : \varphi_1 \wedge \varphi_2}{\Gamma \vdash \pi_1 M : \varphi_1} \ (\wedge E1) \quad \frac{\Gamma \vdash M : \varphi_1 \wedge \varphi_2}{\Gamma \vdash \pi_2 M : \varphi_2} \ (\wedge E2)$$

$$\frac{\Gamma \vdash M : \varphi_1}{\Gamma \vdash \underline{\text{in}}_{1\varphi_1 \vee \varphi_2} M : \varphi_1 \vee \varphi_2} \ (\vee I1) \quad \frac{\Gamma \vdash M : \varphi_2}{\Gamma \vdash \underline{\text{in}}_{2\varphi_1 \vee \varphi_2} M : \varphi_1 \vee \varphi_2} \ (\vee I1)$$

$$\frac{\Gamma \vdash M : \varphi_1 \vee \varphi_2 \quad \Gamma, x_1 : \varphi_1 \vdash N_1 : \varphi \quad \Gamma, x_2 : \varphi_2 \vdash N_2 : \varphi}{\Gamma \vdash \underline{\text{case}} \ M \ \underline{\text{of}} \ [x_1 : \varphi_1] \, N_1, [x_2 : \varphi_2] \, N_2 : \varphi} \ (\vee E)$$

$$\frac{\Gamma, x{:}\varphi_1 \vdash M : \varphi_2}{\Gamma \vdash \lambda x : \varphi_1. M : \varphi_1 \rightarrow \varphi_2} \ (\rightarrow I) \quad \frac{\Gamma \vdash M_1 : \varphi_1 \rightarrow \varphi_2 \quad \Gamma \vdash M_2 : \varphi_1}{\Gamma \vdash M_1 M_2 : \varphi_2} \ (\rightarrow E)$$

$$\frac{\Gamma \vdash M : \varphi}{\Gamma \vdash \lambda X M : \forall X. \varphi} \ (\forall I)^* \quad \frac{\Gamma \vdash M : \forall X. \varphi}{\Gamma \vdash M Y : \varphi[X := Y]} \ (\forall E)$$

$$\frac{\Gamma \vdash M : \varphi[X := Y]}{\Gamma \vdash \underline{\text{pack}} \, M, Y \, \underline{\text{to}} \, \exists X. \varphi : \exists X. \varphi} \ (\exists I) \quad \frac{\Gamma \vdash M_1 : \exists X. \varphi \quad \Gamma, x{:}\varphi \vdash M_2 : \psi}{\Gamma \vdash \underline{\text{let}} \, x{:}\varphi \, \underline{\text{be}} \, M_1 : \exists X. \varphi \, \underline{\text{in}} \, M_2 : \psi} \ (\exists E)^*$$

$$\frac{\Gamma \vdash M : \perp}{\Gamma \vdash \perp_\varphi M : \varphi} \ (\perp E)$$

* Under the eigenvariable condition $X \notin FV(\Gamma, \psi)$.

Fig. 1. The rules of the intuitionistic first-order logic

For the definition of *proof terms* we assume that there is an infinite set of *proof term variables* $\mathcal{X}_{\text{p}}$, usually noted as x, y, z etc. with possible annotations. These can be used to form the following terms.

$$
\begin{aligned}
M, N ::=\ & x \mid \langle M_1, M_2 \rangle \mid \pi_1 M \mid \pi_2 M \mid \\
& \underline{\text{in}}_{1\varphi_1 \vee \varphi_2} M \mid \underline{\text{in}}_{2\varphi_1 \vee \varphi_2} M \mid \underline{\text{case}} \, M \, \underline{\text{of}} \, [x : \varphi_1] \, N_1, [y : \varphi_2] \, N_2 \mid \\
& \lambda x : \varphi. M \mid M_1 M_2 \mid \lambda X M \mid M X \mid \\
& \underline{\text{pack}} \, M, Y \, \underline{\text{to}} \, \exists X. \varphi \mid \underline{\text{let}} \, x : \varphi \, \underline{\text{be}} \, M_1 : \exists X. \varphi \, \underline{\text{in}} \, M_2 \mid \perp_\varphi M
\end{aligned}
$$

where x is a proof term variable, $\varphi, \varphi_1, \varphi_2$ are first-order formulas and X, Y are first-order variables. Due to Curry-Howard isomorphism the proof terms can serve as programs in a functional programming language. Their operational semantics is given in terms of reductions. Their full exposition can be found in the work of de Groote [5]. We omit it here, but give an intuitive account of the meaning of the terms. In particular, $\langle M_1, M_2 \rangle$ represents the product aggregation construct and $\pi_i M$ for $i = 1, 2$ decomposition of the aggregation by means of projections. The terms $\underline{\text{in}}_{1_{\varphi_1 \vee \varphi_2}} M$, $\underline{\text{in}}_{2_{\varphi_1 \vee \varphi_2}} M$ reinterpret the value of M as one in type $\varphi_1 \vee \varphi_2$. At the same time $\underline{\text{case}}\, M \,\underline{\text{of}}\, [x : \varphi_1] \, N_1, \, [y : \varphi_2] \, N_2$ construct offers the possibility to make case analysis of a value in an $\vee$-type. This construct is available in functional programming languages in a more general form of algebraic types. The terms $\lambda x : \varphi.M$, $M_1 M_2$ represent traditional function abstraction and application. The proof terms that represent universal quantifier manipulation make it possible to parametrise type with a particular value $\lambda X M$ and use the parametrised term for a particular case $M X$. At last $\underline{\text{pack}}\, M, \, Y \,\underline{\text{to}}\, \exists X. \, \varphi$ makes it possible to hide behind a variable X an actual realisation of a construction that uses another individual variable Y. The abstraction obtained in this way can be exploited using $\underline{\text{let}}\, x : \varphi \,\underline{\text{be}}\, M_1 : \exists X. \varphi \,\underline{\text{in}}\, M_2$. At last the term $\perp\!\!\!\perp_\varphi M$ corresponds to the break instruction.

The environments (Γ, Δ, etc. with possible annotations) in the proving system are finite sets of pairs $x : \psi$ that assign formulas to proof variables. We write $\Gamma \vdash M : A$ to express that the judgement is indeed derivable. The inference rules of the logic are presented in Fig. 1. We have two kinds of free variables, namely free proof term variables and free first-order variables. The set of free proof-term variables is defined inductively as follows

- $\text{FV}(x) = \{x\}$,
- $\text{FV}(\langle M_1, M_2 \rangle) = \text{FV}(M_1 M_2) = \text{FV}(M_1) \cup \text{FV}(M_2)$,
- $\text{FV}(\pi_1 M) = \text{FV}(\pi_2 M) = \text{FV}(\underline{\text{in}}_{1_{\varphi_1 \vee \varphi_2}} M) = \text{FV}(\underline{\text{in}}_{2_{\varphi_1 \vee \varphi_2}} M) = $
  $\text{FV}(\lambda X M) = \text{FV}(M X) = \text{FV}(\underline{\text{pack}}\, M, \, Y \,\underline{\text{to}}\, \exists X. \, \varphi) = \text{FV}(\perp\!\!\!\perp_\varphi M) = $
  $\text{FV}(M)$,
- $\text{FV}(\underline{\text{case}}\, M \,\underline{\text{of}}\, [x : \varphi_1] \, N_1, \, [y : \varphi_2] \, N_2) = $
  $\text{FV}(M) \cup (\text{FV}(N_1) \backslash \{x\}) \cup (\text{FV}(N_2) \backslash y)$,
- $\text{FV}(\lambda x : \varphi.M) = \text{FV}(X) \backslash \{x\}$,
- $\text{FV}(\underline{\text{let}}\, x : \varphi \,\underline{\text{be}}\, M_1 : \exists X. \varphi \,\underline{\text{in}}\, M_2) = \text{FV}(M_1) \cup (\text{FV}(M_2) \backslash \{x\})$.

Again, the terms that differ only in names of bound proof-term variables are considered α-equivalent and are not distinguished. Note that we can use the notation $\text{FV}_1(M)$ to refer to all free type variables that occur in M. This set is defined by recursion over the terms and taking all the free first-order variables that occur in formulas that are part of the terms so that for instance $\text{FV}_1(\underline{\text{in}}_{1_{\varphi_1 \vee \varphi_2}} M) = \text{FV}_1(\varphi_1) \cup \text{FV}_1(\varphi_2) \cup \text{FV}_1(M)$. At the same time there are naturally terms that bind first-order variables, $\text{FV}_1(\lambda X M) = \text{FV}_1(M) \backslash \{X\}$ and bring new free first-order ones, e.g. $\text{FV}_1(M X) = \text{FV}(M) \cup \{X\}$.

Traditionally, the (*cut*) rule is not mentioned among standard rules in Fig. 1, but as it is common in λ-calculi, it is included it in the system in the form of a β-reduction rule. This rule forms the basic computation mechanism in the system understood as a programming language. We omit the rules due to the lack of space, but an interested reader can find them in the work of de Groote [5]. Still, we want to focus our attention to terms in normal form (i.e. terms that cannot be reduced further). Partly because the search for terms in such form is easier and partly because source code of programs contains virtually exclusively terms in this form. The following theorem states that this simplification does not make us lose any possible programs in our program synthesis approach.

Theorem 1 (Normalisation). *First-order intuitionistic logic is strongly normalisable i.e. each reduction has a finite number of steps.*

The same paper by de Groote contains also (implicitly) the following result.

Theorem 2 (Subject reduction). *First-order intuitionistic logic has the subject reduction property, i.e. if $\Gamma \vdash M : \phi$ and $M \to_{\beta \cup p} N$ then $\Gamma \vdash N : \phi$.*

This theorem speaks about $\to_{\beta \cup p}$ reduction that is the sum of β-reduction and permutation reduction (p stands for permutation), which makes it possible to extensively regulate the shape of normal terms. The resulting regular form defined below is the *long normal form*. As a consequence of the above two theorems we conclude that each provable formula has a proof in this regulated normal form.

2.2   Long Normal Forms

We restrict our attention to terms which are in *long normal form* (*lnf* in short). The idea of long normal form for our logic is best explained by the following example ([12], Sect. 5): suppose $X : r$ and $Y : r \to p \vee q$. The long normal form of YX is $\underline{\text{case}}\,YX\,\underline{\text{of}}\,[a : p]\,\lambda u.\,\underline{\text{in}}_1\,u,\,[b : q]\,\lambda v.\,\underline{\text{in}}_2\,v$.

Our definitions follow those of Urzyczyn, [12]. We classify normal forms into:

- introductions $\lambda X.N$, $\lambda x.N$, $\langle N1, N2 \rangle$, $\underline{\text{in}}_1\,N$, $\underline{\text{in}}_2\,N$, $\underline{\text{pack}}\,N$, $y\,\underline{\text{to}}\,\exists X.\varphi$,
- proper eliminators X, PN, $\pi_i P$, $P(x)$,
- improper eliminators $\perp\!\!\!\perp_\varphi(P)$, $\underline{\text{case}}\,P\,\underline{\text{of}}\,[x : \varphi_1]\,N_1,\,[y : \varphi_2]\,N_2$, $\underline{\text{let}}\,x : \varphi\,\underline{\text{be}}\,N : \exists X.\varphi\,\underline{\text{in}}\,P$

where P is a proper eliminator and N is a normal form. The long normal forms (lnfs) are defined recursively with *quasi-long proper eliminators*:

- A quasi-long proper eliminator is a proper eliminator where all arguments are of pseudo-atom type.[1]
- A constructor $\lambda X.N$, $\langle N_1, N_2 \rangle$, $\in_i N$, $\underline{\text{pack}}\,N$, $y\,\underline{\text{to}}\,\exists X.\varphi$, $\underline{\text{let}}\,x : \varphi\,\underline{\text{be}}\,N_1 : \exists X.\varphi\,\underline{\text{in}}\,N_2$ is a lnf when its arguments N, N_1, N_2 are lnfs.
- A case-eliminator $\underline{\text{case}}\,P\,\underline{\text{of}}\,[x : \varphi_1]\,N_1,\,[y : \varphi_2]\,N_2$ is a lnf when N_1 and N_2 are lnfs and P is a quasi-long proper eliminator. A miracle (*ex falso quodlibet*) $\perp\!\!\!\perp_\varphi(P)$ of a target type φ is a long normal form when P is a quasi-long proper eliminator of type $\perp$.

---

[1] Note that a variable is a quasi-long proper eliminator because all arguments is an empty set in this case.

– An eliminator $\underline{\text{let}}\,x : \varphi\,\underline{\text{be}}\,N : \exists X.\varphi\,\underline{\text{in}}\,P$ is an lnf when N is an lnf and P is a quasi-long proper eliminator.

The usefulness of these forms results from the following proposition, [12].

Proposition 1 (Long normal forms). *If $\Gamma \vdash M : \phi$ then there is a long normal form N such that $\Gamma \vdash N : \phi$.*

The design of automata that handle proof search in the first-order logic requires us to find out what are the actual resources the proof search should work with. We observe here that the proof search process—as it is the case of the propositional intuitionistic logic—can be restricted to formulas that occur only as subformulas in the initial formula. Of course this time we have to take into account first-order variables. The following proposition, which we know how to prove for long normal forms only, sets the observation in precise terms.

Proposition 2. *Consider a derivation of $\vdash M : \varphi$ such that M is in the long normal form. Each judgement $\Gamma \vdash N : \psi$ that occurs in this derivation has the property that, for each formula ξ in Γ and for ψ, there is a subformula ξ' of φ such that $\xi = \xi'[X_1 := Y_1, \ldots, X_n := Y_n]$ where $\mathrm{FV}(\xi') = \{X_1, \ldots, X_n\}$ and $Y_1, \ldots, Y_n$ are some first-order variables.*

Proof. Induction over the size of the term N. The details are left to the reader. □

We can generalise the property expressed in the proposition above and say that a formula ψ *emerged* from φ when there is a subformula ψ_0 of φ and a substitution $[X_1 := Y_1, \ldots, X_n := Y_n]$ with $\mathrm{FV}_1(\psi_0) = \{X_1, \ldots, X_n\}$ such that $\psi = \psi_0[X_1 := Y_1, \ldots, X_n := Y_n]$. We say that a context Γ emerged from φ when, for each its element $x : \psi$, the formula ψ emerged from φ.

3 Arcadian Automata

Our *Arcadian automaton*[2] $\mathbb{A}$ is defined as a tuple $\langle \mathcal{A}, Q, q^0, \varphi^0, \mathcal{I}, i, \mathrm{fv} \rangle$, where

– $\mathcal{A} = \langle A, \leq \rangle$ is a finite tree, which formally describes a division of the automaton control into intercommunicating modules; the root of the tree is written ε; since the tree is finite we have the relation ρ succ ρ' when $\rho \leq \rho'$ and there is no $\rho'' \neq \rho$ and $\rho'' \neq \rho'$ such that $\rho \leq \rho'' \leq \rho'$;
– Q is a set of states;
– $q^0 \in Q$ is an *initial* state of the automaton;
– $\varphi^0 \in A$ is an *initial* tree node of the automaton;
– $\mathcal{I}$ is a set of all instructions;

---

[2] The name Arcadian automata stems from the fact that a slightly different and weaker notion of *Eden automata* was developed before [10] to deal with the fragment of the first-order intuitionistic logic with $\forall$ and $\to$ and in which the universal quantifier occurs only on positive positions.

- $i: Q \rightarrow \mathcal{P}(\mathcal{I})$ is a function which gives the set of instructions *available* in a given state; the function i must be such that every instruction belongs to exactly one state;
- fv $: A \rightarrow P(A)$ is a function that describes the binding, it has the property that for each node v of A it holds that $\mathrm{fv}(v) = \bigcup_{w \in B} \mathrm{fv}(w)$ where $B = \{w \mid v \text{ succ } w\}$.

Each state may be either existential or universal and belongs to an element $a \in A$, so $Q = Q^{\exists} \cup Q^{\forall}$, and $Q^{\forall} = \bigcup_{a \in A} Q_a^{\forall}$ and $Q^{\exists} = \bigcup_{a \in A} Q_a^{\exists}$. The set of states Q is divided into two disjoint sets $Q_{\forall}$ and $Q_{\exists}$ of, respectively, universal and existential states.

Operational semantics of the automaton. An *instantaneous description* (ID) of $\mathbb{A}$ is a tuple $\langle q, \kappa, w, w', S, V \rangle$ where

- $q \in Q$ is the current state,
- κ is the current node in A,
- $w: A \rightharpoonup V$ is the interpretation of bindings associated with κ by $\mathrm{fv}(\kappa)$, in particular we require here that $\mathrm{fv}(\kappa) \subseteq \mathrm{dom}(w)$,
- $w': A \rightharpoonup V$ is the auxiliary interpretation of bindings that can be stored in this location of the ID to implement some operations. w' is the value of a temporary register of the automaton, role of which will be discussed later.
- S is the *store* of the automaton, which is a set of pairs $\langle \rho, v \rangle$ where $\rho \in A$ and $v: A \rightharpoonup V$ and we require that $\mathrm{fv}(\rho) \subseteq \mathrm{dom}(v)$,
- V is the working domain of the automaton, i.e. a set of eigenvariables, which can be represented for example as natural numbers.

Predicate logic is defined in two flavours. In one of them empty structure carriers are allowed in the other one, forbidden. We choose as the initial ID the tuple $\langle q^0, \varphi^0, \emptyset, \emptyset, \emptyset, \emptyset \rangle$. This choice is correct for the version of logic with empty carriers allowed.

Intuitively speaking the automaton works as a device which discovers the knowledge accumulated in the tree $\mathcal{A}$. It can distinguish new items of interest in the domain of the discourse and these are stored in the set V while the facts concerning the elements of V are stored in S. Traditionally, the control of the automaton is represented by the current state q, which belongs to a "module" indicated by κ. We can imagine the automaton as a device that tries to check if a particular piece of information encoded in the tree $\mathcal{A}$ is correct. In this view the piece of information which is being checked for correctness at a given point is represented by the current node κ combined with current interpretation of bindings w. The interpretation of bindings w' is used to temporarily hold an interpretation of some bindings.

We have 7 kinds of instructions in our automata. We give here their operational semantics. Let us assume that we are in a current ID $\langle q, \kappa, w, w', S, V \rangle$. The operation of the instructions is defined as follows, where we assume $q' \in Q$, $\rho, \rho' \in A$.

1. $q : \mathsf{store}\rho, \rho'q'$ turns the current ID into
   $\langle q', \rho', w, \emptyset, S \cup \{\langle \rho, (w' \ll w)|_{\mathrm{fv}(\rho)}\rangle\}, V\rangle$,
2. $q : \mathsf{jmp}\rho, q'$ turns the current ID into $\langle q', \rho, w'', \emptyset, S, V\rangle$, where
   $(w \ll w')|_{\mathrm{fv}(\kappa)} \subseteq w''$ and $\mathrm{fv}(\rho) \subseteq \mathrm{dom}(w'')$,
3. $q : \mathsf{new}\rho, q'$ turns the current ID into $\langle q', \rho, w, \emptyset, S, V \cup \{X\}\rangle$, where $X \notin V$,
4. $q : \mathsf{check}\rho, \rho', q'$ turns the current ID into $\langle q', \rho', w, \emptyset, S, V\rangle$, the instruction is
   applicable only when there is a pair $\langle \rho, v\rangle \in S$ such that $v(\rho) = w(\kappa)$,
5. $q : \mathsf{instL}\rho, \rho', q'$ turns the current ID into $\langle q', \rho', w, \emptyset, S \cup \{\langle \rho, w''|_{\mathrm{fv}(\rho)}\rangle\}, V \cup$
   $\{X\}\rangle$, the instruction is applicable only when there is a node $\rho'' \in A$ such
   that ρ'' succ ρ and where $w'' = ([\rho'' := X] \ll w) \ll w'$ and $X \notin V$,
6. $q : \mathsf{instR}\rho, q'$ turns the current ID into $\langle q', \rho, w'', \emptyset, S, V\rangle$, the instruction is
   applicable only when an additional condition is met that κ succ ρ and where
   $w'' = [\gamma := X] \ll w|_{\mathrm{fv}(\rho)}$ and $\gamma \in \mathrm{fv}(\rho)\backslash\mathrm{fv}(\kappa)$ and $X \in V$,
7. $q : \mathsf{load}\rho, q'$ turns the current ID into $\langle q', \rho, w'', v, S, V\rangle$, where
   $(w \ll w')|_{\mathrm{fv}(\kappa)} \subseteq w''$ and $\mathrm{fv}(\rho) \subseteq \mathrm{dom}(w'')$, and $v : A \rightharpoonup V$.

When an element of the resulting ID is underspecified in instruction semantics
it should be understood that any of the IDs fulfilling the description can be the
result.

These instructions abstract the basic operations associated with the process
of proving in predicate logic. Observe that the content of the additional register
loaded by the instruction load can be used only by the immediately following
instruction as all the other instructions erase the content of the register.

It is also interesting to observe that the set of instructions contains, in addition to standard assembly-like instructions, two instructions instL and instR that
deal with pattern instantiation.

The following notion of acceptance is defined inductively. We say that the
automaton A *eventually accepts* from an ID $a = \langle q, \kappa, w, w', S, V\rangle$ when

1. q is universal and there are no instructions available in state q (i.e. $i(q) = \emptyset$,
   such states are called *accepting states*), or
2. q is universal and, for each instruction i available in q, the automaton started
   in an ID a' eventually accepts, where a' is obtained from a by executing i,
3. if q is existential and, for some instruction i available in state q the automaton started in an ID a' eventually accepts, where a' is obtained from a by
   executing i.

The definition above actually defines inductively a certain kind of tree, the
nodes of which are IDs and children of a node are determined by the configurations obtained by executing available instructions. Actually, we can view the
process described above not only as a process of reaching acceptance, but also
as a process of accepting the ID tree. In this light the automaton is eventually
accepting from an initial configuration if and only if the language of its 'runs' is
not empty. As a result we can talk about the acceptance of such automata by
referring to the *emptiness problem*.

Here is a basic monotonicity property of Arcadian automata.

Structural decomposition instructions

---

(1) $\varphi_1 \to \varphi_2$ $\quad q^\forall_{\varphi_1 \to \varphi_2} : \text{store } \varphi_1, \varphi_2, q^\exists_{\varphi_2}$

$\Rightarrow \langle q^\forall_{\varphi_1 \to \varphi_2}, \varphi_1 \to \varphi_2, w, \emptyset, S, V \rangle \to \langle q^\exists_{\varphi_2}, \varphi_2, w, \emptyset, S \cup \{\langle \varphi_1, w|_{\text{fv}(\varphi_1)} \rangle\}, V \rangle$

---

(2) $\varphi_1 \wedge \varphi_2$ $\quad q^\forall_{\varphi_1 \wedge \varphi_2} : \text{jmp } \varphi_1, q^\exists_{\varphi_1}$

$\Rightarrow \quad \langle q^\forall_{\varphi_1 \wedge \varphi_2}, \varphi_1 \wedge \varphi_2, w, \emptyset, S, V \rangle \to \langle q^\exists_{\varphi_1}, \varphi_1, w, \emptyset, S, V \rangle$

$\quad q^\forall_{\varphi_1 \wedge \varphi_2} : \text{jmp } \varphi_2, q^\exists_{\varphi_2}$

$\Rightarrow \quad \langle q^\forall_{\varphi_1 \wedge \varphi_2}, \varphi_1 \wedge \varphi_2, w, \emptyset, S, V \rangle \to \langle q^\exists_{\varphi_2}, \varphi_2, w, \emptyset, S, V \rangle$

---

(3) $\varphi_1 \vee \varphi_2$ $\quad q^\exists_{\varphi_1 \vee \varphi_2} : \text{jmp } \varphi_1, q^\exists_{\varphi_1}$

$\Rightarrow \quad \langle q^\exists_{\varphi_1 \vee \varphi_2}, \varphi_1 \vee \varphi_2, w, \emptyset, S, V \rangle \to \langle q^\exists_{\varphi_1}, \varphi_1, w, \emptyset, S, V \rangle$

$\quad q^\exists_{\varphi_1 \vee \varphi_2} : \text{jmp } \varphi_2, q^\exists_{\varphi_2}$

$\Rightarrow \quad \langle q^\exists_{\varphi_1 \vee \varphi_2}, \varphi_1 \vee \varphi_2, w, \emptyset, S, V \rangle \to \langle q^\exists_{\varphi_2}, \varphi_2, w, \emptyset, S, V \rangle$

---

(4) $\forall X.\varphi$ $\quad q^\forall_{\forall X.\varphi} : \text{new } \varphi, q^\exists_\varphi$

$\Rightarrow \quad \langle q^\forall_{\forall X.\varphi}, \forall X.\varphi, w, \emptyset, S, V \rangle \to \langle q^\exists_\varphi, \varphi, [\forall X.\varphi := Y] \ll w, \emptyset, S, V \cup \{Y\} \rangle$

where $Y \notin V$

---

(5) $\exists X.\varphi$ $\quad q^\forall_{\exists X.\varphi} : \text{instR } \varphi, q^\exists_\varphi$

$\Rightarrow \quad \langle q^\forall_{\exists X.\varphi}, \exists X.\varphi, w, \emptyset, S, V \rangle \to \langle q^\exists_\varphi, \varphi, [\exists X.\varphi := Y] \ll w|_{\text{fv}(\exists X.\varphi)}, \emptyset, S, V \rangle$

where $Y \in V$

Fig. 2. Structural decomposition instructions of the automaton

Proposition 3. *If the automaton $\mathbb{A}$ eventually accepts from $\langle q, \kappa, w, w', S, V \rangle$ and $w \subseteq \hat{w}$ then the automaton $\mathbb{A}$ eventually accepts from $\langle q, \kappa, \hat{w}, w', S, V \rangle$.*

Proof. Induction over the definition of the configuration from which automaton eventually accepts. The details are left to the reader. □

3.1   From Formulas to Automata

We can now define an Arcadian automaton $\mathbb{A}_\varphi = \langle \mathcal{A}, Q, q^\exists_\varphi, \varphi, \mathcal{I}, i, \text{fv} \rangle$ that corresponds to provability of the formula φ. For technical reasons we assume that the formula is closed. This restriction is not essential since the provability of a formula with free variables is equivalent to the provability of its universal closure. The components of the automaton are as follows.

- $\mathcal{A} = \langle A, \leq \rangle$ is the syntax tree of the formula φ.
- $Q = \{q^\forall_\psi, q^\exists_\psi, q^\forall_{\psi, \vee}, q^\forall_{\psi, \to}, q^\forall_{\psi, \exists}, q^\forall_{\psi, \perp} \mid$ for all subformulas ψ of $\varphi\}$. The states annotated with the superscript $\forall$ belong to $Q^\forall$ while the states with the superscript $\exists$ belong to $Q^\exists$.
- $q^\exists_\varphi$ is the initial state (which reflects that the goal of the proving process is φ).
- The initial state and initial tree node are $q^\exists_\varphi$ and φ, respectively.
- $\mathcal{I}$ and i are presented in Figs. 2 and 3. We describe them in more detail below.
- $\text{fv} : A \to P(A)$ is defined so that $\text{fv}(\psi) = \{\text{bind}_\varphi(\psi, X) \mid X \in \text{FV}(\psi)\}$.

Non-structural instructions

(6) $q_\varphi^\exists : \mathsf{jmp}\ \varphi, q_\varphi^\forall$
$$\Rightarrow\ \langle q_\varphi^\exists, \varphi, w, \emptyset, S, V\rangle \to \langle q_\varphi^\forall, \varphi, w, \emptyset, S, V\rangle$$

(7) $q_{\varphi_i}^\exists : \mathsf{jmp}\ \varphi_1 \wedge \varphi_2, q_{\varphi_1 \wedge \varphi_2}^\exists$ for $i = 1, 2$
$$\Rightarrow\ \langle q_\varphi^\exists, \varphi, w, \emptyset, S, V\rangle \to \langle q_{\varphi_1 \wedge \varphi_2}^\exists, \varphi_1 \wedge \varphi_2, w'', \emptyset, S, V\rangle$$

(8) $q_\varphi^\exists : \mathsf{load}\ \varphi, q_{\varphi, \vee}^\forall$
$$\Rightarrow\ \langle q_\varphi^\exists, \varphi, w, \emptyset, S, V\rangle \to \langle q_{\varphi, \vee}^\forall, \varphi, w, w', S, V\rangle$$

(9) $q_\varphi^\exists : \mathsf{jmp}\ \varphi, q_{\varphi, \to}^\forall$
$$\Rightarrow\ \langle q_\varphi^\exists, \varphi, w, \emptyset, S, V\rangle \to \langle q_{\varphi, \to}^\forall, \varphi, \hat{w}, \emptyset, S, V\rangle \quad \text{where } w \subseteq \hat{w}$$

(10) $q_\varphi^\exists : \mathsf{jmp}\ \forall X.\varphi, q_{\forall X.\varphi}^\exists$
$$\Rightarrow\ \langle q_\varphi^\exists, \varphi, w, \emptyset, S, V\rangle \to \langle q_{\forall X.\varphi}^\exists, \forall X.\varphi, w, \emptyset, S, V\rangle$$

(11) $q_\varphi^\exists : \mathsf{load}\ \varphi, q_{\varphi, \exists}^\forall$
$$\Rightarrow\ \langle q_\varphi^\exists, \varphi, w, \emptyset, S, V\rangle \to \langle q_{\varphi, \exists}^\forall, \varphi, w, w', S, V\rangle$$

(12) $q_\varphi^\exists : \mathsf{jmp}\ \varphi, q_{\varphi, \perp}^\forall$
$$\Rightarrow\ \langle q_\varphi^\exists, \varphi, w, \emptyset, S, V\rangle \to \langle q_{\varphi, \perp}^\forall, \varphi, w, \emptyset, S, V\rangle$$

---

(13) $q_\varphi^\exists : \mathsf{check}\ \varphi, \varphi, q_{\text{axiom}}^\forall$
$$\Rightarrow\ \langle q_\varphi^\exists, \varphi, w, \emptyset, S, V\rangle \to \langle q_{\text{axiom}}^\forall, \varphi, w, \emptyset, S, V\rangle$$

---

(14) $q_{\varphi, \vee}^\forall : \mathsf{jmp}\ \psi_1 \vee \psi_2, q_{\psi_1 \vee \psi_2}^\exists$
$$\Rightarrow\ \langle q_{\varphi, \vee}^\forall, \varphi, w, w', S, V\rangle \to \langle q_{\psi_1 \vee \psi_2}^\exists, \psi_1 \vee \psi_2, w', \emptyset, S, V\rangle$$

(15) $q_{\varphi, \vee}^\forall : \mathsf{store}\ \psi_1, \varphi, q_\varphi^\exists$
$$\Rightarrow\ \langle q_{\varphi, \vee}^\forall, \varphi, w, w', S, V\rangle \to \langle q_\varphi^\exists, \varphi, w', \emptyset, S', V\rangle$$
where $S' = S \cup \{\langle \psi_1, w'|_{\mathsf{fv}(\psi_1)}\rangle\}$

(16) $q_{\varphi, \vee}^\forall : \mathsf{store}\ \psi_2, \varphi, q_\varphi^\exists$
$$\Rightarrow\ \langle q_{\varphi, \vee}^\forall, \varphi, w, w', S, V\rangle \to \langle q_\varphi^\exists, \varphi, w', \emptyset, S', V\rangle$$
where $S' = S \cup \{\langle \psi_2, w'|_{\mathsf{fv}(\psi_2)}\rangle\}$

(15) and (16) should be instantiated with ψ_1 and ψ_2's which were used in (14).

---

(17) $q_{\varphi, \to}^\forall : \mathsf{jmp}\ \psi \to \varphi, q_{\psi \to \varphi}^\exists$
$$\Rightarrow\ \langle q_{\varphi, \to}^\forall, \varphi, w, \emptyset, S, V\rangle \to \langle q_{\psi \to \varphi}^\exists, \psi \to \varphi, w, \emptyset, S, V\rangle$$

(18) $q_{\varphi, \to}^\forall : \mathsf{jmp}\ \psi, q_\psi^\exists$
$$\Rightarrow\ \langle q_{\varphi, \to}^\forall, \varphi, w, \emptyset, S, V\rangle \to \langle q_\psi^\exists, \psi, w, \emptyset, S, V\rangle$$

(18) should be instantiated with ψ and φ's which were used in (17).

---

(19) $q_{\varphi, \exists}^\forall : \mathsf{jmp}\ \exists X.\psi, q_{\exists X.\psi}^\exists$
$$\Rightarrow\ \langle q_{\varphi, \exists}^\forall, \varphi, w, w', S, V\rangle \to \langle q_{\exists X.\psi}^\exists, \exists X.\psi, w', \emptyset, S', V\rangle$$

(20) $q_{\varphi, \exists}^\forall : \mathsf{instL}\ \psi, \varphi, q_\varphi^\exists$
$$\Rightarrow\ \langle q_{\varphi, \exists}^\forall, \varphi, w, w', S, V\rangle \to \langle q_\varphi^\exists, \varphi, w'', \emptyset, S', V\rangle$$
where $w'' = ([\exists X.\psi := X] \ll w') \ll w, S' = S \cup \{\langle \psi, w''|_{\mathsf{fv}(\psi)}\rangle\}$

(19) should be instantiated with ψ and φ's which were used in (20).

---

(21) $q_{\varphi, \perp}^\forall : \mathsf{jmp}\ \perp, q_\perp^\exists$
$$\Rightarrow\ \langle q_{\varphi, \perp}^\forall, \varphi, w, \emptyset, S, V\rangle \to \langle q_\perp^\exists, \perp, w, \emptyset, S, V\rangle$$

Fig. 3. Non-structural instructions of the automaton

Figures 2 and 3 present the patterns of possible instructions in $\mathcal{I}$. Each of the instruction patterns starts with a state of the form $q_\psi^\triangledown$ or of the form $q_{\psi,\bullet}^\triangledown$ where $\triangledown$ is a quantifier ($\forall$ or $\exists$), ψ is a subformula of φ and $\bullet$ is one of the symbols $\vee, \rightarrow, \bot, \exists$. For each of the patterns we assume $\mathcal{I}$ contains all the instructions that result from instantiating the pattern with all possible subformulas that match the form of ψ (e.g. in case $\psi = \psi_1 \rightarrow \psi_2$ we take all the subformulas with $\rightarrow$ as the main symbol). The function $i : Q \rightarrow P(\mathcal{I})$ is defined so that for a state $q_\psi^\triangledown$ it returns all the instructions which start from the state. In addition to the instructions they present the way a configuration is transformed by each of the instructions. This serves to facilitate understanding of the proofs.

As the figure suggests, the instructions of the automaton can be divided into two groups—structural decomposition instructions and non-structural ones. The structural instructions are used to decompose a formula into its structural subformulas. On the left-hand side of each of the structural instructions we present the formula the instruction decomposes. The other rules represent operations that manipulate other elements of configuration with possible change of the goal formula, which is illustrated in the following example.

Example. Consider the formula $\varphi_{\mathrm{pos}} = \forall x(P(x)) \rightarrow \forall y \exists x P(x)$. In order to build the Arcadian automaton for that formula first we have to build the tree A of it, which is shown in Fig. 4.

The instructions available ($\mathcal{I}$) are:

(1) $q_1^\vee$: store2, $4, q_4^\exists$ (19) $q_{1,\exists}^\vee$: jmp5, $q_5^\exists$

(4) $q_2^\vee$: new3, $q_3^\exists$ (19) $q_{4,\exists}^\vee$: jmp5, $q_5^\exists$

(4) $q_4^\vee$: new5, $q_5^\exists$ (19) $q_{5,\exists}^\vee$: jmp5, $q_5^\exists$

(5) $q_5^\vee$: instR6, $q_6^\exists$ (20) $q_{1,\exists}^\vee$: instL5, $1, q_1^\exists$

(10) $q_3^\exists$: jmp2, $q_2^\exists$ (20) $q_{4,\exists}^\vee$: instL5, $4, q_4^\exists$

(10) $q_6^\exists$: jmp2, $q_2^\exists$ (20) $q_{5,\exists}^\vee$: instL5, $5, q_5^\exists$

the instructions available for any $a \in A$ are:

Fig. 4. Syntax tree of the formula ϕ_{pos}.

(6) $q_a^\exists$: jmpa, $q_a^\forall$ (8) $q_a^\exists$: loada, $q_{a,\vee}^\forall$ (9) $q_a^\exists$: jmpa, $q_{a,\rightarrow}^\forall$

(11) $q_a^\exists$: loada, $q_{a,\exists}^\forall$ (12) $q_a^\exists$: jmpa, $q_{a,\bot}^\forall$ (13) $q_a^\exists$: checka, $a, q_{\mathrm{axiom}}^\forall$

(21) $q_{a,\rightarrow}^\forall$: jmp$\bot, q_\bot^\exists$

The set of states can be easily written using the definition. To calculate fv we need to calculate binds first. We have $\mathrm{bind}_1(3, x) = 2$ and $\mathrm{bind}_1(6, x) = 5$; therefore $\mathrm{fv}(3) = \{2\}$, $\mathrm{fv}(6) = \{5\}$ and $\mathrm{fv}(x) = \emptyset$ for $x \neq 3, x \neq 6$. We let $q^0 = q_1^\exists$ and $\varphi^0 = \varphi_{\mathrm{pos}}$. The initial ID is $q = q_1^\exists$, $\kappa = 1$, and the other elements of the description are empty sets. A successful run of the automaton is as follows: jmp1, $q_1^\vee$ (rule (6), initial instruction leads to the structural decomposition of the main connective $\rightarrow$); store2, $4, q_4^\exists$ (r. (1), as the result of the decomposition, the formula at the node 2 is moved to the context, and the formula at 4 becomes the proof goal); jmp4, $q_4^\vee$ (r. (6), we progress to the structural decomposition of $\forall$); new5, $q_5^\exists$ (r. (4), we introduce fresh eigenvariable, say X_1, for the universal quantifier); jmp5, $q_5^\vee$ (r. (6), we progress to the structural decomposition of $\exists$); instR6, $q_6^\exists$ (r. (5), we produce a witness for the existential quantifier, which can be just X_1); jmp2, $q_2^\exists$ (r. (10), we progress now with the non-structural rule that handles instantiation of the universal assumption from the node 2); and now we can conclude with check2, 2, q_{axiom} (r. (13)) that directly leads to acceptance.

Negative example. Consider the formula $\varphi_{\text{div}} = (((\forall x. Q(x)) \to p) \to p) \to p$; its tree is presented in Fig. 5. Obviously it does not have an inhabitant. The run of the corresponding automaton is infinite, and its main loop of states begins from $q_1^\exists$. We proceed first with the instruction (rule 1) store2, 8, $q_8^\exists$, then (r. 9) jmp8, $q_{8,\to}^\forall$. Now one of the applications of (17) results in jmp1, $q_1^\exists$ which closes the loop. Note that there is no other way to construct a run for the automaton.

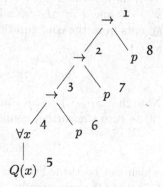

Fig. 5. Syntax tree of φ_{div}.

From derivability questions to IDs. A proof search process in the style of Ben-Yelles [1] works by solving derivability questions of the form $\Gamma \vdash ? : \psi$. We relate this style of proof search to our automata model by a translation of such a question into an ID of the automaton. Suppose that the initial closed formula is φ. We define the configuration of $\mathbb{A}_\varphi$ that corresponds to $\Gamma \vdash ? : \psi$ by exploiting the conclusion of Proposition 2. This proposition makes it possible to associate a substitution w_ψ with ψ and w_ξ with each assignment $x : \xi \in \Gamma$. The resulting configuration is $a_{\Gamma,\psi} = \langle q_{\psi_0}^\exists, \psi_0, w_\psi, \emptyset, S_{\Gamma,\psi}, V_{\Gamma,\psi} \rangle$ where $S_{\Gamma,\psi} = \{ \langle \xi, \psi_\xi \rangle \mid x : \xi \in \Gamma \}$ and $V_{\Gamma,\psi} = \text{FV}_1(\Gamma, \psi)$ as well as $w_\psi(\psi_0) = \psi$.

Lemma 1. *If $\Gamma \vdash M : \psi$ is derivable and such that Γ and ψ emerged from φ then $\mathbb{A}_\varphi$ eventually accepts from the configuration $\langle q_{\psi_0}^\exists, \psi_0, w_\psi, \emptyset, S_{\Gamma,\psi}, V_{\Gamma,\psi} \rangle$, where $w_\psi(\psi_0) = \psi$ and $\text{dom}(w_\psi) = \text{fv}(\psi_0)$.*

Proof. We may assume that M is in the long normal form. The proof is by induction over the derivation of M. We give here only the most interesting cases.

If the last rule is (var), we can apply the non-structural instruction (13) that checks if the formula $w_\psi(\psi_0)$ is in $S_{\Gamma,\psi}$. Then the resulting state $q_{\text{axiom}}^\forall$ is an accepting state.

If the last rule is the $(\wedge I)$ rule then $\psi = \psi_1 \wedge \psi_2$ and we have shorter derivations for $\Gamma \vdash M_1 : \psi_1$ and $\Gamma \vdash M_2 : \psi_2$, which by induction hypothesis give that $\mathbb{A}_\varphi$ eventually accepts from the configurations $\langle q_{\psi_{i0}}^\exists, \psi_{i0}, w_{\psi_i}, \emptyset, S_{\Gamma,\psi_i}, V_{\Gamma,\psi_i} \rangle$ for $i = 1, 2$ where we note that $w_{\psi_i} = w_\psi$, $S_{\Gamma,\psi_i} = S_{\Gamma,\psi}$ and $V_{\Gamma,\psi_i} = V_{\Gamma,\psi}$. We can now use the non-structural rule (6) to turn the existential state $q_\psi^\exists$ into the universal one $q_\psi^\forall$ for which there are two instructions available in (2), and these turn the current configuration into the corresponding above mentioned ones.

If the last rule is the $(\wedge Ei)$ rule for $i = 1, 2$ then we know that $\psi = \psi_i$ for one of $i = 1, 2$ and $\Gamma \vdash M' : \psi_1 \wedge \psi_2$ is derivable through a shorter derivation, which means by the induction hypothesis that $\mathbb{A}_\varphi$ eventually accepts from the configuration $\langle q_{\psi_1 \wedge \psi_2}^\exists, \psi_1 \wedge \psi_2, w_{\psi_1 \wedge \psi_2}, \emptyset, S_{\Gamma,\psi_1 \wedge \psi_2}, V_{\Gamma,\psi_1 \wedge \psi_2} \rangle$ where actually

$w_{\psi_1 \wedge \psi_2}|_{\mathrm{fv}(\psi_i)} \subseteq w_{\psi_i}$ and $\mathrm{fv}(\psi_i) \subseteq \mathrm{dom}(w_{\psi_1 \wedge \psi_2})$ for both $i = 1, 2$. Moreover, $S_{\Gamma, \psi_1 \wedge \psi_2} = S_{\Gamma, \psi}$ and $V_{\Gamma, \psi_1 \wedge \psi_2} = V_{\Gamma, \psi}$. This configuration can be obtained from the current one using respective non-structural instruction presented at (7).

If the last rule is the $(\to E)$ rule then we have shorter derivations for $\Gamma \vdash M_1 : \psi' \to \psi$ and $\Gamma \vdash M_2 : \psi'$. The induction hypothesis gives that $\mathbb{A}_\varphi$ eventually accepts from the configurations

$$\langle q^{\exists}_{\psi'_0 \to \psi_0}, \psi'_0 \to \psi_0, w_{\psi' \to \psi}, \emptyset, S_{\Gamma, \psi' \to \psi}, V_{\Gamma, \psi' \to \psi} \rangle,$$
$$\langle q^{\exists}_{\psi'_0}, \psi'_0, w_{\psi'}, \emptyset, S_{\Gamma, \psi'}, V_{\Gamma, \psi'} \rangle.$$

Note that $S_{\Gamma, \psi' \to \psi} = S_{\Gamma, \psi}$ and $V_{\Gamma, \psi' \to \psi} = V_{F, \psi}$. We can now use the instruction (9) to turn the current configuration into

$$\langle q^{\forall}_{\psi_0, \to}, \psi_0, w_{\psi' \to \psi}, \emptyset, S_{\Gamma, \psi}, V_{\Gamma, \psi} \rangle,$$

which can be turned into the desired two configurations with the instructions (17) and (18) respectively.

If the last rule is the $(\forall I)$ rule then $\psi = \forall X.\psi_1$ and we have a shorter derivation for $\Gamma \vdash M_1 : \psi_1$ (where X is a fresh variable by the eigenvariable condition), which by the induction hypothesis gives that $\mathbb{A}_\varphi$ eventually accepts from the configuration

$$\langle q^{\exists}_{\psi_{10}}, \psi_{10}, w_{\psi_1}, \emptyset, S_{\Gamma, \psi_1}, V_{\Gamma, \psi_1} \rangle,$$

where $w_{\psi_1}(\psi_{10}) = \psi_1$, $S_{\Gamma, \psi_1} = S_{\Gamma, \psi}$ and $V_{\Gamma, \psi_1} = V_{\Gamma, \psi} \cup \{X\}$.

We observe now that the non-structural instruction (6) transforms the current configuration to $\langle q^{\forall}_{\forall X.\psi_{10}}, \psi, w_\psi, \emptyset, S_{\Gamma, \psi}, V_{\Gamma, \psi} \rangle$ and then the new instruction from (4) adds appropriate element to $V_{\Gamma, \psi}$ and turns the configuration into the awaited one.

If the last rule is the $(\exists E)$ rule then we know that $\Gamma \vdash M_1 : \exists X.\psi_1$ and $\Gamma, x : \psi_1 \vdash M_2 : \psi$ are derivable through shorter derivations, which means by the induction hypothesis that $\mathbb{A}_\varphi$ eventually accepts from configurations

$$\langle q^{\exists}_{\exists X.\psi_{10}}, \exists X.\psi_{10}, w_{\exists X.\psi_1}, \emptyset, S_{\Gamma, \exists X.\psi_1}, V_{\Gamma, \exists X.\psi_1} \rangle, \qquad (\mathrm{I})$$
$$\langle q^{\exists}_{\psi_0}, \psi_0, w_\psi, \emptyset, S_{\Gamma', \psi}, V_{\Gamma', \psi} \rangle$$

where $w_{\exists X.\psi_1}(\exists X.\psi_{10}) = \exists X.\psi_1$, $w_\psi(\psi_0) = \psi$ and $\Gamma' = \Gamma, x : \psi_1$, which consequently means that $S_{\Gamma', \psi} = S_{\Gamma, \psi} \cup \{\langle \psi_{10}, w' \rangle\}$ and $V_{\Gamma', \psi} = V_{\Gamma, \psi} \cup \{X\}$ where $w' = ([\exists X.\psi_{10} := X] \ll w_{\exists X.\psi_1})|_{\mathrm{fv}(\psi_{10})}$.

Note that x is a fresh proof variable by definition and X is a fresh variable by the eigenvariable condition.

We observe that the current configuration can be transformed to

$$\langle q^{\forall}_{\psi_0, \exists}, \psi_0, w_\psi, w_{\exists X.\psi_1}, S_{\Gamma, \psi}, V_{\Gamma, \psi} \rangle \qquad (\mathrm{II})$$

by the non-structural instruction (11). This in turn is transformed to the configurations (I) by non-structural instructions (19) and (20) respectively. Note that the correctness of the guess of $w_{\exists X.\psi_1}$ in the step to ID (II) is verified by the step to the first ID in (I) □

We need a proof in the other direction. To express the statement of the next lemma we need the notation Γ_S for a context $x_1 : w_1(\psi_1), \ldots, x_n : w_n(\psi_n)$ where $S = \{\langle \psi_1, w_1 \rangle, \ldots, \langle \psi_n, w_n \rangle\}$.

Lemma 2. *If $\mathbb{A}_\varphi$ eventually accepts from the configuration $\langle q_\psi^\exists, \psi, w, \emptyset, S, V \rangle$ then there is a proof term M such that $\Gamma_S \vdash M : w(\psi)$.*

Proof. The proof is by induction over the definition of the eventually accepting configuration by cases depending on the currently available instructions. Note that only instructions (3), (6), (7), (8), (9), (10), (11), (12) and (13) are available for states of the form $q_\phi^\exists$.

We can immediately see that if one of the instructions (3) from Fig. 2 is used then the induction hypothesis applied to resulting configurations brings the assumption of the respective rule $(\vee Ii)$ for $i = 1, 2$ and we can apply it to obtain the conclusion.

Then taking the non-structural instruction (6) moves control to one of the instructions present in Fig. 2 and these move control to configurations from which the induction hypothesis gives the assumptions of the introduction rules $(\to I), (\wedge I), (\forall I), (\exists I)$ respectively.

Next taking the non-structural instructions (8), (9), (11) and (12) move control to further non-structural rules in Fig. 3 and these move control to configurations from which the induction hypothesis gives the assumptions of the elimination rules $(\vee E), (\to E), (\exists E),$ and $(\bot E)$. At the same time the instructions (7), (10), move control directly to configurations from which the induction hypothesis gives the assumptions of the elimination rules $(\wedge E), (\forall E)$.

At last the non-structural instruction (13) directly represents the use of the (var) rule.

More details of the reasoning can be observed by referring to relevant parts in the proof of Lemma 1 and adapting them to the current situation.   □

Theorem 3 (Main theorem). *The provability in intuitionistic first-order logic is reducible to the emptiness problem for Arcadian automata.*

Proof. Let φ be a formula of the first-order intuitionistic logic. The emptiness problem for $\mathbb{A}_\varphi$ is equivalent to checking if the initial configuration of this Arcadian automaton is eventually accepting. This in turn is by Lemmas 1 and 2 reducible to derivability of $\vdash \varphi$.   □

4   Conclusions

We propose a notion of automata that can simulate search for proofs in normal form in the full first-order intuitionistic logic, which can be viewed by the Curry-Howard isomorphism as a program synthesis for a simple functional language. This notion enables the possibility to apply automata theoretic techniques to inhabitant search in this type system. Although the emptiness problem for such automata is undecidable (as the logic is, [9]), the notion brings a new perspective to the proof search process which can reveal new classes of formulae for which the proof search can be made decidable. In particular this automata, together with earlier investigations [9,10], bring to the attention that decidable procedures must constrain the growth of the subset V in IDs of automata presented here.

Our automata by design find only terms in *total discharge convention* [7], i.e. such that if there is more than one variable of a given type available for use at some point in program, the most recently introduced one is used. This does not influence completeness of the search for inhabitants, but it has an effect on program synthesis. In order to check that it is not a big limiting factor we checked how many of the functions in real world programs are in total discharge convention by analysing the source code of the GHC. It turns out that 74% of the functions defined there are in total discharge convention, so using it does not excessively restrict program synthesis. The code and instructions needed to reproduce our results is available at http://www.mimuw.edu.pl/~maciekz/HaskellTdcStats.

References

1. Ben-Yelles, C.B.: Type-assignment in the lambda-calculus; syntax and semantics. Ph.D. thesis, Mathematics Department, University of Wales, Swansea, UK (1979)
2. Broda, S., Damas, L.: On long normal inhabitants of a type. J. Logic Comput. **15**(3), 353–390 (2005)
3. Düdder, B., Martens, M., Rehof, J.: Staged composition synthesis. In: Shao, Z. (ed.) ESOP 2014. LNCS, vol. 8410, pp. 67–86. Springer, Heidelberg (2014). doi:10.1007/978-3-642-54833-8_5
4. Filiot, E., Talbot, J., Tison, S.: Tree automata with global constraints. Int. J. Found. Comput. Sci. **21**(4), 571–596 (2010)
5. de Groote, P.: On the strong normalisation of intuitionistic natural deduction with permutation-conversions. Inf. Comput. **178**(2), 441–464 (2002)
6. Hetzl, S.: Applying tree languages in proof theory. In: Dediu, A.-H., Martín-Vide, C. (eds.) LATA 2012. LNCS, vol. 7183, pp. 301–312. Springer, Heidelberg (2012). doi:10.1007/978-3-642-28332-1_26
7. Prawitz, D.: Natural Deduction. Almqvist and Wiksell, Sweden (1965)
8. Schubert, A., Dekkers, W., Barendregt, H.P.: Automata theoretic account of proof search. In: Kreutzer, S. (ed.) 24th EACSL Annual Conference on Computer Science Logic (CSL 2015). LIPIcs, vol. 41, pp. 128–143. Dagstuhl (2015)
9. Schubert, A., Urzyczyn, P., Zdanowski, K.: On the mints hierarchy in first-order intuitionistic logic. In: Pitts, A. (ed.) FoSSaCS 2015. LNCS, vol. 9034, pp. 451–465. Springer, Heidelberg (2015). doi:10.1007/978-3-662-46678-0_29
10. Schubert, A., Urzyczyn, P., Walukiewicz-Chrzaszcz, D.: Restricted positive quantification is not elementary. In: Herbelin, H., Letouzey, P., Sozeau, M. (eds.) Proceedings of TYPES 2014. LIPIcs, vol. 39, pp. 251–273. Dagstuhl (2015)
11. Takahashi, M., Akama, Y., Hirokawa, S.: Normal proofs and their grammar. Inf. Comput. **125**(2), 144–153 (1996)
12. Urzyczyn, P.: Intuitionistic games: determinacy, completeness, and normalization. Studia Logica **104**(5), 957–1001 (2016). doi:10.1007/s11225-016-9661-4

Author Index

Printed in the United States
By Bookmasters